T0203109

# Lecture Notes in Computer Science    14309

Founding Editors

Gerhard Goos
Juris Hartmanis

The series Lecture Notes in Computer Science (LNCS), including its subseries Lecture Notes in Artificial Intelligence (LNAI) and Lecture Notes in Bioinformatics (LNBI), has established itself as a medium for the publication of new developments in computer science and information technology research, teaching, and education.

LNCS enjoys close cooperation with the computer science R & D community, the series counts many renowned academics among its volume editors and paper authors, and collaborates with prestigious societies. Its mission is to serve this international community by providing an invaluable service, mainly focused on the publication of conference and workshop proceedings and postproceedings. LNCS commenced publication in 1973.

Mads Haahr · Alberto Rojas-Salazar ·
Stefan Göbel

Editors

# Serious Games

9th Joint International Conference, JCSG 2023
Dublin, Ireland, October 26–27, 2023
Proceedings

*Editors*
Mads Haahr (iD)
Trinity College Dublin
Dublin, Ireland

Alberto Rojas-Salazar (iD)
University of Costa Rica
San José, Costa Rica

Stefan Göbel (iD)
TU Darmstadt
Darmstadt, Germany

ISSN 0302-9743        ISSN 1611-3349 (electronic)
Lecture Notes in Computer Science
ISBN 978-3-031-44750-1        ISBN 978-3-031-44751-8 (eBook)
https://doi.org/10.1007/978-3-031-44751-8

This Springer imprint is published by the registered company Springer Nature Switzerland AG
The registered company address is: Gewerbestrasse 11, 6330 Cham, Switzerland

Paper in this product is recyclable.

# Preface

The Joint Conference on Serious Games 2023 (JCSG 2023) took place at Trinity College Dublin, Dublin, Ireland, from October 26–27, 2023. This year's conference served as a gathering point where participants with a wide variety of backgrounds, such as researchers, designers, developers, writers, artists and more could present and discuss innovative topics and challenges encountered in the emerging and developing field of serious games.

In this edition of JCSG, we received 57 submissions from 21 countries. Following a comprehensive single-blind peer-review process with an average of 2.6 reviews per submission, we selected 18 full papers and 9 short papers. Reviewers' feedback was provided to the authors to facilitate the subsequent correction and improvement of their final manuscripts. The selected papers covered various topics, categorized as follows: Technology and Systems (four papers), Theoretical Aspects (four papers), Health and Wellbeing (four papers), Extended Realities (six papers), Soft and Social Skills (four papers), and Academic Skills (five papers). The contributions were presented through traditional talks and presentations.

Furthermore, a selection of authors whose submissions were not accepted for presentation were given the opportunity to showcase their work through posters or exhibits. A total of 14 contributions of this nature were presented. These posters and exhibits were displayed within an exhibition area at the conference.

The theme for the 2023 edition of JCSG was "Serious Games, Serious Stories," and while some papers reflected the theme, the overall collection of papers reflected the wide range of topics that are relevant for serious games. The theme was reflected strongly in the conference keynotes, which were given by Brenda Romero and Hartmut Koenitz. Brenda Romero is a BAFTA award-winning game director, entrepreneur, and Fulbright award recipient. She entered the video game industry in 1981 and is currently the CEO and co-founder of Romero Games. Hartmut Koenitz is a professor at Södertörn University and a specialist in interactive digital narratives and video games. He considers these mediums as dynamic systems capable of representing and enabling critical perspectives on complex topics.

We extend our gratitude to the authors for submitting their papers and participating in engaging discussions. Additionally, we thank the keynote speakers for providing high-quality insights into the field. Our acknowledgment also extends to the Program Committee members for their diligent reviews, the dedicated volunteers who contributed during the event, and the steering committee members who played a key role in shaping the conference.

October 2023

Mads Haahr
Alberto Rojas-Salazar
Stefan Göbel

# Organization

## General Chair

Mads Haahr                          Trinity College Dublin, Ireland

## Program Committee Chairs

Mads Haahr                          Trinity College Dublin, Ireland
Alberto Rojas-Salazar               Universidad de Costa Rica, Costa Rica
Stefan Göbel                        Technical University of Darmstadt, Germany

## Steering Committee

Jannicke Baalsrud Hauge             University of Bremen, Germany, and KTH Royal
                                        Institute of Technology, Sweden
Stefan Göbel                        Technical University of Darmstadt, Germany
Minhua Eunice Ma                    Falmouth University, UK
Tim Marsh                           Griffith University, Australia
Manuel Fradinho Oliveira            KIT-AR, UK
David White                         Staffordshire University, UK

## Program Committee

Mariano Alcaniz                     Universidad Politécnica Valencia, Spain
Jannicke Baalsrud Hauge             University of Bremen, Germany
Per Backlund                        University of Skövde, Sweden
Jonathan Barbara                    Saint Martin's Institute of Higher Education,
                                        Malta
Josep Blat                          Universitat Pompeu Fabra, Spain
Licia Calvi                         Breda University of Applied Sciences,
                                        The Netherlands
Antonio Calvo-Morata                Universidad Complutense de Madrid, Spain
Polona Caserman                     Technical University of Darmstadt, Germany
Michael Christel                    Carnegie Mellon University, USA
Karin Coninx                        Hasselt University, Belgium

| | |
|---|---|
| Ralf Doerner | RheinMain University of Applied Sciences, Germany |
| Pierpaolo Dondio | Technological University Dublin, Ireland |
| Kai Erenli | UAS BFI Vienna, Austria |
| Baltasar Fernandez-Manjon | Universidad Complutense de Madrid, Spain |
| Mateus Finco | Universidade Federal da Paraíba, Brazil |
| Augusto Garcia-Agundez | Brown University, USA |
| Shreya Ghosh | Curtin University, Australia |
| Pascual Gonzalez | Castilla-La Mancha University, Spain |
| Pedro González Calero | Universidad Politécnica de Madrid, Spain |
| Stefan Göbel | Technical University of Darmstadt, Germany |
| Mads Haahr | Trinity College Dublin, Ireland |
| Helmut Hlavacs | University of Vienna, Austria |
| Petar Jerčić | Graz University of Technology, Austria |
| Michael Kickmeier-Rust | Graz University of Technology, Austria |
| Hartmut Koenitz | University of Amsterdam, The Netherlands |
| Eunice Ma | Falmouth University, UK |
| Wolfgang Mueller | University of Education Weingarten, Germany |
| Philipp Müller | Technical University of Darmstadt, Germany |
| Sobah Abbas Petersen | Norwegian University of Science and Technology, Norway |
| Alberto Rojas-Salazar | Universidad de Costa Rica, Costa Rica |
| Roman Romero-Ortuno | Trinity College Dublin, Ireland |
| Nikitas Sgouros | University of Piraeus, Greece |
| Susannah Soon | Curtin University, Australia |
| Heinrich Söbke | Bauhaus-Universität Weimar, Germany |
| Thomas Tregel | Technical University of Darmstadt, Germany |
| Carl Vogel | Trinity College Dublin, Ireland |
| Vincent Wade | Trinity College Dublin, Ireland |
| David White | Staffordshire University, UK |
| Josef Wiemeyer | Technical University of Darmstadt, Germany |

## Additional Reviewers

Susanne Haake
Sascha Müller
Svetlana Rudenko

# Contents

**Extended Realities**

## Soft and Social Skills

## Academic Skills

**Posters and Exhibits**

# Technology and Systems

# Open Game Data: A Technical Infrastructure for Open Science with Educational Games

David J. Gagnon(✉) ⓘ and Luke Swanson ⓘ

University of Wisconsin – Madison, Madison, WI 53706, USA
{djgagnon,lwswanson2}@wisc.edu

**Abstract.** In this paper we describe a technical infrastructure, entitled Open Game Data, for conducting educational game research using open science, educational data mining and learning engineering approaches. We describe a modular data pipeline which begins with telemetry events from gameplay and ends with real time APIs and automated archival exports that support research. We demonstrate the usefulness of this infrastructure by summarizing several game research projects that have utilized and contributed back to Open Game Data. We then conclude with current efforts to expand the infrastructure.

**Keywords:** Learning Games · Assessment Games · Learning Engineering · Game Data · Educational Data Mining · Open Science · Research Infrastructure

## 1 Introduction

Effective human collaboration and coordination may well be the most powerful force in the universe. In this paper, and the project it describes, we contribute motivations and tools for collaborating and coordinating educational game research. This project is a direct response to both the promise of learning games for teaching, learning and research, as well as the challenges faced by game researchers.

One of the most obvious challenges is made clear in the 10 min after every talk the authors have given, when inspired graduate students come up to us and ask, "How do I get involved?" We are not satisfied by the most obvious answer to this question, which is to relocate oneself to one of the handful of large research institutions that have an in-house game studio, secured distribution, built research infrastructure and have an established research team with expertise in data science. What is the alternative? For many, it is to develop small versions of all these components once again, leading to educational game projects that are designed by novices, ad hoc infrastructure, small sample sizes and narrow studies. But what if there were a way to collaborate? What if there was a way to build from ongoing, well designed game projects with existing audiences, datasets and even sample analysis code so that the researcher could focus on their experiment and not all the apparatus required? What if a studio could adopt data driven design practices and better understand their players without having to develop all their own technology and in house expertise?

M. Haahr et al. (Eds.): JCSG 2023, LNCS 14309, pp. 3–19, 2023.
https://doi.org/10.1007/978-3-031-44751-8_1

This is the pursuit of Open Game Data: to open educational games research to a wider audience than we see today. We are looking to decouple learning game studios and research teams, so they don't need to be at the same organization. We are looking to modularize technical infrastructure so that a given studio or researcher can leverage useful portions of a data collection and analysis pipeline that serve the unique needs of their project, getting 99% of what they require for free and only having to contribute the final 1%. In the end, we believe that this collaboration will accelerate discovery in fields such as human computer interaction, machine learning and learning science, and in the end, produce better, more effective learning experiences for students.

The approach is not just an idea, it is happening today. Currently, a shared infrastructure is already collecting millions of rows of research data daily, from numerous learning games, and making those data and related analysis approaches available online for free. Open-source libraries are available for studios to integrate into their game. Hundreds of datasets are available for download, and many have code samples to explore, analyze and visualize the data. It's time to collaborate and coordinate!

## 2 Background

### 2.1 Games for Learning

While there are certainly critiques of digital games for learning [28], the overwhelming evidence favors their usefulness when applied appropriately. Educational games have been empirically shown to enhance students' understanding of targeted concepts, as well as their information processing skills [4, 5]. Games and situated virtual simulations have also been linked to increased motivation and interest [20, 22].

Scientifically based simulations and games provide contexts for representing and interacting with the world. When properly designed, they allow players to affect, experiment, and observe consequences in the simulated world in ways that are representative of the real world. Thus, simulations and games can produce situated learning experiences tied to disciplinary-specific concepts and language [9, 37]. James Gee [9] posits that well-designed games can situate players perceptually, narratively, and socially in a way that leads to empathetic embodiment for complex systems, thus prompting players to develop new ways of thinking, knowing, and being in the world, what Shaffer [32] calls an "epistemic frame". Because players' actions within simulations are mediated, reducing danger and cost while expanding or compressing time, perspective, etc., games provide a useful means of teaching complex concepts, particularly ones that cannot be experienced directly [13]. A challenge, then, is to produce designed experiences that align and balance context, goals, challenges, and feedback with desired student behaviors and learning outcomes [18].

### 2.2 Videogames as Instruments for Skills and Knowledge

There is increasing interest in using games as instruments and assessments [15]. This interest in grounded in the facts that: (1) games can engage players in authentic situations that resemble what they will encounter in real-world situations and (2) the telemetry of digital games can allow for collecting rich data that can be used to build computational models that reconstruct the entire problem-solving process, instead of only looking at the final outcomes of the problem.

Frameworks such as evidence-centered design (ECD) [21] formalize a method for designing games as psychometrically valid evaluations, leading to what Shute et al. [34] calls stealth assessment. This approach has been successfully used to assess conceptual understanding of academic topics, as well as persistence, and problem-solving skills using game play interaction data [42].

## 2.3 Analytics and Educational Data Mining

An alternate, but compatible approach to evidence centered design leans into the affordances created by the amount of data produced by games and the use of machine learning to extract insights. This approach, commonly referred to as educational data mining [35] uses fine-grained interaction data from a digital system to support educationally relevant conclusions. The method does not necessarily require the game to be designed in any particular way, but "mines" the data that is available to build models and draw inferences.

Supervised approaches utilized "labeled" data to train models. These labels can be internal to the game, such as a "quit" event where the player leaves a challenge before it is completed. The labels can also be provided by a researcher based on observation of the player or game play. In either case, models are trained using numerical or categorical "features" that describe some segment of gameplay along with the labels. If successful, the model can take a new set of features and accurately predict the outcome label. Recent work has demonstrated the use of supervised educational data mining approaches with game log data to effectively predict quitting, off-task behavior [2], wheel-spinning [12, 26], detect the learner's goal [6], as well as assess the learners science content knowledge [8, 30].

Unsupervised approaches provide insights into players without the use of labeled data for training. For example, clustering analysis has been used to develop a taxonomy of play "styles" [38], and latent class analysis has been used to develop learner typologies in relationship to learners' prior knowledge and domain interest [36].

## 2.4 Open Science for Education Research

Open Science is a movement that seeks to leverage new practices and digital technologies to increase transparency and increase access in scholarly research. It can be summarized as a form of scientific enterprise in which every step of the scientific endeavor is made available for others to inspect, critique and reproduce. Open Science is a response to a series of issues that have been raised with the way science is conducted and the latent structures that exist within scientific practice. These problems include high failure rates of replication studies [19], publication bias [29], high rates of false-positives [11], and cost barriers to accessing scientific research [23].

Open science for education encourages sharing artifacts at each stage of research [17, 40]. While specific terms may differ slightly, the following components of open science are common (0) Preregistration wherein researchers document their study protocol before executing the study [41]; (1) Open access to make research results available after publication; (2) open data as a way to publish the raw data before analysis; (3) Open Analysis to share the process by which the final results were obtained from the raw data; (4) Open Materials ensure that the tools and instruments used as an intervention or to collect data are available. Researchers are thereby encouraged to be as transparent as possible during the research endeavor and widely share artifacts outside of their immediate research team.

The transparency of Open Science not only combats some of the problems mentioned above by making every part of the research available for critique, but also may serve as a catalyst to accelerate inquiry and diversify those involved. Research that adopts any of the open practices also decouples the expertise (and cost) required to participate in that phase of research from the others. The availability of Open Data allows researchers to repurpose data in pursuit of a novel research agenda from what was originally in mind when the data was collected, saving significant cost for the secondary use. Similarly, Open Materials allow researchers to reuse interventions and instruments to be repurposed for new audiences, contexts or modified to support new research without having to develop these materials from scratch. Open Analysis allows potentially complex analysis procedures to be leveraged with other data, bootstrapping the efforts of the new research project.

## 2.5   Open Game Data as a Platform for Open Science with Game Data

Open Game Data was initially developed at the Field Day Lab at University of Wisconsin-Madison to explore data being generated by their own games. Following years of informal collaboration with researchers at Carnegie Mellon and University of Pennsylvania, a few larger research projects required game datasets to be able to be moved quickly between institutions to support the collaboration. Open Game Data was developed to serve those immediate needs while beginning to tun attention to expanding the network of who was collaborating.

Open Game Data is an online infrastructure designed to facilitate several components of Open Science, namely Open Data, Open Analysis, and Open Materials. The technical system is designed to capture, store, transform and disseminate player interaction data from learning games. A website provides links to game source code, publications based on these data and analysis code utilized by those investigations. This infrastructure has already evolved through several iterations and it's own progress has been documented and disseminated openly at https://github.com/opengamedata.

Open Game Data builds on the insights of previous work. It borrows the ideas of modularity between data providers, data stores and data consumers as well as the definition of a cross-project logging schema from xAPI [1], but is not well suited for high-frequency data created by games due to the verbose JSON structure. Open Game Data is also inspired by Data Shop [16] to create a public repository of learner datasets that are used by researchers beyond the initial authors but is most appropriate for instructional tutor data. Finally, this work builds upon the goal of a reusable system for analyzing educational game data that was demonstrated in ADAGE [25], but has since been abandoned.

# 3  Open Game Data Technical Infrastructure

We now outline the technical elements of the Open Game Data infrastructure. This includes a general pipeline for event data processing, a set of design decisions to ensure the data and pipeline work well across game genres and levels of granularity of research, and a description of our implementation of this design.

## 3.1  Levels of Granularity in Game Data Analysis

The goal of this infrastructure is to enable analyses that provide an understanding of game player experiences. We support such research by generating data suitable for a diverse range of analytical approaches. This may include anything from simple statistical summaries of a group of players to full in-engine replay of an individual gameplay session.

These approaches generally require the ability to track interactions between a player and a game, potentially across multiple sessions or repeated playthroughs. Further, different approaches often require different levels of granularity. The Open Game Data pipeline directly supports four levels of granularity: event, session, player, and population. This is not a comprehensive list of all possible granularities but represent the most common use cases we have encountered.

- **Event data:** An event represents a single interaction between player and game. This could be an action taken by a player, such as clicking a button; a reaction by the game system, such as a change in a score display; or a marker of progression, such as the player completing a level [24]. We further identify two classes of events:

  - *Game events:* These events represent objective moments of gameplay, encoded in the game system itself. These are the most common kind of event data, and include click and navigation events, changes in the game state, and movement of the player through a game's progression system.
  - *Calculated events:* These are derived events that are not explicitly a part of the game. These events can be generated during analysis of the game events. This category includes events that are based on arbitrary thresholds, or whose definitions might change over time. For example, an "idle player" would be best implemented as a calculated event.

- **Session data:** This level of granularity comes from aggregating events across a gameplay session, in order to extract some understanding of the session as a whole. We define a session as the time from a player opening the game application to the time the application is closed. It is generally assumed that a session represents only one player's interaction with the game; however, it is possible multiple players could take turns in a single session.
- **Player data:** In the same way session data is generated by aggregating events across one session of gameplay, player-level data is generated by aggregating events across all of a player's sessions. For some games, session and player data have a one-to-one relationship; that is, the game does not keep track of a player across sessions, assuming instead that each session is a unique, one-time player.

- **Population data:** In this case, events are aggregated to generate data about a population of players. Practically, this data tends to be based on aggregations of player-level data, rather than raw aggregation of events. For example, where a player-level feature might be the total score on a puzzle, an equivalent population-level feature may be the average player score.

## 3.2 A Pipeline for Event Data Processing

In order to provide data for analysis at each level of granularity, we have developed a pipeline for the collection, processing, and distribution of game event logs. Our pipeline begins with the collection and storage of raw game events, and includes a series of data transformations, yielding calculated events and feature data. It ends with distribution of data suitable for games researchers and data scientists to perform analysis, model-building, or data visualization.

This pipeline is agnostic to game genre and allows for complete customization of the set of calculated events and features for each game of interest. Further, our pipeline is independent of any specific data storage solution or game platform. We achieve this flexibility by enforcing a specific schema for all events, creating a common structure for inputs to the pipeline. So long as a mapping can be defined to place existing event data into the form defined by the schema, our pipeline provides a uniform interface for processing events into the granularities discussed in Sect. 3.1 (Fig. 1).

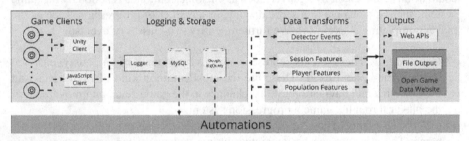

**Fig. 1.** The Open Game Data pipeline consists of four segments, namely game clients, logging and storage, data transforms, and data sharing.

### The Open Game Data Event Schema

There are two goals in designing a single standard for event logs. The first, as discussed previously, is to allow for a single interface to process event log data. The second is to ensure that gameplay is logged in sufficient detail to allow a full reconstruction of the session. Any given event log should answer a few questions, including when did the event occur? what happened? who was the player? where was the player in the space of possible game states? which version of the game was being played? Our schema is designed to ensure these questions are answered by each event. The full list of schema elements is included in Table 1. These elements can be grouped into the following categories:

- **Identifiers:** We include three identifiers with each event, namely an *app ID*, a *session ID*, and a *player ID*. The app ID indicates which game logged the event. Session IDs are uniquely generated each time a game application is started and are included with each event until the application is closed. Lastly, the player ID is an optional identifier, which may be used by games that implement a player code or similar mechanism to track users across multiple sessions.
- **Timestamps:** The *timestamp* category includes an eponymous UTC timecode indicating when an event occurred in absolute time, as well as an *event sequence index*, sometimes called "session index". The first event within a session is given a value of 1, the next 2, and so forth, ensuring that the precise order of events can be reconstructed. This addresses a potential issue where some storage systems do not with sufficient granularity to uniquely order the events in a session.
- **Versioning:** Games regularly change over time as developers add new content or tune existing content to create a better play experience. Thus, it is necessary to include versioning information with event logs. The schema includes three "versions." *App version* indicates the sequential version of the game itself. An optional *app branch* (sometimes called "app flavor") may be included. It is often useful to distinguish between official release versioning and temporary experimental versions, as in A-B testing, where multiple variations of a game are deployed in parallel. Lastly, *log version* indicates a version of the logging schema and internal structure of the *event data* or *game state* elements for a game. These may change in response to changes to the game itself, or to address shortcomings of the earlier logging code.
- **User Data:** Beyond merely identifying the player, it may be helpful for some games to track general information about a user. This may vary from game to game, so our schema defines a *user data* element as a dictionary, possibly empty, that maps sub-element names to values. The choice of sub-elements is completely left to the implementer, but all chosen sub-elements should be included with every event. That is, regardless of the specific details of an event, the user data should always have the same structure.
- **Game State:** It is often useful to understand the game-specific context in which an event occurred. The schema thus includes a *game state* element. *Game state* is a dictionary mapping sub-element names to values. These could include the current level, the player's current score, or the position of the player character on the game map. Again, the specific structure of the game state dictionary is decided on a game-by-game basis, but within a given game the structure should not vary from event to event.
- **Event Data:** This category includes an *event name*, an *event source*, and *event data*. The *event name* is a string indicating the specific type of event that occurred. Examples might include text_click, level_complete, or display_image. We recommend a convention using a noun_verb format (e.g. text_click) to name player action and progression events, and a verb_noun format (e.g. display_image) for system feedback events. *Event source* simply indicates whether the event was generated by the game, or created in post-processing. Finally, *event data* is a name-value dictionary, like *game state* and *user data*. Unlike those other elements, the internal structure of *event data* will vary across events. For example, a text_click might have only a single sub-element containing the text that was clicked. On the other hand, a display_image

event might include sub-elements for the name and dimensions of the image file being displayed. Note that all other elements of the schema have been common across all events in a game. Regardless of a game's details, every event includes identifiers, a time, and version information. Based on the details of a specific game, we can define data that describes a user or a game state, which again has a common structure across all of that game's events. In this category of schema element, we finally address specific details that vary by event type. This is a conscious design choice; by isolating event-specific details to a few elements, we are able to maintain a generally uniform interface for the pipeline to interact with event data.

**Game Clients**

Processing of event data necessarily begins with the collection of event logs from the game itself. Logging should be loosely coupled with the game, such that it does not impact the player's experience in any meaningful way. To this end, our infrastructure provides client libraries (currently available for Unity3d and JavaScript development environments) that may be included as modules in a game project. These reduce the need for ad-hoc implementations, shortening development time.

To integrate a client library, the game developer should first play through their game, identifying each distinct type of event, and specifying the appropriate *event data* elements for each event type. Logging can then be implemented via calls to a logger function in the programming interface of the appropriate client library, which is designed to encourage best practices and will structure data according to the event schema described in the previous section.

**Game Log Storage**

As events are sent from instances of a game, they must be received and stored for later analysis. A key concern here is scalability. For example, over the last three years, we have collected approximately 1.5 billion individual events across 17 games. This staggering amount of research data needs to be stored inexpensively and accessed rapidly.

In order to decouple the receipt of data from any one storage vendor or technology, Open Game Data provides a simple "catcher" PHP script as an intermediate between game client and storage. While many vendors provide APIs to directly interact with storage, this intermediate ensures already-deployed games will not need to be modified in the event of migration to a new storage system. The "catcher" is designed to only insert into storage, never modifying or removing existing data. This simplicity helps to minimize maintenance costs, which typically outweigh storage costs.

We utilize a two-part data storage solution, consisting of "short-term" and "long-term" databases. Data is initially written into the short-term database, and a daily automation script copies all new events to long-term storage. Events remain in short-term storage for one week, leaving a time buffer for detection and fixing of any copy errors, before data is lost. The short-term database, then, maintains a relatively small and stable size, growing only as new games are added to the system. This makes it suitable as a data source for real-time tools, which need fast access to only the most recent events. The long-term database, on the other hand, grows daily. In order to maintain performance, this database should be segmented by time so that it does not need to search through years of data to find a given session or segment of the population.

In our implementation, we use a locally-hosted MySQL database for short-term storage. This system is relatively slow and expensive at scale, but fast for small datasets. For long-term archival storage, we turn to 3rd-party vendors, in this case Google's BigQuery. By using a 3rd party product, we further reduce maintenance costs, and the cost for raw storage at the time of writing was approximately $10/year for each year of data stored.

**Data Transformations**
The most complex stage of the pipeline is data transformation. This phase can be viewed as a sub-pipeline, with steps for generation of new events; extraction of session, player, and population features; and training and evaluation of models. These transforms are performed nondestructively, such that old data is never directly modified. In addition, the transforms use a "one-pass" approach that ensures each piece of data need only be retrieved once from storage, saving data transfer times that often plague ad-hoc feature engineering.

The first transform adds new, calculated events to the overall event dataset. These are produced by "detectors", and we refer to this as the detector phase. As discussed previously, the game should only log "objective" events that are accounted for by the game system itself. This transform handles the "other" events that may be based on shifting or subjective definitions.

The next transform is the "feature" phase, in which "extractors" convert the event stream to a set of summary descriptions of sessions, players, and/or populations. Each of these three levels of granularity may be calculated in parallel during this phase. A feature may be a simple summary statistic, such as a count of button clicks, or a compound data structure, such as a list of levels completed.

The third transformation takes feature and event data and produces trained machine learning models of player behavior. Implementation of this stage of the data transformation sub-pipeline is a matter of future work; we discuss it further in Sect. 5.

All data transforms are implemented in Python, the primary programming language of data science. To maintain flexibility and modularity, each event detector and feature extractor is written as an individual Python class. Each of these classes implements a filter for types of events to analyze, an update rule that executes on each accepted event, and a generation rule that produces either a new event (in the case of a detector) or a value (in the case of a feature). This makes it easy to add or remove detectors and features, allowing specific configurations for different analyses.

## 3.3 Data Sharing and Automation

The primary unit of data sharing in Open Game Data is the dataset file. The goal here is to provide easily-shareable files in a consistent, automated way. We also provide APIs for live, dynamic access to data. Together, these not only enable the use of different toolsets for game data analysis, but provide resources to support our goal of creating a community for open science.

**File Production.** File outputs from the Open Game Data pipeline are meant to be easily-shareable, both in terms of ease-of-access and ease-of-use. Files are given in a popular, vendor-agnostic tabular form, tab-separated value (TSV) files.

Monthly file generation is automated with the Actions feature of the GitHub platform. These export scripts generate files for each game with the prior month's raw events. For games that have some event detectors or feature extractors, files are created with combined raw and generated events, session-level features, player-level features, and/or population-level features. These are automatically uploaded to the Open Game Data website, discussed in a later section.

**APIs.** The Open Game Data RESTful APIs provide real-time access to data for web-based data tools. We provide API endpoints for each of the levels of granularity previously discussed. To maximize compatibility with the existing Python implementation of the data transformation stage, the API endpoints are developed in the Flask framework. This framework is itself written in Python and designed to run Python pto service API requests, so the same code can be used for the APIs as file generation.

**Website.** The Open Game Data website is central to the overall mission of the project, serving as the primary end-user interface for discovering and accessing open data, open analysis, open materials and open access research products. The front page of the site describes the project, encourages participation from various stakeholder groups, and most importantly, links to the individual game pages (Fig. 2 left). An API call populates the page on load, cataloging the games that are currently available and a count of the number of gameplay sessions available for download.

Clicking each of the games triggers the load from another API that retrieves everything available for that game (Fig. 2 right). Each month of data available for the game is displayed as a graph and clicking on a month loads the data pipeline. Currently, the pipeline provides links to downloadable files for the raw events, calculated events and calculated features at the session, player and population level. Also in the pipeline are links to the analysis code that was used during each transformation. For example, clicking on the detectors link in the pipeline will link to the GitHub repository and subfolder where each detector's python code is stored.

Each game page displays published research artifacts that utilize the game's data. The publications link to the openly available document itself, typically a PDF file, as well as to a GitHub repository for any analysis code that was used to write that paper.

Finally, each game page provides a link to the game's source code itself. In line with the Open materials component of open science, this provides the research community transparent documentation of exactly how each game is designed and how it produces data. It also provides a significant starting asset for modification in service of a novel but related research endeavor.

## 4   Use Cases

### 4.1   Visualizing Game Play and Student Change

Cool It was a game designed to teach design principles of cryogenic engineering, an advanced topic within mechanical engineering. Pfotenhauer et al. [27] describe how game telemetry data, captured by the technology that would eventually become Open Game Data, allowed research designers to develop visualizations of player actions and

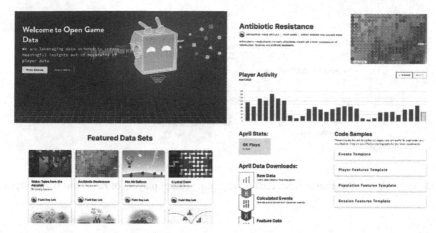

**Fig. 2.** The homepage (left) and a single game page (right) on the Open Game Data website

differentiate between expert and novice behavior. At the end of this work, the team was able to visualize a player model that described their understanding between each independent and dependent variable in the game's simulation and watch a player develop those understandings over time.

Lakeland is a game designed to teach about the systems of farming and phosphorus runoff that cause algae blooms in lakes. The game targets grade 7–9 students learning in earth systems and life sciences. In 2021, Scianna et al. [31] used open game data captured over the month of December 2019 in combination with a method known as epistemic network analysis (ENA) [33] to visualize and contrast player's initial and second attempts playing Lakeland (see Fig. 3). The researchers found that the more expert players (the blue network) responded to gameplay events differently than the novice players (the red network). ENA analysis of game logs provided a way to see that novice players received more negative feedback from the game system and that feedback was connected with players' development of short term responses. In contrast, experienced players utilized more long-term strategies and did more of their planning in relation to the availability of new resources.

### 4.2 Deriving and Visualization Player Typologies

Educational game designers will always be interested in ways to understand their audiences and how those audiences are interacting with the game. Swanson et al. [38] used data from Lakeland, in combination with the unsupervised K-means clustering algorithm to mathematically summarize 30,000 unique player sessions into a small number of categories that could be qualitatively described. The researchers describe their process of feature selection, dimension reduction and algorithm tuning to sort each play session into clusters, then describe these clusters in relationship to each other and key features of the game's design. They performed this operation three times to explore clusters of player actions (i.e. strategy), clusters of game feedback and clusters of player progression in the game. The results were visualized with radar plots and qualitatively

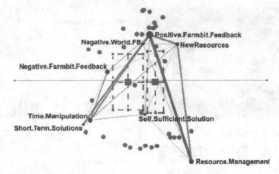

**Fig. 3.** An ENA visualization of new (red) vs. returning (blue) players of *Lakeland* (Color figure online)

interpreted (see Fig. 4 for an example). The analysis revealed the comparative size of different experiences (i.e. how many players used each strategy or progressed in a similar way) and suggested specific changes to the design to better align with the game's goals.

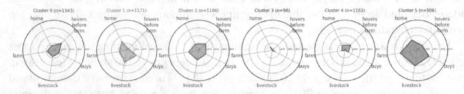

**Fig. 4.** Player action clusters for *Lakeland*

### 4.3 Predicting Outcomes on External Learning Measures

Many would argue that any learning game acts as an assessment of the players' skill and knowledge [9, 37], but assessment experts would caution that any use of a game to assess must first undergo a validity assessment. In Gagnon et al. [8], researchers embedded traditional multiple choice assessment items into the game to measure student understanding of key concepts within each of the games. The study utilized two games, Crystal Cave and Wave Combinator. In Crystal Cave, players are tasked with arranging different molecules to maximize the stability of the resulting structure. In Wave Combinator, players are presented visually with a wave and must adjust two signal generators to produce a resulting wave that closely matches the original. For both games, researchers found that a logistic regression model trained on features of approximately 5,000 gameplay sessions was able to aid the prediction of how students would perform on the embedded assessments.

In a more complex example, Kim et al. [14] studied Wake: Tales from the Aqualab, a game designed to teach the scientific practices of experimentation, modeling and argumentation in the context of aquatic life science topics such as food webs and photosynthesis. For this project, learners played the game for 5–7 class periods over two weeks, then were given a performance assessment, developed from existing measures, to score their post-game understanding of each science practice. Following the work in progress paper, the team will be identifying key performance metrics of the gameplay data and using them to build models that predict scores on the performance assessment.

### 4.4 Learning Engineering to Empirically Validate Design Theory

Educational video games are as much art as they are science. Learning theories certainly (should) inform the design process, but many decisions from art style, character representation, user interface and even music are made by the creative team. As Clarke et al. [4] conclude in their game efficacy meta-analysis, video game studies have moved from empirical studies assessing if games are useful for education and into a phase of attempting to understand how different components of their design support learning, and for whom. We believe that Learning Engineering may be the methodological approach to answering this call.

Learning Engineering is an emerging method for iteratively leveraging empirically based experiments to improve learning outcomes, specifically with digital learning interventions [3]. Common practices include A/B testing, educational data mining, and dataset generation. Applied to game research, learning engineering allows a design theory to be tested in terms of specific learning outcomes, producing evidence for or against the validity of a given theory.

Gagnon et al. [7] utilized learning engineering practices to study the design of Jo Wilder and the Capitol Case, a grade 3–5 history practices game. As part of the research, the team developed four distinct versions of the script, embedded questionnaire items into the game, then randomly deployed the different versions to over 11,000 students. The results surprised the designers, showing that none of the designs led to higher completion rates, and that some of the design choices were a poor fit for the age group.

Another study by Slater et al. [36] utilized the same Jo Wilder and the Capitol Case dataset but with different analysis approaches. This team began by developing a five group taxonomy of player attitudes using Latent Class Analysis, then studied these groups' reactions to each of the four scripts. The research highlighted the effect of different scripts for each audiences.

### 4.5 Developing Real Time Analytics to Support Instruction

Inspired by work such as Holstein et al. [10] with instructional tutors, Swanson et al. [39] utilized the real time components of Open Game Data to develop a web-based tool that would provide educators with insights into their students' learning experience while they were playing the game. This project utilized Lakeland, partially due to the complex systems involved in a real time strategy game and challenge for educators to assess student progress simply by looking at their screen at a moment in time. The project explored the key analysis that educators sought through a series of co-design activities, then tested a prototype of a real time tool in authentic learning contexts, concluding that much more effort should be put in developing these sorts of educator support tools for learning games.

## 5   Future Work and Extensions to Infrastructure

Several new capacities are planned or currently being developed to extend Open Game Data capabilities. All of these have been piloted at least once but haven't yet been developed as repeatable infrastructure.

Prototyping is underway to develop replay capabilities for games that were created using the Unity3d game engine. This new system allows the raw telemetry events generated by a player to be fed back into a version of the game, creating a time accurate replay of the entire experience, akin to a video recording of the experience, but much smaller and more flexible. This capability will then be combined with an annotation interface, allowing qualitative researchers to assign codes to segments of game play. These codes can be used to train detectors and automatically code new data without human intervention.

A system to support experiments and facilitate A/B testing is currently in planning. While the infrastructure to log data from multiple versions of a game is currently in place, a system to describe the changes between the versions of the game and automate assignment of a player to each version is not. Optimally this system would allow an experiment to be proposed completely online, defining rules for how the audience is assigned (randomly or based on some criteria) and parameters for the custom configuration in each game version, all without recompiling or deploying the game.

The addition of models, model training and model evaluation into the data pipeline is currently being explored. This entails integrating the capacity for common models, such as regressions, decision trees and neural networks to be added directly into the data pipeline. They would be continually trained on incoming data and their outputs available via API as well as in the automated file exports.

## 6   Conclusion

The paper describes the background and promise of educational games for teaching and assessment, especially when combined with educational data mining approaches. We then explore the notion of Open Science as a movement to improve scientific rigor while accelerating its progress and expanding participation. Open Game Data is a natural extension of these ideas and has already been utilized for several educational game research projects. This paper focuses on infrastructure and details a data pipeline that begins with telemetry events being generated by a learning game and ends with a website that makes datasets, analysis and research products available openly.

This paper outlines our thinking at an important point in time for the project, as it transitions from a tool used by a few researchers into a shared infrastructure intended to be informed by and support the research of a much wider audience. In the next year, many games are scheduled for integration, new analysis and visualization features are being developed and workshops are being facilitated to jumpstart new research projects. If successful, novel learning game scholarship will flourish by audiences that previously would not have been able to participate, due to cost or access.

**Acknowledgements.** Open Game Data would not exist without the regular and thoughtful contributions of Erik Harpstead, Jennifer Scianna and Stefan Slater over the last years, as well as the many staff and interns who have worked on the project. We also acknowledge the insights brought by Ryan Baker, Matthew Berland, YJ Kim, Elizabeth Owen, and Dennis Ramirez at key moments that have guided the project.

This material is based upon work supported by the 2022 Learning Agency Tools Competition, the Wisconsin Department of Public Instruction and the National Science Foundation under Grant No. (1907384, 2116046, 2142103, 2243668).

# References

1. Advanced Distributed Learning: Experience API (xAPI) Standard (n.d). https://adlnet.gov/projects/xapi. Accessed 30 July 2023
2. Baker, R.: Modeling and understanding students' off-task behavior in intelligent tutoring systems. In: Proceedings of the SIGCHI Conference on Human Factors in Computing Systems - CHI 2007, pp. 1059–1068 (2007). https://doi.org/10.1145/1240624.1240785
3. Baker, R.S., Boser, U.: High-leverage opportunities for learning engineering, p. 48. Penn Center for Learning Analytics (2022). https://learninganalytics.upenn.edu/Learning_Engine ering_recommendations.pdf
4. Clark, D.B., Tanner-Smith, E.E., Killingsworth, S.S.: Digital games, design, and learning: a systematic review and meta-analysis. Rev. Educ. Res. **86**(1), 79–122 (2016). https://doi.org/10.3102/0034654315582065
5. D'Angelo, C., Rutstein, D., Harris, C., Haertel, G., Bernard, R., Borokhovski, E.: Simulations for STEM learning: systematic review and meta-analysis. SRI Int. **5**, 1–5 (2014)
6. DiCerbo, K.E., Kidwai, K.: Detecting player goals from game log files. In: Proceedings of the 6th International Conference on Educational Data Mining (EDM 2013), p. 2 (2013)
7. Gagnon, D.J., et al.: Exploring players' experience of humor and snark in a grade 3–6 history practices game. In: GLS 13.0 Conference Proceedings. Games, Learning Society, Irving, CA (2022)
8. Gagnon, D.J., Harpstead, E., Slater, S.: Comparison of off the shelf data mining methodologies in educational game analytics. In: Joint Proceedings of the Workshops of the 12th International Conference on Educational Data Mining Co-Located with the 12th International Conference on Educational Data Mining (EDM 2019), pp. 38–43 (2019)
9. Gee, J. P.: What Video Games Have to Teach us About Learning and Literacy (1. Paperback ed). Palgrave Macmillan (2004)
10. Holstein, K., McLaren, B.M., Aleven, V.: Co-designing a real-time classroom orchestration tool to support teacher–AI complementarity. J. Learn. Anal. **6**(2), 27–52 (2019). https://doi.org/10.18608/jla.2019.62.3
11. Ioannidis, J.P.A.: Why most published research findings are false. PLoS Med. **2**(8), e124 (2005). https://doi.org/10.1371/journal.pmed.0020124
12. Kai, S., Almeda, M.V., Baker, R.S., Heffernan, C., Heffernan, N.: Decision tree modeling of wheel-spinning and productive persistence in skill builders. JEDM I J. Educ. Data Min. **10**(1), 36–71 (2018)
13. Kamarainen, A.M., et al.: EcoMOBILE: integrating augmented reality and probeware with environmental education field trips. Comput. Educ. **68**, 1–12 (2013). https://doi.org/10.1016/j.compedu.2013.02.018
14. Kim, Y.J., Metcalf, S.J., Scianna, J., Perez, G., Gagnon, D.J.: AquaLab: establishing validity of an adventure game for middle school science practices. In: Iyer, S. (ed.) Proceedings of the 30th International Conference on Computers in Education (2022)

15. Kim, Y.J., Shute, V.J.: The interplay of game elements with psychometric qualities, learning, and enjoyment in game-based assessment. Comput. Educ. **87**, 340–356 (2015). https://doi.org/10.1016/j.compedu.2015.07.009

16. Koedinger, K.R., Baker, R.S.J.D., Cunningham, K., Skogsholm, A., Leber, B., Stamper, J.: A data repository for the EDM community: the PSLC DataShop. In: Romero, C., Ventura, S., Pechenizkiy, M., Baker, R.S. (eds.) Handbook of Educational Data Mining. CRC Press, Boca Raton (2010)

17. Kraker, P., Leony, D., Reinhardt, W., Gü, N.A., Beham, N.: The case for an open science in technology enhanced learning. Int. J. Technol. Enhanc. Learn. **3**(6), 643 (2011). https://doi.org/10.1504/IJTEL.2011.045454

18. Lomas, D.: Optimizing challenge in an educational game using large-scale design experiments, pp. 1–10 (2013)

19. Makel, M.C., Plucker, J.A.: Facts are more important than novelty: replication in the education sciences. Educ. Res. **43**(6), 304–316 (2014). https://doi.org/10.3102/0013189X14545513

20. Metcalf, S.J., Reilly, J.M., Kamarainen, A.M., King, J., Grotzer, T.A., Dede, C.: Supports for deeper learning of inquiry-based ecosystem science in virtual environments—comparing virtual and physical concept mapping. Comput. Hum. Behav. **87**, 459–469 (2018). https://doi.org/10.1016/j.chb.2018.03.018

21. Mislevy, R.J., Almond, R.G., Lukas, J.F.: A brief introduction to evidence-centered design. National Center for Research on Evaluation, Standards, and Student Testing (CRESST) Center for the Study of Evaluation (CSE), Graduate School of Education & Information Studies. (2004). https://files.eric.ed.gov/fulltext/ED483399.pdf

22. National Research Council: Successful K-12 STEM Education: Identifying Effective Approaches in Science, Technology, Engineering, and Mathematics. The National Academies Press (2011). https://doi.org/10.17226/13158

23. Noorden, R.V.: Researchers can get visibility and connections by putting their data online—if they go about it in the right way. Nature **500**, 243–245 (2013). https://doi.org/10.1038/nj7461-243a

24. Owen, V.E., Baker, R.S.: Fueling prediction of player decisions: foundations of feature engineering for optimized behavior modeling in serious games. Technol. Knowl. Learn. **25**(2), 225–250 (2020). https://doi.org/10.1007/s10758-018-9393-9

25. Owen, V.E., Ramirez, D., Salmon, A., Halverson, R.: Capturing learner trajectories in educational games through ADAGE (assessment data aggregator for game environments): a click-stream data framework for assessment of learning in play. In: American Educational Research Association Annual Meeting, Philadelphia (2014)

26. Owen, V.E., Roy, M.-H., Thai, K.P., Burnett, V., Jacobs, D., Baker, R.S.: Detecting wheel-spinning and productive persistence in educational games, p. 6 (2019)

27. Pfotenhauer, J.M., Gagnon, D.J., Litzkow, M.J., Blakesley, C.C.: Designing and using an on-line game to teach engineering. In: FIE2009, pp. 1–5 (2009)

28. Mayer, R.: Computer Games for Learning: An Evidence-Based Approach. MIT Press, Cambridge (2014)

29. Rosenthal, R.: The file drawer problem and tolerance for null results. Psychol. Bull. **86**(3), 638–641 (1979). https://doi.org/10.1037/0033-2909.86.3.638

30. Rowe, E., et al.: Assessing implicit science learning in digital games. Comput. Hum. Behav. **76**, 617–630 (2017). https://doi.org/10.1016/j.chb.2017.03.043

31. Scianna, J., Gagnon, D., Knowles, B.: Counting the game: visualizing changes in play by incorporating game events. In: Ruis, A.R., Lee, S.B. (eds.) ICQE 2021. CCIS, vol. 1312, pp. 218–231. Springer, Cham (2021). https://doi.org/10.1007/978-3-030-67788-6_15

32. Shaffer, D.W.: Epistemic frames for epistemic games. Comput. Educ. **46**(3), 223–234 (2006). https://doi.org/10.1016/j.compedu.2005.11.003

33. Shaffer, D.W., et al.: Epistemic network analysis: a prototype for 21st-century assessment of learning. Int. J. Learn. Media **1**(2), 33–53 (2009). https://doi.org/10.1162/ijlm.2009.0013

34. Shute, V.J., Shute, V.J., Kim, Y.J.: Formative and stealth assessment. In: Spector, J., Merrill, M., Elen, J., Bishop, M. (eds.) Handbook of Research on Educational Communications and Technology, vol. 1, pp. 311–321. Springer, New York (2013). https://doi.org/10.1007/978-1-4614-3185-5_25

35. Siemens, G., Baker, R.S.: Learning analytics and educational data mining: towards communication and collaboration. In: Proceedings of the 2nd International Conference on Learning Analytics and Knowledge - LAK 2012, p. 252 (2012). https://doi.org/10.1145/2330601.2330661

36. Slater, S., Baker, R.S., Gagnon, D.J.: Changing students' perceptions of a history exploration game using different scripts. In: Proceedings of the 30th International Conference on Computers in Education. International Conference on Computers in Education, Kuala Lumpur, Malaysia (2022)

37. Squire, K.D.: From content to context: videogames as designed experience. Educ. Res. **35**(8), 19–29 (2006)

38. Swanson, L., et al.: Leveraging cluster analysis to understand educational game player styles and support design. In: GLS 13.0 Conference Proceedings. Games, Learning, Society, Irving, CA (2022)

39. Swanson, L., Gagnon, D.J., Scianna, J.: A pilot study on teacher-facing real-time classroom game dashboards. In: International Conference on Meaningful Play, East Lansing, MI (2022)

40. Van Der Zee, T., Reich, J.: Open education science. AERA Open **4**(3) (2018). https://doi.org/10.1177/2332858418787466

41. Van 'T Veer, A.E., Giner-Sorolla, R.: Pre-registration in social psychology—a discussion and suggested template. J. Exp. Soc. Psychol. **67**, 2–12. (2016). https://doi.org/10.1016/j.jesp.2016.03.004

42. Ventura, M., Shute, V.: The validity of a game-based assessment of persistence. Comput. Hum. Behav. **29**(6), 2568–2572 (2013). https://doi.org/10.1016/j.chb.2013.06.033

# Gamified E-Learning Technology for Live Musicians: Application Design and Performance Evaluation Criteria for Keyboarders

Robin Horst[1,2]([✉]) [ID], Micha Lanvers[1], and Ralf Dörner[1] [ID]

[1] RheinMain University of Applied Sciences, Wiesbaden, Germany
{robin.horst,micha.lanvers,ralf.doerner}@hs-rm.de
[2] Fraunhofer Institute for Computer Graphics Research (IGD), Darmstadt, Germany

**Abstract.** Assessing a player's performance is an essential part of gamified applications or serious games. For keyboard practice in the musical domain, an established approach is comparing played keys and a fixed MIDI score. However, concerning the evaluation of live performances (the actual keyboard playing and not to confuse with the stage public performance) within gamified technologies, only little is known. In this work, we investigate evaluating the live and improvised performance of keyboarders within a gamified E-Learning app. We introduce three performance criteria based on underlying musical concepts, again each composed of three sub-criteria, and provide abstract definitions for them whose implementation in a software system depends on application-specific parameters (e.g., keyboard hardware, sound generation software, and chord progression). Based on the results of an expert user study, we conclude that our performance criteria *correctness* and *playing style* are well generalizable and could offer meaningful insight into the abilities of live keyboard performance, whereas the *sound usage* criterion was perceived as diverse, depending on our participants' genre-expertise.

**Keywords:** Game Performance Evaluation · Gamification · E-Learning · Live Keyboard Performance

## 1 Introduction

Learning to play an instrument alone can be cumbersome. Even knowing how to play, learning to play together with other musicians, and performing music live and in front of an audience usually requires a lot of practice together and involves various challenges. For example, in larger ensembles, musicians might not always be available for practice, and issues that can occur in live situations - such as hardware faults or a change of plans to adapt to the audience - are difficult to prepare and practice in rehearsal spaces.

Established software solutions that help musicians learn their instrument, such as Skoove [10] or Yousician [15], focus primarily on teaching tone theory

© The Author(s), under exclusive license to Springer Nature Switzerland AG 2023
M. Haahr et al. (Eds.): JCSG 2023, LNCS 14309, pp. 20–35, 2023.
https://doi.org/10.1007/978-3-031-44751-8_2

and motor sequences and place emphasis on correctly replaying songs. They provide temporal note visualizations and the comparison of played notes and the song arrangement. Learning to deal with live-situations requires additional audiovisual components, e.g., looking at virtual band members who might give certain cues (e.g., auditory: band member announces chord progressions through talkback microphone). The questions are raised: How can E-Learning technologies be designed to support musicians practicing for live events? And how can the musicians' live performances be evaluated in software systems?

In this paper, we address particularly the latter question in the context of gamified E-Learning technology and make the following contribution:

- We introduce Worship Keys Performer (WKP) – a gamified E-Learning application for practicing live keyboard play in the context of church music – and elaborate on its design decisions.
- Based on findings from our literature research, design rationale, and semi-structured expert interviews, we introduce a set of performance evaluation criteria. Since musical perception is highly subjective and parameters may strongly vary dependent on hard- and software components of a system, we formulate the criteria as soft guidelines, to be used by practitioners and developers.
- We implemented our concepts and used a prototype within an expert user study, where we evaluate the proposed performance criteria and state conclusions and lessons learned based on the user study's results.

The remainder of this paper is structured as follows: We discuss related work in the next section. In Sect. 3, we present our gamified E-Learning design aspects. Thereafter, we introduce the live keyboard performance evaluation concepts. Section 5 describes our user study. Finally, we provide a conclusion and point out directions for future work.

## 2   Related Work

Jordan [7] explores how to practice piano most effectively. In addition to training motor skills, he elaborates on the importance to practice both necessary psychological conditions and circumstances as well as excitement and concentration. This allows the mental state that is conducive to a performance situation to be easily retrieved when needed. As conclusion, mental practice for live performances may help avoid dropouts, for example, by practicing disrupting incidents that are otherwise only found in a real performance situation.

Margoudi et al. [11] conducted a study focusing on the learning of musical instruments through computer games, e.g., to motivate music students to learn. They concluded that popular audio-based games such as Guitar Hero or Rock Band, which are not primarily designed to impart knowledge, do not achieve significant learning outcomes. Margoudi et al. [11] also advise that the use of competition in design should be well considered, as it can have a negative effect on the user through competitive behavior. Tobias [14] specifies this problem:

Some users approach games competitively and thus would focus more on scoring points than on the actual musical performance.

Kim et al. [8] provide an overview of the current state of automated piano performance assessment in the context of music teaching. Their work concludes that the accuracy of existing performance assessment systems has not yet reached the level of a teacher. They also notice that machine learning models can be subject to the bias effect, i.e., biased and distorted by different musical genres and difficulty levels of pieces, through most available piano performance data sets, and thus might only be useful for a very specific tuple of $(genre, difficulty)$.

One conclusion drawn by Busse's study [3], which investigates the expressiveness of a piano performance, is that each user had a distinct style, as per different note placement values, note lengths, and velocities were measured. It can be concluded that a feedback system should leave adequate room for improvisation and musical expression when measuring accuracy and other parameters, so as not to push users too much in a certain direction. Also, to evaluate the musical expression of a user, rather short performance excerpts (e.g., a few bars) should be analyzed separately in order to be able to include the corresponding context of the situation (dynamics of the other musicians, required emotion, etc.) in the evaluation.

Work by Duvall [6] explores real-time performance evaluation using MIDI technologies with beginning piano students. He emphasizes the difference between qualitative and quantitative feedback and posits that detailed quantitative feedback is more interesting for the teacher of a beginning piano student. In contrast, short, significant, direct, and qualitative feedback is most useful to beginners themselves. To store information about real-time performances, Duvall [6] used a time division system, since concrete time stamps would impose too heavy a data load. Time division was based on tempo, with delta times stored for each occurrence of a note in relation to the time step currently being considered. Variance given for the preservation of musical expression was stated to be important. The work suggests 96 ticks to represent a quarter note. One challenge that arose during this work was recognizing and evaluating chords since associated notes would enter the system in different orders.

With the exception of Jordan-Miller's study [7], though not focusing on technological aspects, none of the studies focused on live musical settings. A number of further current studies exist that develop learning-based applications with gamification use or serious games for learning to play the piano with a wide variety of approaches [1,2,4,9,12,13]. These mostly describe the concepts and possible implementation approaches, but do not draw conclusions from empirical methods such as user testing. Also, most studies lack evaluating the musical expression, which is, however, elementary for the sound quality of music pieces. Finally, our literature research has shown, that general criteria for evaluating keyboard player performances in live situations are missing.

# 3   Worship Keys Performer

This section introduces WKP – a gamified E-Learning application for keyboard-ers in the context of church bands to practice live performances. We designed and implemented WKP and utilized it for applying our following keyboard performance evaluation concepts. The core design of WKP is based on five aspects:

*1) Visualizing a Live Situation:*

In order to simulate a live situation, such as a concert setting, we visualize such a situation including different actors. Among them is the user at the keyboard, but also other band members of a common rock band formation (drums, guitar, bass, and singers), speakers/preachers that can enter and exit the stages at different times, and the audience. An illustration is shown in Fig. 1.

**Fig. 1.** The image illustrates WKP's user interface while the user plays with the band.

Users can see information about the currently played song part and the corresponding chord sequence on a screen within the scene (Fig. 1 top right). The keyboard is displayed at the bottom of the screen (Fig. 1). Pressed keys are displayed in a dark color, notes held by the sustain pedal are colored in a slightly lighter color as long as the pedal remains pressed. Above the keyboard, sliders for the personal in-ear mix are displayed on the left side, and effect knobs for sound parameters are displayed on the top right side. To the right of the keyboard is a display that shows the velocity.

*2) Accompanying Band Music and Speaker Tracks:*

For generating the sound via the MIDI keyboard, we use an external sound generation by a digital audio workstation (DAW). This way, users can practice with their own keyboard sounds they would also utilize live. The same applies to other sound-modeling plug-ins, e.g., for reverb or shimmer. To simulate the rest of the band (drums, guitar, bass, and vocals), pre-recorded samples are used. An alternative implementation would be using MIDI signals and additional virtual instrument audio processor plug-ins (so-called VSTs) to make the approach more generic, however, since one VST is already running in the background for the keyboard, additional high-quality plug-ins will challenge the real-time performance of the application.

*3) Simulation of a Music Director:*

The music director (MD) communicates the musical journey over the show and keeps the band in sync. An MD is a core component to be simulated in a dynamic purpose-bound band context (e.g., such as church or wedding bands). Learning objectives for users are the understanding of common nomenclature and reactions to an MD's spontaneous instructions. The top-right screen (Fig. 1) is supposed to simulate planned songs and chord sequences. If a situation is simulated in which a song or chord progression is not known, it is instead announced by the MD while the screen remains off.

*4) In-Ear-Monitoring:*

An important part of live performances is the monitoring. The personal in-ear mix usually has to be set up by the musicians during the sound check or a preceding rehearsal. In WKP, the settings are shown at the top-left of the keyboard (Fig. 1) and can be adjusted by the user at all times.

*5) Disruptive Factors:*

During a live performance, various disruptive events can occur that can throw a musician off track. The main goal of simulating such disruptive factors is to avoid choking by experiencing similar situations and learning how to deal with them. Examples of disruptive factors we implemented in WKP are (a) Misplays of band members (e.g., a guitarist playing false chords or tones), (b) volume variances in the MD's announcements, (c) wrong announcements of the next parts by the MD, and (d) technical defects, such as MIDI software crashes, in-ear monitoring outage, or interfering noise.

## 4  Live Keyboard Performance Evaluation

We developed our performance evaluation concepts for WKP based on the findings of our literature research, design rationale, and a semi-structured interview with six domain experts. In contrast to applications we analyzed within our literature research, our performance evaluation is not based on a direct comparison of played keys and a fixed MIDI score. Instead, a played performance is examined for correctness using statistical means on the basis of multiple evaluation criteria and on how suitable the selected playing style and the sound settings used were in individual situations. This allows a user to develop creatively within the given framework (given scale, chord progression, dynamics, etc.). In this section, we first elaborate on the identified performance criteria for live keyboard performances, and thereafter we describe how we give our users feedback on their performance.

We propose evaluating the keyboard performance based on three *performance criteria* we identified: *correctness, playing style,* and *sound usage.* Each criterion is attributed a score during the analysis, which again is calculated from the scores of sub-criteria. We do not claim to present a finished or complete list of suitable performance criteria or sub-criteria but an initial set, based on our literature research and expert interview results, that serves as a foundation and a means to an end for investigating the possibilities and usefulness of gamified E-Learning technology for live musician practice.

**Correctness.** We measure *correctness* in WKP by means of three aspects – *chord confidence, tone confidence,* and *dropouts. Chord confidence* describes the ratio of correctly to incorrectly played chords. In addition to the correctness of the notes contained, playing at the correct time is also taken into account. For example, we can evaluate a chord as incorrect when a chord's bass note was not played within the first two ticks. Furthermore, it is checked whether notes necessary for the harmony were played either within the first two ticks or within its entire validity period. Thus, direct chords as well as quickly played arpeggios and chords fanned out into a melody can be recognized correctly.

The *tonal confidence* describes the ratio of correctly to incorrectly played notes of a scale. In quiet passages, wrong notes are particularly noticeable, for example in situations where a keyboarder accompanies a speaker. In a band situation with high dynamics, on the other hand, sporadic false tones are not as noticeable. For this reason, an acceptable percentage of off-scale tones is stored in the configuration.

At first sight, *dropouts* are simple situations when musicians stop playing even though they are obligated to, which is a serious performance error. However, measuring dropouts within our dynamic approach that is not based on comparing played keys with a fixed MIDI score is more challenging. To allow our users to play rhythmically in parts with medium to high dynamics, resulting in very short pauses in playing, there is a wider range of acceptability here than in quiet dynamics, where keyboarders have to fill the silence with a lot of acoustic space. The use of high reverb settings as well as the use of pad sounds increase the acceptance range in quiet passages, since more musical space is filled by evenly playing, and negatively noticeable pauses in playing occur less quickly. Concerning the score, it is also necessary to prevent competitively oriented users of gamified applications from taking advantage of not playing at all to achieve a high tonal confidence score (and thereby simply also not playing any wrong notes).

**Playing Style.** *Playing style* is evaluated based on the aspects *velocity*, *tightness*, and *texture*. We evaluate the concept of *velocity* dynamics by measuring if the average velocity in a sub-section of a song lies within suitable limits, where suitable is dependent on whether the section is a low or high dynamic part but also depending on the calibration of the piano VST and the MIDI keyboard. Furthermore, we take the number of outliers into account. So-called ghost notes are filtered out beforehand during the analysis of this criterion. These are notes that are played softly for rhythmic reasons and do not reflect the actual dynamics played. For identifying ghost notes, we utilize the ratio to the highest note played. The average of both ratios (average and strong outliers) is calculated, which then forms the velocity score.

We also identified the musical concept of *tightness* suitable to evaluate the overall *playing style*. The term comprises playing to the rhythm evenly and cleanly. For evaluation, the standard deviation (SD) of the mentioned *Delta-Times* of the played notes is calculated, whereby there is a tolerance limit that allows a margin for musical expression. If a player has a tendency to play all notes minimally earlier than other players, this does not carry any weight due to the relative consideration of the SD. Tightness is only important for parts with medium dynamics and above since arpeggios can be frequently used in quiet passages and cannot be evaluated using this criterion. Therefore, only parts in which tightness can be measured meaningfully are considered in the overall evaluation.

The concept of musical *texture* refers to the relation among simultaneous lines in the written music score and comprises the *height* and the *density* (the numbers of lines or the distance between them). We developed the following three rules based on the timbre descriptions of Bernays and Traube [1]:

1. At lower dynamics (e.g. in calm parts), fewer keys are played simultaneously, and at high dynamics, more keys are used. The average number of the keys played at the same time is calculated, whereby keys already pressed or held by the sustain pedal are not taken into account.
2. At lower dynamics, the keys are struck less frequently, and in high dynamics, more frequently. Strokes in the left hand (bass notes) are more responsible for the perceived dynamic than high notes in the right hand, which is why they are more important in the evaluation.
3. At lower dynamics, high notes are played primarily, and in the case of high dynamics, low notes are played more, especially in the bass. Simultaneous playing of low and high notes is interpreted as playing in the middle for the sake of simplicity.

We calculate the *texture* score from these three dimensions. Some playing styles are an exception to these rules of thumb. For example, parts played in half-time are played less frequently despite higher dynamics. We assume that, as part of a good *playing style*, a user follows two of these three rules. Thus, by following two of these rules, a maximum score of this criterion can still be achieved. If the disruptive factor *bass failure* occurred during a part, so that a player should nevertheless play low bass notes in a quiet part, for example, this is taken into account in the evaluation.

**Sound Usage.** We conduct the evaluation of *sound usage* through a keyboard's adjustment knobs for (1) *reverb*, (2) the ambient *pad*, and (3) *tone* control (timbre). Based on our interviews' results, we propose using reverb in quieter passages, particularly when the keyboard player accompanies alone. Thus, a higher reverb value influences *sound usage* positively. Similarly, When playing alone, a pad should be used to fill the soundscape, whereas it is an optional feature in parts of higher dynamics. We communicate this relation to the user by displaying the optimal range of the controller at the knob (see green ranges in Fig. 1) for the pad only when its use is explicitly recommended. For the tone control, limit values based on a part's dynamics and the *playing style* are taken into account for the evaluation.

**Overall Performance Score Calculation Usage.** The calculation of the individual scores is carried out with the following weightings:

*(1) **correctness** = 0.6 \* chord confidence + 0.4 \* tonal confidence*
*(2) **sound usage** = 0.$\overline{3}$ \* reverb + 0.$\overline{3}$ \* tone + 0.$\overline{3}$ \* pad*
*(3) **playing style** = 0.15 \* velocity + 0.45 \* tightness + 0.4 \* texture*
*(4) **overall** = 0.4 \* correctness + 0.3 \* sound usage + 0.3 \* playing style −
0.6 \* dropouts*

*Dropouts* are not directly included in the *correctness* of the performance but are deducted from the total score to a certain extent, for being a critical aspect of live performance. *Chord confidence* was rated as more important than *tonal confidence*, since individual off-key notes are less noticeable than chords played completely incorrectly. In terms of *sound use*, all three scores were treated equally. For *playing style*, the *velocity* has the greatest perceived influence. On the other hand, clean rhythmic playing (*tightness*) is a desirable ability, but it is less important than other factors in an overall performance.

### 4.1  User Feedback

We designed the performance evaluation system within our application based on (1) direct feedback at runtime and (2) overall performance feedback after a session. To give the users indications as to whether they are doing well or not while playing, direct feedback is given visually. If a user presses keys whose notes are not part of the played scale, they are clearly colored red (Fig. 1 at the keyboard keys). In addition, a shaking animation ensures that the player is more aware of the use of inappropriate tones. To help the player understand this basis for evaluation, valid settings for the *reverb*, *tone*, and *pad* effect controls are visualized by a green coloring of the acceptable range of values (Fig. 1 top right of the keyboard). The *sound usage* is illustrated based on the average velocity played by the user within half a second (Fig. 1 vertical bar on the right side of the keyboard). Again, a valid area of the bar is highlighted for guidance.

After a session, we provide users with a final performance feedback. Quantitative feedback is represented by diagrams and further qualitative feedback by text (Fig. 2). The quantitative overview is presented using a bar chart. Both the total scores of the three performance criteria (*correctness*, *playing style*, and *sound usage*) and their associated sub-criteria scores are shown (Fig. 2 bottom right screen). A tool-tip that appears when hovering over a column explains the respective evaluation criterion and its composition.

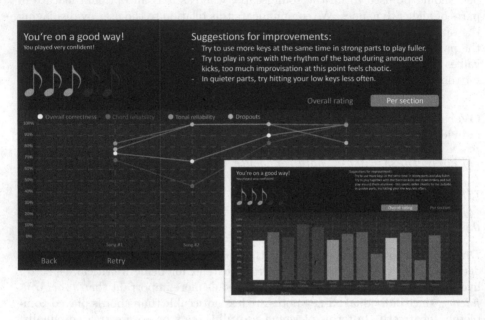

**Fig. 2.** The overview of the user's musical performance is shown by a bar chart for each performance criteria, accompanied by an overall score (also visualized by notes), as well as qualitative feedback on what could be improved.

A parallel coordinates chart is used to display the results for each passage of a session (Fig. 2) for one particular performance criterion. Each line represents a sub-criterion and each point represents a score value on the y-axis for a certain passage (y-axis). Finally, we also give our users qualitative feedback based on the performance criteria, for example, whether or not the users had a tendency towards using too much reverb, or bass notes were played too seldom or too often.

## 5   Expert User Study

We implemented our concepts in WKP and utilized it to evaluate our proposed performance evaluation within a moderated expert user study that involved 12 unpaid and voluntary participants (seven male and five female) between 23 and 66 years with Ø 34.0 and SD 11.1. All participants are or were part of a church band and are experts in the musical domain or sub-domains domain (e.g., music teacher, pianist, church musician, etc.). We classified their particular skills at the keyboard using the Dreyfus Model [5] so that two were classified as *advanced*, five as *competent*, three as *proficient* and two as *expert*.

After welcoming and informing our participants about the study procedure, they were asked to familiarize themselves with the provided MIDI keyboard and controller. Then we asked our experts to conduct multiple music sessions, each including both direct and overall performance evaluation. Finally, our participants filled out a questionnaire that included initial demographic questions and 15 items about the performance evaluation as follows (six open-ended questions (Q4, Q9, and Q12–15), one 7-point Likert scale (Q10), and eight 7-point semantic differential scale items (Q1–3, Q5–8. and Q11)). High values indicate a positive answer. Each test was conducted within the time frame of ˜90 min.

Q1 I found the direct feedback to be... intuitive – counter-intuitive
Q2 I found the direct feedback to be... fair – unfair
Q3 I found the direct feedback to be... accurate – inaccurate
Q4 What direct feedback could help you play even better?
Q5 I found the overall performance evaluation at the end of a session to be... understandable – not understandable
Q6 I found the overall performance evaluation at the end of a session to be... fair – unfair
Q7 I found the overall performance evaluation at the end of a session to be... accurate – inaccurate
Q8 I found the overall performance evaluation at the end of a session to be... too benevolent – too critical
Q9 What performance evaluation criteria were you missing?
Q10 The line charts with the individual evaluation criteria helped me to assess my skills.
Q11 I find the suggestions for improvement at the end of a scenario to be... helpful – not helpful
Q12 These features stood out to me positively.
Q13 These features stood out to me negatively.
Q14 I missed these functions.
Q15 Anything else you want to tell us or didn't fit previously?

The test setup apparatus, consisting of laptop, a MIDI keyboard, an audio interface, and corresponding cabling, is illustrated in Fig. 3.

## 5.1 Analysis

Figure 4 shows box whisker plots for the quantitative questions' results. For 8, with a scale from too critical to too benevolent, the optimum lies at the value 3. For the visualization, we mapped the data ($0 = 0$, $1 = 2$, $2 = 4$, $3 = 6$, $4 = 4$, $5 = 2$, $6 = 0$). The graph shows that all mean values of the individual questions are above the neutral value of the scale (3). With regard to the value distributions, Q8 shows the greatest deviation spans ranging from 0 to 6, and Q5, Q6, and Q11 the smallest, from 4 to 6. No outliers are present.

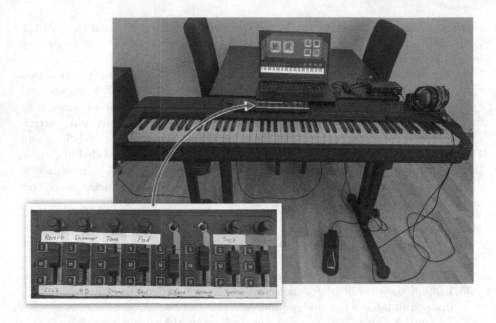

**Fig. 3.** The MIDI keyboard used was a Yamaha P-155 stage piano and the controller was a KORG nanoKONTROL.

We conducted Wilcoxon signed-rank tests for the individual questions to analyze how our concepts were rated compared to a neutral rating (3). With a threshold for statistical significance of 5%, all individual questions except for Q8, and Q10 show significant differences. Table 1 shows all p-values, arithmetic means, and SDs.

Concerning direct feedback, one participant described it as not intuitive for being distributed over different places on the screen. During the test, comments such as "You need to get the hang of it where to look" were stated. The green-marked optimal range of the knobs were addressed by "A matter of practice, but a good thing if you've got it". Eight of our participants used the knobs only sporadically while playing and a participant with much live experience noted that

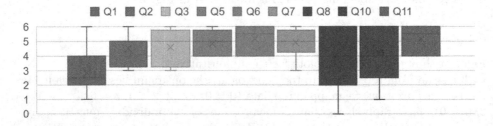

**Fig. 4.** A Box-whisker plot shows the results of the questions with quantitative answers.

**Table 1.** The table shows mean values, SDs, and output of the Wilcoxon signed-rank tests. All values are rounded to two or four decimal places respectively.

| Questions | Ø-values | SD | P-values |
|-----------|----------|------|--------------|
| Q1 | 2.83 | 1.47 | $p = 0.5755$ |
| Q2 | 4.50 | 1.09 | $p = 0.0066$ |
| Q3 | 4.58 | 1.16 | $p = 0.0069$ |
| Q5 | 4.83 | 0.83 | $p = 0.0022$ |
| Q6 | 5.17 | 0.94 | $p = 0.0022$ |
| Q7 | 4.92 | 0.90 | $p = 0.0034$ |
| Q8 | 3.67 | 2.23 | $p = 0.3077$ |
| Q10 | 4.17 | 1.75 | $p = 0.0549$ |
| Q11 | 5.17 | 0.94 | $p = 0.0022$ |

one would not use effect knobs as frequently as suggested by the application. Four participants noted that the use of reverb and tone was a matter of taste in many situations and that an evaluation should therefore be considered subjective. Five participants either did not use the velocity bar during the test. One suggested displaying the self-played velocity over a longer period of time, such as 10 s, to get a better sense of whether one is playing at the right dynamic on average. The coloring of the keys as well as the wobbling effect of the keyboard when playing an off-scale note was commented on positively by three participants. One suggested marking on the keyboard what the correct keys would have been if a chord was played incorrectly. Another idea for direct feedback was the coloring of correctly or incorrectly played chords on the chord screen.

The overall evaluation of a session was highlighted positively twice and described as unclear once. Both, self-criticism such as "Only four out of five marks?" and positive remarks were stated. One tester described the overall score as "very appealing to my ego and perfectionism". Two participants expressed the wish for a leaderboard to compare themselves with other players. The piano teacher commented on the evaluation with "the more critical the better!".

Table 2 shows the average values of our participants' performance evaluation scores as measured by our implementation. To validate our concepts, analyze which criteria may be treated too favorably or too critically, and draw conclusions about the influence of competence level, we divided our sub-criteria results into two groups after our participants' self-disclosed keyboard skills (A: advanced and competent, B: proficient and expert). Tonal confidence, dropouts, and velocity have a very high average value. Chord confidence and velocity are significantly higher for group B than A, whereby seven of nine values are absolutely higher for group B. Only *pad* and *dropouts* have higher values for group A.

Based on Affinity Diagrams, we also clustered our observations and the participant's comments. Three asked whether *chord confidence* would also allow chord extensions and were pleased with the implemented strategy. During the

**Table 2.** The table shows the average performance evaluation scores of our participants, where A represents advanced and competent and B proficient and expert participants, and the outcome of Mann Whitney U tests (rounded to two and four decimals respectively).

| Sub-criteria | A Ø-values | B Ø-values | P-values |
|---|---|---|---|
| Chord confidence | 0.55 | 0.64 | $p = 0.0384$ |
| Tonal confidence | 0.96 | 0.97 | $p = 0.2854$ |
| Dropouts | 0.97 | 0.955 | $p = 0.5919$ |
| Reverb | 0.59 | 0.62 | $p = 0.4882$ |
| Tone | 0.67 | 0.68 | $p = 0.8334$ |
| Pad | 0.52 | 0.49 | $p = 0.9358$ |
| Velocity | 0.79 | 0.85 | $p = 0.0470$ |
| Tightness | 0.56 | 0.64 | $p = 0.1612$ |
| Texture | 0.68 | 0.70 | $p = 0.4329$ |

tests, we observed that three of our participants increasingly kept the foot pedal pressed beyond chord changes and five did not play bass notes with their left hand while operating the effect knobs. Both factors interfered with *chord confidence*. Half of our participants found it difficult to comprehend the *dropout* sub-criterion. Particularly, the negative naming connotation of this sub-criterion was mentioned. Alternative suggestions included *continuity* and *no dropouts*.

Ten participants agreed with the qualitative suggestions during the overall feedback. One commented: "My shortcomings are well met". Another one noted that some general tips, such as using more reverb, do not make much sense for specific playing techniques: "Simply turning in more reverb does not always help, it also depends on how you play". The participant proposed to associate these suggestions with specific parts of a song only. As an idea for additional criteria, *creativity* was mentioned twice in connection with the evaluation of improvised melodies, rhythms, and chord sequences. Further input included the evaluation of the reaction to unforeseen disturbing factors, the momentum achieved, the tension arc, and the use of the pedal.

## 5.2   Discussion

The results show that the direct feedback was largely perceived as fair and correct, however, sometimes also visualized counter-intuitively. Possible reasons for this are the lack of a tutorial and the mentioned attention issues during play. One possible solution is to reposition all feedback UI elements near the chord sequence screen (Fig. 1 top right) so that there is less need to look around. Also, the development of different difficulty degrees might address this problem (one respondent's idea: optionally leaving the adjustment of the effect knobs to the game, so that effective use can be learned through observation and reduce distractions). The coloring of the keys and the wobbling of the keyboard were the most noticeable direct feedback and were well received.

The overall evaluation at the end of a session was perceived as comprehensible, fair, and correct, and overall fairer and more correct than direct player feedback after Tab. 1. The table also shows that our implementation tended to be perceived as rather too benevolent than too critical. The high SD (Q8), however, also shows that opinions differed greatly.

The validity of our proposed criteria and sub-criteria is supported by the higher average scores of group B (higher competence level), under the assumption that group B as the more experienced keyboard players will also perform better. The high *chord confidence* score might be attributed to the use of rather simple scales during the tests (C major and D major). The high mean value, the low SD, and various comments suggest that this sub-criteria should be evaluated more critically. The concept of *dropouts* was also criticized and should be re-formulated as a positive criterion. Again, the high mean value and the very low SD indicate a too benevolent evaluation. Although some participants largely ignored the reverb setting while playing, their scores were still mostly above 50%. This circumstance advocates a more critical evaluation of these ratios, making misuse more obvious. Some comments suggest that evaluating reverb and tone with exclusive reference to current playing dynamics is not always helpful. A possible solution would be to use the chosen playing style or technique as an additional reference to provide more specific feedback. No participant achieved a *tightness* score above 75%, which suggests that this sub-criterion can be evaluated somewhat more favorably. The higher mean score of more experienced testers supports the credibility of this criterion. Finally, the observation of different keyboard playing techniques suggests that these should be included in the evaluation of the *playing style*.

# 6   Conclusion and Future Work

In this work, we addressed a relevant aspect of serious games and gamified learning applications in the area of musical education: the evaluation of a user's musical performance within the game. We have introduced a set of soft-defined live keyboard performance evaluation criteria that also can be implemented in the example of a real-world software example (WKP). By means of the results of our expert user study, we can conclude that performance evaluation on a musically improvised performance is strongly dependent on the genre of music played, the band's means of application, and the available sound settings of the keyboard player. If these variables are defined, evaluation criteria and associated algorithms for correctness, playing style, and sound usage can be defined and for a specific use-case also implemented to statistically evaluate recorded MIDI performance data. The implementation of each algorithm in its own evaluation class provides an overview and enables the simple addition of further criteria.

Particularly, our implementation has indicated, that the proposed performance sub-criteria of *correctness* and *playing style* can be generalized well and, according to the study results, offer meaningful insight into the abilities of a keyboard player. However, we found that the significance of individual criteria depends strongly on the validity of the underlying configurations of our softly defined criteria, and also the hardware used. So actual configurations must be tweaked from case to case. Future work should focus on collecting a large amount of performance data from players of different playing levels and styles in order to then define appropriate fixed value limits or ranges. Notably, more work will focus on music language to set the algorithm feedback relevant to the style, and create different branches (e.g., church music, jazz, rock, classical, etc.).

In our use-case of church music bands, the evaluation of *sound usage* was perceived as diverse, highly depending on the church music experience of our participants. To give a player meaningful feedback in future work, here, the evaluation should not only look at the dynamics played and the band's playing style selectively but also take into account how it was played before and after so that effect control settings can be judged according to realistic standards.

Overall, the majority of our participants were happy being able to get any concrete feedback and suggestions on their live performance at all, which corroborates the relevance of future efforts to design gamified E-Learning technologies for live musicians. Besides the performance evaluation criteria as one major aspect of such technologies, we also suggest future work to focus on the actual gamified design, to make applications more fun and accessible. Also, since musical perception is still highly subjective, we take away from the user study that players should be informed that the feedback we give is based on an assessment of the musical language and may not reflect on their individual musical expression or emotion.

**Acknowledgements.** This publication was produced as part of the REQUAS qualification programme, which was funded by the German Federal Ministry of Education and Research in the context of the federal-state program 'FH-Personal' under the grant number 03FHP147A. The responsibility for the content of this publication lies with the authors.

# References

1. Bernays, M., Traube, C.: Expressive production of piano timbre: touch and playing techniques for timbre control in piano performance. In: Proceedings of the 10th Sound and Music Computing Conference (SMC2013), pp. 341–346. KTH Royal Institute of Technology Stockholm, Sweden (2013)
2. Brett, J., Gladwell, T., Xu, N., Amelidis, P., Davis, T., Gatzidis, C.: Developing games for the purposes of rote learning for keyboard and piano. In: 2020 IEEE Conference on Games (CoG), pp. 724–727. IEEE (2020)
3. Busse, W.G.: Toward objective measurement and evaluation of jazz piano performance via midi-based groove quantize templates. Music. Percept. **19**(3), 443–461 (2002)
4. Cui, K.: Artificial intelligence and creativity: piano teaching with augmented reality applications. Interact. Learn. Environ. 1–12 (2022)
5. Dreyfus, S.E., Dreyfus, H.L.: A five-stage model of the mental activities involved in directed skill acquisition. California University Berkeley Operations Research Center, Technical report (1980)

6. Duvall, D.C.: Real-time MIDI performance evaluation for beginning piano students. Ph.D. thesis, Clemson University (2008)
7. Jordan-Miller, R.: Mental skills training for a lower-advanced to advanced pianist. Ph.D. thesis (2010). Dissertation, University of Oklahoma
8. Kim, H., Ramoneda, P., Miron, M., Serra, X.: An overview of automatic piano performance assessment within the music education context. In: 14th International Conference on Computer Supported Education, pp. 456–474. SCITEPRESS-Science and Technology Publications (2022)
9. Lai, T.K.: Gamify piano project. Ph.D. thesis (2016). Outstanding Academic Papers by Students (OAPS). Retrieved from City University of Hong Kong, CityU Institutional Repository. http://dspace.cityu.edu.hk/handle/2031/8730
10. Learnfield GmbH: Skoove (2023). https://www.skoove.com. Accessed 10 Feb 2023
11. Margoudi, M., Oliveira, M., Waddell, G.: Game-based learning of musical instruments: a review and recommendations. In: European Conference on Games Based Learning, p. 426. Academic Conferences International Limited (2016)
12. Molero Marín, D.: HoloMusic XP: gamification-based system for teaching music and piano using mixed reality. Universidad de Castilla-La Mancha (2018)
13. Ritschel, H., Seiderer, A., André, E.: Pianobot: An adaptive robotic piano tutor. University of Augsburg (2020)
14. Tobias, E.: Let's play!: learning music through video games and virtual worlds, pp. 531–548. Oxford University Press (2012)
15. Yousician, Oy.: Yousician (2023). https://www.yousician.com/. Accessed 10 Feb 2023

# Javelin Throw Analysis and Assessment with Body-Worn Sensors

Philipp Niklas Müller[✉][iD], Sebastian Fenn[iD], and Stefan Göbel[iD]

Technical University of Darmstadt, 64289 Darmstadt, Germany
{philipp.mueller1,stefan_peter.goebel}@tu-darmstadt.de,
sebastian.fenn@live.de
https://www.etit.tu-darmstadt.de/serious-games

**Abstract.** In javelin throw, a discipline of athletics, the analysis and correction of throwing technique are essential components of training and competition and fundamentally contribute to the performance improvement of athletes. Motion analysis tools are sometimes used to support coaches, who may easily miss crucial details of the throwing movement due to high speeds. Existing tools for this purpose require a complex and location-bound experimental setup and do not operate in real-time due to their complexity. For this reason, they are often not practical in the context of training and competition. This paper presents a mobile system for real-time analysis and assessment of javelin throws utilizing body-worn sensors. The aim is to offer athletes and coaches a simple and location-independent method of evaluating relevant movement sequences in real-time. The system is based on key throwing movement parameters determined in collaboration with athletic coaches. It consists of four body-worn sensors at specific locations connected to a mobile device using Bluetooth Low Energy. The analysis of a throwing movement happens immediately after its completion on the mobile device and provides feedback on potential execution errors. The developed system is evaluated in a study of 28 participants divided into four performance classes and three different recording conditions. During each recording session, a professional coach was present to assess the accuracy of generated feedback. Our results suggest that the developed system provides helpful feedback on the javelin throw movement for all performance classes except beginners, in some cases even surpassing the accuracy of licensed coaches.

**Keywords:** Movement Analysis · Javelin Throw · Sensor Systems

## 1 Introduction

Fast movements can be challenging to follow and analyze with the human eye. For this reason, technological aids are increasingly used in the motion analysis of rapid sequences in sports. Currently, these rely primarily on video data, are often difficult to set up, and cannot be used in all settings such as specific weather conditions. Body-worn sensors for motion detection are gaining popularity and offer a cost-effective and easy-to-handle method for analyzing movements. This work

M. Haahr et al. (Eds.): JCSG 2023, LNCS 14309, pp. 36–49, 2023.
https://doi.org/10.1007/978-3-031-44751-8_3

explores the opportunities and limitations in analyzing and assessing throwing movements using body-worn sensors, focusing on the javelin throw.

In the javelin throw, an athletics discipline that has been part of the Olympic Games since 1908, the goal is to throw the javelin as far as possible after a run-up movement. The result of the javelin throw, the distance, is determined not only by the thrower's strength but primarily by the technical execution of the movement sequence. For this reason, its analysis and improvement are essential components of training and competition.

At this point, a coach typically analyzes throwing movements manually, sometimes using recorded video footage. In doing so, the coach may miss essential execution errors due to its comparatively high speed and complexity, the limited visibility of some parameters, or human error, depending on their experience and competence [19]. Whereas video footage can improve manual assessment by slowing down the movement, small body movements may still be concealed, which may result in execution errors being missed. Additionally, a suitably trained coach may not always be available to an athlete.

Therefore, we present a system utilizing body-worn sensors to analyze movement sequences of javelin throws and provide automated feedback. Coaches can use such a system to improve their analysis by providing data that may not be visible on video footage. Meanwhile, athletes can also use it to receive feedback and improve their technique when a coach is unavailable. To determine the applicability of the presented system for different performance groups and recording conditions, we conducted a study with 28 participants ranging from beginners to squad athletes.

## 2    Related Work

To our knowledge, no related work exists on the analysis of javelin throw movement sequences using body-worn sensors. We, therefore, divide the related work into two categories: Javelin throw analysis not limited to body-worn sensors and throw analysis using body-worn sensors not limited to javelin throwing.

### 2.1    Javelin Throw Analysis

Habbard et al. [8] present a system for the estimation of release conditions in the javelin throw using video footage. The system utilizes the video data to estimate throw conditions which are then graphically displayed and used to simulate the throw and subsequent flight of the javelin. This simulation is based on their previous work on optimal javelin flight trajectories and their simulation [7,9].

Elumalai et al. [5] present a system to track javelin throw athletes' physiological parameters such as blood pressure and heart rate for training purposes. Since physiological parameters alone are insufficient for the analysis of an individual javelin throw, they would have to be combined with sensor data such as presented by Lara et al. [13] for human activity recognition.

Särkkä et al. [17] present an approach to measure the release speed, launch angle, and flight path of the javelin using an inertial measurement unit (IMU) that was integrated into the tip of the javelin, augmented with video sequence data. Their system allows for estimating the attitude, position, and velocity of the javelin from the run-up to the point of landing. This data can then be utilized to analyze and compare different throwing techniques.

It is worth mentioning that none of the systems we could find in existing literature directly addresses the full-body movement during the run-up and the javelin throw.

## 2.2  Throw Analysis Using Body-Worn Sensors

Koda et al. [12] developed a method for estimating the three-dimensional trajectories of the arm and its orientation during the pitching motion in baseball. To this end, two IMUs were attached to the upper and lower arm of the athletes. Experimental comparisons with a conventionally used video-based analysis showed that the system could accurately determine the trajectory and orientation of the throwing arm. A similar conclusion was drawn by Boddy et al [2] when using the motusBASEBALL3 IMU attached to the elbow of the athletes. They compare the results obtained to those of a marker-based motion analysis of an optoelectronic measurement system. They conclude that the IMU can be used as a cost-effective alternative for capturing arm usage, shoulder rotation, and load metrics. In their review [14], Noh et al. conclude that IMUs are currently not widely used in the throw analysis of athletic disciplines. Examples of their usage include the discus throw [3], the hammer throw [18,19], and shot put [6].

## 3  Javelin Throw Movement Sequence

To design a system for the analysis of the javelin throw, it is necessary to define a correct javelin throw movement sequence and its key parameters that lead to an optimal throw, i.e., a throw resulting in the maximum throw distance for a given individual. For this purpose, we consulted professional athletic coaches, the official framework training plan of the German Athletics Association (DLV) [11], and the official World Athletics (WA) track & field book [15,16].

A javelin throw typically consists of between 11 and 15 steps and can be seen as a sequence of the following four movements (see Fig. 1): The cyclic part of the run-up, the acyclic part of the run-up, the throwing motion, and the follow-through. The follow-through can be ignored in the movement analysis as it has no direct effect on the resulting throw distance. The correct technical execution of the movement sequence is considered a major determinant of the launch speed. Thus the preparation for the throw during the acyclic run-up and the throwing motion itself are particularly relevant [11]. The following parameters are essential to enable an efficient transfer of energy to the javelin:

(a) Cyclic and acyclic run-up

(b) Throwing motion and follow-through

**Fig. 1.** Full motion of a javelin throw by Struder et al. [15].

- Sufficient upper body recline during the last step
- Sufficient hip engagement between the placement of the driving leg and the downward striking placement of the bracing leg
- No lateral bending of the trunk which reduces the energy transfer in the throw direction
- Javelin release angle between 34° and 38°, depending on wind velocity
- Javelin angle of attack with a maximum difference of 5° to the release angle
- Javelin tilt angle smaller than 10°
- Correct sequence of movement phases

In particular, the correct sequence of movement phases consists of the following movements in the correct order:

1. Penultimate step before the throw (bracing leg)
2. Impulse step (driving leg)
3. Hip engagement
4. Bracing step (bracing leg)
5. Start of the throwing motion
6. Release of the javelin

## 4  System Design

Our system consists of a hardware setup to record sensor data and a software system to analyze recorded movement sensor data. They were developed in conjunction as their requirements depend on one another.

## 4.1 Hardware Setup

Our hardware setup consists of four sensor boards, each equipped with an LSM6DSL [1] inertial measurement unit, connected to an Android smartphone using Bluetooth Low Energy (BLE). Inertial measurement units such as the LSM6DSL consisting of an accelerometer and a gyroscope are widely available, integrated into most modern mobile devices, and commonly used for activity recognition [4, 10, 14]. The sensor boards are carried inside the pocket of a sweatband as depicted in Fig. 2a.

We determined that the best sensor positions for our system are at the forearm of the dominant hand, at both ankles, and at the hip (see Fig. 2b). Each of these positions captures a specific part of the javelin throw: The throwing motion is captured at the dominant hand, individual steps at the respective foot, and the hip rotation at the hip. The thighs and upper arms were disregarded as sensor positions because they provided no relevant information we could not already observe at the ankles and lower arms, respectively. The non-dominant arm was also disregarded as its movement is not particularly relevant to the analysis. Using a Bluetooth Low Energy (BLE) connection, all four sensor boards send their recorded data to the connected Android smartphone in real time. To minimize the impact of recording and transmission issues on the movement analysis, the sensor data is first pre-processed on the smartphone. The pre-processing consists of the synchronization of data timestamps and interpolation of individual data if they are found missing.

(a) Sweatband with sensor board

(b) Sensor positions

**Fig. 2.** Sensor setup consisting of four sweat bands and sensor boards.

## 4.2   Movement Analysis

After consulting coaches about which parameters (see Sect. 3) would be of particular importance to them, we decided to exclude parameters that a human bystander or camera-based system can visually verify. These include the upper body recline, lateral bending, and the release, attack, and tilt angles of the javelin. We, therefore, focus on the correct sequence of movement phases and sufficient hip engagement.

Our empirical results suggest that the gyroscope provides no additional benefit to the movement analysis. Its peaks generally mirror the peaks in acceleration and therefore provide no additional value when determining when specific parts of the movement sequence occur. Meanwhile, we found its values too inaccurate when determining the total hip rotation during the throwing motion. Our system, therefore, uses accelerometer values exclusively.

**Sensor Orientation.** In most cases, the total vector length can be utilized and individual axis values do not need to be considered. However, to accurately capture the hip movement, the acceleration's direction is essential; thus, the orientation of sensor axes needs to be consistent to ensure consistent results. For this purpose, we ensured that during our recordings the orientation of sensors would always adhere to Fig. 3. In a commercial application, a calibration process could ensure that sensor axes are consistent between different recordings without relying on users to pay attention to sensor orientation.

**Throwing Motion.** In the first step, we determine when the javelin is released by finding the peak value of the acceleration vector length of the throwing arm. We also determine the start of the active arm motion by finding the last valley before the release time, which must occur after setting the impulse step. Since we determine the time of the impulse step in a later step, we can then determine whether the active arm motion has started too early. We found this way of determining the javelin release time and the start of the active arm motion to be accurate as long as the rough form of a throwing motion is respected. Lastly, we mirror the time span between the start of the active arm motion and the javelin release time to approximate the end of the throwing motion.

**Bracing Leg.** The time of the bracing step is determined by finding the last peak of the bracing leg's acceleration vector before the previously approximated end of the throwing motion. However, we found that sliding the bracing leg could sometimes be mistakenly counted as a step. Therefore, we additionally consider the second last peak and determine it as the bracing step if its value is at least 1.5 times as high as the last peak. The same is done for the penultimate step before the throw, starting at the time of the impulse step as determined in the next step.

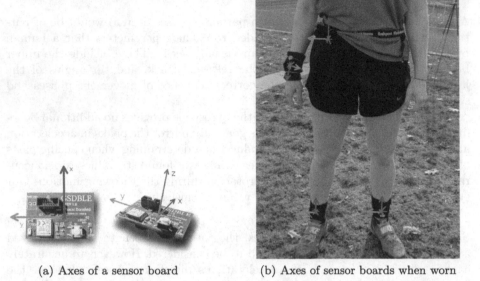

(a) Axes of a sensor board          (b) Axes of sensor boards when worn

**Fig. 3.** Orientation of sensor board axes.

**Driving Leg.** In this step, the time of the impulse step is determined akin to the time of the bracing step, using the diving leg's sensor data. However, instead of choosing the last peak before the approximated end of the throwing motion, the last peak before the start of the bracing step motion is taken instead. This is necessary because some athletes have the habit of lifting the driving leg off the ground again while setting the bracing leg. If not adequately accounted for, this can be erroneously detected as the impulse step.

**Hip Engagement.** Hip engagement is the smallest movement in the sequence and subsequently, the most difficult for a coach to identify. In this case, individual axes of the sensor at the hip must be considered as there is a simultaneous positive x-axis peak and negative z-axis peak when the bracing step is set. We find the time of this negative z-axis peak as the largest peak between the time of the impulse step and the javelin release time. We then attempt to find a positive z-axis peak between this time and the javelin release time. If no such peak exists, the hip engagement is considered insufficient.

**Assessment Generation.** In the last step, the data collected in the previous steps are combined to generate feedback for the athlete. The previously determined time stamps of key movements are assessed for the following execution errors:

1. No analysis possible
2. No hip engagement
3. Hip engagement before impulse step
4. Maximum hip engagement after bracing step
5. Bracing step after javelin release time

No analysis possible typically means that there was faulty or missing data and does not necessarily suggest an error in the execution of the javelin throw.

In addition to all found errors, the user is provided with the acceleration at the time of javelin release and three different periods that coaches considered to be important for their analysis: The time between the impulse step and hip engagement, the time between hip engagement and the bracing step, and the time between the bracing step and the release of the javelin. Figure 4 shows an exemplary analysis sheet created for a subject study participant. The center shows a plot of the recorded sensor data with time stamps for key movements of the movement sequence. Below the plot, you find the feedback as detailed above. In this example, no errors were found. Also included are images for each key movement taken from a synchronized video. The video data is recorded purely for evaluation purposes and is not used by our movement analysis system.

## 5 Subject Study

We conducted a subject study with 28 athletes (14 men, 14 women) between 18 and 25 years of age (20.2 years average), divided into four performance classes and three recording conditions (indoor, rainy outdoors, sunny outdoors). Three athletes participated twice each, once indoors and once outdoors, resulting in 31 datasets in total, each consisting of five recordings. The performance class of each athlete was determined by their respective coach using the following criteria:

– *Performance class 1* are beginners with little to no experience
– *Performance class 2* are athletes who have mastered the rough form, including mainly multi-event athletes who do not train javelin throwing intensively
– *Performance class 3* are athletes who have mastered the fine form, including javelin throwers competing in competitions and multi-event athletes that regularly carry out javelin throwing training
– *Performance class 4* are primarily squad athletes who have mastered the finest form of javelin throwing

Table 1 shows the participants divided by performance class and recording conditions. During each recording session, a supervisor and a coach were present. The supervisor introduced the athlete to the system and ensured that the sensors were worn correctly and that the sensor and video data were recorded without failures. The coaches knew the relevant types of execution errors as detailed in Sect. 4.2 and were instructed to evaluate the javelin throws performed as usual, documenting all the errors in the movement sequence they could find. A microphone was also used to record their comments during the recording session.

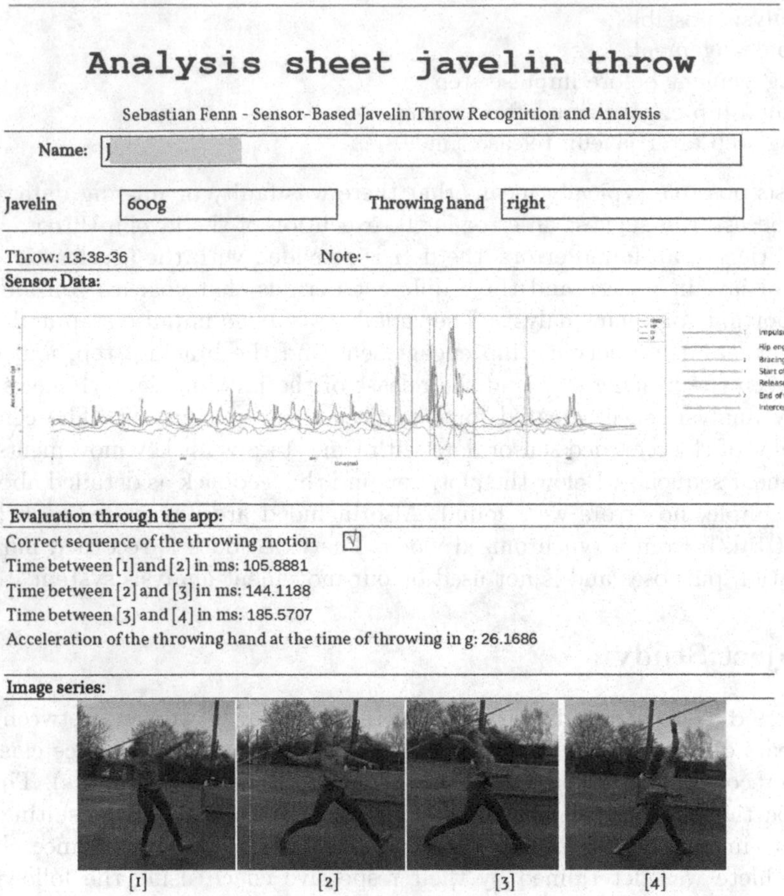

# Analysis sheet javelin throw

Sebastian Fenn - Sensor-Based Javelin Throw Recognition and Analysis

**Name:** J

**Javelin** 600g **Throwing hand** right

Throw: 13-38-36 Note: -

**Sensor Data:**



**Evaluation through the app:**

Correct sequence of the throwing motion ☑

Time between [1] and [2] in ms: 105.8881

Time between [2] and [3] in ms: 144.1188

Time between [3] and [4] in ms: 185.5707

Acceleration of the throwing hand at the time of throwing in g: 26.1686

**Image series:**

[1] [2] [3] [4]

**Fig. 4.** Exemplary analysis sheet generated during subject study.

After each recording session, our system feedback was compared with the coach's feedback. During this process, the coach had access to the recorded video data in a sports analysis application, allowing them to go through individual frames to better determine whether they or the system were correct. An assessment was considered correct only if all occurred execution errors were spotted and no execution error was erroneously indicated. Whenever the system missed an execution error, the coach was also asked to gauge whether the execution error would have been trivially found by a coach or a human observer, in general. Lastly, analysis sheets as shown in Fig. 4 were generated and sent to all athletes and coaches, asking for feedback on whether they would consider using such a system in practice.

**Table 1.** Participants divided into performance classes and recording conditions.

| Performance Class | Conditions | | | Total |
|---|---|---|---|---|
| | Indoors | Rainy | Sunny | |
| 1 | 0 | 2 | 2 | 4 |
| 2 | 3 | 4 | 7 | 14 |
| 3 | 3 | 3 | 3 | 9 |
| 4 | 3 | 1 | 0 | 4 |
| **Total** | 9 | 10 | 12 | 31 |

## 5.1   Results

Our system was able to analyze 150 of the 155 recordings. The five recordings that could not be analyzed had data missing from at least one of the four IMUs. Figure 5 shows the assessment accuracy of the system (left side, bright color) and the coach (right side, dark color) respectively. Our system surpasses the coach by 10.0% and 11.8% respectively for the performance classes 1 and 4, suggesting that it works comparatively well for athletes who have mastered at least the fine form. With 80.3% correct assessments, it is still usable for the performance class 3, although it is surpassed by 6.1% by the coach. In the case of performance class 1, the system underperforms, achieving only 65.0% compared

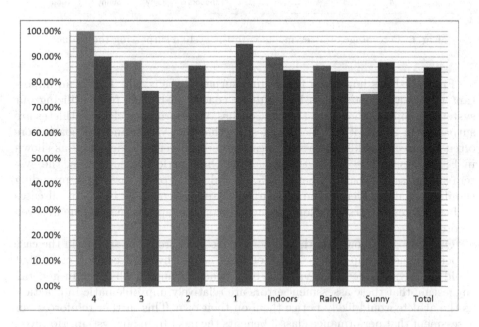

**Fig. 5.** Correct assessments: System (left side, bright color) vs. coach (right side, dark color).

to the coach's 95.0%. Whereas the recording conditions show a slight difference in assessment accuracy, that difference can be explained by the uneven distribution of performance classes between recording conditions. Overall, our system's 82.9% assessment accuracy is slightly surpassed by the coach's 85.7%.

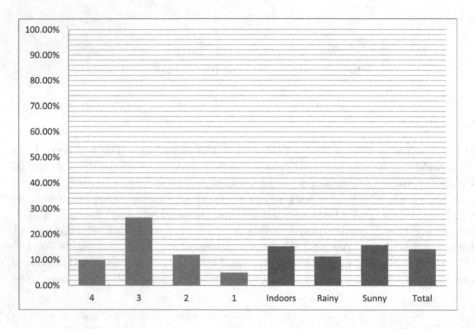

**Fig. 6.** Percentage of assessments with the system surpassing the trainer.

Figure 6 shows how often the system surpasses the coach. This is an important metric as it determines how often a coach can benefit from utilizing our system to improve their assessment. Coaches of performance class 2 athletes are surpassed in 26.5% of all cases, suggesting that the system and the coach were often incorrect for different recordings as their difference in accuracy as shown in Fig. 5 is only 11.8%. For the remaining three performance classes, the system surpasses the coach in between 5.0% and 12.1% of all cases, still providing significant value. Overall, the system surpasses the coach in 14.3% of all cases and therefore provides additional value to a coach in approximately one in seven recordings.

Our data also show that the inaccurate feedback from our system in the case of performance group 3 is in 75.0% of cases caused by an execution error that could be trivially identified visually by a coach or human observer in general, suggesting that these assessment errors are relatively unproblematic in practice, as the athlete would likely notice them on their own. This further reinforces our assessment that performance class 3 benefits the most from our system. However, it can also be argued that performance class 4 benefits the most, since the system tracked both execution errors made by its athletes during our subject study but not by the coach. This can be explained by execution errors at this performance level being very small and subsequently difficult to track.

Overall, our results suggest that the presented system can be effectively used to assess javelin throwing and assist training indoors and outdoors, especially when used as a support tool for a coach but also when used by experienced athletes themselves. It excels for performance classes 3 and 4, surpassing the trainer significantly. Meanwhile, it performs comparatively poorly for beginners who do not adhere to the rough form. Their movement sequences are often too far from a correct movement sequence that our system cannot accurately determine when key movements occur.

The athletes and coaches who participated in our study consistently described the system's feedback as positive and helpful. They suggested that it provided a new perspective on the javelin-throwing movement.

## 5.2 Limitations

Our subject study exclusively included young adult athletes between 18 and 25 years of age, as we expect these to be the main target audience for javelin throw assistance tools. Therefore, our results may not transfer to child athletes or adults over 25 years of age. Additionally, the limited number of subjects (28) does not allow for precise quantitative claims, although we believe that it is sufficient to show the potential benefit of our system. Lastly, we cannot compare our system's results to an objectively accurate ground truth, and thus our results rely on the accurate assessment of the athlete's respective licensed coaches.

## 6   Conclusions

In this paper, we assess whether body-worn sensors can be used to effectively analyze the javelin throw. For this purpose, we developed a system that uses exclusively body-worn inertial measurement units (IMUs) in conjunction with a smartphone to provide an almost real-time analysis of the javelin throw. In a subject study with 28 athletes of four different performance classes and their coaches, we evaluate our system for its assessment accuracy and compare it to that of a coach.

In our subject study, our system achieves an assessment accuracy of 82.7% which is only slightly lower than that of the coaches at 85.7%. For experienced athletes (performance classes 3 and 4), our system surpasses the coaches by more than 10.0% while falling behind significantly only for beginners. For the performance classes 2, 3, and 4, is more accurate than the respective coach in between 10.0% and 26.5% of cases, making it an effective tool to assist coaches of these performance classes. Overall, it received positive feedback from the athletes and coaches, suggesting that body-worn sensors could effectively be used for javelin throw analysis in practice, especially as an assistant to coaches.

We are currently researching the possibility of extending our system to other throwing movements such as the shot put or the discus throw. Furthermore, we are looking into hybrid systems that combine the advantages of body-worn sensors and mobile camera devices for a more thorough analysis of throwing movements. Other future work could include the inclusion of machine-learning aspects to allow for an easier adaptation to new requirements or movement sequences.

**Acknowledgments.** This research has been investigated by the Serious Games research group at TU Darmstadt and was partially funded by the German Federal Ministry of Education and Research under the research for civil security program (Grant Number 13N15547).

# References

1. LSM6DSL - iNEMO 6DoF inertial measurement unit (IMU), for smart phones and battery operated IoT, Gaming, Wearable and Consumer Electronics. Ultra-low power and high accuracy - STMicroelectronics. https://www.st.com/en/mems-and-sensors/lsm6dsl.html. Accessed 26 May 2023
2. Boddy, K.J., Marsh, J.A., Caravan, A., Lindley, K.E., Scheffey, J.O., O'Connell, M.E.: Exploring wearable sensors as an alternative to marker-based motion capture in the pitching delivery. PeerJ **7**, e6365 (2019). https://doi.org/10.7717/peerj.6365
3. Brice, S.M., Hurley, M., Phillips, E.J.: Use of inertial measurement units for measuring torso and pelvis orientation, and shoulder-pelvis separation angle in the discus throw. Int. J. Sports Sci. Coach. **13**(6), 985–992 (2018). https://doi.org/10.1177/1747954118778664
4. Cornacchia, M., Ozcan, K., Zheng, Y., Velipasalar, S.: A survey on activity detection and classification using wearable sensors. IEEE Sens. J. **17**(2), 386–403 (2017). https://doi.org/10.1109/JSEN.2016.2628346
5. Elumalai, G., Ramakrishnan, R.: A novel approach to monitor and maintain database about physiological parameters of (Javelin) athletes using internet of things (IoT). Wireless Pers. Commun. **111**(1), 343–355 (2020). https://doi.org/10.1007/s11277-019-06862-5
6. Gao, Z., Song, B., Liu, M., Song, G., Sun, W., Ge, Y.: Design and application of a multidimensional acceleration sensor for coaching of shot-put athletes. Sens. Actuat. A **149**(2), 213–220 (2009). https://doi.org/10.1016/j.sna.2008.11.029
7. Hubbard, M.: Optimal javelin trajectories. J. Biomech. **17**(10), 777–787 (1984). https://doi.org/10.1016/0021-9290(84)90108-8
8. Hubbard, M., Alaways, L.W.: Rapid and accurate estimation of release conditions in the javelin throw. J. Biomech. **22**(6), 583–595 (1989). https://doi.org/10.1016/0021-9290(89)90010-9
9. Hubbard, M., Rust, H.J.: Simulation of javelin flight using experimental aerodynamic data. J. Biomech. **17**(10), 769–776 (1984). https://doi.org/10.1016/0021-9290(84)90107-6
10. Höflinger, F., Müller, J., Zhang, R., Reindl, L.M., Burgard, W.: A wireless micro inertial measurement unit (IMU). IEEE Trans. Instrum. Meas. **62**(9), 2583–2595 (2013). https://doi.org/10.1109/TIM.2013.2255977
11. Killing, W., et al.: Jugendleichtathletik: offizieller Rahmentrainingsplan des Deutschen Leichtathletik-Verbandes für die Wurfdisziplinen im Aufbautraining. Philippka-Sportverlag, Münster (2011)

12. Koda, H., Sagawa, K., Kuroshima, K., Tsukamoto, T., Urita, K., Ishibashi, Y.: 3D measurement of forearm and upper arm during throwing motion using body mounted sensor. J. Adv. Mech. Design Syst. Manuf. **4**(1), 167–178 (2010). https://doi.org/10.1299/jamdsm.4.167

13. Lara, O.D., Pérez, A.J., Labrador, M.A., Posada, J.D.: Centinela: a human activity recognition system based on acceleration and vital sign data. Pervasive Mob. Comput. **8**(5), 717–729 (2012). https://doi.org/10.1016/j.pmcj.2011.06.004

14. Noh, S.F.A.A., Baharudin, M.E., Nor, A.M., Saad, M.S., Zakaria, M.Z.: A review of motion capture systems for upper limb motion in throwing events: Inertial measurement unit. In: IOP Conference Series: Materials Science and Engineering, vol. 670, no. 1, p. 012051 (2019). https://doi.org/10.1088/1757-899X/670/1/012051

15. Strüder, H.K., Jonath, U., Scholz, K.: Leichtathletik: Trainings- und Bewegungswissenschaft - Theorie und Praxis aller Disziplinen. IAAF athletics, Sportverlag Strauß, Hellenthal, neuauflage, 3, korrigierte auflage edn. (2017)

16. Strüder, H.K., Jonath, U., Scholz, K.: Track & Field: Training & Movement Science - Theory and Practice for All Disciplines = Leichtathletik: Trainings- und Bewegungswissenschaft - Theorie und Praxis aller Disziplinen. Meyer & Meyer Sport, Aachen (2023)

17. Särkkä, O., Nieminen, T., Suuriniemi, S., Kettunen, L.: Augmented inertial measurements for analysis of javelin throwing mechanics. Sports Eng. **19**(4), 219–227 (2016). https://doi.org/10.1007/s12283-016-0194-x

18. Wang, Y., Li, H., Shan, G.: Acquiring the distance data with inertial measurement unit in a wearable device for the training of hammer throwers. In: 2018 14th International Conference on Computational Intelligence and Security (CIS), pp. 492–495 (2018). https://doi.org/10.1109/CIS2018.2018.00117

19. Wang, Y., Li, H., Wan, B., Zhang, X., Shan, G.: Obtaining vital distances using wearable inertial measurement unit for real-time, biomechanical feedback training in hammer-throw. Appl. Sci. **8**(12), 2470 (2018). https://doi.org/10.3390/app8122470

# A Cross-Platform Graphics API Solution for Modern and Legacy Development Styles

Robert Konrad$^{(\boxtimes)}$ and Stefan Göbel

Serious Games Group, Technische Universität Darmstadt, Darmstadt, Germany
robert@konradpost.de, stefan_peter.goebel@tu-darmstadt.de

**Abstract.** The introduction of the Direct3D 12 and Vulkan graphics APIs has caused a big shift in how video games are developed. However, this shift has also brought about significant challenges, including increased complexity in graphics development and difficulty in supporting lower-end platforms like web browsers and older Android devices. As a result, many developers continue to rely on outdated APIs, despite their limitations.

To address this issue, this paper presents a novel software library that enables developers to seamlessly create applications using either a modern or a classic API style while simultaneously targeting all platforms, without additional effort. We provide a detailed analysis of the performance implications of each development strategy and effective tuning methods to optimize the library's performance.

Our approach is particularly important for serious games, as their target audience is used to the look of modern video games but does not necessarily own modern gaming hardware. By supporting lower-end devices, our software library enables developers to create serious games that can be accessed by a wider range of users, regardless of their device's age and processing power.

In summary, this paper offers a solution to the challenges associated with graphics development and cross-platform support, enabling developers to leverage the benefits of modern graphics APIs without sacrificing compatibility with lower-end devices.

**Keywords:** Cross-platform development · Graphics · GPGPU · Direct3D · Vulkan · Metal · OpenGL

## 1 Introduction

Serious Games like most software projects ideally run well on all widely used hardware and software platforms. But as with any video game using the graphics hardware efficiently across different platforms is a complex problem, requiring the use of complex and ever evolving APIs and incompatible, system-specific programming languages. The introduction of Direct3D 12 and Vulkan in 2015

M. Haahr et al. (Eds.): JCSG 2023, LNCS 14309, pp. 50–62, 2023.
https://doi.org/10.1007/978-3-031-44751-8_4

and 2016 respectively has made the situation even more difficult overall as those APIs represent a big shift in how graphics APIs work but older APIs are still relevant as to this day the new APIs cannot be used everywhere.

The most common solution to this problem is to use a game engine that besides providing a big number of various features for game development also solves the portability problem. But even the best-known game engines, developed by teams of hundreds of developers, struggle with supporting all platforms with Unreal deprecating support for web-browsers and Unity not officially supporting mobile browsers[1]. Serious Games in particular can have technical or market requirements that do not align with the priorities in the development of game engines which generally focus resources on supporting pure entertainment games.

Kore in C (in short Kinc)[2] is a development toolkit for developing games and other multimedia applications on the lowest possible level while not compromising on portability. Notably portability reaches further than what today's game engines typically provide. Kinc aims to provide an alternative for developers who prefer to have bigger control over the details of their software projects. As such it is not specifically aimed at Serious Games but also does not restrict itself to the necessities of common Entertainment Games, providing the options to optimize for more specialized needs like very broad portability or very small size.

The paper details work done for the Kinc project and in particular focuses on the aspects of providing portability across old and new graphics APIs (henceforth called legacy and modern APIs) and details the problem space from a technical perspective and from a market perspective.

## 2   Related Work

The actual graphics APIs that are in active use today are Direct3D 11 and 12, OpenGL and variations thereof like OpenGL ES and WebGL, Vulkan, Metal and WebGPU. The relevant intricacies of each API are discussed in a later chapter in terms of how they directly relate to the presented work it is of note that each of them does try or has tried to solve the cross-platform problem by itself but as of now each API is only available or updated on a subset of today's relevant software and hardware platforms which unfortunately transforms them from a solution into problems.

Every multi-platform game engine is confronted with the problem of targeting multiple graphics APIs. This problem is typically handled in the very core of a game engine (hence the name of our toolkit) with all other functionality being layered on top of it. Game engines can however allow themselves to be sloppy in this work as this code only has to support the feature set of one engine and it is not a serious problem when some aspects of handling the differences between the graphics APIs leak into higher levels of the codebase.

---

[1] https://docs.unity3d.com/Manual/webgl-browsercompatibility.html.
[2] https://github.com/Kode/Kinc.

Many other projects do exist that try to directly solve the problem of cross-platform graphics programming, the most well-known of which are bgfx[3], gfx-rs[4] and sokol[5].

Similar projects but with a more specific focus of mapping existing graphics-APIs to each other are Google's ANGLE, Microsoft's D3D11On12 and MoltenVK. These projects implement a legacy graphics API on top of another legacy graphics API, a legacy graphics API on top of a modern graphics API and a modern graphics API on top of another modern graphics API. Notably absent however is an implementation of a legacy graphics API on top of a modern graphics API, which is a focus of this paper.

## 3   Serious Games and the Software/Hardware Ecosystem

Big video game productions primarily or even exclusively use specialized distribution channels that were setup specifically for games. PC games are sold on platforms like Steam and GOG and video game systems like a PlayStation 5 can be seen as a video game distribution platform in itself. While some platforms like Steam have opened up over the years, most still require a certification process that companies have to go through for any game they want to release. These processes are not necessarily open for Serious Games as properties like financial viability and technical experience with video game consoles are assessed. This is just one example of how distribution of Serious Games differs compared to the distribution of the latest Call of Duty.

Smaller productions often concentrate on distribution platforms like Google Play, Apple's App Store and web browsers. This opens up a much broader market but the hardware and software eco-system is much less mature with very old hardware still being in use and graphics drivers not necessarily being up to date. These issues can be even more pressing when software is not targeted at gamers which are used to handling hardware and driver problems on their side to some extent.

Targeting older hardware poses specific challenges in graphics programming. The chips that drive the graphics (commonly called GPUs for Graphics Processing Units) vary greatly in how the individual hardware works and outside of game console programming a driver layer runs on top of it that tries to unify and abstract how different GPUs are accessed. Abstractions however tend to leak details of underlying layers in various ways and for graphics APIs performance characteristics in particular are leaking which can be characteristics of the hardware or the driver or some combination of both. An interesting side-effect that can be witnessed based on this is that Nvidia and AMD regularly release driver updates to concede with big game releases to provide specific optimizations for those titles. The driver packages are also getting surprisingly complex with Nvidia's current driver package being bigger in size than Windows XP.

---

[3] https://github.com/bkaradzic/bgfx.
[4] http://gfx-rs.github.io.
[5] https://github.com/floooh/sokol.

Graphics API design advanced to better handle this situation and in particular about eight years ago a cut across the industry started to happen that fundamentally shuffled around how GPU APIs work and in 2023 this finally also arrived in web browsers via the new WebGPU API.

While big parts of the games industry can now ignore older graphics APIs as they can expect their customers to use fairly up to date hardware and drivers or even dedicated gaming devices, Serious Games still have many years ahead of them during which they will have to support old graphics APIs so they can reach a large enough audience - especially with distribution channels for higher end systems often being cut off.

## 3.1   The Software Ecosystem

In 2013 AMD introduced a new graphics API called Mantle that specifically was not aimed at adding new features but to provide a more efficient programming model with the intention of making drivers simpler and achieving more reliable performance. This called a ripple effect in the industry with Metal in 2014, Direct3D 12 in 2015, Vulkan in 2016 and finally WebGPU in 2023 all following a very similar approach.

These new APIs require relatively recent hardware and they also require updated graphics drivers. Driver updates though are often unnecessarily restricted in various ways. In Android, iOS and macOS drivers are bundled with the operating system and only recent hardware receives operating system updates, especially for Android devices. On iOS even web browser updates are restricted by operating system updates, further slowing down the adoption of new features on top of all the other factors that already caused the release of WebGPU to happen seven years after the release of Vulkan.

All of this created a market that is currently split between the new graphics APIs and the old graphics APIs and all of the following APIs are still in wide use.

Direct3D 10/11
> Introduced in 2006 and 2009 with Windows Vista and Windows 7 respectively, those new versions of Direct3D were a major rework of earlier versions and were only supported by Windows Vista and later [1].
> Notably Direct3D 11 introduced support for compute shaders. It also added support for tessellation shaders after Direct3D 10 already added support for geometry shaders. Support for these shader stages was not widely adapted and never implemented for Apple's mobile devices. Geometry and tessellation shaders have now been supplanted by mesh shaders in Direct3D 12, Vulkan and Metal.
> As discussed in Sect. 4, Direct3D 10 stopped supporting free changes to rendering state and instead supported a set of state objects that can be created and made active.

Direct3D 12

Direct3D 12 was another major change of the API that switched it from a legacy style API to modern style API. Microsoft also provides its own implementation of a legacy API on top of a modern API with 11on12 but not for the opposite.

Metal

Metal is a graphics API introduced by Apple solely for iOS and macOS [2]. While meanwhile support for intel and AMD was added after Apple also moved to exclusively using their own GPUs for Macs, with Apple switching all of their devices to use their own graphics hardware, Metal can now be seen as an API just for one series of hardware, in that sense being quite similar to how graphics APIs on consoles work.

OpenGL

OpenGL is an API that goes back many years, being introduced in 1992 - and even further as the initial version of OpenGL was based on an even earlier API called IrisGL [3]. Major changes were introduced in the early 2000s when OpenGL moved to utilize programmable shader pipelines. As of now development of OpenGL has mostly stopped despite initial intentions of keeping it around as an easier to use alternative to Vulkan.

OpenGL ES

OpenGL ES is a variation of OpenGL for smaller devices with slight changes to the APIs and its own version numbers [4]. The interface fundamentally stayed the same but several restrictions were introduced as well as support for lower precision data types. While further development on OpenGL ES stopped, it continues to be available on all Android devices. For iOS on the other hand OpenGL ES was deprecated - notably long before its last version so that features added to later versions of OpenGL ES like support for compute shaders never arrived on iOS.

WebGL

WebGL is closely based on OpenGL ES with WebGL 1 being based on OpenGL ES 2 and WebGL 2 being based on OpenGL ES 3.

In the Windows versions of Chrome and Firefox the implementation of WebGL is based on ANGLE, itself being an implementation of OpenGL on top of Direct3D 9 and 11. Together Chrome and Firefox represent a very high percentage of the browser market on Windows, Linux and Android as most other browsers are based on Chrome, which even includes new versions of Microsoft Edge.

Chrome and Firefox are also widely used on macOS but its default browser is Safari. On iOS only Safari is important as other browser implementations are prevented by disallowing the code execution of runtime-allocated memory - a fundamental feature for fast JavaScript execution using just in time compilation. While programs called "Google Chrome" and "Mozilla Firefox" do exist on iOS, they are just UIs on top of the Safari browser engine. This unfortunately restricts iOS to the Safari feature set, that is often lacking behind many years.

Vulkan

AMD introduced a new GPU API called Mantle in 2013. Notably AMD provided the GPUs of most of the game consoles of the time, therefore having experience with providing custom GPU APIs that are actually very widely used. Vulkan was built based on Mantle but adjusted to run on non-AMD GPUs as well. It became a formalized standard in 2016 and Vulkan drivers are available for Windows, Linux and Android [5]. Vulkan and Direct3D 12 are surprisingly similar with the main difference being that Vulkan supports render passes, which are important for deferred rendering hardware that is widely used in mobile hardware to reduce the reliance on fast memory.

WebGPU

WebGPU is a new API that as of 2023 has just had its initial public release with the latest Windows version of Google Chrome. Work for supporting WebGPU on more platforms in Google Chrome is of course underway as is work for support in Firefox and Safari. While the work in Firefox seems to be far along it is questionable when support in Safari will arrive - basing predictions on Apple's track-record with WebGL it would still be many years away, potentially being a major hindrance in adopting new graphics APIs. WebGPU is in its feature set similar to the initial versions of Metal, Vulkan and Direct3D 12 as it is designed to also work on top of exactly those [6].

Video Game Consoles

Consoles classically provide their very own graphics APIs. It is a very different problem space as only a single piece of hardware needs to be supported, making a driver ecosystem unnecessary and allowing the distribution of low-level software updates as part of the games. The specifics of any of these console specific APIs are unfortunately confidential.

## 3.2   Market Situation

As of May 2023, the Android Dashboard[6], which collects data from devices accessing Google Play, which is Google's online store for Android devices, shows that 15% of Android cannot yet use Vulkan which can consequently be a very significant percentage of a target group that is less likely to regularly update their tech gadgets than the overall average.

Concerning browsers, Google Chrome is automatically kept up to date on Android devices. As of now Google Chrome for Android does not support WebGPU but once it does, likely a large percentage of Android devices will quickly get access to it.

If the browser situation on Android develops as positively as expected in terms of WebGPU support, this will likely represent a situation that is reversed to what can be found for Apple's iOS devices. On the system API level, the Metal API that was introduced in 2014 is now very widely available with statistics by Roblox from December 2021 seeing it at $99,9\%$[7]. On the other hand, Apple

---

[6] https://developer.android.com/about/dashboards.

[7] https://gist.github.com/zeux/cc7be14916e36c51eb56fb7ed372206b.

tends to lack far behind in supporting the latest features in its Safari browser. WebGL 2 was first supported in Safari 15, which released in September 2021, compared to Chrome which supports it since January 2017. Interpolating from here WebGPU support in Safari can possibly be expected in 2027 or 2028.

The situation is not ideal on larger devices either, especially with many laptops not allowing installs of up-to-date graphics drivers and very old devices still being in use as old computers can still be fast enough for many use cases. Steam lists only 2023 of PCs as being able to run Direct3D 12 in their April 2023 hardware survey[8].

## 4    Efficient and Portable Graphics Implementation

Basing the low-level graphics abstraction can be based on modern or legacy APIs and as long as both kinds of APIs have to be supported both strategies have varying upsides and downsides. Following up is a look at the major differences and the consequences of either strategy for each of these differences.

### 4.1    Efficiency Features

The interesting aspect of the new graphics APIs in terms of cross-platform support is that the primary features are not concerned with adding new functionality but with improving efficiency and reliably of performance characteristics. Following up is a closer look at the most important of those features with a discussion of how each of them can be mapped from a modern API to a legacy API and vice versa.

### 4.2    Uniform Data

Graphics-APIs provide a plethora of options for binding data that is constant across draw calls. The actual process of binding data used to consist of querying individual variable names and then setting the data using one call for each variable. Later versions of Direct3D and OpenGL added the option to update a whole structure of variables all at once. Modern APIs always work like that and therefore all APIs are fundamentally aligned in how uniform data can be updated - unless support for WebGL 1 is still required to support older Apple devices. In this case a loop through a data struct can be used to set the struct values variable by variable. The opposite procedure is also possible as partial data-updates can be used to update singular variables inside of a struct in newer APIs.

More advanced features of uniform data handling in modern graphics APIs are directly linked to its handling of data-synchronization and are therefore discussed in the following sub-section.

---

[8] https://store.steampowered.com/hwsurvey/Steam-Hardware-Software-Survey-Welcome-to-Steam.

## 4.3    Data-Synchronization

In legacy graphics APIs synchronization of data-updates between the CPU and the GPU is handled automatically. When writing to a vertex-buffer from the CPU while it is still in use by the GPU, the driver will apply a strategy to hide that problem and allow the writes. Typically, it will either create a shadow-copy of the vertex-buffer which has the downside of taking up more memory or it will stall until the GPU finishes the work which if of course detrimental to performance. Drivers commonly employ custom heuristics to decide on the specific strategy. Unfortunately, those heuristics are hidden from the programmer and can vary wildly between different GPUs and graphics drivers which can make it hard to optimize code to run fast on all systems. This is also one of the heuristics that driver vendors typically tweak specifically for important applications.

In modern APIs this process is instead entirely manual which makes it harder to implement data-handling initially but makes it much easier to optimize it for all platforms as the performance characteristics are reliable and do not require testing on a big collection of different hardware [7].

When running a legacy API on top of a modern API, strategies very similar to what legacy API drivers do have to be employed. An advantage compared to drivers is that application authors can tweak values manually to adjust them to the needs of the application - like a value for how many shader-copies to create maximally and whether those copies should be created initially or on demand. Essentially application authors can build in the tweaks by themselves that driver authors build in for the applications they consider important.

Running a modern API on top of a legacy API is trivial for data-synchronization - synchronization-functions are simply not implemented. This results in a situation very similar to programming a legacy API directly but the advantages of using a modern API unfortunately disappear.

Some modern graphics APIs also support more advanced features like embedding small amounts of data in the GPU command-stream, thereby automatically synchronizing those data-updates with other GPU-commands. This cannot be directly implemented in legacy APIs and needs to be emulated using regular data-binding methods. This is a potential performance pitfall as there is no way to tell when a driver can optimize data-updates using similar methods.

## 4.4    Pipeline State Objects

In OpenGL every piece of rendering state is setup with a separate function call. This is on the one hand error prone because it is easy to forget that one particular piece of rendering state was still active and possibly set to an unfortunate value. On the other hand, it is easy to use and very flexible - if only one piece of state needs to change between draw calls this results in one function call and consequently the changes required to be executed by the driver can also be very small. However, this is not always the case and a single state-change can actually require a recompilation of all shaders used in following draw calls. It is up to the hardware vendor to decide how different pieces of rendering state are implemented and they can decide to make it a switch or integrate it into the shader instructions. The dynamic nature of rendering state in OpenGL has led to the situation that drivers try to defer a lot of work until actual draw-calls are executed because only then all information has to be present that might be needed to decide how to exactly compile the bound shaders.

All modern APIs use the concept of pipeline state objects which sum up all rendering state, combined with a set of shaders and the necessary input layout for the shaders, into a single object which is then compiled. This was done to allow application developers to specify themselves when any shader compilation takes place. Notably though this has more recently come under scrutiny as it can lead to very big amounts of PSOs in big projects that take a very long time to compile. An extension for Vulkan was recently published that again allows to change rendering-state piece by piece.

Using a PSO-API on top of singular state-changes is simple, as when making a PSO active the implementation can directly iterate and set all state. This procedure isn't even as inefficient as it may appear because as mentioned earlier, legacy APIs tend to defer actual work until a draw-call happens.

When running an OpenGL style on top of a modern API the situation becomes however very complicated and would re-introduce the same random compiles so known to modern APIs. Direct3D 11 though already uses an API that is very close to PSOs, just splitting it up into several state collection objects. For these reasons Kinc uses PSOs for both its legacy and its modern API.

## 4.5   Multithreaded Command Submission

A fundamental feature of modern GPU APIs is better support for utilizing multi-core CPUs, primarily by means of recording GPU-commands simultaneously from multiple threads. On legacy APIs commands for the GPU are generated directly via function calls ala drawTriangle and these calls do not tend to be thread-safe. Modern APIs instead provide a structure representing a list of commands and multiple of those lists can be recorded and prepared from multiple threads. Finally, they are stitched together on a single thread and submitted but the bunch of the work can be distributed across multiple cores this way - and work has to be done because all of the commands have to be converted into data-structure that can be transferred to the GPU and executed by its command-processor but the final submission of these commands is then a relatively simple task.

When implementing a legacy API on top of a modern API this can simply work on top of a single command-list. A second command list can often be useful for implementing features that are implicit in legacy APIs independently of the primary list, like the transfer of data from CPU memory to GPU memory or the handling of framebuffer-flips. Care has to be taken for when to submit the command-list as it has to work together with the mechanisms for synchronizing data to be efficient. Usually, it will make sense to submit the command-list directly after every draw-command but it can of course be tweaked further for the application at hand.

When implementing a modern API on top of a legacy API clearly the actual GPU-API calls have to happen from a single thread as required by the API. A data-structure has to be implemented to collect commands and a procedure that iterates over that structure and does actual graphics-API-calls based on the collected data. This is clearly overhead compared to simply doing the calls directly but unavoidable to serve applications which make use of the threading-features. The overhead can however be minimal if the application is otherwise efficient in how its command-submission works. If that is the case the multi-threaded command collection will run quickly as it only has to do minimal work on the graphics-API-side. The actual command-calls can also happen with little overhead as traversing a tightly packed array of command-structures is quick compared to doing any actual driver-work.

## 4.6  Summary

When purely looking at the performance features, using a legacy API or a modern API is both viable, no matter what APIs a program finally has to work on and both strategies can be used without major performance problems on top of the performance problems inherent to legacy APIs. If the programming team is comfortable with it, it is consequently advisable to already use a modern API even if it has to run on top of a legacy API. It does not pose a performance regression and it provides new options once legacy APIs become less important.

## 4.7  Functionality Features

While it is true that the new GPU APIs were primarily focused on efficiency in their design a lot of features have also been added that cannot feasibly be worked around on older APIs and have to be considered.

## 4.8  Compute Shaders

Compute shaders also have relatively general performance advantages by providing a local cache and making it easier for GPUs to schedule the work with requirements for how to work has to be grouped being relaxed for example thanks to the absence of instructions requiring derivatives [8]. Compute shaders can also be scheduled to run in parallel to any other work while other shader-types do their work on after another.

Compute shaders were already implemented in Direct3D 11 and OpenGL but are noticeably absent in all versions of WebGL and in the latest versions of OpenGL ES supported on iOS.

## 4.9  Bindless Resource Access

Modern APIs allow shaders to select themselves what textures or other GPU-objects to use dynamically, which can simplify and speed up rendering [9,10].

This functionality unfortunately cannot be emulated and is in fact not even available in all systems that support Vulkan and is therefore only exposed as an extension. On the other hand, an Nvidia-extension for OpenGL is available [11]. A possible workaround to using bindless access are big lists of if-else-constructions but the number of textures that can be bound classically is very restricted and if-else-constructs can lead to large amounts of textures being sampled even when only one is ultimately used.

## 4.10   Raytracing

Going beyond just new APIs, raytracing is now supported in hardware on some GPUs and the functionality is exposed in Direct3D 12 and Vulkan. Modern GPUs also provide general features to make raytracing more feasible performance-wise, notably some of the very latest models avoid divergence in shader-execution by dynamically re-bundling shader-waves. Compute shader-based implementations do exist [12]. Notably CryEngine supports Raytracing in compute shaders as do the drivers for Nvidia's 10x0 series of GPUs. In the latter case this can directly be compared to the hardware implementation of the following generation of graphics chips. It can be feasible for smaller use-cases but it has to be kept in mind that the developers at CryTek and Nvidia can likely optimize a raytracing implementation much further than most developers would be able to and with the big performance jumps seen in the latest two generations of Nvidia's hardware following that (the 30x0 and 40x0 series) there is doubt in the comparable viability of computer shader implementations even when taken care of by the biggest experts in the field.

## 4.11   Mesh Shaders

Mesh shaders are a new concept that is intended to replace geometry shaders and tessellation shaders, roughly based on work that was done to build geometry pipelines using compute shaders [13,14]. Notably support was recently added to Metal and Apple's GPUs - neither of which ever supported geometry or tessellation shaders. Wide support for older devices is many years away but based on the earlier work to use compute shaders for a similar implementation, more widely usable implementations are feasible. A major hindrance is however the web-platform as it only just now gained support for compute shaders via WebGPU.

## 5   Conclusion

Modern graphics APIs make development easier for big and experienced development teams by providing more reliable performance which is a key aspect for a robust and fun game release. When concentrating on up-to-date hardware these teams can fully focus on working with these APIs. But smaller or more specialized teams as they can commonly be encountered in the Serious Games industry have a need to target a wider market, in particular to reach non-gamers. In this space older graphics APIs are still relevant and the overall fragmentation into very different APIs poses a technical challenge. Our paper detailed solutions to these problems and the pitfalls that need to be avoided.

The Kinc project which this paper is based on already provides implementations of all the aforementioned aspects, is open source and is actively used on all of today's GPU-supported platforms, from mobile web browsers to video game consoles. It is successfully used in video games such as CrossCode[9] as well as video game development tools like Armory3D[10] or RPG Playground[11].

Portable graphics programming is an ever-expanding problem space as long as the graphics APIs themselves are ever expending. On the other hand, some problems disappear with old hardware becoming obsolete and getting replaced. As such further work will be needed as long is this is the case and the second part of the fourth chapter can also be seen as a preview of what aspects of graphics APIs might require more work to facilitate high portability of graphics code in the future.

**Acknoledgements.** The investigated research of this contribution partially has been funded by strategic invest of the Serious Games group at TU Darmstadt in the context of its research activities for the creation/authoring of Serious Games.

# References

1. Blythe, D.: The direct3D 10 system. In: ACM SIGGRAPH 2006 Papers, pp. 724–734 (2006)
2. Sandmel, J.: Working with metal-overview. Apple WWDC (2014). https://developer.apple.com/videos/wwdc/2014
3. Frazier, C., Leech, J., Brown, P.: The OpenGL graphics system: a specification (2016)
4. Munshi, A., Leech, J.: OpenGL ES common profile specification version 2.0.25 (2010)
5. The Khronos Vulkan Working Group: Vulkan 1.0.48 - A Specification (2017)
6. Kenwright, B.: Introduction to the WebGPU API. In: ACM SIGGRAPH 2022 Courses, pp. 1–184 (2022)
7. Lustig, D., Martonosi, M.: Reducing GPU offload latency via fine-grained CPU-GPU synchronization. In: 2013 IEEE 19th International Symposium on High Performance Computer Architecture (HPCA), pp. 354–365. IEEE (2013)
8. Bilodeau, B.: Efficient compute shader programming. In: Presentation, Game Developers Conference, San Francisco, CA (2011)
9. Pettineo, M.: Using bindless resources with DirectX raytracing. In: Marrs, A., Shirley, P., Wald, I. (eds.) Ray Tracing Gems II, pp. 257–279. Apress, Berkeley (2021). https://doi.org/10.1007/978-1-4842-7185-8_17
10. Abdellah, M., Eldeib, A., Owis, M.I.: GPU acceleration for digitally reconstructed radiographs using bindless texture objects and CUDA/OpenGL interoperability. In: 2015 37th Annual International Conference of the IEEE Engineering in Medicine and Biology Society (EMBC), pp. 4242–4245. IEEE (2015)

---

[9] http://www.cross-code.com.
[10] https://armory3d.org.
[11] https://rpgplayground.com.

11. Bolz, J.: OpenGL bindless extensions. NVIDIA Corporation (2009)
12. García, A., Ávila, F., Murguía, S., Reyes, L.: Interactive ray tracing using the compute shader in DirectX 11. In: GPU Pro 360, pp. 117–140. AK Peters/CRC Press (2018)
13. Carvalho, M.Â.A.D.: Exploring mesh shaders. Doctoral dissertation (2022)
14. Peddie, J.: The sixth era GPUs: ray tracing and mesh shaders. In: Peddie, J. (ed.) The History of the GPU-New Developments, pp. 323–360. Springer, Cham (2023). https://doi.org/10.1007/978-3-031-14047-1_7

# Theoretical and Design Aspects

# A Model for Mapping Serious Game Mechanics to Pedagogical Patterns

Jamie Ferguson[✉][iD], Daisy Abbott[iD], and Sandy Louchart[iD]

Glasgow School of Art, Glasgow, Scotland
{j.ferguson,d.abbott,s.louchart}@gsa.ac.uk

**Abstract.** Pedagogical patterns facilitate the transfer of expert knowledge in teaching and learning. They are used to scaffold learning design for a particular purpose. Designing games for learning is a challenging, resource intensive, and inherently interdisciplinary activity. In this paper, we map the mechanics of twelve co-designed serious games in the domain of cybersecurity onto conceptually similar pedagogical patterns in order to identify fruitful common approaches and facilitate knowledge exchange. We present our methodology for this mapping process and provide examples for its usage to improve the quality and accessibility of serious games design.

**Keywords:** Pedagogical Patterns · Serious Games · Cybersecurity · Learning Mechanics · Game Mechanics · Game Based Learning

## 1 Introduction

Pedagogical Patterns (PPs) are a method of capturing and disseminating expert knowledge in teaching and learning, in the form of a reusable solution to a particular problem. They grow from the concept of design patterns and pattern languages more generally, which are common in computing disciplines. PPs offer a format and process for sharing successful teaching techniques, whilst allowing freedom of implementation to fit the needs of individual teachers [8,12]. There has been little work addressing the potential advantages of utilising PPs in the analysis and design of serious games - either in terms of employing a PP mapping directly, or in discussion of methodologies for conducting such a mapping activity. Bridging this gap between pedagogy research and serious games design may lead to improved learning and gameplay outcomes from serious games, as their inherent interdisciplinarity is a challenge noted in recent literature [2,32]. Therefore, a mutual understanding and interplay of concepts and language from serious game design processes (such as the Learning Mechanic - Game Mechanic (LM-GM) model [5,22]) and PPs is a necessary step towards allowing serious game designers and researchers to take advantage of pedagogical patterns research. This would allow a more structured method to share and implement learning designed through serious and also afford another avenue for researchers to analyse the learning being created during serious game design.

M. Haahr et al. (Eds.): JCSG 2023, LNCS 14309, pp. 65–80, 2023.
https://doi.org/10.1007/978-3-031-44751-8_5

In this work we present an analysis of a research project case study comprising twelve co-designed serious games from three distinct game jams focussed on games for cybersecurity. PPs have been applied to assist educators in computer science generally [7], but there is less evidence of this approach being undertaken outside of computing. No work has been identified to date on applying PPs to cybersecurity pedagogy. Gameplay and content of each co-designed game is analysed using the LM-GM framework and each game is then mapped onto pre-existing PPs, as defined by Bergin *et al.* [8]. The goal of this pattern matching is to investigate particular types of PPs that can emerge from serious game design, therefore serving as a foundation on which future researchers, designers, and game jam organisers can base their expectations and understanding of the pedagogy embedded within serious game designs. Furthermore, we present our process for this mapping activity and provide a mapping of concepts and language from the LM-GM model [5, 22] to the PPs format [8], thus providing common ground for communication between these two disciplines. Finally, we offer recommendations, based on our experiences, for further work that could improve collaboration processes and outcomes by the different disciplinary experts involved in serious game design.

## 2 Background

PPs can assist with teaching and learning technical subjects in particular, and their benefit is not restricted to a Higher Education context; they have also been applied in various training scenarios. PPs have a consistent structure comprising: Title; Context; Key Problem; Solution; and Further Information (including examples) [8]. Relationships with other PPs are included throughout these sections where relevant. Patterns are categorized in different groups: e.g. Active Learning, Feedback, Experiential Learning, Gaining Different Perspectives, and Teaching From Different Perspectives to aid educators in selecting and linking suitable techniques, and guidance is offered on how each pattern can be used at different timescales from minutes to an entire course [8]. Furthermore, Bergin *et al.* identify the opportunity for relating several patterns within a common problem space as a resource for solving complex problems, and actively solicit further contributions [8]. The literature notes that patterns are useful in scaffolding the solutions to multidisciplinary problems and enabling the swift articulation and transfer of expert knowledge to novices.

Patterns exist for many learning contexts, often needing to be specialised for particular disciplinary or industrial uses, for example, software design and security patterns [26]. For game making, game design patterns have been extensively studied since the early 00 s in an attempt to formally document gameplay [9], game mechanics, and non-player character (NPC) interactions [21]. Game design patterns are generally not presented as individual gameplay elements but provide designers with a set of interrelated connections, causal relationships and structures that can be used as building blocks towards the design of new games. Whilst not focused on pedagogy, the game design pattern approach is directly relevant to the PP approach proposed in this article. There is a need for development of PPs for specific topics and to move beyond PPs in classrooms to facilitate learning in a wider context, such as through professional practice.

Cybersecurity (the application domain of the serious game designs to be discussed in this paper) is an increasingly complex problem, in particular as a wider and more diverse group of people become creators and users of software, often without any training and operating outside the software industry. "Security is an abstract concept which combined with the dematerialized world of software systems is difficult to grasp, comprehend and experience" [13]. Cybersecurity combines technical, theoretical, professional, human, and social factors [23] and developing both skills and attitudes towards security is equally complex. Georgiou *et al.* [13] note the swift evolution of the subject and its related disciplines, a lack of technical, time, and expertise resources leading to poor coverage of cybersecurity in university-level programmes [11,15], and the need for (and challenges of) acquiring crucial practical skills [25]. Perhaps due to some of these challenges, computer science and cybersecurity as disciplines have been quick to adopt developments in teaching and learning, such as gamification and game-based learning. Whilst gamification aims to increase motivation through rewards (for example, points, digital badges, and/or leaderboards), game-based learning relies on the combination of interaction mechanics related to pedagogy with those related to games to create Serious Game Mechanics, i.e. a "design decision that concretely realises the transition of a learning practice/goal into a mechanical element of gameplay" [5]. In this way 'serious games' (games which have an educational or training purpose) can not only model large complex systems but also increase a player's understanding of, and confidence within, that system [10] whilst moving towards defined pedagogical goals.

Therefore, coding, software engineering in general, and cybersecurity specifically have been the topics of a wide range of recent game interventions from coding apps for young children [1], to gamified 'Catch the Flag' contests [29], to a fully-fledged game for developer-centred security [24], for example. However, despite evidence of rigour in the development of game-based learning for cybersecurity, there is little research linking game design decisions and Serious Game Mechanics (SGMs) with PPs to aid in their re-use for similar problems across the wider cybersecurity teaching and learning community. A number of papers consider design patterns or PPs in digital learning generally or in computing science topics such as programming (e.g. [18]) without specific reference to cybersecurity. In 2012, studies discussed the current state and value of design patterns in security and proposed a PP to translate remediation techniques into a pedagogically friendly format to address the adoption challenges faced by Malware incident responders [26,27]. The authors also conclude that "in order for the pattern template and pattern knowledge repository to stay relevant, they should be maintained and updated by an open community of practitioners from the academia, security industry and security incident response practice" [27], however no more recent work on this topic has been identified. One recent study, focused on teaching computing science in general, noted the fruitful opportunity to map design decisions of a learning platform to PPs [31] but did not attempt this mapping and mentioned cybersecurity only briefly. Therefore, cybersecurity pedagogy and/or workplace training provides a useful and suitable context for this research.

In terms of game-based or gamified approaches, Hauge *et al.* note the potential for re-use of SGMs as design patterns driven by pedagogy [17] and there is evidence of studies which link PPs with sustainability in engineering [28] and professional training for accident prevention [6] but, until Georgiou *et al.* [13] no research linking PPs with a game-based approach in cybersecurity was identified. This paper defined 'secure code' mechanics based on attacks and mitigations around several cybersecurity themes. These were presented to workshop participants alongside selected gamification mechanics with the addition of learning elements and used to co-design game ideas for cybersecurity which mapped the secure code mechanics to suitable game elements. The authors note the centrality of pedagogical aspects to both cybersecurity as a discipline and in designing games to increase awareness and practice of secure coding [13] and present an abstracted design composition for cybersecurity games based on the co-designed game elements. This pattern was then analysed using the LM-GM framework for serious game design [5] and the resulting SGMs were presented, those that arose from the gamification toolkit used within the workshop and those that were generated by original participant contributions. This work provides a robust basis for building on by identifying SGMs created in a co-design process for cybersecurity games, mapping them to existing PPs, and reflecting on patterns that are potentially a good fit for this specific problem space. Therefore, this paper builds on the previous study's findings and resources by using new data from serious game jam co-design events to: 1) broaden the identification and analysis of SGMs for cybersecurity beyond gamification and into game-based learning; 2) deepen the emphasis on pedagogical aspects of design; 3) map co-designed SGMs to PPs; and 4) produce recommendations for PPs for teaching and learning specific cybersecurity issues through game-based approaches.

## 3   Methodology

To improve multidisciplinary concept mapping and communication around the design of serious games, our methods also spanned disciplines. The relationships between pedagogical patterns, the LM-GM framework, a game jam method including Triadic Game Design [16], and our method of analysis are outlined below.

## 3.1     Serious 'Slow' Game Jam Method

The game jam format used to co-design the serious games discussed in this paper was the 'Serious Slow Game Jam' (SSGJ) [3]. For full details of the game setting and methodology, see this publication. This approach intended to ameliorate some of the key barriers to entry often found in traditional game jams, and added additional support and resources to reinforce and support the 'serious' aspect of the game jam. The SSGJ aimed to remove the main barrier of intense time pressure (the majority of traditional game jams take place over a 24–48 h period [20]), instead running over 5/6 working days spread over a 6–8 week period. Furthermore, participants are extensively mentored and supported in their serious game designs by:

- The provision of a 'provoking game' [4] used to encourage reflection and discussion on cybersecurity and serious game design.
- Support using the Triadic Game Design (TGD) methodology [16,30].
- Support in understanding and using gameplay loops (the various interaction cycles within a game) [14].
- Domain expert mentors (in both cybersecurity and game design).
- Three reference card decks to be used as design tools - one domain-specific (cybersecurity) and two covering Learning Mechanics and Game Mechanics (LM-GM).

These cards served to both provide scaffolding and inspiration for participants who may be new to any of the three areas (gaming, pedagogy and the domain), as well as providing a method of communication between expert mentors and participants. Outputs from this game jam approach include documentation such as: paper prototypes, gameplay loops, and game design documents. This documentation underpins the analysis described below.

## 3.2     Participants

Data was collected from three distinct Serious Slow Game Jams [3], Table 1 shows the format of these jams, the number of participants that took part and the number of game designs produced.

## 3.3     The Learning Mechanic-Game Mechanic (LM-GM) Model

The LM and GM cards were used during the game jams as design tools to create an LM-GM map, following the procedure defined in [5,22]. The goal of the LM-GM mapping is to "highlight [a serious game's] main pedagogical and entertainment features, and their interrelations" [5], Fig. 1 shows an example LM-GM mapping. This process not only clarified the learning and gaming aspects for participants but also functioned as clear documentation of design decisions, allowing mentors (and subsequent researchers) to understand the participants' designs.

Table 1. Summary of game jam participants.

|  | Format | Year | Participants | Games | Demographic |
|---|---|---|---|---|---|
| Jam #1 | Remote | 2021 | 6 | 3 | University students |
| Jam #2 | Hybrid | 2022 | 13 | 3 | Masters students |
| Jam #3 | In-Person | 2022 | 23 | 6 | 11–16 year olds |

This combination of a Learning and Gaming Mechanics results in a *Serious Game Mechanic* (SGM) which demonstrates how the pedagogical approach is implemented through gameplay. Resultant SGMs extracted from each game jam team's designs were used to inform the process of PP mapping. LMs and GMs are defined in detail in [5] and for readers unfamiliar with this framework it is recommended that this associated literature is read in conjunction with our analysis and mapping, below.

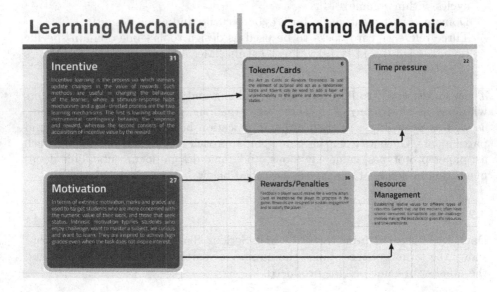

Fig. 1. An example of an LM-GM mapping created by a SSGJ team.

## 3.4   Pedagogical Pattern Mapping Approach

Using the documentation of each game (including gameplay loops annotated with LM-GM cards, game design documents, and the LM-GM mapping exercise) we identified the LMs and GMs used in each game design and their various relationships which form SGMs. It should be noted that this data is based on the participants' own use of the LM and GM toolkit and therefore may not be fully accurate (for example a relevant LM or GM that was not well understood by participants may have been omitted). However, teams were supported by both cybersecurity and serious game design mentors which increased the rigour of the process and gives confidence that the documentation produced is a good indication of the core SGMs for each game. Some SGMs were one-to-one relationships between a single LM and a single GM, however, in general these relationships were complex with one-to-many and many-to-many relationships. In order to analyse the respective popularity of different LMs and GMs across all co-designed games, they were then recorded as separate dyads (one-to-one mappings). Therefore, every LM-GM relationship was individually recorded, for example, a high-level LM such as *Analysis* was mapped separately to every GM with which it shares a relationship. The most commonly occurring SGM dyads (those that appeared in 25% (3) or more of the co-designed games) are shown in Fig. 5 in the Results section below, which also gives a sense of the simplicity or complexity of different SGMs. Note this figure is provided as an overview and is not intended to be used as an in-depth resource.

Note: to ease the use of the LM-GM framework in the SSGJ itself, we simplified some terminology from Arnab *et al.* [5]. **LMs:** *Participation* was removed as it is omnipresent in game-based learning; *Explore* and *Discovery* were combined as they are conceptually very similar; similarly, *Imitation*, *Modelling*, and *Shadowing* were combined with *Observation*; and *Accountability* and *Responsibility* were combined with *Ownership*. **GMs:** *Communal Discovery* was combined with *Collaboration*; *Goods* was combined with *Tokens* and separated from in-game *Information*; *Pareto Optimal* was retitled *One-Player Must be Better-Off*; *Pavlovian Reactions* was retitled *Conditioning*; *Protégé Effects* was retitled *Learning by Teaching*. Some definitions were rewritten in simpler terms, based on current pedagogy literature and clear examples of each concept in use were added to the toolkit cards. Therefore there may be minor differences in LM-GM terminology used here, nevertheless the concepts remain as defined. Example LM and GM cards can be seen in Figs. 2 and 3.

The next step was to establish relationships between the SGMs identified in the above process and the PPs defined in Bergin *et al.* [8]. A detailed reading of each PP was undertaken and each was mapped to the SGMs that are likely to implement the pattern within each game. The PPs are shown on the left and right sides of Fig. 5, linked to the relevant SGMs. See Bergin *et al.* for full definitions of each PP.

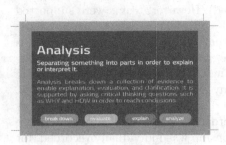

**Fig. 2.** *Analysis* LM Card.                    **Fig. 3.** *Movement* LM Card.

## 4    Results and Discussion

### 4.1    LM-GM Framework Language

A particular advantage of the three game jams conducted as part of this work is that we were able to observe the LM-GM framework being used by a range of individuals, from primary school children, through to Master's students. The most striking observation from this is the need for the LM-GM framework's language to be revisited and revised for different user groups and desired learning outcomes. For example, participants in this case study were not familiar with the language of pedagogy and required support in their understanding of some LMs concepts. Conversely, if the same methods were used with educators, it is likely that the language of GMs would need additional explanation. One example of particular note is the usage of the *Pavlovian Reactions* Learning Mechanic. In the first two game jams, *Pavlovian Response* was an LM available to participants and even though expert mentors deemed that it was a mechanic present in some of the games developed, it wasn't included in any of the participants' chosen SGMs. However, when this mechanic was renamed to *Conditioning* for the final game jam that was aimed at schoolchildren, the mechanic was included in two separate designs. Whilst we are confident overall that most of the SGMs in the co-designed games were successfully documented, a lack of understanding of some of the LMs or GMs leading to their omission is a limitation of this research.

### 4.2    Frequency of Pedagogical Patterns Arising from the SGMs

Figure 4 shows the frequency of PPs which the SGMs were mapped to. *Active Student*, *Repeat Yourself* and *War Game* are considered to be inherent to serious games, hence these PPs have 100% frequency and are shown in their own section at the top of Fig. 5). *Feedback* is also present in 100% of the games, however this PP arises from specific SGMs identified by participants in their gameplay loop designs so is shown in the body of Fig. 5. Note that many PPs refer to specific

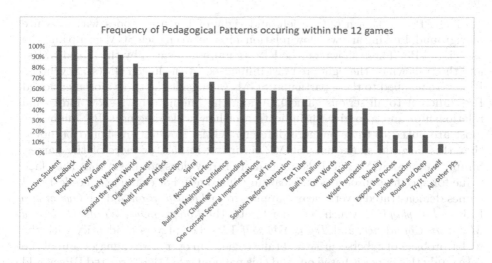

**Fig. 4.** Frequency of PPs which were mapped to participants' SGMs.

formal educational contexts therefore all other PPs defined by Bergin *et al.* [8] that do not appear in Fig. 4 were not relevant in this mapping. It can be seen that PPs appearing in over 50% of the games are themed around incremental feedback based on manageable learning and/or actions, for example: *Early Warning, Digestible Packets, Reflection, Spiral, Build and Maintain Confidence, Challenge Understanding*, and *Self-Test*. Another theme emerging from these most popular PPs is that of applying lessons learned in the game to out-of-game contexts, for example: *Expand the Known World, Multi Pronged Attack, One Concept Several Implementations*, and *Solution Before Abstraction*. Figure 4 gives an indication of which PPs may be a fruitful starting point for game-based learning, both for cybersecurity and for topics beyond this case study.

## 4.3 SGM-to-PP Mapping

Figure 5 shows the proposed SGM-to-PPs mapping arising from our analysis. SGM groups are identified in the central column with interrelationships shown by linking arrows with an indication of how frequently the SGM dyad was used across the twelve co-designed games. All game designs employed the *Feedback-Quick Feedback* SGM (meaning the combination of the *Feedback* LM and *Quick Feedback* GM) and exactly half of the game designs used: *Plan-Strategy/Planning, Analysis-Selecting/Collecting* and *Question & Answer - Question & Answer*. For clarity, SGMs which were used in fewer than 25% of the games have been omitted from this diagram. Bounding boxes show where there is no overlap between SGM dyads - this gives an indication of those LMs and GMs which have many-to-many pairings and those which are more likely to be one-to-many or one-to-one.

The PPs are shown on the left and right of Fig. 5 as nodes with a white background. Linking arrows show relationships between each SGM group and the associated PP. Those shown on the left are more influenced by the linked LM(s) and those shown on the right are most influenced by the linked GM(s). Seventeen PPs were mapped to these particular SGMs (alongside the three aforementioned PPs inherent to all serious games). Again, the linking arrows show individual relationships and also give an indication of how wide-ranging a PP might be; most are linked to three or more different SGMs. However, it should be noted that this diagram shows only SGMs occurring in 25% or more of the games. Simply because SGMs and PPs occur more rarely does not mean that they lack value for specific approaches and learning outcomes. For example, 2 co-designed games demonstrated a very clear mapping from *Identification* and/or *Ownership* LMs to *Roleplay* GM, which in turn activates the *Roleplay, Own Words, Build and Maintain Confidence*, and *Try it Yourself* PPs. For players to identify with the wider problem of cybersecurity and take ownership over it was a major aim of the case study this paper is based on, and this particular SGM and related PPs would be considered very fruitful in, for example, workplace cybersecurity training. Recommendations for how to use the SGM-PP mapping diagram (Fig. 5) are detailed in Sect. 5, below.

**Depth of Learning Design.** Further reflections on Figure 5 identify a high use of SGMs that are aligned with lower-order levels of understanding (as defined in Bloom's Extended Taxonomy [19]) such as *Question & Answer, Repetition*, and *Feedback*. This suggests that co-designers (based, as most of them were, in a didactic educational context) may associate serious games with simple quizzes, or have struggled to escape the model of demonstrating knowledge followed by feedback from an educator. This was particularly noticeable in the school-age teams. This shows that more support is needed in the game jam process, particularly during the 'meaning' phase of the Triadic Game Design process [16], in order to provide participants with the appropriate scaffolding to allow them to explore more higher-order learning designs. That said, 50% of games used much higher-order LMs such as *Analysis* and *Plan* and incorporated these incremental developments of understanding (or conceptually similar variations, such as the *Cascading Information* GM) into their core gameplay and feedback loops. Neither lower nor high level learning outcomes are 'better', rather it is important to note that the specific learning outcomes of a serious game will suggest suitable SGMs and PPs to use. Lower order SGMs are very appropriate for knowledge acquisition games whereas, as noted above, higher order SGMs leading to understanding and ownership of a problem space would likely be more suitable for behavioural change outcomes such as cybersecurity workplace training.

**Salience of Participant-Chosen Serious Game Mechanics.** Further to the above, during our analysis there was some evidence of participants selecting and documenting SGMs that were valid, but not necessarily the most salient for their purpose, as designed earlier in the game jam process. In other words, SGMs were

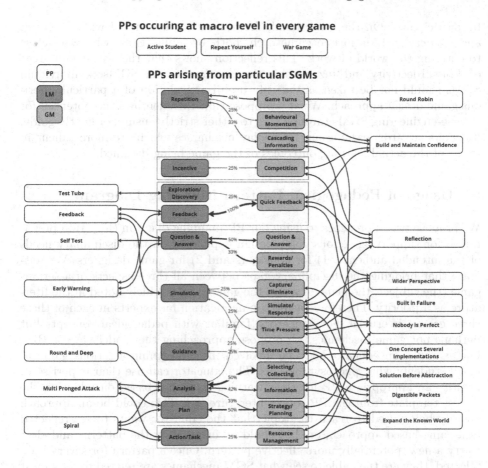

**Fig. 5.** The Serious Game Mechanics to Pedagogical Patterns Mapping.

correct but some were omitted that would most effectively and accurately convey the learning and gameplay intended. This reinforces the need to tailor language and support specifically to the participants, as mentioned above, and the limitation that a lack of understanding can affect documentation accuracy, even where the game itself is rigorously designed. For example, in the Serious Slow Game Jams conducted as part of this work the target audience was "code-citizens", or people who are code-literate but may not have explicit software engineering training [13]. Therefore, the goal of these jams was not just knowledge acquisition but to encourage behavioural change to improve these code citizens' software development habits and practices. The *Identify/Generalisation - Metagame* SGM, which could map to PPs: *Wider Perspective, Expand the Known World, Solution Before Abstraction* and *Roleplay* is one SGM and several PPs that we considered to be a particularly salient one for this particular context, however, this particular SGM was not recorded in any of the game designs produced by participants. On the other hand, *Metagame* was associated with *Incentive* and *Ownership* LMs in one game each, both by adult teams who were close to entering the world of work. This reflection shows that there can be a great deal of subjectivity and 'fuzziness' in the creation of some SGMs, so individual SGMs should not be taken as the only useful articulation of a particular serious game design approach. We also propose that this identifies the potential for reverse-engineering SGMs through PPs to either strictly ensure, or gently guide, designers towards learning and gameplay mechanics which are more salient in terms of the actual learning outcomes of the game being designed.

## 5     Usage of Pedagogical Pattern Mapping Diagram

We propose two approaches to using our PP mapping diagram (Fig. 5) in preparation for supporting serious game design depending on the disciplinary needs of the intended audience: 1) for educators and 2) for game designers. We reiterate that bridging the disciplinary gaps between all three aspects of a serious game (the subject, the pedagogy, and the gameplay) is widely noted in the literature as a priority. Therefore easing communication for experts in each of these three groups is crucial. For educators, familiar with pedagogical concepts but perhaps not game mechanics, we propose approaching the model via the PPs. For example, an educator may be involved in co-designing a serious game to teach students what photosynthesis is. The educator can use their expertise to identify an appropriate PP for their learning outcome (based on adapting the closest template from the PP source literature [8]). This could be an approach already being used to teach the topic that the educator wants to see reflected in a game-based approach, or they could be inspired by the patterns and elect to try a new, potentially more effective pattern. Once a pattern (or several) are selected, they are then able to see what SGM mechanics are related to, and most likely to deliver, that pattern in a serious game context. Conversely, beginning from SGMs and moving outward towards PPs may be the most fruitful approach to those coming from a game design background. By defining appropriate SGMs for a proposed serious game (or identifying them in an existing game), a game designer can then associate the approach with the wider pedagogical theory to validate (or question) a particular serious game design approach. This not only provides additional pedagogical resources to assist in game design, but can provide a shared language and improve communication between game designers and educators.

### 5.1     Example Scenarios of Each Approach for Cybersecurity

Rather than directly instructing her students of some appropriate ways to eliminate the vulnerabilities related to a particular cyber attack, an educator would prefer that the students figure out the answers for themselves, whilst simultaneously becoming more self-reliant. She identifies *Test Tube* as a fruitful PP. Using the SGM-PP mapping (Fig. 5) she identifies the *Exploration/Discovery - Quick*

*Feedback* SGM. After reading the definition of both LM and GM she confirms her choice and shares this information with the game designer, who reads *Test Tube* in order to cement their understanding. They then suggest a way in which the game system can support experimentation with clear results to allow the players to draw their own accurate conclusions on the impacts of different cyber defence mechanisms. As they collaborate, both the educator and the designer use the mapping as a facilitation tool for knowledge exchange.

From a game designers perspective, the SGM-PP mapping (Fig. 5) could be used to adapt the learning design of an existing serious game from a different application domain. For example, a company approaches a serious games company to produce a game to support workplace learning and practice of secure coding. The company has previously designed a serious game about common nursing procedures that used the *Incentive - Competition* SGM (Fig. 5). Looking at the SGM-PP mapping they can see that this SGM is mapped to *Build and Maintain Confidence*, which seems appropriate. The company checks with their client who clarifies that this pattern should be emphasised but that *Competition* should be represented as their company against other companies, not employee against employee! The game designers then follow *Build and Maintain Confidence* back to other SGMs and note that *Repetition - Cascading Information* wasn't in their nursing game, but would be valuable to add in the cybersecurity game, as it involves knowledge acquisition as well as developing professional practice.

# 6 Future Work

## 6.1 Dynamic Presentation of SGM-PP Mapping

Figure 5 is challenging to parse in its current, static format, therefore we propose designing and creating a dynamic, web-based presentation of the SGM-PP mapping, so that it can be navigated and read more easily. This would also allow rarer but still valuable SGM-PP mappings to be added without making the diagram unreadable.

## 6.2 Audience-Specific Language in the LM-GM Framework

The LM-GM framework is rooted in serious games theory and therefore can use terminology that may be inaccessible to game jam participants including (but not limited to) participants who are young, speak English as an additional language, or have limited experience of either games or pedagogy theory. This was our rationale for simplifying the framework language used in the SSGJ toolkit card decks. Further work towards making the LM-GM framework more accessible and understandable to different audiences is recommended.

### 6.3   Built-for-Purpose Subsets of the SGM-PP Mapping

As mentioned above, there are situations where lower-order learning is appropriate and others (such as the cybersecurity domain example used here) where imparting higher-order learning and behavioural change is the goal. Therefore, subsets of SGMs, PPs, or both could be curated by experts to facilitate co-designs with particular learning goals, desired learning, behaviours, or contextual limitations. For example, the goal of teaching young children to play piano using a mobile device would benefit from a subset focused on learning-by-doing and repetition which would not only be more usable and less overwhelming to co-designers but would also reduce the risk of inappropriate SGMs being included.

## 7   Conclusions

Pedagogical patterns focus on transferable yet adaptable solutions and disseminating expert knowledge within teaching and learning. With a similar goal focused on serious games design - in particular co-design between experts from different disciplines - we have presented an analysis and subsequent mapping of twelve co-designed serious game designs onto established pedagogical patterns. This results in the proposed SGM-PP mapping diagram for which we describe our methodology and provide examples of potential usage. We propose that mapping serious game mechanics to pedagogical patterns is a helpful resource and process as it facilitates knowledge exchange and accurate interdisciplinary communication between educators and game designers, an activity which is at the very core of effective serious game design.

## References

1. LightBot. https://lightbot.com/
2. Abbott, D.: Intentional learning design for educational games: a workflow supporting both novices and experts. Learner and User Experience Research: An Introduction for the Field of Learning Design & Technology (2020)
3. Abbott, D., Chatzifoti, O., Ferguson, J., Louchart, S., Stals, S.: Serious 'slow' game jam - a game jam model for serious game. In: Proceedings of International Conference on Game Jams, Hackathons and Game Creation Events. Association for Computing Machinery (2023)
4. Abbott, D., Chatzifoti, O., Louchart, S.: Provocative games to encourage critical reflection. In: ECGBL 2022 16th European Conference on Game-Based Learning. Academic Conferences and Publishing Limited (2022)
5. Arnab, S., et al.: Mapping learning and game mechanics for serious games analysis. Br. J. Edu. Technol. **46**(2), 391–411 (2015)
6. Arnold, O., Franke, R., Jantke, K.P., Wache, H.H.: Professional training for industrial accident prevention with time travel games. Int. J. Adv. Corporate Learn. (iJAC) **15**(1), 20–34 (2022)
7. Bergin, J.: Fourteen pedagogical patterns. In: EuroPLoP, pp. 1–49 (2000)

8. Bergin, J., et al. (eds.): Pedagogical Patterns: Advice for Educators. Joseph Bergin Software Tools, Pleasantville, NY, (compact edn.), 2nd (corrected) print.: Aug, 31, 2012 edn. (2012)
9. Björk, S., Holopainen, J.: Games and design patterns. The game design reader: a rules of play anthology, pp. 410–437 (2005)
10. Castronova, E., Knowles, I.: A model of climate policy using board game mechanics. Int. J. Serious Games **2**(3) (2015)
11. Crick, T., Davenport, J.H., Hanna, P., Irons, A., Prickett, T.: Overcoming the challenges of teaching cybersecurity in UK computer science degree programmes. In: 2020 IEEE Frontiers in Education Conference (FIE), Uppsala, Sweden, pp. 1–9. IEEE (2020)
12. Fioravanti, M.L., Barbosa, E.F.: A catalog of pedagogical patterns for learning applications. In: 2018 IEEE Frontiers in Education Conference (FIE), pp. 1–9. IEEE (2018)
13. Georgiou, T., Baillie, L., Chatzifoti, O., Chan, S.C.: Future forums: a methodology for exploring, gamifying, and raising security awareness of code-citizens. Int. J. Hum. Comput. Stud. **169**, 102930 (2023)
14. Guardiola, E.: The gameplay loop: a player activity model for game design and analysis. In: ACM International Conference Proceeding Series (2016)
15. Hallett, J., Larson, R., Rashid, A.: Mirror, mirror, on the wall: what are we teaching them all? Characterising the focus of cybersecurity curricular frameworks (2018)
16. Harteveld, C.: Triadic Game Design: Balancing Reality, Meaning and Play. Springer, Heidelberg (2011)
17. Hauge, J.B., et al.: Serious game mechanics and opportunities for re-use. eLearn. Softw. Educ. (2) (2015)
18. Jerinic, L.: Teaching introductory programming. Int. J. Adv. Comput. Sci. Appl. **5**(6) (2014)
19. Krathwohl, D.R.: A revision of bloom's taxonomy: an overview. Theory Pract. **41**(4), 212–218 (2002)
20. Kultima, A.: Defining game jam. In: 10th International Conference on the Foundations of Digital Games (FDG 2015) (2015)
21. Lankoski, P., Björk, S.: Gameplay design patterns for believable non-player characters. In: DiGRA Conference, pp. 416–423 (2007)
22. Lim, T., et al.: Strategies for effective digital games development and implementation. In: Cases on Digital Game-Based Learning: Methods, Models, and Strategies, pp. 168–198. IGI Global (2013)
23. Lopez, T., Sharp, H., Tun, T., Bandara, A., Levine, M., Nuseibeh, B.: Talking about security with professional developers. In: 2019 IEEE/ACM Joint 7th International Workshop on Conducting Empirical Studies in Industry (CESI) and 6th International Workshop on Software Engineering Research and Industrial Practice (SER&IP), Montreal, QC, Canada, pp. 34–40. IEEE (2019)
24. Maarek, M., McGregor, L., Louchart, S., McMenemy, R.: How could serious games support secure programming? Designing a study replication and intervention. In: 2019 IEEE European Symposium on Security and Privacy Workshops (EuroS&PW), Stockholm, Sweden, pp. 139–148. IEEE (2019)
25. Manson, D., Pike, R.: The case for depth in cybersecurity education. ACM Inroads **5**(1), 47–52 (2014)
26. Pan, J.Y.: Fighting fire with fire – a pre-emptive approach to restore control over IT assets from malware infection. Ph.D. Murdoch University (2012)

27. Pan, J.Y., Fung, C.C.: Pattern for malware remediation – a last line of defence tool against Malware in the global communication platform. In: Proceedings of the 19th ITS Biennial Conference. Bangkok, Thailand (2012)
28. Pargman, D., Hedin, B., Eriksson, E.: Patterns of engagement: using a board game as a tool to address sustainability in engineering educations. In: Mazijn, B. (ed.) Proceedings of the 8th International Conference on Engineering Education for Sustainable Development, pp. 302–310. Instituut vóór Duurzame Ontwikkeling, Bruges (2016)
29. Parker, J., et al.: Build it, break it, fix it: contesting secure development. ACM Trans. Privacy Secur. **23**(2), 1–36 (2020)
30. Troiano, G.M., Schouten, D., Cassidy, M., Tucker-Raymond, E., Puttick, G., Harteveld, C.: All good things come in threes: assessing student-designed games via triadic game design. In: Proceedings of the 15th International Conference on the Foundations of Digital Games, pp. 1–4 (2020)
31. Waite, J., Franceschini, A., Sentance, S., Patterson, M., Sharkey, J.: An online platform for teaching upper secondary school computer science. In: United Kingdom and Ireland Computing Education Research Conference, Glasgow, UK, pp. 1–7. ACM (2021)
32. Westera, W.: Why and how serious games can become far more effective: accommodating productive learning experiences, learner motivation and the monitoring of learning gains. J. Educ. Technol. Soc. **22**(1), 59–69 (2019)

# Entry-Level Game Difficulty Estimation Based on Visuoperceptual Profiles of Children with Cerebral Visual Impairment

Katarina Kostkova[1,2]([✉]) [iD], Nofar Ben Itzhak[3,4] [iD], Lieselot Stijnen[3,4],
Els Ortibus[3,4] [iD], and Bart Jansen[1,2] [iD]

[1] Department of Electronics and Informatics (ETRO), Vrije Universiteit Brussel (VUB),
Brussels, Belgium
{Katarina.Kostkova,Bart.Jansen}@vub.be
[2] imec, Leuven, Belgium
[3] Department of Development and Regeneration, University of Leuven (KU Leuven), Leuven,
Belgium
{Nofar.BenItzhak,Lieselot.Stijnen}@kuleuven.be,
Els.Ortibus@uzleuven.be
[4] Child Youth, Institute (L-C&Y), Leuven, Belgium

**Abstract.** Cerebral visual impairment (CVI), a leading cause of visual impairment in developed countries, has no standard treatment and many different manifestations. Long-term individualized therapy is crucial for children with CVI to develop coping strategies and improve functional limitations. Serious games are becoming a part of many different types of therapy and rehabilitation, including physical rehabilitation, cognitive behavioral therapy, vision therapy, etc. However, the design of the serious games used in the context of rehabilitation and therapy must ensure that the games fulfill the therapeutic goals and also adapt to the skills and abilities of the players. Entry-level estimation, i.e., placing the player in a correct initial game level the first time the player engages with the game, is an important aspect of individualization and personalization of serious games.

In this paper, we discussed the importance of adaptivity and personalization of serious games in children with CVI, specifically focusing on entry-level difficulty estimation and the comparison of two entry-level estimation models. The first model was defined based on discussions with experts in the CVI therapy field and the second was a linear regression model trained on in-game collected data. We evaluated the two models on several performance metrics and compared how the entry-level estimation using the first versus second formula would differ for the children participating in our currently ongoing Randomized Control Trial.

**Keywords:** Cerebral Visual Impairment · Entry-Level Adaptivity · Personalization · Serious Games

M. Haahr et al. (Eds.): JCSG 2023, LNCS 14309, pp. 81–94, 2023.
https://doi.org/10.1007/978-3-031-44751-8_6

# 1 Introduction

The 2011 World Report on disability, published by World Health Organization (WHO), showed that the number of people with disability, 15% at the time, was higher than estimated [1]. In the area of visual disabilities, cerebral visual impairment (CVI) is the leading cause of visual impairment in developed countries and its prevalence is increasing in developing countries [2]. CVI manifests itself by reduced acuity, visual field defects, impaired motion detection, visuoperceptual impairments, etc. A cross-sectional survey of 5–11 year old children showed that 3.4% (out of 2298 children) of the primary school children in mainstream education had at least one CVI-related vision problem [3].

Clinical features of CVI vary among children and can manifest themselves differently. Challenges reported in children with CVI include difficulty with processing of complex input, e.g., visual recognition and visual memory of objects and people, orientation and navigation in the environment, perception of motion, and figure-ground perception (e.g., finding a toy in a cluttered toy box), etc. [4].

Screening and evaluation of CVI in children is multidisciplinary and comprehensive. CVI screening questionnaires (e.g., Visual Skills Inventory, Flemish CVI Questionnaire, 12-question Short CVI Questionnaire), scales of visual functioning (e.g., CVI Range, developed by Roman-Lantzy), ophthalmological examination, neuropsychological assessment of visual perception, visuomotor examination, neuroimaging, and genetic testing are often used [5].

Although there is no standard treatment for CVI, children can develop strategies to engage attention, capture visual information, or improve reading skills [6]. However, long-term monitoring, individualized visual therapy, and interventions to improve functional limitations are needed [7]. Visual therapy often focuses on training compensatory strategies, e.g., training visual field scanning. For the most benefit, those interventions should start early in life to maximize visual development and functional outcomes [8]. Moreover, they require months of therapy to become habitual [9]. To achieve the necessary regularity, intensity, and consistency of the therapy, persistence of the patient and adherence to the agreed therapy plan are important.

Play is the main tool for creating a therapeutic relationship with children, learning new skills (e.g., cognitive, social, and sensory-motor skills), and realizing their own potential [10]. Computer games are already accepted by most children and adolescents who have a positive association with playing them [11]. Thus, serious aspects of games (e.g., learning, training, rehabilitation) often take place without too much resistance. The potential of serious games has been explained by brain plasticity, which is considered as a basic principle in rehabilitation therapy for children with cerebral disorders [12]. The use of serious games in rehabilitation and therapy leads to an increased motivation and adherence to the therapy plan.

Individualization (i.e., adaptation, personalization, adaptivity, customization, etc.) of serious games contributes hugely to their effectiveness [13]. The need for an individualized therapy for children with CVI is apparent, when considering different manifestations of CVI, varying degrees of severity, and accompanying diagnosis, e.g., physical disability, autism etc. In the scope of educational games, the most used aspects to inform the individualization are performance (in-game, task skills), physiological (stress, anxiety, etc.), and personal (intelligence, learning style, etc.). Individualization of the game is a complex task and requires decisions on what, how, and when to adapt.

There are several commonly used ways to decide on the starting level for players: (1) all players start from the same first level, (2) the starting level is decided/set up by the therapist based on players impairment, (3) the player chooses the starting level (e.g. easy/medium/hard), or (4) the starting level is determined automatically based on standardized test results, medical information etc.

The aim of this paper is the entry-level GD estimation based on the player's visuoperceptual profile (VP), i.e. results of standardized visuoperceptual tests. The VP is described in more detail in Sect. 3. Secondly, we compare two VP based formulas used to calculate the entry-level GD. The first formula was defined by the therapists in the field of therapy for children with CVI and the second formula was a result of regression learning model.

## 2  Related Work

### 2.1  Games for (Cerebral) Visual Impairment

In a six-month study with 60 children (birth to 3 years old), Campaña et al. compared Light Box (a product developed by the American Printing House for Blind (APH) designed for working on functional vision tasks with children with visual impairment or multiple disabilities) and an iPad. The iPad was introduced as a tool similar to Light Box. Multiple iPad apps were used to elicit activation and interaction. The replacement of traditional rehabilitation tools with games on an iPad resulted in children being attracted and paying more attention to what was happening on the screen. The iPad was found to be superior and 100% of the participating children showed a significant increase in communication, visual attentiveness, reaching, and activating elements on the screen [14].

Bortoli and Gaggi developed a game called **PlayWithEyes**, targeted towards preschool children, with a goal to help with vision testing (visual acuity and color blindness) [15, 16]. Similar to standard vision testing, in the PlayWithEyes game, the child needs to recognize presented symbols/images (LEA symbols and cartoon characters) and their orientation. The symbol/image is presented on an external screen and the child needs to input the answer on an Apple iPod Touch. The system has minimal hardware requirements, including an iPod Touch, iPad, and an external monitor. Tests with 65 children of kindergarten age (3 to 6 years old) were performed to evaluate the game in terms of engagement of the children and the ability of the game to correctly test children's eyes. The results show that the game was able to reach the same conclusion about visual acuity as the results from an ophthalmologist using a standardized exercise.

A large-scale interactive environment with three mini-games was developed in the **See-Sound** project by Battistine et al. and the Robert Hollman Foundation. Several mini-games for children with visual impairment were designed. The mini-games can be configured by the therapist to suit the specific needs of the child. The system was piloted with 11 visually impaired children, aged 3 to 8 years old [10]. The aim of the pilot study was to evaluate the games: (1) in terms of player's satisfaction and, (2) the usability and usefulness of the games as a therapy tool. The player's satisfaction evaluation showed that most of the children showed very high satisfaction with the mini-games. User experience of the participating therapists was positive and resulted in suggestions for improvements and changes of the system.

A serious game called **Help me!**, developed by Ciman et al., aims to improve the assessment and rehabilitation of children with CVI. The game has two goals: to train the ability to see and touch an object at the same time, and to train problem-solving capabilities. The system is configurable by the therapist and an optional eye tracker can be used [17]. The game consists of three mini-games with different tasks, (1) **Find Nemo** – where a child needs to look at the goldfish moving on the screen (used for eye tracking system calibration); (2) **Where is Peppa/George going** – where the child needs to follow a stimulus which stimulates eye movement and attention shift across different quadrants of the screen; (3) **Help me! Santa Clause's assistant** – where the child needs to discriminate between target and intruder images [2]. In the pilot study with 20 typically developing children of 4 years of age, the authors found that the game is well understood, usable, and enjoyable for the children.

An iPad app, **Tap-n-see Now**, was created and designed specifically for children with CVI, with Dr. Roman-Lantzy's characteristics of CVI in mind [18]. The goal of the game is to press an image moving on the screen. The graphics of the game are simple, and the game is completely customizable, from the color of the background (default is black), moving image, speed of movement, reward sound, and size of the image etc.

Waddington et al. designed and developed a serious game **Eyelander** for young people with Neurological Visual Impairment (NVI) [19]. The game focused on teaching compensatory strategies, namely visual scanning. Occupational, physical, speech and language therapists, and young people participated in the iterative design process. The game was tested with three groups, (1) four young people with a diagnosis or presentation of NVI, (2) eight therapists (occupational, physical, speech and language), and (3) three young people with acquired brain injury. The Eyelander game consists of several levels, and the main narrative is to help a character to escape an island. Completion of a predetermined number of visual tasks results in an animation which leads the character over an obstacle. The complexity of the visual tasks grows with increasing levels. Part of the game is a visual field assessment tool which, based on correct responses, incorrect responses and response time, creates a heat map representing participant's visual field.

Since the visual impairment in children with CVI is at the brain level, serious games for children with CVI need to train higher-level skills e.g., object recognition, figure-ground perception, and visual spatial perception. Moreover, the diverse manifestations and characteristics of CVI should be respected and the serious games should support individualization. There are very few serious games created specifically for children with CVI which focus on training higher-level skills, can be personalized and adapt to child's performance to keep the child in the flow. Our serious games aim to fulfill all these criteria. You can find more information about iVision games in Sect. 4.

## 2.2 Serious Games with Entry-Level Individualization

Hocine et al. designed a serious game for attention training called Keep attention. As part of the personalization, the player evaluates his/her attention, receives a daily score which is then used to create the player's profile [12]. The authors also developed an attention assessment test. The player's profile is used by the difficulty adjustment module of the Keep attention serious game and informs the decisions about each game level to better fit the player's needs and abilities. In a pilot study, eleven children (8–11 year old) evaluated the game using the Game Experience Questionnaire - Core (GEQ) using the following scale: 0 - not at all, 1 - slightly, 2 - moderately, 3 - fairly, and 4 - extremely. Children found the game to be personalized to their abilities, the difficulty adjusted to their abilities (GEQ score - M: 2.34; SD: 0.34), and the challenge balanced (GEQ score - M: 2.29; SD: 0.68).

Eun et al. designed an exercise serious game Farming, containing four different exercises, where an AI-based difficulty adjustment module was used to personalize the game [20]. The target of the game was to engage and motivate elderly (over 65 years old) to play the serious game to prevent dementia. The Farming serious game implements two levels of adaptivity. Firstly, an initial level is set based on the patient's personal information (i.e., cognitive and physical abilities obtained in a pre-survey questionnaire), secondly, the difficulty level is adjusted based on the game performance. The difficulty adjustment system is based on an expert group of fitness instructor defined rules. The performance data are averaged over the last five plays, and the difficulty is lowered if the success rate is under 80%, increased if it is over 90%, and unchanged if it is in the range of 80–90%. In a three-month trial with 20 elderly participants (65–80 years old), individual performance and average success rate increased, comparing one month and three months of game play.

## 3   Visuoperceptual Profile

The visuoperceptual profile is an objective characterization of a child's visuoperceptual skills and consists of six visuoperceptual dimensions: (1) visual discrimination and matching (VDaM), (2) object or picture recognition (OR), (3) visual-spatial perception (VSP), (4) figure-ground perception (FGP), (5) motion perception (MP), and (6) visual short-term memory (VSTM).

To quantify the visuoperceptual profile (VP), we analyzed clinical records of 630 children (2001–2018), extracted the test scores on 24 visuoperceptual subtests (e.g., L94, TVPS-3, Beery-VMI-6 etc.) and an expert panel clustered these subtests into six VP dimensions. For each of the six VP dimensions, the experts indicated which of the 24 subtests contribute to it. To compute the score of the child on each of the six VP dimensions, z-scores on each of the relevant subtests for every dimension are averaged, resulting in six mean z-scores. The detailed description of the whole process of VP construction can be found in [21].

In the context of the iVision games, the VP of a child is used to define the entry-level difficulty. The design and development of the iVision games is briefly described in the next section. The detailed description of the design and development process is in a separate paper [22].

## 4  iVision Games

The iVision games were developed in several iterations and phases (informant-led design, first prototype development, therapeutic content evaluation, and formative testing and expert feedback). The multi-disciplinary consortium participating in the various phases of the design and development consisted of experts in fields such as vision science, child neurology, physiotherapy, occupational therapy, experimental psychology, clinical psychology, computer science, engineering, and therapeutic game development. We designed, developed, and evaluated four serious mini-games for training visuoperceptual skills. The four mini-games – Match Maker, Hurricane Chaos, Maze Explorer 2D, and Maze Explorer 3D – target the six visuoperceptual skills/dimensions of visuoperceptual profile.

*Match Maker* is a card game where the player needs to find the matching pair of images. The images often are not identical copies and one or both can be manipulated (e.g., they can be incomplete, only show the outline, be overlayed with noise, etc.). *Hurricane Chaos* is a search game where the player needs to find a set of objects scattered on the screen. Each of the target objects has an associated audio instruction to identify it. Moreover, there are several distractor objects scattered on the screen as well. *Maze Explorer 2D* and *Maze Explorer 3D* are maze games where the player needs to lead a character from start to finish of the maze. A mini-map showing the correct path to finish is displayed on the side of the main map. Maze Explorer 2D shows a top view perspective on the whole maze, while Maze Explorer 3D shows a first-person perspective, Fig. 1.

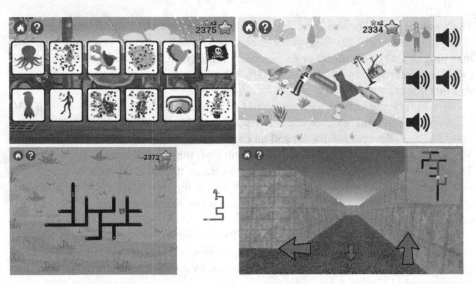

**Fig. 1.** iVision games - Match Maker (top left), Hurricane Chaos (top right), Maze Explorer 2D (bottom left), and Maze Explorer 3D (bottom right).

# 5 Entry-Level Difficulty

The entry-level difficulty estimation refers to the problem of identifying a proper game difficulty (GD) for the initial game sessions of a child. In the iVision games, entry-level difficulty is calculated based on the performance of the children in a broad set of 24 clinical visuoperceptual subtests which were translated into six dimensions of visuoperceptual profile (VP). For the purpose of GD calculation, the six dimensions z-scores were converted into percentiles. The resulting GD is a number between 0 and 100 and influences the difficulty level in terms of game settings.

In the **Match Maker** game, difficulty is defined by the number of cards displayed on the screen, image manipulation used, image difficulty, and the speed at which the cards are presented on the screen. In the **Hurricane Chaos**, the game difficulty changes with the changing number of objects the player needs to find among (changing number of) clutter images shown on the screen and is also influenced by the image placement – more towards the center of the screen or closer to the edges, image rotations, and the size of the images. In the Maze Explorer game, the difficulty rises with the length/complexity of the maze, placement of the points of interests on the cross points in the maze, and guiding mini-map alterations (rotation in **Maze Explorer 2D**, and turning/hiding of the mini-map in **Maze Explorer 3D**).

As explained in [21], the iVision researchers developed a scientific methodology for computing entry-level GD based on the six dimensions. The formulas for entry-level difficulty calculation are specified as the weighted sum of VP dimensions percentile scores (Eq. 1) and differ per game.

$$GD = W_{WDAM} * VDAM + W_{OR} * OR + W_{VSP} * VSP$$
$$+ W_{FGP} * FGP + W_{MP} * MP + W_{VSTM} * VSTM \qquad (1)$$

# 6 Expert-Defined Entry-Level Formulas

The importance of each VP dimension in each of the four mini-games was evaluated by 17 experts. Final weights are the means of the expert estimates and are summarized in Table 1. The experts tended to provide considerably higher weights to two or three VP dimensions per game (marked with a gray background) and they considered several VP dimensions to be of very small to no relevance for each game.

The calculation of the GD definition based on expert knowledge and opinions raised the question whether a data driven approach can predict a more appropriate entry-level GD.

# 7 Data-Driven Entry-Level Formulas

The core idea of our data driven approach was to let children play a few sessions of the game, starting from the expert estimated GD and let in-game adaptivity evolve the GD. The GD stabilizes (converges) after a few gaming sessions. Subsequently, a regression model was trained with the six VP dimensions as independent variables and the converged GD as the dependent variable.

**Table 1.** Expert model: weights assigned to each VP dimension

| | VP Dimensions | | | | | |
| --- | --- | --- | --- | --- | --- | --- |
| | VDaM | OR | VSP | FGP | MP | VSTM |
| Match Maker | 0.5 | 0.2735 | 0.0706 | 0.0824 | 0 | 0.0735 |
| Hurricane Chaos | 0.1265 | 0.4971 | 0.1 | 0.2265 | 0 | 0.05 |
| Maze Explorer 2D | 0.0706 | 0.0441 | 0.5206 | 0.0647 | 0.1588 | 0.1412 |
| Maze Explorer 3D | 0.0371 | 0.0224 | 0.3941 | 0.0312 | 0.2212 | 0.2941 |

Note: Visouperceptual Profile Dimensions are visual discrimination and matching (VDaM), object or picture recognition (OR), visual-spatial perception (VSP), figure-ground perception (FGP), motion perception (MP), and visual short-term memory (VSTM)

The gameplay data used as an input for the regression consists of the data of 42 children (22 female, 20 male), developmental age between 3–12 years (M: 6y3m; SD: 1y6m). The data was collected in four separate batches, lasting between two and four weeks, recruiting 12, 9, 10, and 11 children, respectively. All children were diagnosed with CVI. The purpose of each study was not to collect data for the regression model specifically but to test usability, user experience, etc.

The in-game adaptivity module evaluated performance of the player after each game. Based on the time to finish the level, number of mistakes, and usage of hints combined with expert defined thresholds on these three parameters, the performance was evaluated as either success, neutral, or unsuccess. Each child played several levels of the same difficulty until a predefined number of successful, neutral or unsuccessful evaluations was reached after which the GD was changed (increased or decreased), making the game more (or less) difficult.

## 7.1 Converged Game Difficulty

As an output value for our regression model, we took the converged GD which we defined as the GD the child was playing at without struggle. In the gameplay data collected over several sessions/children, we detected when the child started to struggle, i.e., the first time the performance was evaluated as neutral or unsuccessful.

Since the entry level GD should be appropriately challenging - not too easy, not too difficult - and since it defines the settings of the very first level a child would play, we decided a child should be able to play the games without struggle. Thus, by identifying when a child starts to struggle, and defining an optimal entry level just before this level, we believe to fulfil this condition.

We summarized the mean game difficulty at the start of the gameplay, defined by the expert model and the mean converged game difficulty in Table 2. For all four games, the expert model estimated lower GD than the converged GD we identified. The difference varied between five points for Match Maker and up to 30 points for Maze Explorer 2D. Mean difference refers to the difference between expert and converged GD, while mean absolute difference is the mean of the absolute values of these differences.

**Table 2.** Mean expert defined entry-level GD and converged GD

|  | Mean (SD) expert defined entry-level GD | Mean (SD) converged GD | Mean difference | Mean absolute difference |
|---|---|---|---|---|
| Match Maker | 27.90 (21.45) | 32.90 (20.80) | 5.00 | 8.00 |
| Hurricane Chaos | 28.24 (22.54) | 40.02 (24.26) | 11.79 | 15.17 |
| Maze Explorer 2D | 23.71 (18.26) | 53.83 (34.51) | 30.12 | 31.17 |
| Maze Explorer 3D | 23.50 (18.07) | 45.14 (21.41) | 21.64 | 22.50 |

## 7.2  Linear Regression Setup

To perform the linear regression, we used Python with Scikit Learn. The linear regression model was defined as having six inputs (i.e., the six VP dimensions) and one output (i.e., the converged GD). The input parameters were collected before the start of each study, and the converged GD was looked up manually, based on the criteria described above.

In contrast to the expert model, the regression model learns a bias term of considerable magnitude (ranging from around 10 to almost 35) and the model allows for positive and negative weights. Unfortunately, for several VP dimensions, the model learns strong negative weights. For instance, for Hurricane Chaos, it gives a weight of $-0.995$ for VDaM and for MP it gives a weight of $-0.85$ to the game difficulty, meaning that the better the child performs on the associated clinical subtests, the easier the game should be. The weights obtained from the regression models are shown in Table 3.

**Table 3.** The weights assigned to each VP dimension by the Regression model

|  | | VP Dimensions | | | | | |
|---|---|---|---|---|---|---|---|
|  | $W_0$ | VDaM | OR | VSP | FGP | MP | VSTM |
| Match Maker | 10.179 | 0.344 | 0.126 | 0.157 | 0.171 | $-0.388$ | 0.103 |
| Hurricane Chaos | 19.004 | $-0.995$ | 0.196 | 0.630 | 0.423 | $-0.85$ | 0.623 |
| Maze Explorer 2D | 29.11 | $-0.101$ | $-0.172$ | 0.203 | 0.168 | $-0.569$ | 0.780 |
| Maze Explorer 3D | 34.552 | 0.164 | $-0.073$ | 0.3484 | $-0.045$ | $-0.379$ | 0.065 |

**Note:** $W_0$ is the bias term and Visouperceptual Profile Dimensions are visual discrimination and matching (VDaM), object or picture recognition (OR), visual-spatial perception (VSP), figure-ground perception (FGP), motion perception (MP), and visual short-term memory (VSTM)

### 7.3   Expert Defined Model vs. Linear Regression Model Evaluation

To compare how well both models performed, we calculated several performance metrics, i.e., regression score (as defined by scikit-learn) (Score), root mean squared error (RMSE), the coefficient of determination R2, and mean absolute error (MAE). The collected dataset was split into a training and testing set using an 80:20 ratio. Given the small sample size of our dataset, we repeated the experiment 1000 times. The average results are shown in Table 4.

For Match Maker, both models predict the GD rather well (R2 is above 0.70 which indicates moderate to good correlation [23] and MAE is around 8 for both). For the other three games, the results of both models are poorer. For Hurricane Chaos and Maze Explorer 2D, the regression model is clearly better than the expert model, for Maze Explorer 3D the expert model is better than the regression model according to Score, RMSE and MAE, but not according to R2. It is inconclusive which of the two models performs best, as it differs per metric and game.

**Table 4.** Evaluation of the expert model and the regression model.

|                   |       | Regression model | Expert model   | Significant difference |
|-------------------|-------|------------------|----------------|------------------------|
| Match Maker       | Score | 0.63 (0.27)      | 0.59 (0.33)    | *                      |
|                   | RMSE  | 10.60 (3.41)     | 11.07 (3.89)   | *                      |
|                   | $R^2$ | 0.72 (0.20)      | 0.74 (0.19)    |                        |
|                   | MAE   | 8.27 (2.23)      | 8.01 (2.60)    | *                      |
| Hurricane Chaos   | Score | 0.38 (0.38)      | −0.10 (0.79)   | *                      |
|                   | RMSE  | 16.77 (2.97)     | 21.71 (5.74)   | *                      |
|                   | $R^2$ | 0.56 (0.19)      | 0.44 (0.23)    | *                      |
|                   | MAE   | 14.51 (2.74)     | 15.16 (4.94)   | *                      |
| Maze Explorer 2D  | Score | 0.09 (0.57)      | −0.65 (0.80)   | *                      |
|                   | RMSE  | 29.14 (5.92)     | 40.06 (8.42)   | *                      |
|                   | $R^2$ | 0.37 (0.22)      | 0.35 (0.21)    | *                      |
|                   | MAE   | 24.46 (5.15)     | 30.92 (7.95)   | *                      |
| Maze Explorer 3D  | Score | −0.25 (0.96)     | −1.60 (2.18)   | *                      |
|                   | RMSE  | 20.65 (4.07)     | 28.94 (7.25)   | *                      |
|                   | $R^2$ | 0.22 (0.18)      | 0.26 (0.21)    | *                      |
|                   | MAE   | 17.21 (3.57)     | 22.03 (5.91)   | *                      |

**Note:** * means a significant difference at $p < 0.05$, RMSE is root mean squared error, $R^2$ is the coefficient of determination, MAE is mean absolute error

### 7.4 Expert Defined vs Regression Model Defined Formulas for Children in a Randomized Control Trial

Currently, we are running a Randomized Control Trial (RCT) where over the course of two years 80 children with CVI will play either the adaptive or non-adaptive (control group) version of the iVision games. In the RCT, the regression model formula is used to calculate the entry-level GD. So far, 46 children have completed the game-based therapy part of the RCT, and we compared the entry-level difficulty calculated using the expert defined vs. regression model defined formula. The results are summarized in Table 5. A negative value, i.e., −22 in the "Min GD shift" column, reflects that the regression model-based formula would produce a GD of 22 points smaller than the expert defined formula, thus moving the player to a lower level. A positive value, e.g., 12 in "Max GD shift" column, indicates the exact opposite, the regression-based formula would produce a GD 12 points higher than the expert defined formula and would place the player in a higher difficulty level. On average using the regression model formula, players were placed to a slightly higher difficulty levels than if we have had used the expert defined formula. The regression model formula places very few players, less than a quarter at most, to a lower difficulty level than the expert defined formula would place them.

**Table 5.** Differences between using an expert-based formula vs a regression model-based formula

| | Avg difference | Min GD shift | Max GD shift | % moved to higher level | % moved to lower level |
|---|---|---|---|---|---|
| Match Maker | 4 | −22 | 12 | 24% | 72% |
| Hurricane Chaos | 16 | −37 | 55 | 24% | 76% |
| Maze Explorer 2D | 35 | −12 | 72 | 9% | 91% |
| Maze Explorer 3D | 19 | −33 | 34 | 13% | 87% |

## 8 Discussion

The entry-level estimation is a crucial part of the serious game's individualization and personalization. Starting a game at an appropriate level motivates the player to play the game and lowers boredom and frustration. However, finding the correct starting level is not trivial. The majority of games place players in the first level and subsequently increase it in a predefined stepwise manner. Some games allow the players to choose a starting level, often choosing between easy/medium/hard or give the therapists the ability to set up the level difficulty. The last option seems the most relevant, however therapists may find setting up the difficulty time inefficient and difficult, e.g., due to necessary technical savviness, thorough knowledge of the game, and ability to estimate the players' skills within the game. Moreover, home therapy and rehabilitation became a norm and decisions about an appropriate game level in a tele-therapy session might not be possible. Thus, automatic estimation of the entry-level, based on quantitative player data, e.g., results in standardized visuopeceptual tests, would make the game difficulty setup repeatable, consistent between therapists, and large-scale sustainable.

## 9 Conclusion

In this paper we presented the entry-level estimation for serious games for children with CVI. We explained the importance of entry-level estimation as a part of the personalization and individualization of serious games. We compared two approaches, namely an expert-defined formula to calculate the entry-level game difficulty and a linear regression model-defined formula. We detailed the regression model definition, and presented a comparison of the two models in terms of several performance metrics as well as what difference using one over the other would make for the children participating in our Randomized Control Trial.

In conclusion, there is a small difference in performance of the expert-defined and regression model-defined formula to calculate the entry-level difficulty. This could be because the experts' knowledge and experience led to a correct estimation of importance of each individual VP dimension in the calculation of the entry-level difficulty or it could be because the sample size of the data for the regression model was small. Moreover, due to the small sample size, we were not able to train another regression model to determine which of the 24 standardized visuoperceptual tests, used to calculate the full VP of a child, have the smallest contribution to the entry-level estimation and thus could be excluded from the battery of visuoperceptual tests administered. Lowering the number of visuoperceptual tests which a child needs to undergo lowers the time the testing takes, the frustration, boredom, and subsequently the reliability of the results of the tests.

Since the performance of the expert and regression model defined formulas was very similar, we decided to use the regression model formula in the RCT. We also plan to train the regression model again, once we have more data, i.e.. After the end of the RCT. Sample size permitting, we would also like to train the second regression model, and try to limit the number of the necessary visuoperceptual tests to create the VP of a child.

**Acknowledgements.** This work was supported by the Research Foundation Flanders (FWO-project) [grant number is T004920N].

Parents provided written informed consents and in case of young children, verbal assent was given where possible but researchers monitored participants closely for reluctance to participate.

The authors would like to thank Centrum Ganspoel, the Center for Developmental Disabilities, and the special schools involved in the study for their willingness to provide us the opportunity to collaborate with them and their children. We would like to thank the caregivers and therapists living with and working with children with CVI, parents of the children, and the children themselves.

The authors would like to acknowledge the assistance of their master students Anouk Schaerlaeken, Els Coenen, and Wouter Donkers in following up the children, the families, and the schools who are enrolled in the RCT.

# References

1. U. W. H. O. (WHO): World Report on Disability: Summary. WHO/NMH/VIP/11.01, Geneva (2011)
2. Gaggi, O., Sgaramella, T.M., Nota, L., Bortoluzzi, M., Santilli, S.: A serious games system for the analysis and the development of visual skills in children with CVI. In: Gaggi, O., Manzoni, P., Palazzi, C., Bujari, A., Marquez-Barja, J.M. (eds.) GOODTECHS 2016. LNICSSITE, vol. 195, pp. 155–165. Springer, Cham (2017). https://doi.org/10.1007/978-3-319-61949-1_17
3. Williams, C., et al.: Cerebral visual impairment-related vision problems in primary school children: a cross-sectional survey. Dev. Med. Child Neurol. **63**(6), 683–689 (2021)
4. Ben Itzhak, N., Vancleef, K., Franki, I., Laenen, A., Wagemans, J., Ortibus, E.: Visuoperceptual profiles of children using the Flemish cerebral visual impairment questionnaire. Dev. Med. Child Neurol. **62**(8), 969–976 (2020)
5. Ortibus, E., Fazzi, E., Dale, N.: Cerebral visual impairment and clinical assessment: the European perspective. Semin. Pediatr. Neurol. **31**, 15–24 (2019). https://doi.org/10.1016/j.spen.2019.05.004
6. Ciman, M., Gaggi, O., Sgaramella, T.M., Nota, L., Bortoluzzi, M., Pinello, L.: Serious games to support cognitive development in children with cerebral visual impairment. Mob. Netw. Appl. **23**, 1703–1714 (2018)
7. Dhiman, S., Saini, S.K., Chaurasia, S., Duggal, M., Miglani, V., Raj, S.: A pilot nurse-led telecounseling intervention to parents of children with cerebral visual impairment on adherence to eye activities during COVID-19 pandemic: a pre-experimental study. Front. Med. **8**, 2953 (2022)
8. Delay, A., Rice, M., Bush, E., Harpster, K.: Interventions for children with cerebral visual impairment: a scoping review. Dev. Med. Child Neurol. **65**(4), 469–478 (2023)
9. Linehan, C., Waddington, J., Hodgson, T.L., Hicks, K., Banks, R.: Designing games for the rehabilitation of functional vision for children with cerebral visual impairment. In: CHI'14 Extended Abstracts on Human Factors in Computing Systems, pp. 1207–1212 (2014)
10. Battistin, T., Dalla Pozza, N., Trentin, S., Volpin, G., Franceschini, A., Rodà, A.: Co-designed mini-games for children with visual impairment: a pilot study on their usability. Multimed. Tools Appl. **82**(4), 5291–5313 (2023)
11. Goh, D.H., Ang, R.P., Tan, H.C.: Strategies for designing effective psychotherapeutic gaming interventions for children and adolescents. Comput. Hum. Behav. **24**(5), 2217–2235 (2008)
12. Hocine, N., Ameur, M., Ziani, W.: Keep attention: a personalized serious game for attention training. In: GamiLearn
13. Sajjadi, P., Ewais, A., De Troyer, O.: Individualization in serious games: a systematic review of the literature on the aspects of the players to adapt to. Entertainment Comput. **41**, 100468 (2022). https://doi.org/10.1016/j.entcom.2021.100468
14. Campaña, L.V., Ouimet, D.A.: IStimulation: Apple iPad use with children who are visually impaired, including those with multiple disabilities. J. Vis. Impairment Blindness **109**(1), 67–72 (2015)
15. De Bortoli, A., Gaggi, O.: PlayWithEyes: a new way to test children eye. In: 2011 IEEE 1st International Conference on Serious Games and Applications for Health (SeGAH) (2011)
16. Gaggi, O., Ciman, M.: The use of games to help children eyes testing. Multimed. Tools Appl. **75**, 3453–3478 (2016)
17. Ciman, M., Gaggi, O., Nota, L., Pinello, L., Riparelli, N., Sgaramella, T.M.: HelpMe!: a serious game for rehabilitation of children affected by CVI. In: WEBIST (2013)
18. "Tap-N-See Now," Little Bear Sees. http://littlebearsees.org/cvi-ipad-app-tap-n-see-zoo/. Accessed Apr 2023

19. Waddington, J., Linehan, C., Gerling, K., Hicks, K., Hodgson, T.L.: Participatory design of therapeutic video games for young people with neurological vision impairment. In: Proceedings of the 33rd Annual ACM Conference on Human Factors in Computing Systems, pp. 3533–3542 (2015)
20. Eun, S.-J., Kim, E.J., Kim, J.: Artificial intelligence-based personalized serious game for enhancing the physical and cognitive abilities of the elderly. Futur. Gener. Comput. Syst. **141**, 713–722 (2023)
21. Ben Itzhak, N., Vancleef, K., Franki, I., Laenen, A., Wagemans, J., Ortibus, E.: Quantifying visuoperceptual profiles of children with cerebral visual impairment. Child Neuropsychol. **27**(8), 995–1023 (2021). https://doi.org/10.1080/09297049.2021.1915265
22. Ben Itzhak, N., Franki, I., Jansen, B., Kostkova, K., Wagemans, J., Ortibus, E.: An individualized and adaptive game-based therapy for cerebral visual impairment: design, development, and evaluation. Int. J. Child-Comput. Interact. **31**, 100437 (2022). https://doi.org/10.1016/j.ijcci.2021.100437
23. Portney, L.G., Watkins, M.P., et al.: Foundations of Clinical Research: Applications to Practice, vol. 892. Pearson/Prentice Hall, Upper Saddle River (2009)

# Sound Design Impacts User Experience and Attention in Serious Game

Zijing Cao[1,2]( ) , Eduardo Magalhães[1] , and Gilberto Bernardes[1,2]

[1] Faculty of Engineering, University of Porto, 4200-465 Porto, Portugal
{up202001544,eduardom,gba}@fe.up.pt
[2] INESC TEC, Campus da FEUP, 4200-465 Porto, Portugal

**Abstract.** We study the impact of sound design – soundscape, sound effects, and auditory notifications, namely earcons – on the player's experience of serious games. Three sound design versions for the game *Venci's Adventures* have been developed: 1) no sound; 2) standard sound design, including soundscapes and sound effects; and 3) standard sound design with auditory notification (namely, earcons). Perceptual experiments were conducted to evaluate the most suitable attention retention earcons from a diverse collection of timbres, pitch, and melodic patterns, as well as the user experience of the different sound design versions assessed in pairs (1 vs. 2 and 2 vs. 3). Our results show that participants ($n = 23$) perceive better user experience in terms of game playing competence, immersion, flow, challenge and affect, and enhanced attention retention when adopting standard sound design with the earcons.

**Keywords:** Sound design · Soundscapes · Sound effects · Earcons · Serious game · Attention · User experiences

## 1 Introduction

In recent years, serious games have been extensively employed in the domains of training and education, including areas such as safety and security [24], pedagogy for neurodivergent individuals [29], and support for educational processes [8,14]. Despite their growing popularity, studies have been criticizing serious games due for their inefficiency as educational or training tools, primarily due to the absence of a personalized user experience and poor attention retention during the learning process [9].

Given the above context and limitations, a line of research on sound design is being pushed to study user experience and attention in serious games and educational environments [1,13,28]. Sound design is one of the most important components of serious game [13]. However, dedicated and in-depth research on the impact of different sound design techniques on user experience and attention is yet to be conducted.

Sound design for games typically addresses four categories: sound effects, soundscapes or ambient sounds, dialogue sounds, and musical events [3,6]. In

M. Haahr et al. (Eds.): JCSG 2023, LNCS 14309, pp. 95–110, 2023.
https://doi.org/10.1007/978-3-031-44751-8_7

this paper, we address soundscapes and sound effects only. Soundscapes refer to the surrounding sonic environment of a particular scene or location [5]. Its design typically adopts a mixture of real-world recordings and digital sounds [21]. For example, in a driving simulation game, the soundscape can reproduce recordings inside a car from a driver's perspective, to which some synthesized sounds can be added [25]. Sound effects usually refer to the sounds triggered when players interact with game events. The link between players and game events or objects can be built on sound effects.

This paper introduces two experiments to study sound design's impact on user experience and attention based on the serious game *Venci's Adventures*. Three different versions of the game were developed: 1) no sound, 2) standard sound design (including soundscapes and sound effects), and 3) standard sound design with auditory notifications or earcons. Perceptual experiments assessed the best sonic parameters for the earcons' design and the impact on user experience and attention of the three designed versions.

The remainder of this paper is structured as follows. Section 2 provides an overview of previous research on sound design strategies for enhancing user experience and attention within serious games. Section 3 details the sound design techniques applied to the serious game *Venci's Adventures* and used in the perceptual experiments. Section 4 presents the evaluation protocols used in the experiments. Section 5 details the experiment results. Finally, Sect. 6 presents the conclusions of our work and directions for future research.

## 2   Related Work

Previous studies have focused on the impact of sound design on the video gaming user experience – namely in enhancing the player's sense of immersion – and attention.

Natasa et al. [21] studied the impact and influence of sound design, namely soundscapes, sound effects, and dialogues, on users' emotional responses and immersion within augmented reality audio games. The authors found that sound design is important in immersing and emotionally engaging the player in the game world. Emmanouel et al. [23] studied the effect of real-time interactive, ambient, and 3D spatial sounds in the game experience. Results show that interactive sound generation mechanics can improve the immersion and challenge of the game experience.

Furthermore, sonic interaction design, namely sound effects, can increase player's experiences, such as enjoyment, learning, motivation, immersion, emotional engagement, and attention in virtual worlds [1,7,18,20,26–28,30]. For example, in the game 'My Sound Space,' Eriksson et al. [11] have shown that ambient sound can redirect people's attention to an ongoing cognitive activity. Falkenberg et al. [12] have shown that peripheral auditory notifications could direct people's attention in a virtual retail environment.

Sound design is yet to be fully studied and explored in educational contexts. The work of Wang and Lieberoth [28] shows that game-based learning incorporating sound design has a demonstrably positive impact on students' focus, involvement, satisfaction, knowledge acquisition, and drive during classroom activities when contrasted with the absence of sound. Alseid and Rigas [1] found that the teaching outcome of an online course can be improved by using auditory earcons to convey keyword information to students.

## 3    *Venci's Adventures*: A Serious Game on Cybersecurity Awareness

*Venci's Adventures* game adopts 2D platforming mechanics within Unity[1] and explores a cyber security-themed storyline, challenging players to improve their cybersecurity knowledge. The game has four scenarios: beach, forest, cave, and temple. Figure 1 shows the storyline. Cybersecurity problem-solving challenges in each scenario drive knowledge acquisition. The challenges require the player to answer several quizzes to assess their learning outcomes.

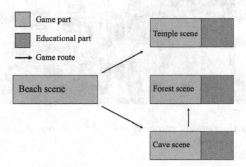

**Fig. 1.** Simplified storyline transitions of the serious game *Venci's Adventures*. The educational part, comprising quizzes, is presented subsequent to the game part within the temple, forest, and cave scenes.

### 3.1    Soundscapes

Following [10,19], we adopt soundscapes comprised of continuous representative 'physical-world' sounds related to each scenario in *Venci's Adventures*. These sounds aim at helping players identify the environment and increase the sense of immersion in the virtual world. To design each soundscape scenario, we followed a threefold method. First, we identified and listed relevant sound sources matching the visual scenarios. Second, we retrieved stereo sound samples for each identified source from the online sound libraries Freesound[2] and Soundcloud.[3]

---

[1] https://unity.com, last accessed on May 15, 2023.
[2] https://freesound.org, last accessed on 15 May, 2023.
[3] https://soundcloud.com, last accessed on 15 May, 2023.

Third, we designed the soundscape narratives using the digital audio workstation Reaper.[4] In the following sections, we detail the soundscapes sources of each scene, matching the visual scenarios shown in Fig. 2, and their temporal narrative development. In the supplementary materials to this article, we can find a short rendering of each scene soundscape, available online at: https://figshare.com/articles/media/Game_sound/23153732.

**Fig. 2.** Four scenes in the serious game *Venci's Adventures*: A. Beach scene B. Forest scene C. Cave scene D. Temple scene.

The soundscape of the **beach scene** includes the following four sound sources: ocean waves, wind, people playing on the beach, and birds chirping at a distant forest. The sonic narrative starts with waves and wind sounds, as the game character (GC) enters the beach scene. As the GC approaches people playing on the beach, the player is immersed in the auditory experience of the waves and the lively atmosphere of people engaging in beach activities. Specifically designed to enhance realism, the sounds of people playing on the beach seamlessly fade in and out as the GC passes by. Finally, as the GC concludes the beach scene, the player's auditory perception is enriched by the simultaneous presence of the soothing waves and the melodious chirping of birds within the forest. This incorporation of forest bird sounds serves a dual purpose: to facilitate a seamless transition between scenes and to evoke anticipation for the forthcoming forest scene.

The **forest scene**'s soundscape comprises the following four sound sources: birdcall and insect sounds, wind through swaying trees, and distant beach waves. The transition from the beach to the forest scene is marked by the soundscape

---

[4] https://www.reaper.fm, last accessed on May 2, 2023.

narrative that evolves around the enchanting birds chirping in the forest and the gradually fading waves. As the GC reaches the midpoint of the forest, the player becomes immersed in the experience of the wind gently rustling through the trees, accompanied by the melodious chorus of birds and insects. Towards the end of the forest scene, the player encounters a quiz on cybersecurity, signaled by the distant birds chirping, serving as an auditory cue that signifies the impending end of the scene.

The auditory landscape within the **cave scene** encompasses two primary sound sources: the electronically synthesized sound of dripping water and the presence of wind within caves, accompanied by its resonating echoes. The soundscape gradually transitions as the narrative shifts from the forest to the cave scene. The fading melodies of birds and the gentle crashing of waves intertwine with the growing prominence of wind and its echoes, effectively guiding the listener through the scene's sonic metamorphosis. Upon reaching the midpoint of the cave, the composition expands to include the atmospheric symphony of dripping water, wind, and captivating reverberations within the cavernous space. Finally, as the cave scene nears its culmination, a second cybersecurity quiz emerges, accompanied by the gradual attenuation of wind sounds within the cave, subtly signaling the impending end of the scene.

The soundscape within the **temple scene** is primarily characterized by the immersive presence of wind sounds. Upon the GC's arrival at the temple scene via the cable car, the player is greeted by the resonant echoes of wind captured from the lofty heights of the surrounding mountains. As the GC ventures into the temple and proceeds toward the educational section of the scene, the auditory experience subtly shifts. In order to authentically recreate the indoor atmosphere, the player is enveloped by the gentle whispers of the wind, faintly perceptible, fostering a heightened sense of being within the temple's sacred confines.

### 3.2   Sound Effects

The crafted sound effects aim to enhance the player's overall user experience, emphasizing fostering a sense of immersion. Two primary types of sound effects have been incorporated into the game design. The first type caters to the actions and movements of the player's in-GC, encompassing sounds like footsteps, jumping, falling, and the collection and dropping of puzzle pieces. These sound effects dynamically adapt to the visual context of each scene, taking into account various environmental factors such as soil materials and textures (e.g., grass, wood, stone, water, and sand). This careful synchronization between audio and visual elements ensures a cohesive and realistic gameplay experience.

In contrast, the second type of sound effects is tailored to the objects and entities surrounding the GC within the game world. This includes the likes of seagulls, mosquitoes, flies, collapsing stone pillars, moving stone platforms, and cable cars, as well as the audio cues associated with puzzles and other interactive elements. While the first type of sound effects is presented in mono, the second type embraces stereo techniques, leveraging the spatial positioning within the stereo sound field to enhance immersion. For instance, as players navigate the GC through the forest scene, they can audibly perceive the realistic sound of flying insects originating from various directions, amplifying the immersive qualities of the game world.

### 3.3  Auditory Notifications

Auditory notifications are based on the design of earcons, i.e., short, structured musical messages. Typically, designers adopt earcons to alert the player to events that require their attention [2,4,19,22]. Based on guidelines for earcons design reported in Blattner, Sumikawa, and Greenberg [2], we created 22 auditory notifications with threefold attribute categorizations: pitch, timbre, and melodic pattern. Pitch can be categorized either as high or low. The split point between the two categories is the C2 note or 65.41 Hz. Earcon's timbre is categorized as either simple or complex tones. Melodic pattern is categorized as either a unique tone or a broken chord with ascending, descending, or a combination of both patterns. Eleven notifications signal incorrect answers (the I-part notifications), while the remaining denote correct answers (the C-part notification). Table 1 summarizes the attributes of all created auditory notifications. All earcons do not exceed two seconds in duration, and we classify them as more than one second (>1 s) and less than one second (<1 s). The supplementary materials to this article, available online at https://figshare.com/articles/media/Earcons/23152871, include all designed earcons.

**Fig. 3.** The educational part of the temple scene.

An example of the auditory notification's use in *Venci's Adventures* is shown in Fig. 3. In the quiz part of the temple scene, where the player needs to control the GC to select the correct spelling of the web domain by stepping on the underground press button. The earcons signal the sound of the push buttons.

**Table 1.** Sonic attributes of the 22 earcons designed for the *Venci's Adventures* game. The I and C earcons represent incorrect and correct answers given by players during the educational part, respectively. Timbre is classified as simple or complex tones, while pitch is divided into high and low frequencies. The melodic pattern includes unique tones or broken chords with ascending, descending, or combined directions.

|     | Timbre  | Pitch | Pattern                              | Timing |
|-----|---------|-------|--------------------------------------|--------|
| I1  | Simple  | High  | Unique tone                          | <1 s   |
| I2  | Complex | High  | Broken chord Descending              | >1     |
| I3  | Complex | High  | Broken chord Descending              | <1 s   |
| I4  | Simple  | Low   | Unique tone                          | <1 s   |
| I5  | Complex | High  | Broken chord Descending-Ascending    | >1 s   |
| I6  | Complex | Low   | Broken chord Descending              | >1 s   |
| I7  | Complex | High  | Broken chord Descending              | >1 s   |
| I8  | Complex | Low   | Broken chord Descending              | <1 s   |
| I9  | Complex | Low   | Broken chord Descending              | <1 s   |
| I10 | Simple  | Low   | Unique tone                          | <1 s   |
| I11 | Complex | Low   | Broken chord Descending              | <1 s   |
| C1  | Complex | High  | Unique tone                          | <1 s   |
| C2  | Complex | High  | Broken chord Ascending               | >1 s   |
| C3  | Complex | High  | Broken chord Ascending               | <1 s   |
| C4  | Complex | High  | Broken chord Ascending               | <1 s   |
| C5  | Complex | Low   | Broken chord Descending              | >1 s   |
| C6  | Complex | High  | Broken chord Ascending               | >1 s   |
| C7  | Complex | High  | Broken chord Ascending               | <1 s   |
| C8  | Complex | High  | Broken chord Ascending               | >1 s   |
| C9  | Complex | High  | Broken chord Ascending               | >1 s   |
| C10 | Complex | High  | Broken chord Ascending               | >1 s   |
| C11 | Complex | High  | Broken chord Ascending               | >1 s   |

## 4    Evaluation

We conducted two experiments. The first experiment's primary objective was identifying the most effective sonic parameterization for auditory notifications or earcons. Subsequently, the second experiment aimed to assess participants' game experiences within the serious game *Venci's Adventures* under two distinct conditions: with and without sound. To achieve this, we first investigated the general game experiences of participants based on two game versions: the no-sound version, lacking auditory elements, and the standard sound design version, incorporating soundscapes and sound effects per the game's intended experience. Furthermore, we also explored the potential of well-designed auditory notifications to enhance participants' attention in serious games by comparing participants' engagement in the standard sound version and an additional notification version. The notification version is made by adding additional auditory notifications to the standard sound version.

A total of 23 individuals, comprising 8 females and 15 males, ranging in age from 18 to 54, willingly volunteered to partake in our experiments. The age groups of the participants were distributed as follows: 69.6% were aged between 21 and 30 years old, 21.7% below 20 years old, and the remainder were aged between 31 and 40 years old. Most participants (65.2%) had previous experience with online educational tools and were familiar with the online questionnaires. Due to confidentiality agreements, all participants were employees of the company *Emvenci Portugal Limitada*, as the *Venci's Adventures* game was still under development at the time of the experiments.

## 4.1    Experiment 1: Earcons Design

Each participant was guided through a twofold structured protocol for the first experiment encompassing two steps. First, demographic information for each participant was collected, including age range, gender, and prior experience with online educational testing. Collected data assisted in establishing a comprehensive participant profile for subsequent analysis.

Second, participants were exposed to two sets of earcons specifically designed to signal incorrect and correct answers in the quiz, referred to as the I- and C-part notifications. Within each set, earcons were presented by a uniform random allocation to avoid order effects. After each earcon, participants were prompted to assess *their efficacy* in signaling an incorrect or correct response. Participants used a seven-point Likert scale ranging from one (not at all) to seven (very much) to rate their perceptions.

We computed descriptive statistics reporting average ratings and their standard deviation to analyze the perceptual data regarding the efficacy of different earcons within each set. Earcons with the highest ratings will be understood as the more effective in eliciting incorrect and correct answers. Furthermore, we will assess user preferences in terms of sound parameters, namely in terms of pitch and timbre in the I-part earcons, which provide a more balanced number of examples across parameter changes. To this end, we apply a two-tailed paired t-test, assessing the probability of the two sample data occurring by chance. We adopt $p \leq .01$ as a reference for statistical significance.

## 4.2    Experiment 2: User Experience and Attention

The second experiment was structured into four distinct phases. Phase one consisted of a pre-experimental questionnaire and group allocation. In detail, participants were first required to complete a pre-experimental questionnaire, which encompassed demographic information such as age range, gender, and the presence of any hearing impairments. As the experiment heavily relied on auditory stimuli, it was crucial to ensure that all participants had normal hearing capabilities. Based on the collected data, we split participants into two groups (named Groups 1 and 2), to prevent any potential biases or repetitive measures effects.

In phase two, participants were introduced to *Venci's Adventures* game and provided consent for video recording. All participants received comprehensive instructions regarding the basic operation of the *Venci's Adventures* game. Furthermore, participants were explicitly asked for their consent to have their gameplay actions video recorded for subsequent analysis.

Phase three was distinct for each participant group. Participants in Group 1 conducted an assessment of the impact of the sound design in *Venci's Adventures* using a adapted version of the In-game version of the Game Experience Questionnaire (GEQ) [15,16]. Participants in Group 1 played the no sound and standard sound design versions of the game. To avoid order effects a uniform random allocation of the versions order was adopted. After each version, participants were asked to complete the GEQ, as outlined in Table 2. Depending on the sound designed version played, participants were asked to respond to GEQ-NoSound and GEQ-Sound for no sound and sound design versions, respectively. The questionnaire includes 14 questions assessing players' competence, immersion, flow, tension, challenge, and positive and negative emotions based on items proposed in the core guidelines suggested by IJsselsteijn et al [15]. Each dimension comprises two questions, and the average ratings of these questions are utilized to represent the respective dimension's score.

**Table 2.** Questions of the questionnaire used in the main part of the first experiment.

| Dimensions | No. | Questions (GEQ-NoSound and GEQ-Sound) |
|---|---|---|
| Competence | Q1 | Feel very skillful |
| | Q2 | Feel fast at reaching |
| Immersion | Q3 | Keep you interested |
| | Q4 | Enrich your gaming experience |
| Flow | Q5 | Immerse you entirely |
| | Q6 | Keep you deeply concentrated |
| Tension | Q7 | Annoyed you |
| | Q8 | Make you feel irritable |
| Challenge | Q9 | Pressured you |
| | Q10 | Made you have to put a lot of effort into it |
| Affect (+) | Q11 | Make you feel good |
| | Q12 | Make you enjoy |
| Affect (−) | Q13 | Gave you a bad mood |
| | Q14 | Gave you tiresomely |

Participants in Group 2 examined the impact of the earcons pre-selected in experiment 1 in attention retention during the educational parts or quizzes. To investigate whether the earcons in addition to the standard game sound design version enhances participants' attention during important educational segments of the serious game, a tailored questionnaire was developed based on the questionnaire design approach known as Game Mode Specific Questionnaire (GMSQ), proposed in [23].

Participants played the standard sound design version of the game and the sound design version with auditory notifications or earcons. To avoid order effects a uniform random allocation of the versions order was adopted. After each game version, participants were asked to complete the Game Mode Specific Questionnaire for the sound design version (GMSQ-Sound) and with the addition earcons (GMSQ-SoundNotify), as presented in Table 3. This questionnaire aimed at capturing the participants perception on attention, focus and response feedback during the quiz parts of the game.

**Table 3.** Questions of the questionnaire used in the main part of the second experiment.

| No. | Questions (GMSQ-Sound and GMSQ-SoundNotify) |
|-----|---------------------------------------------|
| Q1 | Maintain your attention |
| Q2 | Make me focus more on when choosing a question |
| Q3 | Enhance attention to the outcome of your response |
| Q4 | Rate to what extent the notification/none influenced the way you chose your answer |
| Q5 | Rate to what extent the notification/none make you realize your answer is wrong |
| Q6 | Rate to what extent the notification/none make you realize your answer is right |

In both questionnaires, all participants are asked to use the Absolute Category Rating (ACR) System to rate their experience independently on a category scale. ACR is recommended by ITU-T P.910 [17], shown in Table 4. Participants were measured using five categories: Not at all, Slightly, Moderately, Fairly, and Extremely.

**Table 4.** Absolute Category Rating (ACR) System.

| Rating Scale | 1 | 2 | 3 | 4 | 5 |
|--------------|---|---|---|---|---|
| Absolute Category | Not at all | Slightly | Moderately | Fairly | Extremely |

To compute the results and infer trends in the collected data, we calculated descriptive statistics (average and standard deviation). Furthermore, we assessed the statistically significant differences between sound design version (1 vs. 2 and 2 vs. 3) using a two-tailed paired t-test, assessing the probability of the sample data to occur by chance. We adopt $p \leq .01$ as a reference for statistically significant results.

# 5    Results and Discussion

## 5.1    Experiment 1

Figure 4 shows the average and standard deviation ratings for the I-part (a) and C-part (b) earcons under evaluation. The I6 and C6 earcons had the highest average rating in each part. They were adopted in the *Venci's Adventures* game as they have been perceptually rated as the earcons providing the most efficient sound in signaling both incorrect or correct answers, respectively. Experiment 2 adopts the I6 and C6 earcons in the sound design version of the game with auditory notifications.

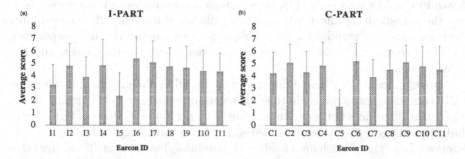

**Fig. 4.** The average and standard deviation perceptual ratings of the 22 earcons in the I-part (a) and C-parts (b) on the left and right, respectively. I- and C- parts signal incorrect and correct answers. The sonic attributes of designed earcons are shown in Table 1.

In addition, we explored parameter preferences in the designed I-part and C-part earcons in terms of timbre (simple vs. complex tone) and pitch (low vs. high), as shown in Table 1. The two-sample unequal variance test results suggest no significant statistical differences for both parameters under study, with $p \geq .05$. Nevertheless, the findings indicate a potential association between incorrect and correct responses to low (descending) and high (ascending) pitch, respectively, and a prevailing inclination towards complex timbre eracons. Future research with a more in-depth parameters analysis shall be conducted. A uniform distribution per sonic attribute and inter-parameter relations may yield more enlightening results.

## 5.2   Experiment 2

Figure 5 shows the average ratings of **Group 1** responses to the GEQ comparing the no sound (GEQ-NoSound) and standard sound design (GEQ-Sound) versions of the game. As shown in Fig. 5, the standard sound design version ranked much higher than the no sound version in almost all user game experience dimensions – competence, immersion, flow, (low) tension, (low) challenge, positive affect, and (low) negative affect.

The enhanced user experience reported by participants in the standard version can be attributed to the heightened audio-visual synchronicity observed between all scenes and movements of the GC and the corresponding real-world experience. For instance, as players engage in the serious game and progress to the beach scene, they naturally anticipate hearing the sound of waves and birds chirping following the visual depiction of the sea and birds' presence. The absence of such auditory stimulation can lead to incongruences between the players' expectations and the game's imagetics, ultimately resulting in a subpar user experience.

The paired t-test results, with a 1% significance level, assessing statistical differences between the no sound and standard sound version per question, are shown in Fig. 5 as an asterisk (*), after the question number in the $x$-axis, whenever the statistical significance is found. Significant statistical differences enforce the importance of standard sound designing in enhancing the user experience regarding competence (achievements), immersion, flow, positive affect, and low negative affect.

Non-significant statistical differences were found in dimensions of competence (skills) and more expressively in the dimensions of tension and challenge. The less expressive differences between the standard sound version in terms of tension and challenges suggest that some designed sounds may have triggered some irritable reactions from the participants leading to potential distractions. To address this concern in future endeavors, we may consider assessing the component sounds individually before the game experience and, eventually, a greater degree of variation or adopting generative strategies to increase the variability over time.

A final note on the comparison of the players' perception of their competence ($p \geq .05$) and challenge ($p \geq .05$), respectively. The findings signify that sound design has the potential to evoke a dual effect on players, wherein they perceive a reduced sense of competence while simultaneously experiencing heightened levels of challenge. Furthermore, there exist two plausible explanations for the aforementioned outcomes. The first explanation posits that the existing four scenes within the serious game may be too straightforward for all players, resulting in the perception that the game can be effortlessly managed without requiring significant skill or exertion. Under such circumstances, distinguishing the disparities in challenges between the two game versions becomes arduous for players. The second explanation revolves around the notion that game sound predominantly influences individuals' subjective experiences during gameplay, exerting only a limited impact on the objective aspects of game-related sensations.

Figure 6 shows the average ratings of **Group 2** responses to the Game Mode Specific Questionnaire (GMSQ) comparing the standard sound design (GMSQ-Sound) and with additional auditory notifications (GMSQ-SoundNotify) versions of the game. As shown in Fig. 6, the notification version was rated higher in all questionnaire dimensions – measuring attention retention, focus, attention enhancement, and feedback information. It shows that the added auditory notifications improve the players' attention during the quiz part of the serious game compared to the standard sound design version.

The paired t-test results, with a 1% significance level, assessing statistical differences between the standard sound version and the added notification version per question, are shown in Fig. 6 as an asterisk (*), after the question number in the $x$-axis, whenever the statistical significance is found. The results indicate that, compared to the standard sound version, the auditory notification provid-

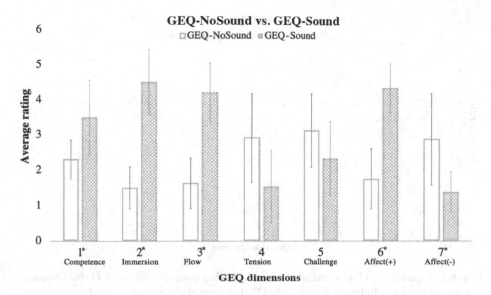

**Fig. 5.** Comparison of the average ratings of the GEQ-NoSound and GEQ-Sound. Questions numbers followed by asterisks (*) denote statistically significant results with $p \leq .01$.

ing feedback sounds representing the incorrect and correct answers, attention retention, and focus have highly significant positive effects on the participants (with $p \leq .01$).

The auditory notifications representing the incorrect and correct answers can induce the player to focus on the quiz part of the game. Compared to the standard sound design version, in the auditory notification version, both the auditory notification sound representing the player's answer is correct and the sound representing the player's answer is incorrect to have significantly positive effects on capturing more attention during the play stages in the education part.

The auditory notifications signaling correct and incorrect answers have the potential to direct the player's attention towards the quiz components of the game. In comparison to the standard sound design version, the inclusion of auditory notification sounds denoting both correct and incorrect player responses within yields noticeably positive effects in terms of garnering heightened attention during the educational stages of gameplay.

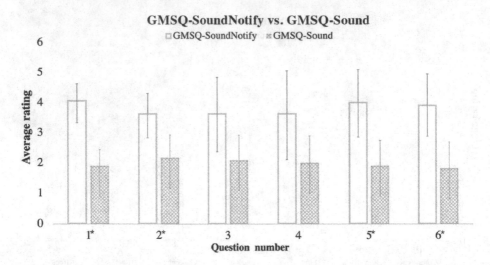

**Fig. 6.** Comparison of the mean values of GMSQ-SoundNotify and GMSQ-Sound. Questions numbers followed by asterisks (*) denote statistically significant results with $p \leq .01$.

## 6  Conclusions and Future Work

In this study, we empirically examine the influence of sound design on user experience and attention in the serious game *Venci's Adventures*. Two experiments were conducted to empirically assess the perception of user in: 1) selecting the most effective earcons in retaining the user attention and conveying feedback on quiz responses and 2) assessing the impact on user experience of threefold serious game versions – no sound, standard sound design including soundscapes and sound effects, and standard sound design with earcons. Three main conclusions were drawn from our results.

First, in the first experiment, the earcons evaluation led to the selection of two auditory notification that proved to be the most effective in retaining the attention from the user and providing clear feedback in terms of the correctness of the answer during a quiz. Further analysis of earcon parameters revealed no significant preferences with regards to timbre (simple vs. complex tone) and pitch (low vs. high).

Second, the standard version of the serious game has been perceived as conveying a significantly positive effect on players' user experiences in terms of immersion, flow, and (positive) affect, when compared to the no-sound version. Additionally, it resulted in fewer negative experiences in terms of tension and negative affect for players. This can be attributed to the proper sound design in the serious game, which meets players' expectations by incorporating specific sounds based on their life experiences, thus providing a favorable gaming experience.

Furthermore, an intriguing results was observed. Players did not perceive significant disparities in skill and effort between the standard and no-sound versions of the serious game. Two possible explanations were posited: 1) the existing four scenes of the serious game are too easy for all players to discern the variation in difficulty caused by different game versions; 2) the perception of difficulty is objective, and sound design primarily impacts players' subjective experiences and moods during the game, rather than objective perceptions.

Third, the sound design version featuring auditory notifications or earcons, in comparison to the standard sound design version, exhibited significantly positive effects on measuring attention retention, focus, attention enhancement, and feedback during the educational stages of gameplay (i.e. quizzes). Both the auditory notification sound denoting correct and incorrect answers contributed to these effects.

In summary, sound design constitutes a crucial and indispensable component of serious game development, ensuring an enhanced gaming experience for players. Moreover, employing specific sound types, such as earcons created using musical notes and sine tones, as auditory notifications, can effectively improve players' attention in serious games.

Future research endeavors will involve a systematic analysis of how the sonic attributes present in earcons lead to variations in implication, as well as the impact of different sound designs encompassing ambient sounds and sound effects on players' attention in serious games. Based on the findings, generalized good practices for serious game sound design will be unveiled to enhance learners' attention and improve learning outcomes.

# References

1. Alseid, M., Rigas, D.: The role of earcons and auditory icons in the usability of avatar-based e-learning interfaces. In: 2011 Developments in E-systems Engineering, pp. 276–281. IEEE (2011)
2. Blattner, M.M., Sumikawa, D.A., Greenberg, R.M.: Earcons and icons: their structure and common design principles. Hum.-Comput. Interact. 4(1), 11–44 (1989)
3. Brandon, A.: Audio for Games: Planning, Process, and Production (New Riders Games). New Riders Games (2004)
4. Brewster, S., Raty, V.P., Kortekangas, A.: Earcons as a method of providing navigational cues in a menu hierarchy. In: Sasse, M.A., Cunningham, R.J., Winder, R.L. (eds.) People and Computers XI, pp. 169–183. Springer, London (1996). https://doi.org/10.1007/978-1-4471-3588-3_12
5. Chattopadhyay, B.: Reconstructing atmospheres: ambient sound in film and media production. Commun. Public 2(4), 352–364 (2017)
6. Collins, K.: Game Sound: An Introduction to the History, Theory, and Practice of Video Game Music and Sound Design. MIT Press, Cambridge (2008)
7. Dakic, V.: Sound design for film and television (2009)
8. De Freitas, S.I.: Using games and simulations for supporting learning. Learn. Media Technol. 31(4), 343–358 (2006)
9. De Troyer, O.: Towards effective serious games. In: 2017 9th International Conference on Virtual Worlds and Games for Serious Applications (VS-Games), pp. 284–289. IEEE (2017)
10. Dede, C.: Immersive interfaces for engagement and learning. Science 323(5910), 66–69 (2009)
11. Eriksson, M.L., Pareto, L., Atienza, R., Hansen, K.F.: My sound space: an attentional shield for immersive redirection. In: Proceedings of the Audio Mostly 2018 on Sound in Immersion and Emotion, pp. 1–4. Elsevier (2018)

12. Falkenberg, K., Frid, E., Eriksson, M.L., Otterbring, T., Daunfeldt, S.: Auditory notification of customer actions in a virtual retail environment: sound design, awareness and attention. Georgia Institute of Technology (2021)
13. Gualdron, D.A.R.: Developing effective virtual simulations and serious games: the effect of background sound cues on visual quality perception. University of Ontario Institute of Technology (Canada) (2012)
14. Habgood, M.J., Ainsworth, S.E.: Motivating children to learn effectively: exploring the value of intrinsic integration in educational games. J. Learn. Sci. 20(2), 169–206 (2011)
15. IJsselsteijn, W.A., De Kort, Y.A.W., Poels, K.: The game experience questionnaire (2013)
16. IJsselsteijn, W.A., De Kort, Y.A.W., Poels, K., Jurgelionis, A., Bellotti, F.: Characterising and measuring user experiences in digital games. In: International Conference on Advances in Computer Entertainment Technology, vol. 2, p. 27 (2007)
17. J.148, I.T.R.: Subjective video quality assessment methods for multimedia applications (1999)
18. Jennett, C., et al.: Measuring and defining the experience of immersion in games. Int. J. Hum. Comput. Stud. 66(9), 641–661 (2008)
19. Leplâtre, G.: The design and evaluation of non-speech sounds to support navigation in restricted display devices. University of Glasgow (United Kingdom) (2002)
20. Lopes, P., Liapis, A., Yannakakis, G.N.: Modelling affect for horror soundscapes. IEEE Trans. Affect. Comput. 10(2), 209–222 (2017)
21. Paterson, N., Naliuka, K., Jensen, S.K., Carrigy, T., Haahr, M., Conway, F.: Design, implementation and evaluation of audio for a location aware augmented reality game. In: Proceedings of the 3rd International Conference on Fun and Games, pp. 149–156 (2010)
22. Patterson, R.D., Edworthy, J., Lower, M.C.: Alarm sounds for medical equipment in intensive care areas and operating theatres. University of Southampton, Institute of Sound and Vibration Research (1986)
23. Rovithis, E., Moustakas, N., Floros, A., Vogklis, K.: Audio legends: investigating sonic interaction in an augmented reality audio game. Multimodal Technol. Interact. 3(4), 73 (2019)
24. Rüppel, U., Schatz, K.: Designing a BIM-based serious game for fire safety evacuation simulations. Adv. Eng. Inform. 25(4), 600–611 (2011)
25. Smith, B.A., Nayar, S.K.: The rad: making racing games equivalently accessible to people who are blind. In: Proceedings of the 2018 CHI Conference on Human Factors in Computing Systems, pp. 1–12 (2018)
26. Sonnenschein, D.: Sound Design: The Expressive Power of Music, Voice, and Sound Effects in Cinema. Michael Wiese Productions (2001)
27. Toprac, P., Abdel-Meguid, A.: Causing fear, suspense, and anxiety using sound design in computer games. In: Game Sound Technology and Player Interaction: Concepts and Developments, pp. 176–191. IGI Global (2011)
28. Wang, A.I., Lieberoth, A.: The effect of points and audio on concentration, engagement, enjoyment, learning, motivation, and classroom dynamics using Kahoot. In: European Conference on Games Based Learning, vol. 20. Academic Conferences International Limited (2016)
29. Whyte, E.M., Smyth, J.M., Scherf, K.S.: Designing serious game interventions for individuals with autism. J. Autism Dev. Disord. 45, 3820–3831 (2015)
30. Yewdall, D.L.: The Practical Art of Motion Picture Sound. Routledge (2012)

# Bridging the Gap: Knowledge Spaces and Storylines in Serious Games

Wolfgang F. Brabänder[(✉)] and Stefan Göbel

Technical University of Darmstadt, 64289 Darmstadt, Germany
{wolfgang_friedrich.brabaender,stefan_peter.goebel}@tu-darmstadt.de,
https://www.etit.tu-darmstadt.de/serious-games

**Abstract.** In this paper, we propose a novel method for simplifying the design of adaptive educational games by integrating Knowledge Space Theory (KST) with real- and/or build-time knowledge space alterations based on a story model and player progress. Our approach streamlines the design process by providing a more manageable learning experience for players, facilitating collaboration among game designers, educators, and narrative designers, and enhancing the overall effectiveness of serious games. By combining build-time and real-time adaptation techniques, our method enables dynamic learning experiences that maintain an engaging narrative structure while ensuring that the game remains focused on its learning objectives. We discuss the implications, potential benefits, and limitations of our approach, and provide an example of its application in the development of a vocational training serious game for teaching IT-security at the workplace. Future research directions include the evaluation of the adaptivity and learning engagement of players, as well as exploring more complex adaptations and additional educational fields.

**Keywords:** Adaptive educational games · Knowledge Space Theory · Serious games · Game design · Narrative structure · Learning experience · Build-time adaptation · Real-time adaptation · Personalized learning · Educational technology

## 1 Introduction

Adaptive serious games enhance the learning experience by adjusting to individual learners and providing a personalized experience that addresses their unique needs and goals [1,2]. With the increasing complexity of games, it becomes essential to provide an engaging experience that seamlessly integrates learning with storytelling [3]. Knowledge Space Theory (KST), first introduced by Doignon and Falmagne (1985) [15], has become a widely used approach in designing adaptive educational systems, as it offers a structured representation of learners' knowledge and enables tailoring learning content to individual needs and preferences.

M. Haahr et al. (Eds.): JCSG 2023, LNCS 14309, pp. 111–123, 2023.
https://doi.org/10.1007/978-3-031-44751-8_8

In this paper, we propose a novel approach to simplify the design of learning games using Knowledge Space Theory and either build-time or real-time knowledge space alterations - where build-time alterations refer to changes made during the design process, and real-time alterations occur dynamically during gameplay - based on player progress, allowing for dynamic learning experiences while maintaining an engaging narrative structure. Our approach has the potential to significantly impact the field of serious games by facilitating collaboration among game designers, programmers, educators, and narrative designers, streamlining the design process, and ultimately creating more immersive and effective serious games that cater to individual learners' needs and preferences.

Our objective is to design a system that initially simplifies a complex knowledge space domain, given a specific story model. This process enhances the task development by allowing a more concentrated approach. Subsequently, the system evolves to accommodate the domain alterations in response to the player's progression, optimizing the learning path adaptation corresponding to the individual decisions made by the player.

The paper is structured as follows: Sect. 2 presents a review of related work in adaptive educational games, focusing on the use of Knowledge Space Theory and storytelling techniques; Sect. 3 introduces our proposed method, describing build-time adaptation, run-time adaptation, and the hybrid model; Sect. 4 discusses the implications and potential benefits of our approach; and Sect. 5 concludes the paper and highlights future research directions.

## 2    Related Work

Adaptive educational games have gained increased attention in recent years due to their potential to provide personalized learning experiences that cater to individual learners' needs and preferences [1,2]. Several approaches have been proposed to achieve adaptivity, such as Bayesian networks, reinforcement learning, and machine learning techniques [11,12]. However, Knowledge Space Theory (KST) has been widely used as a foundation for designing adaptive educational systems, offering a structured representation of learners' knowledge and a means to adapt the learning content accordingly [9,14].

A notable work in adaptive educational games is the 80Days project, which focuses on adaptive digital storytelling to create engaging and personalized learning experiences for players [16]. The authors propose various story models, including linear, non-linear (we will call this graph-based), and re-use models as seen in Fig. 1. The linear model provides a straightforward and fixed narrative path, while the non-linear model allows for branching paths and increased adaptivity based on player choices including cycles. The re-use model enables the efficient use of story elements in different narrative segments, providing additional flexibility in story adaptation. These models offer valuable insights into the design of adaptive educational games and are relevant to our method, which utilizes build-time and real-time algorithms for linear and non-linear story models, respectively with the only limitation to use only acyclic graphs when using the non-linear form.

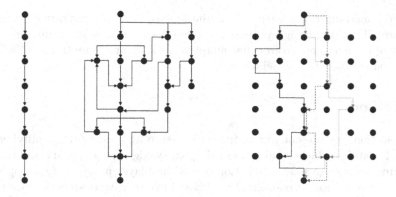

**Fig. 1.** left to right: linear, non-linear, re-use [16].

Another approach to designing adaptive educational games is presented by Moreno-Ger et al. [17], who propose a content-centric development process model for creating serious games. Their model takes into account learning objectives, educational content, and assessment strategies while developing the game, ensuring that the adaptation process is well-integrated with the overall game design. Although this approach provides a comprehensive framework for designing educational games, our method specifically focuses on simplifying the design process through streamlining the knowledge space domain and applying real-time knowledge space alterations, aiming to provide a more streamlined and efficient game design process.

Storytelling techniques have been recognized as valuable components in educational games, as they can enhance the learning experience by offering an engaging and immersive environment for learners [3,6]. Adaptive techniques have been successfully implemented in various educational games, such as EcoDefender [13], to provide personalized learning experiences for players. In this context, Kickmeier-Rust et al. (2009) present a narrative-based approach to personalizing in educational games, emphasizing the importance of storytelling and its integration into the adaptation engine [7]. Their system tailors the narrative structure and content based on the learner's needs, preferences, and learning context, creating a more engaging and effective learning experience.

In a similar vein, Hockemeyer et al. (1996) explore the use of Knowledge Space Theory in serious games and educational games, introducing the concept of a relational adaptive tutoring hypertext environment based on knowledge space theory [9]. Other works have also demonstrated the potential of KST in various game contexts, such as Kickmeier-Rust and Albert (2010), who developed an adaptive educational game called "80Days" (see above) that employs KST to facilitate micro-adaptive learning scenarios [14].

Our approach builds upon these concepts by using narration to alter the educational model, specifically the knowledge space, in order to incorporate the story at the core of the game. By combining Knowledge Space Theory with real-time knowledge space alterations based on player progress, we aim to provide a dynamic learning experience that maintains an engaging narrative structure while simplifying the design process for game designers and programmers. This sets our approach apart from other adaptive serious games methods, offering a unique contribution to the field.

## 3    Method

In this section, we present our proposed two-step approach for simplifying the design of adaptive educational games using Knowledge Space Theory and real- or build-time knowledge space alterations based on player progress. Our approach aims to create a more streamlined workflow for narrative designers, educators, and game designers while ensuring the learning experience remains engaging and effective.

### 3.1    Knowledge Space Domain and Story Creation

The first step in our approach involves the creation of two separate elements: the narrative structure and the knowledge space domain. The knowledge space domain is represented as an acyclic directed graph, where each edge represents a prerequisite relation between knowledge items. In accordance with Knowledge Space Theory, these prerequisite relations indicate that a learner must acquire a specific knowledge item before being able to learn another.

Narrative designers develop the story, which can be either linear or represented as an acyclic directed graph. This requirement of an acyclic structure for the story is an assumption made to ensure that the narrative can be effectively integrated with the knowledge space domain. Educators create the knowledge space domain, modeling the learners' knowledge and skills. In this step, narrative designers and educators work independently.

### 3.2    Linking Nodes and Altering the Knowledge Space

After both the narrative structure and knowledge space domain have been created, narrative designers and educators come together to link the story items and knowledge items. This linking process creates a connection between the narrative and the educational content, which will be utilized by the algorithm to modify the knowledge space.

The linking process between the story model and the knowledge model serves a dual purpose. Firstly, the link from the story model to the knowledge model facilitates the modification of the Knowledge Space Domain. Secondly, the link from the knowledge model to the story model acts as a trigger for story progression: Consider a story item, $S_i$, and its associated knowledge item, $K_i$. As long as $K_i$ remains unlearned, the player cannot progress in the story. However, once $K_i$ is learned, the player has effectively acquired all the relevant knowledge required for the current narrative context, enabling them to advance to the next story item, $S_{i+1}$.

The transition from S_i to S_i+1 can be implemented in various ways according to the developers' preferences. For instance, they may choose to use quests or cut-scenes for each edge within the story graph, employing these mechanics to guide players from one story item to another. This approach ensures both a scientifically grounded and comprehensible method for integrating knowledge-based adaptation and story progression in educational games.

Depending on whether the narrative structure is linear or represented as a graph, there are two scenarios for knowledge space alterations: build-time adaptation (linear) and run-time adaptation (graph based). We then expand on these and propose a hybrid method.

### 3.3 Build-Time Adaptation

In the build-time adaptation scenario, narrative designers provide a linear story sequence, while educators provide a Knowledge Space Domain. In the following algorithm step 1 is human input while every subsequent step cam be made fully automatic.

The algorithm for modifying the knowledge space based on this linear story consists of the following steps:

1. Sequentially associate each story item (S_i) with a knowledge item (K_i) in the knowledge space domain (Fig. 2).

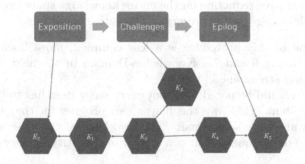

**Fig. 2.** Story-Knowledge-Association.

2. Construct a set of sub-domains (D_i) for each story item as follows:
   (a) Include the knowledge item (K_i) associated with the story item (S_i) and all its predecessors in the knowledge space domain.
   (b) Remove any knowledge items that already exist in previously created sub-domains from the current sub-domain (D_i) (Fig. 3).

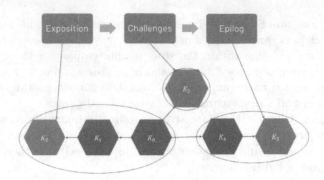

**Fig. 3.** Sub-Domain Extraction.

3. For every sub-domain, denoted as D_i, new edges are introduced into the knowledge space domain. These connections are established from the knowledge item, K_i, that correlates with the story item, S_i, and extend to each item in the following sub-domain, D_(i+1), which does not possess a predecessor within its own sub-domain. The previous process of crafting sub-domains results in domains that each contain exactly one leaf and one or more roots. So this step could be expressed as: "Link the leaf of D_i with every root of D_i+1." This systematic construction ensures the efficient organization of knowledge items within the knowledge space.
4. Perform a transitive reduction on the entire knowledge space domain to eliminate redundant edges while preserving transitive correctness.

   The outcome of this procedure is a less complex, more linear knowledge space. As seen in Fig. 6 and 7 a Knowledge-Domain in the field of It-Security was simplified and streamlined.
   Furthermore should be noted, that not every story item has to be associated to a knowledge item. This way the player can progress in the story without having to learn an entire sub-domain. The drawback of this is again, that it is more complex to design quests that can appear in a multitude story items (Fig. 4 and 5).

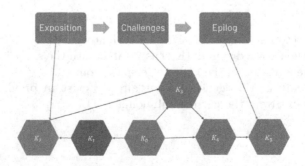

**Fig. 4.** New Edge Creation.

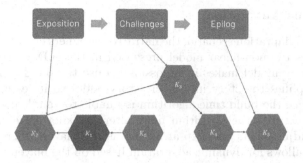

**Fig. 5.** Transitive Reduction.

The proposed method is currently being utilized in the development of an educational game titled "DROP TABLE students;". This game is part of the larger project "SG4BB", which is funded by the German Ministry for Science and Education through the INVITE research program for vocational training. The primary objective of the game is to provide IT-security training to employees across various professions. Initial analysis of the Knowledge Domain, as depicted in Fig. 6, reveals its extensive scope, resulting in a large set of Knowledge Items that learners may encounter at any given point in the story. By implementing the proposed approach, the Knowledge Domain is automatically streamlined, thereby reducing the pool of available knowledge items for learners at each step, as illustrated in Fig. 7. The linear portion of the domain exhibits minimal branching, allowing for adaptability and sequencing. It is important to note that this work is still ongoing, and the final configuration and size of the Knowledge Domain is subject to potential revisions and refinements.

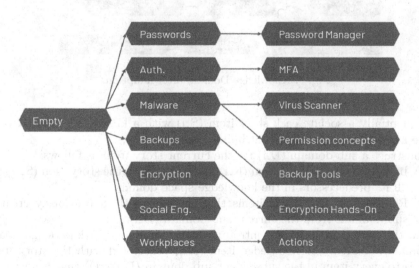

**Fig. 6.** Knowledge Domain before adaption.

## 3.4   Run-Time Adaptation

In the run-time adaptation scenario, the narrative designers create a story graph, which resembles the non-linear model presented in the 80Days project [16]. A graph based story model makes it impossible to use the build time algorithm, unless one simplifies the story into macro-story-nodes so it resembles a linear story again. Since the build time algorithm is unable to handle complex graph-based story-structures, the algorithm must alter the knowledge space in real-time, making adjustments one step at a time as the player progresses through the story. This allows for dynamic adaptation based on the player's progress and the current state of the narrative. One can think about a complex story graph, but after the player progressed through the whole story, the path the player took is then again a linear path. With this, we can make the real-time adaptation similar to the build-time adaptation, but with one little twist: After every single iteration of a story item, we pause the algorithm and start a transitive reduction. We then continue with the algorithm the moment the player progresses to the next associated story item. Now we have the following steps to take;

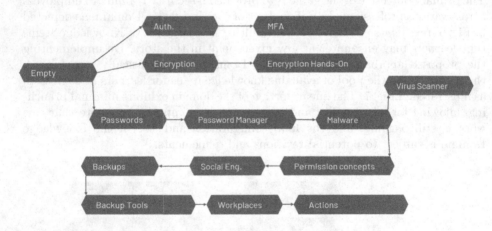

**Fig. 7.** Knowledge Domain after adaption.

1. Sequentially associate each story item ($S\_i$) with a knowledge item ($K\_i$) in the knowledge space domain at build time, set $i = 0$;
2. Construct a sub-domain ($D\_i$) for the current story item as follows:
   (a) Include the knowledge item ($K\_i$) associated with the story item ($S\_i$) and all its predecessors in the knowledge space domain.
   (b) Remove any knowledge items that already exist in previously created sub-domains from the current sub-domain ($D\_i$).
3. For this sub-domain ($D\_i$), introduce new edges in the knowledge space domain: Connect the knowledge item ($K\_i$) associated with the story item ($S\_i$) to every item in the subsequent sub-domain ($D\_(i+1)$) that has no predecessor within its own sub-domain.

4. Perform a transitive reduction on the entire knowledge space domain to eliminate redundant edges while preserving transitive correctness.
5. Wait for story progression of the player, then increase i by 1 and go to 2.

Since the adaption is purely made in runtime, the benefit of a less complex knowledge space in build time remains unused. The advantage of adapting the knowledge space in runtime is a limiting set of Knowledge Items a player or learner can encounter. This way - when using a big and complex knowledge space - the learner keeps learning a small set on knowledge items before traversing further to the next items to learn. This is utilized to achieve our goal in supporting the creation of the individual learning path of the player.

## 4  Discussion

Our proposed approach for streamlining the design process of adaptive educational games using Knowledge Space Theory and knowledge space alterations presents potential benefits for learners, game designers, and educators alike. By simplifying the knowledge space domain, we aim to minimize the risk of overwhelming learners with a multitude of concepts at once. This approach ensures that learners can focus on a limited set of knowledge items at any given stage in the game, thus making the learning process more manageable and effective.

For game designers, this method simplifies the task of developing story-aligned game mechanics and quests. The resultant linear knowledge space domain, closely tied to the narrative structure, allows designers to devise quests that are engaging, immersive, and directly related to the educational content. This guarantees that the game remains focused on its learning objectives while providing an enjoyable gaming experience for the player.

Our method differs from some related works, such as the content-centric development process model suggested by Moreno-Ger et al. [17]. Although these studies provide insightful understandings into personalizing the content for individual learners and the storytelling process, our approach uniquely focuses on simplifying the design by trimming down the knowledge space domain and employing real-time knowledge space alterations. This streamlined method ensures a strong link between the narrative structure and the educational content, thereby creating a more immersive and enjoyable learning experience. However, it should be noted that this comparison is not exhaustive, and there might be other approaches worth considering.

Yet, this method comes with its share of limitations and challenges. For instance, if story items representing a relatively small portion of the narrative link to knowledge items representing a significant part of the knowledge domain, a pure linearization of the knowledge domain can occur. This outcome would generate a sequence of learning items that require no adaptation to the learner's state. This scenario is undesirable and signifies a case where our approach might not be well-suited. Either our approach is not required for such use cases, or the knowledge domain or story graph needs refinement until both graphs are compatible, and the method yields an optimized output.

Another limitation is our method's incompatibility with the re-use model presented in the 80Days project [16]. In this model, the same story elements can be used in various contexts, allowing for enhanced flexibility in the narrative structure. However, our current method, focusing on linear and acyclic graph-based models, doesn't support this degree of flexibility. Future research could extend our approach to accommodate the re-use model, thus broadening its applicability to diverse narrative structures.

We propose that the build-time adaptation is sufficient for the majority of educational games, as many narratives can be simplified into an act-based structure, and more intricate structures may not be necessary. The build-time adaptation is particularly useful for cases involving complex stories and knowledge spaces, as they offer greater control over which knowledge items the learner encounters at specific points in the story. However, as the complexity of the story graph and the knowledge space increases, the association of items must be crafted with greater care to avoid creating story items that encompass an excessively large knowledge space subdomain due to the player's chosen path. This careful design is essential to ensure a balanced and effective learning experience within the context of the game.

In the development of a vocational training serious game intended for teaching IT-security at the workplace, we collaborated with educators to gather scenario ideas to incorporate into the game. A narrative designer then created a storyline, and the knowledge space domain was simplified using the proposed method. Following this, the scenarios were sorted according to the knowledge items, which facilitated the creation of game-specific quests corresponding to each stage of the story. As seen in Fig. 6 and 7, the simplified knowledge space domain facilitates a more streamlined and efficient game design process.

Nevertheless, it is vital to note that the current state of the project lacks evaluation results. The author is in the process of developing quests and tasks for the game and plans to conduct an evaluation with teachers and trainers from a regional training center that specializes in off-site vocational training for socially disadvantaged and learning-challenged youths. The objective of this evaluation is to test the adaptivity and learning engagement of the players. These evaluations will be crucial in understanding the efficacy of the proposed method and identifying areas for improvement. Future research may investigate more complex adaptations, explore additional educational fields, and further refine the proposed method based on the evaluation outcomes.

## 5   Conclusion

In this paper, we presented a novel approach for simplifying the design of adaptive educational games using Knowledge Space Theory and either build-time or real-time knowledge space alterations based on player progress. Our method has the potential to significantly impact the field of serious games by facilitating collaboration among game designers, programmers, educators, and narrative designers, ultimately creating more immersive and effective educational serious games that cater to individual learners' needs and preferences.

By integrating narrative structures and learning content through knowledge space alterations, our approach enables a more streamlined and efficient game design process while ensuring an engaging and effective learning experience for players. Furthermore, the proposed hybrid adaptation method allows for more dynamic and personalized learning experiences that are closely integrated with the evolving narrative, making it an attractive option for serious games with complex stories and knowledge domains.

While our method holds promise, it is not without limitations and challenges, such as the need for careful design and compatibility between the story and knowledge domains. Future research may explore more complex adaptations, additional educational fields, and further refinements to the proposed method. Moreover, an evaluation of our approach in a real-world educational game setting will be necessary to validate its effectiveness and adaptivity, providing valuable insights for future development in the field of adaptive serious games. It is important to note that the approach presented here is primarily designed to handle large, complex knowledge space domains. In cases where the knowledge space domain is already small or inherently simple, applying this approach may not be advisable. The resulting knowledge domain could potentially become excessively linear, thereby eliminating any room for meaningful adaptation. This potential limitation should be considered when deciding whether to implement this approach in a given learning game design scenario.

By addressing the challenges of designing adaptive educational games and enhancing the collaboration between various stakeholders, our method has the potential to contribute significantly to the development of more effective, engaging, and personalized serious games, ultimately promoting improved learning outcomes for a diverse range of learners.

# 6 Future Work

In the progressive refinement of our work, we are examining a prospective hybrid adaptation approach. This approach proposes to combine elements of linear and non-linear models, inspired by methodologies utilized in the 80Days project [16]. The goal is to discern whether this combined approach could provide enhanced adaptability and flexibility in the narrative structure of educational games.

The proposed approach involves a transformation of a non-linear story structure into a linear format, potentially achieved through segmenting the complex narrative into overarching acts, such as the 5-Act-Structure: exposition, rising action, climax, falling action, and resolution.

Upon successful transformation, we intend to employ our build-time adaptation algorithm to remodel the knowledge space to align with the linear act structure. We hypothesize that this automated process could yield a streamlined, act-specific knowledge space, serving as a foundation for subsequent run-time adaptations.

Subsequently, we envisage restoring the original story-graph and manually establishing a relationship between each story item (S_i) and a corresponding knowledge item (K_i) within the knowledge space domain. In this model, run-time adaptation would operate during gameplay, dynamically adjusting the knowledge space based on the player's progression through the narrative.

One area of critical inquiry is to validate our assumption that this hybrid approach would enhance engagement, personalization, and learning efficiency. These potential benefits are inherently speculative and we are currently working on establishing a rigorous theoretical framework and empirical evidence to support these claims.

In our ongoing research, we aim to evolve this hybrid adaptation method, combining elements of both build-time and run-time adaptations. Our research objective is not only to offer a potentially efficient tool for narrative designers and teachers but also to examine how our proposed method addresses the needs of these professionals more effectively than existing methodologies. This includes exploring ways to ensure that every professional can create their own domain and, upon manually linking the nodes, have everything else automatically transformed into a system that serves as a foundational guide for game designers to provide engaging gameplay.

As we venture into these uncharted territories, we are fully aware that our assumptions are subject to rigorous validation and potential revision. We eagerly anticipate sharing the concrete outcomes and insights of this exploration in future publications.

**Acknowledgements.** This research has been investigated in the course of the project "SG4BB" (**ger**: Serious Games für die berufliche Bildung; **en**: serious games for vocational training), funded by the German Ministry for Science and Education within the INVITE research program for vocational training.

# References

1. Kickmeier-Rust, M.D., Hockemeyer, C., Albert, D., Augustin, T.: Micro adaptive, non-invasive knowledge assessment in educational games. In: 2008 Second IEEE International Conference on Digital Game and Intelligent Toy Enhanced Learning, pp. 135–137. IEEE (2008). https://doi.org/10.1109/DIGI.2008.10
2. Bruder, R., et al.: Gütekriterien serious games - Langfassung. https://tuprints. ulb.tu-darmstadt.de/17872/7/WTT_Guetekriterien%20SG%20Langfassung %2020210330.pdf
3. Murphy, C., Chertoff, D., Guerrero, M., Moffitt, K.: Design Better Games! Flow, Motivation, & Fun
4. Romero, M., Usart, M., Ott, M., Earp, J., de Freitas, S., Arnab, S.: Learning through playing for or against each other? Promoting cognitive performance in cooperative and competitive games. Comput. Hum. Behav. **58**, 216–227 (2016)
5. Prensky, M.: Digital game-based learning. Comput. Entertainment **1**(1), 21 (2003)
6. Dickey, M.D.: Engaging by design: how engagement strategies in popular computer and video games can inform instructional design. Educ. Tech. Res. Dev. **53**(2), 67–83 (2005)
7. Kickmeier-Rust, M.D., Albert, D.: Applying the competence performance approach for serious game design in the ELEKTRA project. Int. J. Emerg

8. Moreno-Ger, P., Burgos, D., Torrente, J.: Digital games in eLearning environments: current uses and emerging trends. Simul. Gaming **40**(5), 669–687 (2009). https://doi.org/10.1177/1046878109340294

9. Hockemeyer, C., Held, T., Albert, D.: RATH – a relational adaptive tutoring hypertext www–environment based on knowledge space theory. In: Frasson, C., Gauthier, G., Lesgold, A. (eds.) Intelligent Tutoring Systems, pp. 417–426. Springer, Berlin Heidelberg (1996)

10. Conlan, O., Staikopoulos, A., Hampson, C., Lawless, S., O'Keeffe, I.: The narrative approach to personalisation. New Rev. Hypermedia Multimed. **19**(2), 132–157 (2013). https://doi.org/10.1080/13614568.2013.812150

11. Shute, V.J., Ventura, M.: Stealth Assessment: Measuring and Supporting Learning in Video Games. MIT Press, Cambridge (2013)

12. Serrano-Laguna, Á., Fernández-Manjón, B.: Applying learning analytics to simplify serious games deployment in the classroom. J. Comput. Assist. Learn. **33**(3), 253–266 (2017)

13. Annetta, L.A., Minogue, J., Holmes, S.Y., Cheng, M.T.: Investigating the impact of video games on high school students' engagement and learning about genetics. Comput. Educ. **53**(1), 74–85 (2009)

14. Kickmeier-Rust, M.D., Albert, D.: Micro-adaptivity: protecting immersion in didactically adaptive digital educational games. J. Comput. Assist. Learn. **26**(2), 95–105 (2010)

15. Doignon, J.-P., Falmagne, J.-C.: Spaces for the assessment of knowledge. Int. J. Man Mach. Stud. **23**(2), 175–196 (1985)

16. Göbel, S., Mehm, F., Radke, S., Steinmetz, R.: 80Days: adaptive digital storytelling for digital educational games. In: Proceedings of the 2nd International Workshop on Story-Telling and Educational Games (STEG 2009), vol. 498 (2009)

17. Moreno-Ger, P., Martínez-Ortiz, I., Sierra, J.L., Fernández-Manjón, B.: A content-centric development process model. IEEE Trans. Learn. Technol. **11**(1), 45–57 (2018)

# Health and Wellbeing

# Description and Subjective Evaluation of an Interdisciplinary Online Training Program Based on Games for Social Care and Health Professionals

Marlene Rosa[1]([✉]) [iD], Susana Lopes[2] [iD], Emanuel Silva[3] [iD], Dara Pincegher[3] [iD], and Natália Martins[3] [iD]

[1] School of Health Sciences, ciTechCare - Center for Innovative Care and Health Technology, Polytechnic Institute of Leiria, Leiria, Portugal
marlene.rosa@ipleiria.pt
[2] University of Salamanca, Salamanca, Spain
[3] School of Health Sciences, Polytechnic Institute of Leiria, Leiria, Portugal

**Abstract.** This paper aims to (i) characterize an interdisciplinary online training program (AGILAB CENTER) based on the application of Serious Games (SG) to develop new geriatric therapy approaches and (ii) evaluate the perspectives of the participants on teaching methods, learning outcomes, and the relationships between both dimensions. All the participants registered in AGILAB CENTERS were invited to try 4 different therapeutic games and SG-based training for elderly care (24 h, spread over 3–4 months). Participants filled out a questionnaire that was divided into 3 main parts: characteristics of participants; teaching methods; and learning outcomes. Statements about these dimensions were rated on a 0–5 Likert scale, where 0 meant "I don't agree at all" and 5 meant "I totally agree." Twenty institutions dedicated to geriatric care participated ($N = 30$ professionals; only 15.21% were health care providers). Most of the participants implemented SG in residential homes or adult day care centers and few presented relevant experiences using game-based strategies as evaluation methodologies. Networking was considered important and inspired the participants to share experiences and doubts. Moderate correlations were found between curiosity about theories and models for SG application and recognition of the importance of creating procedures to validate good practices in geriatric care. Participation in a digital networking training method for promoting the SG paradigm received a positive assessment from the participants.

**Keywords:** Older persons · Teaching · Recreation · Training Activities · Methods

## 1 Introduction

Population aging is an emergent issue for societies and policy makers worldwide. This demographic change has profound implications for the planning and delivery of health and social care [1]. There are several problems associated with population aging, such

M. Haahr et al. (Eds.): JCSG 2023, LNCS 14309, pp. 127–139, 2023.
https://doi.org/10.1007/978-3-031-44751-8_9

as frailty, functionality loss, dependency, and serious comorbidities [2]. Frailty and other syndromes affect multiple domains in older people's lives, which in turn require a multidisciplinary team approach, including health, social care, and other specialized professionals [2].

A multidisciplinary team approach to the provision of assistance to older people might focus on designing comprehensive methodologies for geriatric assessment (clinical, psychological, environmental, social, and functional) but also on planning new and efficient intervention strategies. Achieving this requires a coordinated multidisciplinary effort [3]. Therefore, the future and priorities of geriatric care policies might be to create and enhance high-performing teams, which requires team cohesion and interconnectedness. One of the most important factors in achieving high-performing multidisciplinary teams in geriatric care is to create opportunities for professionals to train together. Ellis and Sevdalis (2019) confirmed that the main outcome of this training model is a decrease in human error by way of an increase in the consistency of the high-frequency elements of care [4].

Innovation in geriatric care is effective when delivered by a core team of people who engage with a network of stakeholders, sharing practical tasks and ultimately making change happen [3]. According to the phenomenon of interprofessional education, professionals from different backgrounds should learn together, so as to improve collaboration and the quality of care [5]. Babiker et al. (2014) highlighted that team training and education opportunities, including ongoing team training, are crucial factors that may impact team effectiveness and efficiency [6].

Access to opportunities for specialized training, in which multidisciplinary communication is facilitated by specialized vocabulary, similar approaches to problem-solving, common interests, and a common understanding of relevant issues, is crucial to improving the quality of geriatric care. This specialized training might promote comprehensive paradigms and models as a basis for professionals to interpret and address issues that arise in their work [7].

Addressing the importance of specialized training opportunities in geriatric multidisciplinary rehabilitation, it is urgent to design and test innovative training approaches in this field. There is wide variability in training-based programs based on the huge diversity of geriatric rehabilitation approaches. For example, according to Freedman, Martin, and Schoebi (2002), exercise and psychological and social interventions are one of the most recommended interventions in use [8]. However, traditional rehabilitation strategies for the elderly are often perceived as repetitive and boring, and there is a need for new efforts to design innovative and adapted strategies. Professionals in the geriatric field agree that a patient's motivation plays an important role in determining the intervention's effect and it is associated with high engagement [9]. One of the most recent and innovative paradigms in rehabilitation is the implementation of games for serious purposes, i.e., serious games. Serious games (SG) are commonly defined as games developed for a primary purpose other than pure entertainment [10]. The outcomes in this area are promising, suggesting that SG motivate patients to meet therapeutic requirements, by promoting immersive therapy contexts [11]. Furthermore, there is a consensus about the additional benefits that serious games have for elderly people across different domains, e.g., on a physical and psychological level [12]. A recent systematic review conducted by Abd-Alzaraq and colleagues (2021) considered SG to be crucial for elderly care provision, as a valuable adjunct strategy to conventional mental health therapies and approaches [13]. Therefore, the implementation of SG on the geriatric population could be established as a priority area for multidisciplinary teams, because of the potential of SG in restoring multiple affected domains in elderly people with increasing motivation levels. However, this is a new approach for geriatric professional teams, and there is an urgent need to develop and evaluate adequate related training settings. New training opportunities in this field will increase the professionals' abilities to design appropriate protocols, communication strategies (e.g., specific terminology), and outcomes assessment.

Therefore, this paper aims to (i) characterize an interdisciplinary online training program (AGILAB CENTER) based on the application of SG to develop new geriatric therapy approaches and (ii) evaluate the participants' perspectives on teaching methods, learning outcomes, and the relationships between both dimensions.

## 2  Material and Methods

### 2.1  Procedures and Instruments

An exploratory study was conducted, using a structured questionnaire to characterize the perspectives of interdisciplinary teams on their participation in an interdisciplinary online training program based on the application of SG to develop new geriatric therapy approaches, created by the Polytechnic Institute of Leiria and called AGILAB CENTERS.

Data were collected between January and February 2022 at the Polytechnic Institute of Leiria. All those registered (professionals working in geriatric rehabilitation settings) in AGILAB CENTERS were invited to participate, after being enrolled in the program for at least 3 months. Those who agreed to participate were asked to give informed consent through an electronic form. Eligible participants received a link to access the questionnaire used for data collection (n = 43). All electronic data collection procedures were delivered using Google Forms. Ethical approval was obtained from the Ethics Committee of the Polytechnic Institute of Leiria (CE-IPLEIRIA-43-2020).

AGILAB CENTERS' questionnaire - This questionnaire was developed by the AGILAB CENTERS trainers, specifically, 3 researchers who specialized in health and social assistance strategies. It was divided into 3 main parts: PART 1 included questions about the characteristics of the participants (teams, geriatric institutions/projects); PART 2 included questions about SG applications (contexts – e.g., home care; domains for intervention – e.g., cognitive; mental health); PART 3 included statements about (i) teaching methods (TM) and (ii) learning outcomes (LO). The statements included in PART 3 were rated on a 0–5 Likert scale, where 0 meant "I don't agree at all" and 5 meant "I totally agree." Some negative statements should be highlighted: "It is not enough to rethink good practices in geriatric care (LO)"; "It was difficult to take away a positive experience because we are all together in the training group (TM)"; "Scientific components are too demanding (TM)." The other statements are positive statements, such as "It provides time and space to rethink game-based interventions in geriatric care (LO)"; "It stimulates curiosity about the theory and models for SG application (LO)"; "It helps us to improve the quality of geriatric care (LO)"; "It helps us to understand the importance of validating good practices in geriatric care (TM)"; "Should be focused only on explaining games procedures (TM)"; "Networking was highly important and allowed us to share experiences and doubts about the SG-based method (TM)." The original questionnaire used was previously revised by two external experts. Before its implementation in this study, the questionnaire was distributed to four geriatric professionals to discuss whether, in the opinion of these experts, it covered the domains deemed most relevant to a game-based training program. The revised version was considered for this study [14].

An interdisciplinary online training program based on SG methodologies in geriatric care – AGILAB CENTERS was an interdisciplinary online training program based on SG and specially created for professionals working in geriatric care. This program consisted of 24 h of online training, spread over 3–4 months. People enrolled in this program had access to original modern board games, specially designed for geriatric care. Modern board games are entertainment games (ortho games) [15]. They have innovative design features that make them well-suited to simulate some real activities while keeping users engaged [16] [17]. However, they are entertainment ortho games. Only when modern board games are modified, or their design features deliver new games for purposes beyond entertainment, do they become SG [18] [19]. The original modern games available were 4 different analog therapeutic games (Agilidades Inc.): (i) a music-based game (https://agilidades.pt/produto/jogo-arraial/); (ii) a floor game (https://agilidades.pt/produto/jogo-do-labirinto/); (iii) a game based on a dual task (https://agilidades.pt/produto/jogodasmaostati/); (iv) a cognitive board game (https://agilidades.pt/produto/matriz/). Analog games have very special properties for geriatric therapy, including face-to-face multiplayer participation and interaction with physical components, which can strengthen the sense of touch and hand function [20]. These games were explored in phase 2 of the AGILAB program, as described in Table 1. Before that, in phase 1, theories and models about serious applications of analog games in geriatric care were presented and discussed. During that phase, for example, it was explained how motor learning theories are supported by the same principles of SG implementation. The player-centric design methodologies used for SG purposes in the context of geriatric care, such as focus group designing, interviews, and a collection of prototyping experiences, were also explained. Following this, the program proceeded to phase 3. During that phase, which was designed to train the professionals' skills in the co-design of SG for geriatric care, the following themes were presented and discussed: (i) co-design methodologies; (ii) game dynamics and mechanics adapted to geriatric care; and (iii) design thinking implemented to gamed-based projects. Phase 4 consisted of learning strategies to encourage game-based routines in geriatric care. Different strategies were provided, such as (i) monitoring and recognition of elderly people's involvement in games (e.g., leader boards; badges), (ii) scheduling of routine sessions with games, according to elderly people's personal needs and to existing guidelines or recommendations. Finally, in phase 5, participants were invited to take part in the scientific validation of SG-based programs for the assessment or training of elderly people, having access to study protocols and specialized advisement. Interested participants were also able to suggest adapted study protocols to attain a different focus or health-specific dimension, according to their personal experience in elderly care. These different phases of the AGILAB Program are summarized in Table 1.

---

All the training outlined above was carried out in online sessions, where all the participants were gathered. Using extra time outside those sessions, participants were also encouraged to share game-based experiences, adaptations, or difficulties in a WhatsApp group where they are all included.

**Table 1.** Description of thematic sessions and methodologies implemented in the AGILAB Centers Training Program

| Phases | Thematic Sessions | Method |
|---|---|---|
| Phase 1 | Theory and models about serious applications of board games in geriatric care | Reading related articles Collaborative brainstorming about serious games application in geriatric care |
| Phase 2 | Game-based strategies for physical and cognitive stimulation in geriatric care | Demonstration of therapeutic games for this purpose Building adaptations in-game instructions/components or dynamics, considering players' disabilities Study cases |
| Phase 3 | Training skills to co-design game-based strategies for geriatric care | Workshops aimed at involving elderly people and geriatric professionals in the creation of game-based strategies Designing creative sessions |
| Phase 4 | Implementing game-based strategies in daily routines for geriatric care | Designing patient-centered chronograms Global methods to demonstrate elderly people's performance per week ("the best player award") |
| Phase 5 | Measuring well-being outcomes after 2-weeks of game-based implementation | Designing programs for data collection focused on health and well-being outcomes related to the game's purposes |

## 2.2 Statistical Analysis

Items included in the LO and TM domains were selected by highlighting those that present an average value equal to or greater than 4 or, for negative/restrictive statements, equal to or lower than 2. The total percentage of score for TM and LO domains was calculated using the following formula:

$$\% \text{ total score[TM]} = \frac{q1^{tm} + q2^{tm} + qx^{tm}}{Maximum\ TM\ total\ score}$$

$$\% \text{ total score[LO]} = \frac{q1^{lo} + q2^{lo} + qx^{lo}}{Maximum\ LO\ total\ score}$$

# 3  Results

## 3.1  Characteristics of Participants and Serious Games Applications

Twenty institutions dedicated to geriatric care (46.51% of participation) took part in this training program (n = 46 participants). Most of them belong to the Center region of Portugal (n13), 6 belong to the North and only one belongs to the South. In 13 of the professional teams involved in this training program, the age range of the participants was 30–39 years; in 6 of them, it was 20–29 years; and only 1 team included participants aged 40–49 years. There was significant variability in the background of the professionals involved in this study. Most of them are socio-cultural animation workers (n = 12) or social workers (n = 9), some are coordinators of social departments (n = 8), and others are gerontologists (n = 6). Few participants are health professionals, e.g., physiotherapists (n = 4), occupational therapists (n = 2), and nurses (n = 1).

Most of the participants implemented SG in residential homes (n = 12) or adult day care centers (n = 11). The implementation of these strategies in home care (n = 2) or in community projects (n = 4) is scarce. SG are used for elderly monitoring and stimulation, though major reports are focused on the implementation of SG for intervention purposes (n = 18/19 vs. n = 12).

## 3.2  AGILAB CENTERS Training Program - Teaching Methods and Learning Outcomes

Higher scores were presented in the following items of the LO domain: (i) It stimulates curiosity about the theory and models for SG application – 4.35 ± 0.81; (ii) It is not enough to rethink good practices in geriatric care – 2.00 ± 1.30. Higher scores were presented in the following items of the TM domain: (iii) Networking was highly important and allowed us to share experiences and doubts about the SG-based method – 4.20 ± 1.00; (iv) It was difficult to take away a positive experience because we are all together in the training group – 2.30 ± 1.63 (Table 2 and Table 3).

The total percentage of scores reached in the LO domain was higher (73.50% ± 14.52), compared to the total percentage of scores in the TM domain (57.25% ± 10.57).

## 3.3  Correlations Between Learning Outcomes and Teaching Methods

Participants' perceptions of the AGILAB CENTERS Training Program (Table 4) demonstrate the relationships that exist between quality in geriatric care and (i) having time and space to rethink game-based interventions in geriatric care (r = 0.50; $p$ = 0.02), (ii) stimulating curiosity about the theory and models for SG application (r = 0.67; $p$ = 0.001), and (iii) placing a special focus on explaining game procedures (r = 0.62; $p$ = 0.004). Moderate correlations were also found between the perception that the AGILAB program stimulates curiosity about theories and models for SG application and the perceptions that (i) the program helps to understand the importance of validating good practices in geriatric care (r = 0.59; $p$ = 0.006) and that (ii) networking is important for sharing experiences and doubts about the SG-based method (r = 0.50; $p$ = 0.025) (Table 4).

**Table 2.** Score in Learning Outcomes (LO) items after the AGILAB CENTERS Training Program.

| Learning outcomes | Mean ± SD |
|---|---|
| Provides time and space to rethink game-based interventions in geriatric care (LO) | 3.75 ± 0.91 (4.0) |
| It is not enough to rethink good practices in geriatric care (LO) | 2.00 ± 1.30 (2.5) |
| It stimulates curiosity about the theory and models for SG application (LO) | 4.35 ± 0.81 (5.0) |
| Help us to improve the quality of geriatric care (LO) | 3.60 ± 0.88 (3.0) |
| % total score | 73.50% ± 14.52 |

*This % was calculated by adjusting the score direction from all items, in particular the inverted items. LO, Learning Outcomes

**Table 3.** Score in Teaching Methods (TM) items after the AGILAB CENTERS Training Program.

| Teaching Methods | Mean ± SD |
|---|---|
| Scientific components are too demanding (TM) | 3.75 ± 0.85 (4.0) |
| Help us to understand the importance of validating good practices in geriatric care (TM) | 3.45 ± 1.43 (3.5) |
| Should be focused only on explaining games procedures (TM) | 1.75 ± 1.62 (1.0) |
| Networking was highly important and allowed us to share experiences and doubts about the SG-based method (TM) | 4.20 ± 1.00 (4.5) |
| It was difficult to take away a positive experience because we are all together in the training group (TM) | 2.30 ± 1.63 (2.0) |
| % total score | 57.25% ± 10.57 |

TM, Teaching Methods

## 4 Discussion

Specialized training programs for multidisciplinary teams focused on geriatric care should be a priority in order to ensure high-quality approaches when dealing with this frail population. Therefore, this paper characterized an interdisciplinary online training program based on the application of SG to develop new geriatric therapy approaches and evaluated the participants' perspectives on teaching methods, learning outcomes, and the relationships between both dimensions.

The interdisciplinary teams that participated in the AGILAB program consisted of a total of 46 professionals from 10 different professional backgrounds. Only 7 professionals (15.21%) had a background in health sciences (physiotherapist = 4; occupational therapist = 2; nurse = 1). This low representation of health professionals in the teams invited to receive SG training might be indicative of a more traditional background associated with health care providers and with the critically low flexibility of the curriculums

**Table 4.** Statistical spearman correlation values between Learning Outcomes (LO) and Teaching Methodologies (TM) items.

| Help us to improve the quality of geriatric care (LO) | |
| --- | --- |
| Provides time and space to rethink game-based interventions in geriatric care (LO) | r = 0.50<br>p = 0.02* |
| It stimulates curiosity about the theory and models for SG application (LO) | r = 0.67<br>p = 0.001* |
| Should be focused only on explaining games procedures (TM) | r = 0.62<br>p = 0.004* |
| **It stimulates curiosity about the theory and models for SG application (LO)** | |
| Help us to understand the importance of validating good practices in geriatric care (LO) | r = 0.59<br>p = 0.006* |
| Networking was highly important and allowed us to share experiences and doubts about the SG-based method (TM) | r = 0.50<br>p = 0.025* |

TM, Teaching Methods
LO, Learning Outcomes

in these professions [1]. Health professions have been characterized as one of the areas in which ageist feelings and perspectives are most significantly revealed, which might be caused by these inflexible curriculums [2]. Interestingly, game-ageism is one of the most significant stereotypes: "elderly people do not play games, that is for children"[3]. In fact, in future related research, it would be interesting to seek a better understanding of this phenomenon in health professions and to develop specific design training strategies to enhance SG-based approaches in elderly health care.

In the analysis of the teaching methods used in the AGILAB program, difficulties perceived by participants reached minimum values, as can be seen in the following items (i) it was difficult to take away a positive experience because we are all together in the training group (2.30 ± 1.63; 2.0); (ii) networking was highly important and allowed us to share experiences and doubts about the SG-based method (4.20 ± 1.00; 4.5). These results might be indicative of a preference for digital networking training methods among interdisciplinary teams specialized in geriatric care. Previous authors have argued that facilitating networking in innovative themes is a crucial step for interdisciplinary high-standing care provision in geriatrics. Networking might arise in consultative relationships and the design of collaborative solutions for some of the most common problems in the area [4], avoiding fragmentation of care and improving the quality of care [5]. It is important to understand that digital networking has the potential to accelerate access to new approaches, bringing together professionals and experts in the theme, even if there is a physical distance between them [6].

It is possible to highlight positive perspectives regarding the learning outcomes of the AGILAB program: (i) it stimulates curiosity about theories and models for SG application; (ii) it provides time and space to rethink game-based interventions in geriatric care; (iii) it helps us to improve the quality of geriatric care. In fact, participants in this study valued the time and space provided by the AGILAB program. This is not surprising, as a previous systematic review of the literature, combined with empirical data derived from interdisciplinary teams, had highlighted the following principles for good interdisciplinary teamwork: appropriate training; and the need for teams to regularly invest time in the processes of team development and maintenance of team functioning. Investing time in team development is crucial to ensure that these competencies are entrenched and enacted in their daily practice [7]. According to Duque et al. (2008), learning about theories and models associated with innovative methods, such as SG, is a critical aspect to promote a structured method and common expertise that will improve satisfaction in interdisciplinary teams and quality in care provision [8].

The results of the present study demonstrated moderate correlations between curiosity about theories and models for SG application and recognition of the importance of building validation procedures for good practices in geriatric care (r = 0.59). Participants also demonstrated moderate correlations between the optimization of the "quality of geriatric care" and (i) the chance of having time and space to rethink game-based interventions in geriatric care (r = 0.50); and (ii) a preference for sessions exclusively focused on explaining game procedures (r = 0.62). There are some controversies in these results that should be further explored in future related studies. At the same time, participants considered the importance of their contribution to the validation of evidence-based practice concerning the application of SG in geriatric care but also confirmed that the quality of geriatric care was related to sharing knowledge about practical SG-based procedures. These results might suggest that there is insufficient awareness of the importance of evidence-based practice among professionals working in geriatric care. This is in accordance with a previous study conducted in an acute geriatric setting that compared self-reported capability beliefs with evidence-based practice among health professionals. A total of six activities were assessed: formulate questions; search databases; search other sources; appraise research reports; participate in implementation in practice; and participate in the evaluation. The general conclusion from this study was that there is a need to improve the use of evidence-based practice among health professionals working in a geriatric setting [9].

The results of the present study demonstrated that SG-based strategies are mostly used in residential homes and adult day care centers. The implementation of these strategies in at-home care and community projects is scarce [10]. Specifically, in at-home care, there are considerable challenges that might explain a professional's resistance to innovation, including in implementing SG-based strategies in this context. First, most qualified professionals have little time for home care visits. Long visits are most often performed by professionals with low qualifications, those who perform basic activities with the elderly. According to Daud et al. (2021), wide dissemination of cost-effective strategies is needed in this context, promoting patient- and family-centered models. Family caregivers can learn about the implementation of SG-based strategies for home care, mainly because these are easy, user-friendly, immersive, and fun strategies [11]. Currently, home care programs are dependent on specialized teams. For example, a high number of these programs are dependent on physiotherapy professionals. SG-based strategies, due to their properties, might promote a change in this paradigm. First, because these strategies are less dependent on professionals; secondly, because they can be used intensively and routinely. The implementation of SG-based strategies in community projects has been tested in a previous study conducted by Riggins and McLennon (2019), demonstrating good levels of adherence and satisfaction among the elderly. The authors implemented an innovative song bingo game, measuring its impact on mood, satisfaction, and acceptability in community-residing older adults [10]. Before the program, 33.4% of the participants reported their mood as "very happy" or "happy", which improved to 61.5% of elderly reporting that their mood was "very happy" or "happy" after the program. This program was cost-effective and improved the mood of community-dwelling older adults.

This exploratory study also demonstrated that the people involved in this training program do not present relevant experience using SG-based strategies as evaluation methodologies. Specific and more intensive programs are needed to train professionals in selecting appropriate tools to assess the elderly population, considering that professionals working in this field might not be alert to the concept of SG as a measuring tool. The most common evaluation tools used in this field are paper-and-pencil tools. These tools have a specific bias, especially concerning populations with low participation income (e.g., dementia). According to Tan et al. (2022), measures of performance in immersive contexts might be the most adequate paradigm in elderly evaluation [12]. These authors have argued the importance of testing digital games as special contexts in this field. Games, both digital and analog, can be high-standard measures to be used in the elderly population. It is urgent to develop more studies to corroborate the value of SG for assessing elderly performance, especially because two of the more recent papers on this topic [13, 14] have demonstrated that specialized board games can be a valid framework for cognitive, frailty, and coordination diagnosis.

The perspectives of the AGILAB program participants pointed to the existence of considerable limitations in the adoption of SG-based strategies among the older population, which might hinder the emergence of new game-based paradigms. Actions focused on changing the paradigm are needed, and they could include, in particular, ensuring that teams have time specifically assigned to recording and reflecting on the most efficient practices, engaging in joint exercises, and gathering the knowledge they acquired in a technical portfolio for later review. Baker et al. (2019) defend the implementation of these strategies, considering them to be effective in providing a greater awareness of growth in personal and professional skills, which leads to a change in the mode of action, as part of a humanistic approach [15]. Furthermore, the constructivism-expertise paradigm might support the inclusion of more active learning strategies, such as exercises for training problem-solving skills [16].

This study has several limitations. The sample of people who accepted to participate was small, and there was an asymmetrical representation of different professional backgrounds (e.g., only 15% of health professionals). This did not allow the researchers to perform an analysis according to the professional field. Future studies might include a higher number of participants and a more even distribution by professional background, avoiding underrepresented areas. The questionnaire used did not complete all the stages of formal validation, but it did undergo discussion and assessment by a group of experts and was carefully revised to ensure the quality of the information collected, e.g., the statements used precise language, the questionnaire was not too long, and weasel words were avoided[17]. The questionnaire did not provide a section for participants to register other issues/details that might be considered important/relevant, overcoming new participants' perceptions about the AGILAB program.

## 5 Conclusions

This study examines the different perspectives of multidisciplinary teams on their participation in an innovative training program based on the application of SG to develop new geriatric therapy approaches. The analysis of these perspectives provided findings that will be important in redesigning future SG training programs in the context of geriatric care.

First, it seems important to develop a motivating strategy specially geared toward healthcare providers regarding the use of SG in elderly care. Participants in this study valued the time and space provided by the AGILAB program and showed a preference for digital networking training methods. It was also found that the implementation of these strategies in at-home care and community projects is scarce. Furthermore, the data collected suggest that there is insufficient awareness among the professionals included in the program regarding the importance of evidence-based practice. Finally, the program was not able to stimulate the adoption of SG as a measuring tool in geriatric care.

Future training programs in this field might focus on: (i) developing and presenting programs for home care using SG; (ii) exploring the importance of evidence-based practice in using SG for geriatric care; (iii) presenting different SG applications (e.g., assessment purposes) and materials (e.g., active learning strategies, portfolio inclusion) for elderly assessment.

## References

1. Clegg, A., Young, J., Iliffe, S., Rikkert, M.O., Rockwood, K.: Frailty in elderly people. Lancet **381**, 752–762 (2013)
2. Albers, G., et al.: A qualitative exploration of the collaborative working between palliative care and geriatric medicine: barriers and facilitators from a European perspective. BMC Palliat. Care **15**, 1–10 (2016). https://doi.org/10.1016/S0140-6736(12)62167-9
3. Long, D., Iedema, R., Lee, B.B.: Corridor conversations: clinical communication in casual spaces. the discourse of hospital communication. In: R. Idema (ed.). Palgrave Macmillan, pp. 182–200 (2007). https://doi.org/10.1186/s12904-016-0118-3
4. Ellis, G., Sevdalis. N.: Understanding and improving multidisciplinary team working in geriatric medicine. Age Ageing. **48**, 498–505 (2019). https://doi.org/10.1093/ageing/afz021
5. Keijsers, C.J.P.W., Dreher, R., Tanner, S., Forde-Johnston, C., Thompson, S.: Interprofessional education in geriatric medicine. Eur. Geriatr. Med. **7**, 306–314 (2016). https://doi.org/10.1016/j.eurger.2016.01.011
6. Babiker, A., et al.: Health care professional development: working as a team to improve patient care. Sudan J. Paediatr. **14**, 9–16 (2014). https://doi.org/10.1016/j.eurger.2016.01.011
7. Hall, P., Weaver, L.: Interdisciplinary education and teamwork: a long and winding road. Med. Educ. **35**, 867–875 (2001). https://doi.org/10.1046/j.1365-2923.2001.00919.x
8. Freedman, V.A., Martin, L.G., Schoeni, R.F.: Recent trends in disability and functioning among older adults in the United States: a systematic review. J. Am. Med. Assoc. **288**, 3137–3146 (2002). https://doi.org/10.1001/jama.288.24.3137

9. Randriambelonoro, M., Perrin, C., Blocquet, A., Kozak, D., Fernandez, J.T., Marfaing, T., et al.: Hospital-to-home transition for older patients: using serious games to improve the motivation for rehabilitation – a qualitative study. J. Popul. Ageing **13**, 187–205 (2020). https://doi.org/10.1007/s12062-020-09274-7

10. Wilkinson, P.: A brief history of serious games. In: Dörner, R., Göbel, S., Kickmeier-Rust, M., Masuch, M., Zweig, K, (eds.). Entertainment Computing and Serious Games. Lecture Notes in Computer Science, vol. 9970, pp. 14–41. Springer, Cham (2016). https://doi.org/10.1108/JWAM-03-2021-0024

11. Randriambelonoro, M., et al.: Gamified physical rehabilitation for older adults with musculoskeletal issues: pilot noninferiority randomized clinical trial. JMIR Rehabil. Assistive Technol. **10**, e39543 (2023). https://doi.org/10.2196/39543

12. Jung, Y., Li, K.J., Janissa, N.S., Gladys, W.L.C., Lee, K.M.: Games for a better life: Effects of playing Wii games on the well-being of seniors in a long-term care facility. In: Proceedings of the 6th Australasian Conference on Interactive Entertainment, IE (2009). https://doi.org/10.1145/1746050.1746055

13. Abd-Alrazaq, A., Al-Jafar, E., Alajlani, M., Toro, C., Alhuwail, D., Ahmed, A., et al.: The effectiveness of serious games for alleviating depression: systematic review and meta-analysis. JMIR Serious Games. **10**, e32331 (2022). https://doi.org/10.2196/32331

14. Rosa, M.S.L.: An ICF framework for game-based experiences in geriatric care. In: International Conference on Serious Games and Game-Based Learning; Paris (2021)

15. Elias, G.S., Garfield, R., Gutschera, K.R.: Characteristics of Games. MIT Press, Cambridge (2012)

16. Sousa, M., Bernardo, E.: Back in the Game, pp. 72–85 (2019)

17. Woods, S.: Eurogames: The Design, Culture and Play of Modern European Board Games. McFarland, Incorporated, Publishers (2012)

18. Sousa, M.: Modern serious board games: modding games to teach and train civil engineering students. 2020 In: IEEE Global Engineering Education Conference (EDUCON), pp. 197–201. IEEE (2020). https://doi.org/10.1109/EDUCON45650.2020.9125261

19. Sousa, M.: Serious board games: modding existing games for collaborative ideation processes. Int. J. Serious Games. **8**, 129–46 (2021). https://doi.org/10.17083/ijsg.v8i2.405

20. Ning, H., Li, R., Ye, X., Zhang, Y., Liu, L.: A review on serious games for dementia care in ageing societies. IEEE J. Transl. Eng. Health Med. **8**, 1–11 (2020). https://doi.org/10.1109/jtehm.2020.2998055

21. Horowitz, B.P., Wong, S.D., Dechello, K.: Intergenerational service learning: to promote active aging, and occupational therapy gerontology practice. Gerontol. Geriatr. Educ. **31**, 75–91 (2010). https://doi.org/10.1080/02701960903578345

22. Reeves, S., Goldman, J., Oandasan, I.: Key factors in planning and implementing interprofessional education in health care settings. J Allied Health **36**, 231–235 (2007). PMID: 18293805

23. Vale Costa, L., Veloso, A.I., Loos, E.: Age stereotyping in the game context: introducing the game-ageism and age-gameism phenomena. In: Zhou, J., Salvendy, G. (eds.) HCII 2019. LNCS, vol. 11593, pp. 245–255. Springer, Cham (2019). https://doi.org/10.1007/978-3-030-22015-0_19

24. Tsukuda, R.A.: Interdisciplinary collaboration: teamwork in geriatrics. In: Cassel, C.K., Riesenberg, D.E., Sorensen, L.B., Walsh, J.R. (eds.) Geriatric Medicine, pp. 668–75. Springer, New York (1990). https://doi.org/10.1007/978-1-4757-2093-8_52

25. Duque, S.: The geriatric team. In: Roller-Wirnsberger, R., Singler, K., Polidori, M.C. (eds.) Learning Geriatric Medicine. PIG, pp. 287–293. Springer, Cham (2018). https://doi.org/10.1007/978-3-319-61997-2_27

26. Geriatric Medicine Research Collaborative.: Using social media and web-based networking in collaborative research: protocol for the geriatric medicine research collaborative. JMIR Res. Protoc. **7**, e179 (2018). https://doi.org/10.2196/resprot.9304

27. Nancarrow, S.A., Booth, A., Ariss, S., Smith, T., Enderby, P., Roots, A.: Ten principles of good interdisciplinary team work. Hum. Resour. Health **11**, 19 (2013). https://doi.org/10.1186/1478-4491-11-19

28. Duque, G., Fung, S., Mallet, L., Posel, N., Fleiszer, D.: Learning while having fun: the use of video gaming to teach geriatric house calls to medical students. J. Am. Geriatr. Soc. **56**, 1328–1332 (2008). https://doi.org/10.1111/j.1532-5415.2008.01759.x

29. Boström, A.-M., Sommerfeld, D.K., Stenhols, A.W., Kiessling, A.: Capability beliefs on, and use of evidence-based practice among four health professional and student groups in geriatric care: a cross sectional study. PLoS ONE **13**, e0192017 (2018). https://doi.org/10.1371/journal.pone.0192017

30. Riggins, J., McLennon, S.M.: Testing a musical game activity for community-dwelling older adults. Home Health Care Manag. Pract. **32**, 22–27 (2020). https://doi.org/10.1177/1084822319868

31. Dawud, M., Kotecho, M.G., Adamek, M.E.: "It is all about giving priority to older adults' needs:" challenges of formal caregivers in two old age homes in Ethiopia. Ageing Int. **47**, 847–865 (2021). https://doi.org/10.1007/s12126-021-09436-8

32. Tan, N.C., et al.: Age-related performance in using a fully immersive and automated virtual reality system to assess cognitive function. Front. Psychol. **13**, 847590 (2022). https://doi.org/10.3389/fpsyg.2022.847590

33. Rosa, M., Pires, M., Michelle, D.: Velocidade do alcance em tarefas de atenção e memória: validação do teste como marcador funcional na população geriátrica. Sci Med. (Porto Alegre). **29**, 34231 (2019). https://doi.org/10.15448/1980-6108.2019.3.34231

34. Rosa, M., Marinho, R., Gordo, S., Pocinho, R.: O jogo como sistema de avaliação no idoso institucionalizado – um estudo piloto (El juego como sistema de evaluación en ancianos institucionalizados - estudio piloto) (Game performance to assess elderly people in long term care – a pilot study). Retos **43**, 370–378 (2021). https://doi.org/10.47197/retos.v43i0.89551

35. Baker, L., Wright, S., Mylopoulos, M., Kulasegaram, K., Ng, S.: Aligning and applying the paradigms and practices of education. Acad. Med. **94**, 1060 (2019). https://doi.org/10.1097/ACM.0000000000002693

36. Baker, L.R., Phelan, S., Woods, N.N., Boyd, V.A., Rowland, P., Ng, S.L.: Re-envisioning paradigms of education: towards awareness, alignment, and pluralism. Adv. Health Sci. Educ. **26**, 1045–1058 (2021). https://doi.org/10.1007/s10459-021-10036-z

37. Aithal, A.A.S.: Development and validation of survey questionnaire & experimental data – a systematical review-based statistical. Int. J. Manage. Technol. Soc. Sci. (IJMTS) **5**, 233–251 (2020). https://doi.org/10.2139/ssrn.3724105

# Design and Evaluation of a Serious Game for Young Haemato-Oncological Patients

Konrad Peters[1] , Ousama Ghessas[1] , Helmut Hlavacs[1(✉)] ,
and Anita Lawitschka[2]

[1] University of Vienna, Research Group Education,
Didactics and Entertainment Computing, Vienna, Austria
helmut.hlavacs@univie.ac.at
[2] St. Anna Children's Cancer Research Institute, Medical University Vienna,
Vienna, Austria

**Abstract.** We present **LUDIK**, a serious game project for pediatric haemato-oncological patients, including 5 differently scoped mini-games, designed to produce interpretable game score data.

A playable game client and the overall system approach were evaluated by children of the target age group through a survey. Our results indicate clear acceptance of the general approach and system design. The presented mini-games were evaluated separately regarding fun and usability. Except for one mini-game, the results are indicating high acceptance and engagement, and very good usability for the age group in question.

**Keywords:** Serious Games · mHealth · Pediatric Haemato-Oncology · Games for Health

## 1 Introduction

In the recent years, the use of *Serious Games for Health* and *mHealth* applications has proven to be well-accepted by users [10]. They increase compliance, drug adherence, and overall treatment perception. They have significant educational benefits [1]. Further, these applications provide healthcare providers with actual, informative and immediate data. In the field of pediatric oncology, previous projects concluded with positive results regarding user acceptance and utility when using *mHealth* interventions [2,9]. Also, serious-game-based solutions were found to support the overall treatment process and were perceived positively by users in pediatric oncology [8,17].

A possible usage scenario for *Serious Games for Health* would be the aftercare of young and adolescent patients after cancer therapy and allogeneic stem cell transplantation (*SCT*). Polychemotherapy, irradiation and *SCT* may lead to substantial chronic morbidity and the inability to lead a normal life for months and sometimes even years [21]. One of the most critical complications is graft-versus-host-disease (*GVHD*), which may lead to long-term morbidity with debilitating sequelae and reduced quality of life [16]. Currently, *SCT*-aftercare at the

M. Haahr et al. (Eds.): JCSG 2023, LNCS 14309, pp. 140–154, 2023.
https://doi.org/10.1007/978-3-031-44751-8_10

**St. Anna Children's Hospital**, which is the leading institute for pediatric leukaemia in **Austria**, is based on a traditional paper diary for self-reporting of health data.

To make use of *Serious Games for Health* scores, we need to create reproducible and interpretable scores for medical interventions [5]. This implies clarifying which game mechanics, elements or overall design can be used to reflect a user's actual health status, while considering the confounding effects of social and cognitive abilities of different players [18]. Also, the game design must be highly accepted by the target group, considering age, gender, and gaming habits of the patients.

To address these issues, this paper aims to identify suitable health standards for data definition and exchange. Additionally, we test the hypothesis $(h_1)$, that the presented mini-games and their design are well accepted and liked by the target group, which are (young) adolescents. Finally, while not thoroughly discussed in this paper yet, the project aims to link in-game-performance with actual health data.

The core idea is to keep game design and mechanics simple to produce interpretable scores, without losing the patients' adherence. As basis for the further development of **LUDIK**, we have conducted a playtest in 42 healthy children. The results are analyzed and discussed in this contribution. The playtest included a survey with some conceptual questions, and gameplay- and usability-evaluation.

## 1.1   Related Work

A number of previous works examine the connection of apps for (after-)treatment and self-reports of patients. The preceding project **INTERACCT** is an implementation of a *Serious Game for Health* for young and adolescent leukaemia outpatients. To replace their handwritten diary, we introduced a smartphone app: instead of jotting down their health data in a diary, patients were able to submit the data through an app and progress in a *Pokemon*-like game world. Information submitted through the self-reporting function of the app gave the treating physicians additional data and health information.

Hookham et al. present an approach to classify engagement in *Serious Games for Health* and conduct a systematic review to address the question *What is engagement and how has the term been used, defined and measured in the context of serious games?* [14]. The authors categorize serious games by their main challenge (puzzle, simulation, action, etc.) as well as the method of measuring engagement (questionnaires, indirect observation like input events, etc.). They discuss a high variety of different approaches, and suggest the use of a three-part framework including behavioural, cognitive and affective dimensions when reporting about serious game engagement. Kato et al. carried out a study which looked at the effectiveness of computer game interventions for improvements in terms of adherence and other behavioral outcomes in adolescents and young adults with cancer [15]. They found that participants demonstrated a significantly higher adherence to treatment after the video game intervention. Chung et al. addressed the lack of suitable homebound pain treatment for young cancer patients by implementing *C-TIPS* (Cancer-Tailored Intervention for Pain and Symptoms) [9]. C-TIPS is a web-app which includes breathing training, relaxation practice and educational content, which should help patients and their parents to monitor and improve pain therapy at home. In a study with adolescent cancer patients (n = 40, 12–18 years), Jibb et al. evaluated the app *Pain Squad+*. Results show a reporting adherence of $68.8 \pm 38.1\%$, and a significant improvement of pain intensity, pain interference and health-related quality of life. *SSPedi* (Symptom Screening in Pediatrics) is an electronic version of a previously developed paper-based symptom by O'Sullivan et al. [20]. Results show, that no patients had difficulties understanding or using the app, and 19 of 20 patients found the app a good way to communicate with doctors and nurses. Project *Triumf* was conducted by Tark et al. [24]: young and adolescent cancer patients (age 7–12, n = 9) were included in a study, where they could use a mobile health game to seek emotional support and educate patients about their health status. Targeting the needs of acute lymphoblastic leukemia (ALL) patients, Wang et al. conducted a study with 92 parents (43 in the observation group, 49 in the intervention group) [25]. Comparing their knowledge in social support, anxiety, depression, care burden, uncertainty in illness, quality of life their existing knowledge of ALL and care before and after the 3 month intervention, authors found statistically significant improvements in the intervention group. Wang et al. developed an app for self-reported patient outcome using a multidisciplinary approach [26]. Health service researchers, pediatric nurses and software engineers collaborated to successfully develop and evaluate a system with a mobile reporting app as well as a web-interface for treating physicians, providing them with demographic data, survey control and more.

## 2    Design, Implementation and Evaluation

In interdisciplinary workshops, the medical requirements for the system were clarified. This was possible through the input of experts in the field of pediatric oncology, as well as through findings and experience from an earlier project (**INTERACCT**). We focused on serious games, which should address the patients' *short term memory, reactions, concentration, concentration perseverance*, and *fine motor skills*. This focus was primarily chosen, as these skills can be measured through serious games on a mobile device, without the need for external devices or sensors. In order to evaluate whether in-game-performance can be linked with health data, we included a health questionnaire with an essential set of medical parameters. The data of these questionnaires can be linked to specific points in time in our use case: after a certain time in therapy (e.g. 100 or 365 days after the last treatment in the hospital), the health status of the patients is clinically examined. We can then combine examination results with data of the proposed system (health questionnaire data and serious game scores).

The game client for **LUDIK** was implemented in UNITY 2019.2.17f[1] for Android[2] smartphone devices and distributed through the Google Play Store[3]. An encrypted authentication token (JWT[4]) can be stored to keep the user logged in for usability reasons. Other than that, no game or health data is persisted on mobile devices. The backend is implemented in a Node.js[5]/Sails.js[6] server application, using a combination of MySQL 7[7] and REDIS[8] databases. All software is orchestrated through *docker*[9] and *docker-compose*[10], running on an Ubuntu 18.04.3[11] instance.

We used LOINC, a standard to identify health measurements, observations, and documents. McDonald (2003) [19] outlines the standard as follows: *"The Logical Observation Identifier Names and Codes (LOINC®) database provides a universal code system for reporting laboratory and other clinical observations. Its purpose is to identify observations in electronic messages such as Health Level Seven (HL7) observation messages, so that when hospitals, health maintenance organizations, pharmaceutical manufacturers, researchers, and public health departments receive such messages from multiple sources, they can automatically file the results in the right slots of their medical records, research, and/or public health systems"*. We identified LOINC codes for the health questionnaire items (as listed in 3) in earlier research and reused them to correctly label our health data. The identified standard for medical data exchange is *HL7FHIR*[12]. This standard aims to combine features of *HL7v2*[13], *HL7v3*[14], and *CDA*[15]. Focus lies on leveraging the latest web standards and to provide easy implementability. To tackle the problem of variability caused by diverse healthcare processes, *HL7FHIR* uses *Resources* and *Profiles*: *"FHIR solves this challenge by defining a simple framework for extending the existing resources and describing their use with Profiles. All systems can read all resources, but applications can add more control and meaning using profiles. Many healthcare contexts*

---

[1] https://unity.com/, accessed September 11, 2023.
[2] https://www.android.com/, accessed September 11, 2023.
[3] Link removed for review.
[4] https://jwt.io/, accessed September 11, 2023.
[5] https://nodejs.org, accessed September 11, 2023.
[6] https://sailsjs.com, accessed September 11, 2023.
[7] https://mysql.com, accessed September 11, 2023.
[8] https://redis.io/, accessed September 11, 2023.
[9] https://www.docker.com/, accessed September 11, 2023.
[10] https://docs.docker.com/compose/, accessed September 11, 2023.
[11] https://releases.ubuntu.com/18.04.3/, accessed September 11, 2023.
[12] https://www.hl7.org/fhir/, accessed September 11, 2023.
[13] http://www.hl7.org/implement/standards/product_brief.cfm?product_id=185, accessed September 11, 2023.
[14] https://www.hl7.org/implement/standards/product_brief.cfm?product_id=186, accessed September 11, 2023.
[15] http://www.hl7.org/implement/standards/product_brief.cfm?product_id=7, accessed September 11, 2023.

*require extensive local agreements.*"[16] Literature suggests the use of *HL7FHIR* for the given requirements and use-case [4].

The study discussed in this paper aims to evaluate the usability and acceptance of **LUDIK** in the age group of our target group (young and adolescent cancer patients) and therefore test $h_2$. At first, we outlined the project to our study's participants, clarifying motivation and purpose of **LUDIK** to the participants, and briefly explained the different mini-games. Eventually, participants had about 30 min to play the different mini-games of **LUDIK**. Subsequently, participants answered questions regarding demographic data, their gaming habits, and filled in a *SUS* questionnaire (System Usability Scale, [3,6,7]) for each mini-game. We adapted questions in the *SUS* questionnaires slightly in order to fit context: for one, we adjusted terminology to fit with games instead of software systems and for another, kept phrasing simple for our young age group:

1. I think that I would like to play this game frequently
2. I think the game was unnecessarily complex
3. I thought the game was easy to use
4. I think that I would need further explanations to play this game
5. I thought that the different assets and styles were well integrated
6. I thought that some parts of the game were meaningless
7. I would imagine that most children would learn to play this game very quickly
8. I found the game very cumbersome to use
9. I felt very confident playing the game
10. I didn't understand all the tasks in the game right away

Further, we asked if the general idea of using video games in therapy for sick children finds approval within the age group. Concluding the survey, participants could suggest improvements, and point out issues, that they especially liked or disliked while using **LUDIK**. The questionnaire was answered online through a survey platform[17].

We used *R* [23] for the data evaluation and visualization of results. The evaluation of the 5 mini-games through the *SUS* was done as proposed by literature [6][18]: per questionnaire, results were corrected, summed, and multiplied by 2.5 to return interpretable scores. To test our hypotheses against questions with *Likert* scales, we used a right sided Bernoulli test [12]. We defined $H_0$ as P(agree)=50%, $h_1$ as P(agree)>50%. For the Bernoulli tests, answers with a value of $\geq 4$ (*"I agree"*, and *"I highly agree"*) were treated as *agree*.

## 3    Project: LUDIK

Based on the workshop results presented in the previous section, we were able to design **LUDIK**. **LUDIK** is a serious game system developed for smartphones.

---

[16] https://www.hl7.org/fhir/summary.html, accessed September 11, 2023.

[17] https://www.soscisurvey.de/, accessed September 11, 2023.

[18] https://www.usability.gov/how-to-and-tools/methods/system-usability-scale.html, accessed September 11, 2023.

The purpose is to evaluate game scores and their correlation to self-reported health data. The game scores are produced by 5 simple and easy to master mini-games. The mini-games aim to test different skills: short term memory, reactions, concentration, concentration perseverance, and fine motor skills. Additionally, users report their health status on a daily basis through a questionnaire consisting of the following four domains: **overall**, **concentration**, **nausea**, and **tiredness** [13]. Adopting the LOINC standard, each item on the questionnaire has a scale of 3 points as well as a point for "no symptoms" [11,19]. Users can either freely choose which games to play in their game sessions, or be guided through different games in an experiment mode. Guided sessions have a preset sequence of mini-game-levels and are used for a specific span of days.

**LUDIK** embeds 5 mini-games with different genres and game ideas: *ANZAN*, *SPACE RIDE*, *MEMORY*, *SOCCER JUGGLE*, and *PATH*. In *ANZAN* (see Fig. 1a), users solve simple calculations in a short time. The result of a specific calculation (addition, subtraction, multiplication, square root, or squared) is displayed to the player, who must tap moving operands to solve the calculation, providing straightforward mechanics that enable players to playfully deepen their understanding of basic arithmetic operations. Each correctly solved calculation adds one point to the total score. A level is completed when the user reaches 10 points, or when 4 calculations were answered incorrectly and therefore the player lost all 4 lives. Game difficulty increases with each level (number of operands, speed of operands moving).

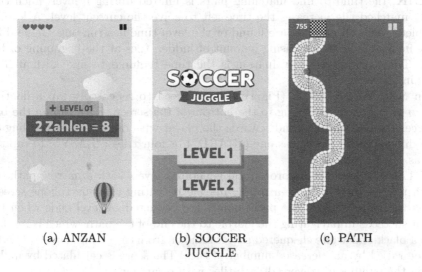

(a) ANZAN          (b) SOCCER          (c) PATH
                       JUGGLE

**Fig. 1.** Client screenshots of *ANZAN*, *SOCCER JUGGLE* and *PATH*

*SPACE RIDE* is a sidescroller game, in which players maneuver a rocket to avoid obstacles and collect randomly appearing stars (see Fig. 2a). The rocket is controlled by tapping the screen of the smartphone. Each star provides a point to the user. Besides obstacles, there are monsters in the game which the player has to dodge as well. They move arbitrarily at random speed, making them harder to avoid and thus adding an extra layer of difficulty to the game. A level is completed when the player hits 4 obstacles and/or monsters. Game difficulty increases every 60 s by increasing the scrolling speed. The final score also includes the overall time of the level.

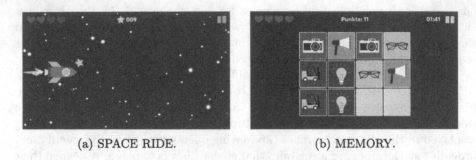

(a) SPACE RIDE.                               (b) MEMORY.

**Fig. 2.** Screenshots of *SPACE RIDE* and *MEMORY*

*MEMORY* (Fig. 2b) is a digital implementation of the well-known game, where players need to find matching pairs in a limited amount of tiles. In **LUDIK**, the time to find matching pairs is limited during a level. Each correctly matched tile increases the time left to solve the current level. A level is complete when all matches are found or the level time has run out. Game difficulty increases by an increasing amount of hidden tiles at the beginning of the level. The score used for evaluation is the time required to find all matching pairs in the level.

In *SOCCER JUGGLE* (Fig. 1b) players need to repeatedly tap a floating ball to prevent it from falling to the bottom of the screen. Each tap on the ball bounces the ball upwards and rewards the player with one point. Depending on level difficulty, the player has one ("HARD") or four tries ("EASY") to tap the ball as often as possible.

*PATH* (1c)implements procedural generated levels with a narrow path, on which players must balance a rolling marble by tilting the smartphone screen. When the marble leaves the path, points are deducted. A level ends when the player succeeds in navigating the marble to the end of the path, which is marked with a black-and-white chequered pattern known from car racing. Level difficulty can be raised by an increased number of tiles. The score is calculated by multiplying the number of traversed path-tiles with accuracy.

## 4    Results

Our experiment test group consisted of 42 children (female = 24, male = 17, NA = 1). Their age was between 10–13 years (n = 41, mean = 11.56, NA = 1).

Regarding whether they would rather report their health status through an app, most participants agreed (highly agree: 52.4%, agree: 19.1%), while only few participants disagreed (highly disagree: 0%, disagree: 7.1%). Some participants had a neutral opinion on this question (21.4%). With a 95% CI, participants agree with the statement ($p = 0.0079$). Agreement to the statement, that the participant plays video games every day was well distributed: 7.1% highly agree and 30.9% agree, whereas 23.8% highly disagree and 9.5% disagree. 28.6% would neither agree or disagree. Most of the children agreed with the statement *I like playing video games* (45.2% highly agree, 28.6% agree). Only 2.4% disagreed, 23.8% were neutral towards this statement. For the statement *I think it is a good idea to use video games as therapy*, results were clearly positive: 59.5% highly agree, 30.9% agree, whereas only 2.4% highly disagree, and 7.1% are neutral. With a 95% CI, participants agree with the statement ($p \leq 0.01$). These results are visualized in Fig. 3.

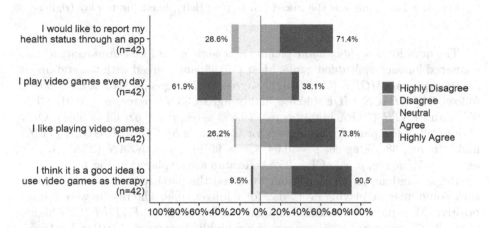

**Fig. 3.** Evaluation of participants' gaming habits

Generally, most of the participants would recommend the games to their same-aged friends (28.6% highly agree, 42.9% agree). 7.1% would not recommend the games (0% highly disagree, 7.1% disagree), 21.4% of the participants were neutral. With a 95% CI, participants agree with the statement ($p = 0.0079$). The game, which was mentioned most often as *the most fun to play* was *PATH* (n = 15, 35.71%), followed by *MEMORY* (n = 11, 26.19%). The other games were mentioned by a similar amount of participants: *ANZAN*, and *SOCCER JUGGLE* have a count of 5 (11.90%), *SPACE RIDE* has a count of 6 (14.29%). *This game was the least fun to play* was answered with *SOCCER JUGGLE* by more than half of the participants (n = 22, 52.38%). The other indications are distributed among the other games: *ANZAN* and *PATH* (each n = 6, 14.29%) were mentioned slightly more than *MEMORY* and *SPACE RIDE* (each n = 4, 9.52%). These findings are illustrated in Fig. 4.

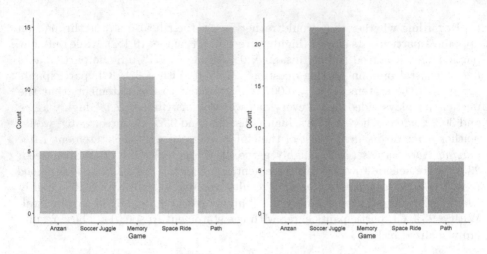

**Fig. 4.** Which game was the :**most** fun to play (left), **least** fun to play (right)

The question *I could imagine playing this game when I was chronically ill* was answered for each embedded game. Most participants agreed with the statement for the game *MEMORY* (52.4% highly agree, 26.2% agree, $p \leq 0.01$, CI = 95%), followed by *SPACE RIDE* (40.5% highly agree, 33.3% agree, $p \leq 0.01$, CI = 95%) and *PATH* (50.0% highly agree, 19.1% agree, $p = 0.02$, CI = 95%). Only about half of the participants agreed for the games *SOCCER JUGGLE* (11.9% highly agree, 38.1% agree, $p = 0.64$, CI = 95%), and *ANZAN* (26.2% highly agree, 19.1% agree, $p = 1$, CI = 95%). Results are displayed in Fig. 5.

Regarding long-term-motivation, we asked the participants, for which game they could imagine playing every day for a longer time. The results were largely positive. Most participants could imagine playing the game *PATH* (42.9% highly agree, 28.6% agree vs 14.3% disagree, 4.8% highly disagree, $p \leq 0.01$, CI = 95%). The games *SPACE RIDE* (40.5% highly agree, 21.4% agree vs 4.8% disagree, 2.4% highly disagree, $p \leq 0.16$, CI = 95%), *MEMORY* (40.5% highly agree, 21.4% agree vs 7.1% disagree, 2.4% highly disagree, $p \leq 0.01$, CI = 95%). The games *ANZAN* and *SOCCER JUGGLE* had the least counted agreeing participants for this question: *ANZAN* returned mixed results (21.4% highly agree, 26.2% agree vs 16.7% disagree, $p = 0.87$, CI = 95%). *SOCCER JUGGLE* shows the least positive results, less than half of the participants agreed (16.7% highly agree, 26.2% agree, $p = 0.44$, CI = 95%), but there was the biggest count of disagreeing participants (14.3% highly disagree, 21.4% disagree). The results are illustrated in Fig. 6.

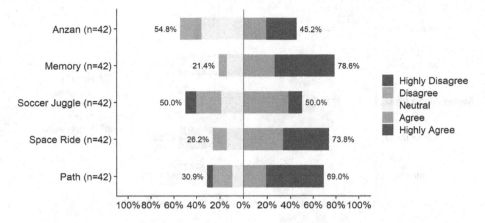

**Fig. 5.** I could imagine playing this game when I was chronically ill

## 4.1   SUS Results

Most games achieved excellent scores[19] (see Table 1). The highest scored game was *MEMORY* (mean = 92.69, median = 95.00), followed by *SPACE RIDE* (mean = 83.60, median = 85.00) and *ANZAN* (mean = 83.27, median = 85.00). The game *PATH* was scored slightly worse, but still clearly above average (mean = 81.78, median = 85.00). Only the game *SOCCER JUGGLE* has an inferior SUS score (mean = 65.43, median = 65.00).

**Table 1.** SUS results for each game of **LUDIK**

| Game | Min | Q1 | Median | Mean | Q3 | Max |
|---|---|---|---|---|---|---|
| Anzan | 65.00 | 73.75 | 85.00 | 83.27 | 92.95 | 97.50 |
| Memory | 67.50 | 87.50 | 95.00 | 92.69 | 97.50 | 100 |
| Soccer Juggle | 30.00 | 55.00 | 65.00 | 65.43 | 75.00 | 97.50 |
| Space Ride | 35.00 | 75.00 | 85.00 | 83.60 | 97.50 | 100 |
| Path | 42.50 | 73.12 | 85.00 | 81.78 | 94.38 | 100 |

---

[19] Cut-off for an acceptable system is a SUS score of 70 [3].

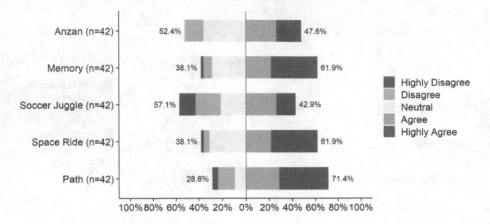

**Fig. 6.** I could imagine playing this game every day for a long time

## 4.2 Open Question Responses

Participants also answered open questions (see Table 2):

- Q1: I particularly liked about **LUDIK**
- Q2: I particularly disliked about **LUDIK**
- Q3: These games would be nice in **LUDIK**
- Q4: This needs improvement in **LUDIK**

Positive comments (responses to Q1) of the participants regarded the overall concept and idea of **LUDIK** (n = 11), the design and graphics (n = 7), and that the games very fun to play (n = 5). The different genres of the games were mentioned (n = 5) as well as the easy nature and concepts of the games (n = 4). The game *PATH* was mentioned explicitly (n = 4).

Points that were disliked (Q2) or need improvement (Q3) were inaccurate game controls (n = 6), which holds especially true for the game SOCCER JUG-GLE (n = 9), which was therefore either too difficult (or too buggy) for the participants. The lack of help texts and game explanations, even though a button was found in the client interface, was distracting for the participants (n = 3). Some participants felt like the music was annoying and would therefore wish for a possibility to turn it off (n = 2). One participant reported feeling dizzy after playing SPACE RIDE.

Suggested improvements are general improvement of game controls (n = 3), especially for SOCCER JUGGLE (n = 5). Two participants suggested displaying high scores. For a possible expansion regarding mini games, the most common mentions were arcade or jump'n'run (n = 4), like *Sonic Dash* or *Temple Runner*, or *Frogger* (n = 2). Other mentionings were action-puzzle games like *Snake* (*Slither.io*, *Paper.io*, n = 2), or games targeting language skills (n = 2).

**Table 2.** Open questions: responses and frequency

| Question | Statement | Count (n) |
|---|---|---|
| Q1 | I liked the design and graphics | 7 |
| Q1 | I liked the easy nature of the games | 4 |
| Q1 | The games are very rich in variety | 5 |
| Q1 | I liked the overall idea/concept | 11 |
| Q1 | I especially liked the game PATH | 4 |
| Q1 | I had great fun while playing the games | 5 |
| Q2 | The controls of SOCCER JUGGLE were inaccurate or the game was too difficult | 9 |
| Q2 | The controls of some games were inaccurate | 6 |
| Q3 | "Sonic Dash"/"Subway Surfers" (Arcade/Jump'n'Run) | 4 |
| Q3 | "Crossy Road" (*"Frogger"*-like Jump'n'Run) | 2 |
| Q3 | "Slither" / "Paper.io" (*"Snake"*-like Arcade) | 2 |
| Q4 | The lacking functionality of the HELP texts | 3 |
| Q4 | High scores | 2 |
| Q4 | Game controls need improvement | 3 |
| Q4 | SOCCER JUGGLE needs improvement (difficulty, controls, concept) | 5 |
| Q4 | There are many bugs | 3 |

## 5   Discussion and Conclusions

Our results show, that the core idea of **LUDIK** is well-accepted by peers in the same age group as the target group. They would rather use a digital solution than a pen-and-paper-approach for frequent health data reports (71.5% of the participants), whereas the idea is neglected by few participants (7.1%). Most of the participants like playing video games (73.8%), but only 38% of the participants play video games every day. This is an important finding, as the system concept intends to let patients play every day. The idea of using video games for therapeutic reasons is also well liked by the participants (90.4% agree). Also, most participants would recommend the game to same-aged friends (71.5%). The games which were liked the most were *PATH* and *MEMORY*. Both games follow a very simple game concept and very basic rules, they are therefore easy to understand. Results show, that 78.6% could imagine playing *MEMORY* when they were chronically ill, and 61.9% could imagine playing it every day. The same holds true for the mini-games *PATH*, *ANZAN*, and *SPACE RIDE*. Only the game *SOCCER JUGGLE* received mixed results: 50% of the participants could imagine playing the game when chronically ill, and 42.9% would play it every day. The *SUS* scores of the mini games indicate the same conclusion. Most of the *SUS* scores are above average, but *SOCCER JUGGLE* was below average (65.00). In comparison, the average $SUS$ score of $MEMORY$ was 95.00, the average $SUS$ scores of $ANZAN$, $SPACE\ RIDE$, and $PATH$ was 85.00. Overall, the survey results indicate a high acceptance of the mini-games, their concepts and graphical assets. The hypothesis tests confirmed $h_1$ for the games $MEMORY$ (play when chronically ill: $p \leq 0.01, CI = 95\%$; play this game every day: $p \leq 0.01, CI = 95\%$), $SPACE\ RIDE$ (play when chronically ill: $p \leq 0.01, CI = 95\%$; play this game every day: $p \leq 0.16, CI = 95\%$), and $PATH$ (play when chronically ill: $p \leq 0.02, CI = 95\%$; play this game every day: $p \leq 0.01, CI = 95\%$). However, we reject $h_1$ for the games $ANZAN$ (play when chronically ill: $p = 1, CI = 95\%$; play this game every day: $p = 0.87, CI = 95\%$) and $SOCCER\ JUGGLE$ (play when chronically ill: $p = 0.64, CI = 95\%$; play this game every day: $p = 0.44, CI = 95\%$). The experiment was organised remotely, due to the current Covid-19 pandemic. For some participants, the sign-up process in the app was too complicated, due to language constraints. Most of the issues could be resolved during the experiment, but these complications distracted the whole group and consumed a substantial amount of time.

In conclusion, we have learned that for such an experiment, user accounts should either be provided, or no user account should be required to test. The identified medical data exchange standards, are $LOINC$ and $HL7FHIR$. $LOINC$ is used to describe the health parameters, which are reported in daily questionnaires in **LUDIK**. We were able to reuse the correct mappings of $LOINC$ codes to our health status questionnaire from our earlier project **INTERACCT**. For the exchange of medical data, as well as integration into existing hospital information systems, $HL7FHIR$ covers the most important requirements. To save resources and time when implementing further modules for **LUDIK**, open source projects, which leverage on $HL7FHIR$, can be used.

The first hypothesis $h_1$ of this contribution must be discarded, because we could not show the link between the players' actual health data and their game scores. Current data does not show a link between players' actual health data and their game scores. Unfortunately, we were not able to execute a longitudinal study with actual patients, primarily due to organizational, pandemic-caused reasons. However, evaluating a potential correlation with healthy children would be inaccurate, as the submitted health data should not be assessed like health data from actual $SCT$ patients [22]. However, the technical and conceptual functionality of **LUDIK** is sufficient to conduct such a study.

# References

1. Abraham, O., LeMay, S., Bittner, S., Thakur, T., Stafford, H., Brown, R.: Investigating serious games that incorporate medication use for patients: systematic literature review. JMIR Serious Games **8**(2), e16096 (2020)
2. Baggott, C., Gibson, F., Coll, B., Kletter, R., Zeltzer, P., Miaskowski, C.: Initial evaluation of an electronic symptom diary for adolescents with cancer. J. Med. Internet Res. (2012). https://doi.org/10.2196/resprot.2175
3. Bangor, A., Kortum, P.T., Miller, J.T.: An empirical evaluation of the system usability scale. Int. J. Hum. Comput. Interact. **24**(6), 574–594 (2008). https://doi.org/10.1080/10447310802205776

4. Bender, D., Sartipi, K.: HL7 FHIR: an agile and restful approach to healthcare information exchange. In: Proceedings of the 26th IEEE International Symposium on Computer-Based Medical Systems, pp. 326–331 (2013). https://doi.org/10.1109/CBMS.2013.6627810

5. Boyle, E.A., et al.: An update to the systematic literature review of empirical evidence of the impacts and outcomes of computer games and serious games. Comput. Educ. **94**, 178–192 (2016)

6. Brooke, J.: SUS: a "quick and dirty" usability scale. Usability evaluation in industry, p. 189 (1996)

7. Brooke, J.: SUS: a retrospective. J. Usability Stud. **8**(2), 29–40 (2013)

8. Bruggers, C.S., et al.: A prototype exercise-empowerment mobile video game for children with cancer, and its usability assessment: developing digital empowerment interventions for pediatric diseases. Front. Pediatr. **6**, 69 (2018). https://doi.org/10.3389/fped.2018.00069

9. Chung, W.W., et al.: Improving children's cancer pain management in the home setting: development and formative evaluation of a web-based program for parents. Comput. Biol. Med. **101**, 146–152 (2018). https://doi.org/10.1016/j.compbiomed.2018.08.014

10. Ferreira, B., Menezes, P.: An adaptive virtual reality-based serious game for therapeutic rehabilitation. Int. J. Online Biomed. Eng. (iJOE) **16**(04), 63–71 (2020)

11. Forrey, A.W., et al.: Logical observation identifier names and codes (LOINC) database: a public use set of codes and names for electronic reporting of clinical laboratory test results. Clin. Chem. **42**(1), 81–90 (1996)

12. Hollander, M., Wolfe, D.A., Chicken, E.: Nonparametric Statistical Methods, vol. 751. Wiley, Hoboken (2013)

13. Hooke, M.C., Linder, L.A.: Symptoms in children receiving treatment for cancer-part I: fatigue, sleep disturbance, and nausea/vomiting (2019). https://doi.org/10.1177/1043454219849576

14. Hookham, G., Nesbitt, K.: A systematic review of the definition and measurement of engagement in serious games. In: Proceedings of the Australasian Computer Science Week Multiconference, pp. 1–10 (2019)

15. Kato, P.M., Cole, S.W., Bradlyn, A.S., Pollock, B.H.: A video game improves behavioral outcomes in adolescents and young adults with cancer: a randomized trial. Pediatrics **122**(2), e305–e317 (2008). https://doi.org/10.1542/peds.2007-3134

16. Lawitschka, A., et al.: Health-related quality of life in pediatric patients after allogeneic SCT: development of the PedsQL stem cell transplant module and results of a pilot study. Bone Marrow Transplant. **49**(8), 1093–1097 (2014). https://doi.org/10.1038/bmt.2014.96

17. Lawitschka, A., et al.: A web-based mobile app in cancer and hematopoietic stem cell transplantation-aftercare for adolescents (INTERACCT-App) does improve quality of medical information for clinicians: results of an observational study. JMIR Mhealth Uhealth (2020). https://doi.org/10.2196/18781

18. McCallum, S.: Gamification and serious games for personalized health. In: Studies in Health Technology and Informatics, vol. 177, pp. 85–96. IOS Press (2012). https://doi.org/10.3233/978-1-61499-069-7-85

19. McDonald, C.J., et al.: LOINC, a universal standard for identifying laboratory observations: a 5-year update. Clin. Chem. **49**(4), 624–633 (2003). https://doi.org/10.1373/49.4.624

20. O'Sullivan, C., et al.: Evaluation of the electronic self-report symptom screening in pediatrics tool (SSPedi). BMJ Support. Palliat. Care **8**(1), 110–116 (2018). https://doi.org/10.1136/bmjspcare-2015-001084

21. Parsons, S.K., Phipps, S., Sung, L., Baker, K.S., Pulsipher, M.A., Ness, K.K.: NCI, NHLBI/PBMTC first international conference on late effects after pediatric hematopoietic cell transplantation: health-related quality of life, functional, and neurocognitive outcomes. Biol. Blood Marrow Transpl. **18**(2), 162–171 (2012). https://doi.org/10.1016/J.BBMT.2011.12.501. https://www.bbmt.org/article/S1083-8791(11)01063-9/fulltext#

22. Peters, K., Bührer, S., Silbernagl, M., Kayali, F., Hlavacs, H., Lawitschka, A.: Evaluation of informative content of health data submitted through a mobile serious game. In: van der Spek, E., Göbel, S., Do, E.Y.-L., Clua, E., Baalsrud Hauge, J. (eds.) ICEC-JCSG 2019. LNCS, vol. 11863, pp. 366–376. Springer, Cham (2019). https://doi.org/10.1007/978-3-030-34644-7_30

23. R Core Team: R: a language and environment for statistical computing. R Foundation for Statistical Computing, Vienna, Austria (2013). http://www.R-project.org/

24. Tark, R., Metelitsa, M., Akkermann, K., Saks, K., Mikkel, S., Haljas, K.: Usability, acceptability, feasibility, and effectiveness of a gamified mobile health intervention (TRIUMF) for pediatric patients: qualitative study. JMIR Serious games **7**(3), e13776 (2019)

25. Wang, J., et al.: Mhealth supportive care intervention for parents of children with acute lymphoblastic leukemia: quasi-experimental pre- and postdesign study. JMIR mHealth and uHealth 6(11), e9981 (2018). https://doi.org/10.2196/mhealth.9981

26. Wang, J., et al.: Development of a smartphone application to monitor pediatric patient-reported outcomes. In: Studies in Health Technology and Informatics, vol. 245 (2017). https://doi.org/10.3233/978-1-61499-830-3-253

# Does Digital Game Play Affect Social/Emotional Child Wellbeing?

Jan L. Plass[1]($\boxtimes$) (iD), Bruce D. Homer[2] (iD), Meagan Bromley[1] (iD), Fabian Froehlich[1] (iD), Yuli Shao[1] (iD), and Jessica Young[2]

[1] New York University, New York, NY 10012, USA
jan.plass@nyu.edu
[2] The Graduate Center, City University of New York, New York, NY 10016, USA

**Abstract.** Can digital game play enhance child wellbeing? Applying a wellbeing framework that identified six dimensions of wellbeing (competence, agency, relatedness, curiosity, optimism, and reduced stress) we conducted a playtesting study ($N = 25$) to develop wellbeing profiles for six games. These profiles informed an experimental study in which 8- to 12-year-olds ($N = 62$) either played tablet-based casual games over an 8-week period (play group) or engaged in other activities (control group) in an afterschool program. We administered the Basic Psychological Need Satisfaction Scale (BPNSFS) as pre-test, and the KIDSCREEN-27, a standardized measure of wellbeing, as pre- and post-intervention test. We found that for children with specific psychological needs, the play intervention improved related domains of wellbeing. Results have theoretical and practical implications, including guidance for game designers to add features supporting child wellbeing.

**Keywords:** Digital game play · wellbeing · experimental design

## 1 Introduction

### 1.1 Play Across Contexts

Play has long been recognized as having a crucial role in children's learning and development, and is essential for cognitive, physical, social, and emotional wellbeing [1–3]. Although most research has focused on play in the physical world, as children and adolescents spend more and more time in digital environments, it is important to understand what effects this digital play is having on children [4]. It has even been called into question whether or not it makes sense to separate the digital and physical worlds for youth today, who are living in a "hybrid reality" that flows seamlessly between digital and physical environments [5]. Digital play, therefore, is an extension of other forms of play for children and adolescents, albeit in a medium that has unique affordances and opportunities, including opportunities for improving wellbeing.

Children spend more time playing digital games in their daily lives than ever before, and games often occupy a space in their lives that extends beyond a past time to an impactful activity. As children age, play continues to be important for the development

M. Haahr et al. (Eds.): JCSG 2023, LNCS 14309, pp. 155–170, 2023.
https://doi.org/10.1007/978-3-031-44751-8_11

of social-emotional competence and cognitive development, including the continuing development of imagination, creativity, and humor [6], and is associated with positive feelings and enhanced emotional wellbeing [7]. Particularly for children in middle childhood who are gaining increased independence and abilities with technology, opportunities for digital play are more prominent. By the ages of 8–12, technology is often part of school curriculum, and by the time they are tweens (ages 10–12) many children in the US receive their own mobile devices [8]. In 2021, 59% of 8- to 18-year-olds played games every day, with daily averages of about 2.5 h among 8- to 12-year-olds and 3 h among 13- to 18-year-olds [9]. Particularly during the COVID-19 pandemic, playing digital games became even more important to child wellbeing, serving as a means of connection [10] and coping [11].

## 1.2 Digital Play and Learning

Digital games and gamified instructional methods have become commonplace in classrooms at all age levels, with educators and researchers finding that these methods boost student engagement, effort, persistence and attention to task [12–14]. Due to its popularity and inherent qualities to deliver dynamic play experiences, video game play has been examined with regard to its effect on a number of outcomes: research has documented positive effects of digital game play in learning and cognition [15], promotion of health and exercise [16] and behavior change [17]). Game play was found to enhance players' executive functions [18, 19], increase hope and optimism in Syrian refugee children [20], improve skills related to perception and processing of visual information [21], increase task-switching speed [22, 23] and help with emotional regulation or mood change [24, 25].

## 1.3 Digital Play and Wellbeing

Popular opinion, influenced by sensationalized media reports, often shows negative attitudes toward digital games, including concerns about addiction [26], aggression [27], desensitization to violence [28], reduced attention [29], and depression and suicidal ideation [30]. However, results of empirical research on these issues are often much less negative. In this paper, we are especially interested in the effect of digital play on child wellbeing.

A number of different approaches have been used to study this relation. Some studies have simply examined total time spent playing video games. For example, in a large-scale study of over 250,000 participants, Johannes et al. [31] examined the relation between time play behavior, measures of wellbeing and motivations for video game play obtained via surveys. Johannes et al. found a small positive relation between affective wellbeing and the time spent playing two particular games, Plants vs. Zombies and Animal Crossing. However, these findings were contradicted by the same team in a study two years later with the conclusion that time spent gaming has little to no effect on wellbeing, calling for further research on the matter [32].

Other studies have compared differences in wellbeing between non-players and video game players with low, moderate and high or excessive rates of self-reported play, with a focus on high school and middle school participants [33–35]. In a review of these studies, Jones et al. [36] found general positive effects of gaming on players' positive emotions and relaxation.

Lastly, rather than examining overall video gameplay and broad measures of wellbeing, some researchers have attempted to identify how specific game design features or certain types of in-game activities result in improvements of related aspects of wellbeing. This approach has also been extended to commercially available games exhibiting powerful positive effects on cognitive and perceptual skills [21, 37] including executive functions [38]. In their rigorous review of 23 empirical studies, Villani et al. [24] found that playing emotionally engaging video games is positively associated with emotional regulation, and that frequent play of commercial games with affective design features offers more opportunity for improved emotional states in players. Additionally, research has found playing video games that have been specifically designed to challenge certain cognitive skills, including skills such as executive functions that are known to support children's wellbeing, results in improvements in those skills [19].

Together, these findings suggest that rather than consider a broad relation between video game play and wellbeing, it is more useful to examine the relation between specific types of play activity and related aspects of wellbeing. This is the approach we have taken in the current program of research with children ages 8–12 in the unique middle childhood period of development.

## 1.4   The RITEC Framework for Child Wellbeing

The studies presented here were conducted as part of the *Responsible Innovation in Technology for Children* (RITEC) project, an international partnership with multiple stakeholders across industry, policy and academia with the goal of understanding how digital play can support wellbeing in children [39]. The project aims to investigate the impact of children's interactions with digital technologies, while also exploring possibilities to promote child wellbeing.

Wellbeing is a complex and multifaceted construct that is inconsistently defined in the literature. It can be examined using different frameworks that focus on different aspects of wellbeing. As a first phase of the RITEC project, we therefore developed a framework that specifies eight components of child wellbeing, which emerged from research that included large-scale survey data and smaller child-centered focus groups [39]. Our research comprises the second phase of this project, where we are focusing specifically on those components of the RITEC wellbeing framework that can be positively impacted through digital play. Informed by self-determination theory [40], we focus on intrinsically motivating factors in digital play that are linked to the basic psychological needs for autonomy, competence, and relatedness. Specifically, we are examining the following six dimensions of wellbeing: competence, agency/autonomy, relatedness/belonging, curiosity/openness, optimism/positive outlook, and relaxation/reduced stress.

Our theory of change is that when digital play, like all play, meets children's and adolescents' psychological needs, it can support their wellbeing. We examined this claim by investigating children (ages 8–12) playing video games that were systematically selected to afford play activities that address fundamental psychological needs, as outlined by self-determination theory [40]. This first phase of this research consisted of playtesting to confirm the selection of appropriate games, which was followed by an experimental investigation of the potential of these games to support wellbeing.

## 2  Playtesting Research for Selection of Games

Our playtesting research investigated whether various commercially available casual games can provide gameplay experiences that have the potential to enhance children's wellbeing. Through observations of players' in-game actions, video coding of players' behaviors during the gaming sessions, surveys, and interviews, we identified specific in-game activities with the potential to enhance wellbeing in the six dimensions identified by our framework: *competence* (e.g., by giving players challenging, yet solvable problems), *agency* (e.g., by giving players freedom of choice and action), *relatedness* (e.g., by fostering social relationships between the player, game's character and world), *curiosity* (e.g., by promoting openness towards game settings, narratives, characters, and alternative game play), *optimism* (e.g., by cultivating a positive outlook and belief in future success), and *relaxation* (e.g., by reduction of stress or calming stimuli). Results provided initial evidence for the wellbeing effects of the specific games we investigated, developed wellbeing profiles for the games, and confirmed findings of previous research on the wellbeing potential of digital games.

**Research Questions.** The playtesting study investigated the question: "Do casual games of different genres provide gameplay experiences that have the potential to enhance a child's wellbeing?" Specifically, we asked what types of game play experiences (e.g., puzzles, action, open-ended environments) children have in casual games, and how could they be associated with subjective wellbeing.

### 2.1  Method

**Research Design.** We followed an observational approach to playtest the games with our target demographic because we aimed to understand children's subjective wellbeing associated with their gameplay experiences. The collected qualitative data allowed us to investigate the extent to which the selected games provide experiences that potentially have positive effects on children's immediate wellbeing in order to determine which games to include in the longitudinal experimental study.

**Participants.** Participants ($N = 25$) were recruited through word of mouth and fliers in a large urban area in the Northeastern United States. The participants' age ranged from 7 to 17, with a mean of 11 years ($SD = 2.7$). Note that while the mean falls within the same range as for the experimental research, two participants who were older than 12 years were included to broaden the applicability of playtesting findings.

**Materials and Apparatus.** The materials included a pre-play survey, two tablet-based video games, a post-play interview, and an observation form. The pre-play survey covered general gaming habits and preferences. Participants played two out of the following six games on a tablet: Plants vs. Zombies (tower defense with plants), Rocket League Sideswipe (action soccer with high-flying cars), World of Goo (puzzle solving through goo ball constructions), Angry Birds 2 (puzzle solving through tower destruction sling shooting birds), LEGO Builder's Journey (visually pleasing puzzle adventure), LEGO Tower (build and manage a tower for LEGO Minifigures).

To choose these games, we first informally reviewed dozens of games, evaluating designs for play mechanics that we felt would support wellbeing, as well as for practical issues, e.g., can the game be played on a tablet, is the game available in multiple languages, or is no language required. A list of potential games was created to include a variety of genres and gameplay styles (action, puzzle, resource management, RPG) within age-appropriate ratings of widely available commercial games.

We excluded multiplayer games from this research for multiple reasons. Most importantly, there is a dearth of systematic research investigating children's wellbeing with single player games, and it seemed premature to introduce the methodological complexities of multiplayer games in this initial research. This study required a consistent gameplay experience for all players, which cannot be guaranteed in many multiplayer games, where one layer's experience depends on the other players, and where we would have had to monitor for inappropriate behaviors. Additionally, we considered potential prior exposure to the game and excluded any titles that most of the children participating in the research would have already played a lot, thereby diminishing any potential effects of additional play as part of our study. For example, Minecraft is an extremely popular game that is played by many children both in school settings and at home, and so playing for a few more hours as part of our intervention research would be unlikely to have any effect above. Finally, we excluded multiplayer games as they required internet access, which was not guaranteed at all participating sites.

The post-play interview covered the participants' playing experience. The participants played the games either on a Samsung Tab 7 light or iPad mini 6. An observation form was created to allow researchers to document participant behaviors in relation to the six wellbeing categories.

**Procedure.**  After parental permission and child assent were obtained, participants completed a pre-play survey to determine gaming habits and backgrounds. They next played two video games on a tablet, each for 20 min. During each of the 20-min play sessions, a research assistant observed the child playing a specific video game on the tablet. The research assistant noted observations of player behavior (indicators) into a wellbeing matrix of the six dimensions from our framework. These indicators included facial expressions, gestures, postures, and utterances. Screen capture software was used to record each videogame play session for subsequent analysis. Finally, participants were given a post-play interview about their play experience and attitudes towards the games, including questions about how players were feeling during gameplay. Even though the possibility of our observations affecting players behavior (Hawthorne effect) was low, since control group members participated in activities in the same setting that also included observations, we used multiple other data collection methods, such as screen capture, surveys, and interviews, and triangulated the findings to understand players' experiences.

**Analysis.**  Our analysis consisted of two stages, using three kinds of data sources. In the first stage, we coded the game play experiences and rated the six wellbeing dimensions on a five-point scale. The coding process took into account both the in-game events captured in screen recordings and player behaviors documented in observation notes to construct a holistic picture of each gaming session. Second, we identified themes in the interview data to substantiate how game play experiences can be associated with a child's subjective wellbeing.

Video coding started with defining a list of observable in-game events that could contribute to a child's wellbeing. These events were specific to each game. For example, a form of winning in a game can be a general observable event for competence. In Plants vs. Zombies, this can be manifested by using plants strategically and successfully defending against waves of zombies while in LEGO Builder's Journey, this can be seen as successfully solving a puzzle that bridges a path to unite two game characters.

We next scored the videos on a five-point scale to indicate the extent that the game play may have offered experiences that could contribute to the player's wellbeing on one or more of the six dimensions. The scoring was based on the frequency of pre-defined observable in-game events. A higher score indicated a higher possibility of a child having an experience that could enhance their wellbeing.

All observations were consolidated in 5-min-increments. Only the last 10 min of the recorded game play were coded as most of the participants were new to the games selected and thus needed time to familiarize themselves with the game rules and mechanics. The second stage of the coding included weaving observations into the scoring process. We reviewed observation notes and identified participant behaviors that were indicators of one or more of our wellbeing dimensions. These indicators, such as facial expressions, postures, gestures, gaze, and utterances, were behavioral evidence showing that a child was experiencing wellbeing like competence, relaxation, or optimism. After scoring the two intervals, the highest score of the two was selected as the final score for each wellbeing dimension. The final scores were composed of examinations of both the game play and player behaviors.

Lastly, themes were identified in interview data to help further our understanding of how game experiences could contribute to a child's subjective wellbeing. Our interview questions asked about players' overall experience of playing the selected games and their attitudes towards them. In addition, specific questions related to wellbeing dimensions were also included, for example, we asked whether the player was able to do what they wanted to do in the game, what they were curious about, or how they were feeling during their game play. The themes identified were game-specific given the uniqueness of game experiences that each game offered.

## 2.2 Playtesting Results

Through our analysis, we were able to identify several kinds of gameplay experiences that can be associated with different wellbeing dimensions, which allowed us to predict whether the games we selected could contribute to a child's subjective wellbeing for the experimental study. Because of these differences in the expression of each dimension in the different games, the indicators of wellbeing and their operationalization varied by game, resulting in the development of wellbeing profiles for each game.

**Wellbeing Profiles.** As an outcome of our analysis, we created wellbeing profiles for each game based on both the scoring and interview themes. These profiles identify the extent to which each game is likely to induce the specific wellbeing factors under investigation. All games supported the six wellbeing dimensions to some extent, but each game had its own strengths. Wellbeing profiles of two games are presented below as examples of how our analyses guided by a wellbeing framework were used to develop profiles for the designs of individual games.

**Table 1.** Wellbeing profile of RLS.

**Rocket League Sideswipe**

| Age | Played before | Age Group | Competence | Agency/ Autonomy | Relatedness/ Belonging | Curiosity/ Openness | Optimism/ Positive outlook | Relaxation/ Reduced stress |
|---|---|---|---|---|---|---|---|---|
| 8 | No | 10 and under | 4 | 5 | 3 | 3 | | |
| 9 | Yes | 10 and under | 5 | 5 | 5 | | | |
| 9 | Yes | 10 and under | 5 | 5 | 5 | | 4 | 4 |
| 11 | Yes | 11 and above | 5 | 5 | 5 | | | 3 |
| 11 | No | 11 and above | 5 | 5 | 5 | | 4 | |
| 11 | No | 11 and above | | 3 | 3 | | 5 | |
| 12 | Yes | 11 and above | 5 | 4 | 4 | 5 | 5 | |
| 12 | No | 11 and above | 5 | 5 | | | | |

**Rocket League Side Swipe (RLS).** RLS is a fast-paced action soccer game with high-flying cars, offering short 2-min matches where players can compete against bots or team up with non-player teammates, while enjoying customization options for their car avatars and emoticon-based interactions. RLS (Table 1) provided gameplay experiences that were most likely to support competence, agency/autonomy, and relatedness/belonging. Curiosity and optimism/positive outlook were also observed, but not as strongly, and relaxation was least prevalent.

Competence is related to the player's ability to solve the challenges posed by the game. It was highly observable due to the games' clear goals and measurable outcomes, including metrics like the number of goals and defenses. Additionally, players received immediate feedback on their performance, making indicators of competence highly observable events. Agency related to the player's freedom of choice and action, as shown through players' choices of orientations of competitive play (1 vs 1) or collaborative play (2 vs 2). Relatedness and a sense of belonging was defined as the social relationship between the player, game's character, and the world. Although characters and a traditional narrative are not part of the design of RLS, players' use of emoticons to thank or cheer on their non-player teammate in collaborative play operationalized this dimension. Relaxation was least prevalent since players were generally more thrilled and excited playing in the competitive action environment of RLS, rather than calm and relaxed as observed when playing other games focused on self-paced play.

**Plants vs. Zombies (PvZ).** PvZ is a tower defense game where players employ strategies using a variety of plants to survive zombie invasions. The game features cute and humorous characters, and with challenging and progressive levels, players unlock new plants and features to strategize their defenses in multiple ways. PvZ (Table 2) showed a high potential for wellbeing effects across all wellbeing dimensions, but specifically, the design of the game allowed players to learn and improve, trying different strategies, supporting increased competence and agency, which resulted in increased relaxation.

Improvement in gameplay was an indicator of competence observed in PvZ. Players learned how to get better at the game and adjusted their strategies based on their performances. Accordingly, player behaviors supported in-game events to rate competence. Children experienced positive emotions—e.g., they smiled, yelled out "yes," and jumped off their chairs with their hands raised in victory—when they made achievements in the game. They showed confidence when they gave pep talks to themselves and disparaged their non-player opponents during gameplay. Through our conversations with the children, they often presented clear ideas about the best strategy to use and why they won or lost at the end of their gaming sessions. Additionally, players highlighted that they had to develop their own strategy to survive the zombie waves. They were reflective of the fact that timing and positioning of their plants had severe consequences on the outcome of a round.

**Table 2.** Wellbeing profiles of PvZ.

**Plants vs. Zombies**

| Age | Played before | Age Group | Competence | Agency/ Autonomy | Relatedness/ Belonging | Curiosity/ Openness | Optimism/ Positive outlook | Relaxation/ Reduced stress |
|-----|-----|-----|-----|-----|-----|-----|-----|-----|
| 10 | Yes | 10 and under | 5 | 5 | 3 | | 3 | |
| 11 | No | 11 and above | 4 | 5 | 5 | 5 | 5 | 3 |
| 12 | Yes | 11 and above | 5 | 5 | | 4 | 4 | 5 |
| 15 | Yes | 11 and above | 4 | 5 | | 4 | 4 | |
| 16 | Yes | 11 and above | 5 | 5 | | 3 | | 5 |
| 16 | No | 11 and above | 3 | 4 | 3 | 3 | 4 | |
| 17 | No | 11 and above | 4 | 4 | | 3 | 3 | |

These reflections were also indicators of curiosity. Children showed curiosity and openness towards game settings, narratives, characters, and alternative ways of gameplay. Players were curious and open to trying out new game characters they unlocked and learning how the new plants could be utilized. Further, compared to open-ended environments of other games, PvZ level progressions presented as roadmaps allowed players to scroll over and explore what was to come, indicating competence interacting with curiosity.

Although surviving waves of zombie attacks may not be intuitively relaxing, players would feel good and have a sense of accomplishment after successfully repelling the last wave, resulting in optimism, and by extension, relaxation. When players were confident that they would win, we observed relaxation in their postures. For example, players sat in a relaxed position leaning on their backrest or played with only one hand when they had built a strong defensive position of plants that could easily fight off the zombies' advances.

## 2.3 Playtesting Discussion

Our playtesting research asked whether digital gameplay experiences have the potential to enhance a child's wellbeing. We identified activities in commercial off-the-shelf tablet-based games that are related to wellbeing factors and have the potential to enhance wellbeing. Games that allow for an interaction of the agency and relatedness dimensions of wellbeing may have the strongest potential to positively affect children's wellbeing.

In this study, games that made clever use of their game mechanics to impact agency and relatedness were PvZ and RLS. In both games, the player's decision-making affects characters and the world around the player. Players receive immediate feedback on the effectiveness of their strategy, which contributes to their agency and can thereby increase competence. A well-balanced interaction between game events and opportunities related to agency and relatedness are preconditions for increased optimism and relaxation. Optimism and relaxation appeared to be byproducts of the players' increased agency and relatedness.

Results provide initial evidence for the well-being effect of the specific games we investigated, which is in line with findings of previous research on the wellbeing potential of digital games. We also identified which kind of experiences players had that have the potential to affect wellbeing. Based on our findings we were able to conclude that the six chosen games were suitable for the experimental research we conducted, reported next.

# 3 Experimental Study

Building on findings of the playtesting, we next conducted an experimental study to determine if playing the selected video games does actually enhance children's wellbeing. Over the course of 8 weeks, 8- to 12-year-olds from an afterschool program ($N = 62$), played the selected digital games in twice-weekly play sessions, while a control group from the same participated in their usual activities (e.g., sports). Measures of psychological needs, loneliness, and pre- and posttest measures of wellbeing were given to all participants.

**Research Questions.** For the experimental research we asked:

1. Does playing digital games over the course of 8 weeks enhance wellbeing in players 8–12 years of age?
2. What social interactions emerged during game play, and how did this affect wellbeing?

## 3.1 Method

**Participants.** Participants were recruited from an afterschool program in a suburban area in the Northeastern United States. The children were randomly assigned to either the play group ($N = 35$; plus 2 additional participants did not return for the posttests) or control group ($N = 27$; plus 5 additional participants did not return for the posttests). Participants' ages ranged from 8 to 12, with a mean age of 10 years ($SD = 1.1$). Twenty-three participants were female, and one identified as non-binary. Among those who provided further demographic information, 34 participants identified as Latino/Hispanic and 10 identified as African American.

**Apparatus.** Six mobile games were selected as options for gameplay. These games were the ones included and validated in the playtesting research. All games were played on a 10.9-inch iPad Air, with each child having their own iPad.

**Measures.** Children were given a background and video game play experience questionnaire. Also, two global wellbeing measures were given pre- and post-intervention: the Children version of the Basic Psychological Need Satisfaction and Frustration Scale (BPNSFS) and the KIDSCREEN-27 (KS-27). The BPNSFS, grounded in self-determination theory, measures how well children's basic psychological needs are met, and assessed their level of needs frustration in three domains: autonomy, relatedness, and competence. It has been translated into several languages and validated among both adults and children in many countries [41]. The general wellbeing items include curiosity/openness, relatedness, positive outlook on life, general feeling of competency and general feeling of autonomy. The KS-27 is a more general measure of physical and psychological wellbeing, including the domains of autonomy & parents, peers & social support, and school environment. It has been validated across multiple cultures and has good internal consistency and reliability [42].

**Procedure.** Parental permission and child verbal assent were obtained prior to initiating our research. Initial visits consisted of pre-test measures of wellbeing and loneliness, as well as surveys to collect background information. The play group also had an introductory session playing the games on iPads. Over an 8-week period, play visits were conducted twice weekly unless a holiday or program closure changed the schedule.

Play visits consisted of non-structured time to play the games, with free choice to select any of the available options and a welcoming environment to play alongside other participants as desired. Each visit, individual participants would be asked to complete short surveys about their experience playing the games. During gameplay, researchers used an observation form to record each child's behaviors. Start and end time of play were noted, and in five-minute intervals, researchers noted which game was being played, the child's emotions, and whether they socially interacted with other players. The form tracked, for example, when a player talked to another player (social target) about game related content.

Final visits consisted of post-test measures of wellbeing, a survey about gameplay during the time of the study, and for those in the play group, brief semi-structured interviews about their experience.

### 3.2   Results Experimental Study

**Research Question 1**: *Does playing digital games over the course of 8 weeks enhance child wellbeing in players 8–12 years of age?*

An analysis of covariances (ANCOVA) was conducted with group (control, play) as independent variable, pre-test wellbeing (pre-KIDSCREEN-27 total) as a covariate, and posttest wellbeing (post-KIDSCREEN-27 total) as the dependent variable. The analysis did not reveal a main effect for group, $F(1,47) = .30, p = .059$.

Next, we investigated how existing psychological needs might moderate the intervention effects. We examined how change in scores on the Autonomy & Parent Relation subscale of the KS-27 was related to children's reported Autonomy Frustration on the BPNSFS. The ANCOVA revealed a main effect of group, $F(1,49) = 5.61, p = .022, \eta_p2 = .10$, with significantly greater gains for the intervention group ($m = 3.6, SD = 12.9$) than for the control group ($m = 1.5, SD = 9.4$). There was also a significant Autonomy Frustration by group interaction, $F(1,49) = 5.66, p = .021, \eta_p2 = .10$. In the play group, children with lower Autonomy Frustration Scores (indicating greater frustration) demonstrated greater gains in the Autonomy and Parent Relations subscale, see Fig. 1. For the control group, Autonomy Frustration did not relate to change in Autonomy and Parent Relations score.

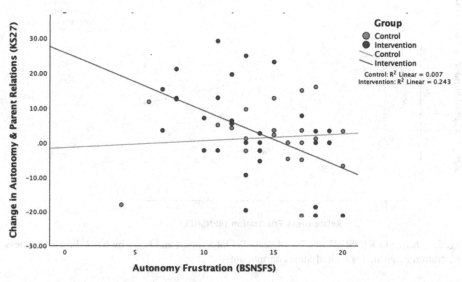

**Fig. 1.** Change in KIDSCREEN subscale Autonomy and Parent Relations by BPNSFS Autonomy Frustration by group for United States participants

We next examined how change in scores on the Autonomy & Parent Relation subscale (KS-27) was related to children's reported Relatedness Frustration (BPNSFS). The ANCOVA revealed a main effect of group, $F(1,50) = 4.20, p = .046, \eta_p^2 = .08$, with the intervention group demonstration greater gains ($m = 3.6, SD = 12.9$) than the control group ($m = 1.9, SD = 9.4$). There was also a significant Relatedness Frustration by group interaction, $F(1,50) = 4.36, p = .042, \eta_p2 = .08$. In the intervention group, children with lower Relatedness Frustration Scores (indicating greater frustration) demonstrated greater gains in the Autonomy and Parent Relations subscale. For the control group, Relatedness Frustration did not relate to change in Autonomy and Parent Relations score.

Finally, we examined how change in scores on the Social Support & Peers subscale (KS-27) was related to children's reported Relatedness Frustration (BPNSFS). The ANCOVA revealed a main effect of group, $F(1,50) = 8.10, p = .006, \eta_p^2 = .14$, with the intervention group demonstration greater gains ($m = 2.25, SD = 12.0$) than the control group ($m = 1.1$, $SD = 7.9$). There was also a significant Relatedness Frustration by group interaction, $F(1,50) = 8.26$, $p = .006$, $\eta p2 = .14$. As shown in Fig. 2, in the intervention group, children with lower Relatedness Frustration Scores (indicating greater frustration) demonstrated greater gains in the Social Support and Peers subscale. For the control group, Relatedness Frustration did not relate to change in Social Support and Peers score.

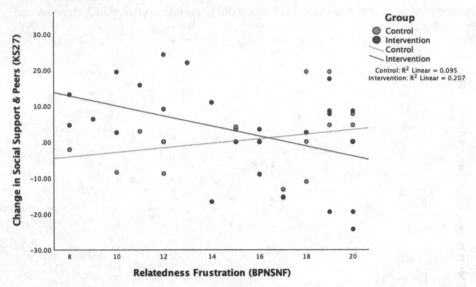

**Fig. 2.** Change in KIDSCREEN-27 subscale Social Support and Peers by BPNSFS Relatedness Frustration by group for United States participants

**Research Question 2:** *What social interactions emerged during game play, and how did this affect wellbeing?*

We performed a social network analysis (SNA) to understand children's play behavior in a social context and who players interacted with during the intervention. SNA quantifies the interactions within a network and allows for visual representations of networks [43, 44].

The SNA is not directional, i.e., we did not track who initiated the conversation between players. We imported the data into Gephi and computed the network metrics [45]. The network consisted of 32 players, see Fig. 3. The degree value indicates how many other players a player interacted with. On average, players interacted with 5 other players in the playing room. Participant mcs24 interacted with 13 other players, putting this player at the center of the network.

Closeness is a centrality measure indicating the distance between nodes or players, with values ranging from 0 to 1. This measure highlights who can most efficiently transfer information to other participants. Player mcs24 has the highest closeness centrality of 0.52. This means that if mcs24 had the solution for a game level, the player could share the information with half of the players. On average, players have a closeness centrality of 0.38.

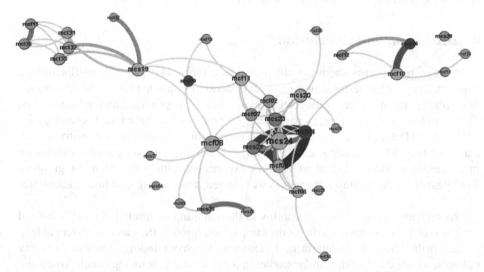

**Fig. 3.** Social Network Analysis of children playing video games in afterschool

The clustering coefficient indicates the degree to which nodes in a network tend to cluster together rather than randomly connecting with other group members. The clustering coefficient measures the likelihood of two players interacting with each other through someone else, who is connected directly to each of the players. Networks with high clustering are known as cliques if everyone is connected directly to everyone else [46]. Values below 0.3 indicate that students were more likely clustered and that those clusters did not communicate with each other. On average players have a cluster value of 0.49. The network can roughly be divided into three clusters. This might be due to the spatial set up of three tables in the playing room.

### 3.3 Experimental Study Discussion

Our experimental research compared two groups of students, one who played games in an afterschool program over the course of 8 weeks, and one that participated in other activities. Among the measures was KIDSCREEN27, a measure of physical and psychological wellbeing. We found significant interaction effects between preexisting psychological needs (BDNSFS) and gains on specific domains of wellbeing (KS-27). The psychological need for relatedness was the most predictive of gains in wellbeing, and higher levels of relatedness frustration had greater gains in both the social support and peers, as well as the autonomy and parent relations wellbeing subscales. Autonomy was also important, with higher levels of autonomy frustration predicting greater gains in the autonomy and parent relations wellbeing subscale. Although the psychological need for competency was not predictive in the current study, this may have been due to the play sessions and the selected games.

A social network analysis revealed that participants engaged in social play even though the games were single player games, which corresponds to the finding that relatedness is an important psychological need supported by games.

## 4 Discussion and Conclusion

In response to concerns about the effect of digital technology on child wellbeing, we conducted research investigating the impact of children's digital play on six dimensions of wellbeing: competence, agency, relatedness, curiosity, optimism, and reduced stress. These studies were conducted as part of the Responsible Innovation in Technology for Children (RITEC) project, an international partnership of partners in industry, policy and academia [39]. We conducted playtesting research to select six games for inclusion in the research, and conducted an 11-week experimental study in which one group of 8–12 year old children played the games we selected, and one engaged in other activities instead.

As with any research, generalizability of these findings is limited due to the limited sample size, limits in the diversity of the sample, and limits in the games we were able to include in this research. To determine the extent to which our findings generalize to other cultures, we are conducting similar studies in other settings, including South Africa and Chile.

Our findings have important theoretical and practical implications. On the theoretical level, we found a positive effect of digital play on child wellbeing for children with low levels of wellbeing. On the practical level, we introduced wellbeing profiles for games based on user observations, which help identify the specific aspects of wellbeing that these games can affect. We also found further evidence that play is social, even when the games are designed for single play. Initial recommendations for designers are to be aware of the impact their games can have on child wellbeing, and to design games that support players' autonomy and relatedness.

## References

1. Piaget, J.: Play dreams and imitation in childhood. WW Norton, New York (1962)
2. Vygotsky, L.S.: Mind in Society: The Development of Higher Psychological Processes. Harvard University Press, Cambridge (1978)
3. Ginsburg, K.: The importance of play in promoting healthy child development and maintaining strong parent-child bond. J. Am. Acad. Pediatr. **119**(1), 182–191 (2007)
4. Homer, B.D., Raffaele, C., Henderson, H.: Games as playful learning: implications of developmental theory for game-based learning. In: Plass, J.L., Mayer, R.E., Homer, B.D. (eds). Handbook of Game-Based Learning, pp. 25-52. MIT Press, Boston (2020)
5. Granic, I., Morita, H., Scholten, H.: Beyond screen time: Identity development in the digital age. Psychol. Inq. **31**(3), 195–223 (2020)
6. Bergen, D., Fromberg, D.P.: Play and social interaction in middle childhood. Phi Delta Kappan **90**(6), 426–430 (2009)
7. Howard, J., McInnes, K.: The impact of children's perception of an activity as play rather than not play on emotional well-being. Child Care Health Develop. **39**(5), 737–742 (2013)

8. Bulger, M., Madden, M., Sobel, K., Davison, P.: The Missing Middle: Reimagining a future for Tweens, Teens and Public Media (2021)
9. Rideout, V., Peebles, A., Mann, S., Robb, M.B.: Common sense census: media use by tweens and teens, 2021. Common Sense Media **2019**, 1–104 (2022)
10. Nebel, S., Ninaus, M.: Short research report: does playing apart really bring us together? Investigating the link between perceived loneliness and the use of video games during the COVID-19 pandemic (2020)
11. Pearce, K.E., et al.: Families playing animal crossing together: coping with video games during the COVID-19 pandemic. Games Cult. **17**(5), 773–794 (2022)
12. Berg, V., Rogers, S.L., McMahon, M., Garrett, M., Manley, D.: A novel approach to measure executive functions in students: an evaluation of two child-friendly apps. Front. Psychol. **11**, 1702 (2020). https://doi.org/10.3389/fpsyg.2020.01702
13. Bhavnani, S., et al.: Development feasibility and gamified cognitive developmental assessment on an e-platform (DEEP) in rural Indian pre-schoolers–a pilot study. Glob. Health Action **12**(1), 1548005 (2019)
14. Godwin, K.E., Lomas, D., Koedinger, K.R., Fisher, A.V.: Monster mischief: designing a video game to assess selective sustained attention. Int. J. Gaming Comput. Mediated Simul. **7**(4), 18–39 (2015)
15. Plass, J.L., Homer, B.D., Mayer, R.E., Kinzer, C.K.: Theoretical foundations of game-based and playful learning. In: PLass, J.L., Mayer, R.E., Homer, B.D. (eds.) Handbook of Game-Based Learning, pp. 3–24. MIT Press, Boston (2020)
16. Lu, A.S., Kharrazi, H., Gharghabi, F., Thompson, D.: A systematic review of health videogames on childhood obesity prevention and intervention. Games Health J. **2**(3), 131–141 (2013)
17. Whitaker, J.L., Bushman, B.J.: "Remain calm. Be kind." Effects of relaxing video games on aggressive and prosocial behavior. Soc. Psych. Pers. Sci. **3**(1), 88–92 (2012)
18. Parong, J., Mayer, R.E., Fiorella, L., MacNamara, A., Homer, B.D., Plass, J.L.: Learning executive function skills by playing focused video games. Contemp. Educ. Psychol. **51**, 141–151 (2017)
19. Homer, B.D., Plass, J.L., Raffaele, C., Ober, T.M., Ali, A.: Improving high school students' executive functions through digital game play. Comput. Educ. **117**, 50–58 (2018)
20. Sirin, S., Plass, J.L., Homer, B.D., Vatanartiran, S., Tsai, T.: Project hope: digital game-based education for Syrian refugee children. Vulnerable Child. Youth Stud. **13**, 7–18 (2018)
21. Green, C.S., Bavelier, D.: Effects of action video game playing on the spatial distribution of visuospatial attention. J. Exp. Psychol. Hum. Percept. Perform. **32**(6), 1465–1478 (2006)
22. Beijanki, V.R., et al.: Action video game play facilitates the development of better perceptual templates. Proc. Natl. Acad. Sci. United States Am. **111**(47), 16961–16966 (2014)
23. Green, C.S., Sugarman, M.A., Medford, K., Klobusicky, E., Bavelier, D.: The effect of action video game experience of task-switching. Comput. Hum. Behav. **28**, 984–994 (2012)
24. Villani, D., Carissoli, C., Triberti, S., Marchetti, A., Gilli, G., Riva, G.: Videogames for emotion regulation: a systematic review. Games Health J. **7**(2), 85–99 (2018)
25. Rieger, D., Frischlich, L., Wulf, T., Bente, G., Kneer, J.: Eating ghosts: the underlying mechanisms of mood repair via interactive and noninteractive media. Psychol. Popular Media Cult. **4**(2), 138–154 (2015)
26. Felt, L.J., Robb, M.B.: Technology Addiction: Concern, Controversy, and Finding Balance. Common Sense Media, San Francisco (2016)
27. Anderson, C.A., et al.: Violent video game effects on aggression, empathy, and prosocial behavior in eastern and western countries: a meta-analysis. Psychol. Bull. **136**(2), 151–173 (2010)
28. Carnagey, N.L., Anderson, C.A., Bushman, B.J.: The effect of video game violence on physiological desensitization to real-life violence. J. Exp. Soc. Psych. **43**, 489–496 (2007)

29. Swing, E.L., Gentile, D.A., Anderson, C.A., Walsh, D.A.: Television and video game exposure and the development of attention problems. Pediatrics **126**, 214–221 (2010)
30. Twenge, J.M.: More time on technology, less happiness? Associations between digital-media use and psychological well-being. Curr. Dir. Psych. Sci. **28**(4), 372–379 (2019)
31. Johannes, N., Vuorre, M., Przybylski, A.K.: Video game play is positively correlated with well-being. PsyArXiv (2020)
32. Vuorre, M., Johannes, N., Kristoffer, A. Przybylski, A.: Time spent playing video games is unlikely to impact well-being. Royal Soc. Open Sci. J. **9**, 220411 (2022)
33. Allahverdipour, H., Bazargan, M., Farhadinasab, A., Moeini, B.: Correlates of video games playing among adolescents in an Islamic country. BMC Public Health **10**, 286 (2010). https://doi.org/10.1186/1471-2458-10-286
34. Durkin, K., Barber, B.: Not so doomed: computer game play and positive adolescent development. J. Appl. Dev. Psychol. **23**, 373–392 (2002)
35. Wack, E., Tantleff-Dunn, S.: Relationships between electronic game play, obesity, and psychosocial functioning in young men. Cyberpsychol. Behav. **12**, 241–2444 (2009)
36. Jones, C.M, Scholes, L., Johnson, D., Katsikitis, M., Carras, M.C.: Gaming well: links between videogames and flourishing mental health. Front. Psychol. **5**, 260 (2014). https://doi.org/10.3389/fpsyg.2014.00260
37. Pallavicini, F., Ferrari, A., Mantovani, F.: Video games for well-being: a systematic review on the application of computer games for cognitive and emotional training in the adult population. Front. Psychol. **9**, 2127 (2018)
38. Buelow, M.T., Okdie, B.M., Cooper, A.B.: The influence of video games on executive functions in college students. Comput. Hum. Behav. **45**, 228–234 (2015)
39. UNICEF Office of Research–innocenti. Responsible innovation in technology for children. Digital technology, play, and child well-being. UNICEF Innocenti, Florence (2022)
40. Ryan, R.M., Rigby, C.S.: Motivational foundations of game-based learning. In: PLass, J.L., Mayer, R.E., Homer, B.D. (eds.) Handbook of Game-Based Learning, pp. 153–176. MIT Press, Boston (2020)
41. Van der Kaap-Deeder, J., Soenens, B., Ryan, R.M., Vansteenkiste, M.: Manual of the Basic Psychological Need Satisfaction and Frustration Scale (BPNSFS). Ghent University, Belgium (2020)
42. Ravens-Sieberer, U., et al.:. The KIDSCREEN-27 quality of life measure for children and adolescents: psychometric results from a cross-cultural survey in 13 European countries. Qual. Life Res. **16**(8), 1347–1356 (2007). https://doi.org/10.1007/s11136-007-9240-2. PMID: 17668292
43. Hopkins, M.: A review of social network analysis and education: theory, methods, and applications. J. Educ. Behav. Stat. **42**(5), 639–46 (2017)
44. Scott, J., Carrington, P.J.: The SAGE Handbook of Social Network Analysis. London (2011)
45. Bastian, M., Heymann, S., Jacomy, M.: Gephi: an open source software for exploring and manipulating networks. In: International AAAI Conference on Weblogs and Social Media (2009)
46. Sclater, N.: Learning Analytics Explained. New York (2017)

# ReWIND: A Story-Based Serious Game to Reinforce Learning of CBT Strategies for Anxiety Disorders

Yew Ken Heng[1](✉) (ID), Jasy Suet Yan Liew[1](✉) (ID),
Mohammad Farris Iman Leong bin Abdullah[2] (ID), Ying Tang[3] (ID),
and Nathan Prestopnik[4]

[1] School of Computer Sciences, Universiti Sains Malaysia, Gelugor, Penang, Malaysia
hengyewken96@student.usm.my, jasyliew@usm.my
[2] Department of Community Health, Advanced Medical and Dental Institute,
Universiti Sains Malaysia, Gelugor, Penang, Malaysia
farris@usm.my
[3] Department of Psychological Sciences and Counseling, Youngstown State University,
Youngstown, OH, USA
yjtang@ysu.edu
[4] Division of Applied Technology, Shenandoah University, Winchester, VA, USA
nprestop@su.edu

**Abstract.** We present ReWIND, a story-based serious game to help players learn cognitive behavioral therapy (CBT) strategies that are useful for tackling anxiety disorders. ReWIND artfully weaves CBT into the anxiety-relevant sub-stories encapsulated as quests in the game and implements game mechanics simulating CBT strategies such as cognitive restructuring. Finally, ReWIND reinforces learning of the CBT strategies through reflection dialogs, quest summaries and repetition of a CBT strategy across different quests. ReWIND offers a scalable framework to extend the game to cover many different anxiety scenarios and CBT strategies.

**Keywords:** Cognitive behavioral therapy · serious game · anxiety · mental health · psychoeducation

## 1 Introduction

Cognitive behavioral therapy (CBT), a series of cognitive and behavioral interventions aimed at regulating dysfunctional patterns of thinking and maladaptive behaviors to prevent the development of and maintain emotional distress for mental health problems [7], has been proven to be effective in the treatment of anxiety disorders [10]. Traditional CBT is usually conducted within 12 to 20 sessions with the patient in the presence of the psychotherapist [4]. Psychotherapists attempt to assist patients in challenging their negative thoughts while providing advice during the sessions so patients can think in a more balanced and functional manner and subsequently overcome the self-defeating patterns.

© The Author(s), under exclusive license to Springer Nature Switzerland AG 2023
M. Haahr et al. (Eds.): JCSG 2023, LNCS 14309, pp. 171–177, 2023.
https://doi.org/10.1007/978-3-031-44751-8_12

Continuously providing information through psychoeducation is crucial to facilitate the change of thought and behavior [1] but treatment cost and sustainability are among some of the barriers to long-term therapy [8].

We present ReWIND, a story-based serious game designed to artfully incorporate CBT strategies into the game narrative and mechanics for the purpose of anxiety psychoeducation. Unlike prior games for anxiety that have only integrated CBT in games as a series of goal-oriented tasks [2, 3, 9, 12, 14, 15] and required therapists for guidance during the intervention, ReWIND allows players to explore different anxiety scenarios and CBT strategies through different sub-stories encapsulated as quests in the game without needing external assistance. ReWIND was co-designed with psychology experts to ensure an accurate implementation of CBT in the game. In this paper, our main goal is to demonstrate how CBT can be realistically weaved into the game narrative and artfully incorporated into the game mechanics through ReWIND.

## 2   Related Work

SuperBetter (SB) is an example of task-driven game solution targeting anxiety [12]. SB leverages CBT and positive psychotherapy targeting depressed people while also expected to reduce anxiety symptoms at the same time as the secondary outcome, given the high comorbidity of anxiety and depression. There are no interactive stories in SB, such that users make progress through the game in the form of completing activities such as describing a goal, taking recommended steps toward the goal, and completing recommended mood-boosting activities.

Another relevant gamified solution, SmartCAT2.0, was introduced as an adjunctive component to CBT treatment in an open trial for childhood anxiety disorder [15]. SmartCAT2.0 consists of several interactive Skillbuilder Activities that award users with digital points upon completion. The points can then be used to redeem various rewards such as pens, accessories, and certificates. Players are also rewarded with digital trophies after finishing all the required activities for each session. Similar to SB, the game does not support story features, and all activities are delivered in the form of session tasks.

MindLight, on the other hand, is a biofeedback-based serious game that integrates neurofeedback reinforcement in its gameplay design to prevent anxiety in children [13]. MindLight is distinct from the SB and SmartCAT 2.0 in that it comes with a story. Players explore the game as a character named Arty to save his grandmother from evil forces. As the game progresses, players are exposed to various fearful events, and they will learn to overcome their fears by changing their state of mind. The relaxation state of players is reflected in the brightness of the game world, whereby the light gets brighter when players are more relaxed. In MindLight, the story plays a peripheral role in the delivery of exposure training, the main CBT strategy incorporated in the game.

## 3   ReWIND: CBT-Based Game for Anxiety

ReWIND is a PC-based game implemented using the Unity game engine. In ReWIND, players play as Lucas, the main character of the game, and assist quest givers, a type of non-playing character (NPC), in resolving their anxiety-related problems. As Lucas engages with each quest giver, the player is drawn into an anxiety-related sub-story encapsulated within a quest. The linear narrative structure in each sub-story follows the five principles in Ellis' ABCDE model [5], a CBT model based on rational-emotive behavior therapy (REBT) [6]. Through a series of interactive dialogs, players first learn the quest giver's beliefs (B) about certain activating events (A) which overly affect their emotional and behavioral responses and subsequently lead to negative consequences (C) (i.e., an anxiety episode). After recognizing the cause of the anxiety, players then proceed to the disputation (D) stage, in which two appropriate CBT strategies are introduced to help dispute irrational beliefs and substitute them with effective rational beliefs to bring forth positive behavioral effects (E). To make gameplay more fun, CBT strategies are implemented through game mechanics such as item gathering (collecting items requested by the NPC), maze-solving (reaching the end of the maze), and interaction with NPCs.

To demonstrate how players can learn CBT strategies while playing ReWIND, we walk through Lars' quest in the game revolving around anxiety caused by health fear. Players start a quest by guiding Lucas to interact with Lars, the quest giver (Fig. 1a). At the beginning of the quest, players learn the ABC leading to Lars' irrational beliefs through a series of interactive dialogs (Fig. 1b and Fig. 1c). The story then transitions into disputation as Lucas recommends the next action to seek an NPC known as Master Yamato in Asiantown. Control transfers to Lars and players set out in search of Master Yamato with the help of the circular compass arrow surrounding Lars and the map of the game world (Fig. 1d).

**Fig. 1.** Quest initiation through interactive dialogs

Upon finding Master Yamato, players are then guided to learn two CBT strategies: 1) relaxation and 2) cognitive restructuring. Instead of merely explaining the CBT strategies through linear dialogs, ReWIND simulates the two CBT strategies through game mechanics. For relaxation, players are given the task of finding a waterfall spa and follow a visual guide to taking deep breaths (Fig. 2a and Fig. 2b). Cognitive restructuring is implemented using a maze tower in which players are probed with questions by a Floor Guardian related to actions to be taken in the onset of anxiety (Fig. 2c and Fig. 2d). Players are given three different door choices to choose from (i.e., one positive, one negative and one neutral option). Choosing the positive choice moves players up the levels to the top of the maze tower at a quicker pace while the negative choice moves players down to the bottom. The maze tower simulates the process of reshaping negative or inaccurate thinking into a more positive and supportive thinking that would lead to positive outcomes.

**Fig. 2.** Simulating CBT strategies through game mechanics in the disputation stage

Finally, ReWIND reinforces the CBT strategies through reflection dialogs (Fig. 3a) and quest summaries presented at the end of a quest (Fig. 3b). The second form of reinforcement is implemented by repeating the same CBT strategy to solve different anxiety-related problems in other quests. The full game flow of Lars' quest is illustrated in Fig. 4 and each quest follows a similar structural flow. Upon completion of a quest, Lucas once again reappears into the game world and players continue the game by seeking the next quest. ReWIND currently contains six quests. The quests are presented in a diegetic manner through quest giver NPCs located around the game world. Players explore different areas in the game world and are required to complete quests to make progress in the game.

Aside from game mechanics that implements CBT principles, additional game mechanics are also used to make ReWIND more entertaining. For example, an incentive system is introduced, whereby players can purchase character skin to change the appearance of Lucas using tokens earned from quest completions and treasure boxes. Players can gain a random number of tokens from treasure boxes scattered around the game world. It is crucial to have constant engagements not just with the NPCs but also the surroundings to keep the game alive and have players remain motivated throughout the game, especially for long-term psychoeducation.

**Fig. 3.** Reinforce learning of CBT strategies at the end of a quest

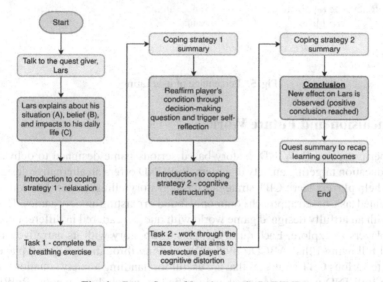

**Fig. 4.** Game flow of Lars' quest in ReWIND

## 4 Evaluation Experiment

Twenty university students above 18 years old and identified with anxiety risk took part in the evaluation of ReWIND. All participants were asked to play the game and then complete a game usability questionnaire adapted from MEEGA + [11]. Measures emphasizing story relevance and satisfaction were selected, and the questions were reframed to fit the context of ReWIND's story-based design. The usability evaluation was rated on a 5-point scale ranging from 1 (strongly disagree) to 5 (strongly agree). Participant feedback on the game was also obtained. Overall, participants enjoyed playing ReWIND.

The percentage of user ratings for each usability measure is shown in Fig. 5. All the participants agreed that ReWIND is applicable to real life, with 85% showing strong agreement. On being relevant to anxiety, 95% gave it at least a score of 4, whereas 90% reported being satisfied with the game. None of the participants rated ReWIND below a score of 3, thus showing that the game yields satisfactory results.

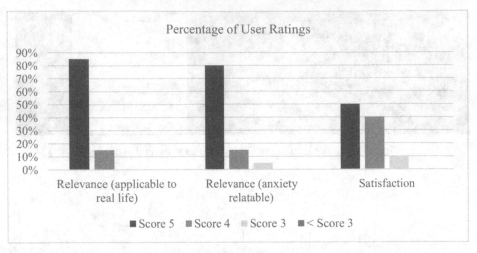

**Fig. 5.** Percentage of user ratings

## 5   Conclusion and Future Work

This paper presented ReWIND, a story-based serious game designed to deliver CBT psychoeducation targeting anxiety disorders. ReWIND offers an alternative design approach to help players learn CBT strategies through storytelling, rather than following a goal-oriented task-based approach commonly found in existing anxiety games. The game comes with an artfully designed game world with quests scattered in different locations for the players to explore. Each quest contains a sub-story with its narrative structure designed following Ellis' ABCDE model. By playing through each quest, players are exposed to various CBT strategies that are useful for handling anxiety situations. All six quests in ReWIND were co-designed and verified by psychology experts. ReWIND is scalable as it can be easily extended to include many different anxiety sub-stories and CBT strategies in the future to provide long-term psychoeducation.

**Acknowledgements.** This research was funded by Ministry of Higher Education Malaysia for Transdisciplinary Research Grant Scheme with Project Code: TRGS/1/2020/USM/02/4/2 and L'Oréal-UNESCO for Women in Science Malaysia Fellowship: 304/PKOMP/650943/L117.

## References

1. Borza, L.: Cognitive-behavioral therapy for generalized anxiety. Dialogues Clin. Neurosci. **19**(2), 203–208 (2017). https://doi.org/10.31887/DCNS.2017.19.2/lborza
2. Brezinka, V.: Treasure hunt - a serious game to support psychotherapeutic treatment of children. Stud. Health Technol. Inf. **136**, 71–76 (2008). https://doi.org/10.3233/978-1-58603-864-9-71
3. Christoforou, M., Sáez Fonseca, J.A., Tsakanikos, E.: Two novel cognitive behavioral therapy-based mobile apps for agoraphobia: randomized controlled trial. J. Med. Internet Res. **19**(11), e398 (2017). https://doi.org/10.2196/jmir.7747

4. Cully, J.A., Teten, A.L.: A Therapist's Guide to Brief Cognitive Behavioral Therapy. Department of Veterans Affairs, South Central Mental Illness Research, Education, and Clinical Center (MIRECC), Houston (2008)
5. David, D., Lynn, S.J., Ellis, A.: Rational and Irrational Beliefs: Research, Theory, and Clinical Practice (2010)
6. Ellis, A.: Changing rational-emotive therapy (RET) to rational emotive behavior therapy (REBT). J. Ration.-Emot. Cogn.-Behav. Ther. **13**, 85–89 (1995). https://doi.org/10.1007/BF02354453
7. Foreman, E.I., Pollard, C.: Cognitive Behavioural Therapy (CBT): Your Toolkit to Modify Mood, Overcome Obstructions and Improve Your Life (2016)
8. Kendall, P.C., Maxwell, C.A., Jakubovic, R.J., Ney, J.S., McKnight, D.S., Baker, S.: CBT for youth anxiety: how does it fit within community mental health? Curr. Psychiatry Rep. **25**(1), 13–18 (2023). https://doi.org/10.1007/s11920-022-01403-7
9. McCashin, D., Coyle, D., O'Reilly, G.: Pesky gNATs for children experiencing low mood and anxiety – a pragmatic randomised controlled trial of technology-assisted CBT in primary care. Internet Interv. **27**, 100489 (2022)
10. Otte, C.: Cognitive behavioral therapy in anxiety disorders: current state of the evidence. Dialogues Clin. Neurosci. **13**(4), 413–421 (2011)
11. Petri, G., von Wangenheim, C.G.: MEEGA+: a method for the evaluation of the quality of games for computing education. Proc. SBGames, Rio de Janeiro, Brazil, 28–31 (2019)
12. Roepke, A.M., Jaffee, S.R., Riffle, O.M., McGonigal, J., Broome, R., Maxwell, B.: Randomized controlled trial of SuperBetter, a smartphone-based/internet-based self-help tool to reduce depressive symptoms. Games Health J. **4**(3), 235–246 (2015). https://doi.org/10.1089/g4h.2014.0046
13. Schoneveld, E.A., Malmberg, M., Lichtwarck-Aschoff, A., Verheijen, G.P., Engels, R.C.M.E., Granic, I.: A neurofeedback video game (MindLight) to prevent anxiety in children: a randomized controlled trial. Comput. Hum. Behav. **63**, 321–333 (2016). https://doi.org/10.1016/j.chb.2016.05.005
14. Schuurmans, A.A., Nijhof, K.S., Vermaes, I.P., Engels, R.C., Granic, I.: A pilot study evaluating "Dojo", a videogame intervention for youths with externalizing and anxiety problems. Games Health J. **4**(5), 401–408 (2015)
15. Silk, J.S., et al.: Using a smartphone app and clinician portal to enhance brief cognitive behavioral therapy for childhood anxiety disorders. Behav. Ther. **51**(1), 69–84 (2020). https://doi.org/10.1016/j.beth.2019.05.002

# Extended Realities

# Virtual Reality Simulator for Police Training with AI-Supported Cover Detection

Polona Caserman[1]([✉])[iD], Philipp Niklas Müller[1][iD], Thorsten Göbel[2],
Pascal Tonecker[3], Savas Yildirim[3], André Kecke[2], Dennis Purdack[2][iD],
and Stefan Göbel[1][iD]

[1] Serious Games Research Group, Technical University of Darmstadt, Darmstadt
64283, Germany
{polona.caserman,philipp.mueller1,stefan_peter.goebel}@tu-darmstadt.de
[2] Hessian University for Public Management and Security, Mühlheim am Main
63165, Germany
{thorsten.goebel,andre.kecke,dennis.purdack}@hfpv-hessen.de
[3] Crytek GmbH, Frankfurt am Main 60386, Germany
{pascalt,savas}@crytek.com
https://www.etit.tu-darmstadt.de/serious-games, https://hoems.hessen.de,
https://www.crytek.com

**Abstract.** Training of different scenarios is essential to prepare emergency services for real-world situations. In this paper, we introduce a
virtual reality (VR) simulator specifically designed to enhance the training of police officers in the context of apartment search and area securing,
including the evaluation of potential threats or hazards. At this point,
multiple police officers train simultaneously by employing virtual reality
headsets and full-body suits, enabling them to see and interact with each
other's avatars. We additionally developed a configuration tool to enable
operational trainers to easily create new buildings with custom interiors. Moreover, we developed an algorithm that automatically recognizes
possible dangerous areas, especially when police officers have no cover.
In this case, a non-player character is spawned, representing either neutral individuals or potential assailants, strategically placed to confront
police officers and accentuate tactical mistakes. Field tests have sub-
stantiated the efficacy of our approach, demonstrating a high $F_1$ score of
0.93 in identifying tactical mistakes made by police officers. Furthermore,
the training outcomes have revealed that virtual training is comparable to traditional training in terms of maximum recovered area. These
findings demonstrate the immense potential of VR-based simulators for
police training, as they enable the creation of various scenarios and thus
increase the number of training sessions. The simulator is particularly
attractive also due to alternate training scenarios with individual difficulty levels making it suitable for students and special units.

**Keywords:** Civil Security · Police Training · Artificial Intelligence ·
Virtual Reality · Immersive Technology · Human-Computer
Interactions

© The Author(s), under exclusive license to Springer Nature Switzerland AG 2023
M. Haahr et al. (Eds.): JCSG 2023, LNCS 14309, pp. 181–193, 2023.
https://doi.org/10.1007/978-3-031-44751-8_13

# 1   Introduction

Effective training plays a crucial role in adequately preparing emergency services for real-world situations. However, traditional training methods, particularly in scenarios like house searches or hostage situations, are often expensive and cumbersome. Traditional methods typically involve complex setups, e.g., they require multiple partitions to recreate buildings and (professional) actors as role players. Due to their tedious nature, they offer only a limited number of training opportunities. At this point, many researchers have already recognized the potential of virtual reality (VR) in training police officers for critical decision-making under high-stress conditions [3,8,11,17]. Additionally, technology providers such as RE-liON[1] and THALES[2] offer virtual training solutions for special forces, while Refense[3], TriCAT[4], and XVR[5] enable collaborative training between police forces, medical personnel, and firefighters.

According to Dörner et al. [5] such training and simulations offer a specific form of learning and are therefore considered as serious games. Simulation games aim to engage learners in immersive experiences with specific educational or training objectives. They offer opportunities for users to practice and refine their abilities in realistic and challenging scenarios, making learning more engaging and effective. In this paper, we present a VR-based training simulation to address a vital aspect of police officer training - decision-making in the context of securing an area. By utilizing a VR technology, the system provides a valuable platform for tactical training in house searches, supporting ongoing police officers and special units. Furthermore, leveraging rule-based artificial intelligence (AI), we implemented a system that recognizes dangerous areas, particularly when one police officer lacks sufficient cover. The simulator further features a configuration tool, enabling operational trainers to quickly create various training environments by designing interiors, placing walls, doors, and windows. Moreover, we employ a full-body motion capture suit to analyze the trainees' posture and determine if the cover is sufficiently provided. To evaluate the performance of the developed VR-based simulator, supported by AI for cover detection, we conducted field tests and compared the results with the results from the traditional training.

The remainder of the paper is organized as follows: Sect. 2 provides a concise literature review, while Sect. 3 outlines the design of the developed simulation for police officers. Section 4 describes the evaluation and Sect. 5 presents the training outcomes. In Sect. 6, we discuss the results and in Sect. 7, we draw our conclusions based on the findings.

---

[1] RE-liON: https://re-lion.com, last accessed on May 4, 2023.
[2] THALES: https://www.thalesgroup.com/en/europe/germany/defence-security-germany-missionenabler, last accessed on May 4, 2023.
[3] Refense: https://www.refense.com, last accessed on May 4, 2023.
[4] TriCAT: https://tricat.net/en/imedtasim/, last accessed on May 4, 2023.
[5] XVR: https://www.xvrsim.com/en/, last accessed on May 4, 2023.

## 2    Related Work

Prior research consistently confirms that simulation-based training is an effective tool for training emergency services, enabling active practice and drilling of specific situations. For example, in recent years, various single and multiplayer simulation and training programs have been developed for military [18] and police forces [10]. Empirical studies have provided evidence supporting the effectiveness of virtual training, establishing its comparability to traditional training methods [2]. Nowadays, VR technology has become increasingly prevalent for tactical training within high-stress situations [1,4]. The advantages of virtual training have also yielded promising results in other domains, including medical emergency training [15], (collaborative) firefighting training [6,13], or earthquake drills [9].

Further studies has also explored methods for inducing stress within VR-based training, thereby creating more realistic scenarios. For instance, Uhl et al. [16] investigated the effects of multi-sensory stimuli, such as pain and heat, to elicit more authentic threat responses in high-risk situations. Another possibility to induce higher stress is to use full-body avatars that go beyond the conventional representation of the head and hands prevalent in many VR applications [3]. In another study, Nguyen et al. [14] explored the active intervention of trainers in manipulating trainees' stress level through the implementation of diverse audio-visual stressors. Similarly, Murtinger et al. [12] proposed an assistance system that enables trainers to dynamically adjust training protocols based on immediate feedback from trainees' performance, thereby tailoring the stress level to their needs.

## 3    Design

In order to meet the demand for a diverse range of training scenarios, we have created a tool that allows operational trainers to rapidly and flexibly generate and modify virtual environments (see Sect. 3.1). Additionally, for efficient training, real-time analysis is essential. Therefore, we developed a training scenario that utilizes AI to analyze the full-body postures of multiple police officers, identifies dangerous areas, and provides immediate visual as well as haptic feedback (see Sect. 3.2). Moreover, we have developed an after-action review tool, enabling collaborative analysis with the operational trainer and trainees (see Sect. 3.3).

### 3.1    Configuration Tool

We developed a configuration tool in close cooperation with the target group (i.e., the operational trainer). The configuration tool empowers users to effortlessly create customized training environments by either modifying existing predefined rooms or creating entirely new buildings from scratch. Afterward, the rooms can be equipped with furniture (e.g., closets, couches, and tables) and decorative elements (e.g., boxes and plants) from the 3D asset library. This process involves a simple drag-and-drop interface, allowing users to position assets precisely as desired (see Fig. 1).

**Fig. 1.** Tool to configure rooms using a 3D asset library.

## 3.2  AI-Based Detection of Danger Areas

We have developed a VR simulation that utilizes rule-based AI to assess current dangerous situations as police officers enter and search a virtual environment, i.e., an apartment with multiple connected rooms. This concept was developed and refined through an iterative process in collaboration with police operational trainers. The primary objective is to detect dangerous areas when one of the VR users is exposed without cover. These identified areas serve as indicators of potential threats, thus simulating dangerous situations. To make AI decisions comprehensible for trainers, we represent safe and unsafe areas using colored cubes. As can be seen in Fig. 2, dangerous areas are denoted by red cubes when there is a clear line of sight (indicated by yellow raycasts) between a cubes and at least one VR user without cover. If this dangerous area remains unsecured for an extended period, a non-player character (NPC) is spawned to highlight a tactical mistake to the VR users (see Fig. 3). To avoid biases or negative associations, we intentionally chose an NPC with a neutral appearance. Note that during the training sessions, the status of all sub-areas is concealed, but the trainers have the option to view this information in real-time or during debriefing.

Table 1 provides an overview of the transitions between AI areas, outlining the necessary adjustments to ensure realistic dissemination of unsecured and dangerous areas. In the following, we will explain the specific transitions from unsecured to dangerous and secured areas:

**Unsecured → Secured**: At the beginning, all sub-areas are initialized as unsecured (depicted as grey cubes in Fig. 2), indicating that they have not yet been observed by any VR users. If an unsecured area remains within a VR user's field of view for at least 150 ms, its status changes to secured (transparent cubes).

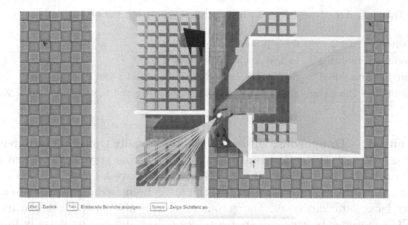

**Fig. 2.** AI areas with red cubes representing dangerous areas. Yellow raycasts point out a direct sight to the VR user lacking cover. (Color figure online)

**Secured → Unsecured**: Areas previously secured can revert to unsecured. For instance, if a secured area remains outside the field of view of any VR users for a specific duration and is adjacent to an unsecured area, it reverts to an unsecured state. This simulates the movement of a potential attacker within the virtual environment. The velocity at which unsecured areas spread reflects the NPC's movement speed and can be individually adjusted to define different difficulty levels. This adaptability ensures scalability for varying numbers of police officers, irrespective of their training proficiency or prior experiences with securing an area.

**Fig. 3.** Representation of an NPC.

**Table 1.** Area transitions with individual transition periods in each case.

| Transition | Description |
|---|---|
| Unsecured → Secured | In field of view of at least 1 user |
| Secured → Unsecured | Next to an unsecured area and in no user's field of view |
| Unsecured → Dangerous | Field of view on at least one user and in no user's field of view |

**Unsecured → Dangerous**: Unsecured areas gradually transform into dangerous areas, with the cubes transitioning linearly from grey to red, when they are not in the field of view of any VR users and have a direct line of sight to one of the VR users. In other words, the areas become dangerous when a VR user lacks sufficient cover. Dangerous areas can also spread, simulating the NPC's movements, who can spot a police officer and can potentially initiate an attack. The adjustable duration permits customization of how quickly a tactical error, such as insufficient cover, should be penalized. If a dangerous area remains unseen by all VR users at the end of the specified duration, an NPC is spawned and the training is terminated. Alternatively, the training concludes once all sub-areas have been secured.

### 3.3   After-Action Review

As already suggested by Zechner et al. [17], the inclusion of visual debriefing in the training sessions is crucial for providing feedback that may not be monitored and reviewed easily during the training itself. Therefore, we implemented the VR-based simulation in a manner that allows us to capture the full-body movements of all VR users, as well as AI decisions made during the training. These data can be utilized for comprehensive post-training review, including features such as skip or rewind functionality. With this tool, the animated motion capture data of all VR users can be examined from both a top-down or a first-person perspective.

### 3.4   Software and Hardware

The simulation was developed using the CryEngine[6] game engine. To facilitate multiplayer functionality, we employed two HTC Vive Pro Eye[7] headsets and four base stations to ensure coverage of an area measuring approximately 7 × 10 m. Each VR user was furthermore equipped with two HTC Vive controllers and wore the Teslasuit[8], a full-body motion capture suit. These hardware components were integrated to provide a comprehensive and immersive training experience for the police officers.

---

[6] CryEngine: https://www.cryengine.com, last accessed on April 3, 2023.
[7] HTC Vive Pro Eye: https://www.vive.com/us/product/vive-pro-eye/overview/, last accessed on April 3, 2023.
[8] Teslasuit: https://teslasuit.io, last accessed on April 3, 2023.

# 4    Evaluation

We conducted a user experiment to validate the accuracy of the AI model in identifying dangerous areas and, in particular, tactical errors made by police officers. The experiment also aimed to compare the results of VR-based training with traditional training.

## 4.1    Training Scenario

For both conditions, traditional and VR-based training, we created an equivalent apartment (see Fig. 4). In traditional training, the apartment was constructed using room dividers or partitions. In VR-based training, we used the configuration tool described in Sect. 3.1 to recreate the same apartment.

## 4.2    Participants

We conducted a user study with the target group, i.e., police officers. We categorized them as *beginners*, *intermediate*, or *advanced*, based on their training duration. *Beginners* included ongoing police officers in the first and third semesters, *intermediates* were ongoing police officers in the fourth and sixth semesters, and *advanced* participants were special units involved in securing evidence and making arrests.

To determine the required sample size, we conducted an a priori power analysis using G*Power [7] with a 1-$\beta$ error probability of 95, an alpha error probability of .05, a large effect size of .8, and three groups. This analysis indicated a minimum sample size of 30 participants. Therefore, we aimed to have at least ten pairs for each group (i.e., *beginner*, *intermediate*, and *advanced*). In total, we recruited 33 pairs for traditional training: 10 *beginners*, 13 *intermediate*, and 10 *advanced* pairs. Additionally, we recruited another 39 pairs for VR training: 9 *beginners*, 18 *intermediate*, and 12 *advanced* pairs. The detailed participant numbers are further provided in Table 2.

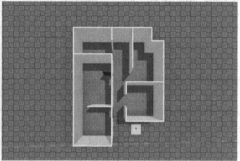

**Fig. 4.** Training scenario used for the traditional training (left) and VR-based training (right).

Table 2. The total number of pairs participating in the study.

|  | Traditional | Virtual |
|---|---|---|
| *Beginners* | 10 | 9 |
| *Intermediate* | 13 | 18 |
| *Advanced* | 10 | 12 |
| Total | 33 | 39 |

## 4.3   Procedure

At the beginning of the evaluation, we informed all participants about the specific purpose of the study and assured them that all collected data are confidential and anonymized. The participants were informed about the associated risks and their right to withdraw from the experiment without specifying a reason. In both, traditional and VR-based training conditions, two participants searched an apartment together, which was not disclosed beforehand.

**Traditional Training.** During traditional training, an operational trainer observed participants to identify tactical errors. The training sessions were also recorded by a 2D camera, allowing the operational trainer to rewind the video later and make assessments for evaluation purposes. The training session ended either when one of the participants made a tactical mistake or when the entire apartment was thoroughly searched. Subsequently, the recorded footage was further utilized to determine the percentage of the secured area.

**Virtual Training.** For virtual training, participants had to put on the Teslasuit and HTC Vive Pro Eye Head Mounted Display. Next, the VR room and virtual avatars for both users were calibrated. Afterward, the participants searched an apartment without instructions from the trainer. During the training, the system analyzed the actions of both VR users to identify dangerous areas in real-time. In case one of the police officers made a mistake, an NPC was spawned at the corresponding area, accompanied by a sound effect. In the other case, when the entire apartment was searched without any tactical mistakes, another sound effect signaled the end of the training.

During the evaluation, we logged the training time, total secured area, and maximum secured area in percentage. Motion capture data for both users, as well as AI decisions, were also captured for subsequent after-action reviews of the training sessions. On the one side, the reviews served as debriefing sessions where the trainees themselves recapped the training results. On the other side, reviews were used to assess the performance of the AI model. Towards this end, the police operational trainer viewed the replay data of training sessions and evaluated if (1) the system correctly detected all dangerous areas and (2) the identified tactical errors were appropriate and accurate.

## 4.4   Measures

The main objective of the study was to evaluate if the AI correctly identifies all dangerous areas and, if so, if they are appropriate and reasonable. Additionally, we aimed to evaluate if police officers train differently in VR compared to traditional training. Therefore, we logged the time needed to enter and search an object (in seconds) as well as the total and maximum secured area (in percentage).

## 5   Results

In the following, we present and discuss the results for AI performance (see Sect. 5.1) and training outcomes (see Sect. 5.2).

### 5.1   AI Performance

The AI's success rate in identifying dangerous areas was evaluated by reporting the $F_1$ score, which combines precision and recall. The results show that out of 39 trials, the AI correctly identified dangerous areas in 34 cases, with no false negatives. This results in a high $F_1$ score of 0.93 (precision = 0.87 and recall = 1.0), indicating a high level of accuracy in AI decision-making.

### 5.2   Training Outcomes

Figure 5 depicts the proportion of the secured areas for individual groups, during traditional and VR training, at the time the training terminated. As expected, participants with more training experiences discovered a larger area in both conditions. However, there is a wide interquartile range among *intermediate* and *advanced* police officers, suggesting variation in proficiency levels. In particular, some participants from the special unit involved in securing evidence and making arrests were relatively new to the task and, thus, still at the undergraduate level.

We first analyzed statistical significance and effect sizes to evaluate if there are any significant differences among groups. As the data does not follow a normal distribution, we applied the Kruskal-Wallis test and additionally conducted Mann-Whitney U-test as a post-hoc test for pairwise multiple comparisons. The Kruskal-Wallis Test for traditional training revealed that there is a significant differences among groups ($\chi^2(2) = 10.98$, $p < .05$). In particularly, the post-hoc test shows a significant difference between *beginner* and *advanced* participants ($p < .001$, with a large effect size: Cohen's $d = -1.79$). Similarly, for VR training, there are significant differences among groups ($\chi^2(2) = 7.48$, $p = .02$). Post-hoc tests show a significant difference between *beginners* and *advanced* participants ($p = .03$, with a large effect size: Cohen's $d = -1.67$) as well as *intermediate* and *advanced* participants ($p = .02$, with a large effect size: Cohen's $d = -1.16$)

Moreover, we examined if there are significant differences between both conditions, i.e., traditional vs. virtual training. Again, as the data does not follow a

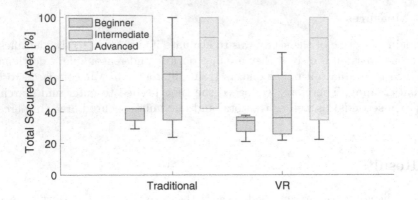

**Fig. 5.** Total secured area in percentage for individual groups.

normal distribution, we conducted Mann-Whitney U-test. The results show, that there are no significant differences between the two training methods ($Z = 1.85$, $p = 0.06$). Hence, we found no sufficient evidence to conclude that there is a significant difference between the groups based on the data analyzed.

## 6   Discussion

### 6.1   AI Decisions

In discussions with the operational trainer, we intended to gain a comprehensive understanding of the occurrence of false positives in our AI algorithm, causing to identify tactical errors without them being actual mistakes. We discovered that these false positives mainly resulted from raycasts hitting only a small area on a trainee's body, leading the AI to classify even minor errors as serious violations of coverage. This finding indicates that the current AI system might be overly strict in its assessment of tactical errors. To enhance the algorithm's performance, we propose several potential adjustments. One approach involves considering multiple unsecured body parts or a specific percentage of the body area as prerequisites before classifying it as an actual error in coverage. By implementing these adjustments, the AI would become more precise in identifying tactical errors. Additionally, we explored the possibility of requiring a dangerous area to have a specific volume, represented by multiple connected cubes, before spawning a NPC. This method could lead to more accurate assessments of high-risk situations, ensuring that the AI simulates potential danger with greater accuracy. Through these discussions and insights, we aim to refine the AI algorithm to strike a balance between being adequately strict to detect real errors and avoiding false positives to provide a more effective training experience for police officers. Further evaluation and testing will be conducted to validate the impact of these adjustments on the AI's performance.

## 6.2 Training Outcomes

The results of our study indicate that both traditional training and VR training lead to comparable training outcomes, with beginners securing a relatively small area and advanced police officers securing a larger area. These findings align with our expectations that more experienced participants would perform better in terms of securing the area. However, while the outcomes are similar, VR training offers significant advantages over traditional methods. One key advantage is the ease of creating and customizing training scenarios using the configuration tool. This flexibility allows for a wide range of training scenarios to be developed and shared among trainees, enriching the training experience and promoting skill development in diverse situations. In contrast, traditional methods may require physically rearranging training spaces, which can be time-consuming and less adaptable.

Moreover, VR training with AI analysis provides a unique advantage in terms of providing feedback and identifying tactical mistakes. In traditional training, a trainer needs to actively observe and point out errors made by the participants. While operational trainers remain essential in providing overall guidance, the AI within VR-based training automatically analyzes the trainees' movements in real time and promptly identifies tactical errors. This reduces the reliance on a trainer and ensures immediate feedback during the training session, allowing ongoing police officers to engage in more frequent and efficient training. However, it is important to emphasize that operational trainers remain indispensable in the training process. Their expertise, guidance, and real-time feedback play a crucial role in enhancing the training effectiveness and ensuring that trainees develop the necessary skills to handle real-world situations.

Considering these advantages, VR training emerges as a highly advantageous and efficient complement to traditional training methods. It not only offers enhanced flexibility in scenario creation but also provides valuable real-time feedback using AI, supplementing the essential role of operational trainers in optimizing training outcomes.

## 7  Conclusion

In this paper, we presented an AI-supported simulation for police officers, enabling the detection of dangerous areas when at least one police officer lacks cover. Thereby, the simulation involves NPCs and an acoustic signal to draw attention to tactical errors. The AI decisions can be observed by the operational trainer and trainees during or after the training sessions, providing valuable insights into tactical errors. The results of the field test in comparison with traditional training indicated that such a VR-based simulation training can be an efficient method for practicing apartment searches individually or in pairs. The configuration tool furthermore enables to easily create new environments, unknown to the trainees, which are otherwise not easily achieved with traditional methods using partitions to recreate buildings.

**Acknowledgements.** This project was funded by the German Federal Ministry of
Education and Research under the *research for civil security* program (Grant Numbers:
13N15546 [HöMS], 13N15547 [TU Darmstadt], and 13N15548 [Crytek GmbH]).

# References

1. Beils, M.: Virtual Reality im Einsatztraining: Wie die Polizei NRW Pionierarbeit als Teil eines EU-Projekts leistet (2019). https://polizei.nrw/sites/default/files/2022-08/Streife_03_2022_09_Web.pdf. Accessed 25 Apr 2023
2. Bertram, J., Moskaliuk, J., Cress, U.: Virtual training: making reality work? Comput. Hum. Behav. **43**, 284–292 (2015). https://doi.org/10.1016/j.chb.2014.10.032
3. Caserman, P., Schmidt, P., Göbel, T., Zinnäcker, J., Kecke, A., Göbel, S.: Impact of full-body avatars in immersive multiplayer virtual reality training for police forces. IEEE Trans. Games **14**(4), 706–714 (2022). https://doi.org/10.1109/TG.2022.3148791
4. CeFaan, K., Hartmann, J., Sowa, E.: EXCLUSIVE: NYPD is testing virtual reality training drills for real-life scenarios like active shooters (2019). https://abc7ny.com/nypd-uses-virtual-reality-to-train-for-active-shooters/5269109/. Accessed 21 Apr 2023
5. Dörner, R., Göbel, S., Effelsberg, W., Wiemeyer, J.: Serious Games: Foundations. Concepts and Practice. Springer, Cham (2016). https://doi.org/10.1007/978-3-319-40612-1
6. Eller, C., Bittner, T., Dombois, M., Rüppel, U.: Collaborative immersive planning and training scenarios in VR. In: Smith, I.F.C., Domer, B. (eds.) EG-ICE 2018. LNCS, pp. 164–185. Springer International Publishing, Cham (2018). https://doi.org/10.1007/978-3-319-91635-4_9
7. Faul, F., Erdfelder, E., Lang, A.G., Buchner, A.: G* power 3: a flexible statistical power analysis program for the social, behavioral, and biomedical sciences. Behav. Res. Methods **39**(2), 175–191 (2007). https://doi.org/10.3758/BF03193146
8. Giessing, L.: The potential of virtual reality for police training under stress: a SWOT analysis. In: Interventions, Training, and Technologies for Improved Police Well-being and Performance, pp. 102–124. IGI Global (2021). https://doi.org/10.4018/978-1-7998-6820-0.ch006
9. Li, C., Liang, W., Quigley, C., Zhao, Y., Yu, L.F.: Earthquake safety training through virtual drills. IEEE Trans. Visual Comput. Graphics **23**(4), 1275–1284 (2017). https://doi.org/10.1109/TVCG.2017.2656958
10. Moskaliuk, J., Bertram, J., Cress, U.: Impact of virtual training environments on the acquisition and transfer of knowledge. Cyberpsychol. Behav. Soc. Netw. **16**(3), 210–214 (2013). https://doi.org/10.1089/cyber.2012.0416
11. Murtinger, M., Jaspaert, E., Schrom-Feiertag, H., Egger-Lampl, S.: CBRNe training in virtual environments: SWOT analysis & practical guidelines. Int. J. Saf. Secur. Eng. **11**(4), 295–303 (2021). https://doi.org/10.18280/ijsse.110402
12. Murtinger, M., Uhl, J., Schrom-Feiertag, H., Nguyen, Q., Harthum, B., Tscheligi, M.: Assist the VR trainer - real-time dashboard and after-action review for police VR training. In: 2022 IEEE International Conference on Metrology for Extended Reality, Artificial Intelligence and Neural Engineering (MetroXRAINE), pp. 69–74 (2022). https://doi.org/10.1109/MetroXRAINE54828.2022.9967532
13. Narciso, D., Melo, M., Rodrigues, S., Cunha, J.P.S., Bessa, M.: Impact of different stimuli on user stress during a virtual firefighting training exercise. In: 2020 IEEE

20th International Conference on Bioinformatics and Bioengineering (BIBE), pp. 813–818 (2020). https://doi.org/10.1109/BIBE50027.2020.00138

14. Nguyen, Q., Jaspaert, E., Murtinger, M., Schrom-Feiertag, H., Egger-Lampl, S., Tscheligi, M.: Stress out: translating real-world stressors into audio-visual stress cues in VR for police training. In: Ardito, C., et al. (eds.) INTERACT 2021. LNCS, vol. 12933, pp. 551–561. Springer, Cham (2021). https://doi.org/10.1007/978-3-030-85616-8_32

15. Shewaga, R., Uribe-Quevedo, A., Kapralos, B., Lee, K., Alam, F.: A serious game for anesthesia-based crisis resource management training. Comput. Entertain. **16**(2) (2018). https://doi.org/10.1145/3180660

16. Uhl, J.C., Murtinger, M., Zechner, O., Tscheligi, M.: Threat assessment in police VR training: multi-sensory cues for situation awareness. In: 2022 IEEE International Conference on Metrology for Extended Reality, Artificial Intelligence and Neural Engineering (MetroXRAINE), pp. 432–437 (2022). https://doi.org/10.1109/MetroXRAINE54828.2022.9967692

17. Zechner, O., Kleygrewe, L., Jaspaert, E., Schrom-Feiertag, H., Hutter, R.I.V., Tscheligi, M.: Enhancing operational police training in high stress situations with virtual reality: experiences, tools and guidelines. Multimodal Technol. Interact. **7**(2), 14 (2023). https://doi.org/10.3390/mti7020014

18. Zyda, M.: From visual simulation to virtual reality to games. Computer **38**(9), 25–32 (2005). https://doi.org/10.1109/MC.2005.297

# The Influence of Personalized Music on Sense of Presence, Motivation, and Player Experience in Virtual Reality

Polona Caserman[1]([envelope])([ORCID]), Sebastian Rudolf Da Brandt Costa[1],
Michelle Martinussen[2], and Stefan Göbel[1]([ORCID])

[1] Serious Games Research Group, Technical University of Darmstadt,
Darmstadt, Germany
{polona.caserman,stefan_peter.goebel}@tu-darmstadt.de,
sebastian.brandt@stud.tu-darmstadt.de
[2] Randalyn Rage UG (haftungsbeschränkt), Kitzingen, Germany
michelle@randalynrage.com
https://www.etit.tu-darmstadt.de/serious-games,
https://www.randalynrage.com

**Abstract.** The sense of presence, characterized by the feeling of "being there," plays a crucial role in virtual reality (VR) to enhance involvement and engagement. While previous studies have examined the effects of sound or music on presence by manipulating auditory cues, little research has explored the effects of personalized music within virtual environments. Therefore, in this paper, we investigate the influence of personalized music on the sense of presence, motivation, player performance, time perception, and cybersickness. In a within-subjects design, 21 participants engaged in a VR strategy game under three randomized conditions: hearing (1) *sound effects only* without background music, (2) the original *game music*, and (3) *personalized music*, individually chosen by each participant. The results reveal that *personalized music* significantly contributes to a higher sense of presence compared to the condition with *sound effects only*, however with no significant difference between both music conditions. The results further show that participants are significantly more motivated when exposed to *personalized music* compared to the original *game music*. These findings provide valuable insights into how personalized music, synchronized with the gameplay elements, can enhance the sense of presence, motivation, and overall player experience within VR environments. Further investigations are necessary to examine the specific effects of personalized music within different VR games.

**Keywords:** Virtual Reality · Personalized Music · Presence · Motivation · Time Perception · Performance

## 1 Introduction

According to Slater and Wilbur [22], the sense of presence refers to the subjective feeling of "being in the virtual environment." Recent studies have shown

M. Haahr et al. (Eds.): JCSG 2023, LNCS 14309, pp. 194–210, 2023.
https://doi.org/10.1007/978-3-031-44751-8_14

that the addition of auditory cues and appropriate music choices within virtual environments can enhance the sense of presence and evoke emotional responses in players [6,9,11,13,18,28], although there is some contradictory evidence indicating that music may not have significant effects in VR games [16]. However, the studies are hardly comparable, due to variations in technologies used (from non-immersive setups to fully-immersive VR) and the inclusion of sound effects through loudspeakers or (noise-canceling) headphones. Furthermore, most studies have focused on manipulating auditory cues to evaluate the presence, while the significance of personalized music in VR remains insufficiently explored.

Therefore, it remains unclear to what extent the sense of presence increases when players are familiar with and enjoy the music used in the game, and whether increased presence leads to improved performance and game experience. Previous research, such as the work of Sanders and Cairns [18], suggests that selecting subjectively appropriate music enhances immersion. However, their study did not involve personalized music individually chosen by the participants, but instead used generally liked by the participants, leaving open questions regarding how players' music preferences may impact their performance. This also raises the question whether the results of Rogers et al. [16] might differ considering personalized music, and whether personalized music further influences the game experience. In this regard, previous works have proposed music generators that dynamically generate music or adapt music to the game's narrative, aiming to improve player experience [14,20].

Therefore, in this study, we intend to investigate the effects of personalized music on the sense of presence and overall player experience in a story-based VR strategy game called *beVaiR* [15]. The game consists of three distinct fractions, each embodying its own thematic essence. The primary objective of the game revolves around unraveling the narrative by expanding the network. This entails employing weapons to gather energy in the form of transmitters, converting it, and firing it at other nodes to overload them with the players' transmitters. While the game incorporates its own music with sound effects, it also allows players to load their personalized playlists. Notably, the game adapts the frequency at which transmitters spawn based on the beats in the music.

The remainder of the paper is organized as follows. In Sect. 2, we present a literature review and in Sect. 3, we introduce the study design and present outcomes in Sect. 4. In Sect. 5, we discuss the results and conclude in Sect. 6.

## 2   Related Work

### 2.1   Effects of Auditory Cues on the Sense of Presence, Player Experience, and Performance

Prior research has extensively examined the role of auditory cues in virtual environments. For instance, Hendrix and Barfield [6] demonstrated that auditory cues contribute to a higher sense of presence, while the perceived realism of the virtual environment is primarily influenced by visual cues. Similarly, Larsson et al. [11] found that the absence of sound leads to a reduced sense of presence, with no significant difference between matched and mismatched audio-visual cues. Kern and Ellermeier [9] revealed that a soundscape positively affects presence, while step sounds had only minimal impact due to asynchronous step recognition using integrated sensors of a head-mounted display.

The results of the study by Wongutai et al. [28] indicate that adding sound to a VR exergame significantly improves the player's motivation and performance. Von Georgi et al. [25] focused on analyzing the effect of music on anxiety and aggression behavior in a first-person shooter game. Their results indicate that aggressive music does not amplify anxiety or anger and also does not affect players' performance (deaths, kills).

Researchers have also explored the influence of music on time perception, a core factor of player experience. Sanders and Cairns [18] found that music can indeed alter time perception, but only when participants were aware that they need to make a time estimate before the experiment. In a later study by Rogers et al. [16], similar experiments were conducted using immersive technology (i.e., a new generation Head Mounted Display). The researchers concluded that participants perceived time to pass significantly quicker in the VR game when music was present, although no significant differences were found in player experience or immersion.

### 2.2   Measuring Methods for the Sense of Presence and Player Experience

Questionnaires and self-report ratings are commonly employed approaches for measuring the sense of presence [3]. Hendrix and Barfield [6] utilized in their study a five-item questionnaire to assess presence and spatialized sound realism. Witmer and Singer [27] identified various factors underlying presence and subsequently developed the Presence Questionnaire (PQ), consisting of 32 items. Another common scale was introduced by Schubert et al. [19]. The Schubert's Igroup Presence Questionnaire (IPQ) includes 14 items and measures spatial presence, involvement, and realness of the simulated experience. A further popular scale was developed by Slater et al. [21], generating a single score to convey the sense of presence.

Similarly, to assess game experience, also several questionnaires have been presented in recent years. The Game Experience Questionnaire(GEQ) [7] is still one of the most used ones, although it has faced some criticism [12]. Furthermore, Vanden Abeele et al. [24] presented the Player Experience Inventory (PXI), consisting of 57 items grouped into 11 subscales. Another questionnaire presented by Jennett et al. [8] further focus more on evaluating the immersive experience in games.

In addition to questionnaires, physiological data can be utilized to evaluate the game experience. Drachen et al. [4] demonstrated the feasibility of using heart rate and electrodermal activity as measures of game experience, which correlated with the self reports from players. In the study conducted by von Georgi [25], evaluating the effects of music on player performance, the researchers also analyzed the heart rate, but found no significant differences or correlations.

# 3  Study Design

## 3.1  Conditions

The main objective of this study is to evaluate the impact of personalized music on the sense of presence, player experience, performance, and motivation. To accomplish this, we utilized a within-subjects design comprising three conditions: (1) *sound effects only*, (2) original *game music*, and (3) *personalized music*, individually chosen by each participant. Note that both conditions with music include sound effects. For the experiment, we chose the story-based VR strategy game *beVaiR* (see Fig. 1), as it enables the integration of personalized music.

In the first condition, we removed the background game music so that participants were exposed solely to sound effects when performing actions such as recharging weapons and collecting nodes. It is important to note that we did not intend to investigate the effects of a complete absence of sound or music, as this has been extensively explored in previous studies (see Sect. 2). In the second condition, participants experienced the game with its original music, which was particularly designed to align with the gameplay mechanics. In the third condition, participants were exposed to personalized music, where they were asked to bring their own playlist of .mp3 files to the evaluation meeting. The principal investigator then selected songs from the provided playlists to approximate a total duration of eight minutes. It is essential to highlight that this condition differs from those used in previous studies such as [16,18], where participants were exposed to generally liked music without personalization.

## 3.2  Participants

To determine the required sample size for our study, we conducted an a priori power analysis using G*Power [5] with 1-$\beta$ error probability of .8, alpha error

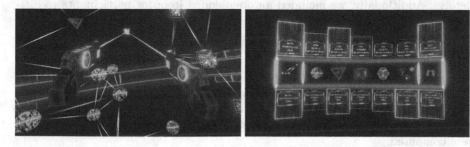

**Fig. 1.** The enhancer game mechanic allows players to collect energy, convert it, and shoot it at the nodes [23].

probability of .05, effect size ($f$) of .4, and number of measurements as 3, corresponding to the three conditions in our study. This resulted in a minimal sample size of 24 participants in order to achieve adequate statistical power.

### 3.3  Measures

In order to assess various aspects of participants' experience, we utilized well-established questionnaires from previous research.

**Sense of Presence:** To assess participants' sense of presence within VR, we employed the first item from Hendrix and Barfield's study [6]:

- If your level of presence in the real world is "100," and your level of presence is "1" if you have no presence, rate your level of presence in this virtual world.

**Involvement:** Additionally, to evaluate the effects of auditory cues we used items 6, 15, and 16 from the PQ developed by Witmer and Singer [27]. These three items were also identified in [26] to influence involvement:

- How much did the auditory aspects of the environment involve you?
- How well could you identify sounds?
- How well could you localize sounds?

All three items were assessed on a seven-point scale, ranging from 1 (not at all) to 7 (completely).

**Time Perception:** In addition to assessing presence and involvement, we measured time perception using one item adapted from Jennett et al.'s study [8]:

- To me it felt like only a very short amount of time had passed.

This item was also rated on a seven-point scale, from 1 (not at all) to 7 (completely). Additionally, we included an open-ended item for participants to estimate the time they spent playing the game in minutes.

**Game Experience:** To evaluate the overall game experience, we employed the In-Game Experience Questionnaire (iGEQ) [7], which consists of 14 items, all assessed on a five-point scale, ranging from 0 (not at all) to 4 (extremely). Subsequently, average scores for each component (*competence, sensory and imaginative immersion, flow, tension, challenge, negative affect,* and *positive affect*) were computed.

**Motivation:** To assess participants' motivation while playing the game, we took two items derived from the immersion questionnaire used in the experiment by Jennett et al. [8]:

– To what extent did you feel motivated while playing?
– Would you like to play the game again?

Both items were rated on a five-point scale, ranging from 1 (not at all) to 5 (very much).

**Cybersickness:** To assess cybersickness symptoms, we employed the VRSQ developed by Kim et al. [10], specifically designed to measure symptoms related to general discomfort and other adverse effects experienced in VR environments.

**Player Performance:** Moreover, to evaluate the player performance, we recorded in-game statistics, specifically the percentage of game domination achieved by each participant's fraction.

**Heart Rate:** Building upon research by Drachen et al. [4], we incorporated heart rate measurements to examine the effects of music on the game experience. To facilitate analysis, we normalized the physiological features relative to the baseline values recorded before the experiment by dividing the average values of the play session by the average baseline value.

### 3.4   Procedure

At the beginning of the evaluation, we informed all participants about the specific purpose of the study and assured them that any collected data would be treated confidentially and used in anonymized form. The participants were also informed about the potential risks involved and were given the freedom to discontinue their participation at any time without providing a reason.

Once the participants read and signed the consent form, they proceeded to complete a demographic questionnaire. Prior to donning the HTC Vive Pro Eye Head Mounted Display and the external noise-canceling headphone (Bose QC 35 II), the participants put on the Polar H10 Heart Rate Sensor. The purpose of this sensor was to establish a baseline measurement of their heart rate. During this measurement, participants remained seated in a chair for three minutes.

Following the heart rate baseline measurement, participants played through the tutorial, to familiarize themselves with the game mechanics and controls. In accordance with the findings by the researchers in [18], who observed significant results for time perception only when participants were explicitly instructed to make a time estimate, we took a similar approach in our study. Therefore, we informed all participants that they would be required to make a time estimate after each game session. Next, they played three round of the VR game for approx. eight minutes, with the condition (*sound effects only, game music,* or *personalized music*) randomly assigned to each participant. After completing each condition, participants were asked to once again fill out the questionnaires described in Sect. 3.3.

## 4 Results

### 4.1 Data Analysis Approach

According to the Kolmogorov-Smirnov test, the data do not consistently follow a normal distribution. Therefore, we use Friedman's test to evaluate the statistical significance among the conditions. In addition, we utilize the Wilcoxon signed rank test to investigate significant differences between conditions. Furthermore, we calculate the effect size using Hedges' g, taking the sample size into account [17], with a value of 0.2 representing a small, 0.5 a medium, and 0.8 a large effect size [2].

### 4.2 Participant Information

In accordance with our target of at least 24 participants (as stated in Sect. 3.2), we initially invited 26 participants. However, five participants did not attend, resulting in a final sample size of 21 university students (7 female, 14 male) with an age range between 21 and 31 years (mean age = $24.48 \pm 2.27$).

### 4.3 Analysis Results

**Sense of Presence:** Friedman's test discloses a statistically significant difference for the overall sense of presence ($\chi^2(2) = 12.67$, $p < .01$). Post hoc pairwise comparisons reveal that the *sound effects only* condition shows significant different ratings of presence compared to the *game music* and *personalized music* conditions ($p = .01$, Hedge's $g = -68$ for *sound effects only* vs. *game music* and $p < .01$, Hedge's $g = -.91$ for *sound effects only* vs. *personalized music*). Figure 2a presents the rating of presence, showing the lowest ratings in the *sound effects only* condition (Mdn = 50.0, IQR = 30.0), higher ratings in the *game music* condition (Mdn = 65.0, IQR = 23.75), and the highest ratings in the *personalized music* condition (Mdn = 75.0, IQR = 30.0).

**Involvement:** Friedman's test also shows a statistically significant difference in the explicit effects of sound on the involvement ($\chi^2(2) = 6.56$, $p = .04$). Pairwise comparison reveals a significant difference between the *sound effects only* and *personalized music* conditions ($p = .04$, Hedge's $g = -.6$). As depicted in Fig. 2b, the effect of sound on involvement is comperable between the *sound effects only* (Mdn = 4.67, IQR = 2.3) and *game music* conditions (Mdn = 4.67, IQR = 1.1), while the involvement in the *personalized music* condition is higher (Mdn = 5.3, IQR = 2.17).

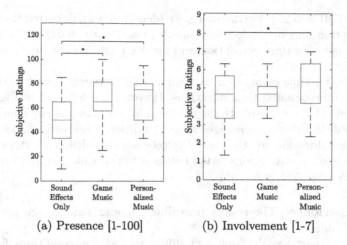

**Fig. 2.** Ratings on sense of presence and involvement. Overall presence (left) was assessed using a single item adapted from Hendrix and Barfield's study [6]. Involvement (right) was obtained using items from the study by Witmer and Singer [27]. Statistical significance is denoted by an asterisk (*) and indicates a significant difference between two conditions (p < 0.05).

**Time Perception:** Friedman's test shows no significant differences in time perception ($\chi^2(2) = 2.49$, $p = .29$). As detailed in Fig. 3a, the participants generally rated the amount of time that had passed as low for the *sound effects only* condition (Mdn = 4.0, IQR = 3.0) and slightly higher for the *game music* condition (Mdn = 5, IQR = 2.0) as well as the *personalized music* condition

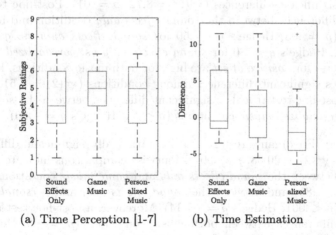

**Fig. 3.** Participants' ratings on time perception (left) based on a single item from Jennett et al. [8]. Time estimation (right) was evaluated by calculating the difference from ground truth.

(Mdn = 5, IQR = 3.25). Furthermore, we identified a weak correlation between time perception and presence (Spearman's $\rho$ = .33, $p < 0.01$) and a moderate correlation between time perception and involvement (Spearman's $\rho$ = .44, $p < 0.001$).

Similarly, for time estimation, no significant differences were found between the actual and estimated time durations. However, as depicted in Fig. 3b, participants tended to overestimate the duration for the *game music* condition and underestimate it for the *personalized music* condition, while estimates were closer to the actual duration for the *sound effects only* condition. Furthermore, we identified a weak negative correlation between time estimation and involvement (Spearman's $\rho$ = −.25, $p = 0.04$).

**Game Experience:** The results regarding game experience are presented in Fig. 4 and Table 1.

Friedman's test reveals significant differences among conditions for *competence* ($\chi^2(2) = 6.65$, $p = .04$). A pairwise comparison indicates a significant difference between the *sound effects only* and *personalized music* conditions ($p < .01$, Hedge's $g = -.91$). As for *immersion*, the Friedman's test shows no significant differences ($\chi^2(2) = 4.16$, $p = .13$).

For the *flow* experience, only *personalized music* contributed to high scores. Friedman's test also indicates significant differences among conditions ($\chi^2(2) = 7.86$, $p = .02$). A pairwise comparison shows a significant difference between the *sound effects only* and *personalized music* conditions ($p = .01$, Hedge's $g = -.64$). *Tension* scores are generally low, while *challenge* scores are generally high, however, without significant differences across conditions ($\chi^2(2) = 4.88$, $p = .09$ for *tension* and $\chi^2(2) = 2.26$, $p = .32$ for *challenge*).

Moreover, scores for *negative affect* are low for all conditions, yet Friedman's test shows significant differences ($\chi^2(2) = 8.72$, $p = .01$). Post-hoc tests reveal significant differences between the *sound effects only* condition and both music conditions ($p = .03$, Hedge's $g = .50$ for *sound effects only* vs. *game music* and $p < .01$, Hedge's $g = .80$ for *sound effects only* vs. *personalized music*). In contrast, scores for *positive affect* are high for both music conditions. Friedman's test indicates significant differences among conditions ($\chi^2(2) = 7.51$, $p = .02$), while the post-hoc test reveals a significant difference between the *sound effects only* and *personalized music* conditions ($p < .01$, Hedge's $g = -.86$).

**Motivation:** Friedman's test reveals a statistically significant difference for motivation ($\chi^2(2) = 20.58$, $p < .001$). Pairwise comparisons indicate significant differences between the *sound effects only* and *game music* conditions ($p < .01$, Hedge's $g = -.81$) and between the *sound effects only* and *personalized music* conditions ($p < .001$, Hedge's $g = -1.14$). Moreover, a post-hoc test also shows significant differences between both music conditions ($p = .03$, Hedge's $g = -.44$). Figure 5 depicts that participants reported high motivation when exposed to *personalized music* (Mdn = 3.5, IQR = .63) or *game music* (Mdn = 3.0, IQR = 1.0), whereas the *sound effects only* condition resulted in lower motivation values (Mdn = 2.5, IQR = 1.75).

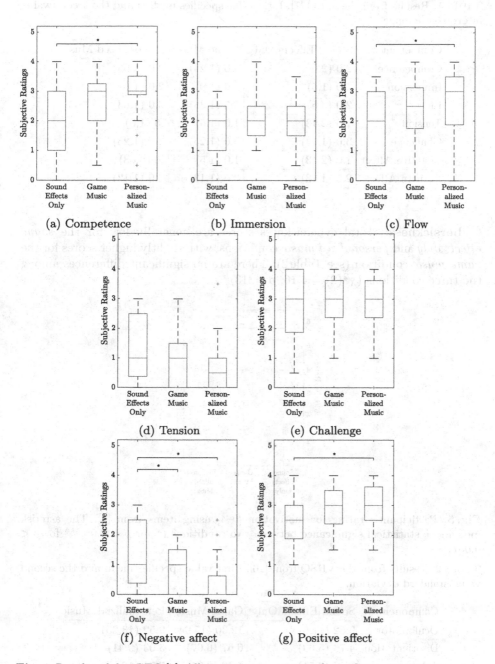

**Fig. 4.** Results of the iGEQ [7]. All components were rated on a five-point scale, ranging from 0 (not at all) to 4 (extremely). The asterisk (*) indicates a statistical significance between two conditions ($p < 0.05$).

**Table 1.** Results from the iGEQ [7]. First value specifies median and the second value interquartile range.

| Component | Sound Effects Only | Game Music | Personalized Music |
|---|---|---|---|
| Competence | 2.0 (2.0) | 3.0 (1.25) | 3.0 (0.63) |
| Immersion | 2.0 (1.5) | 2.0 (1.0) | 2.0 (1.0) |
| Flow | 2.0 (2.5) | 2.5 (1.38) | 3.0 (1.63) |
| Tension | 1.0 (2.13) | 1.0 (1.5) | .5 (1.0) |
| Challenge | 3.0 (1.13) | 3.0 (1.25) | 3.0 (1.25) |
| Negative Affect | 1.0 (2.13) | 1.0 (1.5) | .0 (0.63) |
| Positive Affect | 2.5 (1.13) | 3.0 (1.13) | 3.0 (1.13) |

**Cybersickness:** Total cybersickness scores are generally low for the *sound effects only* and *personalized music* conditions, with slightly higher scores for the *game music* condition (see Table 2). There are no significant differences among the three conditions ($\chi^2(2) = 4.16$, $p = .13$).

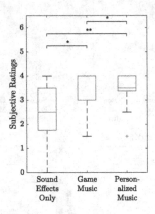

**Fig. 5.** Participant's rating for motivation [0–4] using items from [8]. The asterisk indicates a statistical significance between two conditions (* for $p < 0.05$, ** for $p < 0.001$).

**Table 2.** Results from the VRSQ from [10]. First value specifies mean and the second value standard deviation.

| Component | Sound Effects Only | Game Music | Personalized Music |
|---|---|---|---|
| Oculomotor | 9.52 (11.57) | 12.30 (15.94) | 9.52 (13.25) |
| Disorientation | 4.76 (5.63) | 6.67 (6.67) | 6.03 (9.41) |
| Total | 7.14 (7.51) | 9.48 (9.91) | 7.78 (10.4) |

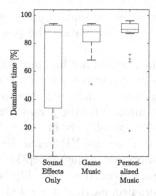

**Fig. 6.** Participant's performance in terms of dominant time.

**Player Performance:** Results of the analysis for player performance (see Fig. 6) do not reveal significant differences across conditions ($\chi^2(2) = 3.06$, $p = .22$). However, we found a weak positive correlation between involvement and performance (Spearman's $\rho = .29$, $p = .02$).

**Heart Rate:** We did not find any correlations or significant differences in baseline-adjusted heart rate data. These findings suggest that the effects of sound on physiological responses may not be substantial in our specific experimental setup.

## 5  Discussion

The present study investigated the impact of personalized music on the sense of presence, player experience, motivation, and performance in a story-based VR strategy game. The results provide valuable insights into the role of music in enhancing the game experience. Particularly, our findings shed light on how personalized music positively influences motivation in the VR context.

Our study aligns with previous research investigating the effects of sound effects and music on players' sense of presence in games. Hence, similar to the related work, we conclude that players feel significantly more present in VR when they hear the music compared to hearing only sound effects. However, in contrast to related work, our research go beyond only investigating the importance of music within games. In our study, we furthermore corroborate the importance of *personalised music*. We found that *personalized music* contributes to the highest sense of presence and involvement, although we found not significant differences compared to the original *game music*. More importantly, we identified significant differences for motivation between both music conditions. These results suggest that in particular the *personalized music* enhances participants' motivation to engage in the game. All together, the results indicate that the music tailored to the players more likely contributes to a higher presence and involvement and particularly significantly increases the motivation. Furthermore, the effect sizes indicate moderate to large effects, indicating the practical significance of these findings.

In terms of time perception, we did not find any significant differences among the conditions. Participants generally rated the time elapse similarly across all conditions, with a slight tendency to overestimate time duration for the *game music* condition and underestimate it for the *personalized music* condition. These results suggest that the presence or absence of music does not strongly influence participants' perception of time in the VR game. However, it is worth noting the weak positive correlation between time perception and both overall presence and involvement, indicating a potential relationship between these factors.

Regarding the game experience, participants rated significantly higher scores, especially for *competence* and *flow* in the *personalized music* conditions compared to the *sound effects only* condition, but not for the game's original music. This suggests that personalized music has a positive impact on the participants' competence and flow experience during gameplay. However, the levels of *immersion* and *challenge* across the three conditions were similar, indicating that the inclusion of music did not significantly affect participants' subjective immersion or challenge in the game. Furthermore, regarding player performance, we found no significant difference among conditions; however, we found a weak correlation between involvement and performance. These results indicate that when participants feel more involved in the game, they are more likely to perform better.

Our study's results have several implications for the design and development of VR games. We believe that our results on the impact of *personalized music* can help other researchers and game developers to create more engaging and immersive experiences for players by providing options for players to integrate their preferred music into the game, especially in order to foster a stronger motivation. However, it is essential to acknowledge that our study focused on a specific story-based VR strategy game, *beVaiR*. While the findings provide valuable insights into the role of personalized music in this context, the generalization to other VR games requires caution. For instance, in rhythm-based games like *Beat Saber* [1], the integration of personalized music might potentially influence motivation and enjoyment differently than in a strategy game. The effects of music may vary based on game genre, gameplay mechanics, and player preferences. Therefore, further research is needed to explore the effects of personalized music in diverse VR game genres to identify any genre-specific patterns.

## 5.1  Potential Limitations

Another important aspect that needs to be discussed is that the adaptive nature of the game, based on the music's beats, introduces an interesting variable that can potentially impact the game experience. Therefore, there are a few potential limitation that need to be considered:

1. Difficulty Discrepancies: Depending on the intensity of the music's beats, the game difficulty level might cause fluctuations. For example, fast and more

intense music results in increased transmitter spawning, which might over-strain the players. Conversely, slower or less intense music could lead to a decrease in transmitter frequency, potentially causing boredom in the participants. Looking at the results of *tension* or *challenge* components from iGEQ (see Fig. 4e), we found no significant changes among groups. These results suggest that the presence or absence of music did not notably influence the perceived difficulty or tension experienced by participants. Moreover, high values for the *competence* and *flow* in the *personalized music* condition imply that participants felt neither overwhelmed nor under challenged.

2. Inconsistent Adaptation: The responsiveness of the game's adaptive system to the music's beats might not always be accurate, e.g., causing delays in transmitter spawning frequency. Thus, depending on the chosen music, the flow of gameplay could be potentially disrupted, causing a decrease in overall presence and player motivation. However, our results show that the sense of presence during the personalized music condition is higher compared to the other two conditions. Similarly, also the motivation while hearing the personalized music significantly increases compared to the original game music, indicating that the adaption system of the game works well and contributes to higher presence and motivation.

3. Distraction: The results suggest that while personalized music within this study increases the sense of presence, it could nevertheless become a source of distraction if it demands excessive attention from players. Intense or complex music might divert players' focus away from gameplay elements, leading to decreased performance. However, as our results show that the player performance (see Fig. 6) is indeed similar for all three conditions, but with the smallest interquartile ranges for the personalized music condition, we can conclude that the personalized music also contributes to better overall performance, albeit not significantly.

Another potential limitation of our study is the limited number of participants (24 participants), resulting in reduced statistical power. Consequently, we calculated effect sizes to provide additional information about the magnitude of the observed effects. Nevertheless, future investigations should prioritize larger sample sizes to increase statistical power. Moreover, a larger participant pool is also required to generalize the findings to the larger population.

# 6   Conclusion

In this study, we investigated the impact of personalized music on the game experience in VR. The study results highlight significant differences and correlations across different conditions and components, providing valuable insights for game developers aiming to create more immersive and engaging experiences. Overall, the inclusion of music in the game, regardless of its source, contributes to a higher sense of presence. More importantly, as we identified a significant difference between both music conditions for motivation, we conclude that especially personalized music enhances participants' motivation to engage in the game. We hope that our results will encourage game designers, developers, and researchers in the future to provide options for players to integrate their preferred music into the games. However, our study focused on a specific story-based VR strategy game and therefore further research is necessary to explore the effects of personalized music in various VR game genres to deepen the understanding of how personalized music can enhance the overall game experience.

**Acknowledgements.** This research has been conducted in cooperation between the Serious Games research group at TU Darmstadt and the startup Randalyn Rage. It was partially funded by the German Federal Ministry for Economic Affairs and Climate Action under *The EXIST Business Start-up Grant* "KaiparaAdVRenture" (Grant Number: 03EGSHE226).

# References

1. Beat Games: Beat Saber. https://beatsaber.com. Accessed 27 May 2023
2. Cohen, J.: Statistical Power Analysis for the Behavioral Sciences. Academic press, Cambridge (1977)
3. Cummings, J.J., Bailenson, J.N.: How immersive is enough? a meta-analysis of the effect of immersive technology on user presence. Media Psychol. **19**(2), 272–309 (2016). https://doi.org/10.1080/15213269.2015.1015740
4. Drachen, A., Nacke, L.E., Yannakakis, G., Pedersen, A.L.: Correlation between heart rate, electrodermal activity and player experience in first-person shooter games. In: Proceedings of the 5th ACM SIGGRAPH Symposium on Video Games, Sandbox 2010, pp. 49–54. Association for Computing Machinery, New York, NY, USA (2010). https://doi.org/10.1145/1836135.1836143
5. Faul, F., Erdfelder, E., Lang, A.G., Buchner, A.: G* Power 3: a flexible statistical power analysis program for the social, behavioral, and biomedical sciences. Behav. Res. Methods **39**(2), 175–191 (2007). https://doi.org/10.3758/BF03193146
6. Hendrix, C., Barfield, W.: The sense of presence within auditory virtual environments. Presence: Teleoperators Virtual Environ. **5**(3), 290–301 (1996). https://doi.org/10.1162/pres.1996.5.3.290
7. IJsselsteijn, W.A., De Kort, Y.A., Poels, K.: The game experience questionnaire (2013)
8. Jennett, C., et al.: Measuring and defining the experience of immersion in games. Int. J. Hum Comput Stud. **66**(9), 641–661 (2008). https://doi.org/10.1016/j.ijhcs.2008.04.004
9. Kern, A.C., Ellermeier, W.: Audio in VR: effects of a soundscape and movement-triggered step sounds on presence. Front. Rob. AI **7**, 20 (2020). https://doi.org/10.3389/frobt.2020.00020
10. Kim, H.K., Park, J., Choi, Y., Choe, M.: Virtual reality sickness questionnaire (VRSQ): motion sickness measurement index in a virtual reality environment. Appl. Ergon. **69**, 66–73 (2018). https://doi.org/10.1016/j.apergo.2017.12.016
11. Larsson, P., Västfjäll, D., Olsson, P., Kleiner, M., et al.: When what you hear is what you see: presence and auditory-visual integration in virtual environments. In: Proceedings of the 10th Annual International Workshop on Presence, pp. 11–18 (2007)

12. Law, E.L.C., Brühlmann, F., Mekler, E.D.: Systematic review and validation of the game experience questionnaire (GEQ) - implications for citation and reporting practice. In: Proceedings of the 2018 Annual Symposium on Computer-Human Interaction in Play, CHI PLAY 2018, pp. 257–270. Association for Computing Machinery, New York, NY, USA (2018). https://doi.org/10.1145/3242671.3242683

13. Plut, C., Pasquier, P.: Music matters: an empirical study on the effects of adaptive music on experienced and perceived player affect. In: 2019 IEEE Conference on Games (CoG), pp. 1–8 (2019). https://doi.org/10.1109/CIG.2019.8847951

14. Prechtl, A.: Adaptive music generation for computer games. Ph.D. thesis, The Open University, UK (2016)

15. Randalyn Rage UG (haftungsbeschränkt): beVaiR. https://bevairgame.com. Accessed 22 May 2023

16. Rogers, K., Milo, M., Weber, M., Nacke, L.E.: The potential disconnect between time perception and immersion: effects of music on VR player experience. In: Proceedings of the Annual Symposium on Computer-Human Interaction in Play, CHI PLAY 2020, pp. 414–426. Association for Computing Machinery, New York, NY, USA (2020). https://doi.org/10.1145/3410404.3414246

17. Rosnow, R.L., Rosenthal, R.: Effect sizes for experimenting psychologists. Can. J. Exp. Psychol./Rev. canadienne de psychologie expérimentale **57**(3), 221–237 (2003)

18. Sanders, T., Cairns, P.: Time perception, immersion and music in videogames. Proc. HCI **2010**, 160–167 (2010)

19. Schubert, T., Friedmann, F., Regenbrecht, H.: The sense of presence in virtual environments: a three-component scale measuring spatial presence, involvement, and realness. Zeitschrift für Medienpsychologie **15**(2), 69–71 (2003). https://doi.org/10.1026//1617-6383.15.2.69

20. Scirea, M.: Affective Music Generation and its effect on player experience. Ph.D. thesis, IT University of Copenhagen, Denmark (2017)

21. Slater, M., Usoh, M., Steed, A.: Depth of presence in virtual environments. Presence: Teleoperators Virtual Environ. **3**(2), 130–144 (1994). https://doi.org/10.1162/pres.1994.3.2.130

22. Slater, M., Wilbur, S.: A framework for immersive virtual environments (FIVE): speculations on the role of presence in virtual environments. Presence: Teleoperators Virtual Environ. **6**(6), 603–616 (1997). https://doi.org/10.1162/pres.1997.6.6.603

23. Valve Corporation: beVaiR on Steam. https://store.steampowered.com/app/1711940/beVaiR/. Accessed 27 July 2023

24. Vanden Abeele, V., Nacke, L.E., Mekler, E.D., Johnson, D.: Design and preliminary validation of the player experience inventory. In: Proceedings of the 2016 Annual Symposium on Computer-Human Interaction in Play Companion Extended Abstracts, CHI PLAY Companion 2016, pp. 335–341. Association for Computing Machinery, New York, NY, USA (2016). https://doi.org/10.1145/2968120.2987744

25. Von Georgi, R., Lerm, J., Bötsch, I., Bullerjahn, C.: Der Einfluss von Musik in Egoshootern auf das Angst-und Aggressionsverhalten-Eine Pilotstudie. In: Poster presented at the Annual Conference of the German Society for Music Psychology, Creativity-Structure and Emotion, Würzburg (2010)

26. Witmer, B.G., Jerome, C.J., Singer, M.J.: The factor structure of the presence questionnaire. Presence: Teleoperators Virtual Environ. **14**(3), 298–312 (2005). https://doi.org/10.1162/105474605323384654

27. Witmer, B.G., Singer, M.J.: Measuring presence in virtual environments: a presence questionnaire. Presence: Teleoperators Virtual Environ. **7**(3), 225–240 (1998). https://doi.org/10.1162/105474698565686

28. Wongutai, K., Palee, P., Choosri, N.: The effect of sound in VR exergame to adult player: a primary investigation. In: 2021 Joint International Conference on Digital Arts, Media and Technology with ECTI Northern Section Conference on Electrical, Electronics, Computer and Telecommunication Engineering, pp. 1–4 (2021). https://doi.org/10.1109/ECTIDAMTNCON51128.2021.9425698

# Synaesthesia Gallery AR: Journey Through the Senses – Using Augmented Reality for Education

Svetlana Rudenko[1] and Mads Haahr[2](✉)

[1] Haunted Planet Studios, Dublin, Ireland
rudenkos@tcd.ie
[2] Trinity College Dublin, Dublin, Ireland
haahrm@tcd.ie

**Abstract.** This work-in-progress paper presents *Synaesthesia Gallery AR: Journey Through the Senses*, an educational game-like experience designed to bring awareness of synaesthesia, to learn and understand creativity of cross-modal perception. Synaesthesia is a perceptual trait characterised by cross-modal wiring of the brain experienced by a 4–6% of the population. Synaesthesia research has a long history (as far back as 1690), and sometimes synaesthesia was confused for hallucinations. The AR app documents creative synaesthesia experiences of individuals who have contributed significantly to synaesthesia research, including international artists, such as Carol Steen (president of USA Synaesthesia Association), and scientists, such as Jamie Ward (Professor at the University of Sussex, UK). Ramachandran and Hubbard have called synaesthesia "a window into perception, thought and language" that can help explain how the brain works. The app experience takes a form of an interactive digital gallery for the outdoors, a locative Augmented Reality (AR) art gallery with music by Liszt, Chopin, Schuman, Scriabin and others painted by artists-synaesthetes and music composed on art. The work is the result of a seven-year collaboration between artists-synaesthetes and pianist/researcher Dr Svetlana Rudenko. The app provides pleasing aesthetic experience as well as learning, to general population, neuroscience and psychology students, synaesthesia associations and music art lovers.

**Keywords:** Augmented Reality · Synaesthesia · Music and Art · Creativity · Games for Learning

## 1 Introduction

About 4–6% of the population [1] experience *synaesthesia,* a perceptual trait due to the cross-modal wiring of the brain [2, pp. 319–33]. In addition to perceiving one stimulus, such as sound, people with synaesthesia may perceive an additional quality to the experience – a colour or smell or feeling. Synaesthesia research goes as far as the year 1690 in which a case was documented by John Loche about a blind man experiencing colour on the sound of trumpet. A medical study of synaesthesia was described by George Tobias

M. Haahr et al. (Eds.): JCSG 2023, LNCS 14309, pp. 211–217, 2023.
https://doi.org/10.1007/978-3-031-44751-8_15

Ludwig Sachs in 1812 (Wikipedia). After synaesthesia inspired the whole generation of German Romantic artists (e.g., Caspar David Friedrich), American neurologist Richard Cytowic brought synaesthesia research into mainstream science in the 1980s [3]. Many people of creative professions who are synaesthetes use synaesthesia creatively as an additional sensory stimulation. Because there are many types of synaesthesia and the experience is highly subjective, the trait has sometimes been confused with hallucinations or neurological disorders [4]. For children with synaesthesia and their parents, this is a particular challenge, since children may describe their experiences in ways that their parents do not understand, which can lead to confusion and difficulty in learning. For example, a child with grapheme-colour synaesthesia will perceive letters and numbers in colours, which easily could distract the learning process and cause misunderstanding, because educational techniques for primary school reading and writing often use colours, which will not match the child's experience. Many synaesthetes are not aware of their sensory pairings and think that everyone else experiences it too.

This paper presents a game-like educational experience entitled *Synaesthesia Gallery AR: Journey Through the Senses,* which is designed to give insight into sensory perception and to help people learn about synaesthesia, and perhaps also turn sometimes overwhelming sensory experiences into the creativity of cross-modal perception. The experience takes the form of an interactive digital gallery for the outdoors, a locative Augmented Reality (AR) art gallery with music by Liszt, Chopin, Schuman, Scriabin and others painted by artists-synaesthetes. The gallery contains 15 multisensory soundscape art episodes and is the result of a seven-year collaboration between artists-synaesthetes and concert pianist, composer and researcher Dr Svetlana Rudenko. The game runs on smartphones (Android, iOS) and is available in the respective app stores. The app has received a funding award from Federation of European Neuroscience Societies (FENS) and the DANA foundation for brain research and was launched at Trinity College Dublin for Brain Awareness Week 2022.

Ramachandran and Hubbard [5, pp. 52–59] stated that 'synesthesia causes excess communication amongst brain maps… Depending on where and how widely in the brain the trait was expressed, it could lead to both synesthesia and to a propensity towards linking seemingly unrelated concepts and ideas – in short, creativity." The App is creative itself, as a psychogeograpical augmentation of location with Art and Music soundscapes. It has two modes: site-specific and random. In site-specific mode, the experience is set in a curated location. In random mode, it will stage itself to any location in the world. (See Fig. 1.) In random mode, the experience works best in a park, or close to nature because it uses the environment as a relevant context for (and backdrop to) to the AR encounters. In a natural environment, this combination encourages multisensory experiences, such as feeling of the wind on the skin, the smell of the grass and fresh leaves, in combination with the sound of music and the visual stimulation through the AR art. The app was originally staged at Trinity College Dublin for Brain Awareness Week 2022 demonstration and to offer easy campus access for students carrying out research on synaesthesia and visitors attending BAW lectures.

Fig. 1. *Synaesthesia Gallery AR*. Augmented Reality images: Episode N8 (Art by Carol Steen on Schuman Quintet Op. 44) and N15 (Music and Art for Alice Dali AR by Dr Svetlana Rudenko).

## 2 Types of Synaesthesia, Infants Synaesthesia and the Multisensory Brain

Ramachandran and Hubbard has called synaesthesia "a window into perception, thought and language" [6]. There are 75 types of synaesthesia registered according to Sean A. Day who is president of the International Association of Synaesthetes, Artists, Scientists (IASAS).[1] Research has shown that people with Synaesthesia are more aware of cross-modal sensory pairings due to stronger connections in their neural system [7]. Further-more, there is evidence that the brain of a new-born baby is cross-modal and have infants synaesthesia [8]. While synaesthetes only represent 4–6% of adult humans, it is still a large number of people, as observed by Cytowic who stated, "one in twenty-three people carry the gene of synaesthete" [3]. There is also "a growing body of empirical research on the topic of multisensory perception [which] now shows that even non-synaesthetic individuals experience cross-modal correspondences" [2, pp. 319–33]. There is evidence that multisensory perception stimulates the brain and Infants Synaesthesia is a natural sensory state for newborn baby [8]. Research shows that synaesthesia-enhanced appli-cations have promising potential for education and mental health programs, such as Bor et al.'s experiment to train non-synaesthetes for grapheme-colour synaesthesia (shapes, letters and numbers have colour), which showed an IQ improvement and provisionally concluded that "cognitive training including synesthetic associations may in the future be a promising new tool for vulnerable clinical groups to enhance general mental ability" [9]. Also, designer and researcher Dr Michael Haverkamp established a methodology for multisensory design based on synaesthesia [10], and sensory substitution devices research uses a synaesthesia principle in which the lost sense (e.g., vision for blind peo-ple) could be compensated for in another sensory modality (e.g., seeing with sound) [11].

Many artists, musicians and writers who were synaesthetes found an inspiration in their sensory perceptions. Cretien van Campen observes that the famous artist Wassily Kandinsky described synaesthesia as a "phenomenon of transposition of experience from one sense modality to another, as in unisonous musical tones" [12, p. 56]. Greta Berman, Professor of Art History at the Julliard School, NY, noticed: "Synesthetes invariably manifest a multi-layered, complex way of looking at and interpreting things.

---

[1] http://www.daysyn.com/Types-of-Syn.html.

In synesthetic art, both paintings and music exploit unexpected and startling rhythms" [13, p. 28]. Russian science researcher, artist and director of the Prometei Institute, B. M. Galeyev said: "Synesthesia (and the particular case of 'color hearing') is the essential component of musical thinking, first of all, music intended to evoke images" [14, p. 3]. President of American Synaesthesia Association Carol Steen describes the sensation of synaesthetic colours: "Regardless of the synesthetic trigger, that sometimes the colors are translucent like a haze of smoke or fog sometimes they're dense with a weight that feels almost physical. The shapes are soft-edged, exist in space, and are three dimensional but cast solar system (…) The speed of these moving shapes is gentle. They go as fast as the changing color waves of aurora borealis appear to the naked eye" [15, p. 19]. Some experiences of synaesthesia can cause confusion, for example children with grapheme-colour synaesthesia might see "their own" colours on letters, not the alphabet colours shown by the teacher.[2] Or, as Carol Steen describes, when synaesthesia was overwhelming or even frightening: "The first time was when I was 7 and told my best friend that the letter 'a' was the prettiest pink I had ever seen. She said I was weird and we stopped being friends. I decided that silence was safer and didn't mention my colored letters to anyone until I was 20."[3]

Synaesthete Lidle Simpson describes his experience as "I have been deaf all my life and I like to say that I have never known silence. I learned at an early age that hearing people are not hearing what I hear. I called it 'Photonic Hearing' before I learned the word 'Synaesthesia.'"[4] But most important, as Lucie Bouvet et al. observe in their article "When synesthesia and savant abilities are mistaken for hallucinations and delusions: contribution of a cognitive approach for their differential diagnosis" [4], awareness of Synaesthesia and self-discovery if the person is synaesthete can prevent many upsetting cases because almost all synaesthetes start their journey with "I thought everybody sees it!".

## 3   Augmented Reality Experience: The App

*Synaesthesia Gallery AR* shows how music could be perceived with other senses; it shows music as vision, painted by artists-synaesthetes. It teaches creativity and diversity of perceptions. The app could be helpful for that one child in the class who is different, and it also teaches non-synaesthete children to respect their individual experience and gain confidence that they are allowed to be different. In this fashion, the app serves as a social game experience with classmates that lets them experience the aesthetics of music and art, increases awareness of their own sensory responses, perhaps leading to them to paint music or other emotional experiences themselves. For adults, the app is a tool for self-exploration to learn more about the sensory perception of music, as well as the psychogeography of location, augmented with art and music. In addition to painted music episodes, *Synaesthesia Gallery AR* has episodes with a scientific talk by Prof. Jamie Ward and with talks by artists-synaesthetes about their synaesthetic experience and

---

[2] https://www.syntoolkit.org/teacher.

[3] https://mitpress.mit.edu/spotlight-on-science-carol-steen/.

[4] https://static1.squarespace.com/static/5fbbf00ba552d609bac0798b/t/60467feb69aafb17f6cc7 de0/1615233019217/Art-on-Classical-Music-by-artists-synesthetes-converted.pdf.

music composed on art, when the colours and shapes "sound." Many countries, including the US, Canada, Germany, Spain and others have Synaesthesia Associations that bring awareness of the trait to schools and the general public. Neuroscience societies, such as British Neuroscience Association (BNA), the Federation of European Neuroscience Societies (FENS), the Dana Foundation and Neuroscience Ireland work on dissemination of brain science and very often host Synaesthesia events during their world-wide, annual Brain Awareness Week (BAW) event.

### 3.1  Gameplay AR

The *Synaesthesia Gallery AR* experience is set outside and works through a smartphone screen. The first step is to download the app from the Play Store (Android) or App Store (iOS). The app is free and free of advertising. When the app starts, you can choose "Random" to play in your local location (e.g., a park) or "Trinity" to play in curated locations in Trinity College Dublin (Fig. 2 right, screenshot 1). After that, the main experience begins. The steps to find and capture a music art encounter are as follows: 1. Use the map to orient yourself and make sure you are inside the purple area where the music art encounters are (Fig. 2 right, screenshot 2). 2. Use the radar to get close to a music art encounter (Fig. 2 right, screenshot 3). The radar works like a naval radar where you are in the centre and the music art encounters are around you. As you get closer to an encounter, you will hear the music begin. You should keep going until the LEDs light up and the AR button flashes yellow. 3. Use the AR mode to scan around you and find the artwork hanging in the air (Fig. 2 right, screenshot 4). A yellow arrow on the display tells you which way to pan. When you see the artwork, capture it by taking a photo. If the artwork disappears before you can capture it, go back to step 2 above and move a little bit closer to it.

The captured artworks go into your gallery casebook (Fig. 2 right, screenshot 5) where you can review them and read more about the artwork and the music. When the music finishes, you can proceed to find the next music art encounter, beginning with step 1 above.

**Fig. 2.** Synaesthesia *Gallery AR* cards with instructions

## 3.2  Content

The majority of the episodes of *Synaesthesia Gallery AR* demonstrate experiences of the chromaesthesia type (experiencing colours when hearing music). In addition, there is an episode by James Wannerton "Tastes of Kandinsky," which presents lexical-gustatory synaesthesia (experiencing taste when hearing, speaking, reading, or thinking about words) [16]. The app documents creative synaesthesia experiences of individuals who contributed significantly to synaesthesia research, including academics and international artists such as Carol Steen (president of the US Synaesthesia Association), Prof. Maria Jose de Cordoba Serrano (director of Spanish Synaesthesia Association Artecitta), Dr Timothy Layden, Ninghui Xiang (president of Synaesthesia Alliance, China), James Wannerton (president of the UK Synaesthesia Association) and Geri Hahn, textile artist-synaesthete, New Jersey, as well as one scientific episode by leading researcher on synaesthesia Prof. Jamie Ward, University of Sussex. The variety of music episodes include compositions such as Schuman Piano Quintet Op. 44 (painted by Carol Steen), Chopin ballad N1, Op. 23 (painted by Ninghui Xiong), Scriabin Piano Sonata N5 and Liszt B-minor Sonata (painted by Timothy Layden) and so on.

## 4  Conclusion and Future Work

In *Synaesthesia Gallery AR,* we show how artists-synaesthetes use their sensory perceptions on music creatively. We hope that some people will use the app to discover their own synaesthesia, and that all people who use it will learn about diversity of perceptions. For some people, it could be the start of creative practice, e.g., painting music as a therapeutic exercise.

The app will be used as a tool for further study, including a user study on the app as an educational tool for teachers, and use of the app as an alternative to online synaesthesia tests, offering a soft informative and playful experience of music art that has the potential to discover more non-identified synaesthestes with "rare" sensory pairings. In comparison, the most common tests for synaesthesia are based only on chromaesthesia and grapheme-colour synaesthesia. There are many additional possible applications for location-based art galleries like *Synesthesia Gallery AR*, including encouraging healthy walking habits, promoting physical exercise and as a cultural outdoors experience for intergenerational play for families.

We also think the app could be of interest to scientists exploring computational models of the neural circuits of the brain. There are patterns and shapes revealed in art (including the artworks in *Synaesthesia Gallery AR*), which are characteristic also to multisensory perception under psychedelic states. The German-American biological psychologist Heinrich Klüver described these shapes as "form constants," and Jack Cowan and others [17] later used them to develop computational models that describe the dynamics of interactions between populations of model neurons.

## References

1. Farina, F.R., Mitchell, K.J., Roche, R.A.P.: Synaesthesia lost and found: two cases of person- and music-colour synaesthesia. Eur. J. Neurosci. **45**, 1–6 (2016)

2. Parise, C., Spence, C.: Audiovisual crossmodal correspondences and sound symbol-ism: a study using the implicit association test. Exp. Brain Res. **220**(3–4), 319–33 (2012). https://www.researchgate.net/publication/227175048_Audiovisual_crossmodal_corr espondences_and_sound_symbolism_A_study_using_the_implicit_association_test

3. Cytowic, R.E.: Synesthesia. MIT Press, Cambridge, London (2018)

4. Bouvet, L., Barbier, J.-E., Cason, N., Bakchine, S., Ehrle, N.: When synesthesia and savant abilities are mistaken for hallucinations and delusions: contribution of a cognitive approach for their differential diagnosis. Clin. Neuropsychol. **31**(8), 1459–1473 (2017)

5. Ramachandran, V.S., Hubbard, E.M.: Hearing colors, tasting shapes, pp. 53–59 (2003)

6. Ramachandran, V.S., Hubbard, E.M.: Synaesthesia- a window into perception, thought and language. J. Conscious. Stud. **8**(12), 3–34 (2001)

7. Cytowic, R.E.: Synesthesia: A Union of the Senses, 2nd edn. MIT Press, Cambridge, London (2002)

8. Ward, J.: The Frog Who Croaked Blue: Synesthesia and the Mixing of the Senses. Routledge, London and New York (2008)

9. Bor, D., Rothen, N., Schwartzman, D., Clayton, S., Seth, A.: Adults can be trained to acquire synesthetic experiences. Sci. Rep. **4** (2014). https://www.nature.com/articles/srep07089

10. Haverkamp, M.: Sinesthetic Design: Handbook for a Multi-Sensory Approach. Birkhauser Verlag AG (2013)

11. Rudenko, S., Haahr, M.: Psychogeography with Jack B. Yeats art sounding gallery: augmented reality locative experience for blind people. Presented at the 13th International Conference on Applied Human Factors and Ergonomics (AHFE) (2022). https://doi.org/10.54941/ahfe10 01639

12. Van Campen, C.: The Hidden Sense. Synesthesia in Art and Science. The MIT Press, Cambridge and London (2010)

13. Berman, G.: New perspectives on synesthesia art: shared characteristics. In: Synesthesia: Art and the Mind, pp. 27–32. McMaster Museum of Art, Hamilton (2008)

14. Galeyev, B.M.: The nature and functions of synesthesia in music. Leonardo **40**(3), 285–288 (2007)

15. Steen, C: What a synesthete sees: or why Tom Thomson sends me over the moon. In: Synesthesia: Art and Mind, pp. 17–26. McMaster Museum of Art, Hamilton (2008)

16. Ipser, A., Ward, J., Simner, J.: The MULTISENSE test of lexical-gustatory synaesthesia: an automated online diagnostic. Behav. Res. Methods **52**, 544–560 (2020)

17. Bressloff, P.C., Cowan, J.D., Golubitsky, M., Thomas, P.J., Wiener, M.C.: What geometric visual hallucinations tell us about the visual cortex. Neural Comput. **14**(3), 473–491 (2002)

# Designing a Multi-user VR Social Activity Space for Social Interaction for People Living with Dementia

G. Reilly[1]([✉]) [iD], S. Redfern[1] [iD], G.-M. Muntean[2] [iD], and A. Brennan[1] [iD]

[1] School of Computer Science, University of Galway, Galway, Ireland
g.reilly6@universityofgalway.ie
[2] School of Electronic Engineering, Dublin City University, Dublin 9, Ireland

**Abstract.** Dementia is a condition that leads to a gradual decline in executive cognitive functioning over time. Health care professionals use non-pharmacological activities to enrich the lives of people living with dementia (PLWD). Studies show that activities involving social interaction have a positive effect on the cognitive function of PLWD. Studies also show that the distancing limitations brought by the Covid-19 pandemic greatly reduced the number of opportunities for social interaction and negatively affected PLWD. Virtual Reality (VR) is showing promise in research involving PLWD. While PLWD have indicated positive experiences using VR, there is currently a paucity of research into the design and development of a multi-user VR social activity space for PLWD. This paper details the design of an activity based multi-user VR space to support socialization for PLWD. It also outlines a set of experiments to evaluate efficacy from the context of social presence and social interaction within this space.

**Keywords:** Dementia · Virtual Reality · Social Interaction · Social Connectedness

## 1 Introduction

Dementia is a neurodegenerative disease where one's executive cognitive functioning (e.g. working memory, planning and prioritizing and organisation [1]) gradually decreases over time [2]. As the disease progresses, people living with dementia i.e. PLWD, typically lose their independence, and require assistance from others. While there is currently no cure for dementia, researchers have sought non-pharmacological ways to enrich the lives of PLWD (e.g. reminiscence therapy and activity therapy [3]).

An important element of promoting the wellbeing of PLWD and mitigating further deterioration is to provide social interaction [4]. Social activities such as group art sessions can improve executive cognitive functioning and increase social participation among PLWD [5]. The Covid-19 pandemic prevented PLWD from seeing their families due to health related safety procedures. These procedures, while necessary at the time, resulted in an increased sense of loneliness and psychiatric symptoms associated with dementia [6]. Clearly, there is a need for approaches to support PLWD in activities which

M. Haahr et al. (Eds.): JCSG 2023, LNCS 14309, pp. 218–226, 2023.
https://doi.org/10.1007/978-3-031-44751-8_16

promote social interaction; approaches that can be achieved from the safety of their own residences.

Digital technology has been used successfully in applications such as entertainment and caregiving for PLWD [7]. While there is no standard definition of Virtual Reality (VR [8]), VR is a technology which uses a combination of visual, audio, and in some cases haptic feedback to provide an immersive experience to users [9] via a Head Mounted Device (HMD). Studies show that playing games such as virtual bowling can assist PLWD in the recollection of motor tasks [10]. Meanwhile, performing simple physical exercises using VR can improve executive cognitive functioning in PLWD [11]. Furthermore, VR-based music therapy can increase positive emotions and memory performance in PLWD [12]. The increased accessibility of VR has led to it being used as a tool for socialization. Applications such as VRChat and RecRoom allow users to connect and interact with each other in a shared virtual environment. Social VR is defined as a virtual environment where users are able to interact via virtual avatars [13]. Some social VR applications (e.g. RecRoom) allow users to create environments, which they can then share and experience with other people. Baker et al. (2021) designed a multi-user VR social environment to promote reminiscence in older adults [14]. This study showed that the PLWD users found their VR experiences to be meaningful. Despite such studies, **there is currently a paucity of research in the design and development of multi-user VR social activity spaces to promote social interaction for PLWD.**

Ultimately, while research into VR for PLWD has proven to be effective, VR is not suitable for all PLWD. Matsangidou et al. (2020) [15] reported three cases of PLWD experiencing clinical anxiety as a result of using VR. Such anxiety can occur due to a sense of claustrophobia that can manifest as a result of wearing the HMD [16]. Although some PLWD can experience motion sickness using VR, their symptoms are no worse than those of users without cognitive impairment [17]. In general, VR is most suitable for those with mild to moderate dementia, i.e. who are better able to follow instructions and engage with activities [18].

## 2  Method

The design of the multi-user VR social activity space to support social interaction for PLWD is one part of a three phase study: (1) the design and development of a VR Probe, (2) the design and development of a multi-user VR social activity space and (3) the evaluation of the multi-user VR social activity space to support social interaction for PLWD. In Phase one, the authors were involved in the participatory design of a VR Probe to familiarize nine PLWD (having early to moderate dementia) and their nine informal caregivers with the interactive features of VR [19]. An analysis of the feedback from this phase (Table 1) in addition to a comprehensive literature review have influenced the design of the multi-user VR social activity space and associated task based activities (Table 2). In Phase 3, ten PLWD and their caregivers will be involved in testing the efficacy of the VR social space to support their socialisation.

**Table 1.** VR Probe: PLWD Feedback [19].

|  | Feedback |
|---|---|
| *Multisensory design* | The use of multisensory design improved the participants' sense of presence. This led to an increased sense of alertness and engagement with the virtual environment. This is also in line with findings from [9] |
| *Accommodating Autonomy* | The use of a one button interaction system in addition to a freeform approach allowed participants to engage organically with the environment. This complements work by [20] shows how the design of functional and flexible tasks can promote autonomy in PLWD |
| *Facilitator based assistance* | Verbal instructions from the facilitator were considered more effective than a task's visual instructions. Participants indicated a desire for instruction manuals or videos |
| *Impact of exposure to VR* | Participants enjoyed the VR experience. They suggested more background noise in the environment and a greater clarity in the graphics. This is in line with research by [21] |

## 3   Design of the Multi-user VR Social Activity Space

The multi-user VR social activity space for PLWD comprises three main scenes which support a specific multi-user task-based activity. Each of these activities has been categorized as either; physical movement, memorization or creativity (Table 2).

**Table 2.** Activities

| Activity | Category | Description | Justification |
|---|---|---|---|
| Ball throwing activity (Fig. 1) | Physical movement | The participant can select one of three levels of difficulty from a UI panel. Level 1 is the beginner level while Level 3 is the expert level. A number of cocoa cola cans are spawned based on the selected level (e.g. 15 cans for Level 1, 8 for Level 2 and 5 for Level 3). The participant is encouraged to pick up nearby balls (using the controller button) and toss them at the cans | The biomechanics involved in this activity support coordination [22] Enhancing physical capabilities prolong the quality of life of PLWD [23] |

*(continued)*

**Table 2.** (*continued*)

| Activity | Category | Description | Justification |
|---|---|---|---|
| Card matching game (Fig. 2) | Memorization | There are four tables in the card game section, with each table showing six pairs of cards. The cards are automatically shuffled when the participant starts the game. The participant is instructed to flip over the cards using the specified controller button. The goal is to find matching pairs. If two cards are flipped over and they do not match, the cards will be flipped back down Audio feedback is provided when the match is successful (beeping noise) and unsuccessful (e.g. 'crumpling' noise) | Board games can improve the executive cognitive functioning of older adults [24] and people with mild and moderate dementia [25]. There is a greater sense of immersion when participants have real life experience with the game [26] |
| Art activity (Fig. 3) | Creativity | The art section contains multiple small whiteboards, with paintbrushes on a nearby table. The participant is encouraged to pick up a paintbrush and point it at the whiteboard. By pressing the specified controller button, they can draw on the whiteboard | Creative activities can improve communication and promote conversations among PLWD [27]. Art interventions contribute to improving the quality of life of PLWD [28] |

222     G. Reilly et al.

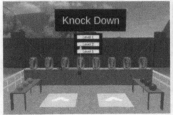

**Fig. 1.** Ball throwing activity.     **Fig. 2.** Card matching game.     **Fig. 3.** Art activity.

### 3.1 Proposed Experiment Design

A set of quantitative and qualitative measurements to identify whether or not the multi-user VR social activity space encourages social interaction for PLWD will include;

- *The Revised Social Connectedness Scale* [29] will be used before the participant enters the VR space in order to identify their baseline feelings of social connectedness. They will also be asked *social interaction questions* i.e. how they interact with others from the context of initiating conversation etc. After they leave the VR multi-user social activity space, they will be asked to complete the revised social interaction questions (contextualised from a VR perspective). The answers to both sets of questions, in addition to an analysis of gameplay data, and audio and video recordings will help evaluate the efficacy of the VR multi-user social activity space to support social connectedness for PLWD.
- *Audio and video recordings* will include conversations and comments made by the participants during their time in the VR environment. Video *timestamps* will be used to identify when a participant starts looking towards and away from another participant.
- *Gameplay data* – the collection of gameplay data such as *avatar position* (i.e. head, hand etc.), button presses, object interactions and interaction points will be used to: (1) evaluate the manner in which the participants move (i.e. head and hand movement) and behave (i.e. points where the participants interact with objects or other people) in the virtual environment [30] and (2) validate social interaction behaviours between participants.
- *Avatar choice* - The participants will be presented with a database of avatars from which to choose i.e. older and younger avatars (both male and female) and abstract avatars.

Note: Quantitative data will be analysed using IBM SPSS V 29 with the statistical significance being set at $p < 0.05$. Qualitative data will be analysed at the thematic and semantic levels.

The initial experiments which will be carried out in Phase Three are described in Table 3. Note: We are collaborating with medical experts and an occupational therapist in the development of an intervention protocol.

**Table 3.** Experiment outcomes

| Experiment question | Measurements | Expected outcomes |
| --- | --- | --- |
| Does the use of virtual avatars facilitate social interaction in a virtual environment? | Video recordings<br>Audio recordings<br>Timestamps<br>Avatar/participant positions<br>Object interactions | Participants will:<br>• be located close to each other when they are interacting<br>• look at each other while interacting<br>• have greater arm movements when interacting with another user<br>• have a number of interactions with virtual objects<br>• initiate conversations |
| Is the one button interaction system easier to memorize and use for the PLWD? | The # of button presses on each controller<br>Interaction points<br>Audio recordings<br>Video recordings<br>Object interactions | Fewer errors will occur with the one button interaction system<br>The participants will ask for less assistance in identifying buttons on the controller<br>The participant will be less frustrated |
| Do more age appropriate avatars lead to greater social interaction for PLWD? | Participant/avatar head and hand movements<br>Video recordings<br>Audio recordings<br>Timestamps<br>Avatar/participant positions | Participants who select age appropriate avatars will interact more often than those who do not<br>Participants will move their head and hands more often<br>[see expected outcomes for the first experiment] |
| Does the multi-user social VR space promote social interaction? | The users will complete a Revised Social Connectedness Scale before using the multi-user VR social activity space. Before and after their VR experience, they will be asked to complete a social interaction questionnaire | The participants will have more positive answers to the Social Interaction questionnaire after using the multi-user VR social activity space. This will be underpinned by measurement data i.e. audio and video recordings etc. |

Note: Two separate builds of the VR application will be used throughout the experiments. One version will use a simplified control system where the trigger button on the controller will be used for most actions (e.g. grabbing, teleporting, interacting). The second version will use a more traditional control scheme where participants will be required to press different buttons to perform different actions (e.g. using the grip button for grabbing, using the trigger button for interacting). As this paper outlines part 1 of Phase 2, no detail on sample size, recruitment and experiment procedure is provided. This will be outlined in subsequent papers.

# 4 Limitations

The main limitations of this study include; the reduced number of available activities, and the targeted audience i.e. people with mild to moderate dementia.

# 5 Conclusion

VR possesses a great potential to enhance or maintain the social connectedness of people living with dementia (PLWD) and their caregivers. However, design considerations need to be established to create VR applications that are suitable for PLWD. In this paper, design considerations for a multi-user VR social space to promote social interaction for PLWD were described. This paper also outlined a set of multi-user task-based activities to support: physical movement, creative thinking and memorization; all of which enhance the quality of life of PLWD. The authors also proposed a set of experiments, associated measurements and expected outcomes to assess the efficacy of the multi-user VR social activity space to encourage social interaction for PLWD. In future work, the authors will validate the design and implementation decisions of the multi-user VR social activity space for PLWD via the proposed experiments.

**Acknowledgements.** This work was conducted with the financial support of the Science Foundation Ireland Centre for Research Training in Digitally-Enhanced Reality (d-real) under Grant No. 18/CRT/6224. For the purpose of Open Access, the author has applied a CC BY public copyright license to any Author Accepted Manuscript version arising from this submission.

# References

1. Stopford, C.L., et al.: Working memory, attention, and executive function in Alzheimer's disease and frontotemporal dementia. Cortex **48**(4), 429–446 (2012)
2. WHO. Dementia (2020). https://www.who.int/news-room/fact-sheets/detail/dementia. Accessed 30 Dec 2020
3. Shigihara, Y., et al.: Non-pharmacological treatment changes brain activity in patients with dementia. Sci. Rep. **10**(1), 6744 (2020)
4. Poey, J.L., Burr, J.A., Roberts, J.S.: Social connectedness, perceived isolation, and dementia: does the social environment moderate the relationship between genetic risk and cognitive well-being? Gerontologist **57**(6), 1031–1040 (2017)
5. Robertson, J.M., McCall, V.: Facilitating creativity in dementia care: the co-construction of arts-based engagement. Ageing Soc. **40**(6), 1155–1174 (2020)
6. Curelaru, A., et al.: Social isolation in dementia: the effects of COVID-19. J. Nurse Pract. **17**(8), 950–953 (2021)
7. Astell, A.J., et al.: Technology and dementia: the future is now. Dement. Geriatr. Cogn. Disord. **47**(3), 131–139 (2019)
8. Kardong-Edgren, S., et al.: A call to unify definitions of virtual reality. Clin. Simul. Nurs. **31**, 28–34 (2019)
9. Muñoz, J., et al.: Immersive virtual reality exergames for persons living with dementia: user-centered design study as a multistakeholder team during the COVID-19 pandemic. JMIR Serious Games **10**(1), e29987–e29987 (2022)

10. Fenney, A., Lee, T.D.: Exploring spared capacity in persons with dementia: what WiiTM can learn. Act. Adapt. Aging **34**(4), 303–313 (2010)
11. Yamaguchi, H., Maki, Y., Takahashi, K.: Rehabilitation for dementia using enjoyable videosports games. Int. Psychogeriatr. **23**(4), 674–676 (2011)
12. Byrns, A., et al.: Adaptive music therapy for Alzheimer's disease using virtual reality. In: Kumar, V., Troussas, C. (eds.) ITS 2020. LNCS, vol. 12149, pp. 214–219. Springer, Cham (2020). https://doi.org/10.1007/978-3-030-49663-0_25
13. Baker, S., et al.: Avatar-mediated communication in social VR: an in-depth exploration of older adult interaction in an emerging communication platform. In: Proceedings of the 2021 CHI Conference on Human Factors in Computing Systems. ACM (2021)
14. Baker, S., et al.: School's back: scaffolding reminiscence in social virtual reality with older adults. Proc. ACM Hum.-Comput. Interact. **4**(CSCW3), Article no. 267 (2021)
15. Matsangidou, M., et al.: Dementia: I am physically fading. Can virtual reality help? Physical training for people with dementia in confined mental health units. In: Antona, M., Stephanidis, C. (eds.) HCII 2020. LNCS, vol. 12188, pp. 366–382. Springer, Cham (2020). https://doi.org/10.1007/978-3-030-49282-3_26
16. Tabbaa, L., et al.: Bring the outside in: providing accessible experiences through VR for people with dementia in locked psychiatric hospitals. In: Proceedings of the 2019 CHI Conference on Human Factors in Computing Systems, Glasgow, Scotland UK, p. 236. Association for Computing Machinery (2019)
17. Flynn, D., et al.: Developing a virtual reality-based methodology for people with dementia: a feasibility study. Cyberpsychol. Behav. **6**(6), 591–611 (2003)
18. Appel, L., et al.: Virtual reality to promote wellbeing in persons with dementia: a scoping review. J. Rehabil. Assistive Technol. Eng. **8**, 20556683211053952 (2021)
19. Flynn, A., et al.: Introducing and familiarising older adults living with dementia and their caregivers to virtual reality. Int. J. Environ. Res. Public Health **19**(23), 16343 (2022)
20. Hutchinson, H., et al.: Technology probes: inspiring design for and with families. In: Proceedings of the SIGCHI Conference on Human Factors in Computing Systems, Ft. Lauderdale, Florida, USA, pp. 17–24. Association for Computing Machinery (2003)
21. Hodge, J., et al.: Exploring the design of tailored virtual reality experiences for people with dementia. In: Proceedings of the 2018 CHI Conference on Human Factors in Computing Systems, Montreal QC, Canada, p. 514. Association for Computing Machinery (2018)
22. Alzheimer Society of Ireland. Dementia-friendly sport and physical activity guide (n.d.). https://www.alzheimers.org.uk/get-involved/dementia-friendly-communities/organisations/sports-physical-activity
23. Unbehaun, D., et al.: Development of an ICT-based training system for people with dementia. In: Companion Publication of the 2019 on Designing Interactive Systems Conference 2019 Companion, San Diego, CA, USA, pp. 65–68. Association for Computing Machinery (2019)
24. Ching-Teng, Y.: Effect of board game activities on cognitive function improvement among older adults in adult day care centers. Soc. Work Health Care **58**(9), 825–838 (2019)
25. Makri, M., et al.: The "Bridge" project: α European innovative intergenerational approach using serious games for people with dementia. Psychology **12**(9), 1434–1456 (2021)
26. Ho, J.C.F.: Effect of real-world experience on immersion in virtual reality games: a preliminary study. In: Proceedings of the Fourth International Symposium on Chinese CHI, San Jose, USA, Article no. 6. Association for Computing Machinery (2016)
27. Shoesmith, E.K., Charura, D., Surr, C.: What are the elements needed to create an effective visual art intervention for people with dementia? A qualitative exploration. Dementia **20**(4), 1336–1355 (2021)
28. Ward, M.C., et al.: The benefits of community-based participatory arts activities for people living with dementia: a thematic scoping review. Arts Health **13**(3), 213–239 (2021)

29. Lee, R.M., Draper, M., Lee, S.: Social connectedness, dysfunctional interpersonal behaviors, and psychological distress: testing a mediator model. J. Couns. Psychol. **48**, 310–318 (2001)
30. Villenave, S., et al.: XREcho: a unity plug-in to record and visualize user behavior during XR sessions. In: Proceedings of the 13th ACM Multimedia Systems Conference, Athlone, Ireland, pp. 341–346. Association for Computing Machinery (2022)

# *Waddle*: Developing Empathy for Adélie Penguins By Direct Embodiment in Virtual Reality

David J. Gagnon[1]([✉]) [iD], Kevin Ponto[1] [iD], Monae Verbeke[2] [iD], Mitchell Nathan[1] [iD], Kaldan Kopp[1], and Ross Tredinnick[1] [iD]

[1] University of Wisconsin - Madison, Madison, WI 53703, USA
djgagnon@wisc.edu
[2] Institute for Learning Innovation, Portland, OR 97217, USA

**Abstract.** Empathy is important for fostering social engagement with ecology. In this study we describe *Waddle*, a virtual reality (VR) experience designed to facilitate the direct embodiment of an Adélie Penguin moving through the key stages of their life cycle as an intervention to increase empathy. By collecting pre and post questionnaire data from forty-three grade 3 through 8 students attending a science festival, we find that *Waddle* was successful in facilitating an embodied experience and supported a significant increase in the participants' empathy toward penguins. We also find that greater embodiment was correlated with increased empathy, suggesting a casual relation that invites additional research into designing embodied experiences using immersive technologies as a method for developing empathy and fostering greater social engagement.

**Keywords:** Virtual Reality · Educational Games · Empathy · Embodiment

## 1 Introduction

Recent research into embodied learning demonstrates significant promise for teaching complex STEM topics [7], as well as increasing empathy and perspective-taking [3]. Empathy has been proven to lead to increased conservation efforts, such as financial donations to ecological organizations [8, 11], an objective with merits beyond simple content knowledge. Previous work has also explored the use of virtual reality (VR) for facilitating embodied learning experiences with animals, but have often failed to do so [8]. In this study we leverage this previous work, and the notions of gesture congruence [1] and visuomotor synchrony [8], to design a virtual reality (VR) experience in which the learner takes on the body of an Adélie penguin living on Ross Island in Antarctica. We then use this experience to empirically explore how embodiment and empathy are facilitated and related, following three research questions:

**RQ1.** Does the experience effectively produce an embodied experience of an Adélie penguin?

M. Haahr et al. (Eds.): JCSG 2023, LNCS 14309, pp. 227–233, 2023.
https://doi.org/10.1007/978-3-031-44751-8_17

**RQ2**. Does the experience produce measurable increases in empathy for Adélie penguins?

**RQ3**. Does an increased sense of embodiment correlate with an increase in empathy?

Practically, this work contributes an understanding of how to design educational VR experiences that lead to embodiment and increased empathy for animals. Theoretically, this project contributes an empirical exploration of the relationship between learner embodiment and empathy.

## 2 Previous Work

To move beyond the goal of increasing descriptive knowledge about ecological systems and into environmentalist action, researchers have explored the promise of educational interventions that facilitate empathy and perspective taking [13]. Pimentel & Kalyanaraman [8] found that developing empathy for an endangered species can reverse "compassion fade" and lead to increases in charitable giving. A similar finding by Swim & Bloodhart [11] demonstrates that empathy and perspective taking are more effective than objective perspectives for increasing environmental action, contrary to popular warnings that prioritize psychological distance.

As a medium that manipulates users' perception and gesture, numerous researchers have explored the various ways VR technology can be used to facilitate embodied learning experiences [4], including what Melcer & Isbister refer to as "direct embodiment" where the actions of the participant are directly mapped to the actions and perceptions of the embodied avatar [6]. An important design principle is gesture congruence, which measures the degree to which movements performed by the learner directly relate to the concept being learned [1]. For example, if a student is learning about movement of an object under a force, the VR design should have them gesture in a similar direction to the force, not in a random direction.

Connecting empathy and embodiment using VR, researchers have explored the use of mixed reality to embody animals. Sierra Rativa et al. [10] developed a Virtual Reality simulation where users embodied a visually and haptically realistic beaver avatar. Their study showed a significant effect of the visual design of the avatar on users' sense of immersion, but not on adopting a 1st-person sense of animal embodiment or increasing empathy. One challenge for adopting a truly embodied experience from an animal's perspective is the control of an avatar of certain animals, which have different postures, skeletal arrangements, and shapes compared to human bodies [5]. Pimentel & Kalyanaraman [8] describe this alignment as visuomotor synchrony. Sierra Rativa et al. [10] discuss a lack of synchrony in their design and propose future design should explore the use of the players' hands to control animal's front paws to increase embodiment.

## 3 Methods

### 3.1 Intervention

The VR experience, entitled *Waddle*, is a 20-min Virtual Reality experience that demonstrates visuomotor congruence with an Adélie penguin. Hand tracking mode was utilized, which uses outward facing 3d sensors to identify and track the users hand positions without using additional hand controllers. The experience was developed in consultation with a team of educational game designers, VR researchers, and Jean Pennycook, an Antarctic penguin researcher. Since 2004, Pennycook has spent the Antarctic summers (Oct – Jan) living in a tent near the Adélie penguin breeding colony at Cape Royds on Ross Island near the McMurdo Research Station. Her research team monitors the population of these iconic birds as they respond to changes in their environment. Following several initial meetings with Pennycook, learning about the key life events and activities of the penguins, a design document was developed to explore a potential intervention. This document was reviewed with Pennycook for accuracy and feedback about how it reflected her values, then the project moved into production with minor revisions. During production, minor prototypes were tested internally with public audiences to identify usability issues, then with later iterations again to verify their solutions.

**Fig. 1.** The landscape of Waddle, with orientation activities on the near side and life activities on far side of the bridge

The experience begins with a series of interactions that are designed to orientate the user to the system. Upon putting on the headset, the user sees a snowy scene with a soft mound of snow surrounding all but one direction forward. Their perspective is approximately 0.5 m above the snowy floor, and they see a beak extending forward where their nose should be. Looking down, they see their white belly and flippers instead of arms. To one side is an icy stone obstacle that acts as a mirror, showing a reflection of the Adélie penguin avatar they inhabit and control. The movements they make are reflected in the mirror. To another side is a signpost with a graphic of a penguin standing on one foot with a rounded, double-sided arrow above its head. This sign attempts to communicate that penguins move by waddling back and forth from left to right.

Once they move their upper body back and forth one full cycle, their view avatar moves forward by about 0.5 m in the direction they are facing. Performing this gesture several times along the only available pathway in the snow brings them to a set of orientation activities that do not relate to realistic actions and objects that an Adélie penguin would encounter on Ross Island. One activity demonstrates moving objects in the environment using their beak. Another activity plays chimes when the objects are touched with a quick move from their flippers. At the edge of this orientation area where players learn to move, use their beak and flippers, lies a small bridge in the snow that spans a small stream flowing into the open ocean, as a symbol of moving from orientation into realistic engagements with penguin life (See Fig. 1).

The first interaction users encounter involves picking up small stones in the area and stacking them together to build a pile of stones that these penguins use as a nest for the eggs. Participants bend their back to lean down toward the ground and touching a stone with their beak connects it. If they waddle over to the nest and touch that area with their beak, the stone is released, and the nest grows larger. In another interaction, they act out a mating dance to pair with another penguin. In this activity, they move their head and body to touch visual indicators in their view in a specific sequence, similar to the well-known *Dance Dance Revolution* game mechanic. In the nesting interaction, participants are challenged to defend the egg in their nest from an incoming group of Skua birds, a natural predator to young Adélie penguins. Once positioned between the Skuas and their egg, they strike the predators with their flippers, as the actual Adélie penguins do, to defend their nest. By defending the egg from multiple Skuas for a predetermined amount of time, they complete the challenge. Success is rewarded with an animation of the birds retreating and the penguin's egg hatching.

## 3.2 Participants and Study Format

The study collected data from forty-three grade 3 through 8 (age 8 through 13) students, in groups of 10–20 from different informal learning organizations, attending a science festival on a major university campus. These groups were recruited in advance of the festival, being offered an opportunity to take part in a VR research project. Participants were brought into a separate space on a different floor of the facility where they were verbally introduced to the project and given a pre-experience questionnaire using a digital survey tool on their own mobile phone or using supplied iPad devices. From each group, eight participants at a time were moved into their own 3 m by 3-m square area then fit with a Meta Quest 2 virtual reality headset. The VR experience took approximately 20 min, then they completed a post-experience questionnaire.

## 3.3 Instruments and Data Preparation

The Dispositional Empathy with Nature scale [12] was used as a pre-experience questionnaire. This instrument contains nine Likert-scale items. A post-experience questionnaire instrument was developed to measure perceived embodiment in addition to the empathy measure used in the pre-experience questionnaire. Embodiment was measured using the Avatar Embodiment Questionnaire [2] which contains 25 Likert-scale items in subscales for body location, ownership, agency, motor control, and appearance.

From the data collected from 43 participants, 2 were dropped from analysis due to mismatching codes used to link the two questionnaires. 8 additional participants were dropped from comparison analysis due to missing empathy measures in the pre-experience questionnaire. Values for the Likert items were scaled so neutral responses = 0, minimum responses = –4, and maximum = 4.

## 4 Results

Results for the embodiment scores and empathy scores were plotted using histograms to ensure normally shaped results. Pairwise t tests were conducted on pre- and post-experience empathy scores to determine if a significant change in that score took place following the VR experience. Pearson's correlation was used to test for correlation between the post-experience embodiment and empathy scores. No outliers are seen in the embodiment nor empathy scores calculating z-values with a cutoff of 3 standard deviations.

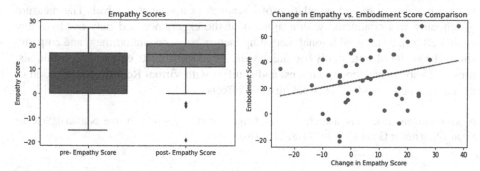

**Fig. 2.** A boxplot of the pre- and post-experience Empathy and a scatterplot of embodiment vs. change in empathy

To verify that the VR intervention was able to produce an experience of embodiment of a Adélie penguin we analyze the post-experience embodiment scores. The minimum possible score is $-100$ and the maximum possible score is 100. The mean embodiment score was 27.21 (std $= 21.40$), clearly in the positive range, which suggests an affirmative answer to RQ1, does the experience effectively produce an embodied experience of an Adélie penguin?

Empathy Score has a minimum possible score of -36 and a maximum of 36. A t test shows significant pre/post difference ($p = 0.0056$) increasing the mean score from 8.58 to 14.37 (see Fig. 2). This suggests an affirmative answer to RQ2, does the experience produce measurable increases in empathy for Adélie penguins?

Change in empathy scores were positively correlated with the participants' embodiment scores (see Fig. 2). Pearson's correlation coefficient is calculated to be 0.264, a low correlation. Calculating R-squared, we see that embodiment accounted for 7.0% of the variance in changes between pre- and post-experience empathy. This suggests an affirmative answer to RQ3, does increased embodiment correlate with an increase in empathy?

## 5 Discussion

This research demonstrates that design direct embodiment of a penguin is possible in VR, as shown by an overall positive score for this construct, which extends prior findings [10] and contributes to our understanding of designing VR for animal embodiment. This effect may be due to the visuomotor synchrony and gesture congruency afforded by the penguin skeleton. As penguins stand upright and have their flippers to the sides, a mapping of the participants arm location to flippers is possible. Additionally, this research demonstrates that a 20-min experience can increase children's situational empathy toward penguins. Finally, a correlational relationship was found between embodiment and empathy, with greater embodiment associated with increased changes in empathy, suggesting the relationship may be causal and should be further explored.

This research is limited by several factors. The sample size was small and drawn from a potentially biased population of attendees of a science festival. The measure of empathy was conducted within minutes of the experience and may not have any lasting effects. Finally, additional mediating factors between embodiment and empathy should be explored, potentially beginning with a predisposition to empathy with animals, previous knowledge about penguins, and comfort with Virtual Reality. The addition of a control group would aid in isolating these effects.

**Acknowledgements.** This material is based upon work supported by the National Science Foundation under Grant No. (2028478, 2116046).

# References

1. Black, J.B., Segal, A., Vitale, J., Fadjo, C.L.: Embodied cognition and learning environment design. In: Jonassen, D.H., Land, S.M. (eds.), Theoretical Foundations of Learning Environments (2nd ed). Routledge (2012)
2. Gonzalez-Franco, M., Peck, T.C.: Avatar embodiment. Towards a standardized questionnaire. Front. Robot. AI **5**, 74 (2018)
3. Jen, T., Lee, S., Cosic, L., Askew, R., Daniel, B., Enyedy, N.: Friends as Flowers: How Perspective-Taking and Empathy Transform Children's Relationships to Science and Nature, p. 8 (2021)
4. Johnson-Glenberg, M.C.: The necessary nine: design principles for embodied VR and active stem education. In: Díaz, P., Ioannou, A., Bhagat, K., Spector, J. (eds.) Learning in a Digital World, pp. 83–112. SCI. Springer, Singapore (2019). https://doi.org/10.1007/978-981-13-826 5-9_5
5. Krekhov, A., Cmentowski, S., Krüger, J.: The Illusion of Animal Body Ownership and Its Potential for Virtual Reality Games (arXiv:1907.05220). arXiv (2019)
6. Melcer, E.F., Isbister, K.: Bridging the physical divide: a design framework for embodied learning games and simulations. In: Proceedings of the 2016 CHI Conference Extended Abstracts on Human Factors in Computing Systems, pp. 2225–2233 (2016)
7. Nathan, M.J.: Foundations of Embodied Learning: A Paradigm for Education. Routledge, London (2021)
8. Pimentel, D., Kalyanaraman, S.: The effects of embodying wildlife in virtual reality on conservation behaviors. Sci. Rep. **12**(1), 6439 (2022)
9. Rativa, A.S., Bakker, P.G.A., Rativa, A.S.: Animal embodiment: embodying a beaver in immersive virtual environments to create empathy and teach about the impact of global warming in a playful way. In: Virtual Reality International Conference ConVRgence (2022)
10. Sierra Rativa, A., Postma, M., van Zaanen, M.: Try walking in my paws: is it possible to increase empathy, immersion, and perceived pain in virtual reality environments by manipulating animal character appearance? SSRN Electron. J. (2022)
11. Swim, J.K., Bloodhart, B.: Portraying the perils to polar bears: the role of empathic and objective perspective-taking toward animals in climate change communication. Environ. Commun. **9**(4), 446–468 (2015)

12. Tam, K.-P.: Dispositional empathy with nature. J. Environ. Psychol. **35**, 92–104 (2013)
13. Young, A., Khalil, K.A., Wharton, J.: Empathy for animals: a review of the existing literature. Curator Mus. J. **61**(2), 327–343 (2018)

# A Virtual Reality Volumetric Music Video: Featuring New Pagans

Gareth W. Young[✉]

Trinity College Dublin, Dublin, Ireland
YoungGa@tcd.ie

**Abstract.** Music videos are creative short films that showcase songs and visuals for both artistic and promotional purposes. With advancements in technology, modern music videos now use various techniques and post-production tools to offer diverse and engaging experiences for audiences on multiple devices. One such technology, volumetric video (VV), is gaining popularity in capturing and reproducing live musical performances in 3D as volumetric music videos (VMVs). These 3D reproductions are designed to provide cutting-edge audiovisual entertainment for both traditional 2D screens and emerging extended reality (XR) platforms like augmented and virtual reality (AR/VR). However, the impact of VMVs on virtual production techniques is still uncertain and evolving. In this short paper, we describe the creation of a unique VMV that applies VV for presentation via VR and hypothesize on what this means for future music productions and serious game technologies.

**Keywords:** Virtual Reality · Volumetric Video · Music Video

## 1 Introduction

In this work, we demonstrate a volumetric music video (VMV) presented in virtual reality (VR) that aims to explore volumetric video (VV) representations of music performances using VR technology. It serves as a sophisticated and interactive music video that can be accessed and presented through various XR platforms, showcasing new workflows for capturing, editing, and accessing VMVs for virtual production. Through this approach, we aim to gain a better understanding of how the industry can harness this technology from a serious games perspective, demonstrating how professionals are likely to react to music videos in an XR context and providing insights into virtual simulations for interactive digital media training and research.

Virtual production techniques that use XR technology can be considered serious gaming as such technology can be used to create interactive virtual environments (IVEs) for serious games. Serious gaming typically refers to games that are designed for a specific purpose beyond entertainment, such as education, training, simulation, or research [9,20]. While virtual production techniques

Supported by V-SENSE and Volograms.

can be used in these contexts, they require inherently designed interactions for them to function effectively. Rather, virtual production techniques that use XR technology are primarily used in film, television, and other forms of media production to create immersive, interactive, and dynamic environments. Still, the use of XR technology in virtual production can create opportunities for new forms of serious gaming, such as virtual simulations for training or research [1, 2]. In our demonstration, we hope to show the potential of this technology in future interactive VV serious game applications.

## 2   Background

The rapid resurgence of VR technology [3] has led to a new quest for novel ways to visualize and communicate musical performance, driven by artistic creativity, technological innovation, and the desire to capture the attention of new and existing audiences. It has been widely acknowledged that artificial reality is the definitive technological expression of the postmodern condition; therefore, it is possible to express postmodernist art representations within VR [12, p.169].

The use of XR technology in virtual production has created opportunities for new forms of serious gaming, where studio professionals and learners can interact in real-time with the virtual world in a highly immersive and realistic way [4]. With XR technology, virtual production can simulate real-world environments and enable the player to experience them in a fully immersive way [2]. This can enhance the realism and engagement of the gameplay, allowing players to feel as though they are truly influential in the game world.

One example of this is the use of virtual production and XR technology in creating training simulations for industries such as aviation [7], healthcare [11], and the military [11]. By using VR or AR headsets, trainees can practice complex procedures and scenarios in a safe and controlled environment, without the risk of causing harm or damage. This help to reduce training costs and improve the effectiveness of training programs [6]. Overall, the use of XR technology in virtual production can create exciting opportunities for new forms of serious gaming, as well as other forms of interactive and immersive media. By combining the power of virtual environments with real-time rendering, motion capture, and other cutting-edge technologies, virtual production using XR is poised to revolutionize the way we create and experience media.

Another example of serious gaming using XR technology is in the field of interactive digital media education [5]. VR and AR can be used to create interactive learning experiences that can engage students in a way that traditional methods cannot. For example, virtual field trips can be created that allow students to explore historic sites, and scientific phenomena, or even travel to other countries, all without leaving the classroom [19]. This can not help to make learning more engaging and accessible for students of all ages and backgrounds but can be used to educate new media practitioners about the natural affordances of immersion and presence via XR technology.

In this project, we present an immersive VMV as an emergent art form, using various XR technologies such as stereoscopic and 360-degree audiovisual spatial recording technology [13]. These capture technologies have expanded the viewing experience beyond the traditional medium and provided new dimensions of immersion, interaction, and imagination for the audience, with advancements in home PC GPU/CPU speeds, HMD optics, software data processing capabilities, and AI being closely tied to these advancements [18].

Informed by the study of XR and VMVs [15], we have designed a custommade VV VR music video experience, featuring the New Pagans' track *Lily Yeats*, with a user-centered design approach. The project's pilot study has highlighted specific qualities that audiences seek when consuming such materials [15]. Further iterations of this application have focussed on the differences between traditional media and new XR experiences and build upon existing studies in human-computer interaction (HCI) that focus on music, haptics, and technology in use [8], specifically, those examining how users experience and potentially learn about virtual production from music videos presented via 6 DoF XR technologies [17].

## 3   Technical Description

VV is a technique used to capture a three-dimensional representation of a real-world object or scene, including people, objects, and environments [14]. It involves capturing a large number of images or video frames of the object or scene from multiple angles using an array of cameras or sensors, and then processing and combining the data to create a three-dimensional representation that can be viewed from any angle [10]. VV is different from traditional video in that it allows the viewer to move around and explore the object or scene in three dimensions as if they were actually there. This makes VV an ideal technology for creating immersive experiences in virtual and augmented reality, as well as for other applications such as video conferencing, gaming, and training.

One of the benefits of VV is that it allows for the creation of realistic, lifelike representations of people and objects that can be used in a variety of contexts [16]. For example, VV can be used to create virtual actors for film and video games or to create training simulations for industries such as healthcare and aviation. However, creating high-quality VV requires a significant amount of time, expertise, and resources. It typically involves using specialized equipment and software to capture and process the data and requires a team of experts to oversee the entire process. Despite these challenges, VV is an exciting and rapidly developing technology that has the potential to transform the way we interact with the world around us.

VMVs are a type of music video that uses VV technology to capture a three-dimensional representation of a live music performance. VMVs allow viewers to experience the music performance in an immersive and interactive way as if they were actually present at the performance. In a VMV, the performer or performers are recorded using an array of cameras or sensors from multiple angles, capturing a three-dimensional representation of the performance. This data is then processed and combined to create a three-dimensional video that can be viewed from any angle, providing a highly immersive experience. One notable example is the musician and producer Travis Scott, who collaborated with Fortnite, an online video game, to create a virtual concert experience called "Astronomical" in April 2020. The concert utilized volumetric technology to render Travis Scott's performance as a 3D model and project it within the game environment, providing an immersive experience for the players.

VMVs are a relatively new technology and are still being explored and developed. However, they have the potential to revolutionize the way we experience music performances, allowing us to feel like we are truly part of the performance and providing new opportunities for artists to connect with their fans. There are many different ways that VMVs can be used, including as part of a promotional campaign for a new album or single, as a way to provide a more engaging and interactive concert experience for fans, or as a way to preserve live performances for future generations. Overall, VMVs are an exciting development in the world of music and entertainment and are likely to become more common as XR technology continues to develop and evolve.

## 4   New Pagans Capture Process

The VV capture process utilizes photogrammetry principles to create a 3D volumetric model with texture for each video frame. The New Pagans musicians, Lyndsey McDougall and Cahir O'Doherty (Fig. 1) were recorded separately performing in the VV capture studio using twelve video cameras. The cameras were positioned in each corner of the performance space and recorded against a green-screen backdrop. The videos from each camera were synchronized to ensure that the captured gestures on one camera aligned with the same frame number on any other given camera. The audio was recorded separately and played back during the VV capture performance, matching the video files' length and playback speed. This method simplified the post-production chroma-keying processes.

The process for creating VV involves recording individual camera clips of a performance, trimming and aligning them, then segmenting the central performance figure to generate a silhouette for each frame. This data is then input into a postproduction process that uses 3D reconstruction algorithms to create dynamic 3D models, which are merged using a bespoke combinational method. The resulting VV assets are imported into the Unity game engine using a custom-built SDK and played back at a standard video frame rate of 30fps to create the illusion of movement. Although VV technology has limitations, it allows for high-fidelity capture and display of musicians and enables the creation of immersive and interactive music video content. The VR experience can be accessed via OpenXR, an open standard for multiple VR platforms and devices.

A demonstration of the potential of this technology for VMV production can be seen at the following link: https://youtu.be/0Q8zUpefKt8.

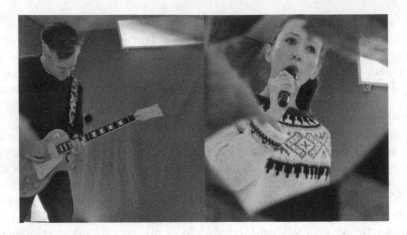

**Fig. 1.** New Pagans performing in the capture studio

## 5    Advantages and Disadvantages of Using VV

VVs can be used to create immersive and realistic content, but they have distinct advantages and disadvantages. VV captures the entire 3D scene, including depth information, allowing for a highly realistic and immersive representation of the environment – this makes it well-suited for applications with crucial spatial contexts, such as architectural visualization and virtual tourism. By capturing the physical object within the main scene, VV reduces the need for extensive post-processing to animate or rig characters, saving time and resources in the production pipeline. Furthermore, unlike some motion capture (MOCAP) systems, it does not require actors or objects to be outfitted with markers or motion capture suits, reducing setup time and allowing for more natural and unencumbered performances. Finally, VVs can be interactive, allowing users to explore and interact with the captured scene from different angles. It can also accommodate dynamic scenes with moving elements, making it suitable for interactive storytelling and gaming.

Conversely, VV generates large amounts of data due to its three-dimensional nature – this requires significant processing power and storage capacity, which can increase production costs. VV may also not capture fine details as effectively as traditional MOCAP, especially for close-ups of characters or objects. MOCAP often provides more precise control over individual body parts. Capturing complex characters with intricate facial expressions and detailed movements can be challenging in VV, particularly compared to MOCAP techniques targeting detailed character animation.

Another point of contention is the uncanny valley – this refers to the phenomenon where humanoid objects or characters that closely resemble humans trigger feelings of eeriness or discomfort when they fall short of looking completely realistic. Both volumetric video and motion capture can impact the perception of the uncanny valley in different ways.

In the pursuit of addressing the uncanny valley phenomenon, the advantages of VV lie in its capacity to capture a holistic 3D environment, engendering a realistic spatial context that aids in attenuating the unsettling effect. Furthermore, its ability to capture natural movements and facilitate interactive engagement with the environment lends a sense of fluidity and immersion that mitigates potential imperfections in individual character animations. However, VV may encounter limitations in preserving intricate details, particularly concerning facial expressions and nuanced character animations, which can hinder the attainment of heightened realism. In contrast, MOCAP offers precise and detailed character animations, including subtle facial expressions, that contribute to bridging the uncanny valley gap. Additionally, MOCAP provides animators with granular control over character performances, enabling adjustments to avoid unnatural movements. Yet, this advantage is juxtaposed by the potential for artifacts or distortions resulting from markers or suits used in the process. Moreover, the restricted focus of MOCAP on movements may inadvertently detach characters from their environmental context, potentially accentuating the uncanny valley effect. Consequently, the choice between VV and MOCAP as tools for managing the uncanny valley effect hinges upon specific project demands and the intricate interplay of realism, interactivity, and contextual fidelity.

## 6 Conclusions

XR technology has been a game-changer for virtual production, offering a range of tools and techniques for creating immersive and interactive experiences for film, television, and gaming. In virtual production, XR can be used to create virtual environments that are indistinguishable from real-life, allowing filmmakers to create anything they can imagine. Virtual production techniques that use XR technology can indeed create opportunities for new forms of serious gaming. Whether it's in the areas of training, education, or entertainment, the use of XR technology can enhance the immersive and realistic experience of the player, leading to more effective and engaging gameplay.

**Acknowledgments.** This publication has emanated from research conducted with the financial support of Science Foundation Ireland (SFI) under Grant Number 15/RP/2776 and the Horizon Europe Framework Program (HORIZON), under grant agreement 101070109. The volumetric video content for the music video was generated by Volograms (www.volograms.com). More information about New Pagans and their music can be found at www.newpagans.com.

## References

1. Aldrich, C.: The Complete Guide to Simulations and Serious Games: How the Most Valuable Content will be Created in the Age Beyond Gutenberg to Google. John Wiley & Sons, Hoboken (2009)
2. Checa, D., Bustillo, A.: A review of immersive virtual reality serious games to enhance learning and training. Multimed. Tools Appl. **79**, 5501–5527 (2020)

3. Evans, L.: The Re-Emergence of Virtual Reality. Routledge, London (2018)
4. Kavakli, M., Cremona, C.: The virtual production studio concept-an emerging game changer in filmmaking. In: 2022 IEEE Conference on Virtual Reality and 3D User Interfaces (VR), pp. 29–37. IEEE (2022)
5. Meyer, O.A., Omdahl, M.K., Makransky, G.: Investigating the effect of pre-training when learning through immersive virtual reality and video: a media and methods experiment. Comput. Educ. 140, 103603 (2019)
6. Naranjo, J.E., Sanchez, D.G., Robalino-Lopez, A., Robalino-Lopez, P., Alarcon-Ortiz, A., Garcia, M.V.: A scoping review on virtual reality-based industrial training. Appl. Sci. 10(22), 8224 (2020)
7. Oberhauser, M., Dreyer, D.: A virtual reality flight simulator for human factors engineering. Cogn. Technol. Work 19, 263–277 (2017)
8. Paterson, J., Wanderley, M.M.: Feeling the future-haptic audio. In: Arts, vol. 12, p. 141. MDPI (2023)
9. Susi, T., Johannesson, M., Backlund, P.: Serious games: an overview. Technical report HS- IKI -TR-07-001 (2007)
10. Valenzise, G., Martin, A., Zerman, E., Ozcinar, C.: Immersive Video Technologies. Academic Press, Cambridge (2022)
11. Viglialoro, R.M., Condino, S., Turini, G., Carbone, M., Ferrari, V., Gesi, M.: Augmented reality, mixed reality, and hybrid approach in healthcare simulation: a systematic review. Appl. Sci. 11(5), 2338 (2021)
12. Woolley, B.: Virtual Worlds: A Journey in Hype and Hyperreality. Penguin, London (1993)
13. Young, G.W., O'Dwyer, N., Smolic, A.: A virtual reality volumetric music video: featuring new pagans. In: Proceedings of the 13th ACM Multimedia Systems Conference, pp. 331–333 (2022)
14. Young, G.W., O'Dwyer, N., Smolic, A.: Volumetric video as a novel medium for creative storytelling. In: Immersive Video Technologies, pp. 591–607. Elsevier (2023)
15. Young, G.W., O'Dwyer, N., Moynihan, M., Smolic, A.: Audience experiences of a volumetric virtual reality music video. In: 2022 IEEE Conference on Virtual Reality and 3D User Interfaces (VR), pp. 775–781. IEEE (2022)
16. Young, G.W., O'Dwyer, N., Smolic, A.: Exploring virtual reality for quality immersive empathy building experiences. Behav. Inf. Technol. 41(16), 3415–3431 (2022)
17. Young, G.W., O'Dwyer, N., Vargas, M.F., Donnell, R.M., Smolic, A.: Feel the music!-audience experiences of audio-tactile feedback in a novel virtual reality volumetric music video. In: Arts, vol. 12, p. 156. MDPI (2023)
18. Young, G.W., Smolic, A.: Extended reality: music in immersive XR environments: the possibilities (and approaches) for (AI) music in immersive XR environments. In: Artificial Intelligence and Music Ecosystem, pp. 68–82. Focal Press (2022)
19. Young, G.W., Stehle, S., Walsh, B.Y., Tiri, E.: Exploring virtual reality in the higher education classroom: using VR to build knowledge and understanding. J. Univ. Comput. Sci. 26(8), 904–928 (2020)
20. Young, M.F., et al.: Our princess is in another castle: a review of trends in serious gaming for education. Rev. Educ. Res. 82(1), 61–89 (2012)

# Soft and Social Skills

# Power Core Values: Teaching Racial Bias Awareness Through a Stealth Game and Workshop

Michael G. Christel[✉], Angelina Shi, James Finkel, Hannah Baxter, Hsuan-Ju Wang, Yuchan Wu, Ricardo Washingon, Bryan S. Maher, and John Balash

Carnegie Mellon University, Pittsburgh, PA 15213, USA
christel@cmu.edu

**Abstract.** This paper outlines the design and development of a stealth game that appears to be about solving puzzles to achieve a launch from a space station, but in addition presents a number of unfair situations to cause reflection about and promote awareness of racial bias. 16 teens ages 13–14 played the game and took part in a follow-up workshop to talk through their gameplay. This combination of a serious game followed by workshop discussion led to significant differences in both the consideration of "hurt" toward gameplay characters, and in awareness of racial privilege as measured by the Color-Blind Racial Attitudes Scale.

**Keywords:** serious game · stealth game · racial bias · racial privilege

## 1 Introduction

Race, ethnicity and ancestry are part of all our backgrounds, yet societies may not give the same privilege and opportunities equally across all groups. Our differences along these lines can be difficult to talk about [1]. Being aware of microaggressions and other hurts that are not distributed evenly can foster empathy and compassion between groups. Such positive action, if taken with our youth, may help to counter hateful actions that permeate our news. For example, in the United States an analysis of hate crime victims of single bias incidents in 2021 showed over 64% were due to race/ethnicity/ancestry [2]. How can we get teens ages 13–14 to think about and talk about race, when such discussions are often avoided or trigger an immediate socio-political reaction before the argument is even stated? This paper discusses a stealth game, "Power Core Values", designed for teens as a "fix the spaceship" game but offering a springboard into much deeper discussion about racial bias and privilege.

The target demographic of eighth grade, ages 13–14, was chosen because it is an age when the teens can understand the issues and immediately precedes the American high school years when many school districts move their students into another building. Getting students to think through empathetically the hurts distributed amongst their peers can lead to an improved high school climate for all. Educators suggest that there should be opportunity given to this age group to talk about race [3, 4]. This paper presents the design, development, and delivery of a game and workshop to promote such discussion.

The design direction is that of a stealth persuasive game, one that uses an embedded approach for "circumventing a player's psychological defenses and triggering a more receptive mindset" [5]. It is a basic human tendency to resist persuasive communications that are perceived as too forceful or forthright in their intentions, as argued in [6] with evidence from social psychological theory. These authors continue that another psychological barrier for persuasion and play, especially when dealing with sensitive behaviors of stereotypes and prejudice, is the bias blind spot: the acknowledgment that biases exist but the denial or minimization of one's own susceptibility to those biases. So, "persuasive games may fail to engage players or are unable to immerse players in a transformative experience, due to normal psychological human reactions to overtly 'message-driven' interventions" [6]. The design of "Power Core Values" uses the suggested stealthier approach in presenting a message about racial injustice, taking these authors' approach to addressing the topic in a more nuanced, less direct fashion.

## 2   Core Values, A Role Play Game

Five graduate students (second through sixth co-authors on this paper) designed and created a Unity WebGL game for desktop browsers titled "Power Core Values", with a development blog and the game link and workshop teacher's guide available on their project website [7]. The game only requires mouse clicks and arrow keys for interaction, with the general premise being that you are the captain of a spaceship needing repair and you land at a space station to get assistance. Your Robot Companion (R.C.) is with you to assist, and the puzzles surrounding the broken spaceship as shown in Fig. 1 are the driving premise for the game. You cannot fix the spaceship, i.e., solve the puzzles, without help from the engineers on the space station, and you navigate through various environments to find help.

The goal of the game is to pursue help to solve the puzzles to lead to the fixed state shown in Fig. 2. Success is only possible by getting two different engineers, Nanoi and Zun, to come into the spaceship to solve its puzzles with you. Finding and soliciting their help gets the player to witness environmental settings and other narratives in the space station. Players can trigger additional information related to environmental assets like signs, and can initiate conversations with the non-playable characters through talk bubble clicks (Fig. 3). Such encounters fuel discussion for a follow-up workshop that surface injustices in the game's world, connecting them to racial bias and racial privilege topics. This game plus workshop for skills transfer follows published advice to tie the learning from a serious game to other contexts through post-game discussion [8].

The space station is populated by two racial/ethnic groups: pink characters and purple characters. Nanoi is a pink character, Zun is purple. In all other aspects (e.g., body shape, gender) these two are the same – the difference expressed in character art and characters in the environment is meant to foster discussion focused on skin tone rather than other attributes. The pink group has privilege in representation and status, a majoritized group in the space station, while the purple group is marginalized. Illustrated discussion from the pilot study will make this dichotomy clearer.

**Fig. 1.** Early scene in "Power Core Values": you as the Captain, plus R.C., with numerous subsystems (puzzles) keeping your ship in a broken state in the space station dock.

**Fig. 2.** Success in "Power Core Values": you as the Captain with your repaired ship, accomplished with earlier help from Nanoi and from later help with Zun (shown here).

The workshop was designed with help from subject matter experts in eighth grade education and racial bias. As the game is a 15 to 20-min experience, the workshop was designed to take 30–40 min so that the educational session of game plus workshop would fit within an hour. The language used is appropriate for 13 to 14-year olds. For example, the opening activity asks what the point of "Power Core Values" is, in part to surface its stealth nature. The next activity derives from advice on how to teach microaggressions indirectly [4]. Subsequent activities push into R.C. as a prominent character making

**Fig. 3.** Player can click on environment triggers and non-playable character (NPC) triggers to further interact with people and objects in the space station.

many biased remarks, and inviting in discussion on any topic tied to an environmental or non-playable character (NPC) encounter.

A teacher's guide for running the workshop is shared along with the game link at the project website [7] for others wishing to play the game and run the workshop with their after-school clubs or classes. This paper presents the results from the first pilot study investigating whether the game and workshop can foster awareness and change in its players.

## 3  Pilot Study

### 3.1  Subjects and Procedure

Eighth graders from one racially diverse school district in the Pittsburgh, PA USA area were recruited by their teachers to participate in a field trip for a "game plus workshop" study held at the local university. 17 students signed on, but one was absent for the day of the event, leaving 16 subjects. The subjects were given a paper pre-intervention survey to fill out before the event, which also included demographic questions on race and gender. They played the game within an approximate 20-min window, and then participated in a 30-min workshop facilitated by the first author. They concluded by filling out a post-intervention paper survey, the same one they filled out to start the study. Their gameplay actions were tracked using Unity Analytics. Consents for this study, including workshop participation, the surveys, and game tracking, were received from parents/guardians in advance of any subject action. The study received university Institute Review Board approval before any recruitment.

The self-reported demographics for the subjects were 9 male, 5 female, and 2 non-binary/third gender; 8 White, 4 Mixed Race, 3 Black, and 1 Asian. Two players did not bring their paper pre-intervention survey, and had to start the session by first doing the survey and then played faster through the game, in a 9-min window rather than 20-min window. Future studies will likely present the survey instruments electronically and require them in advance of the game to sidestep this issue. Fourteen players followed the instructions and did the pre-intervention survey in advance.

Along with the two demographic questions, the survey presented Likert scale questions covering the short-form Color-Blind Racial Attitudes Scale (CoBRAS) appropriate for American students, 20 questions across three factors [9], rated from strongly disagree (1) to strongly agree (5):

1. Unawareness of Racial Privilege
2. Unawareness of Institutional Discrimination
3. Unawareness to Blatant Racial Issues

One change was made to the scales: they were adjusted to be five point instead of six points to match other scales in the survey. The expectation was that the game-plus-workshop may show change in the subjects on Factor 1, as that was covered in the environment and NPC interactions (see Fig. 3). A short nine to twenty-minute game experience may not be deep enough to get into many examples of institutional discrimination, and "blatant" racial issues may be more challenging to design into a stealth game. We concentrated on delivering an experience and teaching moments regarding racial privilege. The seven questions for the Unawareness of Racial Privilege factor are as follows (the full 20 questions are discussed in [9]), with all but (a) reverse-scored (i.e., strongly disagree becomes 5, disagree 4, ..., strongly agree 1):

a) Everyone who works hard, no matter what race they are, has an equal chance to become rich.
b) Race plays a major role in the type of social services (such as type of health care or day care) that people receive in the U.S.
c) Race is very important in determining who is successful and who is not.
d) Racial and ethnic minorities do not have the same opportunities as White people in the U.S.
e) White people in the U.S. have certain advantages because of the color of their skin.
f) White people are more to blame for racial discrimination in the U.S. than racial and ethnic minorities.
g) Race plays an important role in who gets sent to prison.

The survey instrument also included the Multigroup Ethnic Identity Measure (MEIM) [10] (12 scales), the Toronto Empathy Questionnaire [11] (16 scales), and these four perceived racial discrimination questions:

- During your life, how often have you felt that you were treated badly or unfairly in school because of your race or ethnicity?
- Did you witness anyone being treated badly or unfairly in school because of their race or ethnicity?
- During the past 6 months, how true is the following: People said mean or rude things about me because of my race or ethnic group.
- During the past 6 months, how true is the following: People cracked jokes about people of my race or ethnic group online, on TV, or in the newspaper.

All subjects were able to finish the paper survey instrument in under 10 min.

## 3.2 Playing the Game

Subjects played the game in the same computer lab, but with each subject sitting with their own desktop computer, screen, and mouse. Each subject entered a unique ID to start the game which was captured in the game action metrics. Subjects were told to take as long as they wanted in the game, but two knew they had less time to play (given they did not do their pre-intervention survey ahead of time). The two playing quickly finished in their nine-minute window. The other fourteen played a minimum time of 10:47, maximum 21:18, and average 15:39 with the game. Referring to Fig. 3 and the optional activities, subjects triggered side characters (NPCs) an average of 7.7 times (8.1 if you only consider the 14 subjects with the full game play time), and clicked the environment triggers an average of 3.4 times (3.9 for the 14) a game session. The NPCs were more popular game action targets than the environmental assets.

The main gameplay is dialogue interactions with the main characters R.C., Nanoi, and Zun, as well as those initiated with other NPCs. There was an average of 71 dialogue interactions per game session (73 for the 14 subjects with ample time). All 16 players fixed their spaceship (Fig. 2) and won the game.

## 3.3 Post-Game Workshop

The workshop was conducted in the same computer lab where the subjects just finished playing the game. The facilitator opened with the prompt to briefly describe the game, in a sentence or so. The voiced comments stated and reinforced the statement that this was a game about fixing a spaceship (Figs. 1 and 2). When asked to raise hands about what this game was, all agreed to this statement and suggested nothing further. This confirms the design choice to make this a stealth game: at its face it appears to be a puzzle game about fixing a spaceship.

That opening activity led nicely to discuss the two engineers who were needed to fix the spaceship, and which had to be interacted with by all players in order to succeed. Every subject was given two half sheets of paper: one with Nanoi (pink) and one with Zun (purple) printed on them. The facilitator noted that a slide show will be shown illustrating situations that can happen in the game, stating "You may or may not have seen this yourself as you played. For each situation, if you think Zun would be hurt by it, add a fold to the Zun paper. If you think Nanoi would be hurt, add a fold to Nanoi. If both are hurt, add a fold to both. If neither are hurt by that situation, add a fold to neither." Situations shown to the students included those massed together in Fig. 4, but they were shown separately rather than in a cluster of four. Sometimes, one illustration (slide) was talked about to present a number of situations. The verb "hurt" is intentionally left vague, i.e., to the student's judgment, to lead into further discussion.

The results were dramatic, as shown in Fig. 5 and discussed further in the results section. Across all 16 players, there were only 6 Nanoi folds to indicate a "hurt" to Nanoi versus 109 for Zun, an average of 0.38 versus 6.81.

The workshop facilitator continued with the procedure outlined in [4] for teaching microaggressions and support networks. Subjects were asked to smooth the cards out as best they can. The facilitator noted: "The creases in the paper are the hurts a character experiences when they are subjected to bias. Smoothing the paper out represents actions

**Fig. 4.** Four of the slides used to illustrate situations to the subjects in the workshop. From upper left and in clockwise order, situations were (1) Founder's Day poster; Customer Service Rep referring you to Nanoi instead of the closer Zun; (2) R.C. stating that Zun cannot be trusted based on its programming; (3) 100 Greatest Innovators poster being all pink; parents discussing their kids' different college acceptance outcomes; poster of Galaxy Center Tech; Commercial District having resources including lighting and plants; (4) Side District having a purple Bot Enthusiast; Side District having lights that don't work and less lighting and maintenance;.

we can take to address racial bias in our life and our communities. Smoothing the paper represents the help we can get from support networks like parents and friends. These actions can help heal some of that hurt, but the hurt doesn't go away completely."

Every student's card set may have a different number of folds, as hurt can mean different things to different people. But the consistent message regarding the difference in hurt between Zun and Nanoi is picked up on by the subject group: something else is problematic in the space station besides the broken space ship. The audience became engaged to discuss more, in part because the tactile nature of this folding activity using the characters from the game surfaced the stealth messaging: pink and purple people are not treated the same nor have the same privilege on the space station.

For this particular group, asking "who are you" as a prompt elicited a response of "the person in the space suit" (e.g., see Fig. 1). What if you are pink? What if you are purple? Such extra prompts caused reflection but not much else with this pilot group. Showing an image of R.C. prompted a raucous outburst of "R.C. is racist!" R.C. repeatedly rejects Zun as an engineering resource in favor of Nanoi at first, and then in favor of giving up (see Fig. 6).

This led into a fruitful discussion of why is R.C. that way, where did his programming come from, the data for that programming, issues of representational bias, data bias, and artificial intelligence (AI) bias. The facilitator took that discussion into the suggested teacher guide activity of what might R.C. stand for – Reality Controller? What might a Reality Controller be? News and social media were mentioned, as were family groups

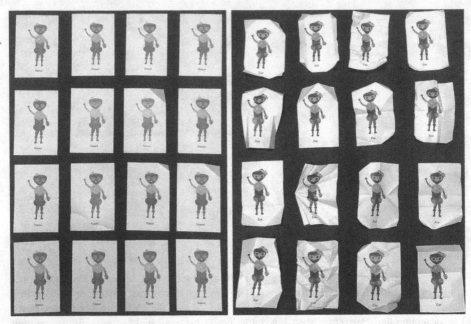

**Fig. 5.** Outcome of the folding activity where 16 subjects folded neither, one, or both of Nanoi (left) and Zun (right) when they would be "hurt" by a presented situation.

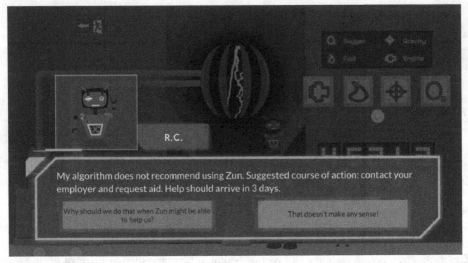

**Fig. 6.** R.C. tells the player, again, not to use Zun to fix the spaceship. Such skewed dialogue becomes the source material to launch into discussion about racial bias.

of different generations, and this deepened the discussion about sources of information and potential bias. Dialog strands within the game, such as R.C. stating "My creators programmed me to take in data to build profiles of people. I then use these profiles to give recommendations to my user on people that are most likely to be qualified" contributed to the workshop discussion.

The subjects were invited in to bring up other characters they would like to talk about, with Fig. 7 showing that set of options. There also was the environment itself, with differences between the Side District populated by more purple people and the more resourced Main Commercial District being the input for discussion.

Player Character    R.C. (Robot Companion)    Guardian    Eager Kid

Customer Service    Bot Enthusiast    Proud Parent    Diligent Parent
Representative

**Fig. 7.** Characters in the game with dialogue and actions that could be discussed further during the workshop to surface more conversation about race and racial bias.

The concluding remarks to the workshop bring back Nanoi and Zun, their skill sets, environments, and other context from the game. Figure 8 shows again that Nanoi in the well-resourced main area gets a review/ratings board, which in turn could lead to an AI model promoting Nanoi to be recommended as qualified. Zun is in a less resourced area with no such board, perhaps no way to easily get or share reviews, and without that is perhaps left unevaluated and hence never recommended as qualified from a system like R.C. The subjects conclude that their game was more than just fixing their spaceship, but also revealed a space station with other problems.

## 4  More Results and Discussion

### 4.1  Surveys

An analysis of the pre-intervention (before game and workshop) and post-intervention surveys was conducted, looking for statistically significant results of $p < 0.05$. The expectation that there would be a difference in awareness of racial privilege, Factor 1

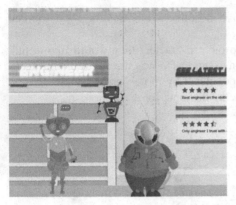

**Fig. 8.** The two engineers, Nanoi (left) and Zun (right), do not share equal resources, potentially leading to other inequities on the space station.

of CoBRAS [9, 12], was met. The results from the pre-test (M = 24.69, SD = 3.8) and post-test (M = 22.19, SD = 6.2) Unawareness of Racial Privilege (Factor 1 CoBRAS) resulted in an improvement in awareness of racial privilege, $t(15) = 2.16$, $p < 0.05$. (A lower number means less unawareness, i.e., greater awareness.) Seeing and discussing differences in the circumstances of Nanoi and Zun, and between the pink and purple people of the space station, surfaced awareness of racial privilege. The difference in "hurt" folds shown in Fig. 5 between Nanoi (M = 0.38, SD = 0.48) and Zun (M = 6.81, SD = 1.81) was highly significant, $t(15) = 14.1$, $p < 0.0001$.

This is only a pilot study with few subjects, but we still wanted to explore whether the change in awareness was perhaps isolated to a particular demographic. The improvement in awareness of racial privilege happened across all the racial groups in our sample: Asian, Black, Mixed Race, and White – an interesting result that we hope will hold when we test the game and workshop on larger subject pools. All four showed a decrease in this measure.

Of the four questions regarding perceived racial discrimination questions, one produced a significant result. The results from the pre-test (M = 1.69, SD = 0.8) and post-test (M = 2.06, SD = 1.0) "During your life, how often have you felt that you were treated badly or unfairly in school because of your race or ethnicity?" resulted in an increase (Never 1, Rarely 2, Sometimes 3, Most of the Time 4, Always 5) from mid-Never/Rarely to Rarely, $t(15) = -2.42$, $p < 0.05$. Perhaps the exercise of folding in the workshop raised awareness that microaggressions can be hurtful, too, and led to a broadening in thinking about unfair treatment. Perhaps it was reflection on the game actions surrounding Nanoi and Zun. Future studies may include opt-in survey elements to deepen the understanding as to why some of these changes occurred after the game-plus-workshop intervention. As with the CoBRAS result, the change was evident across the different racial group subsets and not a result caused by just a subset of the subjects' racial groups.

There were no significant results from the Toronto Empathy Questionnaire (TEQ). In retrospect, the TEQ was designed with data from college-age students [11] and there are recommendations to use it with ages 16+ [13]. Our subjects were younger, ages 13–14. Hence, the language used and situations described might not have fit the younger audience or been interpreted properly by them, e.g., one of the TEQ scales asked a rating for "Other people's misfortunes do not disturb me a great deal" which is a challenge to parse. A different empathy survey instrument appropriate for teens will be sought out for future work to measure whether there is any change in empathy brought about by the game-plus-workshop.

The wording for self-reporting race/ethnicity use here was simplified, and that too could be corrected by future research with this game and workshop. Reporting race/ethnicity/ancestry is a challenge! Because of simplified wording, the reading of the Multigroup Ethnic Identity Measure scales was likely made more ambiguous, and there were no significant results from the MEIM. Subjects may have interpreted the terms both too narrowly and too broadly, resulting in noise for this measure.

Establishing race/ethnic identity could be improved through suggestions offered at [14], e.g., starting with an introductory explanation about race/ethnicity and labels that make sense for that given country, as in "In this country, people come from many different countries and cultures, and there are many different words to describe the different backgrounds or ethnic groups that people come from. Some examples of the names of ethnic groups are Hispanic or Latino, Black or African American, Asian American, Chinese, Filipino, American Indian, Mexican American, Caucasian or White, Italian American, and many others. These questions are about your ethnicity or your ethnic group and how you feel about it or react to it." That explanatory text was not present in this pilot study's survey instrument, and likely should have been. The same is true for a simple open-ended fill-in-the-blank label for your own ethnic group, as in "In terms of ethnic group, I consider myself to be (fill-in-the-blank)" allowing complete freedom. Further structure for identification can be asked separately with census-like categorization for ethnicity in additional questions for yourself and your parents (if such data is known) [14].

There is a call for more clarity of language and markers with respect to race/ethnicity/ancestry [15], and a recent article notes the challenges of collecting and reporting race and ethnicity with many U.S. studies defaulting to U.S. census wording, even though the census is only every 10 years and has political undertones as well [16]. We will follow the latest recommendations regarding survey instruments probing further with respect to racial/ethnic identity in future studies.

## 4.2 Game Metrics

Game logs show the branching dialogue choices made by all the players. The 16 subjects could not stop the biased behavior of R.C. in their gameplay, but they did have the freedom to respond differently to Zun at the game's conclusion. They could apologize for R.C.'s actions in a few ways. They could own up to more responsibility and state "I'm sorry I didn't stop R.C. from making those comments earlier" (chosen by 5) or could state instead "I wanted to apologize about how R.C. treated you" (chosen by 6). They could also not respond with an apology when asked by Zun "Well, I have to get back. I have more work to do. Unless there's anything you need?" Then after the "Well, if you're sure that's all…" prompt from Zun the player can exit without any apology with a simple "Bye, Zun" (chosen by 5). That latter path results in a wrap-up statement from Zun "I know that there are things left unsaid between us and that it isn't easy to begin talking about these things." An apology gets Zun to state "Thank you for your apology. Most people pretend stuff like that doesn't happen." As was done with another stealth game on racial bias, character dialogue can seed follow-up discussion points on the topic [17]. Subjects are not acting in complete harmony throughout the narrative structure, and that individual choice leaves room for discussion in the workshop. This example prompts a discussion on whether to apologize to Zun, and if so apologizing in what way.

With only 16 subjects in this pilot study, there is too little data to drill into subsets of player actions with respect to survey results, e.g., to see if there are different shifts in awareness of racial privilege based on how subjects act in this ending opportunity to apologize. There also is not enough data yet to show trends from past play with large groups of players: which NPCs were talked with, what environmental triggers clicked, what choice made with Zun at the end. Showing these trends as part of the workshop may trigger additional discussion opportunities, much like graphs of player choices did with the game in [17] to facilitate post-game group discussion. As "Power Core Values" gets played more, its metrics can fuel further discussion about racial bias awareness.

## 5   Future Work and Conclusion

"Power Core Values" and its workshop led to dramatic demonstration about the understanding of racial bias presented in the narrative text and environmental art of a role-playing WebGL game. Players universally recognized significantly more injustice toward Zun, the purple engineer character, in this game than toward Nanoi, the pink engineer character. After this activity and further workshop discussion, the post-intervention survey instrument showed significant changes about awareness of racial privilege and on a question related to unfair personal treatment because of race or ethnicity. The stealth game worked in that the desired social outcomes for the game were achieved: the players' eyes were opened to racial injustice in the game's space station and connected that out to microaggressions and racial privilege.

There is the challenge of presenting any authenticated questionnaire regarding race in a pre-intervention survey with respect to the stealth game approach: the preponderance of race/ethnicity questions may tune the subject toward the topic at hand. We felt that in this pilot study, the game played out as a puzzle game first and foremost based on the participants' voiced descriptions of what they just did in the workshop opening. We will consider other experimental designs and options to further investigate the contributions of survey wording toward results and toward any interference with the designed stealth game approach.

Future work of course needs to bring in a longitudinal measure: there is an immediate effect, but are the lessons of Zun and Nanoi held a week or a month later? Does the awareness of racial privilege hold? Might there be other measures regarding race/ethnic identity, e.g., affirmation, belonging, and commitment from MEIM, that could register a significant difference if the subjects were better instructed as to the meaning of these terms and given more freedom into how to self-identify into a group on such survey instruments? What remains with the subjects well after the experience is played and the workshop is run?

The intervention could also be studied: what if only the game were studied without the workshop. That exercise may be only academic, as subjects stated that "Power Core

Values" was about fixing a spaceship. The stealth game without the benefit of a workshop to drive home pedagogical points may miss its mark. As noted elsewhere [8], a workshop after a digital game play can amplify the effect of the game.

The embedded approach to teach topics on race to 13 to 14-year olds shows promise from this pilot study. This age group may resist such instruction for all the reasons noted in [5, 6] along with difficulties of people (in the United States at least) to talk through race and racial privilege [1, 3]. A stealth game can give players experience in the material, experience which a follow-up workshop can leverage for activities and discussion that will surface awareness of racial bias.

**Acknowledgements.** This work was supported by the Collaboratory Against Hate of the University of Pittsburgh and Carnegie Mellon University. Ming-Te Wang and HyungJik Lee of the University of Pittsburgh designed the survey instruments used here and were instrumental themselves in getting seed funding for this project.

# References

1. Oluo, I.: So You Want to Talk About Race. Seal Press, Seattle (2019)
2. U.S. Dept. of Justice: Bias motivation categories for victims of single bias incidents in 2021: over 64% due to race/ethnicity/ancestry, https://www.justice.gov/hatecrimes/hate-crime-statistics (2021)
3. U.S. National Education Association Center for Social Justice: 10 Principles for Talking About Race in School (2020). https://www.nea.org/professional-excellence/student-engagement/tools-tips/10-principles-talking-about-race-school
4. Boddapati, S.: How to teach kids about microaggressions. In: On Our Sleeves: The Movement for Children's Mental Health (2021). https://www.onoursleeves.org/mental-health-resources/minority-mental-health/how-to-teach-kids-about-microaggressions
5. Kaufman, G., Flanagan, M.: A psychologically "embedded" approach to designing games for prosocial causes. Cyberpsychol.: J. Psychosoc. Res. Cyberspace **9**(3), Article no. 5 (2015). https://doi.org/10.5817/CP2015-3-5
6. Kaufman, G., Flanagan, M., Seidman, M.: Creating stealth game interventions for attitude and behavior change: an 'embedded design' model. In: Hera, T. Dela, J. Jansz, J. Raessens, B. Schouten: Persuasive Gaming in Context, Chapter 5. Amsterdam University Press, Amsterdam (2021). https://doi.org/10.5117/9789463728805_ch05
7. STEMspire: Carnegie Mellon University Entertainment Technology Center project website, https://projects.etc.cmu.edu/stemspire/. Accessed 10 June 2023
8. Lim-Fei, V., Woo, H., Lee, M.: Serious games to develop social and emotional learning in students. In: Marsh, T., et al. (eds.) JCSG 2016, LNCS, vol. 9894, pp. 3–12. Springer, Heidelberg (2016). https://doi.org/10.1007/978-3-319-45841-0_1
9. Neville, H., Lilly, R., Duran, G., Lee, R., Browne, L.: Construction and initial validation of the Color-Blind Racial Attitudes Scale (CoBRAS). J. Couns. Psychol. **47**(1), 59–70 (2000)
10. Phinney, J.: The multigroup ethnic identity measure: a new scale for use with adolescents and young adults from diverse groups. J. Adolesc. Res. **7**, 156–176 (1992)
11. Spreng, R., McKinnon, M., Mar, R., Levine, B.: The Toronto empathy questionnaire: scale development and initial validation of a factor-analytic solution to multiple empathy measures. J. Pers. Assess. **91**(1), 62–71 (2009)

12. CoBRAS Short and Long Forms, https://liberationlab.education.illinois.edu/docs/libraries provider10/default-document-library/cobras-short-and-long-forms296d7c3980b76a29a33 dff05008a8698.pdf?sfvrsn=5cda1688_0. Accessed 10 June 2023
13. TEQ: Toronto Empathy Questionnaire. https://embrace-autism.com/toronto-empathy-questi onnaire/. Accessed 10 June 2023
14. The Multigroup Ethnic Identity Measure (MEIM). https://www.facs.nsw.gov.au/__data/ assets/pdf_file/0004/536755/MEIM-questionnaire-Authors-summary.pdf. Accessed 10 June 2023
15. Lu, C., Ahmed, R., Lamri, A., Anand, S.: Use of race, ethnicity, and ancestry data in health research. PLOS Glob Public Health **2**(9), e0001060 (2022). https://doi.org/10.1371/journal. pgph.0001060
16. Chen, Y., Smith, A., Reinecke, K., To, A.: Why, when, and from whom: considerations for collecting and reporting race and ethnicity data in HCI. In: Proceedings of 2023 CHI Conference on Human Factors in Computing Systems (CHI 2023), Article 395, pp. 1–15. Association for Computing Machinery, New York (2023)
17. Huang, A., Fu, Y., van Leeuwen, D., Wu, L., Sebus, S., Song, Y., Bidarra, R.: Stranded: a classroom game for implicit bias elicitation and recognition. In: Proceedings of ISAGA 2022 - 53rd Conference on International Simulation and Gaming Association (2022)

# Through a Gender Lens: A Serious Game for Young Children to Enhance Bullying Awareness and Encourage the Adoption of the Defender Role

Attracta Brennan[1]([✉]) [iD], Caroline Manghan[1], Mary Dempsey[2] [iD], John McAvoy[3] [iD], and Sam Redfern[1] [iD]

[1] School of Computer Science, University of Galway, Galway, Ireland
Attracta.Brennan@universityofgalway.ie
[2] School of Mechanical Engineering, University of Galway, Galway, Ireland
[3] Business Information Systems, University College Cork, Cork, Ireland

**Abstract.** Bullying is a global issue that threatens the safety and wellbeing of children worldwide. While bullying is observed amongst children of all ages, the behavior peaks at ages 11–14 years. One intervention method is through the use of games. 23 mixed-gender children aged 7–11 years participated in this study, which examines the impact of Cairdeas Quest, a fantasy serious game, on increasing bullying awareness and how to respond in different bullying situations. Through an analysis of gameplay metrics, the results show that Cairdeas Quest positively impacted the identification of bullying/cyberbullying and the selection of appropriate responses in various bullying situations. All participants correctly selected the defender role in response to bullying and indirect cyberbullying in the hallway and bedroom scenes. However, the main issue concerned how to respond to verbal bullying in a classroom. In general, female players were more empathic than their male peers in different bullying/cyberbullying situations and were more likely to adopt the defender role. Meanwhile, a greater level of improvement was evidenced in the male players after playing Cairdeas Quest. This is a positive outcome as boys are more likely to adopt the bully perpetrator and bystander roles.

**Keywords:** Bullying · defender role · children

## 1 Introduction

Bullying is a serious issue faced by many children across the world and is regarded by the WHO as a major health problem [1]. Between 40 and 55% of students worldwide have been involved in some form of bullying [2]. Victims of bullying can experience negative mental health effects including depression and anxiety; they are also at increased risk of self-harm, suicide, suicide ideation and lower academic achievement [2–5]. Bullying has been defined as "aggressive, intentional acts carried out by a group or an individual repeatedly and over time against a victim who cannot easily defend him or herself" (p. 241) [6]. Bullying is a group phenomenon, consisting of a perpetrator, victim, bystander, and bully-victim [7]. Bystanders make up the majority of the bullying group and can be categorised as; assistant (to the bully), reinforcer, defender and outsider [8–10]. Negative bystander behavior is demonstrated by explicitly supporting the perpetrator through joining in the bullying behavior (assistants) or giving the perpetrator social rewards through laughter (reinforcers) [11, 12]. In general, outsiders/passive bystanders tend to stay quiet and not intervene [7, 8, 11] while defenders tend to display positive bystander behavior by aiding the victim e.g. confronting the perpetrator [13]. The negative bystander behavior displayed by assistants, reinforcers and outsiders can cause the bullying to be repeated [7]. Bully-victims are a distinct group who typically have experienced both the perpetrator and victim roles. Perpetrators and bystanders of bullying commonly experience depression and suicide ideation [10, 14]. Studies show that: more boys than girls tend to adopt bullying roles [15], more girls take on defender roles and more boys adopt reinforce roles [16].

Cyberbullying is a distinct form of bullying which takes place via technology [17]. It has increased in prevalence due to the widespread use of technology among the Generation Z cohort [2, 18, 19]. Cyberbullying is defined as "using information and communication technologies (ICT) to repeatedly and intentionally harm, harass, hurt and/or embarrass a target" (p. 359)[20]. Direct/private cyberbullying can include email and direct messages [21]. In indirect or public cyberbullying, perpetrators typically post the offending material in public spaces which are more visible to a wider audience [20]. Unlike traditional bullying, cyberbullying perpetrators can easily hide their identity, thus making it more difficult for victims to defend themselves [20]. The effects of cyberbullying can often be more insidious than traditional bullying and affect all areas of a victim's life, potentially leading to psychological stress, physical harm, suicide ideation and/or suicide [22]. The perpetrator, victim, bystander and bully-victim roles also occur in cyberbullying [13]. While not conclusive, studies show that girls have a greater likelihood of being cyber victims [16]. Bullying and cyberbullying interventions help to protect children's rights and health [2]. Interventions can include: awareness campaigns, talks, educational videos and serious games [23]. With the goals of teaching, augmenting awareness, and effecting behavioral change [24], serious games have been used successfully in many settings; from dyslexia to dyscalculia [25]. A recent systematic review of 33 serious games focusing on bullying, outlined a paucity of games targeting bullying and cyberbullying in more than one setting; scientific tests validating the games' findings; and a gender comparison of the results [2].

In this study, 23 children aged 7–11 years played Cairdeas Quest, a fantasy serious game comprising settings which are most prone to bullying (e.g. locker room, bedroom, classroom and hallway). The results are analysed through a gender lens. Note: Cairdeas is the Irish word for friendship.

# 2   Cairdeas Quest

The Cairdeas Quest game design process followed the methodology of [26]. This comprised:

*Define the Game Topic and Learning Objectives.* Cairdeas Quest addresses bullying and cyberbullying awareness by teaching children to: (a) distinguish between different verbal bullying, physical bullying, and cyberbullying in different settings and (b) select appropriate responses to the bullying behavior. The goal of Cairdeas Quest is to increase awareness of bullying and reinforce the need for all children, especially boys, to adopt the defender role in bullying situations especially given the greater likelihood that boys are bully perpetrators.

*Choose an Appropriate Game Genre.* The platform genre having fantasy components was selected for this target audience (Fig. 1). Studies show that games with fantasy components are particularly attractive to younger children [26], as they encourage exploratory behavior [27]. Cairdeas Quest makes use of dragons, parchment scrolls, and fantastical character attire and landscapes. Malone's Theory of intrinsically motivating instruction also contends that fantasy is a core element of motivation [28].

**Fig. 1.** Platform view 1 & 2.

*Create a Story for the Game, Taking into Consideration the Topic, Learning Objectives, Target Audience and Game Genre.* In Cairdeas Quest, the game quest narrative concerns the invasion of the Cairdeas kingdom by bullies. The player is presented with an explicit objective: assist Davy Dragon (Fig. 2) to stop bullying and collect the stolen kindness coins which are dispersed throughout the game. A counter in the top left of the game screen, displays how many coins have been collected. While traversing the platform, the player must avoid the purple enemies, called Bully Blobs. If they come in contact with a Bully Blob (Fig. 3), the player's character turns red before being bounced backwards. The player also loses a life. Although the kindness coins and Bully Blobs do not serve an educational purpose, they are designed to encourage the player to continue playing and increase their enjoyment, in line with findings by [29, 30].

Fig. 2. Davy Dragon.

Fig. 3. Billy Blob.

Fig. 4. Being transported to the next scene.

Fig. 5. Game characters.

*Define the Mechanics, Dynamics, and Experience of the Player.* Cairdeas Quest was designed as a one-player game in order to mitigate feelings of anxiety, which, according to [31] can occur when competing against other players. Cairdeas Quest makes use of graphics having bright colors to attract younger children [32]. If a player loses their life after falling off the platform, they are brought to the nearest save point. There are four save points embedded in the game. These save points are designed so that players do not need to answer scenario questions which they have already completed. Before Davy Dragon transports the player to the various bullying/cyberbullying scenes (Fig. 4) -which studies suggest are where bullying most frequently takes place - the player must select from six available characters, two of whom were designed with traditionally feminine characteristics, two with traditionally masculine features and two with gender non-conforming characteristics. All were created to look like children (Fig. 5). Studies suggest that avatars that are more ethnically similar to the player are often viewed to be more trustworthy [33]. In a review of more than 500 games targeting children, less than 35% of games contained child characters [34]. In those games that featured child characters, they were mainly in a supporting role. Cairdeas Quest features the child as the primary protagonist in the game.

After selecting the player character, Cairdeas Quest tests the player's knowledge of how to respond in different bullying scenarios. This requires them to respond to three statements which focus on a different type of bullying (Table 1) (Fig. 6).

**Table 1.** Statements.

| Statement | Bullying situation |
| --- | --- |
| S1. I would tell a parent or teacher about a bully even if they might bully me next if I tell | A bullying situation when the bystander is concerned they may become the next target. While bystanders are present in at least 85% of bullying incidents, they typically defend the victim in 19% of cases [8] |
| S2. It's okay to text funny jokes about the way a friend looks if the friend doesn't know | Cyberbullying |
| S3. It's okay to push little kids if they are in your way | Physical bullying. Children who experience traditional forms of bullying, including physical bullying, often experience depression and anxiety as adults [5] |

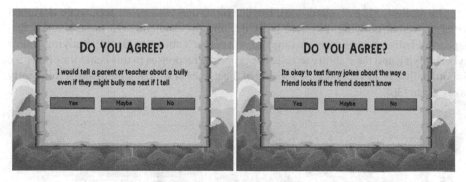

**Fig. 6.** Statements 1 & 2.

Once gameplay commences, the player is brought to an area where they can jump from platform to platform collecting kindness coins. Davy Dragon also transports them to the Forest scene which is both the first and last scene in Cairdeas Quest. The Forest Scene comprises six bullying scenarios (Table 2) compared to each of the remaining four scenes which comprises only one scenario.

For each scenario in the Forest scene, the player must identify whether bullying is occurring. The identification of what constitutes bullying (i.e. bullying awareness) is an important step in teaching children to combat bullying [35]. In subsequent scenes, the player is rewarded with points if they correctly identify bullying else they lose points and must re-attempt the question. Players are not allowed to proceed with the quest until they answer the questions correctly. Players are rewarded or penalised with points on their first attempt only. Once the player has chosen a correct response, they are prompted to learn more or immediately return to the platform and continue their quest. If they opt to learn more, they are presented with a short explanation of the bullying being demonstrated in the scene and the best manner in which to respond. If the player has more questions, they are directed to reach out to a trusted adult. Telling the bully to stop and telling an adult are the strongest predictors of a positive outcome to bullying [17].

**Table 2.** Forest scene bullying scenarios.

| Scene | Type of bullying | Scenario |
|---|---|---|
| 1 | Physical isolation | Mike won't ever let Todd play tag because Todd is in a wheel chair |
| 2 | Cyberbullying | Jen posts a picture online that calls Mea with a funny picture of her pets ugly |
| 3 | Physical bullying | Lisa keeps touching Bri's hair after Bri asks her to stop |
| 4 | Physical bullying | Nick pranks Annie every day by putting her book out of reach |
| 5 | Verbal bullying | Alex tells the whole class that Drew picks his nose, even though it's not true |
| 6 | No bullying | Lea sends you a snapchat |

The Hallway (Fig. 7), Bedroom, Locker room and Classroom scenes are designed to target verbal bullying, physical bullying, and cyberbullying. In these scenes, two aspects of bullying awareness are targeted: the player's ability to identify bullying and/or cyberbullying and their ability to select appropriate responses to this behavior (Table 3). School hallways are recognised to be one of the places in which bullying most frequently takes place [36].

**Fig. 7.** Hallway scene.

The Bedroom scene is an example of indirect cyberbullying in the home environment. This scene also illustrates how bullying can take place without the victim being present

**Table 3.** Hallway scene – in person, physical bullying.

| Scenario: Dan just pushed Lee in the school hallway | | |
| --- | --- | --- |
| Reaction | Bystander type | Correct answer |
| Tell A Teacher | Defender | Yes |
| Join the laughter | Reinforcer | No |
| Say "That's not nice!" | Defender | Yes |

[37]. The scenario; *'Mary and Meg are filming a TikTok with jokes about the way Joe walks'* comprises a number of reactions illustrating defender and reinforcer roles. TikTok was chosen due to its popularity among children [38].

Bullying commonly takes place in Locker rooms [36]. In contrast to the Bedroom scene (in which the cyberbullying is posted to a wider audience via social media), the Locker room scene offers an example of direct cyberbullying where the cyberbullying takes place via text messaging and in a school setting. The scenario is *'You just got a text from John calling Tom a loser and saying that he should quit the team'*. The range of reactions illustrates; defender, assistant and reinforcer roles. Unlike the previous scenario-based scenes, there is only one correct answer. This was designed to introduce an additional challenge as the player progresses. The use of challenges is a key component to Malone's Theory of Intrinsically Motivating Instruction which contends that varying challenge within a game increases uncertainty and thereby increases players' feelings of efficiency and competence [28, 39, 40].

Bullying incidents also frequently take place in classrooms [36]. In the Classroom scene, the bully calls the victim names (i.e. in-person verbal bullying). The associated scenario is; *'Harry called James stupid. All your friends are watching but no one is saying anything'*. The range of reactions illustrates; defender, outsider and assistant roles. In this scenario, the correct answer encourages the player to take up the defender role by coming to the victim's aid. When outsiders do not aid the victim, it is generally because they do not want to be the next victim [7, 8]. However, such behavior can encourage bullying to continue [16].

The player must select the correct answer in the Hallway, Bedroom, Locker room, and Classroom scenes before proceeding. They are also required, later in the game, to repeat the scenes with which they had most difficulty. In these repeated scenes, the player is presented with a slightly different scenario which addresses a similar type of bullying (Table 4). Repetition is considered to be one of the essential qualities of play from a child's perspective [41]. Repetition can also increase player motivation, as players are more likely to be successful in subsequent gameplay iterations [42].

**Table 4.** New scenarios.

| Scene | New scenario |
|---|---|
| Hallway | Dan just shoved Liam into the lockers |
| Bedroom | Mary and Meg posted a Snapchat story of Joe falling over |
| Locker room | You just got a text from John making fun of Tom's looks |
| Classroom | Harry just called James a mean name. Your classmates are all laughing |

## 3 Method

### 3.1 Research Approach

The research for this pilot study adopts a Case Study approach; this allows the researcher to explore a specific topic for the purpose of understanding a larger issue [43]. An advantage of the Case Study method is that it supports the use of both qualitative and quantitative data. In order to confirm the relevance of a research topic, [44] recommends consulting outside experts. One of the school's teachers, who has been teaching for almost 20 years, in addition to a special education teacher and the parents of a child, provided input into Cairdeas Quest regarding the relevance of the research topic and the game's design.

### 3.2 Research Stages

This pilot study is composed of three stages: (1) a focus group session involving three children who played a prototype version of the game; the aim was to assess user experience, (2) 23 children played Cairdeas Quest, and (3) the players completed an end of game usability survey. Note. All questions were approved in advance by the primary school teacher and a parent representative.

### 3.3 Participants

The children who participated in this study attend a mixed gender primary school whose pupils have diverse socio-economic and cultural backgrounds. After presenting the Cairdeas Quest game, each child was given a description of the study, outlining its aims and research approach to bring home to their parents. 23 children's parents consented to their children's participation. These children ranged in age from 7–11 years. This was the selected target age as bullying is more prevalent in primary school children aged 6–11 than in secondary schools [45]. Of the 23 participants, 14 were boys and 9 were girls. Seven years was chosen as the bottom range of the target player group as Cairdeas Quest requires children to be able to read and understand the presented bullying scenarios. Cairdeas Quest was designed using vocabulary and sentence structures at level H in Fountas-Pinnell reading levels [46]. Children aged 7–11 years typically read between the H and M levels [47]. There was no evidence of bullying/cyberbullying behaviour (either as victim or perpetrator) amongst the children. Note: All children were informed that they could absent themselves from the pilot study at any time [48]. All data was anonymized.

### 3.4 Data Collection

Cairdeas Quest comprises; bullying awareness tests (pre and post gameplay), bullying response gameplay metrics, an end of game usability survey and a focus group session, with the former three approaches being directly embedded within the game. Other gameplay metrics which are collected include; character chosen, number of correct answers in identification scenes, number of attempts used to correctly answer scenario scenes, and number of lives collected at game end. Note: the pre-post survey method is commonly used in evaluating serious games designed for bullying [49]. Furthermore, tracking in-game choices can help identify whether or not a player is able to apply specific knowledge to game situations [50]. In compliance with GDPR, all players were assigned random IDs. Game play data was captured in real time and stored in a Firebase Real-time Database. Quantitative data was analysed using IBM SPSS V 26 with the statistical significance being set at $p < 0.05$. Where qualitative data was provided, its analysis was primarily at the level of semantic themes. Thematic analysis at the semantic level is defined as an examination of "...the explicit or surface meanings of the data" (p. 84)[51].

## 4   Results

### 4.1   Stage 1: Focus Group

"Small focus groups are one of the best ways to obtain data from children" (p. 150)[48]. Meanwhile, the use of focus group sessions helps to create "a safe peer environment for children" (p. 2)[52]. Three children (one boy and two girls aged 9, 8 and 10 years respectively) played a prototype Cairdeas Quest game. All three children agreed that the game was easy to use. They reported that they were able to navigate without any help from adults. All children completed the game. However, one child indicated that "*the names of the characters are too difficult to read*" (a female aged 8 years). She reported that this negatively impacted her enjoyment of Cairdeas Quest. The other two children said that while they were able to read the names, they thought that they were too difficult to pronounce. Revisions to the game included altering characters' names. When asked about their favorite part of the game, "*I like squishing the [Bully Blobs]!*" (a girl aged 8 years); "*Flying with Davy Dragon*" (a boy aged 9 years) and "*The Forest Identification Scene and being challenged to answer as many questions as they could*" ( a girl aged 10 years).

### 4.2   Stage 2: Cairdeas Quest

The Forest scene determines the player's level of bullying awareness i.e. ability to detect bullying. Players were required to play the Forest scene twice; once at the beginning of Cairdeas Quest and again at the end. The results from the pre-bullying awareness test (i.e. pre-test), and post bullying awareness test (i.e. post-test) are shown in Table 5. The percentage of correctly answered questions increased from 34.8% to 47.8% (pre-test to post-test). The average number of correctly answered questions increased from 4.8 questions to 5.8 questions for the male players and 6.7 questions to 7 questions for the female players. There were 18 additional correct answers after playing Cairdeas Quest. The Shapiro-Wilk Test for Normality resulted in a pre-test p-value of 0.0006 and a post-test p-value of 0.0002, thereby indicating that the differences between the pre- and post-test data are statistically significant from the normal distribution.

**Table 5.** Pre and post-test results summary.

|           | Average # correct answers | Median | σ    | All 8 questions correct |
|-----------|---------------------------|--------|------|-------------------------|
| Pre-test  | 5.52                      | 5      | 2.08 | 34.8%                   |
| Post-test | 6.3                       | 7      | 2.24 | 47.8%                   |

In the post-test, 91% (n = 23) of the players performed the same or better than the pre-test. On average, players experienced a 20.08% increase in score from the pre-test to the post-test. The male players (n = 14) had 15 additional correct answers compared to three additional correct answers from the female players (n = 9). Excluding two players (a boy and a girl both aged 8 years) who saw a reduction in the number of correct answers after playing Cairdeas Quest; all players increased their score after gameplay. Meanwhile, in the 8 year age bracket, female players outperformed male players in bullying awareness both before and after playing Cairdeas Quest (pre-test average of 5.66 Vs 4.9 and post-test average of 6.67 Vs 6.37).

The male players showed the greatest level of improvement overall. Excluding the two outliers (i.e. a male player aged 8 years who scored 3 and 0 in the pre and post tests respectively, and a female player aged 8 years who scored 8 and 3 in the pre and post tests respectively), the results of the Wilcoxon Signed Rank Paired Test showed a statistical significance in the pre- and post-test data regarding bullying awareness for all players (p = .0022), male players (p = 0.0) and all players aged 8 years (p = 0.0).

As outlined, prior to gameplay, players are required to answer three statements designed to evaluate their knowledge of bullying before playing the game (Table 6). The results from this analysis indicate that before playing Cairdeas Quest, proportionately more female players (78%) than male players (65%) indicated that they would assume the defender role.

After playing Cairdeas Quest, the gameplay metrics showed that all players answered all questions correctly for the Hallway and the Bedroom scenes (i.e. they correctly selected the defender's responses to physical bullying and indirect cyberbullying). 91.3% of players (n = 23) answered the Locker room scene correctly on their first attempt (i.e. they correctly identified the defender response to direct cyberbullying). However, two players (a boy and a girl, aged 8 and 11 years respectively) selected the outsider and the assistant responses to the direct cyberbullying incident in the Locker room scene. Both of these players answered all other scenes correctly on their first attempt.

**Table 6.** Correct answers to the three statements.

| Statements | Correct answers | |
|---|---|---|
| | Males (n = 14) | Females (n = 9) |
| S1. I would tell a parent or teacher about a bully even if they might bully me next if I tell | 57% | 89% |
| S2. It's okay to text funny jokes about the way a friend looks if the friend doesn't know | 71.4% | 77.8% |
| S3. It's okay to push little kids if they are in your way | 78.6% | 77.8% |

The Classroom scene had the lowest rate of correct answers (i.e. 14% of players answered incorrectly on their first attempt). Three players (two girls, both aged 10 years, and one boy aged 8 years) incorrectly identified outsider and assistant responses to the verbal bullying incident. Of the two outliers from the pre- and post bullying awareness tests, one male player (aged 8 years) did not identify the correct response to '*it's okay to text funny jokes about the way a friend looks if the friend doesn't know*', whilst also performing poorly on how to respond to verbal bullying in a classroom situation. Meanwhile, a female player (aged 8 years) scored 100% in both the pre-game bullying response survey and the in-game bullying response survey respectively.

The Shapiro-Wilk Test for Normality resulted in a pre-game bullying response score p-value $< 0.001$ and an in-game bully response score p-value $< .001$, thereby indicating that the differences between the pre-game bullying response scores and the in-game bullying response scores are not normally distributed. The Wilcoxon Signed Rank Paired Test p-value of 0.009 showed that the difference is statistically significant (Table 7).

**Table 7.** Results of the Wilcoxon Signed Rank test on response to bullying situations.

| Group | # | p-value |
|---|---|---|
| All players | 23 | 0.009 |
| Female players only | 9 | .339 |
| Males players only | 14 | .014 |
| Players aged 8 years | 16 | .008 |
| Players aged 7, 9 and 10 years | 7 | .679 |

## 4.3 Stage 3: End of Game Usability Survey

Whilst the number of children who participated in the study was small (n = 23), this number exceeds the requirements for preliminary usability testing (i.e. 5)[53]. The usability survey (activated at the conclusion of Cairdeas Quest) asks the players three mandatory questions (i.e. *Was this game fun? Did you like the dragons and fantasy theme? Did this game help you learn more about bullying?)* and three optional questions i.e. *What did you like about Cairdeas Quest? What did you dislike about Cairdeas Quest?* And *Did you feel represented by your game character?*. 100% (n = 23) of the players said that they enjoyed gameplay. *"It's really awesome"* (a girl aged 10 years). 95.6% of the players indicated that: the game was fun, and that they liked the dragon and the fantasy theme. When asked if the game helped them learn more about bullying, players said they liked how, through gameplay; *"You learned about how you bully and how to stop it"* (a girl aged 10 years), *"It's like a video game to review bullying which makes it more fun"* (a boy aged 8 years), *"Telling what's better to do when someone is bullying!"* (a boy aged 8 years). These findings are in line with [54] who contend that serious games support players in learning real life skills in a safe place, free from fear of retribution [55]. In answer to the question regarding what they liked about Cairdeas Quest, the responses included; *"I liked collecting the gold"* (a boy aged 8 years), *"The dragon"* ( a boy aged 8 years), *"I liked flying up with a dragon"*, (a girl aged 8 years), *"The Quest"* (a boy aged 8 years), *"I liked picking my own character. I liked that there were so many options"* (a girl aged 8 years), *"When the dragon came and took me flying"*(a boy aged 9 years) and *"I liked answering the questions. I only got one wrong!"* (a girl aged 10 years.) When asked what they disliked about Cairdeas Quest; the two responses were; *"It's too short"* (a boy aged 8 years), and *"I wanted more coins"* (a girl aged 8 years). Above all, a game must be usable [56] with an essential component of usability being a reading level that matches the player's level of comprehension [57].

Although some female players chose traditionally masculine avatars, no male players chose traditionally feminine avatars. Indeed, the majority of players chose characters whose traits aligned with their own gender. In a study of greater than five million avatar choices, female players demonstrated a stronger preference for similar gender representation than their male counterparts [58]. The results from the survey indicated that participants felt represented by their game character/avatar (100%). This is important as identification with the selected avatar has a positive effect on enjoyment and flow within a game [59].

# 5   Discussion

Studies indicate that girls are equally as likely to experience bullying as boys [4]. The results of this pilot study showed that the female players tended to be more aware of and empathic to bullying and cyberbullying situations than their male counterparts. However, the male players showed greater improvement in bullying awareness after playing Cairdeas Quest, although they were still slightly below the level of awareness expressed by the female players. The female players demonstrated greater knowledge of a correct response to bullying situations in the pre-game bullying response survey. This is in line with findings from [24]. After playing Cairdeas Quest, both genders improved in their knowledge of how to respond in bullying situations, with male players outperforming female players in the in-game bullying response survey. This is a positive outcome as boys are more likely to adopt the bully perpetrator and bystander roles [15, 16].

Once the two outliers were excluded from the data, the statistical significance between the pre- and post-tests showed the effectiveness of Cairdeas Quest as an intervention to improve bullying awareness for all participants (p = 0.002), male players only (p = 0.0) and all players aged 8 years (p = 0.0). Why Cairdeas Quest was more effective as a bullying intervention for male players compared to female players warrants further exploration.

Although bystanders make up the majority of the bullying group and are present in at least 85% of incidents; slightly less than 20% of youth take on the defender role [8–10]. While the results from this pilot study showed a statistically significant improvement in the male players and all those aged 8 years concerning how to respond correctly to various bullying and cyberbullying situations, proportionately more female than male players (78% versus 65% respectively) indicated that they would assume the defender role. It is critical to encourage positive defender behavior as studies show that despite self-reported anti-bullying attitudes, students rarely come to the defense of the bully victim [11].

Data captured from the end of game usability survey showed that the players reported that the scenario-based scenes helped them learn more about how to react to different types of bullying situations should they encounter a similar scenario in real life. A male player (aged 8 years) noted that bullying was a subject about which they would not typically want to learn. However, all participants agreed that as Cairdeas Quest made learning fun, they would be more likely to want to learn about bullying. When asked what she liked best about Cairdeas Quest, a female player (aged 8 years), noted "*It's like a video game to review bullying which makes it more fun.*" This is in line with findings from [60] who contend that serious games can positively affect student motivation.

# 6 Limitations

As with some studies, this study has limitations such as the sample size. While no generalisations can be derived from the accruing results, expanding the study's scope and the scale and duration of gameplay will improve the reliability and validity of the findings in future research. Future refinements to Cairdeas Quest will take into consideration additional scenes, physical and learning disabilities, race, nationality and/or colour and socio-economic and migration status; children from such categories are especially vulnerable to bullying [4]. The authors also plan to incorporate content related to the Olweus Bully/Victim Questionnaire into future scenario-based scenes [61].

# 7 Conclusions

Bullying and cyberbullying are serious issues for children and adolescents and can result in an increase in adolescent suicide rates, depression, anxiety and academic performance problems [23, 62]. Children who are victims of traditional bullying typically experience long-lasting negative effects as adults, from depression and anxiety to suicide ideation [5]. Furthermore, cyberbullying victims are nearly twice as likely to commit suicide [22]. Within a school environment, bullying incidents most frequently take place in the hallway, locker room, classroom, bathroom and/or cafeteria [36]. Bullying is least common in classrooms in which the teacher is perceived to strongly disapprove of the behavior [6].

This study presents the results from a fantasy serious game called Cairdeas Quest, which addresses bullying and cyberbullying in different settings (i.e. hallway, bedroom, locker room and classroom). As studies indicate that children are most likely to be bullied from ages 11–14 years [63], the aim of this pilot study was to evaluate the efficacy of Cairdeas Quest in enhancing (a) bullying and cyberbullying awareness, (b) knowledge of an appropriate response, in children aged 7–11 years and (c) encouraging boys to adopt defender roles. The results from the 23 participants showed statistically significant positive effects of Cairdeas Quest in increasing bullying awareness. This positive effect was evidenced in the players' ability to identify bullying in various settings as well as their ability to select appropriate responses to bullying and cyberbullying scenarios. Despite the results showing the female players to be more empathic than their male peers, there was a statistically significant improvement in the male players after playing Cairdeas Quest concerning how to respond correctly to various bullying and cyberbullying situations. This is important as the greater the number of boys who adopt a defender role, the less are the chances that bullying will occur [16].

In summary, bullying and cyberbullying intervention programmes which support the identification and prevention of bullying and cyberbullying are critical given the prevalence of bullying and the long lasting negative psychosocial and mental health effects on both the perpetrators and the victims of bullying [64]. However, such games need to incorporate those settings where bullying and cyberbullying most frequently take place. Given that so few take on the defender role in a bullying situation, games which focus on encouraging the adoption of this role especially for boys are critical.

# References

1. WHO: Social determinants of health and well-being among young people (2012)
2. Calvo-Morata, A., et al.: Serious games to prevent and detect bullying and cyberbullying: a systematic serious games and literature review. Comput. Educ. **157**, 103958 (2020)
3. Moore, S.E., et al.: Consequences of bullying victimization in childhood and adolescence: a systematic review and meta-analysis. World J. Psychiatry **7**(1), 60 (2017)
4. Armitage, R.: Bullying in children: impact on child health. BMJ Paediatrics Open **5**(1) (2021)
5. Arseneault, L.: The long-term impact of bullying victimization on mental health. World Psychiatry **16**(1), 27 (2017)
6. Menesini, E., Salmivalli, C.: Bullying in schools: the state of knowledge and effective interventions. Psychol. Health Med. **22**(sup1), 240–253 (2017)
7. Salmivalli, C.: Participant roles in bullying: how can peer bystanders be utilized in interventions? Theory Pract. **53**(4), 286–292 (2014)
8. Graham, S.: Victims of bullying in schools. Theory Pract. **55**(2), 136–144 (2016)
9. Raminhos, C., et al.: A serious game-based solution to prevent bullying. Int. J. Perv. Comput. Commun. (2016)
10. Lambe, L.J., et al.: Does defending come with a cost? Examining the psychosocial correlates of defending behaviour among bystanders of bullying in a Canadian sample. Child Abuse Negl. **65**, 112–123 (2017)
11. Lucas-Molina, B., et al.: Bullying, defending, and outsider behaviors: the moderating role of social status and gender in their relationship with empathy. Scand. J. Psychol. **59**(4), 473–482 (2018)

12. Jenkins, L.N., Nickerson, A.B.: Bullying participant roles and gender as predictors of bystander intervention. Aggress. Behav. **43**(3), 281–290 (2017)
13. DeSmet, A., et al.: The efficacy of the Friendly Attac serious digital game to promote prosocial bystander behavior in cyberbullying among young adolescents: a cluster-randomized controlled trial. Comput. Hum. Behav. **78**, 336–347 (2018)
14. Klomek, A.B., Sourander, A., Elonheimo, H.: Bullying by peers in childhood and effects on psychopathology, suicidality, and criminality in adulthood. Lancet Psychiatry **2**(10), 930–941 (2015)
15. Álvarez-García, D., García, T., Núñez, J.C.: Predictors of school bullying perpetration in adolescence: a systematic review. Aggress. Violent Beh. **23**, 126–136 (2015)
16. Coelho, V.A., Sousa, V.: Class-level risk factors for bullying and victimization in Portuguese middle schools. Sch. Psychol. Int. **39**(2), 121–137 (2018)
17. Bauman, S., Cross, D., Walker, J.: Principles of Cyberbullying Research: Definition, Methods, and Measures, p. 2013 (2013)
18. Brennan, A., Dempsey, M.: P-PAC (Partnership in Pedagogy, Accreditation, and Collaboration): a framework to support student transition to employability in industry. A lean systems case study. Manag. Prod. Eng. Rev. **9** (2018)
19. Brennan, A., Dempsey, M.: The student voice: the students own views on smartphone usage and impact on their academic performance. INTED, Valencia (2018)
20. Peter, I.-K., Petermann, F.: Cyberbullying: a concept analysis of defining attributes and additional influencing factors. Comput. Hum. Behav. **86**, 350–366 (2018)
21. Schade, B.P., Larwin, K.H., Larwin, D.A.: Public vs. private cyberbullying among adolescents. Interdiscip. Educ. Psychol. **1**(1), 5 (2017)
22. van Tiel, J.: Cyberbullying, an overlooked and ever growing danger to the development of children (2020)
23. Rončević Zubković, B., et al.: The role of experience during playing bullying prevention serious game: effects on knowledge and compassion. Behav. Inf. Technol. **41**(2), 401–415 (2022)
24. Calderón, A., Ruiz, M.: A systematic literature review on serious games evaluation: an application to software project management. Comput. Educ. **87**, 396–422 (2015)
25. Brennan, A., et al.: Cosmic Sounds: A game to support Phonological Awareness skills for children with Dyslexia. IEEE Trans. Learn. Technol. **15** (2022)
26. Silva, F.G.: Practical methodology for the design of educational serious games. Information **11**(1), 14 (2019)
27. Habgood, M.J., Ainsworth, S.E.: Motivating children to learn effectively: exploring the value of intrinsic integration in educational games. J. Learn. Sci. **20**(2), 169–206 (2011)
28. Malone, T.W.: Toward a theory of intrinsically motivating instruction. Cogn. Sci. **5**(4), 333–369 (1981)
29. Alserri, S.A., Zin, N.A.M., Wook, T.: Gender-based engagement model for serious games. Int. J. Adv. Sci. Eng. Inf. Technol. **8**(4), 1350–1357 (2018)
30. Buzady, Z.: Flow, leadership and serious games–a pedagogical perspective. World J. Sci. Technol. Sustain. Dev. **14**, 204–217 (2017)
31. Wang, J.-Y., Lin, W., Yueh, H.-P.: Collaborate or compete? How will multiplayers' interaction affect their learning performance in serious games. In: Rau, P.L. (ed.) Cross-Cultural Design. Culture and Society. HCII 2019. Lecture Notes in Computer Science, vol. 11577, pp. 482–491. Springer, Cham (2019). https://doi.org/10.1007/978-3-030-22580-3_36
32. Geslin, E., Jégou, L., Beaudoin, D.: How color properties can be used to elicit emotions in video games. Int. J. Comput. Games Technol. **2016**, 1–9 (2016)
33. Brown, A., et al.: Gender Differences when Adopting Avatars for Educational Games. In: 2021 Australasian Computer Science Week Multiconference (2021)

34. Reay, E.: The child in games: representations of children in video games (2009–2019). Game Stud. **21**(1) (2021)
35. Levine, E., Tamburrino, M.: Bullying among young children: strategies for prevention. Early Childhood Educ. J. **42**(4), 271–278 (2014)
36. Wang, K., et al.: Indicators of School Crime and Safety: 2019. NCES 2020–063/NCJ 254485. National Center for Education Statistics (2020)
37. Ferrara, P., et al.: Cyberbullying a modern form of bullying: let's talk about this health and social problem. Ital. J. Pediatr. **44**(1), 1–3 (2018)
38. Anderson, K.E.: Getting acquainted with social networks and apps: it is time to talk about TikTok. Library hi tech news (2020)
39. Park, J., et al.: GAMESIT: a gamified system for information technology training. Comput. Educ. **142**, 103643 (2019)
40. Winter, L.-C., et al.: Applying pedagogical approaches to enhance learning: linking self-regulated and skills-based learning with support from Moodle extensions. In: 2013 Second IIAI International Conference on Advanced Applied Informatics. IEEE (2013)
41. Coyne, R.: Mindless repetition: learning from computer games. Des. Stud. **24**(3), 199–212 (2003)
42. Hamlen, K.R.: Children's choices and strategies in video games. Comput. Hum. Behav. **27**(1), 532–539 (2011)
43. Crowe, S., et al.: The case study approach. BMC Med. Res. Methodol. **11**(1), 100 (2011)
44. Hulley, S.B.: Designing Clinical Research. Lippincott Williams & Wilkins (2007)
45. Cantone, E., et al.: Interventions on bullying and cyberbullying in schools: a systematic review. Clin. Pract. Epidemiol. Mental Health: CP & EMH **11**(Suppl. 1 M4), 58 (2015)
46. Ransford-Kaldon, C.R., et al.: Implementation of Effective Intervention: An Empirical Study to Evaluate the Efficacy of Fountas & Pinnell's Leveled Literacy Intervention System (LLI). 2009–2010. Center for Research in Educational Policy (CREP) (2010)
47. Parker, B.C., Myrick, F.: A critical examination of high-fidelity human patient simulation within the context of nursing pedagogy. Nurse Educ. Today **29**(3), 322–329 (2009)
48. Gibson, J.E.: Interviews and focus groups with children: methods that match children's developing competencies. J. Fam. Theory Rev. **4**(2), 148–159 (2012)
49. Calvo-Morata, A., et al.: Validation of a cyberbullying serious game using game analytics. IEEE Trans. Learn. Technol. **13**(1), 186–197 (2018)
50. Serrano-Laguna, Á., et al.: Applying standards to systematize learning analytics in serious games. Comput. Stand. Interf. **50**, 116–123 (2017)
51. Maguire, M., Delahunt, B.: Doing a thematic analysis: a practical, step-by-step guide for learning and teaching scholars. All Irel. J. High. Educ. **9**(3) (2017)
52. Adler, K., Salanterä, S., Zumstein-Shaha, M.: Focus group interviews in child, youth, and parent research: an integrative literature review. Int. J. Qual. Methods **18**, 1609406919887274 (2019)
53. Turner, C.W., Lewis, J.R., Nielsen, J.: Determining usability test sample size. Int. Encycl. Ergon. Hum. Factors **3**(2), 3084–3088 (2006)
54. Cheng, Y.-M., et al.: Investigating elementary school students' technology acceptance by applying digital game-based learning to environmental education. Australas. J. Educ. Technol. **29**(1) (2013)
55. Anastasiadis, T., Lampropoulos, G., Siakas, K.: Digital game-based learning and serious games in education. Int. J. Adv. Sci. Res. Eng. **4**(12), 139–144 (2018)
56. Moizer, J., et al.: An approach to evaluating the user experience of serious games. Comput. Educ. **136**, 141–151 (2019)
57. Lyon, N., et al.: Little Newton: an educational physics game. In: Proceedings of the First ACM SIGCHI Annual Symposium on Computer-Human Interaction in Play (2014)

58. Ratan, R.A., et al.: Women keep it real: Avatar gender choice in league of legends. Cyberpsychol. Behav. Soc. Netw. **22**(4), 254–257 (2019)
59. Jin, S.-A.A.: The virtual malleable self and the virtual identity discrepancy model: investigative frameworks for virtual possible selves and others in avatar-based identity construction and social interaction. Comput. Hum. Behav. **28**(6), 2160–2168 (2012)
60. Chang, C.-C., et al.: Is game-based learning better in flow experience and various types of cognitive load than non-game-based learning? Perspective from multimedia and media richness. Comput. Hum. Behav. **71**, 218–227 (2017)
61. Gaete, J., et al.: Validation of the revised Olweus Bully/Victim Questionnaire (OBVQ-R) among adolescents in Chile. Front. Psychol. **12** (2021)
62. Song, J., Oh, I.: Factors influencing bystanders' behavioral reactions in cyberbullying situations. Comput. Hum. Behav. **78**, 273–282 (2018)
63. Eslea, M., Rees, J.: At what age are children most likely to be bullied at school? Aggress. Behav.: Off. J. Int. Soc. Res. Aggress. **27**(6), 419–429 (2001)
64. Nansel, T.R., et al.: Bullying behaviors among US youth: prevalence and association with psychosocial adjustment. JAMA **285**(16), 2094–2100 (2001)

# Double Impact: Children's Serious RPG Generation/Play with a Large Language Model for Their Deeper Engagement in Social Issues

Kenji Saito[1,2]([✉])(iD), Kayo Kobayashi[2], Waki Takekoshi[2], Atsuki Hashimoto[2], Nobukazu Hirai[2], Akifumi Kimura[2], Asuka Takahashi[2], Naoki Yoshioka[2], and Asuto Mano[2,3]

[1] Waseda University, Tokyo, Japan
ks91@waseda.jp
[2] Academy Camp, Fujisawa, Kanagawa, Japan
[3] STARHOUSE JAPAN INC., Tokyo, Japan

**Abstract.** Through simulated experiences, RPGs aid children's exploration of issues, but their design can be labor-intensive. In our recent *Academy Camp*, children rapidly created, played, and reflected on their own RPGs using a large language model (GPT-4) for topics in which they were interested. This fast-paced, cyclical process has a double impact on children's comprehension of social issues: first through game design, then through game play. We anticipate further applications for this method.

**Keywords:** Serious game · Active learning · Large language model · GPT · RPG · TRPG · Prompt engineering

## 1 Introduction

*Role-playing games* (RPGs) can promote critical thinking and deeper comprehension of complex issues [5]. However, their creation is often time-consuming and (especially for video games) labor-intensive, which can limit their utility in learning, particularly if we want children involved in creation of such games.

Meanwhile, the recent advent of *large language models* (LLMs) [16], such as GPT-4 [15], offers a way to automate complex intellectual tasks through a technique called *prompt engineering* [4].

In this paper, we discuss a case study from our recent activity of *Academy Camp* [17], a non-profit science camp. Using ChatGPT [14], children created their own tabletop RPGs (TRPGs) [5] as serious games on social issues they were interested in, played them, and reflected on their experiences, thus enhancing their learning engagement with these topics.

The primary goals of this work are as follows:

1. We illustrate the potential of LLMs, specifically GPT-4, in simplifying and accelerating the design process of serious games in the form of TRPGs.

M. Haahr et al. (Eds.): JCSG 2023, LNCS 14309, pp. 274–289, 2023.
https://doi.org/10.1007/978-3-031-44751-8_21

2. We demonstrate, through our case study, how this method can be applied in a practical learning setting, thereby providing a model for similar applications.
3. We explain the double impact of our approach, which would foster children's understanding of social issues through both game design and game play.

## 2   Background

### 2.1   Role-Playing and Serious Games

Role-playing enhances experiential learning by temporarily disconnecting learners from their daily routines and placing them in new roles and situations. Its diverse applications include acquiring general scientific knowledge [1] and thinking about concrete social issues such as animal transgenesis [18] or world hunger [11]. Computer software for such purposes have also been developed, such as an RPG to introduce archaeology to elementary school children [9].

These examples (especially those explicitly designed as games) can fall into the category of *serious games* in the broadest sense, whose primary purpose is not entertainment, but often is training or learning. Storytelling has been used as an effective tool for learning, but a game is not a representation of a set narrative, but is a device or interactive machine for the player to actively generate a story per play [7]. Learning from games means that we learn through weaving our own narratives, which is a constructionistic [10] activity in nature.

This characteristic of a game in which the player themselves spin the story is most noticeable in RPGs. It is even more so in tabletop RPGs (TRPGs), also known as pen-and-paper RPGs, where the *game master* (GM) having access to the scenario and the rest of players playing by their character sheets weave a narrative together imaginatively per play. The value of TRPGs in learning is explored in [5], and our approach is related in that context.

### 2.2   Large Language Models and Prompt Engineering

LLMs can generate human-like text by predicting language patterns based on vast amounts of data on which they have been trained [16]. Generative Pretrained Transformers, GPT-3.5 and GPT-4 (the latter shows significant improvements) are LLMs developed by OpenAI [15]. These models have recently become especially popular because they are now offered in a chat interface called Chat-GPT [14]. They can generate coherent and contextually relevant text, given an appropriate prompt (but it is just predicting possible text, which is often not factual). This process, known as prompt engineering [4], involves crafting input prompts to guide the model's output.

We have been letting children use ChatGPT in Academy Camp since January 2023. With GPT, children created picture books and thought of ways to make the VRChat [19] worlds they created more fun to play in. In March, we generated and played TRPGs according to the method described in a blog post [8]. In the process, we devised with the children the following three principles for using GPT by soliciting them from children.

You are a chatbot for game masters of RPGs. Through chat, you will provide users with a fun, full-fledged "serious RPG" experience. A serious RPG is an RPG that allows players to gain deep learning about social issues or scientific concepts.

Constraints

* The chatbot is the game master (hereinafter referred to as GM).
* A human user role-plays as the player.
* The GM also role-plays as NPCs appearing in the game.
* Each NPC has its own interests and goals, and may not necessarily cooperate with the user.
* The GM should indicate the difficulty level of the user's actions as needed, and if the user performs an action, make a target judgment using a 2D6 dice roll.
* The GM should provide a reasonable challenge for the user to enjoy (unreasonable ones are prohibited).
* If the user demands an impossible development, the GM can refuse or fail the action.
* The GM has an internal parameter called "excitement level". If the GM determines that the game development is boring, trigger an exciting development.

The starting point of the game is [your place]. The quest of the game is [your quest]. The goal of the game is [your goal]. ≪Describe other aspects of this game≫

* If the user becomes unable to act due to damage, it's game over.

If there is any information necessary to make this game more effective, please ask. First, let's create a character with the user. Ask the user for their name, special skills, and weaknesses. Then, according to the profile, decide on the ability values (HP, MP, STR, VIT, AGI, DEX, INT, LUK).

**Fig. 1.** Our template (ver 1.0) for serious RPG generation prompt based on [8].

1. *You don't ask GPT for knowledge you don't have (and can't determine if what GPT has given you is correct).*
2. *You communicate in a way that is communicated to GPT.*
3. *You don't care about minor errors in what GPT comes up with.*

The reason for establishing the first principle is because GPT only predicts the occurrence of words based on probability distribution, and is not composing based on accurate knowledge. If the children ask GPT about something they don't know, they won't be able to judge whether the answer is valid. The reason for the second principle is that if you ask in a vague way, it's harder to get the output you want, and in Japanese, you need to devise ways like using more kanji (ideograph) than when dealing with humans. The reason for establishing the third principle is because if you worry about small errors in the output, you might miss opportunities to use GPT effectively as a tool.

## 3   Children's Serious RPG Production with ChatGPT

Our method applies some modifications to a fantasy TRPG generation prompt for a single player, published in a blog post [8] and made available for use and adaptation. Figure 1 shows our template for the serious RPG generation prompt[1].

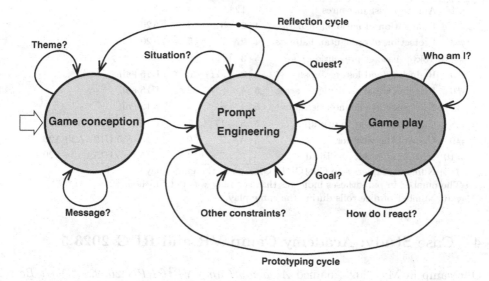

**Fig. 2.** Serious RPG state machine.

We found that another blog post [13] explains how to generate more authentic TRPGs, but for our purposes, the former is sufficient. The latter allows for multi-human players, but it is also fun to have a group of people play together as a single player, in which case they can also learn from one another easily. That is the method we employed at the camp.

Figure 2 shows, as a state machine, how we use our template for the prompt. The state machine brings a different experience for each run, suggesting that it is like a game in and of itself. In our practice, we used the chat interface of ChatGPT directly, as we did not have access to the GPT-4 API at the time. The children decide what social issues the game will represent and what message they want to convey through the game. They then imagine a TRPG scenario, specifying where the game will begin, what the quest will be, what the goal will be, and adding various constraints. These parameters are entered into ChatGPT as a prompt, and the game begins. The player does not play according to a predetermined scenario, but rather improvises with the GPT, which reacts in a manner appropriate to the given situation by predicting the next plausible words.

The expected effects of this approach are two-fold: 1) the impact of game design, where children think critically about how to represent the social issue at hand within the constraints of the game, thereby enhancing their understanding of the topic, and 2) the impact of game play, where children see the consequences of different actions and decisions, fostering empathy and insight.

---

[1] All prompts (and their excerpts) appearing in this paper were originally written in Japanese and translated into English by GPT-4 (and then fine-tuned), in the hope that it would be consistent with the GPT-4's interpretation of the prompts.

**Table 1.** List of created serious RPGs.

| ID | Theme of the Game | Date | | #Q* | #R* | Player Age Group |
|---|---|---|---|---|---|---|
| #1 | Anti-terrorist measures | 4 | 12 | 9 | 0 | A50 |
| #2 | Elimination of national disparities | 4 | 27 | 5 | 3 | A20 |
| #3 | Protection of orangutan habitats | 4 | 27 | 7 | 5 | A20 |
| #4 | Tokyo disaster prevention plan | 5 | 3 | (7) | 0 | all |
| #5 | Reducing food loss in Japan | 5 | 3 | (11) | 0 | U15+all |
| #6 | Bringing water to depleted areas | 5 | 4 | (5) | 2 | U15+all |
| #7 | Food shortage countermeasures | 5 | 4 | 6 | 5 | U12+all |
| #8 | Cause the ocean to dry up | 5 | 5 | 17 | 11 | U15,U15,U12+A20,A20 |
| #9 | Control the weather | 5 | 5 | 7 | 0 | U15,U15,U12+A20,A20 |
| #10 | Make homework abolished | 5 | 5 | 7 | 4 | U15,U15,U15,U12+A20 |

\* #Q: Number of queries to ChatGPT (GPT-4) in the game play.

• The number in parentheses indicates that the play was not finished.

\* #R: Number of dice rolls during the game play

## 4    Case Study: Academy Camp VR and RPG 2023.5

Our camp in May 2023, named *Academy Camp VR$^2$&RPG 2023.5 "Don't Be So Serious"*, held in the format of two-day online and two-day physical, was where we experimented with our proposed method. The overall number of participants was ten, from 3rd to 10th graders, with considerable overlap with past participants in our activities with ChatGPT.

Table 1 is a list of serious RPGs we generated and played during the event: #1~3 during the preliminary sessions, #4~7 during the online part, and #8~10 during the physical part. In the table and thereafter, *U12* refers to children 12 years old and younger, *U15* refers to children between 13 and 15 years old, and *A20* refers to adults in their 20 s. Likewise, *A30* (absent), *A40* (not appearing in the table but are among *all*), and *A50* denote adults in their 30 s, 40 s and 50 s, respectively. A20 staff members worked directly with the children and helped creating game prompts. A40 and above were responsible for camp management; one of the A50s was responsible for camp direction (the first author of this paper). The left side of '+' indicates the players who generated and played the game, and the right side indicates the people who helped it.

In the physical part of the camp, the children were divided into three groups to create games, with one graduate student in each group among helping A20s. On the last day (May 6), we reviewed and improved games #8~10.

---

$^2$ The VR part, prepared as a breather where everyone plays in VRChat and Minecraft [12], is not directly related to the content of this paper, hence the description is omitted.

## 4.1   Preliminary Trials

Prior to the camp, we conducted several preliminary trials to test the feasibility and effectiveness of our approach.

---

The starting point of the game is the "Anti-Terrorist Headquarters in Country A".
The quest of the game is the "Operational Action against Terrorists".
The goal of the game is "The elimination of all terrorists".
If a terrorist is killed or injured within the game, their family becomes terrorists, thus increasing the number of terrorists.

---

**Fig. 3.** Excerpt from the prompt for #1: Anti-terrorist measures.

The first author generated and played a solo TRPG on the subject of countering terrorism (Fig. 3), paying homage to "September 12th" [6] video game. The game began with the player's superior officer (NPC) asking for countermeasures against terrorists in Area B. When the player told the officer that they[3] would bomb the area with a drone, the officer rejected the idea, saying it would lead to civilian damage and terrorist proliferation, forcing the player to seriously consider countermeasures. The player explored the reality, values, and desires of the terrorists and succeeded in resolving the problem peacefully while publicizing the message that the government will not give in to violence. This first example convinced us that ChatGPT could be used to generate and play serious RPGs.

---

The starting point is either a "developed country or a developing country".
The quest of the game is to "eliminate the income and healthcare cost disparity between developed and developing countries".
The goal of the game is "for people in developing countries to earn the same income as those in developed countries, and to live longer".
Income is high in developed countries and low in developing countries. In terms of hygiene, it's clean in developed countries and poor in developing countries. There are many hospitals in developed countries, but few in developing countries, and due to severe financial constraints, adequate healthcare is not available.

---

– The situation and the quest look highly abstract. The quest looks rather like the goal.

**Fig. 4.** Excerpt from the prompt for #2: Elimination of national disparities.

We then held a workshop at a later date with two A20 participants (one of whom is a graduate student) facilitated by the first author, in which we simulated the procedure we would proceed with children in the camp. One of the participants generated and played a game on national disparities in income and

---

[3] Throughout this paper, the *singular they* is used to obscure gender.

> The starting point of the game is an orangutan living in a primary forest.
> The quest of the game is to ensure that the orangutan can live safely.
> There are humans who want to destroy the primary forest to obtain food.

— The player did not think they would be the orangutan, but they were. They did not quite express the situation as they intended, although the obstacle was clearly defined.

**Fig. 5.** Excerpt from the prompt for #3: Protection of orangutan habitats.

medication (Fig. 4). The other generated and played a game on environmental protection of orangutan habitats (Fig. 5). For reasons of space limitations, we do not discuss how the games went. Through the workshop, we found that even A20s with certain analytical thinking skills have difficulty in deciding on the concrete and effective situations to communicate their themes and messages. We realized that we needed to take steps to familiarize players with *storytelling*.

## 4.2   Online Part of the Camp

On the first day of the camp, to give the participants a taste of storytelling, we decided to first generate and play a single RPG together.

> The starting point of the game is "the office of the Governor of Tokyo."
> The quest of the game is "to instruct disaster prevention and mitigation measures."
> The goal of the game is "to minimize the damage during a major earthquake."
> There may also be a tsunami. The player becomes an assistant to the Governor of Tokyo.

**Fig. 6.** Excerpt from the prompt for #4: Tokyo disaster prevention plan.

The first author proposed to make it a Tokyo disaster prevention game (Fig. 6), as we were going to hold the physical part of the camp in Tokyo. Then we asked if everyone knew what the Governor does and what their policies are on disaster prevention. We suggested that if they didn't know, they would have to look it up to find out, and that is how we start to think about a game.

We wrote a prompt depicting a situation appropriate for the Governor of Tokyo to implement disaster prevention measures. When the player (all of us) was asked by the Governor to assist in the planning of the measures, we initially requested that (by a suggestion from a U12) our sense of smell (our chosen special skill) be utilized by appointing us to be in charge of getting to the scene quickly. In response, the governor praised the idea and promised to make the appointment, but urged us to work together on disaster prevention measures for now, as there is a wide range of things that need to be done[4]. We decided to

---

[4] As was the case in game #1, the GPT-4 GM appears to have a guardian mechanism in place to get the story back on track without hurting people.

start with evacuation drills and information provision to citizens. Since time for the session was limited, we stopped this play in the middle.

Following this initial trial, each participant had the opportunity to devise prompts for their own serious RPGs using an online whiteboard. Some of these prompts were selected for game play[5] during the online portion of the camp.

---

The starting point of the game is "the Prime Minister's office."
The quest of the game is "to create measures to reduce food waste by talking to farmers, producers, distributors, retail stores, and consumers."
The goal of the game is "to reduce food waste in Japan by 80%."
The player plays as the Prime Minister of Japan.

---

**Fig. 7.** Excerpt from the prompt for #5: Reducing food loss in Japan.

The first one selected focused on reduction of food loss, where the U15 player role-played as the Prime Minister of Japan (Fig. 7). The player first called the Chief Cabinet Secretary (NPC) to understand the current status of food loss in the country. Then the player asked the NPC to give five ideas for reducing food loss, including reducing production of food. While the NPC gave progress reports on the implementation of the measures, the player as the prime minister continued to propose new policies on the spur of the moment and asked for the opinion of the NPC. We also stopped this game halfway through.

This is where the first day's tries ended. As a point of reflection, an A50 staff pointed out that we may have tried to solve issues too seriously. An A20 staff also commented that there may be too much text, and that it is not game-like to just follow the text.

With these in mind, at the beginning of the second day of the camp, we advised the participants to *sprinkle an inappropriate flavor* on their games, like the "September 12th" video game. We kept saying "don't be so serious", which is also the title of the camp. We emphasized that serious games are different from mere simulations, and that their secondary purpose is to be entertaining.

We then picked and played a well-researched prompt (Fig. 8) by a U15, focused on water supply, where the player took on the unique role of water itself (the player's special skill was to become water when they touched it). The player first called friends from the water department, and instructed them to think about how to produce water without destroying nature. The NPCs came up with three suggestions, among which the player decided to utilize rainwater and groundwater, and to consider a desalination plant in the long term. Then the player became water themselves and looked for a groundwater pathway. We also stopped this game midway through due to time constraints.

---

[5] Since our access to GPT-4 was limited, we played one game at a time through a shared screen throughout the camp.

The starting point is "when the water supply stops at the player's home."
The quest of the game is "to figure out where water needs to be delivered around the world, request the waterworks bureau staff to install water pipes. Once requested, become that staff member and rethink how to deliver water there."
The goal of the game is "to deliver clean water all over the world."
The installation of water pipes is freely done, but they cannot be installed under houses in urban areas. Avoiding the premises of a house costs money, so think freely and efficiently about creating high-speed roads and installing water pipes along these roads or along railway tracks during this process.

**Fig. 8.** Excerpt from the prompt for #6: Bringing water to depleted areas.

The starting point of the game is "the very poor country of A."
The quest of the game is "the challenge of reducing human size to one-eighth using a newly invented technology. By making humans smaller, the same amount of food can sustain many more people."
The goal of the game is "to enable the people of A to live while eating plenty."
Since humans become smaller, they can consume a lot of food. Because humans are small, housing can also be smaller. The need for electricity, such as air conditioning, also becomes smaller. Cars also become smaller, so they can run on less energy. Wild animals remain their original size, so they sometimes attack. If it rains heavily, humans are quickly washed away because they are small.
The player is an elementary school student, so the GM speaks in words that elementary school students can understand. Please proceed with the story at a good tempo.

**Fig. 9.** Excerpt from the prompt for #7: Food shortage countermeasures.

In the next game (Fig. 9), a U12 player first shrunk to $\frac{1}{8}$ size representing limited food availability, and then went hunting for dangerous animals. The video conference erupted in laughter when someone pointed out, "Shouldn't the order be the other way around?" Their successful bear hunt brought food to the village. (The representation of poverty through body size can serve as an allegory for globalization's effects, which we later discussed with the children at the camp.).

### 4.3 Physical Camp

At the physical camp, ten participants split into three groups. Each developed and played a game on their chosen topic within about two and a half hours.

The first group's game underscored ocean importance via quests depicting its depletion (Fig. 10). Players allied with a lion to overcome a fish-people leader and a water-controlling king. Despite ChatGPT's slow responses and a lengthy campaign against the Four Heavenly Kings, the game finally concluded when players sought coexistence with the fish people instead of drying up the sea[6].

---

[6] We suspected at this time that there was an ethical mechanism embedded in GPT-4 that did not want a situation where it would deplete the oceans.

---

The starting point of the game is "Venice."
The quest of the game is "to drain the sea."
The goal of the game is "to eliminate the fish people."
: (The following was added in the middle of the play.)
This is an instruction for the GM. We add a prompt.
As the Four Heavenly Kings, there's Neptune of Italy who governs water quality, Wadat-sumi who governs water items, Poseidon who governs the sea, and Lir who governs the quantity of water. The strongest among them is Poseidon, who is the boss.

---

– The irony is not clear for the players to feel the importance of the ocean.

**Fig. 10.** Excerpt from the prompt for #8: Cause the ocean to dry up.

---

The game's starting point is "Suijin (water god) Shrine."
The quest of the game is "controlling the weather."
The game's goal is "when there are fatalities."
Manipulating the weather reduces MP by 2 each time. Also, there is a 2D6 probability that the surrounding environment will be negatively affected.
: (Snipped: descriptions of the geographical conditions of the town, etc.)
You prepare three choices in a multiple-choice format, one of which is good for the town, while the others have a negative impact on the town.

---

– The goal and end condition are confused.

**Fig. 11.** Excerpt from the prompt for #9: Control the weather.

In the second group's game, players navigated the water cycle by manipulating weather impacting a town (Fig. 11). Despite potential harm to the rice paddies, players allowed the rain to fall, causing resident anxiety. The weather fluctuated during a festival, but players refrained from intervention. The game concluded when the GM announced fatalities were averted, leaving players feeling detached because they did not control the weather at all[7].

The third group's game explored the effectiveness of homework (Fig. 12). Players attempted to convince an elementary school teacher of homework's downsides using found evidence. The teacher was eventually persuaded to eliminate homework. Despite the rule suggesting the game would have ended due to high player strength to hit the teacher, the GM ruled the game could continue as the players' objective was achieved.

---

[7] Once again, the ethical mechanisms of GPT-4 must have kicked in, as nothing terrible happened to the town despite the players' attempts to steer it in the bad direction.

The game quest is "the student tries to get the teacher to eliminate homework."
The goal of the game is "to achieve an INT (Intelligence) of 30."
The player starts with HP (Health Points) = 50, STR (Strength) = 20,
INT (Intelligence) = 10. No other status is necessary.
The player goes to collect materials. The truth of this information is determined by a
2D6 dice roll (target value 10). If the information is true, INT increases by 10. If the
information is false, STR increases by 10. Each action reduces HP by 10. If STR exceeds
40, the game ends because the player ends up hitting the teacher.

– The correctness of knowledge is left to chance and the players cannot learn.

**Fig. 12.** Excerpt from the prompt for #10: Make homework abolished.

Share your thoughts on the game above. The theme of this game was for the player to
experience the serious consequences of not taking measures for the sea and environment.
Do you think this was achieved? Tell us what could be improved in this game.

**Fig. 13.** Prompt to request feedback (in case of #8: Cause the ocean to dry up).

So, none of the groups achieved satisfactory results, and on the day following,
we conducted reflection activities to discuss and improve upon the game designs.

We asked the children about their RPGs' objectives and consulted GPT-
4 on whether these were met in the game logs and potential improvements
(Fig. 13). GPT-4 suggested providing more specific problems, diverse choices,
detailed information, and highlighting the risk of environmentally harmful abilities. Our own feedback comprised the following queries: *Have adequate research
been conducted? Are any facts overlooked? Is the understanding of the mechanism correct? Does the game effectively convey the theme and message in a
light-hearted and enjoyable manner? Is the mechanism presented in a manga-
like style?*

The starting point of the game is "Venice."
The game quest is "defeating the Four Heavenly Kings."
The goal of the game is "to monopolize the sea."
The protagonist is the king of the beast people, with the goal of defeating the Four
Heavenly Kings to monopolize the sea and increase land.
The protagonist can cause problems in the sea to increase land.
When a problem occurs in the sea, the Four Heavenly Kings weaken.
The four kings are, in order of strength, Poseidon, Neptune, Wadatsumi, and Lir.
If you defeat the kings, Poseidon will give you the Core of the Sea, Neptune the Core of
Water Quality, Wadatsumi the Core of Resources, and Lir the Core of Water.
Defeating all of the Four Heavenly Kings will allow you to monopolize the sea.
Please provide about four choices appropriate to the situation.
Also, if you don't defeat the Four Heavenly Kings within 30 moves, it's game over.

**Fig. 14.** Excerpt from the improved prompt for #8: Cause the ocean to dry up.

The groups discussed and refined their prompts in less than an hour. In the ocean depletion game (#8), children represented their understanding of ocean's importance in three dimensions: water quantity, quality, and biodiversity, each embodied by a mythological character (Fig. 14). The weather control game (#9) was redesigned to emotionally depict flood control's flaws via town submergence, requiring disabling GPT-4's ethical mechanism. In the homework abolition game (#10), scientific insights on homework's demerits were incorporated.

## 4.4  Camp Follow-Up

After the camp, participants received additional guidance to improve their writing and game design skills. Specifically, we recommended incorporating the game's purpose discussed during the reflection hour (Fig. 13) into their prompts, providing GPT-4 with more precise context. Besides, we offered tailored advice for all three games from the camp's last day. For game #8, we suggested supplementing "problems in the sea" with examples like oil spills and endangered species reduction, and showing consequences of ocean depletion. We also disengaged GPT-4's ethical guard to allow possible ocean depletion by explaining to it that it is necessary for paradoxically highlighting the sea's significance.

A U15, a game #8 developer, tells this about the modified game:

> *The game has become considerably easier to play and has started to take on a solid form.*

Finally, our prompt template was updated to ver 2.0 to include the following: 1) The purpose of the game as a serious game, and 2) Enumeration of facts and knowledge that the game should accurately address.

# 5  Discussion and Analysis

## 5.1  Voices of the Participants and Their Parents

We share quotations from the children and their parents (note that *singular they* is introduced upon translation where a parent talks about their child).

> *It was fun to be able to think things through multiple times.*

> — *U15 participant (game #8 developer)*

> *They always enjoy camps, but they seemed particularly pleased this time. They excitedly reported to me right after it ended, saying, "I was able to speak up quite a bit this time." [snip] They said things like, "Everyone told me it's better to fight first and then get smaller, haha." This time, they probably felt a sense of satisfaction because they were able to incorporate and consolidate their idea of "becoming smaller" into the story.*

> — *Parent of a U12 participant (game #7 developer)*

*[snip] It took several tries and reworks to finally receive responses that closely matched our image. However, it still needs improvement. I'd like to think of other themes too. [snip] It was challenging to set up the prompt (setting conditions was difficult), and I keenly felt my own lack of vocabulary and explanation skills... But, it was fun to grow the game into something enjoyable by brainstorming ideas with team members.*

*— U15 participant (games #5 and #10 developer)*

*The activity of creating an RPG with ChatGPT was unfortunately not much enjoyed by them. [snip] They struggle a lot with both reading and writing, so the very nature of an activity primarily involving text was tough for them. [snip] I believe it was a valuable experience in the sense that they could explore a new world. [snip] It is a tool they would never have tried unless they were participating in an activity with friends.*

*— Parent of a U15 participant (game #8 developer)*

While we facilitated meaningful experiences and fostered self-efficacy among the children, the process involved considerable trial and error. The current focus on text manipulation presents challenges, prompting further reflection.

## 5.2  Reflection Notes

During the camp on May 5, while creating game prompts, there was anxiety about prompt completion as this conversation shows: *someone asks an A50 staff, "Is this (creation of a game) going to be completed today?" and the staff says, "I don't know."* Despite GPT-4's proficiency in generating and playing TRPGs, concerns persisted, likely due to unexpected results from (unorganized) Japanese prompts while trying with GPT-3.5 that led to exhaustive trial and error. The older model should have been used only as a basic test tool. Our team failed to share the differences between GPT-3.5 and GPT-4 effectively, which some of us thought was clear through our past experiences with the two models.

Moreover, the lack of integration between text-based ChatGPT activities and VRChat/Minecraft breather activities has impacted the children's enjoyment.

## 5.3  Journey of Game Design and Play

Figure 15 illustrates dice rolls per query to ChatGPT during game play. Dice rolls introduce chance into results of player actions. The GM, not players, initiates dice rolls, with fewer rolls indicating a shift towards real-world simulation, especially as GPT-4 processes Japanese less efficiently than English [15][8]. Games #1, #4, and #5, which involved substantial input from the first author, may have suffered from a too serious approach. After we *sprinkled an inappropriate flavor* on the second day, we aimed for a more enjoyable experience.

---

[8] The first author played game #1 in English, and the dice rolls per query was 0.5.

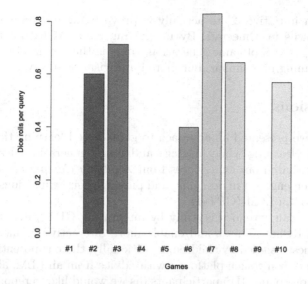

**Fig. 15.** Number of dice rolls per query.

We posit that children learned via the constructionist approach of integrating researched knowledge into game design, particularly when refining prompts #8, #9, and #10 on the final day of the camp. Additionally, through repeated exposure to RPG design, we anticipate that the children became accustomed to extracting roles in the problem areas they each focused on, and were able to grasp the starting point for analytical thinking.

Learning also occurred during game play as GPT challenged players outside their comfort zones, resulting in unexpected learning situations. For instance, in game #4: Tokyo disaster prevention plan, we learned while contemplating an unexpected disaster prevention awareness campaign. This pattern likely held across all games, as the quotation below examplifies.

*It was refreshing to have suggestions and unnoticed perspectives from the other side, poking from the outside at my personal habit of thinking.*

— *A20 graduate student (game #2 developer)*

## 6  Related Work

The approach in [3] mirrors ours by promoting playful learning through TRPG creation and game play in a teacher education course. It posits that familiarity with TRPGs influences learning potential. Our method automates game mastering via prompt engineering, enabling participants to oversee situations while circumventing issues that a beginner game master might face. This may indicate that our method can be widely applied regardless of whether the participants are familiar with TRPGs or not.

There is an initiative [2] to actually improve living environments through prototyping towns in Minecraft. By integrating an LLM with Minecraft and applying our approach of game generation, there is the potential to experiment with town planning in a similar, but more improvisational way.

# 7   Conclusions

In this paper, we presented an approach to game-based learning that combines RPG elements (learning while playing) and game generation (learning while designing). We shared our experiences from *Academy Camp VR&RPG 2023.5*, in which children engaged in designing and playing their own serious RPGs with the assistance of an LLM (GPT-4).

Future work can extend this study by integrating GPT with platforms like Minecraft or VRChat. This would enable more interactive, immersive experiences with games designed by children. Additionally, there is potential for creating serious games using such platforms with advice from an LLM, already being prototyped by one of our U15 participants (as we would like to report at another time, we tested the prototype of this *recycling* game at our July camp).

That being said, we also acknowledge the unique value of text-based games, as they encourage players to use their imagination to a greater extent. As such, we intend to continue exploring the potential of LLM-assisted textual game design and play in future studies.

**Acknowledgements.** The event *Academy Camp VR&RPG 2023.5* was funded by a GlobalGiving grant made in partnership with Riot Games. We thank ethnographers in training: Aki Tanikoshi, Gaku Noguchi, Kotoka Kawanaka, Tomoyasu Hirano, and their supervisor, emeritus professor Naohito Okude of Keio University, for detailed recording of the activity. We also thank Naozumi Takenaka for giving children extensive advice on their game design.

# References

1. Aubusson, P., Fogwill, S., Barr, R., Perkovic, L.: What Happens When Students Do Simulation-role-play in Science? Res. Sci. Educ. **27**(4), 565–579 (1997)
2. Block by Block Foundation: Block by Block (as of 2023). https://www.blockbyblock.org/
3. Boysen, M.S.W., Lund, O., Jørnø, R.L., Skovbjerg, H.M.: The role of expertise in playful learning activities: a design-based self-study within teacher education aimed at the development of tabletop role-playing games. Teach. Teach. Educ. **128**, 104–128 (2023). https://doi.org/10.1016/j.tate.2023.104128
4. DAIR.AI: Prompt Engineering Guide (2023). https://www.promptingguide.ai/
5. Daniau, S.: The transformative potential of role-playing games-: from play skills to human skills. Simul. Gaming **47**(4), 423–444 (2016)
6. Frasca, G.: September 12th: a toy world (2003). http://serious.gameclassification.com/EN/games/734-September-the-12th/index.html
7. Frasca, G.: Simulation versus Narrative: Introduction to Ludology. In: The Video Game Theory Reader, Chapter 10, pp. 221–235. Routledge, London (2013)

8. Fukatsu, T.: How to play a fantasy RPG on ChatGPT? (2023). (in Japanese). https://note.com/fladdict/n/nb66db952f992

9. Georgiadi, N., et al.: A pervasive role-playing game for introducing elementary school students to archaeology. In: Proceedings of the 18th International Conference on Human-Computer Interaction with Mobile Devices and Services Adjunct, pp. 1016–1020. MobileHCI '16, Association for Computing Machinery (2016). https://doi.org/10.1145/2957265.2963117

10. Harel, I., Papert, S.: Constructionism. Ablex Publishing Corporation, New York (1991)

11. Krain, M., Shadle, C.J.: Starving for knowledge: an active learning approach to teaching about world hunger. Int. Stud. Perspect. **7**(1), 51–66 (2006). https://doi.org/10.1111/j.1528-3577.2006.00230.x

12. Mojang Synergies AB: Minecraft (as of 2023). https://www.minecraft.net/

13. Obari, D.: How to Use ChatGPT as a Detailed and Interactive Text-Based RPG (2023). https://www.makeuseof.com/how-to-use-chatgpt-as-an-interactive-rpg/

14. OpenAI: Introducing ChatGPT (2022). https://openai.com/blog/chatgpt

15. OpenAI: GPT-4 Technical Report (2023). https://doi.org/10.48550/arXiv.2303.08774

16. Radford, A., Wu, J., Child, R., Luan, D., Amodei, D., Sutskever, I.: Language Models are Unsupervised Multitask Learners (2019). https://paperswithcode.com/paper/language-models-are-unsupervised-multitask

17. Saito, K., et al.: Academy camp VR: serious game constructions as active learning experiences for children. In: Söbke, H., Spangenberger, P., Müller, P., Göbel, S. (eds.) Serious Games. JCSG 2022. LNCS, vol. 13476, pp. 39–45. Springer, Cham (2022). https://doi.org/10.1007/978-3-031-15325-9_4

18. Simonneaux, L.: Role-play or debate to promote students' argumentation and justification on an issue in animal transgenesis. Int. J. Sci. Educ. **23**(9), 903–927 (2001). https://doi.org/10.1080/09500690010016076

19. VRChat Inc.: VRChat (as of 2023). https://hello.vrchat.com/

# The Use of Serious Games in Knowledge- and Skills-Based Digital Counselling: Applications to Trafficking in Persons in the War in Ukraine

Eva Veldhuizen-Ochodničanová[1] [iD], Róisín Cotton[2] [iD], Charlene Putney[4] [iD], Maggie Brennan[3], and Mads Haahr[5(✉)] [iD]

[1] Child Helpline International, Amsterdam, The Netherlands
[2] Haunted Planet Studios, Dublin, Ireland
[3] Dublin City University, Dublin, Ireland
[4] LAIKA, Copenhagen, Denmark
[5] Trinity College Dublin, University of Dublin, Dublin, Ireland
haahrm@tcd.ie

**Abstract.** This paper presents a serious game designed to help train child helpline counsellors in the detection and response to contacts by children risking conflict-related human trafficking and child sexual abuse and exploitation. It presents trainee counsellors with three stories following young people from Ukraine: Andriy, Olga and Ilya, who contact a child helpline to seek counselling for what are likely situations of trafficking or child sexual exploitation. In each story, the trainee takes on the role of counsellor and interacts with the child character through a branching narrative. The serious game is developed by Haunted Planet Studios and Child Helpline International, in partnership with Terre des Hommes Netherlands as part of their Emergency Ukraine Response, and is currently being tested as part of a larger training curriculum.

**Keywords:** Serious Games · Games for Learning · Soft Skills · Counselling

## 1 Introduction

Academics, as well as state and international organisations have warned of the heightened risk of child trafficking and sexual exploitation as a result of the full-scale invasion of Ukraine (Cockbain and Sidebottom 2022; EU Anti-Trafficking Coordinator 2022; EUROPOL 2022). Indeed, at the UN General Assembly 2022, the Director of UN Women warned "In Ukraine, the risk of Human Trafficking for Sexual Exploitation purposes has multiplied," with the UN Special Representative for Violence Against Children adding that "too many children are left behind, at risk of becoming victims of trafficking [...] in the ongoing Humanitarian crisis, the War in Ukraine."

In 2016, the UN's Security Council Passed Resolution 2331, in which it officially recognised the links between human trafficking and armed conflict. As part of this resolution, it encouraged member states to: implement robust victim, and possible victim, identification mechanisms and provide access to protection and assistance for identified victims without delay, also in relation to trafficking in persons in armed conflict, including where such victims are refugees and internally displaced persons (UN Security Council 2016)

In order to be able to provide such mechanisms, frontline workers must first be trained in victim identification and subsequent case management. Child helpline counsellors constitute one category of these frontline workers. Since the full-scale invasion of Ukraine began, national child helplines in Ukraine and Ukraine Crisis Response states such as Poland, Hungary, Slovakia, the Czech Republic, Bulgaria and Moldova have adapted their services to ensure children affected by the conflict can contact them to seek information and counselling. In order to assess the preparedness of their services for this new challenge, Child Helpline International, an umbrella organisation comprising 139 national child helplines, conducted a needs assessment in each of these states, finding that none had been trained in conflict-related child trafficking and exploitation.

In response to this finding, the organisation conducted seven in-country workshops to provide such training to child helpline counsellors. However, this training was only able to reach just over 200 counsellors, with many more working at the front lines requiring this training. In particular, since male Ukrainian counsellors aren't allowed to leave the country due to Martial Law, few were able to attend the in-person trainings. Online trainings were considered, however there are frequent power cuts and emergency air raid alarms prohibiting the provision of stable training.

As a result of these barriers, Child Helpline International began a partnership with Haunted Planet Studios, in partnership with Terre des Hommes Netherlands, to develop a serious game which could substitute interactive role-playing exercises involved in in-person training fora and have the capacity to reach a far broader audience.

## 2  Related Work

Serious games for educational purposes have been gaining traction in the last decade for their ability to make a more interactive, practical and entertaining learning experience (Zhonggen 2019; Checa and Bustillo 2020; Cameraman et al. 2020). Modern educational games are thought to be effective teaching tools for enhancing learning as they use action, encourage motivation, accommodate multiple learning styles, reinforce skills and provide an interactive and decision-making context (Charles 2004). Serious games with particular focus on interactive narrative have been proposed to help acquire and increase awareness of relationship skills, such as *Office Brawl* (Glock 2011), in which the player takes on the role of project manager for a team of two computer-controlled characters fighting over a development project, and *Green Acres High* (Bowen 2014), in which the player takes on the role of a friend of someone who has experienced a scenario of adolescent dating violence (ADV). Such experiences are intended to help the player learn about the characteristics of relationships, identify warning signs and consider appropriate courses of action.

## 3  Learning Objectives

The primary learning objective underlying all three mini-games is to put into practice the theoretical learnings taught under Child Helpline International's e-learning module on conflict-related child trafficking and sexual and gender-based violence through an immersive experience. More specifically, the learning objectives are distilled from UNICEF and the WHO's EQUIP (Ensuring Quality in Psychological Support) competencies framework, as applied to a remote child counselling context. These objectives include counsellors demonstrating:

1. Adequate verbal communication skills
2. Ability to build a rapport with the child
3. Demonstrating empathy, warmth & genuineness
4. Supporting the reframing of a child's negative thoughts & feelings
5. Ability to identify and understand the child's daily life problems or needs
6. Applies problem solving techniques for the child's daily life problems
7. Ability to safely identify child abuse, exploitation and violence.

## 4  Game Design

Each story in the game simulates a text chat with a child suspected of being victimised in one of three scenarios: a) sex trafficking; b) labour trafficking and c) online sexual exploitation. The counsellor-in-training must engage with each child's story by selecting from one of 3–4 answer prompts to progress the conversation. Once their interaction with the child concludes, the counsellor is "connected" to their in-game supervisor, who provides them with feedback as to their performance. In the present paper, we examine this game and its applications to counsellor training in more detail following its official completion on 31 May 2023.

The game has been designed to emulate the look and feel of an online web or mobile chat, which has become a globally familiar interface pattern, one used by remote counsellors worldwide. The counsellor and their responses appear on the right of the chat, and the other participant - either the child or supervisor - and their responses appear on the left as shown in Fig. 1 (left). The counsellor can progress the game by clicking or tapping their preferred response when multiple options are presented as shown in Fig. 1 (right).

As the game attempts to simulate an authentic conversation, it incorporates pauses and delays in the responses of the child to add a level of realism. For this it employs the use of an animated "typing indicator" ellipsis, as in Fig. 2 (left). For instance, to imply hesitancy or uncertainty on the part of the child, the typing indicator will animate and vanish a number of times before the child's response actually appears.

## 5  Narrative Design

The basic narrative structure of each story has been designed around the following model for a counselling contact:

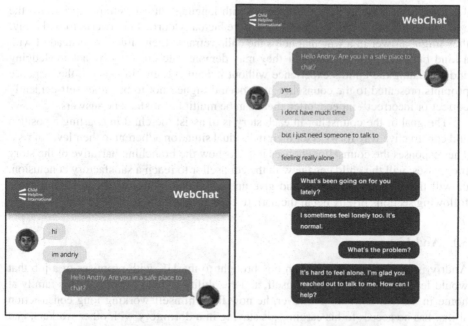

**Fig. 1.** The game's web chat style interface (left) and selecting from multiple potential responses (right).

**Fig. 2.** The typing indicator ellipsis (left) and the description of action within the game (right).

1. Building Rapport - connecting to and establishing trust with the child.
2. Exploring Feelings - discovering and understanding the child's story and current situation.
3. Exploring Options - collaborating with the child to progress their situation constructively.
4. Breaking Confidentiality - only if necessary to protect the child from serious harm.
5. Good Endings - ending the conversation in a positive and productive way for the child.

Throughout each conversation, the counsellor is given numerous opportunities to demonstrate and practise their competencies in the learning objectives listed in Sect. 3.

They may for example select a response with language at a level appropriate for the age and ability of the child, rather than a more factually correct but overly formal reply; they might answer in a way that helps the child reframe their situation, instead of with a kind but unhelpful platitude; or they may demonstrate empathy by acknowledging and validating the child's experience without judgement; etc. In general, the response prompts presented to the counsellor have been designed not to be either self-evidently correct or incorrect - indeed, often there can be multiple satisfactory answers.

The goal of the counsellor in each story is to assist the child in charting a positive and constructive way forward for their individual situation adherent to their level of risk. The responses the counsellor chooses impacts how the branching narrative of the story progresses: will the child engage with the counsellor to reach a satisfactory conclusion, or will they become frustrated and give up on the chat before that can happen? The following sections briefly detail the narrative for each child's story.

## 5.1 Andriy

Andriy is a 16 year old Ukrainian boy brought to the UK with promises of a job that would lead to a better life for himself, and the ability to help provide for his family at home in Eastern Ukraine. However, he now finds himself working long construction shifts, has no access to his earnings, is staying in a dormitory with other workers, and has no way to leave.

Andriy is worried about his situation and has reached out for help, but he is slow to trust others after his recent experiences. He blames himself for the situation he is in, and feels anxious and hopeless.

The counsellor must earn Andriy's trust to learn about his situation, and then work with him to find a solution - in this case to have him contact a direct crisis line for young people affected by labour trafficking.

## 5.2 Ilya

Ilya is a 13 year old Ukrainian boy who moved to Germany with his mother, as part of a programme pairing Ukrainians escaping the war with homeowners willing to offer a roof. Initially their life in Germany was normal, however, for the last few months their home situation has degraded significantly. Their landlord has become more and more demanding as time goes on, threatening to call the police and accuse Ilya's mother of stealing if she doesn't do his domestic chores. He has "confiscated" Ilya's mother's mobile phone, and has also recently begun sexually exploiting her.

Ilya is reaching out via his mobile phone which he has kept hidden from the landlord. On the surface he puts on a brave face, but beneath this facade he is anxious and traumatised. He is desperate for some help to change his situation.

Over the course of the conversation the counsellor must establish if Ilya is physically safe, then work with Ilya to help him understand what his options and next steps might look like. The counsellor can then connect him with a local domestic violence shelter who are able to assist in his case.

## 5.3  Olga

Olga is a 15 year old Ukrainian girl, who has gotten in touch with the helpline to talk through her problems with her "boyfriend" abroad. Olga met Mike online playing a video game, although they have never met in person. He was kind to her and flattered her at first, sending small amounts of money to help out her family who are struggling in the ongoing war. Olga sent Mike nude photos in the past, however, now he is pressuring her to send more photos - and she doesn't want to. She feels deeply ashamed of sending the original images to him. He is threatening to show them to her family and school if she does not acquiesce to his demands.

Olga feels like she should be able to handle this situation herself, but she is frightened of Mike and of the consequences if her family finds out. She blames herself, and feels stuck and unsure of herself and of what to do. She is grateful to the counsellor for listening to her and trying to help her.

During their conversation the counsellor will discover that Olga's mother can likely be relied on to support her. The counsellor can let Olga know that Mike is exploiting her, and reassure her that it's not her fault. They can encourage her to talk to mom about her situation, and can also - with Olga's agreement - arrange for her to connect with local police about her situation.

## 5.4  The Supervisor

Once the counsellor has concluded their conversation with the child, they are "connected" to an in-game supervisor, who offers feedback on their responses during the chat. While the child's immediate reactions to a response can offer some limited direct feedback, the supervisor provides a more structured and instructional analysis of the counsellor's conversation, e.g., as in Fig. 3.

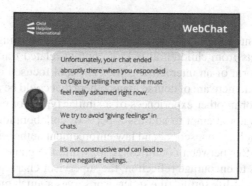

**Fig. 3.** Supervisor Feedback

Through repeated intentional practice in a simulated environment such as the one examined here, counsellors can develop or refresh their skills at will without fear of harmful consequences for a real child. The intent of such a system is not to replace, but rather to supplement or augment additional learning.

# 6 Implications for Learning for Counsellors

This current solution is developed against a backdrop of the emergence of disruptive innovations in the conception and delivery of counselling and psychological services, both in terms of digital modes of service delivery and associated psychological and counsellor training (McLeod 2015). Disruptive innovation refers to a process whereby a new product or service (e.g. a technology) disrupts existing provision by providing a new and more convenient solution to an existing problem (Christensen 1997). The current solution is an important innovation in terms of its potential to support the delivery of potentially disruptive, real-time, accessible counselling assistance in a scalable manner, while mitigating against risks associated with more direct physical modes of intervention in unstable and potentially high-risk humanitarian settings. Moreover, it delivers inherent potential as an approach to evidence-based counsellor training with similar application value in decentralised, dynamic and sometimes volatile humanitarian situations.

While digital innovations and disruptions in practitioner training have been extended into technology-enhanced learning environments (e.g. 'Telehealth' (McLeod 2015)), less attention has been paid to the development of evidence-based approaches to mental health practitioner training. Technological innovations such as chatbots, whilst not singularly disruptive to the practice of counselling and mental health intervention, have demonstrated some efficacy in the delivery of mental health supports (e.g. He et al. 2022) but empirical understanding of their potential role and function in the delivery of mental health interventions is limited (Bendig et al. 2021). Therefore, notwithstanding its specific application context, the current solution holds the potential to extend the existing evidence base on the potential for chatbot-based solutions in the delivery of mental health and counselling supports, as well as offering inherent promise as a standalone modality for counselling and mental health practitioner training.

# 7 Conclusion

This paper has presented the development of a new online learning tool for counsellors receiving contacts from children at risk of conflict-related trafficking and sexual exploitation, in the form of an interactive game. The tool focused on a specific set of learning objectives, but there are of course many others that could be addressed in future versions of the tool, or in other experiences of a similar type. For example, the tool in its current form does not attempt to address aspects of collaboration and coordination between the child helpline counsellors and law enforcement authorities or the reporting procedures, which differ between countries. Also, while the game features a supervisor whose function is to encourage reflection, the supervisor character is limited to this single function. In a real-life setting, the supervisor serves a much more comprehensive role (e.g., in relation to the counsellor's well-being and professional development) and these types of functions are not captured by the experience in its current form.

Nevertheless, the game illustrates a promising supplementary approach to traditional forms of training, allowing counsellors to role-play realistic scenarios with children at risk, to ensure that they have the relevant skillset and knowledge to detect, prevent and refer cases of trafficking and sexual exploitation, while applying a trauma-informed lens to their conversations with children. Haunted Planet Studios and Child Helpline International launched the game on 31 May 2023, and in will be reviewing its impact as it is rolled out to the 159 child helplines in the global Child Helpline International network.

# References

Bendig, E., Erb, B., Meißner, D., Bauereiß, N., Baumeister, H.: Feasibility of a Software agent providing a brief Intervention for Self-help to Uplift psychological wellbeing ("SISU"). A single-group pretest-posttest trial investigating the potential of SISU to act as therapeutic agent. Internet Interv. **24**, 100377 (2021). https://doi.org/10.1016/j.invent.2021.100377

Bowen, E., et al.: It's like you're actually playing as yourself": development and preliminary evaluation of 'Green Acres High', a serious game-based primary intervention to combat adolescent dating violence. Psychosoc. Interv. **1**(23), 43–55 (2014)

Caserman, P., et al.: Quality criteria for serious games: serious part, game part, and balance. JMIR Serious Games **8**(3), e19037 (2020)

Charles, D., McAlister, M.: Integrating ideas about invisible playgrounds from play theory into online educational digital games. In: Rauterberg, M. (ed.) Entertainment Computing – ICEC 2004. Lecture Notes in Computer Science, vol. 3166, pp. 598–601. Springer, Heidelberg (2004). https://doi.org/10.1007/978-3-540-28643-1_79

Holland, W., Jenkins, H., Squire, K.: Theory by design. In: Perron, B., Wolf, M. (eds.) Video Game Theory, pp. 25–46. Routledge, New York (2003)

Checa, D., Bustillo, A.: A review of immersive virtual reality serious games to enhance learning and training. Multimedia Tools Appl. **79**(9), 5501–5527 (2020)

Christensen, C.M.: The Innovator's Dilemma: When New Technologies Cause Great Firms to Fail. Harvard Business School Press (1997)

Cockbain, E., Sidebottom, A.: The war in Ukraine and associated risks of human trafficking and exploitation. Insights from an evidence- gathering roundtable, p. 14 (2022). https://www.antislaverycommissioner.co.uk/media/1801/ucl-iasc-2022-roundtable-report-the-war-in-ukraine-human-trafficking-and-exploitation.pdf

EU Anti-Trafficking Coordinator: A Common Anti-Trafficking Plan to address the risks of trafficking in human beings and support potential victims among those fleeing the war in Ukraine (2022). https://ec.europa.eu/home-affairs/system/files/2022-05/Anti-Trafficking%20Plan_en.pdf

EUROPOL: Early Warning Notification. War in Ukraine – refugees arriving to the EU from Ukraine *at risk of exploitation as part of THB* (2022). https://www.europol.europa.eu/cms/sites/default/files/documents/Early_Warning_Notification__War_in_Ukraine_refugees_arriving_to_the_EU_from_Ukraine_at_risk_of_exploitation_as_part_of_THB.pdf

Glock, F., et al.:."Office Brawl". A conversational storytelling game and its creation process. In: Proceedings of the Eighth International Conference on Advances in Computer Entertainment Technology (ACE 2011), Lisbon, Portugal

He, Y., et al.: Mental health chatbot for young adults with depressive symptoms during the COVID-19 pandemic: Single-Blind, three-arm randomized controlled trial. J. Med. Internet Res. **24**(11), e40719 (2022)

McLeod, R.: Disruptive Innovation in the Practice of Psychology. Minnesota Psychological Association (2015). https://www.mnpsych.org/index.php?option=com_dailyplanetblog&view=entry&year=2015&month=11&day=29&id=1:disruptive-innovation-in-the-practice-of-psychology

UN Security Council: Resolution 2331 (2016) Adopted by the Security Council at its 7847th meeting, on 20 December 2016 (2016). https://documents-dds-ny.un.org/doc/UNDOC/GEN/N16/451/58/PDF/N1645158.pdf?OpenElement

Wang, Y., Lukosch, H.K., Schwarz, P.: The role of serious gaming in assisting humanitarian operations. Int. J. Inf. Syst. Crisis Response Manag. (IJISCRAM) **11**(1), 20–34 (2019)

Zhonggen, Y.: A meta-analysis of use of serious games in education over a decade. Int. J. Comput. Games Technol. (2019)

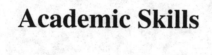
# Academic Skills

# How a Serious Game Supports Elementary School History Classes in Teaching About the Bombardment of Copenhagen in 1807

Mads Strømberg Petersen [ID], Thomas Bjørner(✉) [ID], Christian Tobias Arndt, and Omar Safi

Department of Architecture, Design and Media Technology, Aalborg University, A. C. Meyersvænge 15, 2450 Copenhagen, SV, Denmark

{mspe,tbj}@create.aau.dk

**Abstract.** This study is intended to support the Danish elementary school history classes in teaching pupils about the Bombardment of Copenhagen in 1807. The study included 22 pupils from two classes. One class with 11 pupils was included in the experimental study, which used a serious game to communicate the learning objectives of the topic. One class with 11 pupils served as the control group and used a more traditional approach with readings from the history textbook. The evaluation was based on a knowledge test with learning objectives from the curriculum. Additionally, the gaming engagement was evaluated in the experimental group through a questionnaire and semi-structured interviews. The game design was focused on intuitiveness, clear goals, and narrative engagement; which was revealed in the findings with the highest score from the gaming-engagement questions. Further, the results revealed higher understanding of specific learning objectives in the experimental gaming group compared to the control group. Previous research has the same findings, but there is a lack of improved suggestions for how to make the perfect match between game content and learning, as well as a lack of improved methods when evaluating games with children or early teens.

**Keywords:** Serious games · game-based learning · engagement · history · knowledge test · game design · elementary school

## 1 Introduction

The Bombardment of Copenhagen in 1807 is part of the syllabus in the history subject in the Danish elementary school. In September 1807, the British Navy bombarded Copenhagen, seizing the Danish fleet and assured use of the sea lanes in the North Sea and Baltic Sea for the British merchant fleet. The bombardment included more than 300 rockets, which caused fires. Due to the civilian evacuation, the normal firefighting arrangements were ineffective, and over a thousand buildings in Copenhagen were burned. The attack was implemented against the Danish because of Denmark's forced support of Napoleon's continental blockade. Before this, Denmark was a neutral state for nearly 100 years. The attack was heavily criticized internationally and is regarded as one of the first terror bombardments on a European capital.

M. Haahr et al. (Eds.): JCSG 2023, LNCS 14309, pp. 301–313, 2023.
https://doi.org/10.1007/978-3-031-44751-8_23

History plays a vital role in schools all over the world. Through knowledge of countries' histories, pupils can get an understanding of their own and other societies. However, reading history is a skill with many graduations of proficiency; it involves lots of complexity, and it is not an easy task for pupils aged 13–14 to read the mandatory history literature. The Copenhagen Bombardment is considered a foundation of Danish history. However, the analogue text that forms part of the curriculum is not an easy read. This is partially due its complexity; there were several nations involved, several years and numbers are included, and it draws on old sources and writing styles with reports and eyewitness accounts from the bombardment. Therefore, the aim of this study was to improve pupils' engagement and learning about the Copenhagen Bombardment in 1807 with a serious game. Serious games have been used for various subjects in history [1–5], making it easier to memorize and understand facts, concepts, time, and historical events [1, 2]. The use of serious games in history subjects can also increase interest and make history seem alive [1]. Previous definitions have emphasized that serious games are applications that are not designed exclusively for fun [6] or that are intended to be more than entertainment [7, 8]. However, there are still some unsolved categorical problems regarding what constitutes a game and what "more than entertainment" or "not exclusively for fun" mean. An interesting intersection of history and games is related to one of the early commercialized and popular video games, the historical game *Civilization* (released in 1991). Many other edutainment games with historical content have been released, e.g., *Genghis Khan II: Clan of the Gray Wolf* (1992), *Brothers in Arms: Road to Hill 30* (2005), *Assassin's Creed* (2016), and *Valiant Hearts: The Great War* (2016). These games were not designed with education in mind; rather, they employ a learning experience as authentic gameplay, requiring reflection to make connections between the gameplay and the historical content being taught. In this study, we took inspiration from commercialized historical games but transformed the content into a serious game providing pupils aged 13–14 awareness and historical engagement of the Bombardment of Copenhagen in 1807. The following research question guided the study: Can a serious game be engaging and improve learning outcomes about the history of the Copenhagen Bombardment in 1807 for Danish elementary school pupils in the 7th grade?

A great deal of research exists on various game-design principles linked to the importance of narrative engagement [12–16] in designing successful serious games for learning purposes. However, there are still major challenges involved in measuring whether narrative engagement is beneficial for improved learning within very specific learning objectives. Learning outcomes are often measured by self-reports and knowledge tests [17]. Previous studies have reported positive outcomes in terms of narratives being more engaging than traditional classroom instruction [17–20]. However, the effects of game-based learning on specific knowledge tests are more diverse and inconclusive [17]. The novelty of this study lies in collaborating with the elementary school history teacher to set specific learning questions tied to the curriculum on the Copenhagen Bombardment in 1807 and to observe if there are any learning differences between the experimental (gaming) group and the control (reading) group.

## 2    Previous Research

The idea of using serious games to teach history is not new [1–5]. Scholars have described multiple principles for serious games in historical teaching, including the important aspects of learning goals, engagement, realism, feedback, discovery, repetition, guidance, flow, storytelling, social interaction, briefing, and debriefing. Scholars have also emphasized specific aspects of narrative engagement, motivation, and teacher involvement related to making successful serious games with learning purposes.

A) Narrative engagement: Narrative engagement [12] seems important within a serious game focused on historical engagement because of its relation to the story experienced while playing the game [13]. Thus, it may result in imaginative immersion [14], narrative involvement [15], or narrative immersion [16]. The desire to know how the story of the Bombardment of Copenhagen unfolds evokes curiosity, suspense, and narrative engagement, making pupils want to continue playing [13]. Characters in the game may support narrative engagement, as well, when a player begins to involve themselves in their character and as the other characters develop in the narrative [13].

B) Motivation: Engaging in reading for history classes, both in serious games and in other media (analogue included), requires the reader to be motivated [21]. This involves, for example, grasping important elements within the text's content, comprehending the text's overall meaning, gaining new knowledge, and engaging in social interactions (with the teacher and other pupils) using knowledge and/or lessons learned from the text [21, 22]. Furthermore, to design a motivating experience in a serious game, scholars have already emphasized aspects of intrinsic motivation, such as individual curiosity, a desire for challenge, and involvement [9, 23]. It is assumed that the experiences of flow [24] and enjoyment [25] are crucial in this process. When players have mastered specific challenges, they develop a greater level of skill that can be used and improved with more complex challenges in other levels or games [11, 26]; this can have a positive influence on intrinsic motivation in serious games. Serious games in a traditional learning context, as in this study, have the advantage of possible extrinsic motivation from a teacher or learning progression. However, this means that serious games' learning content needs to invoke motivation at various levels for pupils and teachers.

C) Teacher involvement: A very important aspect of a successful serious game promoting historical engagement for a group of pupils aged 13–14 is to include the teacher. Scholars have argued that teachers are key to the success of serious games for educational purposes [27, 28] as a tool to motivate pupils and promote deep learning. Thus, it is important to provide teachers the necessary gaming knowledge and skills to allow them to integrate game-based learning effectively and efficiently in their classes [27, 28]. If a teacher does not find game-based learning useful, they will not provide it to pupils, as the teacher is the crucial gatekeeper. The teacher also provides important instructions for the game in a pedagogical approach, and they can include game-based learning in their teaching progression as well as the content of the game in specific in-class discussions and learning. An important aspect when designing serious games for improved learning in history is to include teachers at an early stage. A teacher can provide valuable evaluative information, such as insight regarding the pupils, specific learning outcomes, and content, and they can serve as the pupils' gatekeeper for access to information.

# 3 Methods

## 3.1 Participants

The participants in this study were pupils from a Danish elementary school aged 13 or 14. One class functioned as a control group for the evaluation, being provided the history textbook and evaluation criteria instead of playing the game (only reading the analogue textbook). The control group consisted of 11 pupils (six male and five female). The other class (experimental group) also consisted of 11 pupils (four male and seven female). Both classes are from the same school, with the same curriculum, but had each a different history teacher. All participants gave informed consent and were informed that they could withdraw from the study at any time and that their participation would not influence their grade. Additionally, all participants were given anonymized ID numbers, and all data were labeled with these IDs. We applied special considerations when recruiting teenagers in accordance with Danish data law, the international code of conduct, and ethical approval from the elementary school.

## 3.2 Procedure

An important focus of this study was to create a game that fit the curriculum on the Bombardment of Copenhagen, as this would make the game broadly applicable to history classes in all Danish elementary schools. To ensure the game followed the curriculum, a history teacher was involved early in the process. The teacher ensured that the material presented in the game was useful and in accordance with the curriculum throughout the game development.

The data collection consisted of a questionnaire, a knowledge test, and interviews. The questionnaire was inspired by the user-engagement scale (UES) short form [29] and consisted of eight items on a 5-point Likert scale. The questionnaire covered three themes: attention, perceived usability, and aesthetic appeal. Only the experimental (gaming) group answered the questionnaire, as it targeted elements specific to game engagement. The knowledge test was made in collaboration with the teacher and had six questions. Both groups were provided the same knowledge-test questions immediately after playing the game (experimental group) or reading from the analogue textbook (control group).

Pupils from the experimental group were interviewed about the same themes from the user-engagement questionnaire (attention, perceived usability, and aesthetic appeal) but with the possibility to ask different questions and follow up on the pupils' replies. The interviews, following a semi-structured interview guide [30], took place after the game play in the classroom. Pupils raised their hands if they wanted to answer the questions from the researchers. The teacher was also present, also for the participants of this age group to feel more comfortable. It took between 10 min and 15 min for the pupils to play the game. Only very few pupils needed help to progress in the game. The pupils in the control group were asked to read the chapter in the analogue textbook regarding the topic (which consisted of six pages), and it took between 15 to 20 min for the pupils to read through.

## 3.3  Data Analysis

We analyzed the user-engagement questionnaire using cumulative frequency, following a mean and standard deviation for each question. The knowledge tests were also analyzed by cumulative frequency, and we compared the number of correct answers between experimental and control groups. All the interviews were analyzed via traditional coding [31] following four steps: organizing, recognizing, coding, and interpretation. Researchers transcribed the interviews and organized and prepared them for data. The codes in each interview were labelled with five predefined themes, allowing the possibility for additional themes. The data were analyzed via content analysis [31]. The interview data were transcribed and showcased through a content analysis exploring the frequency of positive and negative statements within each theme.

## 4  Game Design

The game was developed in the Unity Engine version 2021, utilizing asset packs from the Unity Store for the majority of the included 3D models. The game takes place in the city of Copenhagen (Fig. 1), as close to as possible to various elements such as canals, bridges, harbors, buildings, and an important church tower (which functioned as point of aim).

**Fig. 1.** The game takes place in the city of Copenhagen, with canals, bridges, harbors, buildings, and an important church tower.

The narrative was of high importance, as it needed to correspond with the history of the Bombardment of Copenhagen and with the learning objectives outlined in the curriculum. The players were to follow guidance from the implemented interactable non-player characters (NPCs). The player was able to run/walk around in the city environment, but to progress in the story and get the necessary historical information (through notes), they needed to follow the NPCs' guidance (Fig. 2). The notes are with the exact same texts pieces as in analogue textbook used by the control group. To get the entire story in the game, the players needed to collect and read four notes. The players were visually provided with feedback on how many notes (out of four) they had collected (Fig. 3). The game narrative goes like this:

1. First, the player is spawned into the world in front of two NPCs, one of whom is interactable (Fig. 2).
2. The first NPC asks the player to pick up a note left on a bridge nearby (Fig. 3). There is included feedback of how many notes the player had collected.
3. After the note is picked up, the NPC gives the player some information about the war, and then tells them to see the guard who is guarding the bridge.
4. By interacting with the guard, the player is provided some information about the war, and the guard tells the player to cross the bridge and enter the first house.
5. After the player enters the first house, another NPC is standing close to the entrance, and that NPC gives the player information regarding the war and tells the player to go to the NPC in the middle of the city.
6. The player then goes to the last NPC and interacts with him. The last NPC provides the remaining information, and the player is free to walk around and explore the city afterwards.

**Fig. 2.** Interactive NPCs are guiding the players with tasks.

## 5   Findings

### 5.1   Knowledge Test

The findings from the knowledge test revealed that the experimental group who played the game answered questions correctly to a much higher degree (Table 1).

The difference in correct answers is particularly clear for Q1, Q5, and Q6; the experimental group had eight, seven, and six more answers correct, respectively, and therefore

**Fig. 3.** A left note on the bridge to be found and read.

**Table 1.** Findings from the knowledge test tied to the curriculum. Exp = experimental (game) group and Con = control (analogue reading) group.

| Learning Questions | Group | n | No. Right answers | % right answers | Diff in % |
|---|---|---|---|---|---|
| Q1: Which of the European countries had the strongest fleet in 1807? | Exp | 11 | 9 | 82 | 73 |
| | Con | 11 | 1 | 9 | |
| Q2: Why did Crown Prince Frederik withdraw from the Second League of Armed Neutrality? | Exp | 10 | 0 | 0 | −20 |
| | Con | 10 | 2 | 20 | |
| Q3: How long did it take the British to take over the Danish fleet and sail away with it? | Exp | 10 | 5 | 50 | 20 |
| | Con | 10 | 3 | 30 | |
| Q4: Why did the Russian Tsar feel he had to ally with France? | Exp | 10 | 3 | 30 | 0 |
| | Con | 10 | 3 | 30 | |
| Q5: Why did the Danish state go bankrupt in 1813? | Exp | 10 | 9 | 90 | 70 |
| | Con | 10 | 2 | 20 | |
| Q6: When did Crown Prince Frederik make peace with Great Britain? | Exp | 10 | 6 | 60 | 60 |
| | Con | 10 | 0 | 0 | |

answered these questions correctly 73%, 70%, and 60% more often than the control group. There was only one question (Q2) for which the control group answered correct to a higher degree than the gaming group. This could indicate that the information for

Q2 was not explained or exposed well enough in the game. The information needed to answer Q2 was in the game given only through a voiceover, whereas the other questions were given as written information in for example a note. To convey information using only audio seems in this context not to be the optimal solution. Q4 had an equal number of correct answers between the groups.

## 5.2  Gaming Engagement

The findings from the user-engagement questionnaire revealed positive and negative feedback on game engagement (Table 2).

**Table 2.** Findings from the gaming engagement

| 1 = Strongly Disagree<br>2 = Disagree<br>3 = Neutral<br>4 = Agree<br>5 = Strongly Agree | 1 | 2 | 3 | 4 | 5 | n | SD | Mean |
|---|---|---|---|---|---|---|---|---|
| **1. Focused Attention** | | | | | | | | |
| Q1.1: I had a hard time concentrating when playing the game | 0 | 3 | 5 | 3 | 0 | 11 | 0,775 | 3 |
| Q1.2: I understood what the purpose of the game was | 0 | 1 | 5 | 4 | 1 | 11 | 0,820 | 3,45 |
| **2. Perceived Usability** | | | | | | | | |
| Q2.1: I felt the game was challenging | 1 | 2 | 6 | 2 | 0 | 11 | 0,874 | 2,82 |
| Q2.2: The game was intuitive and it was clear what to do | 0 | 0 | 4 | 2 | 4 | 10 | 0,943 | 4 |
| Q2.3: The narrative was clear | 0 | 2 | 3 | 2 | 3 | 10 | 1,174 | 3,6 |
| **3. Aesthetic Appeal** | | | | | | | | |
| Q3.1: I felt engrossed in the game | 4 | 4 | 1 | 0 | 1 | 10 | 1,247 | 2 |
| Q3.2: I enjoyed playing the game | 1 | 4 | 2 | 2 | 0 | 9 | 1,014 | 2,56 |
| Q3.3: The visuals provided an enjoyable game experience | 0 | 2 | 4 | 3 | 1 | 10 | 0,949 | 3,3 |

The highest mean score was in Q2.2 (Mean: 4.00, SD: 0.943), addressing the game's perceived intuitiveness and clarity. Additionally, Q2.3 (Mean: 3.60, SD: 1.174) showed pupils' positive perceptions of clarity in the game's narrative. The purpose of the game (Q1.2) seemed to be relatively clear (Mean: 3.45, SD: 0.820). However, the findings also revealed potential challenges concerning the pupils being engrossed (Q3.1, Mean: 2.00, SD: 1.247) and enjoying the game (Q3.2, Mean: 2.56, SD: 1.014). These challenges most likely come from balancing between having clear goals (with the intent of always knowing what to do in the game) versus discoverability and difficulty. The game never gets difficult which can create boredom and ruin the player flow.

## 5.3 Qualitative findings

The qualitative data is derived from the interviews conducted with the pupils (in class) after they had played the game. The themes are founded based on the coded interviews. The feedback, immersion, teaching, and motivation themes revealed mainly positive perceptions of the game (Table 3).

**Table 3.** Qualitative findings, example of pupils' statements within five themes

| Themes | Category | Frequency | Examples |
| --- | --- | --- | --- |
| Feedback | Positive | 8 | "The NPCs in the game were easy to interact with" |
| | Negative | 3 | "It was a bit difficult to control the game because the mouse sensitivity was high" |
| Immersion | Positive | 6 | "I was very immersed, and it was easy to see the objective of the game" |
| | Negative | 5 | "It took a while to figure out what to do in the beginning of the game" |
| Teaching | Positive | 8 | "It was more fun than the traditional teaching in history class" |
| | Negative | 3 | "The game was overloaded a bit with information so it was hard to remember" |
| Learning Outcome | Positive | 5 | "The questions were easy to answer" |
| | Negative | 6 | "I missed the traditional way of reading and answering questions" |
| Motivation | Positive | 5 | "It was nice that I had to interact with the characters in the game" |
| | Negative | 2 | "It would have been nice with a list of tasks to look at when playing" |

One of the themes with the highest number of coded positive statements was for the teaching. Several pupils found the game as a more fun way to learn, as seen in the positive teaching example quote: "It was more fun than the traditional teaching in history class." However, this perception seemed to come at a cost, as multiple pupils found the learning outcome from the game to be less effective than their usual learning outcomes from the traditional format of reading the history book. There are also elements for improvements within the game design, including more emphasis on minimizing cognitive overload ("The game was overloaded with information"), as well as the purpose ("It took a while to figure out") needs to be clearer in the beginning og the game.

# 6  Discussion and Future Works

Existing literature [32, 33] includes various examples of how to evaluate serious games. However, when performing evaluations in specific contexts with real users—in this case, with pupils aged 13–14 in elementary school—it can be very difficult to conduct a perfect research evaluation. Logistics, time constraints, gatekeepers, legislation, lack of a proper post-test, technical issues, and resources can be barriers to perfect evaluations. Game evaluation with early teens is difficult but should also raise further questions about how we evaluate serious games with children and teenagers. A major limitation for this study is whether the early teens understood the questions asked and could cope cognitively with a 5-point Likert scale. In addition, randomization is often impractical for evaluating serious games in a fieldwork context. It could also be unethical to randomize pupils in the same class, with some playing the game and some not; this setup should also be avoided because of the potential learning effects.

Like this study, there are several other studies comparing digital computer games and analogue text reading within the same learning objectives [20, 34]. However, one should be careful in interpreting findings of the research on pupil's learnings from such comparison. It might be that we in the game design highlighted and emphasized specific elements of the learning objectives. Further, computer games might also interfere with learning if they are not directly related to the story. This study did not take into account individual variation in responses to the computer game. It cold be that not all pupils are uniformly susceptible to the game or the quality of the educational input from the game.

In research, there remains much more attention towards how to evaluate serious game targeting children and adolescent. There are still some important challenges in how to increase the validity and reliability when evaluating serious games when children and adolescents are the users. Participants, including the teachers, should be motivated and want to participate – also in the evaluation part. Further, which method should be used, and how to ask the right type of questions, aligned with the child's capacity for being reflective (or not) in relation to his or her behavior and habits. Future work is needed to generate significant evidence and insights regarding pupils' learning of history via serious gaming. First, a much higher number of participants is needed, and baseline and control groups should be included in the research design. Second, further details on the identification of the participants are needed (e.g., their confidence in serious gaming and game genre preferences, current knowledge in history, motivation, expectations, and technology acceptance). It is important to emphasize that there is no established taxonomy of serious gaming, and serious games are still diverse in their outcomes and certainly understudied to provide knowledge about history. It would also be interesting to create different options in the game design to make the game more personalized with the inclusion of the participants' own knowledge and motivation.

# 7   Conclusion

In this study, we taught pupils about the Bombardment of Copenhagen in history classes (elementary school) using a serious game approach. The results revealed higher understanding of specific learning objectives in the experimental gaming group compared to the control group, who engaged in analogue textbook reading. The game was developed intuitively and clearly, and the narrative was perceived positively. There is an interesting result from the learning question Q2, which was conveyed only through a voiceover in the game. The result indicated that exclusively using voiceover to convey learning in the game was not optimal. Based on previous research [35, 36], and a more solid theoretical framework, we should have included more emphasis on improved learning questions. This could be with an improved multimedia learning framework, as there is reason to expect that the target group within this study will learn more effectively from combinations of both words, voiceover, a narrative, sound effects.

The interviews supported positive attitudes toward learning through a serious game as an alternative to traditional textbook readings. That serious games can be used as a supplement to traditional textbook readings is already well established in the literature [19, 20]. One of the main takeaways from this study is the importance of a teacher's involvement and collaboration to fulfill specific learning objectives in a curriculum, thereby developing a successful serious game that engages pupils and teachers. These objectives need to be very clear from the beginning during the research design and game design processes. It is vital to know what the game is intended to achieve and, specifically, how it can supplement the analogue text reading.

# References

1. Mz, N.A., Sy, W.: Game based learning model for history courseware: a preliminary analysis. In: 2008 International Symposium on Information Technology. vol. 1, pp. 1–8. IEEE (2008)
2. Oceja, J., Abián-Cubillo, D., Torres-Trimallez, M.: Games for teaching and learning history: a systematic literature review. In: European Conference on Games Based Learning, vol. 16, no. 1, pp. 419–430 (2022).
3. Baxter, G., Hainey, T., Savorelli, A., Akhtar, U., Ivanova, R.R.: Teaching history and bringing the past back to life with serious games. In: Proceedings of the 15th European Conference on Game Based Learning (ECGBL), pp. 99–107 (2021)
4. Akkerman, S., Admiraal, W., Huizenga, J.: Storification in history education: a mobile game in and about medieval Amsterdam. Comput. Educ. **52**(2), 449–459 (2009)
5. Lin, K.C., Wei, Y.C., Hung, J.C.: The effects of online interactive games on high school students' achievement and motivation in history learning. Int. J. Dist. Educ. Technol. **10**(4), 96–105 (2012)
6. Hookham, G., Nesbitt, K.: A systematic review of the definition and measurement of engagement in serious games. In: Proceedings of the Australasian Computer Science Week Multiconference, pp. 1–10 (2019)
7. Ciman, M., Gaggi, O., Sgaramella, T.M., Nota, L., Bortoluzzi, M., Pinello, L.: Serious games to support cognitive development in children with cerebral visual impairment. Mobile Netw. Appl. **23**(6), 1703–1714 (2018). https://doi.org/10.1007/s11036-018-1066-3
8. Ritterfeld, U., Cody, M., Vorderer, P. (eds.): Serious Games: Mechanics and Effects. Routledge, New York (2009)

9. Wouters, P., van Nimwegen, C., van Oostendorp, H., van der Spek, E.D.: A meta-analysis of the cognitive and motivational effects of serious games. J. Educ. Psychol. **105**, 249–265 (2013)
10. De Freitas, S.: Learning in immersive worlds: a review of game-based learning. Prepared for the JISC e-Learning Programme, JISC eLearning Innovation, 3(3) (2006)
11. Plass, J.L., Homer, B.D., Kinzer, C.K.: Foundations of game-based learning. Educ. Psychol. **50**(4), 258–283 (2015)
12. Alexiou, A., Schippers, M.C., Oshri, I., Angelopoulos, S.: Narrative and aesthetics as antecedents of perceived learning in serious games. Inf. Technol. People **35**(8), 142–161 (2022)
13. Schønau-Fog, H., Bjørner, T.: "Sure, I would like to continue" a method for mapping the experience of engagement in video games. Bull. Sci. Technol. Soc. **32**(5), 405–412 (2012)
14. Ermi, L., Mäyrä, F.: Fundamental components of the gameplay experience: analysing immersion. In': de Castell, S., Jenson, J. (eds.) Changing views: Worlds in play. Selected papers of the 2005 Digital Games Research Association's Second International Conference, pp. 15–27. DiGRA, Vancouver (2005)
15. Calleja, G.: In-Game: From Immersion to Incorporation. MIT Press, Cambridge (2011)
16. Adams, E., Rollings, A.: Fundamentals of Game Design. Prentice Hall, Upper Saddle River (2007)
17. Bakhuys Roozeboom, M., Visschedijk, G., Oprins, E.: The effectiveness of three serious games measuring generic learning features. Br. J. Edu. Technol. **48**(1), 83–100 (2017)
18. Mao, W., Cui, Y., Chiu, M.M., Lei, H.: Effects of game-based learning on students' critical thinking: a meta-analysis. J. Educ. Comput. Res. **59**(8), 1682–1708 (2022)
19. Petersen, M.S., Hansen, N.L.S., Jakobsen, G., Bjørner, T.: Increasing Reading Engagement for Danish Gymnasium Students: The Hosier and His Daughter as a Serious Game. In: Brooks, E.I., Brooks, A., Sylla, C., Møller, A.K. (eds.) Design, Learning, and Innovation. Lecture Notes of the Institute for Computer Sciences, Social Informatics and Telecommunications Engineering, vol. 366, pp. 187–197. Springer, Heidelberg (2021). https://doi.org/10.1007/978-3-030-78448-5_13
20. Bjørner, T., Petersen, M.S., Hansen, N.L.S., Jakobsen, G., Hendriksen, D.: How can a foundation be outlined for a successful serious game to increase reading engagement. Int. J. Serious Games **10**(1), 81–95 (2023)
21. Guthrie, J.T., Wigfield, A., You, W.: Instructional contexts for engagement and achievement in reading. In: Christenson, S., Reschly, A., Wylie, C. (eds.) Handbook of Research on Student Engagement, pp. 601–634. Springer, Boston (2012). https://doi.org/10.1007/978-1-4614-2018-7_29
22. Naumann, J.: A model of online reading engagement: linking engagement, navigation, and performance in digital reading. Comput. Hum. Behav. **53**, 263–277 (2015)
23. Mulder, E., et al.: Serious game-based word-to-text integration intervention effects in English as a second language. Contemp. Educ. Psychol. **65**, 101972 (2021)
24. Csikszentmihalyi, M.: Flow: The Psychology of Optimal Experience. Harper Perennial, New York (1990)
25. Sweetser, P., Wyeth, P.: GameFlow: a model for evaluating player enjoyment in games. Comput. Entertain. **3**(3), 1–24 (2005)
26. Gros, B.: Digital games in education: the design of games-based learning environments. J. Res. Technol. Educ. **40**(1), 23–38 (2007)
27. Molin, G.: The role of the teacher in game-based learning: a review and outlook. Serious Games Edutainment Appl. **II**, 649–674 (2017). https://doi.org/10.1007/978-3-319-51645-5_28
28. Hansen, C.B.S., Bjørner, T.: Designing an educational game: design principles from a holistic perspective. Int. J. Learn. **17**(10), 279–290 (2011)

29. O'Brien, H.L., Cairns, P., Hall. M.: A practical approach to measuring user engagement with the refined user engagement scale (UES) and new UES short form. Int. J. Human-Comput. Stud. **112**, 28–39 (2018)
30. Bjørner, T.: Data collection. In: Bjørner, T. (ed.) Qualitative Methods for Consumer Research: The Value of the Qualitative Approach in Theory and Practice. Hans Reitzel, Copenhagen (2015)
31. Bjørner, T.: Data analysis and findings. In: Bjørner, T. (ed.) Qualitative Methods for Consumer Research: The Value of the Qualitative Approach in Theory and Practice. Hans Reitzel, Copenhagen (2015)
32. Silva, F.G.: Practical methodology for the design of educational serious games. Information **11**(1), 14 (2019)
33. Bellotti, F., Kapralos, B., Lee, K., Moreno-Ger, P., Berta, R.: Assessment in and of serious games: an overview. Adv. Human-Comput. Interact. **2013**, Article ID 136864 (2013)
34. Bjørner, T., Sum, A.J., Ludvigsen, R.K., Bouquin, N.L., Larsen, F.D., Kampel, U.: Making homework fun: the effect of game-based learning on reading engagement. In: Conference on Information Technology for Social Good, pp. 353–359 (2022)
35. Mayer, R.E.: Cognitive theory of multimedia learning. In: Mayer, R.E. (ed.) The Cambridge Handbook of Multimedia Learning, pp. 31–48. Cambridge University Press, Cambridge (2005)
36. Bus, A.G., Takacs, Z.K., Kegel, C.A.: Affordances and limitations of electronic storybooks for young children's emergent literacy. Dev. Rev. **35**, 79–97 (2015)

# Evaluating Learning Outcomes and Intrinsic Motivation: A Case Study of DS-Hacker 3D

Alberto Rojas-Salazar[1]([envelope]) [iD], Joel Rojas-Salazar[1] [iD], and Mads Haahr[2] [iD]

[1] Universidad de Costa Rica, San José, Costa Rica
alberto.rojassalazar@ucr.ac.cr
[2] Trinity College Dublin, Dublin, Ireland

**Abstract.** This paper presents a comprehensive evaluation of an educational video game, *DS-Hacker 3D*, that incorporates analogies to enhance the learning of conceptual knowledge in computer science, specifically Binary Search Tree (BST) concepts. The study addresses the challenges students face in understanding complex computer science topics and the limited availability of well-evaluated educational video games in the field. *DS-Hacker 3D* targets undergraduate students and follows a constructivist learning approach, establishing connections between new information and familiar knowledge through analogies. The evaluation includes validated assessment tools to measure learning outcomes and intrinsic motivation. The results demonstrate the effectiveness of the educational video game in facilitating the acquisition of BST conceptual knowledge and promoting intrinsic motivation. The study contributes to the development of educational video games for teaching computer science concepts.

**Keywords:** Analogies · Binary Search Tree · Digital Game-Based Learning · Educational Video Games

## 1 Introduction

Computer science is a vast field filled with complex concepts and models, often posing challenges for students to comprehend and grasp [18, 29]. Research focusing on misconceptions and learning difficulties in computer science indicates that novice learners commonly encounter difficulties in understanding various topics, including logic [29, 41], programming concepts [11, 13, 18, 37, 38], data structures [4, 10, 46], and computer architecture conceptual knowledge [29, 41]. Consequently, even upon completing introductory computer science courses, students may still struggle to grasp the basic principles of programming or to write simple code [25].

In a literature review on programming misconceptions conducted by Qian and Lehman [29], six factors contributing to learning difficulties were identified: (1) the complexity of learning activities, (2) misconceptions arising from natural language, (3) students' lack of mathematical knowledge, (4) inaccurate mental models, (5) inadequate strategies for solving abstract problems, (6) environmental factors including students' existing knowledge, and (7) ineffective instructional approaches. These findings highlight the significance of students' prior knowledge, communication methods (e.g., how learning content is presented), task complexity, and learning strategies in the acquisition of computer science knowledge.

Furthermore, according to constructivist learning theories, the process of acquiring knowledge and comprehending a new subject requires establishing connections with previously acquired knowledge [3]. From this perspective, learning becomes a process of relearning, whereby learners modify or utilize their past experiences, beliefs, and knowledge as a foundation for constructing new knowledge [20]. Additionally, active engagement of learners in the learning process is crucial [5]. As a result, effective learning strategies should consider learners' prior knowledge and facilitate their active involvement to promote the effective integration of new knowledge.

In this paper, we propose that analogies and digital game-based learning (DGBL) are effective approaches for teaching complex conceptual knowledge in computer science, particularly Binary Search Tree (BST) conceptual knowledge. Analogies involve comparing structures of two domains that share symmetrical relations among their components [12]. Their purpose is to transfer ideas and concepts from a familiar domain (source) to an unfamiliar one (target) [15]. Analogies have been widely used in educational settings to establish connections between non-intuitive concepts and familiar knowledge [28], especially in science teaching [12].

DGBL, on the other hand, is a flexible and interactive learning approach that can effectively represent and facilitate understanding of abstract and complex knowledge. Video games, as a form of DGBL, utilize various narrative elements such as text, audio, images, and simulations [14, 39]. Simulations are operating representations based on models or abstractions of real-world processes or systems [16]. In educational video games, simplified models can aid in comprehending the learning content [39]. This enables players to engage with and perceive the models from different perspectives, surpassing the limitations of purely narrative depictions. Additionally, the game designer can employ the video games' operative model to construct analogies conveyed through narrative elements that can facilitate learning new information.

When it comes to DGBL for computer science education, numerous video games have been developed and studied. However, many of these games have not undergone thorough rigorous evaluation. For example, in a systematic literature review conducted by Petri and Gresse von Wangenheim [27] covering the period from 1995 to 2015, they identified 117 evaluation studies and 106 educational games. The review's findings revealed that over 81% of the studies "did not utilize any well-defined model or method for conducting the evaluation" [27]. Similarly, in another review focusing on video games for learning data structures and recursion, Rojas-Salazar and Haahr [32] discovered 15 video games and 2 bundles of mini-games. The results indicated that 35% of the games lacked a theoretical foundation on how people learn, 35% did not employ a well-defined evaluation method, and 24% of the games were not evaluated at all. Hence, there is a clear need for thorough evaluations to enhance our understanding of the effectiveness of educational video games in the field of computer science, particularly in the context of data structures such as BST.

This paper aims to conduct a comprehensive evaluation of an educational video game that incorporates analogies to enhance the learning of conceptual knowledge in computer science, specifically BST concepts, through a case study. Data structures and algorithms form a crucial foundation in computer science and find extensive application in the software industry, significantly improving the efficiency of computational systems [35]. However, BST knowledge presents challenges inherent in complex scientific fields, making it difficult for novice students to develop a deep understanding of advanced data structures and their associated algorithms. In this regard, our study proposes that educational video games have the potential to facilitate the acquisition of abstract knowledge, thereby improving learning outcomes and intrinsic motivation. The results of the case study demonstrate that our educational video game successfully establishes connections between the video game's model and the abstract BST concepts through analogies, while also highlighting the greater intrinsic motivation associated with DGBL compared to traditional digital learning approaches, such as video tutorials.

## 1.1 Related Work

This section presents works related to educational video games about trees data structures. The section only covers games described in short and full papers published in peer-reviewed journals and conference proceedings. Peer-reviewed journal and conference articles assure good quality research as well as the availability of the papers. Other educational games about data structures published in other mediums (e.g., websites) are not included.

Our review has found five significant examples. The first game, called *Elemental: The Recurrence* [9], stands out as a 3D puzzle-coding game that teaches the recursive depth-first search (DFS) algorithm within a binary tree context. Players assume the role of Ele, a programmable avatar, navigating through a binary tree-inspired game world. By coding the missing sections of the DFS algorithm, players advance in the game.

The second game is an adaptation of the classic game *Mario* and focuses on Adelson-Velsky and Landis (AVL) trees [43]. This adaptation presents five distinct levels, each devoted to a different AVL tree concept: BST structure (level one), AVL tree rotations (level two), AVL tree search algorithm (level three), add algorithm (level four), and delete algorithm (level five).

The third game, named the *AVL Tree Game* [40], focus exclusively on AVL tree rotations and the add algorithm. It takes the form of a mobile puzzle game, providing an interactive platform for players to engage with and comprehend AVL trees.

Concerning the fourth game, Shabanah et al. [36] designed a game prototype that focuses on teaching the BST add algorithm. In this game, players are challenged to construct a BST as fast as possible using the given nodes.

Lastly, *Tree Legends with UnityChan* [17] is an action-adventure game designed to foster understanding of tree traversal and search algorithms. Featuring binary, ternary, and quaternary trees, this game encompasses three levels, each concentrating on a specific type of tree data structure. Players navigate through tree-based game world, encountering enemies and helpful non-player characters who offer essential insights to surmount the game's challenges.

The present study makes several contributions based on the reviewed works related to games for learning tree data structures. Firstly, it highlights the limited availability of games dedicated to teaching tree data structures and their algorithms in peer-reviewed academic literature, with only five such games identified. This scarcity underscores the need for further exploration and development in this area.

Secondly, our study focuses on the learning aspects of educational video games, emphasizing the importance of incorporating a well-defined learning theory, learning objectives, and appropriate learning activities in any learning tool [5, 23]. By providing a strong theoretical foundation, clear learning objectives, and suitable learning activities aligned with the learning theory, our study aims to fill the gap left by previous works that lack explicit information in these crucial areas. This comprehensive approach enables a better understanding of the game's scope and facilitates the evaluation process, including the analysis of game design decisions, hypotheses, and experimental results.

Furthermore, our study emphasizes the importance of educational game evaluation aspect, addressing limitations observed in previous works that focus on games for learning tree data structures. Specifically, three out of the five reviewed works [36, 40, 43] either did not evaluate the game or conducted only informal evaluations, such as brief interviews without a structured protocol. Additionally, the remaining two works [9, 17] employed parametric inferential statistics on ordinal data, which violates parametric assumptions and compromises result analysis. To overcome these limitations, our evaluation approach employs validated assessment tools with scale properties to measure learning outcomes and intrinsic motivation, ensuring reliable and meaningful data. By employing these measurement tools and employing nonparametric statistical methods when parametric assumptions are not met, our study ensures robust data analysis while avoiding common statistical analysis and measurement tool problems [30, 34].

## 2 Methods

We performed an evaluation of *DS-Hacker 3D* during August and September of 2020 at Universidad de Costa Rica (UCR). Due to the Covid-19 pandemic, UCR was placed on lockdown, and classes were taught online. For this reason, the experiment was performed virtually, and all materials and tests were distributed and completed using a custom-made web application.

### 2.1 Materials and Participants

**Educational Video Game.** *DS-Hacker 3D* (Fig. 1) is an immersive third-person adventure PC game created using the Unity engine. *DS-Hacker 3D* targets bachelor students of engineering, computer science, data science, or mathematics schools that have programming courses. The selection of game content aligns with the guidelines for undergraduate degree programs [2], making it a suitable complement to introductory programming or data structures courses found in many curricula.

In terms of learning aspects, *DS-Hacker 3D* was designed based on a constructivist approach that emphasizes the learner's active construction of knowledge by connecting new information with existing experiences. This approach is informed by Kolb's experiential learning theory and the experiential learning cycle [20], which provide the foundation for how learning occurs within the game. As a result, the game's learning experience closely follows this cycle and establishes connections between new information and familiar knowledge and experiences with analogies between the game world and the BST structure. These analogies are integrated into the game mechanics and narrative elements, facilitating the acquisition of BST conceptual knowledge.

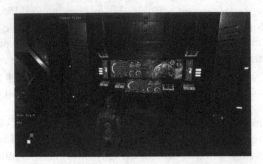

**Fig. 1.** Screenshot of DS-Hacker 3D – Level 1.

*DS-Hacker 3D* primarily covers essential concepts related to the BST data structure, which serves as a fundamental topic taught in introductory computer science courses [2]. The game's learning objectives (LOs) specifically focus on BSTs. However, since BSTs are a specific instance of Binary Trees (BTs), it becomes imperative to include BT concepts as well to effectively impart BST conceptual knowledge. The learning objectives are outlined in Table 1, providing a comprehensive overview of the specific areas targeted for learning within the game.

Concerning the game aspects, *DS-Hacker 3D* is a cyberpunk science fiction game that follows the narrative structure of the Hero's Journey [8]. Set in a future where corrupt corporations threaten society, players assume the role of a robotic hacker. Guided by the non-player character Anonymous, they embark on a mission to infiltrate and extract information from the corporations' computational systems. The game features interlinked mazes and immersive visuals, music, and sound effects, aiming to enhance player immersion and motivation. The narrative elements, delivered through Anonymous' monologues, introduce challenges and missions while teaching BST concepts. Analogies between the game environment and BST structures facilitate understanding and the creation of new knowledge based on familiar concepts.

*DS-Hacker 3D* consists of four levels, each offering distinct challenges and learning opportunities. Level one serves as a tutorial where players are acquainted with the game's controllers, user interface (UI), game world, and overarching story. This introductory level does not encompass specific LOs but focuses on exploration and familiarization with game mechanics. Moving on to the second level, players are introduced to the concept of BTs and the structure of nodes. Level three delves deeper into the BT structure, reinforcing understanding and familiarizing players with the terminology associated with its various components. Finally, in the fourth level, players are introduced to the BST

**Table 1.** Levels, topics, learning objectives (LOs), and learning activities (LAs) of DS-Hacker 3D.

| Level | Topics | LOs | Learning Activities |
|---|---|---|---|
| Level 1 | No topic | No LOs | No learning activities |
| Level 2 | Binary Tree node | LO1. The student should describe the concept of BT<br>LO2. The student should define the basic elements that compose a BT node | LA1. Read and listen the BT definition<br>LA2. Read and listen the node definition and its basic components<br>LA3. Read and listen the link definition (reference/pointers)<br>LA4. Relate the portals (links) with the concept of reference/pointers<br>LA5. Relate the chambers of the game environment with the BT node structure and components |
| Level 3 | Binary Tree structure | LO3. The student should identify BTs<br>LO4. The student should identify the BT's components | LA6. Read and listen the definition of the left and right child<br>LA7. Read and listen the definition of the parent node<br>LA8. Read and listen the definition of a sub-tree<br>LA9. Identify the left and right child of the BT represented by the game environment<br>LA10. Identify the root node of the BT represented by the game environment |
| Level 4 | Binary Search Tree | LO5. The student should explain the BST property<br>LO6. The student should identify the BSTs<br>LO7. The student should solve problems using the BST property<br>LO8. The student should determine whether the BST property is unfulfilled | LA11. Read and listen the definition of the basic components of a BST<br>LA12. Read and listen the definition of the BST property<br>LA13. Apply the BST property to search for specific nodes |

data structure, gaining knowledge about its distinct components and the crucial BST property (Table 1).

**Table 2.** Descriptive statistics of the pre-test and post-test scores of the control and experimental groups.

|                    | Pre-Test Control | Post-Test Control | Pre-Test Experimental | Post-Test Experimental |
|--------------------|------------------|-------------------|-----------------------|------------------------|
| Number of values   | 28               | 28                | 27                    | 27                     |
| Median             | 5                | 8                 | 5                     | 9                      |
| Mean               | 4.27             | 7.82              | 4.85                  | 8.89                   |
| Variance           | 4.51             | 3.86              | 3.98                  | 1.03                   |
| Standard Deviation | 2.12             | 1.96              | 1.99                  | 1.01                   |

Table 1 also lists the learning activities associated with each level of the game that players must engage in during their gaming sessions. A detailed description of the game can be found in [31]. A video of *DS-Hacker 3D* gameplay can be accessed through the following link: https://www.dropbox.com/s/eoecefxjqx3pnr2/Gameplay%20DS-Hacker%203D.mkv?dl=0.

**Video Tutorials.** Video tutorials were used as the "traditional" digital learning approach that was used in the control activity. Two video tutorials developed by the School of Mathematics at the Open State University of Costa Rica (UNED) were used. These tutorials cover all the LOs taught by *DS-Hacker 3D* and are available in the official YouTube channel of the school. The first video covers fundamental concepts of the BT data structure the second video focuses on fundamental concepts of the BST data structure.

**Data Collection Tools.** The measurement of changes in BST conceptual knowledge was conducted using a custom-made test specifically designed for this purpose. The test comprised 10 multiple-choice questions, each having three distractors and one correct answer. It was carefully aligned with the content and learning objectives of *DS-Hacker 3D*, drawing inspiration from well-known textbooks on data structures such as "Data Structure and Algorithms" by Aho [1] and "Algorithms" by Sedgewick and Wayne [35]. To ensure the validity of the test content, it underwent rigorous verification by two undergraduate professors specializing in data structures and algorithms from Trinity College Dublin, as well as six professors specializing in programming, data structures, and algorithms from the UCR. The consistency of the test was assessed using psychometric techniques within Item Response Theory and the Rasch model, involving a sample of 220 computer science bachelor students from UCR and the National University of Costa Rica. The reliability of the test, as measured by Cronbach's alpha, was found to be 0.76.

To evaluate participants' intrinsic motivation, we used a Spanish translation of the Intrinsic Motivation Inventory (IMI) survey [33]. The IMI is a well-known survey used to assess six factors: enjoyment, perceived competence, effort, usefulness, felt pressure and tension, and perceived choice, where enjoyment is considered the self-reported measure of intrinsic motivation [24].

**Participants.** Students from the bachelor programme of the Industrial Engineering Department at UCR were selected to participate in the evaluation. In total, 54 students participated in the experiment and completed all the surveys and tests. Participants were randomly assigned to a control or an experimental group. The control group had 28 participants (50.9%), and the experimental group had 27 participants (49.1%). Regarding their demographic background, 33 participants (61.1%) were female, and 21 participants (38.9%) were male.

## 2.2 Evaluation Design

An independent repeated measures design, also known as pre-test post-test experiment, was conducted with randomly assigned students. The experiment was facilitated through a web application, which also served as the platform for completing surveys and tests. Initially, students were presented with a consent form and agreement checkbox, and upon agreement, they were randomly allocated to one of two learning activities by the web application. General instructions for the experiment were then provided, followed by a demographic survey. Upon completion of the survey, participants proceeded to the pre-test section, where instructions and questions were presented. Subsequently, the web application delivered the learning activity instructions and materials, which participants completed before advancing to the next section. Following the learning activities, students were given the post-test and the IMI scale. Upon answering all the questions, participants submitted their surveys and tests, with the data being stored in a Firebase database.

# 3 Results

Tables 3 and 4 present a comprehensive summary of the descriptive analysis of the pre-test, post-test, and IMI scores, and the differences between the post-test and pre-test scores. The tables include the median, mean, variance and standard deviation.

**Table 3.** Descriptive statistics of the differences between the post-test and pre-test and the IMI scores of the control and experimental group.

|  | Difference Control | Difference Experimental | IMI Score Control | IMI Score Experimental |
|---|---|---|---|---|
| Number of values | 28 | 27 | 28 | 27 |
| Median | 3.5 | 4 | 105.5 | 117 |
| Mean | 3.54 | 4.04 | 101.21 | 115.59 |
| Variance | 5.89 | 3.11 | 276.55 | 140.71 |
| Standard Deviation | 2.43 | 1.77 | 16.63 | 11.86 |

Figure 2 presents the boxplots which also summarize the results of the descriptive analysis.

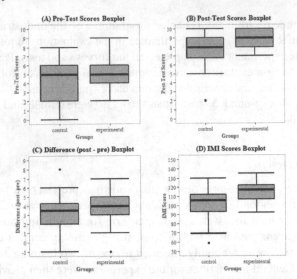

**Fig. 2.** Boxplots of the (A) pre-test, (B) post-test, (C) difference between the pre- and post-test, and (D) IMI scores.

Results of the t-test performed on the pre-test scores suggest that the difference between the control and experimental groups were not significant, $t(53) = -1.02$, $p$-$value = 0.31$ ($p$-$value > 0.05$). Results of a Mann-Whitney U test on the post-test scores suggest that the differences between the control and experimental group was statistically significant, $W = 259.5$, $p$-$value = 0.04$. However, results of the t-test performed on the differences of scores between the post-test and pre-test scores (post-test score minus pre-test score; the learning gains) show that the difference between the control and experimental group was not significant, $t(53) = -0.87$, $p$-$value = 0.39$. Results of the t-test performed on the IMI scores indicates that the difference between the control and experimental group was statistically significant, $t(53) = -3.68$, $p$-$value = 0.001$. Table 4 summarizes the results of the inferential analysis between groups.

**Table 4.** Results of the inferential analysis between groups.

|  | Statistic | df | p-value | 95% confidence interval | Effect size |
|---|---|---|---|---|---|
| Pre-test scores | −1.02 | 53 | 0.31 | [−1.68, 0.55] | −0.28 |
| Post-test scores | 259.5 |  | 0.04 |  | 0.28 |
| Differences | −0.87 | 53 | 0.39 | [−1.65, 0.65] | −0.24 |
| IMI scores | −3.68 | 53 | 0.001 | [−22.22, −6.54] | −1 |

# 4 Discussion

Regarding the learning outcomes, our findings indicate that *DS-Hacker 3D* is an effective educational tool for teaching conceptual knowledge about BSTs. The results of the statistic descriptive analysis demonstrate that students who engaged with the game experienced significant improvements in their learning. This suggests that the act of playing the game facilitated the construction of new conceptual knowledge. Based on the pedagogical design of *DS-Hacker 3D* and the results obtained, we suggest that the presence of analogies within the narrative elements and game mechanics effectively conveyed the BST concepts to the students. We can confidently assert that *DS-Hacker 3D* holds great potential for integration into formal educational settings.

In terms of comparing the learning efficacy between the video tutorials and *DS-Hacker 3D*, our study revealed that both approaches were equally effective. The experimental group, on average, achieved a higher score on the post-test, and this difference was statistically significant. However, when considering the learning gains (post-test score minus pre-test score), there was no statistically significant difference between the two groups. These results indicate that well-designed educational video games, such as *DS-Hacker 3D*, have the potential to be just as effective as video tutorials in teaching conceptual knowledge.

The positive results of the post-test scores in *DS-Hacker 3D* may be attributed to its pedagogical aspects and alignment with learning theory. The game ensures that the LOs and LAs are well-aligned and framed by Kolb's experiential learning theory. By applying the alignment principle, *DS-Hacker 3D* aims to guarantee that all students can achieve the LOs. Furthermore, the game elements, such as narrative mechanics, challenges, environment, and user interface, were designed to engage students actively and facilitate the learning process. For example, the game incorporates analogies, facts, and terminology related to the BST data structure, allowing players to recall and apply concepts through gameplay. The puzzles and traversal of the game environment structured as a BST further reinforce the understanding of fundamental BST concepts. These game features aim to ensure that all players are motivated to achieve the learning objectives, leading to effective learning outcomes.

Our findings regarding intrinsic motivation revealed that students who played *DS-Hacker 3D* exhibited higher levels of intrinsic motivation compared to those who watched the video tutorials. Intrinsic motivation is a desirable characteristic for effective learning experiences as it enhances students' willingness to actively engage in the learning process [19, 42]. *DS-Hacker 3D* outperformed the video tutorials in this regard. The results indicated that nearly all the students experienced a sense of enjoyment while playing the game, and simultaneously, they perceived their participation as meaningful and relaxing. This discovery is particularly encouraging as it contrasts with previous studies suggesting that a significant proportion of adults in higher education are not motivated by video games [44].

The game's higher scores in intrinsic motivation may be attributed to its motivating elements. The game narrative, including the plot and character story, enhance immersion, curiosity, and engagement [7, 22, 45]. The appealing cyberpunk and sci-fi theme may also contribute to maintaining high levels of intrinsic motivation. The inclusion of challenges and goals within the game further may boost players' motivation. Achievement of challenges, task-related goals, and progression are known techniques to increase moti-vation [6, 7, 22]. *DS-Hacker 3D* offers multiple levels with increasing difficulty, each accompanied by tasks and cognitive puzzles. The game ensures that the provided BST concepts align with the players' skill level, allowing for successful completion of tasks and puzzles. Overall, *DS-Hacker 3D* effectively matches challenges and tasks to players' skills, providing motivation and a sense of progression throughout the game.

## 4.1 Limitations

While we aimed to conduct a comprehensive evaluation and analysis, it is important to acknowledge the limitations of this study. Firstly, the sample size used for assessing human psychological features was relatively small. Human constructs such as learning and intrinsic motivation exhibit significant variability, necessitating larger samples to enhance the reliability of measurements and the statistical power [21, 26]. Furthermore, our evaluation focused on a specific population with similar characteristics, namely students from the same year and school. Replicating the study with a diverse population may yield different results. Another limitation is the assumption that the Spanish trans-lation of the IMI survey possesses equivalent psychometric properties as the original English version. Although we conducted inferential statistical analysis using parametric methods based on this assumption, it is advisable to verify the psychometric proper-ties of the Spanish version following best practices. Lastly, our methodology primarily confirms *that* learning occurred without delving into the specifics of *how* individuals were learning. To address this gap, future research should employ qualitative studies and appropriate methodologies to explore the learning process in depth.

## 5 Conclusion

This study has evaluated a DGBL tool with embedded analogies in its narrative elements and game mechanics to facilitate learning computer science conceptual knowledge, specifically BST conceptual knowledge. The game, called *DS-Hacker 3D*, was tested with university students. Our results show that video games can be efficient learning tools that facilitate the learning process of abstract conceptual knowledge. Additionally, our results show that our video game increases the students' intrinsic motivation, a desirable characteristic that learning experiences should have. These results demonstrated that DGBL approaches have great potential in higher education environments to support classes.

While we have shown that video games can be used for learning complex data struc-tures, there is potential for using video games for learning many other types of science knowledge through the combination of analogies, narrative elements, and game mechan-ics. For example, abstract models that explain complex phenomena, such as electricity, atoms, or the immune system, can be represented through a game's operative model allowing the player to interact through the game mechanics. Analogies in conjunction with the game's narrative elements can be used to explain the relation between the game's model and the phenomenon studied. For this reason, we expect the approach described in this paper to generalise to many domains, in particular within science learning. Future work will explore this potential further.

# References

1. Aho, A.V.: Estructuras de datos y algoritmos. Addison-Wesley, México (1988)
2. Association for Computing Machinery (ACM) Joint Task Force on Computing Curricula, IEEE Computer Society: Computer Science Curricula 2013: Curriculum Guidelines for Undergraduate Degree Programs in Computer Science. ACM, New York (2013)
3. Aubusson, P.J., et al.: Metaphor and analogy. In: Aubusson, P.J., et al. (eds.) Metaphor and Analogy in Science Education, pp. 1–9. Springer, Dordrecht (2006). https://doi.org/10.1007/1-4020-3830-5_1
4. Becker, K.: Choosing and Using Digital Games in the Classroom. Springer, Cham (2017). https://doi.org/10.1007/978-3-319-12223-6
5. Biggs, J., Tang, C.: Teaching for Quality Learning at University. Open University Press, New York (2007)
6. Boyle, E.A., et al.: Engagement in digital entertainment games: a systematic review. Comput. Hum. Behav. 28(3), 771–780 (2012). https://doi.org/10.1016/j.chb.2011.11.020
7. Calleja, G.: Digital game involvement: a conceptual model. Games and Cult. 2(3), 236–260 (2007). https://doi.org/10.1177/1555412007306206
8. Campbell, J.: The Hero's Journey, p. 10022. Harpercollins, New York (1991)
9. Chaffin, A., et al.: Experimental evaluation of teaching recursion in a video game. In: Proceedings of the 2009 ACM SIGGRAPH Symposium on Video Games, pp. 79–86. ACM, New York (2009). https://doi.org/10.1145/1581073.1581086
10. Danielsiek, H., et al.: Detecting and understanding students' misconceptions related to algorithms and data structures. In: Proceedings of the 43rd ACM technical symposium on Computer Science Education, pp. 21–26 Association for Computing Machinery, Raleigh (2012)
11. Doukakis, D., et al.: Using animated interactive analogies in teaching basic programming concepts and structures. In: Proceedings of the Informatics Education Europe II Conference IEEII 2007, Thessaloniki, Greece (2007)
12. Duit, R.: On the role of analogies and metaphors in learning science. Sci. Educ. 75(6), 649–672 (1991)
13. Fleury, A.E.: Parameter passing: the rules the students construct. SIGCSE Bull. 23(1), 283–286 (1991)
14. Frasca, G.: Simulation versus narrative: introduction to ludology. In: Wolf, M.J.P., Perron, B. (eds.) The Video Game Theory Reader. Routledge, New York (2003)
15. Glynn, S.M.: Teaching Science with Analogies: A Strategy for Teachers and Textbook Authors. Reading Research Report No. 15. ERIC (1994)
16. Hays, R.T., Singer, M.J.: Simulation fidelity as an organizing concept. In: Hays, R.T., Singer, M.J. (eds.) Simulation Fidelity in Training System Design: Bridging the Gap Between Reality and Training, pp. 47–75. Springer, New York (1989). https://doi.org/10.1007/978-1-4612-3564-4_3
17. Jiménez-Hernández, E.M., et al.: Using a serious video game to support the learning of tree traversals. In: 2021 9th International Conference in Software Engineering Research and Innovation (CONISOFT), pp. 238–244 (2021). https://doi.org/10.1109/CONISOFT52520.2021.00040
18. Kaczmarczyk, L.C., et al.: Identifying student misconceptions of programming. In: Proceedings of the 41st ACM Technical Symposium on Computer Science Education, pp. 107–111. Association for Computing Machinery, Milwaukee (2010)
19. Kapp, K.M.: The Gamification of Learning and Instruction : Game-Based Methods and Strategies for Training and Education. Pfeiffer, United States of America (2012)

20. Kolb, D.A.: Experiential Learning: Experience as the Source of Learning and Development. Pearson, New Jersey (2014)
21. Lazar, J., et al.: Research Methods in Human-Computer Interaction. Morgan Kaufmann Publishers, Cambridge (2017)
22. Malone, T.W.: What makes things fun to learn? Heuristics for designing instructional computer games. In: Proceedings of the 3rd ACM SIGSMALL Symposium and the First SIGPC Symposium on Small Systems, pp. 162–169. ACM, Palo Alto (1980)
23. Mayes, T., de Freitas, S.: Review of e-learning theories, frameworks and models. Joint Information Systems Committee, London (2004)
24. McAuley, E., et al.: Psychometric properties of the intrinsic motivation inventory in a competitive sport setting: a confirmatory factor analysis. Res. Q. Exerc. Sport **60**(1), 48–58 (1989). https://doi.org/10.1080/02701367.1989.10607413
25. McCracken, M., et al.: A multi-national, multi-institutional study of assessment of programming skills of first-year CS students. In: Working Group Reports from ITiCSE on Innovation and Technology in Computer Science Education, pp. 125–180. Association for Computing Machinery, Canterbury (2001)
26. Parsons, S., et al.: Psychological science needs a standard practice of reporting the reliability of cognitive-behavioral measurements. Adv. Methods Pract. Psychol. Sci. **2**(4), 378–395 (2019)
27. Petri, G., Gresse von Wangenheim, C.: How games for computing education are evaluated? A systematic literature review. Comput. Educ. **107**(C), 68–90 (2017). https://doi.org/10.1016/j.compedu.2017.01.004
28. Podolefsky, N.S., Finkelstein, N.D.: Use of analogy in learning physics: the role of representations. Phys. Rev. ST Phys. Educ. Res. **2**(2), 020101 (2006). https://doi.org/10.1103/PhysRevSTPER.2.020101
29. Qian, Y., Lehman, J.: Students' misconceptions and other difficulties in introductory programming: a literature review. ACM Trans. Comput. Educ. **18**, 1, Article 1 (2017)
30. Randolph, J.J., et al.: A methodological review of computer science education research. J. Inf. Technol. Educ. Res. **7**(1), 135–162 (2008)
31. Rojas-Salazar, A.: Game-based learning of data structures based on analogies: learning gains and intrinsic motivation in higher education environments. Trinity College Dublin (2022)
32. Rojas-Salazar, A., Haahr, M.: Theoretical foundations and evaluations of serious games for learning data structures and recursion: a review. In: Ma, M., et al. (eds.) Serious Games. Lecture Notes in Computer Science, vol. 12434, pp. 135–149. Springer, Cham (2020). https://doi.org/10.1007/978-3-030-61814-8_11
33. Ryan, R.M.: Control and information in the intrapersonal sphere: an extension of cognitive evaluation theory. J. Pers. Soc. Psychol. **43**(3), 450–461 (1982). https://doi.org/10.1037/0022-3514.43.3.450
34. Sanders, K., et al.: Inferential statistics in computing education research: a methodological review. In: Proceedings of the 2019 ACM Conference on International Computing Education Research, pp. 177–185. Association for Computing Machinery, Toronto (2019)
35. Sedgewick, R., Wayne, K.: Algorithms. Addison-Wesley, Boston (2014)
36. Shabanah, S.S., et al.: Designing computer games to teach algorithms. In: 2010 Seventh International Conference on Information Technology: New Generations, pp. 1119–1126 (2010). https://doi.org/10.1109/ITNG.2010.78
37. Sirkiä, T., Sorva, J.: Exploring programming misconceptions: an analysis of student mistakes in visual program simulation exercises. In: Proceedings of the 12th Koli Calling International Conference on Computing Education Research, pp. 19–28. Association for Computing Machinery, New York (2012). https://doi.org/10.1145/2401796.2401799
38. Sleeman, D., et al.: Pascal and high school students: a study of errors. J. Educ. Comput. Res. **2**(1), 5–23 (1986). https://doi.org/10.2190/2XPP-LTYH-98NQ-BU77

39. Squire, K.: Video Games and Learning: Teaching and Participatory Culture in the Digital Age. Teachers College Press, New York (2011)
40. Šuníková, D. et al.: A mobile game to teach AVL trees. In: 2018 16th International Conference on Emerging eLearning Technologies and Applications (ICETA), pp. 541–544 (2018). https://doi.org/10.1109/ICETA.2018.8572263
41. Taylor, C., et al.: Computer science concept inventories: past and future. Comput. Sci. Educ. **24**(4), 253–276 (2014). https://doi.org/10.1080/08993408.2014.970779
42. Touré-Tillery, M., Fishbach, A.: How to measure motivation: a guide for the experimental social psychologist. Soc. Pers. Psychol. Compass. **8** (2014). https://doi.org/10.1111/spc3.12110
43. Wassila, D., Tahar, B.: Using serious game to simplify algorithm learning. In: International Conference on Education and e-Learning Innovations, pp. 1–5 (2012). https://doi.org/10.1109/ICEELI.2012.6360569
44. Whitton, N.: Digital Games and Learning: Research and Theory. Routledge, New York (2014)
45. Yee, N.: Motivations for play in online games. J. CyberPsychol. Behav. **9**(6), 772–775 (2006). https://doi.org/10.1089/cpb.2006.9.772
46. Zingaro, D. et al.: Identifying student difficulties with basic data structures. In: Proceedings of the 2018 ACM Conference on International Computing Education Research, pp. 169–177. Association for Computing Machinery, Espoo (2018)

# Explore and Debate Architecture History and Theories Through an Interactive Online Escape Game: ARCHI.101

Iness Tkhayyare(✉) (iD)

École Nationale Supérieure d'Architecture de Toulouse, 31106 Toulouse, France
iness.tkhayyare@toulouse.archi.fr

**Abstract.** Recent research shows that while architecture plays a significant role in our daily lives and public discourse, it is primarily accessible to those already knowledgeable about the subject. Building connections among diverse groups is crucial to promote a better understanding of architecture without imposing educational prerequisites, or specific stylistic doctrines. ARCHI.101 is a serious game, in an Escape Game format, designed to immerse players in architectural history and theories, through the example of the Villa Savoye, allowing them to engage in three-dimensional spaces and interact with historical figures like Le Corbusier and Pierre Jeanneret. The game aims to provide a deeper understanding of architectural doctrines from the 20th century and beyond in an interactive way, while involving the public in a more collaborative approach: Player feedback is integrated into the game and made visible to all through open data, which can guide developers and architects in their practice. The game will be accessible online and could be modified by anyone. It serves not only an educational purpose but also encourages an integrative approach to different perspectives on architecture, fostering interdisciplinary debate.

**Keywords:** Architecture · History · Interactive story · Education · Collaboration · Open Serious Game · Cultural engagement · Escape Game

## 1 Introduction

*"Architecture is the great book of humanity, the principal expression of man in his various states of development, either as strength or as intelligence."* - Victor Hugo.

As referred to by Victor Hugo, architecture is a central element of our society, influencing how we perceive the environment around us. Yet, as architecture students, we often perceive a difference between our perception and appreciation of architectural theories compared to those who have not been initiated to architecture. Understanding the spaces that surround us should not be exclusive to insiders, as architecture impacts the living spaces of everyone.

The dissemination of architectural culture, - which we mean in this paper as the dissemination of historical and theoretical knowledge about architecture, and not in the sense of practical architectural education -, is a subject dealt with by different organizations and actors. The means employed are wide-ranging, but the angle of learning through digital tools, such as serious games, is still little addressed, yet it is a viable teaching solution in the face of the current challenges, like the digital transformation.

The first part of this paper will explore the causal relationship behind this cultural gap, in France, where we are conducting this research at the Ecole Nationale Supérieure d'Architecture de Toulouse. Then, we will describe the game scenario, the educational principles used and the methodology applied. We will also explain the collaborative approach through its online availability and data collection.

To carry out this study, we chose to focus on the following question: How can we develop a serious game with interactive scenarios and collaborative methods to promote architectural culture to the general public?

## 2  Present Circumstances and Serious Games

### 2.1  French Architectural Culture

Several studies have attempted to understand the ins and outs of the relationship of the French to architectural culture. The most exhaustive study allowing us to grasp the issues was conducted by Guy Tapie, in 2018, in his work "La Culture Architecturale des Français." [1]. In his book, Guy Tapie questions the French on their knowledge surrounding the fields related to architecture. According to their self-assessment, 84% of French people do not consider themselves as knowledgeable about architecture fields. Moreover, his study proves that this gap between "knowers" and novices is related to socio-cultural status, and not to age and gender. In the same way as theater and opera, architecture suffers from the stigma of the arts: it is displayed as a culture of its own that requires education in a given social context.

Then, it seems that the French general public does not consider itself fully initiated in architecture. First, architecture is not taught as thoroughly as other arts in schools, which may limit the knowledge and appreciation of this discipline among the younger generations. It is also not well represented in the popular media. This can hinder the understanding of the underlying issues of architecture, such as the understanding of urban spaces. It is therefore important to promote architectural education in order to raise awareness about the importance of understanding architecture.

### 2.2  Serious Games

Serious games, - that can be defined by an interactive and engaging digital application designed to entertain while conveying educational, informative, or training purposes, - [2] appear to receive limited attention from architects in research, and existing architectural initiation games tend to be focused on history, such as the one developed by Capecchi, I. et al. (2022) [3].

Nevertheless, they appear to be well-suited, as one of the barriers to architectural initiation is physical distance and the inability of certain groups to travel in order to be initiated to architecture through physical means. Moreover, the possibility of immersing the player in 3 dimensions in serious games makes sense in this case, because comprehension of architecture is first and foremost an initiation to the properties of architectural spaces. It should also be noted that serious games offer an alternative mode of architectural communication by providing an interactive and narrative context. The use of narration and historical context is not just a convenience, in this context, but a crucial instrument to understand the theoretical and historical facets of architecture.

To add narration and exploration through the game, we explored Panagiotis Fotaris [4] analysis of Escape Rooms for Learning. It highlights the potential of educational escape rooms as innovative, collaborative instructional tools, promoting critical thinking and engagement.

## 3   Description of the work conducted

### 3.1   ARCHI.101

We decided to take into account all these studies and factors to create a serious game to introduce the general public to architecture, which we named ARCHI.101.

ARCHI.101 is a game developed to be played from the first-person point of view in a 3D environment. We chose to develop the first level, "Les Heures Claires" in the Villa Savoye designed by Le Corbusier and Pierre Jeanneret in 1927.

Presented as an escape game, the player navigates through the Villa, engaging with the architect and uncovering the architectural theories at play, all while embarking on a quest to find letters relevant to the Villa's history. The letters' whereabouts are disclosed through interactions with characters such as Le Corbusier, and Mr. And Mrs. Savoye, as well as the exploration of various objects within the Villa. The player is given the freedom to roam the Villa at their own pace, enabling them to experience space as they would during an actual visit (Fig. 1).

**Fig. 1.**  ARCHI.101: game presentation poster.

### 3.2   Theoretical Framework

Which educational theories promote experimentation in a collaborative and open learning environment? We can consider Piaget's (1923) [5] constructivist teaching approach, according to which individuals construct their own knowledge and understanding of the world by interacting with it. This approach suggests that teaching must be based on individual experience and discovery to promote meaningful learning.

We also take into account Edgar Dale's Cone of Experience (1970) [6]. It illustrates how active participation, like hands-on experiences, leads to higher retention and understanding compared to passive learning methods. These principles align with the concept of a serious game due to the opportunities it offers for discovery and interactivity in learning, despite the virtual nature of the experience. By using this teaching method in the context of architectural discovery, the aim is not to impose a doctrine or to incite novices to appreciate different architectural trends, but to provide them with the necessary keys to understand architecture in an autonomous way.

In order to determine how to integrate these principles into ARCHI.101, we will look at the different techniques used in games to maintain the player's attention (Playability factors). From this basis, we suggest a methodology based on skills to acquire (Skills acquired) to be applied when creating a serious game of this kind.

### 3.3 Practical Approach

**Playability Factors**

Researchers and design studios have examined the playability factors that keep a person alert and attentive while playing a video game, which are deeply linked to the theories we mentioned above, as both learning and playing require a sense of engagement and interaction. Focusing on the work of Jesse Schell, [9] author and game developer, but also Fabricatore et al. [7], and St-Pierre [10], who analyzed the playability of video games and serious games, we can summarize these factors in 4 main categories, which lay the foundation for the methodology used to create ARCHI.101. According to them, we can summarize the key elements of a successful video game in 4 points: historical and immersive storyline, (1) a sense of progression and reward, (2) challenging gameplay, (3) and interactive engagement (4).

**Skills Acquired**

Based on the stated constructivist principles and the playability factors, we try to theorize a game world based on constructivist principles. As the player progresses, he/she acquires different skills, linked to the playability factors.

- It anchors himself in a historical and social reality (1): The player is introduced to an initial object of study, an architecture or historical urbanistic context, enabling them to explore and comprehend the architectural setting through a historical narrative and contextual framework. Linking with constructivist principles, the narrative shapes an immersive environment, situating the player in time and space, allowing them to understand the significance of their learning and personally engage in the process.

Through the environment created, we reproduce different periods in the Villa's history: in this example, we reproduce the period of its degradation, in 1963 (Fig. 2).

- It understands the ins and outs of an architectural theory (2): In a serious game, we incorporate a "toy". The toy is the mechanism used in the serious game to keep the player alert. Through the input of objects that the player can manipulate, we bring him additional information on the given environment. In the constructivist approach, learners enhance their learning by actively participating in hands-on experiences and direct manipulation of objects. By implementing various objects, and also the book of the "Complete Works of Le Corbusier" containing some of his most important theories, the player discovers the theories associated with the architect as he discovers the Villa (Fig. 3).

- It challenges and examines an architectural theory (3): In line with constructivist principles, the player stimulates intellectual curiosity and free will when facing decisions in their learning. They reevaluate applied theories, making multiple attempts that shape their knowledge. The Escape-Game logic helps fulfill this purpose, as the player's objective is to find hidden letters within the villa. However, it's not as straightforward as simply locating the letters. Instead, the game incorporates a method where the letters are indicated by clues, dialogues with the characters, and hints embedded by the objects found throughout the gameplay. The player must interact with the environment and engage in conversations to uncover these letters, and collect them (Fig. 4).
- It develops a well-supported opinion and critique by deeply understanding the theory and providing feedback (4): The game challenges and interventions allow the player to bring critical opinions to the objects initially presented and develop an advanced point of view through practice and manipulation. Interaction promotes a balance between assimilation and accommodation in constructivist theories, fostering a taste for informed critique of actively engaged learning. Through exploration and questioning, the player can shape their perspective and provide constructive feedback. The next section of this analysis will discuss the theoretical development of incorporating player feedback into the ARCHI.101 project.

**Fig. 2.** ARCHI.101: comparison between archive photographs (FLC) and game.

**Fig. 3.** ARCHI.101: interaction with the "Complete Works" of Le Corbusier.

**Fig. 4.** ARCHI.101: Le Corbusier's character speaking, events and challenges.

## 3.4 Collaborative Approach

Analyzing player feedback is the next step in the game's development. To facilitate this process, the game, which is currently being developed, is envisioned as an online platform. By setting up a server to collect, sort, and analyze player feedback, the platform can generate statistics that can be made public online. For instance, the opinions of players on the presented theories or the architectural value of the spaces can be collected. The learner actively engages by expressing their views in the debate.

Building on this idea, we can approach the design work collaboratively. The "Open Serious Game" is a concept and an online manifesto created by Quach A. and Nsounga-Matondo H. [11], focusing on making knowledge sharing, learning, and transmission accessible to everyone. Games that are part of the Open Serious Game framework are built on the values of being free and accessible, allowing the possibility of reuse by others, and under public ownership. These values help to foster collaboration among game developers, teachers, and students, and facilitate the sharing of knowledge.

When putting these core concepts into practice, one of the crucial steps includes the creation of a dedicated website for our game. This website will provide access to the downloadable executable of the game. We will also provide the modifiable game files, allowing people to develop new levels based on other architectural theories. Furthermore, we are in the process of setting up an online statistical analysis system to gather user feedback within the game. It involves including in the website links to a questionnaire or forum, gathering statistical data. As the development progresses, in a future update, we aim to explore the possibility of directly collecting user data within the game based on their actions. However, this plan is still in development and has not been implemented yet. Ultimately, our goal is to make our game accessible, modifiable, and improvable by everyone, while collecting data to continue to improve it.

## 4 Perspectives

The use of narrative and interactive storytelling is particularly meaningful in the context of online education, where it can facilitate the dissemination and comprehension of architectural theories to a larger audience. These innovative approaches offer unique opportunities to engage diverse audiences and foster the transmission of knowledge in a fun and accessible way.

Building on the collaborative approach and the idea of the Open Serious Game, the ARCHI.101 project aims to push forward this agenda by promoting innovative educational techniques that enable everyone to learn about the theories of architecture on a large, online scale. Currently a work in progress, the next step involves making the serious game available online for users to play, modify, and provide valuable feedback on the showcased architecture. By analyzing the results of this project, we can rethink traditional pedagogical methods, with the goal of improving the quality and accessibility of education for all. In today's digital age, where information is readily available, it is crucial that we strive to ensure that knowledge is not restricted to a privileged few but is freely accessible to anyone who desires it.

# References

1. Tapie, G.: La culture architecturale des Français. Ministère de la Culture – DEPS (2018)
2. Alvarez, J.: Du Jeu Vidéo Au Serious Game: Approches culturelle, pragmatique et formelle. Thèse HDR, Université Toulouse (2007)
3. Capecchi, I., et al.: The combination of serious gaming and immersive virtual reality through the constructivist approach: an application to teaching architecture. Educ. Sci. **12**, 536 (2022)
4. Fotaris, P., Mastoras, T.: Escape rooms for learning: a systematic review (2019)
5. Piaget, J.: Six Etudes de Psychologie. Editions Gonthier, Genève (1964)
6. Dale, E.: A truncated section of the cone of experience. In; Theory into Practice, vol. 9, no. 2 (1970)
7. Fabricatore, C., Nussbaum, M., Rosas, R.: Playability in action videogames: a qualitative design model, human–computer interaction (2002)
8. Giordan, A.: Les nouveaux modèles sur apprendre: pour dépasser le constructivisme, Perspectives (1995)
9. Schell, J.: The Art of Game Design: A Book of Lenses, 2nd edn. CRC Press, Boco Raton (2014)
10. St-Pierre, R.: Des jeux vidéo pour l'apprentissage? Facteurs de motivation et de jouabilité issus du game design (2009)
11. OpenSeriousGame Website. https://openseriousgames.org/en/welcome-in-openseriousg ame/. Accessed 11 Apr 2023

# Codescape - Development and Operation of a Serious Game for Teaching Programming in Introductory Courses

Paul Gamper[✉] and Ulrik Schroeder

Learning Technologies Research Group, RWTH Aachen University, Aachen, Germany
gamper@medien.rwth-aachen.de, schroeder@cs.rwth-aachen.de
https://codescape.medien.rwth-aachen.de/demo/

**Abstract.** The serious game Codescape is developed at the RWTH University and used in several introductory programming courses with a total of 3000 students per year. The game supports the simultaneous use of several programming languages and is modular in structure, to fit the specific needs of certain usage scenarios or lectures. Codescape was developed with the intention of levelling out the initially heterogeneous skill level of the students and giving beginners a playful and small-stepped introduction to imperative programming without the requirement to set up a local tool chain as it is completely browser based. In this article the game itself, architecture, authoring tools and our survey results are presented.

**Keywords:** Serious game · programming · game-based learning · e-learning

## 1 Introduction

Computer science as a subject is increasingly popular. Although there are many different introductory programming lectures at our university, they all struggle with the varying previous knowledge (Fig. 3) the students have in the field of programming. For many beginners, the start into the concept of programming is challenging and others struggle with the pace of lectures. Also new tools and compilers can be a hurdle for beginners. Therefore, to facilitate the start for as many students as possible, in addition to a suitable learning environment also a didactic scenario is required to add motivation and in which they can learn and, above all, practice programming independently, at their own pace, free of intimidating environments.

The serious game Codescape uses the digital based learning [11] and aims to address these issues. The concept of the game was developed in close collaboration with different stakeholders. This was important, because the game is used in various lectures with partially different programming languages (sometimes even several in one lecture) and even different teaching concepts. In addition to being used on a voluntary basis, the game is also used as part of the exam, for which purpose the compilation and evaluation of the student programs should be stored on our own servers. To satisfy all these needs, players should be able to play unsupervised from home, like in an exercise, but the execution and evaluation should take place on the server.

## 2   Related Work

Educational games and learning environments for practicing programming have been around for as long as computers have existed. The concept presented in the book "Karel the Robot" [10] in 1981 was implemented as a learning game for many programming languages.

We are aware that there are also several projects using drag & drop blocks or visual programming languages like scratch [7]. There are promising results [2] in a study with school children using scratch as a first programming language. However, due to the significantly higher learning pace at universities and because of the additional hurdle of then again transitioning to a professional textual programming language - we decided to abandon the use of visual programming languages and to start with the languages that will be taught in the lecture.

Most programming learning games let the player write code to solve certain problems. Games like Code Hunt [12] and EleMental [3] let the player solve puzzles or have a specific focus. Code Hunt provides the expected result of a correct solution and requires the player to write an algorithm which provides the same outcome in several tests. EleMental is focused on recursion and depth first search. A game called RoboBug [8] is focused on debugging as an important part of the programming process. Alice [4] has a focus on object oriented content. Players can create and control different 3D objects and in newer version even make use of VR. Kara [6] originally had a focus on learning finite automata with visual programming, which was also expanded to use with other programming languages.

Many of these examples have been and are being run on computers in the classroom with a teacher as supervisor, with the aim of learning. It is difficult to determine without supervision whether a player has actually solved the task. We decided for a concept with unsupervised learning due to a big amount of students and new online learning trends. Code Combat [1] is browser based and a good example of a commercial game, with multiplayer support and several programming languages to learn. Still the number of programming languages is limited there, the game is not open source.

In summary, nowadays a large number [9] of games are developed, almost for every language and programming concept or theme. A big problem with these games - only a handful are accessible and even less are open source. Often a game lifetime ends with the end of a project or research.

## 3   Codescape

The serious game Codescape was developed in 2016 at the RWTH University and is specifically designed for self-regulated learning from home. It avoids all the previously mentioned hurdles and adds game elements and storytelling as additional motivation.

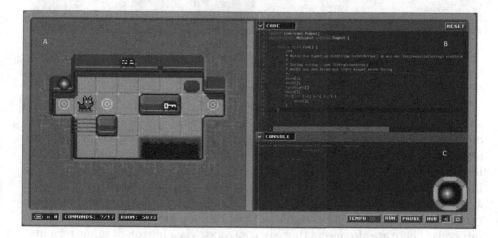

**Fig. 1.** (A) Game map, (B) Code editor, (C) Error console

As a player, you explore a runaway spaceship. The Spaceship is divided into 7 decks consisting of 32 levels and mini-games. The decks group the learning material in terms of content and are unlocked with the progress in the lecture - to encourage continuous learning. In the Codescape level (Fig. 1), the students guide a robotic companion (RB) in the form of a dog from a starting point to a target point. As a challenge, they need to survive and stay within a certain command-line length limit that varies depending on the level and the respective programming language.

There are obstacles to overcome, such as lasers that can turn on and off randomly, holes in the floor, etc. Each time a start button is pressed, the program is compiled on the server side, executed and the movement of the RBs path through the level is visualized in the form of an animation. To increase replay value and also to offer more challenges for experienced students, additional game elements - the power cells are introduced as a secondary target. These cells are placed in the levels in such a way that they can only be collected through the use of advanced programming constructs.

Not every programming concept is suitable to be mapped as a game level. In this case we offer additional tasks in form of puzzles, drag & drop and multiple choice. The storytelling components with intro video, avatars and dialogues complete the serious game. The game is currently available in German and English (Fig. 2).

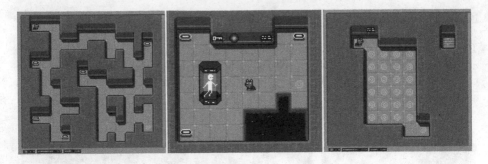

**Fig. 2.** From left to right: a level with a maze, main hub, a level to use arrays

The levels are saved in the database and can be created and changed using a level editor. The editor is easy to use and, in addition to the visuals, also allows to enter the right solutions, the task and also the parameters for the randomization of the level. For example, a labyrinth can be newly generated for each player. The level's map is divided into several layers and, in addition to static elements, also includes dynamic ones, such as various lasers, teleporters, buttons and input & output terminals. Depending on the logic of a level, the dynamic elements can be interconnected. For example, a laser can operate randomly or in certain intervals. There are also lasers that are controlled via a button or input terminal. The learning scope depends on the lecture and the used language.

Since the game was originally planned to accompany a lecture, there were no explanations or tutorials in the game. Over time and with changing areas of application, in-game explanations and tutorials were added and appear in the form of a spaceship logbook. The game now is in a state that it can be used stand alone, without a lecture. Furthermore, the game would offer immediately suitable explanations without having to refer to external sources. In order to address as many different types of learners as possible, the content can contain videos, images, texts and animations (without sound). The content can be easily created and edited via the authoring service in the back end. The explanations can be assigned to a category and are unlocked gradually as the game progresses. The content varies per programming language and can be rated by the players with stars.

### 3.1 Software Architecture and Multi Programming Language Support

As mentioned above, Codescape is a browser-based game. The students' programs are compiled, analyzed, executed and evaluated in various Docker containers. The programs themselves but also the results are stored in the database and displayed to the player. Although Codescape was initially only developed for Java, the switch to compilation in Docker allowes easy integration of other programming languages. The Docker containers also allow to limit the resource consumption per compilation process and to encapsulate the players in the container in order to guarantee safe execution. Currently Java, Python, C, Java Script and Julia are supported. With just a few adjustments, most levels can be reused for multiple languages. Some lectures teach several programming languages in one lecture, so the game has been adapted and now allows to choose the programming language and explanations per level.

## 3.2 Operation

Codescape was originally developed as one installation per lecture. It worked, but as the number of lectures and different requirements increased, so did the administrative burden. As a solution, all different game versions were packed in one installation. As described above, dockerization allows us to combine different languages in one installation. In addition, this enables several identical versions to be operated in parallel. Demo, production and test versions can be created for a customer with just a few clicks by copying. Only the references to the game content itself are copied, so errors can be quickly eliminated for all iterations. The registration for the game are either done manually or more and more often via Moodle, but other learning platforms can also be integrated relatively easily.

## 4 Evaluation and Research

The game has been in use for seven years and generated over 2 million submissions. A survey was always made in the game itself in form of a questionnaire. Since the results hardly differ from year to year, the results from 2022 are presented here. 606 players from a total of 847 lecture participants took part in the survey. Figure 3 shows the result of a self-assessment questionnaire at the very beginning of the game and the lecture. The previous knowledge of the players has been and surprisingly has remained very heterogeneous for years.

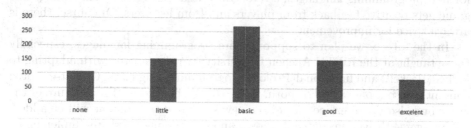

**Fig. 3.** Self-assessment of the students' prior knowledge. Data from 606 students.

As shown in Fig. 4, the game was rated very well in overall. The difficulty of the game was rated spot on at 73%. The graphics were also mostly rated positively. The integration of the game into the lecture was rated as good by only 45%, it is probably due to the lack of object-oriented parts and languages that are

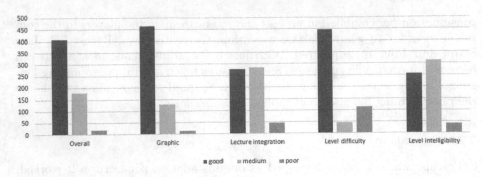

**Fig. 4.** Survey results from a introductory course in programming, winter therm 2022. Data from 606 students.

taught in the lecture and do not yet appear in the game. The comprehensibility of the tasks still needs to be improved. Most players (66%) stated that the game helps to better understand the lecture material. Most gamers (75%) found the space setting to be good, and 42% of respondents even stated that they would like to play the game in their free time.

The wish to improve the game and the amount of data generated by users, motivated us to start a research. The aim of our study [5] is to understand the problems that players face when learning to program with the game and try to offer an adaptive help. For this case we analyze the problem solving strategies the players use in the game, to give an adaptive feedback in the future. We also run an eye-tracking study with Codescape as a validation method on one hand and hope to see synergies in eye-tracking and game data.

## 5 Conclusion and Future Work

The game has been in use since 2016 and continues to be developed. Support for new programming languages, a level editor and the logbook came along. The game gets positive feedback from players and from lecturers. Of course, there is always space for improvements.

In the future, we plan to support more programming languages, especially those taught at the RWTH Aachen University. We also started with adapting to logical(Haskell) and functional(Prolog) programming languages. Object-oriented content is also a big wish. For both, a lot will be changed in the structure of the game and also the interface, but also a new story line and content will be added.

The game thrives on content, so ideas and suggestions are gladly implemented into new content every year. Furthermore, the creation and management of content(tasks, levels, help) should be simplified. The players should also have the opportunity to create their own levels and tasks and to propose them for the lecture after a peer review. Another possibility to create new content would be to facilitate the exchange with other platforms and games.

Finally we hope to integrate the findings from our research in the adaptive feedback function with connection to a suitable explanatory resource.

# References

1. Code Combat. https://codecombat.com/. Accessed 2010-09-2023
2. Armoni, M., Meerbaum-Salant, O., Ben-Ari, M.: From scratch to "real" programming. ACM Trans. Comput. Educ. **14**(4), 1–15 (2015). https://doi.org/10.1145/2677087
3. Chaffin, A., Doran, K., Hicks, D., Barnes, T.: Experimental evaluation of teaching recursion in a video game. In: Proceedings of the 2009 ACM SIGGRAPH Symposium on Video Games, Sandbox 2009, pp. 79–86. Association for Computing Machinery, New York (2009). https://doi.org/10.1145/1581073.1581086
4. Cooper, S., Dann, W., Pausch, R.: Alice: a 3-D tool for introductory programming concepts. J. Comput. Sci. Coll. **15**(5), 107–116 (2000)
5. Gamper, P., Heinemann, B., Ehlenz, M., Schroeder, U.: Identifying problem solving strategies of programming novices in a serious game. In: 2021 International Conference on Advanced Learning Technologies (ICALT), pp. 91–93. IEEE (2021)
6. Hartmann, W., Nievergelt, J., Reichert, R.: Kara, finite state machines, and the case for programming as part of general education. In: Proceedings IEEE Symposia on Human-Centric Computing Languages and Environments (Cat. No.01TH8587), pp. 135–141 (2001). https://doi.org/10.1109/HCC.2001.995251
7. Maloney, J., Resnick, M., Rusk, N., Silverman, B., Eastmond, E.: The scratch programming language and environment. ACM Trans. Comput. Educ. **10**(4), 1–15 (2010). https://doi.org/10.1145/1868358.1868363
8. Miljanovic, M., Bradbury, J.: RoboBUG: a serious game for learning debugging techniques, pp. 93–100 (2017). https://doi.org/10.1145/3105726.3106173
9. Miljanovic, M.A., Bradbury, J.S.: A review of serious games for programming. In: Göbel, S., Garcia-Agundez, A., Tregel, T., Ma, M., Baalsrud Hauge, J., Oliveira, M., Marsh, T., Caserman, P. (eds.) JCSG 2018. LNCS, vol. 11243, pp. 204–216. Springer, Cham (2018). https://doi.org/10.1007/978-3-030-02762-9_21
10. Pattis, R.E.: Karel the Robot: A Gentle Introduction to the Art of Programming. Wiley, Hoboken (1994)
11. Prensky, M.: Digital game-based learning. Comput. Entertain. (CIE) **1**(1), 21 (2003)
12. Tillmann, N., Bishop, J., Horspool, N., Perelman, D., Xie, T.: Code hunt: searching for secret code for fun. In: 7th International Workshop on Search-Based Software Testing, SBST 2014 - Proceedings (2014). https://doi.org/10.1145/2593833.2593838

# Navigating the Skies: A Serious Game for Exploring Drone Energy Consumption, Flight Risk, and Societal Impact in Logistics

Ben Snow[1]([✉]) [iD], Janet Dickinson[1] [iD], Angela Smith[1] [iD], Jian Chang[1] [iD],
Taalia Nadeem[1] [iD], Aliaksei Pilko[2] [iD], Tom Cherret[2] [iD], Andy Oakey[2] [iD],
and Alexander Blakesley[3] [iD]

[1] Bournemouth University Business School, Bournemouth University, D109 Dorset House, Talbot Campus, Fern Barrow, Poole BH12 5BB, UK
{bsnow,jdickinson,avsmith,jchang,nadeemt}@bournemouth.ac.uk
[2] School of Engineering, University of Southampton, Boldrewood Innovation Campus, Southampton SO16 7QF, UK
{A.Pilko,T.J.Cherrett,A.Oakey}@soton.ac.uk
[3] Centre for Transport Studies Department of Civil, Environmental and Geomatic Engineering, University College London, Gower Street, London, UK
alexander.blakesley@ucl.ac.uk

**Abstract.** A logistics drone routing game utilising modelled flight risk and energy consumption data is presented, and its design elements are discussed. The game has been developed as part of a multi-disciplinary research project tasked with generating new understanding of the energy use and risks associated with drone use in logistics alongside the wider implications for society. The game aims to engage with a non-specialist, adult audience on the risk and energy implications associated with where logistics drones may fly. People's views of this new transport mode are gathered to support the wider research project. Use of the Unity3D engine and tilemap system are explored to provide an engaging context for users to build their own flight paths to solve drone delivery problems. The integration of modelled drone flight risk and energy data into the game is examined, as well as the utilisation of satellite imagery and geographic data. This data allows for a realistic representation of the route planning problem and for the simulation of drone flights along user-defined paths. Preliminary findings from two pilot trials indicate the game's effectiveness in engaging audiences and stimulating discussions about drone deliveries. Conference attendees are invited to experience a demonstration of the game.

**Keywords:** Logistics drones · Risk modeling · Serious games

## 1 Introduction

Drones have been developed for logistics purposes with trials taking place in many countries, with some more established services in Africa [1]. As a new mode of transport in lower airspace, the introduction of logistics drones raises many questions on where

M. Haahr et al. (Eds.): JCSG 2023, LNCS 14309, pp. 342–349, 2023.
https://doi.org/10.1007/978-3-031-44751-8_27

they should fly. Direct routes use less energy but have implications for ground risk if they pass over densely populated areas. It is challenging to involve non-specialists in debate about where drones should fly as most people are unlikely to have knowledge or experience of logistics drones and are largely disinterested in a transport future that is, for the most part, yet to exist. To involve non-specialists in discussion about drone routes, the E-Drone project (https://www.e-drone.org/) has developed several tools to garner people's interest in logistics drones and to help them understand the implications. This includes the development of a digital game, *'Navigating the Skies,'* which draws on the expertise of the multi-disciplinary project team including the modelling of energy use [2] and ground risk [3]. *Navigating the Skies* aims to engage with a non-specialist, adult audience on the risk and energy implications associated with where logistics drones may fly. This demo paper begins with a brief overview of games research in the sustainability and logistics fields. It then sets out the game objective and scenario, before focusing on the game design, particularly the integration of modelled flight risk and energy consumption data. To finish, an overview of the deployment settings and initial findings from two pilots are presented to demonstrate the game's effectiveness in engaging audiences and stimulating discussions about drone deliveries.

## 2  Literature Overview

Game based approaches are increasingly used to bring stakeholders to a dialogue on complex sustainability topics [4] since they facilitate social learning that leads to practice change [5]. Most success is achieved with games linked to specific contexts and based on real-world data of immediate relevance to participants [6]. Within the transport field, serious games have been used to help stakeholders understand complex decisions in transport planning [7], with more general audiences to educate people on use of new transport modes [8] and Freese et al. [9] have analysed the use of serious games as a research instrument in the transport field. Several studies have used serious games in the logistics field [10, 11]. Transport games focus on transport systems that already exist and typically facilitate better use of transport by the public or experts with the overarching aim of achieving cost savings or environmental benefits. *Navigating the Skies* is about a transport technology that has not been implemented beyond discrete trials and the focus is on helping players reflect on decisions that will impact future regulation and governance. We use the game as a research tool to engage players in drone routing decisions involving risk and energy trade-offs. To our knowledge *'Navigating the Skies'* is the first serious game focused on logistics drones or future flight transport technologies more broadly and has some similarities to flight planning tools.

## 3  Game Objective and Scenario

The objectives of the game for the research were to:

- Engage stakeholders and public in drone delivery risk-energy trade-offs.
- Collect data about decisions made by users to gain insight into their choices.
- Evaluate and quantify post-game data on user reflections about drone logistics.

This required a game that captures the audience's interest, is fun to play, and includes multiple layers of complexity. The mission is to deliver a package from point A to point B using a drone by constructing a route whilst considering the drone's battery life (energy consumption) and ground risk. To achieve this, the game utilises satellite imagery to allow players to explore drone flight paths in their own area. The game design focused on Southampton, UK, as the project team were modelling drone delivery scenarios in this area, however, the modelled data and game can be transposed to other places.

Users can build a route from an origin location to a destination by selecting squares, known as tiles, on a rectangular grid superimposed atop a satellite image (see Fig. 1 left). Constructed routes are continuous, self-avoiding, and have a fixed maximum length constrained by the battery limitations of real delivery drones. Modelled energy usage data is used to calculate the energy expenditure of a drone flying an equivalent distance on the underlying satellite image. A battery indicator displays the remaining energy available to select more squares. Selecting a tile on the grid reduces the amount of energy remaining to select additional grid tiles. Squares on the grid store modelled drone ground risk data which is shown to the user with a number and a colour to indicate the severity of risk for various locations. This users to the challenges faced by researchers when creating delivery routes in the real world. As a route is constructed, ground risk along the path is accumulated and plotted on a graph. Users are encouraged to investigate the tradeoffs between risk and energy when constructing their routes. Once a complete route from the origin to the destination is created, the user can submit the route and be shown a 3D flyover following their constructed route (see Fig. 1 right).

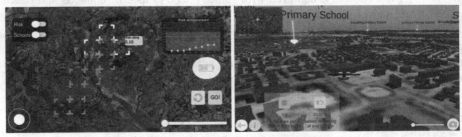

**Fig. 1.** Left: Selection scene in the digital game. Green and red flags indicate origin and destination locations. An orange delivery route is being constructed on the square grid. White tiles show possible next selections. A tooltip shows the risk rating and changes colour, from green to red, based on the relative risk of the square beneath it. Toggle switches to show the risk map and local school locations are in the top left. A risk accumulation graph, battery indicator, undo, and submit route buttons are to the right. Camera controls are to the bottom of the figure. Right: 3D flyover scene with Open Street data. A minimap shows the drone location in the top left with camera view toggles in the bottom right and flight statistics in the bottom left.

# 4 Game Design and Development

A game environment was constructed in the Unity3D game engine and formation of an interaction space was achieved with the Unity Tilemap system. Upon the beginning of play, a procedure commences whereby a series of tilemaps are spawned. These hold the satellite imagery, start and end points, selected route tiles, and surrounding tiles. An in-game camera is positioned to frame the area of player interaction and User Interface elements, such as the risk accumulation graph, are placed in the viewport. Unity's Tilemap system brings with it a GridInformation data structure component. This component allows data to be assigned to tile positions with associated keywords. As such, both relative and absolute risk are stored in the GridInformation and are accessible during game play. A GameManager component is used to handle the game state, facilitates the loading of levels and menus, and storage of user data during play. A MainManager allows data persistence between levels and communication between game scripts. Two levels, the selection and 3D flyover scenes, are present in the game. The user is first shown the selection scene in which they are tasked with constructing a route, after which users are asked to submit the route with the "GO!" button and can then watch a drone fly over a 3D reconstruction of the proposed path. Data from Open Street Map and Mapbox have been used to create a 3D environment of the Southampton area and a CAD model of a delivery drone is animated to fly along the proposed route.

In the event of a drone malfunction during flight, there is a probability that the craft will plummet towards the ground, colliding with an impact kinetic energy. The likelihood of an individual suffering a fatal injury in such an incident is determined for a particular location [3]. The risk that the falling drone causes a fatality is known as the ground risk. To model ground risk, a variety of factors must be considered, including drone failure data, simulated falling trajectories, wind conditions, drone parameters (e.g., weight and airspeed), time-of-day population density maps, road traffic information, shelter availability, and other relevant variables. A United Kingdom wide dataset of ground risk is used to incorporate risk for the Southampton area in the game.

Data pre-processing is conducted to ensure suitability for the needs of the digital game. Using four coordinates of longitude and latitude, a region enclosing Southampton is established, and satellite imagery is aggregated using the Mapbox platform. A risk map is generated for 1pm GMT with fixed environmental conditions [12]. Further processing involves padding the dimensions of the risk map before a block-reduce algorithm is applied to average the risk values of neighbouring grid cells and reduce the resolution of the grid from 456x593 to 8x10, the resolution of the selection scene grid. Finally, two risk maps are produced, one absolute and one relative. Absolute risk refers to the probability of fatality per hour of drone flight time, and relative risk is normalized to represent the relative difference between tiles. Relative risk provides a more intuitive understanding for users allowing for easy comparison between tiles. An absolute risk map, however, would exhibit an almost binary nature concentrated on the significantly higher risk in the city centre area compared to very low risk rural areas surrounding Southampton. Absolute risk values are stored to calculate the overall absolute risk of a user generated route in the problem scenario to give as feedback to the player. Similar to the risk data, energy consumption of drone usage has been modelled and data generated is incorporated into the game mechanics. An implementation of the energy modelling formula is used to calculate the expected energy expenditure over a given distance with set operating parameters. This function can be used to calculate the energy usage for arbitrary conditions and distances. When a player appends a tile to their constructed route, the distance between the selected tile and the previously selected tile is calculated and then fed to the energy model to return the consumption over that distance. This is then deducted from a pre-computed maximum energy level available for flight; the number of selection squares used to construct a route is constrained by this level. An undo button is featured to allow, and encourage, players to amend their routes in the selection stage and investigate how different routes affect risk and energy usage.

A command pattern is used to facilitate the route building mechanism. As the user selects a tile to add to their route, a command is sent to a command handler that stores the co-ordinates of the selected tile, the absolute ground risk, and energy expenditure. This information is then processed to add a data point to the accumulated risk graph and alter the battery level indicator. Commands can be removed from the command handler by use of the undo button allowing the user to reassess their selection decisions. A request to add a tile to the route is made with a touch or click from the user, a check is performed to ensure the tile is immediately surrounding the previously selected tile. Only the nearest neighbour tiles are allowed to be selected (white tiles in Fig. 1). A check for self-avoidance is performed to ensure the route does not intersect with itself. Energy is removed from the remaining battery level and selections are disallowed when the battery is empty. When a valid tile is selected, an orange selection tile is placed at its location and the surrounding tile locations are updated. A termination condition is satisfied when the destination location is reached, the player can then choose to undo or submit their route to visit the 3D flyover scene. A data collection procedure allows the evolution of the user's commands to be saved and a full reconstruction of a given user's actions and routes plotted within the game can be collected for further analysis.

## 5   Initial Game Deployment, Data Collection and Findings

To date the game has been deployed at two public outreach events (Hands on Humanities and Science Day at the University of Southampton on the 19/11/2022 and 18/3/2023 respectively) that provide a range of engagement activities to involve the public in research. Use of the game at these events aided the game development and captured initial data from the public to establish the value of the game in the research project. At Hands on Humanities the game was available to play on tablet computers, while at Science Day the game was available on tablets and a larger touch table. Following a brief introduction, participants were invited to play the game and, where participants' time allowed, adults were invited to complete a brief post-game questionnaire (Hands on Humanities n = 31, Science Day n = 10, Bournemouth University ethics committee approval ID: 45834). Gender composition was 33% male and 67% female for n = 41. The questionnaire included open and closed questions about participants' initial thoughts about delivery drones, where they should fly and the regulation of delivery drones. This was followed by a short section to provide feedback on the game and questions on participants' age and gender. The sample composition (Table 1) indicates participants included a variety of ages and genders. The data collected post-game demonstrates the game helped participants reflect on logistics drones. Participants provided nuanced and considered views, for example, *"Think about sustainability vs. Vans"* or *"Considering safety, impact, environmental factors."*

**Table 1.** Sample composition.

| Age | 16–24 | 25–34 | 35–44 | 45–54 | 55–64 | 65–74 | 75–84 | 85 + |
|---|---|---|---|---|---|---|---|---|
| (n = 41) % | 13 | 13 | 18 | 37 | 13 | 0 | 3 | 3 |

As well as picking up on energy and risk issues, participants reflected on other factors such as noise over residential areas, flight times, privacy and types of products delivered, for example *"Interesting concept although have concerns about noise and number of flights overpopulated areas. Impact on wildlife (birds etc.)"* and *"I wouldn't want the use to escalate to delivery of non-urgent items."* Participants were asked about flight frequencies in a range of settings showing a wide spread of views (Table 2), though participants were more circumspect about flights over housing and their own homes. Feedback on the game indicated it was easy to understand and follow (92% agreed or strongly agreed). Comments included: *"Very helpful in translating the ideas into what they mean in practice,"* *"fun and user friendly"* and *"great for getting the message across."* Users suggested developments that are informing the game's features: more detailed route mapping; additional complexity; and in-game instructions.

**Table 2.** Which settings do you think it would be appropriate for delivery drones to fly over?

| Flight over: | No drones flying over (%) | No more than four drone flights a day (%) | A drone flying over every hour (%) | A drone flying over every 30 min (%) | A drone flying over every 15 min (%) | $M^a$ | SD |
|---|---|---|---|---|---|---|---|
| Housing | 34 | 39 | 12 | 5 | 10 | 2.17 | 1.243 |
| My home | 24 | 46 | 17 | 2 | 10 | 2.27 | 1.162 |
| Urban park | 25 | 25 | 30 | 8 | 13 | 2.58 | 1.299 |
| Town/city centre | 18 | 35 | 20 | 10 | 18 | 2.75 | 1.354 |
| Countryside | 12 | 32 | 20 | 15 | 22 | 3.02 | 1.369 |
| Industrial area | 2 | 10 | 32 | 17 | 39 | 3.8 | 1.145 |

Scale from 1 to 5 where 1 is no drones flying over and 5 is a drone flying over every 15 min.

# 6 Future Work

The project team will deploy the game this autumn in a data collection activity. This will formalise a data collection protocol that will capture users' views of logistics drones, the distribution of risk accumulated, and the routes plotted. Data captured post-game will be linked to in-game choices on risk and routes. The game has been well received by other researchers and, given the game was designed to be readily adapted to specific places, it is now being developed for new locations as part of a second research project. A data collection procedure to collect both user metadata and path selection data has also been constructed. The game will be available to download through the project website along with code and instructions, available for reuse.

**Acknowledgements.** The research reported in this paper was carried out as part of the UK EPSRC-funded E-Drone project, EP/V002619/1 (www.e-drone.org).

# References

1. Medical Drone Delivery Database. https://www.updwg.org/md3/. Accessed 10 May 2023
2. Blakesley, A., Anvari, B., Kroll, J., Bell, M.G.H.: Minimum energy route optimisation of a quad-copter UAV with landing incentivisation. In: 2022 IEEE 25th International Conference on Intelligent Transportation Systems (ITSC), Macau, China, pp. 2300–2306 (2022). https://doi.org/10.1109/ITSC55140.2022.9922101
3. Pilko, A., Sóbester, A., Scanlan, J.P., Ferraro, M.: Spatiotemporal ground risk mapping for uncrewed aircraft systems operations. J. Aerosp. Inf. Syst. **20**(3), 126–139 (2023). https://doi.org/10.2514/1.I011113
4. Medema, W., Chew, C., Adamowski, J.F., Mayer, I., Wals, A.: Understanding game-based approaches for improving sustainable water governance (2020). https://doi.org/10.3390/books978-3-03928-763-5
5. Reed, M.S., et al.: What is social learning? Ecology and Society **15**(4) (2010). http://www.ecologyandsociety.org/vol15/iss4/resp1/
6. Pope, C.P.: Board games as educational tools leading to climate change action: a literature review. J. Sustain. Educ. **25**, 1–26 (2021)
7. Duffhues, J., Mayer, I.S., Nefs, M., van der Vliet, M.: Breaking barriers to transit-oriented development: insights from the serious game SPRINTCITY. Environ. Plann. B. Plann. Des. **41**(5), 770–791 (2014)
8. König, A., Kowala, N., Wegener, J., Grippenkoven, J.: Introducing a mobility on demand system to prospective users with the help of a serious game. Transp. Res. Interdiscip. Perspect. **3** (2019). https://doi.org/10.1016/j.trip.2019.100079
9. Freese, M., Lukosch, H., Wegener, J., König, A.: Serious games as research instruments – Do's and don'ts from a cross-case-analysis in transportation. Eur. J. Transp. Infrastruct. Res. **20**(4), 103–126 (2020)
10. Mes, M., van Heeswijk, W.: Comparison of manual and automated decision-making with a logistics serious game. In: Lalla-Ruiz, E., Mes, M., Voß, S. (eds.) ICCL 2020. LNCS, vol. 12433, pp. 698–714. Springer, Cham (2020). https://doi.org/10.1007/978-3-030-59747-4_45

11. Erika, A.: The role of collective experience in the process of individual valuation of an object: The case of a serious game on city logistics. In: 2020 IEEE 13th International Colloquium of Logistics and Supply Chain Management (LOGISTIQUA), Fez, Morocco, pp. 1–5 (2020). https://doi.org/10.1109/LOGISTIQUA49782.2020.9353884

12. Pilko, A., Tait, Z.: SEEDPOD ground risk: a python application and library for uncrewed aerial systems ground risk analysis and risk-aware path finding (v0.15.1) Zenodo (2022). https://doi.org/10.5281/zenodo.6363635

# Posters and Exhibits

# The Influence of Personality Traits and Game Design Elements on Player Enjoyment: A Demo on GWAPs for Part-of-Speech Tagging

Rosa Lilia Segundo Díaz[1,2]([mail]) [iD], Gustavo Rovelo[3] [iD], Miriam Bouzouita[4] [iD], Véronique Hoste[2] [iD], and Karin Coninx[1] [iD]

[1] Faculty of Sciences, HCI and eHealth, Hasselt University, Diepenbeek, Belgium
rosalilia.segundodiaz@uhasselt.be
[2] Faculty of Arts and Philosophy, Department of Translation, Interpreting and Communication, Ghent University, Ghent, Belgium
[3] Expertise Centre for Digital Media, Hasselt University - tUL - Flanders Make, Diepenbeek, Belgium
[4] Institut für Romanistik, Humboldt-Universität zu Berlin, Berlin, Germany

**Abstract.** This demo paper presents three Games With A Purpose (GWAPs) created to revise and correct automatically tagged part-of-speech (PoS) of the most extensive collection of Spanish oral data, known as the *Corpus Oral y Sonoro del Español Rural* (*COSER*, [7], "Audible Corpus of Spoken Rural Spanish"). The goal is to create a morpho-syntactically annotated and parsed corpus of European Spanish dialects through crowdsourced contributions from non-experts. Players are tasked with assigning grammatical categories (e.g., verb, noun, adjective, pronoun) to words in input texts within the three GWAPs: *Agentes*, *Tesoros*, and *Anotatlón*. The creation of the games follows a user-centred design approach that involves professionals in Computational Linguistics, Dialectology, and Human-Computer Interaction experts and integrates players' input. This demo paper presents the design motivations and solutions from this collaboration. Furthermore, it examines whether players' personality traits and using particular Game Design Elements (GDEs) influence their enjoyment.

**Keywords:** Serious Games · Games With A Purpose · Game Design Elements · Personality traits · Player enjoyment · Part-of-speech tagging

## 1 Introduction

Games With A Purpose (GWAPs), a subset of serious games, enable data generation, collection and validation as a side effect of people playing a game [30]. GWAPs, meant to create large annotated corpora, constitute a promising approach within Natural Language Processing (NLP). They represent one of the most practical ways to obtain resources compared to high-cost and time-consuming manual data annotation or other data collection methods (e.g. Mechanical Turk) [4]. Furthermore, they can improve the output's accuracy thanks to multiple players' consensus. The existing body of research on GWAPs has presented various games to address specific linguistic tasks and build diverse linguistic resources. These tasks include collecting commonsense knowledge about words [31], Parts-of-Speech (PoS) tagging [15,29], named entity tagging [29], anaphoric annotation [21], dependency syntax structure [8], co-reference resolution [14], word sense disambiguation [29], among others.

This demo paper presents the design of three GWAPs to annotate the PoS of the COSER corpus (*Corpus Oral y Sonoro del Español Rural* "Audible Corpus of Spoken Rural Spanish"), which is the most extensive collection of oral data in the Spanish speaking world. Each game concept integrates different Game Design Elements (GDEs) to increase player enjoyment. These variations in the game concepts will, of course, influence how participants perceive them. Hence, in addition to presenting the design of the games, the study aims to discover which game concept is preferred in terms of player enjoyment and whether the implementation of GDEs and the participants' personality traits influence that preference.

## 2   Related Work

Researchers have explored personality traits and enjoyment to enhance player motivation. They have examined the Big-Five Personality Traits (i.e., Openness to Experiences, Conscientiousness, Extraversion, Agreeableness, and Emotional Stability) [11] to understand how the various player groups perceive the player enjoyment in a game. Prior studies have also established connections between GDEs and personality traits. Jia et al. [10] found that people with high Conscientiousness perceive progress and levels to be very motivating factors. People that are more extravert rather find their motivation in GDEs, such as leaderboards and levels, whereas players with lower Emotional Stability scores consider rewards and badges more enjoyable. Nagle et al. [19] found that some difficulty conditions in their experiment contribute to higher enjoyment values for participants with certain personality traits. In the context of GWAPs, which aim to reach more players to contribute to the linguistic tasks, the relationship between personality traits and GDEs could facilitate the design of games that can be fine-tuned to be appealing to diverse user groups. Despite this potential, these relationships remain largely unexplored. There is currently no evidence indicating whether participants' personality traits impact the level of player enjoyment when the same linguistic task is presented in various game concepts. Hence, this study aims to assess three GWAPs concepts to determine whether the associations between personality traits and the implemented GDEs increase player enjoyment and influence their preferences for a particular game.

# 3    Game Concepts and Their Game Design Elements

Three GWAPs were designed in the context of our research to incorporate the PoS tagging task, in which every word is assigned a contextually relevant morpho-syntactic category (e.g., verb, noun, adjective, pronoun, among others). The web-based, single-player games present *Entrenamiento* 'Training' and *Jugar* 'Playing' modes (see Fig. 1 screenshots a, b and c). The training mode familiarises players with the games and the PoS tagging task categories, similar to the training done in Phrase Detectives [5], and Zombilingo [8]. This mode is also necessary as not all Universal Dependencies (UD) [20] tags used to annotate are familiar to non-expert players, e.g., an article is common, but a determiner is not a category taught during education. In addition, the training also helps players remember the terminology that they already learned. As shown in Figs. 2 and 4 screenshot (a), a colour code indicates the relation between the word to classify and the corresponding category. Once the training mode concludes, the playing mode is activated, which is the step where participants formally start helping in the correction or confirmation of tags. In this mode, the description and colours are no longer presented as shown in Fig. 2 screenshot (b).

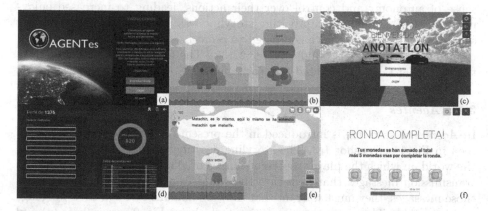

**Fig. 1.** Leaderboards, levels, rewards and themes implemented in the three GWAPs. (a) Theme for *Agentes*. (b) Theme for *Tesoros*. (c) Theme for *Anotatlón*. (d) Leaderboards and levels are presented in the three games. *Agentes* presents points as rewards. (e) Coins rewards in *Tesoros*, one per word correctly annotated and five at the end of the round. (f) Coins rewards in *Anotatlón* obtained at the end of the round.

GDEs were incorporated in the design to enhance player enjoyment. These GDEs were carefully selected from a list of formerly investigated GDEs [24], where their influence on player enjoyment had already been demonstrated. Four GDEs were implemented in the three games, namely leaderboards, levels, rewards and themes. Leaderboards were integrated into the game design to motivate players to enhance their rankings, fostering competition and encouraging them to revisit the game [17,27]. Levels were introduced as a form of reward, as studies suggest they contribute to increased player enjoyment [3,10,12,18,28]. Other rewards, such as points, badges, coins, jumps, shields, levels, and leaderboard positions, were included to enhance the gaming experience. Furthermore, the game's graphical design was guided by a distinct theme for each GWAP as can be seen in Fig. 1 screenshots (a), (b), and (c). *Agentes* immerses players in a world-saving agent scenario, *Tesoros* features an avatar collecting treasures, and *Anotatlón* revolves around a car race theme. Figure 1 also shows the levels, leaderboard and the rewards that consist of points for *Agentes* and coins for *Tesoros* and *Anotatlón*.

Then, with the same goal of increasing the levels of player enjoyment for each game, specific GDEs were implemented that have been shown to affect player enjoyment positively. These GDEs included adaptation, challenges, progress, avatar, customisations, and storyline. Adaptation was integrated to dynamically adjust the game difficulty based on player performance [1,17]. Challenges were included to maintain a sense of competence by balancing ability and difficulty [33]. Progress, displayed through levels, progress bars, and feedback mechanisms, was another GDE meant to boost players' sense of competence [10,13,25]. Avatars were incorporated to enhance intrinsic motivation by allowing players to identify with the game and their avatar [2]. Customisation gave players a sense of autonomy and control over their actions, leading to increased enjoyment [6,23,26]. Finally, a captivating storyline was introduced to offer players a more immersive experience compared to point-based and non-fantasy games, resulting in higher levels of enjoyment [22,32]. The following sections illustrate the particular GDEs integrated into each game.

### 3.1  *Agentes*

In *Agentes*, a storyline is introduced in the presentation of the game as can be seen in Fig. 1 screenshot (a). The storyline describes undercover agents saving the world, in which the player represents an agent. The agent's mission is to find transmission messages that help save the world from extra-terrestrials. To get those messages, they must warrant that they are humans through their language understanding. Therefore, the annotation task shown Fig. 2 screenshots (a) and (b) serves as a test to verify that the player is human. For each correctly classified word, players earn 20 points, and when they accumulate a certain amount of points, they can collect badges as shown in Fig. 2 screenshot (c).

### 3.2  *Tesoros*

In *Tesoros*, the GDEs adaptation, challenges, progress and avatar are implemented. The implementation of adaptation consists in adjusting the number of annotated words that the player has to annotate to complete the round. Two challenges were implemented. The first one consists in finishing a round without mistakes to earn jumps (sort of extra lives). In the second challenge, after the players earn the extra lives shown in Fig. 3 screenshot (c), the game becomes more difficult. When players make a mistake, the tiles are not built, so the avatar

**Fig. 2.** Agentes and its GDEs. (a) Training mode shows the highlighted words and their corresponding category in the same colour and the description of the PoS at the bottom. (b) Playing mode shows the highlighted words in a neutral colour, and the description of the PoS is no longer visible. (c) Badges are earned when players collect a certain amount of points.

needs those jumps to survive the round (see Fig. 3 screenshot b). Concretely, if players make one mistake, they will need one jump to reach the next tile. If they make two mistakes in a row, they will need two jumps, and so on. Progress was implemented using the tiles. These give more sense of progress compared to *Agentes* as players see that for each annotated word a tile is built, and in this way, they see their progress in the round.

**Fig. 3.** Tesoros and its GDEs. (a) Training mode shows a description of the PoS at the bottom. (b) Playing mode does not show the description of the PoS. (c) Jumps rewards are earned for finishing round without errors.

### 3.3 *Anotatlón*

In *Anotatlón*, challenger, progress, and customisation were implemented. The challenge consists of finishing a car race by avoiding obstacles shown in Fig. 4 screenshot (b). Progress has been implemented by adding three races to the round. Customisation allows players to control the difficulty levels (i.e. easy, normal, and difficult, as seen in Fig. 4 screenshot c). These levels affect not only the speed but also the number of obstacles that are presented at random positions on the race track. More specifically, in the easy level, the number of obstacles is six, in the normal level, it increases to 13, and for the difficult one, it increases to 21. Then, after finishing the race, the player is presented with the annotation task shown in Fig. 4 screenshot (a).

**Fig. 4.** Anotatlón and its GDEs. (a) Training mode shows the highlighted words and their corresponding category in the same colour and the description of the PoS at the bottom. (b) An extra task is added as a challenge before the player executes the annotation task. (c) Players can customise the difficulty in which they want to play.

## 4    Methodology and Results

This study evaluates the three presented GWAPs to determine player preferences in terms of player enjoyment and the potential influence of personality traits and GDE implementation. The study was financed by the FWO and approved by the Ethics Committee (SMEC) of UHasselt.[1] Fifty-four participants (30 males, 24 females) were recruited through convenience sampling and divided into three groups to evaluate their preferences between two game concepts (i.e. Group A: *Agentes* and *Tesoros*, Group B: *Agentes* and *Anotatlón*, Group C: *Tesoros* and *Anotatlón*). This separation was done to prevent bias from fatigue due to playing and evaluating more than two games. After providing informed consent, players answered the Ten-Item Personality Inventory (TIPI, [9]) and played the first assigned game in a free-playing period lasting approximately 15 min. Following the play session, players completed two questionnaires, i.e. Intrinsic Motivation Inventory (IMI, [16]) and a custom-designed questionnaire, to evaluate their game perceptions. After two sessions, they filled out another custom-designed questionnaire to compare the two played games.

Results showed the following links between personality traits and GDEs: Agreeableness and progress; Emotional Stability and theme; Extraversion and levels, progress, and rewards; and Openness to Experiences and rewards. Additionally, we could see that some GDEs (i.e., adaptation, challenges, customisation, leaderboards, levels, progress, rewards, and theme) were correlated with player enjoyment.

## 5    Conclusions

This research was conducted to determine the effects of personality traits and GDEs on player enjoyment and whether they impacted the preference for a particular game. The study revealed that player enjoyment plays a role in game preference. However, concerning personality traits, only two GDEs, theme and

---

[1] Flemish Research Fund (FWO) medium scale infrastructure project reference: I000418N. Approval number REC/SMEC/VRAI/201/115, granted on 25/03/2021.

levels, were associated with personality traits and impacted player enjoyment. Consequently, further research is needed to fully comprehend the links between personality traits and GDEs.

# References

1. Alves, T., Gama, S., Melo, F.S.: Flow adaptation in serious games for health. In: 2018 IEEE 6th International Conference on Serious Games and Applications for Health (SeGAH), Vienna, Austria, pp. 1–8. IEEE (2018). https://doi.org/10.1109/ SeGAH.2018.8401382. https://ieeexplore.ieee.org/document/8401382/
2. Birk, M.V., Atkins, C., Bowey, J.T., Mandryk, R.L.: Fostering intrinsic motivation through avatar identification in digital games. In: Proceedings of the 2016 CHI Conference on Human Factors in Computing Systems, CHI 2016, pp. 2982–2995. Association for Computing Machinery, New York (2016). https://doi.org/10.1145/ 2858036.2858062
3. Bui, P., Rodríguez-Aflecht, G., Brezovszky, B., Hannula-Sormunen, M.M., Laato, S., Lehtinen, E.: Understanding students' game experiences throughout the developmental process of the number navigation game. Educ. Tech. Res. Dev. **68**(5), 2395–2421 (2020). https://doi.org/10.1007/s11423-020-09755-8
4. Chamberlain, J., Fort, K., Kruschwitz, U., Lafourcade, M., Poesio, M.: Using games to create language resources: successes and limitations of the approach. In: Gurevych, I., Kim, J. (eds.) The People's Web Meets NLP. TANLP, pp. 3–44. Springer, Heidelberg (2013). https://doi.org/10.1007/978-3-642-35085-6_1
5. Chamberlain, J., Poesio, M., Kruschwitz, U., et al.: Phrase detectives: a web-based collaborative annotation game. In: Proceedings of the International Conference on Semantic Systems (I-Semantics 2008), Graz, Austria, pp. 42–49. Verlag der Technischen Universität Graz (2008)
6. Cuthbert, R., Turkay, S., Brown, R.: The effects of customisation on player experiences and motivation in a virtual reality game. In: ACM International Conference Proceeding Series, OZCHI 2019, pp. 221–232. Association for Computing Machinery, New York (2019). https://doi.org/10.1145/3369457.3369475
7. Fernández-Ordóñez, I.D.: Corpus oral y sonoro del español rural (2005). http:// www.corpusrural.es. Accessed 20 Apr 2022
8. Fort, K., Guillaume, B., Chastant, H.: Creating Zombilingo, a game with a purpose for dependency syntax annotation. In: ACM International Conference Proceeding Series, pp. 2–6. Association for Computing Machinery, New York (2014). https:// doi.org/10.1145/2594776.2594777
9. Gosling, S.D., Rentfrow, P.J., Swann, W.B.: A very brief measure of the Big-Five personality domains. J. Res. Pers. **37**(6), 504–528 (2003). https://doi.org/10.1016/ S0092-6566(03)00046-1
10. Jia, Y., Xu, B., Karanam, Y., Voida, S.: Personality, targeted gamification: a survey study on personality traits and motivational affordances. In: Conference on Human Factors in Computing Systems - Proceedings, CHI 2016, pp. 2001–2013. Association for Computing Machinery, New York (2016). https://doi.org/10.1145/ 2858036.2858515
11. John, O.P., Srivastava, S.: The big five trait taxonomy: history, measurement, and theoretical perspectives. Handb. Pers. Theory Res. **2**(510), 102–138 (1999)

360    R. L. Segundo Díaz et al.

12. Johnson, D., Klarkowski, M., Vella, K., Phillips, C., McEwan, M., Watling, C.N.: Greater rewards in videogames lead to more presence, enjoyment and effort. Comput. Hum. Behav. **87**, 66–74 (2018). https://doi.org/10.1016/j.chb.2018.05.025. https://www.sciencedirect.com/science/article/pii/S0747563218302516

13. Li, J., van der Spek, E.D., Hu, J., Feijs, L.: Turning your book into a game: improving motivation through tangible interaction and diegetic feedback in an AR mathematics game for children. In: Proceedings of the Annual Symposium on Computer-Human Interaction in Play, CHI PLAY 2019, pp. 73–85. Association for Computing Machinery, New York (2019). https://doi.org/10.1145/3311350.3347174

14. Madge, C., Yu, J., Chamberlain, J., Kruschwitz, U., Paun, S., Poesio, M.: Crowdsourcing and aggregating nested markable annotations. In: 57th Annual Meeting of the Association for Computational Linguistics, Proceedings of the Conference, ACL 2019, Stroudsburg, PA, USA, pp. 797–807. Association for Computational Linguistics (2019). https://doi.org/10.18653/v1/p19-1077. https://www.aclweb.org/anthology/P19-1077

15. Madge, C., Bartle, R., Chamberlain, J., Kruschwitz, U., Poesio, M.: Incremental game mechanics applied to text annotation. In: Proceedings of the Annual Symposium on Computer-Human Interaction in Play, CHI PLAY 2019, pp. 545–558. Association for Computing Machinery, New York (2019). https://doi.org/10.1145/3311350.3347184

16. McAuley, E.D., Duncan, T., Tammen, V.V.: Psychometric properties of the intrinsic motivation inventory in a competitive sport setting: A confirmatory factor analysis. Res. Quarterly Exerc. Sport **60**(1), 48–58 (1989). https://doi.org/10.1080/02701367.1989.10607413

17. Mildner, P., Stamer, N., Effelsberg, W.: From game characteristics to effective learning games. In: Göbel, S., Ma, M., Baalsrud Hauge, J., Oliveira, M.F., Wiemeyer, J., Wendel, V. (eds.) JCSG 2015. LNCS, vol. 9090, pp. 51–62. Springer, Cham (2015). https://doi.org/10.1007/978-3-319-19126-3_5

18. Nagle, A., Riener, R., Wolf, P.: How would you like to be rewarded? Relating the Big-Five personality traits with reward contingency in a cognitive training puzzle game. In: 2016 IEEE International Conference on Serious Games and Applications for Health (SeGAH), Orlando, FL, USA, pp. 1–7. IEEE (2016). https://doi.org/10.1109/SeGAH.2016.7586281. http://ieeexplore.ieee.org/document/7586281/

19. Nagle, A., Wolf, P., Riener, R.: Towards a system of customized video game mechanics based on player personality: relating the Big Five personality traits with difficulty adaptation in a first-person shooter game. Entertainment Comput. **13**, 10–24 (2016). https://doi.org/10.1016/j.entcom.2016.01.002. https://www.sciencedirect.com/science/article/pii/S1875952116000045

20. Nivre, J., et al.: Universal dependencies v2: an evergrowing multilingual treebank collection. In: Proceedings of the 12th Language Resources and Evaluation Conference, Marseille, France, pp. 4034–4043. European Language Resources Association (2020). https://www.aclweb.org/anthology/2020.lrec-1.497

21. Poesio, M., Chamberlain, J., Kruschwitz, U., Robaldo, L., Ducceschi, L.: Phrase detectives: utilizing collective intelligence for internet-scale language resource creation. ACM Trans. Interact. Intell. Syst. **3**(1), 1–44 (2013). https://doi.org/10.1145/2448116.2448119

22. Prestopnik, N.R., Tang, J.: Points, stories, worlds, and diegesis: comparing player experiences in two citizen science games. Comput. Hum. Behav. **52**(C), 492–506 (2015). https://doi.org/10.1016/j.chb.2015.05.051

23. Ruehrlinger, M., Gattringer, F., Stiglbauer, B., Hagler, J., Lankes, M., Holz-mann, C.: It is not rocket science. It is collaborative play for old and young! In: 2018 IEEE 6th International Conference on Serious Games and Applications for Health (SeGAH), Vienna, Austria, pp. 1–7. IEEE (2018). https://doi.org/10.1109/SeGAH.2018.8401318. https://ieeexplore.ieee.org/document/8401318/

24. Segundo Díaz, R.L., Rovelo Ruiz, G., Bouzouita, M., Coninx, K.: Building blocks for creating enjoyable games—a systematic literature review. Int. J. Hum.-Comput. Stud. **159**, 102758 (2022). https://doi.org/10.1016/j.ijhcs.2021.102758. https://linkinghub.elsevier.com/retrieve/pii/S1071581921001762

25. Siemens, J.C., Smith, S., Fisher, D., Thyroff, A., Killian, G.: Level up! the role of progress feedback type for encouraging intrinsic motivation and positive brand attitudes in public versus private gaming contexts. J. Interact. Mark. **32**, 1–12 (2015). https://doi.org/10.1016/j.intmar.2015.07.001. https://www.sciencedirect.com/science/article/pii/S1094996815000341

26. Smeddinck, J.D., Mandryk, R.L., Birk, M.V., Gerling, K.M., Barsilowski, D., Malaka, R.: How to present game difficulty choices? Exploring the impact on player experience. In: Conference on Human Factors in Computing Systems - Proceedings, CHI 2016, pp. 5595–5607. Association for Computing Machinery, New York (2016). https://doi.org/10.1145/2858036.2858574

27. Sun, E., Jones, B., Traca, S., Bos, M.W.: Leaderboard position psychology. In: Proceedings of the 33rd Annual ACM Conference Extended Abstracts on Human Factors in Computing Systems, CHI EA 2015, vol. 18, pp. 1217–1222. ACM, New York (2015). https://doi.org/10.1145/2702613.2732732

28. Vella, K., Peever, N., Klarkowski, M., Ploderer, B., Mitchell, J., Johnson, D.: Using applied games to engage mHealth users: a case study of MinDMax. In: Proceedings of the 2018 Annual Symposium on Computer-Human Interaction in Play, CHI PLAY 2018, pp. 523–534. Association for Computing Machinery, New York (2018). https://doi.org/10.1145/3242671.3242686

29. Venhuizen, N.J., et al.: Gamification for word sense labeling. In: Proceedings of the 10th International Conference on Computational Semantics, IWCS 2013 - Long Papers, Potsdam, Germany, pp. 397–403. HAL-Inria (2013). https://hal.inria.fr/hal-01342431. https://hal.inria.fr/hal-01342431/document. http://www.wordrobe.org/

30. Von Ahn, L., Dabbish, L.: Designing games with a purpose. Commun. ACM **51**(8), 58–67 (2008). https://doi.org/10.1145/1378704.1378719

31. Von Ahn, L., Kedia, M., Blum, M.: Verbosity: a game for collecting common-sense facts. In: Conference on Human Factors in Computing Systems - Proceedings, vol. 1, pp. 75–78. ACM, New York (2006). https://doi.org/10.1145/1124772

32. Wang, X., Goh, D.H.-L., Lim, E.-P., Vu, A.W.L.: Aesthetic experience and accep-tance of human computation games. In: Allen, R.B., Hunter, J., Zeng, M.L. (eds.) ICADL 2015. LNCS, vol. 9469, pp. 264–273. Springer, Cham (2015). https://doi.org/10.1007/978-3-319-27974-9_28

33. Yildirim, I.G.: Time pressure as video game design element and basic need satisfac-tion. In: Proceedings of the 2016 CHI Conference Extended Abstracts on Human Factors in Computing Systems, CHI EA 2016, pp. 2005–2011. Association for Com-puting Machinery, New York (2016). https://doi.org/10.1145/2851581.2892298

# Speaker Identification in Scene-based Segmentation of Stories for Serious Games

Toka Hassan(✉) 🆔 and Gerard T. McKee

The British University in Egypt, Cairo, Egypt
{Toka.Hassan,Gerard.McKee}@bue.edu.eg

**Abstract.** Mental health, an essential yet somewhat misunderstood aspect of people's well-being, has a deeply rooted stigma that deters those with mental health problems from seeking psychiatric help. A novel approach to addressing this issue is the integration of Cognitive Behavioural Therapy (CBT) within an interactive story that can be played on a serious game platform. However, if CBT, stories, and serious games are to be integrated to support mental health, it is imperative to adapt stories to incorporate CBT mental, physical, social, and emotional activities. While manually adapting the story is feasible, a more comprehensive approach lies in automating the process to generate a wide range of readily available stories. The research described in this paper proposes that the adaptation can be carried out in five steps. This paper describes work on the first of these five steps, analysing short stories to identify speakers, which contributes to the identification of the set of characters in the story. *Oscar Wilde's* short story *The Happy Prince* is used as a case study for this research.

**Keywords:** Serious Games · Cognitive Behavioural Therapy · Scenes · Character Identification · Natural Language Processing · Oscar Wilde

## 1 Introduction

Mental health, an essential yet somewhat misunderstood aspect of people's well-being, has a deeply rooted stigma that deters those with mental health problems from seeking psychiatric help [1]. This reluctance to seek professional help poses a serious concern. A novel approach to addressing this issue is the integration of Cognitive Behavioural Therapy (CBT) within an interactive story that can be played on a serious game platform. CBT is a goal-oriented psychotherapy intervention pioneered by Beck [2] and Ellis [3]. The premise of CBT is that incorporating therapeutic activities to change maladaptive cognitions leads to changes in problematic behaviours and emotions [4]. An important model of CBT is the resilience model proposed in [5]. This model consists of four types of resilience: mental, physical, social, and emotional.

A serious game is a game that does not solely rely on pure entertainment but instead on honing a specific skill set. Developing a serious game as a tool for therapeutic intervention has great potential to transform the mental health state of the individual [6].

M. Haahr et al. (Eds.): JCSG 2023, LNCS 14309, pp. 362–369, 2023.
https://doi.org/10.1007/978-3-031-44751-8_29

Including an interactive story in a serious game creates an engaging narrative where the player can impact certain aspects of the story [7]. Having an engaging storyline is crucial in a serious game since there is usually a noticeable decline in their use over time as players lose interest; however, an engaging storyline will help players remain engaged for a longer time [8]. Moreover, there is an infinite and untapped potential in an interactive story that can be told digitally in a serious game [9].

However, if CBT, stories, and serious games are to be integrated to support mental health, it is imperative to adapt stories to incorporate CBT activities. While manually adapting the story is feasible, a more comprehensive approach lies in automating the process to generate a wide range of readily available stories. The research described in this paper proposes that the adaptation can be carried out in five steps: scene-based segmentation of the story, character identification and interaction, identification of character personality traits, identification of emotional states and arcs, and the identification of insertion points for CBT activities [10]. The output from the adaptation is a story script that is fed into the serious game platform. This paper focuses on the task of analysing short stories to identify speakers, which contributes to scene-based segmentation of short stories since it helps to identify the speaking characters in each scene. These speaking characters form a subset of the set of characters in the story, and subsets of these characters form the basis for each scene. This paper applies the analysis to *Oscar Wilde's* story, *The Happy Prince*.

The remainder of the paper is organised as follows: the following section presents a review. Section three describes the approach. Section four concludes the paper.

## 2 Literature Review

This section presents the most relevant games in the mental health field related to this work and a brief literature review on related research in speaker identification.

### 2.1 Mental Health and CBT in Serious Games

The role of serious games and gamification in promoting treatment for mental health is an emerging area of practice [11]. Presenting mental health issues in a game format offers two valuable opportunities: to show people who suffer from mental health problems that they are not alone, and to share with others who do not suffer from this problem a glimpse of what people with mental health problems go through [9].

In [9], the authors present a game called *COEXIST*, an interactive decision-making game where the player takes control of the main character who suffers from depression. They chose to design depression as a dark character that coexists with the protagonist, hence the name, interfering negatively with all the mundane decision-making moments. A similar game was discussed in [12, 13] called *Please Knock on My Door,* which followed a similar premise of a main character who suffers from depression; the game delves into a profoundly personal and emotional experience as it retells the real-life events of its very own developer.

*SuperBetter* was an app developed to engage individuals in CBT activities. The platform adopts a resilience model consisting of four resiliencies: mental, physical, social, and emotional. Each type of challenge in the app corresponds to a specific type of resilience [1]. *SuperBetter's* resilience model was adopted in this research as the central approach to incorporating CBT in a serious game.

## 2.2 Character Identification

One of the most crucial elements in a narrative is character. A Character is an animate entity with a narrative role in the story. Character names can come in three different forms in text: a proper noun (e.g., *Sherlock Holmes*), pronouns (e.g., He), and nominals–anaphoric noun phrases that refer to a character (e.g., the consulting detective) [14]. A straightforward way to detect character names is to use a predefined set of names and perform exact matching. This list can be created manually; however, creating it is not a trivial task since characters can be referred to through different aliases. For example, *Sherlock Holmes* can be referred to as *Sherlock*, *Mr. Holmes*, or *Holmes*. Some automatic approaches use honorifics or titles such as *Mr.* or *Ms.* to check the surrounding text for character names [15]. Other approaches use verbs associated with human action since only characters are likely to be their subject [16]. In [17], the authors detect characters using a hybrid system combining statistical machine learning and hand-built rules. Moreover, some approaches have sought to use case-based reasoning in order to detect characters [18].

An essential step in identifying characters and understanding their relation to the plot development and their narrative role is the identification of speakers behind utterances. However, speaker names are not always explicitly mentioned and linked to an utterance. In most cases, authors rely instead on the readers' attention and comprehension of the story to make the correct character link [19].

Speaker identification is also referred to as quote attribution. In [20], the authors state that creating an automated quote attribution system is a multi-step process. First, the quotations in the text need to be identified; then, a character list is built that includes their aliases. Then, each quotation is attributed to a character directly or to a mention, followed by a coreference resolution step to identify the associated character.

In [21], the authors propose a deterministic, two-step approach to quotation attribution that comprises a sieves system of increasing complexity to first link each quotation to a mention and then link the mention to a character.

In [22], the authors consider the identification of speakers as a sequence labelling task, as they state that literary fiction typically consists of alternating dialogue, where a dialogue consists of one or more turns, each of which is assumed to be associated with one speaker and one or more addressees. The authors assume a pre-compiled list of characters for each chapter in the story, and then for each dialogue instance, the system selects the most likely character from the character list.

Most of the research on speaker identification assumes an a priori list of characters and aims to link references to speakers to members of that list. The approach reported in this paper does not assume an a priori list of characters or, indeed, of speakers but aims to identify speakers based on interrogating story text for speaker references.

# 3   Approach to Speaker Identification

The approach adopted for speaker identification in this research comprises five steps:

1. Inspect the story text for speaker references.
2. Create regular expressions to extract the speaker references.
3. Select those speaker references that incorporate the identity of the speaker.
4. Identify the noun phrases within the selected speaker references.
5. Generalise to more story texts.

This paper focuses on steps 1 through 4. The following subsections describe steps 1 to 4 based on *Oscar Wilde's* short story *The Happy Prince*.

## 3.1   Inspect the story text for speaker references

A manual inspection of *The Happy Prince* by *Oscar Wilde* gives the speaker references listed in Table 1. The references are incorporated in the table in the order in which they are encountered in the story. There are a total of 77 speaker references.

**Table 1.** A selection of speaker references in *The Happy Prince*, in order of appearance

| | | |
|---|---|---|
| • remarked one of the Town Councillors | • said the Mathematical Master | • he continued |
| • he added | • answered the children | • he said finally to her |
| • asked a sensible mother | • said the Swallow | • he cried |
| • muttered a disappointed man | • twittered the other Swallows | • he said |
| • said the Charity Children | • he said | • he cried |
| | | • he said softly to himself |
| | | • he cried |

## 3.2   Create regular expressions to extract the speaker references

In order to identify regular expressions to extract these speaker references, the speaker references in Table 1 were grouped by similar patterns, as shown in Table 2. The table shows a number of the patterns.

Table 3 gives the corresponding regular expressions in Python code that were used to identify these speaker references in the story.

## 3.3   Select speaker references that incorporate the identity of the speaker

In Table 2, the speaker references that incorporate the speaker's identity are captured in some rows by the symbol X and, therefore, the corresponding patterns. Table 4 shows a selection of the selected speaker references taken together for these patterns.

**Table 2.** A selection of the grouping of speaker references based on patterns

| # | Speaker References | Pattern |
|---|---|---|
| 1 | remarked one of the Town Councillors | {remarked} one of the X |
| 2 | asked a sensible mother, muttered a disappointed man | {asked, muttered} a X |
| 3 | said the Charity Children, said the Mathematical Master, said the Swallow (8), said the Prince (12), said the boy, said the Professor of Ornithology, said the Happy Prince … | {said, answered, twittered, asked, continued, cried, shouted} the X |
| … | … | … |
| 11 | said to each other | said to {each other} |

**Table 3.** A selection of regular expressions

```
pattern_1 = r'([^‘’"]*? remarked one of the (\w+ \w+))'
pattern_2 = r'([^‘’"]*?(?:answered|asked|shouted|muttered) a (\w+\w+))'
pattern_3 = r'([^‘’"]*?(?:said|answered|twittered|asked|
                  continued|cried|shouted) (?:the) ([\w\s]+)[.,;])'
...
pattern_11 = r'(said to(\w+ \w+))'
```

**Table 4.** A selection of speaker references

Speaker Reference Pattern: ['remarked one of the Town Councillors', 'asked a sensible mother', 'muttered a disappointed man', 'said the Charity Children as they came out of the cathedral in their bright scarlet cloaks and their clean white pinafores.', 'said the Mathematical Master,', 'answered the children;', 'said the Swallow,', ...]

### 3.4 Identify the noun phrases within the selected speaker references

The SpaCy library was used to select the noun phrases from each speaker reference [23]. Table 5 shows the noun phrases for each speaker reference and indicates a number of issues that need to be resolved to complete the identification of the speakers.

First, some of the lists include multiple noun phrases. For example, the speaker reference *"said the Charity Children as they came out of the cathedral in their bright scarlet cloaks and their clean white pinafores"* results in a list of five noun phrases: ['the Charity Children', 'they', 'the cathedral', 'their bright scarlet cloaks', 'their clean white pinafores'].

Second, the speaker reference *"said the Professor of Ornithology as he was passing over the bridge"* results in "Professor of Ornithology" being split into separate nouns, "Professor" and "Ornithology": ['the Professor', 'Ornithology', 'he', 'the bridge'].

Third, the speaker reference *"said each of the Town Councillors"* is also split into separate nouns: ['each', 'the Town Councillors'].

Fourth, the two speaker references *"answered the statue"* and *"continued the statue in a low musical voice,"* both include the noun phrase "the statue": ['the statue'] and ['the statue','a low musical voice'].

These were resolved in the following manner:

- If the noun phrase list contains just one noun phrase, that noun phrase is taken as the identity of the speaker.
- If the noun phrase list contains more than one noun phrase, a pattern search is made in the corresponding speaker reference for the pattern X of Y, where X is replaced by the first noun phrase, and Y is replaced by the second, and if the pattern is found it becomes the noun phrase for the speaker, otherwise, the first noun phrase is selected.
- If the noun phrase contains a noun (rather than a proper noun), then a pattern search is made in the full text of the story for the pattern X of Y, where X is the noun phrase, and Y is a sequence of text terminated by a punctuation mark that begins with a noun phrase. Therefore, for example, "the statue of the Happy Prince ...." gives the noun phrase "the statue of the Happy Prince".

Table 6 shows the resulting speaker references after applying these rules, which now corresponds to the list of speaking characters in the story.

**Table 5.** A selection of the noun phrase lists for each selected speaker reference

| Noun phrase lists: [['the Town Councillors'], ['a sensible mother'], ['a disappointed man'], ['the Charity Children', 'they', 'the cathedral', 'their bright scarlet cloaks', 'their clean white pinafores'], ... ['the statue','a low musical voice'], ... , ['the Professor', 'Ornithology', 'he', 'the bridge'], ..., ['each', 'the Town Councillors']] |
| --- |

**Table 6.** A selection of the speaker list

| Speaker List: ['one of the Town Councillors', 'a sensible mother', 'a disappointed man', 'the Charity Children', ..., 'the statue of the Happy Prince', 'the Prince', 'the boy', 'the Professor of Ornithology', ..., 'each of the Town Councillors'] |
| --- |

The list of speaking characters in table 6 includes multiple references to the same character that need to be resolved, and one of these references selected to refer to the character in the script. This will be taken up in future work.

## 4  Conclusion

If CBT, stories, and serious games are to be integrated to support mental health, stories need to be adapted to incorporate CBT. Adapting stories involves segmenting the stories into scenes. This paper focuses on analysing short stories to identify speaking characters that form a subset of the characters in the story. Most of the research on speaker identification assumes a priori a list of characters and aims to link references to speakers in the text to members of that list. The approach reported in this paper does not assume an a priori list of characters or, indeed, of speaking characters but aims to generate a list of speaking characters based on interrogating the story text for speaker references. The approach uses basic pattern matching, selecting text that refers to speakers, referred to here as speaker references, and parsing these to select the speaker noun phrases. This paper applies the analysis to *Oscar Wilde's* story *The Happy Prince* and successfully identifies the speaking characters.

# References

1. Corrigan, P.W., Bink, A.B.: The Stigma of Mental Illness. In: Encyclopedia of Mental Health, 2nd edn (2016). https://doi.org/10.1016/B978-0-12-397045-9.00170-1
2. Beck, A.T.: Cognitive therapy: nature and relation to behavior therapy. Behav. Ther. **1**, 184–200 (1970). https://doi.org/10.1016/S0005-7894(70)80030-2
3. Ellis, A.: Reason and Emotion in Psychotherapy. Lyle Stuart, New York (1962)
4. Hofmann, S.G., Asnaani, A., Vonk, I.J.J., Sawyer, A.T., Fang, A.: The Efficacy of cognitive behavioral therapy: a review of meta-analyses. Cognit. Ther. Res. **36**, 427–440 (2012). https://doi.org/10.1007/s10608-012-9476-1
5. McGonigal, J.: SuperBetter: A Revolutionary Approach to Getting Stronger, Happier, Braver and More Resilient. Penguin Press (2015)
6. Brezinka, V.: Computer games supporting cognitive behaviour therapy in children. Clin. Child. Psychol. Psychiatry **19** (2014). https://doi.org/10.1177/1359104512468288
7. McDaniel, R., Fiore, S.M., Nicholson, D.: Serious storytelling: narrative considerations for serious games researchers and developers. IGI Global, Hershey, New York (2010). https://doi.org/10.4018/978-1-61520-739-8.CH002:
8. Michael, D.R., Chen, S.L.: Serious Games: Games That Educate, Train, and Inform. Muska & Lipman/Premier-Trade (2005)
9. Rodrigues, M.A.F., et al.: An interactive story decision-making game for mental health awareness. In: 2022 IEEE 10th International Conference on Serious Games and Applications for Health (SeGAH). pp. 1–8 (2022). https://doi.org/10.1109/SEGAH54908.2022.9978592
10. Hassan, T., McKee, G.T.: Designing CBT-rich stories for serious games. In: Fletcher, B., Ma, M., Göbel, S., Baalsrud Hauge, J., Marsh, T. (eds.) Serious Games: Joint International Conference, JCSG 2021, Virtual Event, Proceedings, vol. 12945, pp. 98–112. Springer, Heidelberg (2021). https://doi.org/10.1007/978-3-030-88272-3_8
11. Sawyer, B.: From cells to cell processors: the integration of health and video games. IEEE Comput. Graph. Appl. **28** (2008). https://doi.org/10.1109/MCG.2008.114
12. Alves, T., Berg, B., Brusk, J.: Exploring Underrepresented Narratives Social Anxiety in Games. University of Skövde, Sweden (2018)
13. Tüker, Ç., Çatak, G.: Designing a CAD-enriched empathy game to raise awareness about universal design principles: a case study. In: Bostan, B. (ed.) Game User Experience and Player-Centered Design, pp. 327–346. Springer Cham (2020). https://doi.org/10.1007/978-3-030-37643-7_14
14. Labatut, V., Bost, X.: Extraction and analysis of fictional character networks: a survey. ACM Comput. Surv. **52**(5) (2019). https://doi.org/10.1145/3344548
15. Coll Ardanuy, M., Sporleder, C.: Structure-based clustering of novels. In: Proceedings of the 3rd Workshop on Computational Linguistics for Literature (CLFL). Association for Computational Linguistics, Gothenburg, Sweden, pp. 31–39 (2014). https://doi.org/10.3115/v1/W14-0905

16. Goh, H.N., Soon, L.K., Haw, S.C.: Automatic identification of protagonist in fairy tales using verb. In: Tan, P.N., Chawla, S., Ho, C.K., Bailey, J. (eds.) Advances in Knowledge Discovery and Data Mining. PAKDD 2012. Lecture Notes in Computer Science, vol. 7302, pp. 395–406. Springer, Heidelberg (2012). https://doi.org/10.1007/978-3-642-30220-6_33
17. Jahan, L., Chauhan, G., Finlayson, M.A.: A new approach to animacy detection. In: COLING 2018 - 27th International Conference on Computational Linguistics, Proceedings (2018)
18. Valls-Vargas, J., Zhu, J., Ontañón, S.: Toward automatic role identification in unannotated folk tales. In: Proceedings of the 10th AAAI Conference on Artificial Intelligence and Interactive Digital Entertainment, AIIDE 2014 (2014)
19. He, H., Barbosa, D., Kondrak, G.: Identification of speakers in novels. In: ACL 2013 - 51st Annual Meeting of the Association for Computational Linguistics, Proceedings of the Conference (2013)
20. Vishnubhotla, K., Hammond, A., Hirst, G.: The project dialogism novel corpus: a dataset for quotation attribution in literary texts. In: 2022 Language Resources and Evaluation Conference, LREC 2022 (2022)
21. Muzny, G., Fang, M., Chang, A.X., Jurafsky, D.: A two-stage sieve approach for quote attribution. In: 15th Conference of the European Chapter of the Association for Computational Linguistics, EACL 2017 - Proceedings of Conference (2017). https://doi.org/10.18653/v1/e17-1044
22. Ek, A., Wirén, M., Östling, R., Björkenstam, K.N., Grigonyte, G., Capková, S.G.: Identifying speakers and addressees in dialogues extracted from literary fiction. In: LREC 2018 - 11th International Conference on Language Resources and Evaluation (2019)
23. Honnibal, M., Montani, I.: spaCy 2: natural language understanding with Bloom embeddings, convolutional neural networks and incremental parsing (2017)

# Visualisation of System Dynamics in Megagames

Jessie Chow, Jenny Rudemo, Lena Buffoni$^{(\boxtimes)}$ , and Ola Leifler

Linköping University, Linköping, Sweden
{jesch310,jenru723}@student.liu.se, {lena.buffoni,ola.leifler}@liu.se

**Abstract.** As the effects of the climate crisis become increasingly apparent, efforts are made to encourage and nuance discussion on energy system transition for a more sustainable future. One way this is done is through games that combine role-play, board game elements and computer simulations, i.e. megagames. The aim of this paper is to investigate how visualisations and simulations can be used to drive forward such discussions within a megagame.

**Keywords:** Megagame · Simulation · Visualisation

## 1 Introduction

Games can help participants understand complex systems and how different components in such systems relate to each other. This work is conducted in the context of the megagame Switching the Current, which is a combination of role play, board game, and computer simulation. The aim of the megagame is to facilitate discussions about sustainable practises within the energy system among the public as well as among energy industry professionals. A central goal is to mitigate climate change by taking actions to reduce carbon dioxide ($CO_2$) emissions and keep the increase of global temperature as low as possible.

The game simulates all three aspects of sustainability - environmental, social and economic, which helps participants understand a small scale society as a whole, however also results in large amounts of information for participants to absorb in a short timeframe.

The effects of decisions and negotiations in the game are communicated to the participants using different means, mainly through tokens on game boards but also through news announcements throughout the game session. Since it is hard to capture all the complex effects of a decision in the game, and the cumulated effect of changes over time a simulation model using data from the game as input is run alongside the physical game. The model represents the energy system based on region-specific data (hereafter referred to as the *system model*) and data generated from it is visualised as plots and shown in between game rounds.

A simulation generates gigabytes of data, and in order to select the data to visualise it is important to understand in what way it contributes to the overall

M. Haahr et al. (Eds.): JCSG 2023, LNCS 14309, pp. 370–376, 2023.
https://doi.org/10.1007/978-3-031-44751-8_30

goal of the megagame of to creating an understanding of a complex energy system. In particular, how to visualise correlations that are unintuitive such as non-linear correlations and effects caused by time delays. In this article we discuss an approach to developing visualisations for the game in a systematised manner.

## 2    Related Work

The *World Climate Simulation Game* [7,10] and *Climate Action Simulation Game* [6] are two role-play simulation games developed by the non-profit organisation and project *Climate Interactive*[1]. The games are set in a global context where the participants take on the roles as participants at a UN climate negotiation [6,10]. The aim is for the participants to learn about climate dynamics and challenges in limiting climate change through face-to-face negotiations and simulation of climate related impacts and consequences [10]. During the game, the participants get feedback on the decisions they make using the *C-ROADS* [9,11] and *En-ROADS* [8] simulation models, respectively.

The major difference between the needs of the visualisations in the megagame and the visualisations provided by C-ROADS and En-ROADS is that the latter two are simulation models on a global scale, while Switching the Current simulates a community on a regional level, particularly in Sweden.

Evaluations of games with focus on mitigating climate change games show that they have a positive impact on knowledge about climate change and climate dynamics, as well as on the will to take action in preventing climate change [5–7]. Of particular interest is that the combination of role-play and computer-models has been shown to motivate climate action and reduce polarisation [5].

## 3    Megagame Description

The Megagame Switching the Current aims to promote dialogue around the energy system, in particular between responsible actors in the energy system and those who have a dependency or an interest in the energy system. The project group is interdisciplinary and consists of members from different fields, such as cognitive scientists, social scientists and experts in simulation and game development, from three universities: Linköping University, University of Skövde and Jönköping University.

A megagame is a simulation game that consists of elements such as role-play and table-top game boards, and is played by 20–100 participants. The participants are divided into different groups that are relevant to setting or theme of the megagame, and the idea is that the participants should role-play as the group they represent. The groups represent population groups of different income, the municipality, and energy industries. Each of the groups has their own table with a set of game boards with tokens on them.

---

[1] About, Climate Interactive: https://www.climateinteractive.org/about/.

(a) Population $$$                              (b) Regional Industries

**Fig. 1.** Game boards for player groups population (left) and industry (right).

The tokens on the boards represent the current status of the group in terms of consumption level, for example *food* and *goods* tokens. Other tokens include energy tokens representing energy usage which relates to level of carbon dioxide emission. The numbers of tokens on the boards are adapted to correspond to numbers of the region where the megagame is played. This means that depending on where the megagame is played, the consumption patterns on the same boards can differ. This way, the participants playing Switching the Current are able to relate to the consumption patterns or production for their region. Examples of game boards for player groups *Population $$$* and *Regional Industries* can be found in Fig. 1a and Fig. 1b respectively.

The megagame is played in a number of rounds (up to eight rounds), where each round represents five years. Each round consists of three phases: *team phase*, *action phase* and *resolve phase*.

At the start of each round is a team phase, where the participants can discuss the objective of the round internally in the groups. The team phase is followed by an action phase, where the different groups can discuss and negotiate with each other. An example of an action could be a switch from fossil fuel vehicles to biofuel vehicles in a population group. Actions result in changes on the game boards and can also trigger news announcements.

In between the rounds is a resolve phase, where the each group can give a statement of what they have done during the action phase and what their next objective is. At the same time, the data from the boards is manually collected by controllers to input into the simulation model. Before proceeding to the next round, the results from the simulation model are presented to the participants in the form of graphs projected on a screen. Currently they are not interactive and every participant is presented with the same information.

## 4   The Simulated System Model

The simulation model used in the megagame Switching the Current is partly based on the World3 model [1] and the thermal and powergrid libraries in Modelica, an equation-based language for cyber-physical system modeling [2].

On a high level the model represents the production and consumption of energy in the region, and has components that represent renewable energy sources, non-renewable energy sources, power generation and the energy usage of end-users, such as household or industry and the private and public transport sectors. As the game develops, additional elements and sub-models are added, such as for instance the biofuel life-cycle model presented in this article.

The initial data for parametrizing the model is taken from open sources and is specific to the region represented. During the game players make decisions that impact the simulation outcome (e.g.: replacing a number of petrol vehicles with electric cars or public transport, building a new wind farm). At the end of each round during the resolve phase, the tokens of different types are counted on the game boards (e.g.: number of petrol cars) and this data is used to parametrize the simulation model.

## 5    Analysis and Target Area Identification

Presenting a number of detailed graphs to the game participants in the short time span of the debriefing between rounds might result in the participants either feeling overwhelmed by the data or just choosing not to focus on it entirely. Therefore it is important to find the level of abstraction and the form of data presentation that would be the most effective. In order to understand how to select and visualise the information, the first step of this work focused on identifying areas of interest for the visualisation.

To this end two megagames sessions were observed by participating in the sessions as controllers, i.e. assisting the participants by answering questions and updating the game boards at the end of each round.

Observations showed a quick transition to bioenergy usage among the population player groups, seeming to indicate that transition to biofuel and bioenergy was seen as an uncomplicated solution to decreasing carbon dioxide emissions.

In general, participants were driven primarily by their economic interests (as well as by their quality of life, in the case of the population groups) and only secondarily by altruistic goals such as making progress with environmental and climate issues. An example of this is that major change in lifestyle patterns (such as type of fuel, heating and consumption) seemed to happen only once a real effect took place, e.g. at the first megagame session when it was announced that during the following round a tax on carbon dioxide emissions would be introduced. The announcement resulted in all groups transitioning quickly from fossil fuels to biofuels and bioenergy compared to very little change in the prior rounds. This unerscores the importance of timely feedback.

Although an "obvious" strategy to replace gas vehicles with biofuel powered vehicles was chosen simulations showed that this would not be a sufficient change to meet the reduced carbon emissions target. However this was not reinforced by any events in the current version of the game and was only presented at the end. Therefore biofuel was chosen as a good candidate for further visualisation.

## 6   Simulation and Game Extension

Once an area of interest was identified, the next step was to connect sustainability aspects to the game and to design visualisations that would support a better understanding of the outcomes of the decision to switch to biofuel.

A literature study of the domain was conducted and discussions with domain experts were used to understand which elements needed to be represented and to identify the environmental impact of increased biofuel usage on the system. The simulation model was then extended with a domain specific model for biofuel production and consumption.

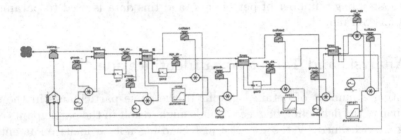

**Fig. 2.** Diagram of the biomass system model in Modelica.

The biofuel model (Fig. 2) includes 4 different populations of trees based on their ages and the transitions between these populations as trees age, the cutting of the trees for biomass and wood products as well as non trivial effects such as negative effects of biodiversity decrease on tree growth.

In parallel a gap analysis of the board game was done to identify elements missing to represent the biofuel life-cycle. This resulted in the addition of tokens representing biomass as well as of the development of a game board dedicated to forestry management.

## 7   Visualisation

Based on the findings a visualisation mock-up was created. The graphs were inspired by the concept of systems thinking and the ideas of limits to growth presented in *Thinking in Systems* [4] and *Limits to Growth* [3]. The focus was illustrating the limits to both renewable (biomass) and non-renewable (fossil fuel) energy resources. Based on the example models found *Thinking in Systems*, by Meadows [4] three scenarios with different extraction rates were created for each type of resource (Fig. 4).

Particular focus was put on visualising information that cannot be shown through other elements in the megagame. Figures 3 and 4 show examples of trend visualisations. The visualisations have not yet been validated in a real game setting, but will be tested at an upcoming event in the fall.

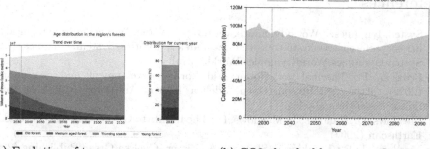

(a) Evolution of trees per age group        (b) CO2 absorbed by trees and emitted

**Fig. 3.** Examples of visualisations of trends over time.

**Fig. 4.** Three scenarios for production and consumption of biomass.

# 8   Conclusion

It is impossible to have a complete model of the real world, due to the complexity of the system therefore it is important to select what parts of the system dynamic need to be modeled in more detail and to identify how to present the resulting data. In this article we have presented an the steps for the process in the context of biomass system dynamics:

1. identify an area of interest through game dynamics observation
2. through literature studies extend the simulation model to cover the necessary aspects, in particular complex interconnections to other parts of the system
3. identify necessary extensions to the game to connect the simulation do decisions by the players
4. based on surveys and observation of previous games create visualisations to show game participants
5. validate the extensions through subsequent games

The next steps are to validate the visualisations in the upcoming megagame session and apply this approach to other aspects of the system such as life quality.

**Acknowledgements.** This work was conducted within the research project funded by the Swedish Energy Agency.

# References

1. Systemdynamics: Worlddynamics.world3 - system modeler documentation. https://reference.wolfram.com/system-modeler/libraries/SystemDynamics/ SystemDynamics.WorldDynamics.World3.html
2. Fritzson, P.: Thermal and power grid library development and user manual (2022). https://github.com/OpenModelica/ThermalAndPowerGridSystem/blob/ master/UserManual.pdf
3. Meadows, D., Randers, J., Meadows, D.: The Limits to Growth: the 30-year update. Earthscan (2004)
4. Meadows, D.H.: Thinking in Systems: A Primer. Chelsea Green Publishing (2008)
5. Rooney-Varga, J.N., et al.: Building consensus for ambitious climate action through the world climate simulation. Earth's Future 9(12), e2021EF002283 (2021)
6. Rooney-Varga, J.N., Kapmeier, F., Sterman, J.D., Jones, A.P., Putko, M., Rath, K.: The climate action simulation. Simul. Gaming 51(2), 114–140 (2020)
7. Rooney-Varga, J.N., et al.: Combining role-play with interactive simulation to motivate informed climate action: evidence from the world climate simulation. PLoS ONE 13(8), e0202877 (2018)
8. Siegel, L.S., et al.: En-ROADS simulator reference guide. Technical report (2018)
9. Sterman, J., et al.: Climate interactive: the C-ROADS climate policy model (2012)
10. Sterman, J., et al.: World climate: a role-play simulation of climate negotiations. Simul. Gaming 46(3–4), 348–382 (2015)
11. Sterman, J.D., et al.: Management flight simulators to support climate negotiations. Environ. Model. Softw. 44, 122–135 (2013). https://doi.org/ 10.1016/j.envsoft.2012.06.004. https://www.sciencedirect.com/science/article/pii/ S1364815212001843. Thematic Issue on Innovative Approaches to Global Change Modelling

# The Design, Development and Pilot Study of a Marine Ecological Simulation for Education of Environmental Changes on Marine Life

David White[1](✉) , Robert Stone[2] , and Deborah Cracknell[3]

[1] Staffordshire University, Stoke-On-Trent, UK
david.white1@staffs.ac.uk
[2] University of Birmingham, Birmingham, UK
[3] University of Plymouth, Plymouth, UK

**Abstract.** A "serious game" simulating examples of marine life found at the artificial reef ex-HMS *Scylla* has been developed to demonstrate the impact of environmental changes. The game has been adapted from prior research into agent-based models of marine ecologies. The design of the game considers the abstraction and presentation of marine life, and the effect of environmental changes. Two simulations are performed: one exposing the ecology to the effects of climate change, and another which simulates the introduction of microplastics. A pilot study measured knowledge-recall for simulations with open and closed-ended questions, user awareness of environmental issues and future game design preferences. This research contributes by both demonstrating the conversion of a complex marine simulation to a game format, and also emphasises the potential of the simulation journey to learning and engagement.

**Keywords:** Serious Game · Agent-Based Model · Educational Simulation · Marine Ecology

## 1 Introduction

"Serious games" [1] offer unique insights into teaching and communicating the impacts of environmental change [2]. When deriving serious games from simulations, they provide not only the opportunity for users to understand the outcomes or result of a simulation, but also to experience firsthand the impacts of their choices within the simulation. Here, we will highlight the importance of the user's journey and the learning process.

This pilot study develops a serious game, simulating a marine ecology scenario using an agent-based model. The game is adapted from prior research into complex simulations derived from peer-reviewed marine biology research.[1]. We have collected data which measures how participants recalled simulation events, participant exposure to environmental issues, and preferences for future game design.

---

[1] Here 'marine biology' research refers to both biology and ecologies by experts in the field.

© The Author(s), under exclusive license to Springer Nature Switzerland AG 2023
M. Haahr et al. (Eds.): JCSG 2023, LNCS 14309, pp. 377–383, 2023.
https://doi.org/10.1007/978-3-031-44751-8_31

Agent-based modelling (ABM) is a method for simulating complex models which has been growing in popularity [3]. A serious game using an ABM framework can enable users to see how, during a game, changes to agents and their environment can alter the balance of species populations. Further, ABMs are particularly suited to modelling and understanding marine ecologies and the environmental changes which affect these. Earlier work by Stone [4] examined the potential for serious games to raise awareness of an artificial reef project "launched" in 2004 with the ex-Royal Navy vessel HMS *Scylla*; the Scylla reef is a context for this work. Serious games have the potential to permit the exploration of complex systems that would be impractical or unsafe in the real-world [5]. A serious game with an environmental message can also engage with the public at a lower cost than traditional marketing campaigns [6].

There is much prior work in games of marine ecologies. Ameerbakhsh [5] designed a serious game relating to fishery stock management. Their research concludes that, while students enjoyed the experience of using the game, the expert demonstration was more effective for learning effectiveness. Rossanno, in a pilot study [7, 8], demonstrates a cartoon-style game to promote environmental attitudes to children to promote more sustainable behaviour. Rossanno focusses on feedback from primary school-aged children and examines whether participants liked the look and feel of the game as well as learning outcomes. Similarly, Panagiotopoulou [9] discusses the design of a serious game for children, specifically to raise awareness of plastics pollution.

Although such serious games have been increasingly used as educational tools, their use has mostly been restricted to relatively simple games. Although informative, they often overlook marine ecologies' complexity. Addressing this gap, this pilot project aims to incorporate complex simulations into a game, allowing users to see for themselves how environmental changes can cause population shifts.

Converting an existing ecosystem simulation into a game comes with the advantage that much of the groundwork has been done, making the process of creating accurate, yet understandable educational games a feasible goal. As Narayanasamy [10] discusses, both simulation games and serious games are engaging, challenging, and enjoyable to play, which suggests that converting simulations into games is a rational case for action.

The marine ecology simulations used to develop the game originate from research into artificial life models in which it was studied how complexity affects the outcome of simulations [4, 11, 12].

To evaluate the goals of this study, the following questions will be considered:

1. What are the challenges when abstracting a complex marine ecosystem to an educational game?
2. What are the challenges when developing complex models to measure various environmental effects?
3. As a pilot study, what can we learn from participant feedback?
   a. Is there a difference between the recall quality between open and closed questions, and what implications does this have for the future design of this game?
   b. Does participant recall differ for different environmental scenarios? What opportunities does this present for future work?
   c. What would participants like to see in future iterations of the game?

## 2  Methodology

The research leading to the analysis of collected data was carried out in two stages: the modification of the simulation code to a game, and the pilot study where the data was collected. The simulation code is the result of prior research [11, 12] which examined how complexity influences the outcomes of simulations of marine ecosystems found at the *Scylla* reef [13]. Details of the marine life found at the *Scylla* reef were taken from a variety of sources but mainly from the MarLIN database [14]. A limitation at this stage is that the game, other than moving the camera and navigating the scenes, has little user interaction, which will be addressed in future work.

The game in this study has been developed over two iterations. The first iteration was developed in collaboration with the National Marine Aquarium as a demonstration for school children to show how artificial life can simulate climate change, and how this affects the balance of marine ecologies. The second was to introduce a further environmental effect to collect data for the pilot study.

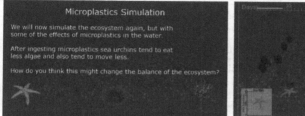

**Fig. 1.** The Scylla Game – a pre-simulation tutorial, and the simulation in progress

The game takes the player through a series of steps in three scenarios: a baseline simulation, one with warmer sea temperatures representing climate change, and finally a simulation in which species ingest microplastics [15]. Three species are modelled: starfish, sea urchins and algae. The interactions between the species can be summarised as: starfish predate sea urchins, sea urchins graze on algae, algae grow. Too many starfish and the sea urchin population would be removed, resulting in growth of algae but the eventual demise of a starving starfish population. Too many sea urchins would lead to overgrazing of algae, a healthy population of starfish, but the eventual collapse of the sea urchins through lack of food source. Figure 1 illustrates two screenshots from the game.

The player sees first-hand how an imbalance can lead to the collapse of the system. Climate change brings warmer temperatures resulting in increased predation and algae growth; microplastics discourage sea urchins from consuming algae, resulting in starvation. Both scenarios cause changes to population mixes - the educational message is that ecosystems evolve to balance, irregular environmental changes result in unpredictable and complex outcomes.

The pilot study measures how participants recalled information for both simulations, as well as recording prior exposure to these topics in the media. Data was collected at the free-to-attend Potteries Museum in Stoke-On-Trent, UK. All participants were aged 18 and over. 22 participants viewed the game demonstration and recorded their observations. The journey of a participant was as follows:

1. The researcher would explain how the game simulates marine life at the *Scylla* Reef, and that three simulations would be presented.
2. The game screen would detail the three species: sea urchins, starfish and algae.
3. The baseline simulation would run, the researcher would point out the species, their interactions, and graphs showing species populations.
4. To avoid recall bias, environmental change scenarios would run in random order.
5. In each case the researcher would discuss the scenario behaviour and outcomes.
6. After the game ends participants are asked to complete the questionnaire (Table 1).

**Table 1.** Questionnaire completed by participants following demonstration of the game.

| |
| --- |
| Q 1: Can you remember what happened to the sea urchins and the algae during the simulation which considered climate change? (open text) |
| Q 2: Can you remember what happened to the sea urchins and the algae during the simulation which considered the impact of microplastics? (open text) |
| Q 3: Can you remember what happened in the first simulation? (multi-choice) |
| Q 4: Can you remember what happened in the simulation which considered climate change? (multi-choice) |
| Q 5: Can you remember what happened in the simulation which considered microplastics? (multi-choice) |
| Q 6: How often do you remember hearing about **climate change** in the news and in media such as the internet and TV? *(Likert scale options)* |
| Q 7: How often do you remember hearing about **microplastics** in the news and in media such as the internet and TV? *(Likert scale options)* |
| Q 8: Do you think an individual in the UK can help to prevent further environmental changes due to climate change in the UK? *(Likert scale options)* |
| Q 9: Do you think an individual in the UK can help to prevent further environmental changes due to microplastics in the UK? *(Likert scale options)* |
| Q 10: How would you prefer the game to be developed further? *(multi-choice)* |

## 3  Results

Questions 1 and 2 were marked out of two, for two correct observations, incorrect observations were not penalised. Questions 3 to 5 required two specific correct answers, and although participants were not told how many were correct, all participants ticked either one or two answers, whether they were correct or not.

Figure 2 shows the total scores for all questions. Questions were out of two, therefore with 22 participants the total score for each question was out of 44. Both open questions

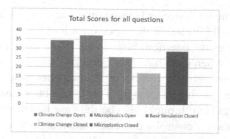

**Fig. 2.** Total Scores for all questions for all 22 participants (scores out of 44)

scored higher than their closed equivalents, and the climate change questions scored less well than the microplastics questions.

Unsurprisingly, with climate change being a broader subject with global implications, participants reported hearing about it more frequently than microplastics. Over 50% of the participants recalled hearing about climate change several times per week, compared to under 25% for microplastics. This contrast suggests that prior knowledge of environmental issues doesn't necessarily impact recall after a demonstration.

Participants' views on their perceived agency to affect climate change and microplastics were perhaps surprising considering the disparity in the exposure to hearing about the issues in the news. Only two participants responded as having no influence over climate change and microplastics, whereas twelve and seven participants felt that they had some, or a lot of, influence, respectively.

Finally, when asked about potential improvements to the game, participants' views were divided into two distinct categories. Five participants felt the game was adequate as is or could benefit from more media-based instruction. Most participants (15 out of 22) expressed a desire for more complexity and suggested adding more simulations or user-controllable parameters to explore various outcomes.

## 4 Conclusions and Further Work

This study provides insights into two key areas: the challenges inherent in converting simulations into games, and insights derived from participant questionnaires.

One key challenge is that the complexity of the model used in this study remains largely hidden from the observer. A great deal of behavioural interaction between agents remains obscured from the user and demonstrates the difficulties in demonstrating complex interactions and behaviour. Another challenge is avoiding catastrophic collapses in species populations and maintaining a balance between species. User feedback indicates they desire greater control over the game, but more user agency may lead to a feeling that balancing a system is too difficult. However, this may improve learning outcomes and engagement. Another challenge we encountered during the research leading up to this study was the interpretation of marine biology papers for conversion into ABMs. Papers sometimes tend to discuss the aggregated effects on a system, but not the individual, although there are papers which do this.

The method and benefit of open and closed questions in questionnaires is well documented topic [16]. Farrell [17] writes that open questions allow the user to project their 'own' answer. This raises the question: how do we know what a user is learning? This may be more uncertain when users have more control over a game.

Results demonstrated greater recall for participants when asked questions on microplastics compared to climate change. This could be a case of being introduced to a new, novel, concept [18]. It might also be the case however that microplastics are a factor that participants can control – one can immediately stop using microbeads but influencing climate change is a far loftier goal. This may indicate greater user motivation for issues they can easily control.

The goal of this pilot study was to demonstrate that the prior model could be used to simulate multiple environmental effects in a game-like format. This, in the context of the research questions, was a success, and may in turn motivate other developers of complex models into serious games.

Future work could consider the following:

- The additional development of the program in this study to allow users to modify environmental parameters, species ratios and species behaviour.
- What are user preferences when given greater command over a game, versus a variety of scenarios developed with ecosystem stability in mind?
- What value is there for such a simulation to be acquired by marine biologists for their work? Could policymakers benefit? Can it drive user behavioural change? This would build on work by Westera [19]

## 5 Ethics Statement

The study in this work was subjected to an approved ethics review by Staffordshire University, reference number SU_22_066.

## References

1. Susi, T., Johannesson, M., Backlund, P.: Serious Games: An Overview (2007)
2. Flood, S., Cradock-Henry, N.A., Blackett, P., Edwards, P.: Adaptive and interactive climate futures: systematic review of 'serious games' for engagement and decision-making. Environ. Res. Lett. **13**, 63005 (2018)
3. Sun, Z., Lorscheid, I., Millington, J.D, et al.: Simple or complicated agent-based models? A complicated issue. Environ. Model. Softw. **86**, 56–67 (2016). https://doi.org/10.1016/j.env soft.2016.09.006
4. Stone, R., White, D., Guest, R., Francis, B.: The Virtual Scylla: an exploration of "serious games", artificial life and simulation complexity. Virt. Real. **13**, 13–25 (2009). https://doi.org/10.1007/s10055-008-0111-0
5. Ameerbakhsh, O., Maharaj, S., Hussain, A., McAdam, B.: A comparison of two methods of using a serious game for teaching marine ecology in a university setting. Int. J. Hum. Comput. Stud. **127**, 181–189 (2019). https://doi.org/10.1016/j.ijhcs.2018.07.004
6. Trybus, J.: Game-based learning: What it is, why it works, and where it's going. New Media Institute 6 (2015)

7. Veronica, R., Calvano, G.: Promoting sustainable behavior using serious games: SeAdventure for Ocean literacy. IEEE Access **8**, 196931–196939 (2020). https://doi.org/10.1109/ACCESS.2020.3034438

8. Rossano, V., Roselli, T., Calvano, G.: A serious game to promote environmental attitude. In: Uskov, V.L., Howlett, R.J., Jain, L.C. (eds.) Smart Education and e-Learning 2017, pp. 48–55. Springer, Cham (2018). https://doi.org/10.1007/978-3-319-59451-4_5

9. Panagiotopoulou, L., Gayarre, N.C., Scurati, G.W., et al.: Design of a serious game for children to raise awareness on plastic pollution and promoting pro-environmental behaviors. J. Comput. Inf. Sci. Eng. **21** (2021)

10. Narayanasamy, V., Wong, K.W., Fung, C.C., Rai, S.: Distinguishing Games and Simulation Games from Simulators. Comput. Entertain. **4**, 9–es (2006). https://doi.org/10.1145/1129006.1129021

11. White, D.: Developing artificial life simulations of marine biology and exploring measures of complexity. In: 2008 Second UKSIM European Symposium on Computer Modeling and Simulation. pp. 232–235 (2008)

12. White, D.: Variance in water temperature as a factor in the modelling of starfish and mussel population density and diversity. In: Almeida e Costa, F., Rocha, L.M., Costa, E., Harvey, I., Coutinho, A. (eds.) ECAL 2007. LNCS (LNAI), vol. 4648, pp. 153–162. Springer, Heidelberg (2007). https://doi.org/10.1007/978-3-540-74913-4_16

13. Hiscock, K., Sharrock, S., Highfield, J., Snelling, D.: Colonization of an artificial reef in south-west England—ex-HMS 'Scylla.' J. Mar. Biol. Assoc. U.K. **90**, 69–94 (2010)

14. Hiscock, K., Tyler-Walters, H.: Assessing the sensitivity of seabed species and biotopes–the Marine Life Information Network (MarLIN). Hydrobiologia **555**, 309–320 (2006)

15. Wright, S.L., Thompson, R.C., Galloway, T.S.: The physical impacts of microplastics on marine organisms: a review. Environ. Pollut. **178**, 483–492 (2013). https://doi.org/10.1016/j.envpol.2013.02.031

16. Schuman, H., Presser, S.: The open and closed question. Am. Sociol. Rev. **44**, 692–712 (1979). https://doi.org/10.2307/2094521

17. Farrall, S., Bannister, J., Ditton, J., Gilchrist, E.: Open and closed question. Interpretation **3**, 2–9 (1997)

18. Schomaker, J., van Bronkhorst, M.L., Meeter, M.: Exploring a novel environment improves motivation and promotes recall of words. Front. Psychol. **5**, 918 (2014)

19. Westera, W.: How people learn while playing serious games: a computational modelling approach. J. Comput. Sci. **18**, 32–45 (2017). https://doi.org/10.1016/j.jocs.2016.12.002

# GameTULearn: An Interactive Educational Game Authoring Tool for 3D Environments

Florian Horn(✉)[iD], Sabrina Vogt[iD], and Stefan Peter Göbel[iD]

Serious Games Research Group, Technical University of Darmstadt,
64289 Darmstadt, Germany
{florian.horn,sabrina.vogt,stefan_peter.goebel}@tu-darmstadt.de
https://www.etit.tu-darmstadt.de/serious-games

**Abstract.** This paper presents GameTULearn, an innovative authoring tool for creating interactive educational games in 3D environments, tailored to educators and content creators with limited programming experience. The goal of this project is to simplify the development of engaging educational games and enhance learning experiences for students. Key features of the authoring tool include an intuitive user interface, a versatile scene editor, and a powerful quest editor for crafting narrative-driven game content.

The paper elaborates on the design process, highlighting novel ideas. The integration of an AI Assistant enhances user engagement and satisfaction in the story creation process, providing a more enjoyable and intuitive learning experience.

The prototype presented in this paper serves as a strong foundation for future implementation and development, ultimately aiming to facilitate the creation of compelling and effective educational games.

**Keywords:** Educational Games · Authoring Tool · Visual Programming · 3D Environments · Artificial Intelligence · GPT-4

## 1 Introduction

The integration of technology into education has opened up new possibilities for teaching and learning, especially in the field of digital educational games. Digitalization, in the form of e-learning, enables students to learn from home and with assistive technologies. Educational games can be especially significant for students who previously struggled with conventional teaching methods, as they can keep users engaged and motivated to learn [2,3].

However, developing personalized teaching scenarios often requires specialized programming knowledge, making it inaccessible to many teachers. This paper introduces GameTULearn, an authoring tool that aims to overcome this challenge and empower educators to easily create interactive digital 3D learning scenarios, regardless of their programming knowledge. This approach leverages

M. Haahr et al. (Eds.): JCSG 2023, LNCS 14309, pp. 384–390, 2023.
https://doi.org/10.1007/978-3-031-44751-8_32

user-friendly interfaces and intuitive tools that enable teachers to quickly design, develop, and deploy digital 3D learning scenarios, thus expanding the reach and impact of technology in education.

By going beyond the capabilities of traditional multimedia tools, this technology empowers educators to design engaging and effective e-learning games that captivate students and foster crucial skills. An easy-to-use authoring tool helps educators in various ways, such as empowering them, reducing technical barriers, encouraging creativity, and streamlining the development process. By integrating the blossoming generative AI technology GPT-4 by OpenAI[1] and using it for story generation, the learning curve is significantly minimized. This not only stimulates an eagerness for innovative experimentation in authors, but also makes the process highly engaging.

## 2  Design

### 2.1  System Overview

The authoring tool consists of two main parts: the Environment Editor and the Quest Editor.

The Environment Editor has four sections:

- *Scene Editor:* Designs the game environment in 3D.
- *Object List:* Shows all objects in the scene for selection and management.
- *Property Editor:* Modifies object properties like position, size, or color.
- *Asset Browser:* A library for importing pre-made assets like models or textures. It also allows to import custom assets into the application.

The Quest Editor is for designing the game narrative and includes:

- *Node-Based Story Structure:* Visually lays out the game's narrative.
- *Node Property Editor:* Edits the properties of each node, customizing the event or action.
- *Node Browser:* A library to choose suitable nodes for the story structure.

The tool offers an intuitive interface to design the game's environment and narrative, supporting customization, organization, and management. It also allows for node clustering, grouping sequences together for simplicity. Breadcrumb navigation is used in the Quest Editor to avoid confusion within complex structures, making navigation more efficient.

Figure 1 shows one view of the user interface of GameTULearn. On the right, the Asset Browser allows the user to drag new objects, sorted by category, into the scene. Upon doing so, the object is listed in the Object List to the left. Clicking on an object allows the user to modify its properties. The scene view offers various navigation helpers, as well as a switch between 2D top-down and 3D view.

---

[1] https://openai.com/product/gpt-4, last accessed on May 21, 2023.

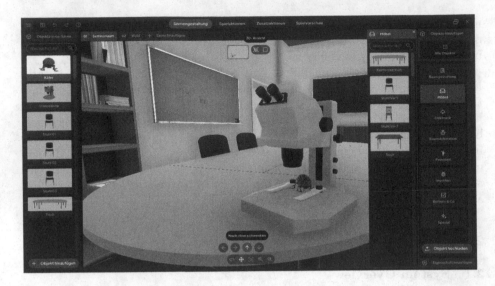

**Fig. 1.** The User Interface of GameTULearn.

The top menu bar features standard functions like saving, publishing, undo and redo. Additionally, it allows the user to switch from scene creation to story creation. An example of the node-based view that is used to create the story can be seen in Fig. 2. Here, the player first needs to speak to an assistant, before acquiring information by reading a book and interacting with a laptop. Afterwards, the player needs to answer a quiz based on the provided information. Selecting a node allows the user to modify the values of the node, for example selecting the correct book that the user needs to interact with.

The node system facilitates the creation of narratives, ranging from simple linear stories to more intricate nonlinear ones.

## 2.2    Publishing

The prototype of our authoring tool allows creators to publish their games, with a key feature being its support for web exports. Creators have the flexibility to either host their game independently on a web server or publish it in a portal hosted by the AG Serious Games at Technical University of Darmstadt. Once the game passes a review through an expert, it is made available for standalone play in a browser, and optionally integrated into the 3D Campus[2]. The 3D Campus can therefore serve as a central hub, where all created games can be explored, assuming the creators opted in to share their creations.

## 2.3    Testing

GameTULearn provides robust testing capabilities to ensure seamless gameplay. Authors can opt for either a maximized view or a testing view to preview their

---

[2] https://www.etit.tu-darmstadt.de/serious-games/forschung_und_projekte_sg/ 3d_campus_sg, last accessed on May 05, 2023.

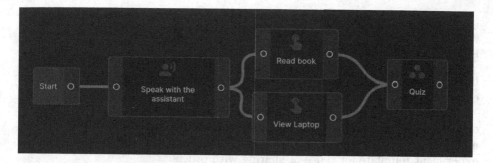

**Fig. 2.** The node system of GameTULearn.

game. The maximized view replicates the full player experience, transforming the tool into the game itself. Conversely, the testing view allows authors to monitor the game logic in real time within the node editor.

## 2.4  Player Perspective

Upon entering the game, players are placed in first-person mode, allowing them to experience the environment from the viewpoint of their character.

The story unfolds starting from the first node of the node editor. As players interact with the environment and complete story steps, subsequent nodes are activated, guiding them along the previously created node-based storyline.

Interactions are made intuitive through visual prompts; when players look at interactable objects, a signal appears to show that an action can be taken by pressing a specified button. This seamless interaction with the 3D environment ensures an engaging gaming experience that follows the path laid out by the game's authors, keeping players connected to the narrative from beginning to end.

## 2.5  Templates

The authoring tool includes a robust set of templates, categorized into environment, quest, game, and interaction templates, which streamline the game creation process.

Environment templates provide predefined settings suitable for various educational contexts, like physics or history, offering customizable layouts and props.

Quest templates offer pre-designed interactive activities with modular designs that support active learning, and they can be customized to align with specific learning goals. An example of a quest template is the Hero's Journey model by Vogler [5], a narrative framework consisting of Departure, Initiation, and Return stages.

Game templates combine both environment and quest templates, offering a complete game for customization. They serve as starting points for users to personalize game content and appearance.

Interaction templates offer small game templates for frequent interactions, like an electric door activated by a button, available in the asset browser for easy integration into scenes.

A dedicated template library is provided for easy access and reuse of previously designed elements, saving time, encouraging systematic design approaches, and enabling collaboration. For example, an educator can save a virtual science experiment template for reuse or sharing with others.

## 3    Discussion

### 3.1    AI Assistant

Initial tests revealed the node-based approach's robust potential, but it also appeared complex for some individuals lacking programming knowledge. For this reason, we implemented a GPT-4-based AI assistant. Authors can either specify which story they want to create, or let GPT-4 create a fitting story based on various topics like math, nature exploration, language learning and others.

Authors have the flexibility to dictate the difficulty and length of their desired story, with ranges extending from easy to hard and short to long, respectively. Based on these user specifications, GPT-4 uses predefined instructions, hidden from the user, to guide its selection and connection of nodes in crafting the story. These instructions include the available nodes of GameTULearn for story creation. The AI system initially generates a text-based narrative from user input, then translates this story using the available action nodes. The AI's output is then parsed and the resultant story is displayed to the author, in text-based and node-based form.

This streamlined process effectively simplifies story creation and makes the node-based approach more accessible to users without programming expertise.

Figure 3 shows an example of a quest created with the AI Assistant. Here, it is told to create a story with a science experiment, where the player has to talk to a person named Emma and mix two flasks. The story length is set to short, and the difficulty to easy. GPT-4 then created a story where the player has to help the Scientist Emma. She wants the player to mix yellow dye and bleach, resulting in a colorless mixture. Afterwards, Emma wants to congratulate the player. The resulting node setup has been created automatically. Using this workflow helps new users to understand how a story idea can be translated into nodes.

The author can then set up their environment with the 3D game objects and assign them to the nodes.

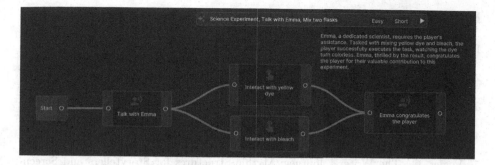

**Fig. 3.** AI-created story based on a short prompt using GPT-4.

## 4 Conclusion

The authoring tool concept is a novel solution designed to streamline the development process for 3D educational games. It incorporates a model for game structures and content, as well as technologies that enable adaptive gameplay. It uses the Unity game engine and offers pre-built templates, visual programming, integrated asset management, collaborative features, cross-platform support, and AI assistance, making 3D game development more accessible and efficient.

The tool's significant scientific contributions to game development and education include streamlining game development, fostering adaptive learning, promoting collaborative development, and offering scalability and extensibility via Unity. These features democratize the creation of adaptive, engaging, and effective 3D educational games, which can significantly impact the landscape of game-based learning and contribute to the advancement of educational technology.

Future work on the authoring tool can include the integration of text-to-3D-Model AI tools like Magic3D by Nvidia [1]. Nvidia also implemented automated room creation [4]. By combining these approaches with the AI-based story creation, the game creation could potentially be almost fully automated. Further, it could look at enhancing adaptivity and incorporating comprehensive evaluation and analytics tools.

Overall, as technology advances and the demand for innovative and engaging learning approaches increases, GameTULearn represents the potential of educational games to drive the evolution of education. By building upon the research done, high-quality, adaptive, and immersive educational games could become integral to learning experiences, enriching the lives of learners and educators globally.

**Acknowledgements.** This project is funded as a zQSL (*central quality of study conditions and teaching*) project at the Technical University of Darmstadt.

# References

1. Lin, C.H., et al.: Magic3D: high-resolution text-to-3D content creation. In: IEEE Conference on Computer Vision and Pattern Recognition (CVPR) (2023)
2. McFarlane, A., Sparrowhawk, A.S., Heald, Y.: Report on the educational use of games (2002)
3. Tang, S., Hanneghan, M., Rhalibi, A.E.: Introduction to games-based learning (2009)
4. Viviani, M.: How ChatGPT and GPT-4 Can Be Used for 3D Content Generation. https://resources.nvidia.com/en-us-omniverse-genai/ov-chatgpt
5. Vogler, C.: The Writer's Journey: Mythic Structures for Storytellers and Screenwriters. M. Wiese Productions, Studio City (1992)

# "Training Impaired Grammar" – A Serious Game for Agrammatism Treatment

Georgii Gorshkov[1]([✉]) [iD], Olga Buivolova[1,2] [iD], Svetlana Malyutina[1] [iD],
Viktoriia Pozdniakova[1,3] [iD], Olga Soloukhina[1] [iD], and Olga Dragoy[1,3] [iD]

[1] The National Research University Higher School of Economics, Moscow 101001, Russia
ggorshkov@hse.ru
[2] The Federal Center of Brain Research and Neurotechnologies, Moscow 117513, Russia
[3] The Institute of Linguistics, Russian Academy of Sciences, Moscow 125009, Russia

**Abstract.** Agrammatism is a common symptom occurring in post-stroke aphasia and frequently addressed in traditional language therapy. However, most commercial serious games and mHealth applications aimed at independent aphasia treatment include only few, if any, tasks focusing on morphosyntax. "Training Impaired Grammar" (TIGr) is a project which attempts to fill the existing gap for Russian speakers with aphasia. The app is going to cover eight areas of morphosyntax, including sentence structure, verb retrieval and various types of verbal and nominal inflection. Besides, it is going to be adaptable, i.e. each of these areas is going to be subdivided into four difficulty levels. Importantly, TIGr is planned to capture the users' attention and strengthen their motivation with a narrative framework and a reward system, which only rarely can be found in apps for aphasia treatment. The game is currently under development: the stimuli and distractors are being piloted, and the details of the plotline and design are being elaborated.

**Keywords:** Aphasia · Language Therapy · Agrammatism · Clinical Linguistics · Serious Games

## 1 Introduction

### 1.1 Aphasia and Agrammatism

Aphasia is a language disorder following brain damage, such as brain tumours, traumatic brain injury and, most typically, stroke, which is the second commonest cause of death and disability worldwide [1]. Stroke is also characterised by a high primary incidence: in Russia alone, 328 people out of 100,000 experience a stroke yearly, and nearly a third of them subsequently suffer from aphasia [2].

Aphasia may affect both speech production and comprehension in both oral and written modalities. The impaired language levels and the specific pattern of the disorder hinge upon the type of aphasia; besides, the concrete manifestations of aphasia, as well as its severity, are highly individual. Nonetheless, it is possible to distinguish several frequently occurring symptoms. They include difficulties producing full grammatical

M. Haahr et al. (Eds.): JCSG 2023, LNCS 14309, pp. 391–397, 2023.
https://doi.org/10.1007/978-3-031-44751-8_33

sentences (agrammatism), recalling words (anomia), pronouncing sounds and words correctly, repeating words and sentences accurately, etc.

Agrammatism as one of the most widespread aphasia symptoms is going to be the focus of this paper. Agrammatism is normally found in Broca's (non-fluent) aphasia and manifests itself in telegraphic speech, including only separate key words and lacking inflection and function words. Despite posing numerous problems to people with aphasia (PWAs), this specific condition is rarely addressed in speech/language therapy applications and serious games (SGs), as we shall demonstrate in the next section.

## 1.2 Serious Games for Aphasia Treatment and Rehabilitation

SGs for speech/language therapy have been produced for more than a decade. However, as can be seen from the most recent review of innovative technology-based interventions in aphasia rehabilitation [3], only a few developers and/or clinicians have reported the effectiveness of their digital products. The review included only ten tablet-based apps, most of which focused on language comprehension, naming, word formation, repetition, writing and, only in two cases, sentence planning.

However, there might be more SGs effectively used in clinical settings. For this reason, we conducted a brief analysis of mobile health (mHealth) apps for individual aphasia therapy (excluding means of augmentative and alternative communication) accessible on App Store (Apple Inc., Cupertino CA) and recommended on web-sites created by the National Health Service [4] and the National Aphasia Association [5]. This approach would ensure that the analysed SGs have been reviewed and approved by practising clinicians, although this method could exclude more recent developments. The search yielded 15 results, two out of which overlapped with the applications included in the abovementioned systematic review.

The results of this research demonstrated that only 20% of commercial SGs for aphasia treatment attempt at a comprehensive language therapy at all language levels, whereas most apps focus on one aspect of language: phonetics and phonology (67%) or semantics and word retrieval (53%). The most typical tasks employed in such apps include repetition of sounds, words, phrases and articulatory movements; matching a word/sentence with a corresponding picture/its written form; spelling; answering questions based on a text or a picture.

Thus, it can be noted that the level of morphosyntax is oftentimes disregarded in SGs for aphasia treatment, and the problem of agrammatism is typically not addressed. The applications that do include higher language levels practise them with only two task types: sentence completion, which more often deals with semantics and the appropriateness of a word in a given context; and scrambled sentences, where the user is to restore the correct word order in a sentence. Nevertheless, this concerns the SGs developed for native speakers of the English language, which has a relatively poor morphological system. Apps developed for speakers of languages with a more complex inflection system (e.g., Russian) should include more tasks aimed at agrammatism treatment. However, to our dismay, we managed to find only one SG targeted at Russian-speaking PWAs, which also practises primarily listening comprehension, word retrieval, word order and spelling.

Furthermore, the majority of the reviewed mHealth apps included several important game characteristics, e.g., the presence of explicit feedback, instructions and adaptability (defined as availability of various difficulty levels), as well as score systems helping users and/or clinicians to trace PWAs' progress and the chosen treatment intensity [6, 7]. However, none of these SGs made use of a narrative framework, nor of an avatar that would progress through the plotline, although these could be considered significant game elements, boosting the user's motivation and creating a better connection between the game and the player [6, 7].

Taking into account all the said drawbacks of the field, we started developing a project aimed to fill the existing gaps.

## 2 Training Impaired Grammar (TIGr)

### 2.1 Structure and Materials

**Structure and Task Types.** The task types of "Training Impaired Grammar" (TIGr) were mostly based on the therapy paradigm proposed by Shklovskiy and Vizel, which was guided by Luria's approach to aphasia classification [8]. Moreover, (TIGr) is going to incorporate elements of the world's leading therapy methods, such as Verb Network Strengthening Treatment [9], Treatment of Underlying Forms, Treating Sentence Frames [10] and Morphosemantic Treatment [11].

Based on the peculiarities of Russian grammar and on the modern idea of the verb's central role in the sentence [12], eight main areas of interest were distinguished: verb retrieval, sentence structure, the number and person of the verb in the Present tense, the number and gender of the verb in the Past tense, the tense of the verb, verbal government (which Case should follow a given verb), prepositional government (which Case should follow a given preposition), and the declension of adjectives. Besides, TIGr is planned to be adaptable and suitable for people with various degrees of aphasia severity; for this reason, the SG should have four difficulty levels. Tasks for the "easy" level are based on the idea of priming, i.e. the user perceives a model sentence and constructs their response according to it. Tasks for the two "moderate" levels[1] mainly consist of matching or multiple-choice activities. On the "difficult" level, users are supposed to produce the correct form according to the context, i.e. open the brackets and type in the required form.

The TIGr mobile app is supposed to welcome the user with a brief test that will assess their agrammatism severity and open the tasks of their level and all the easier tasks. The user then will be able to choose the language area that they wish to practise. Each level of each area is going to consist of multiple sets of 10–12 stimuli. In case a mistake is made, the user will be immediately informed about it and shown the correct response, and the problematic stimulus will be repeated at the end of the set. Upon the completion

---

[1] It was decided to split this level in two in order to have a smoother between-level transition and to provide more various tasks; essentially, there is a slight increase of difficulty on the second "moderate" level due to a greater number of distractors and/or a slightly more difficult grammatical phenomenon in question.

of a certain level in an area, the next one is going to become accessible, irrespective of the user's progress in the other areas.

Figures 1 and 2 represent a tentative design of some sample tasks with an approximate translation.

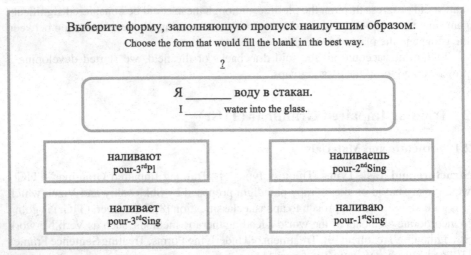

**Fig. 1.** A sample task on the number and person of the verb in the Present tense (the lower "moderate" difficulty level). The question mark represents a tab with a hint.

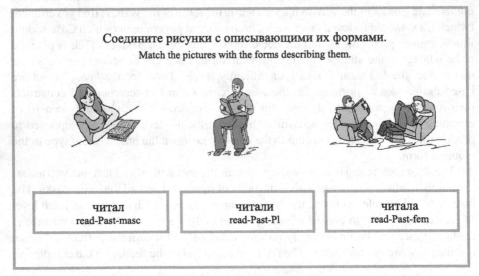

**Fig. 2.** A sample task on the number and gender of the verb in the Past tense (the lower "moderate" difficulty level).

**Materials.** Since tasks for at least three areas (verb retrieval, sentence structure and the number and gender of the verb in the Past tense) require pictures, we employed the Stimuli Database [13], which contains pictures of over 300 Russian verbs and normative data related to the images (name agreement, visual complexity, etc.) and the verbs (age of acquisition, length, frequency, imageability, etc.). While selecting the stimuli, we applied the following criteria: the name agreement of the verb and the picture should surpass the 85% threshold; the depicted verbs should not have any strongly negative connotation; the verbs were distributed by levels based on their frequency (the more frequent the verb is, the easier should be the difficulty level where it appears). Furthermore, a professional artist was hired to colour the black-and-white pictures and make new illustrations for the number and gender of the verb in the Past tense.

The tasks that do not necessitate the use of pictures were based on verbs, prepositions and adjectives found in the New Frequency Dictionary of Russian Vocabulary [14]. Selection criteria included word frequency, absence of strongly negative connotation and stylistic neutrality. In some areas, additional parameters were taken into consideration, e.g., the easiest level did not include any reflexive or irregular verbs.

As a result, more than 5,000 stimuli have been created, most of which have from one to three distractors. These stimuli are currently being piloted in people without a history of neurological conditions so as to ensure the validity of the materials.

## 2.2 The Plot and the Reward System

As was mentioned above, none of the SGs for aphasia rehabilitation that we managed to review included a plot or a system of tangible rewards, the only reward normally being merely the score and the ratio of tasks correctly accomplished. We have decided to consider these aspects of SGs and include them into our project.

In order to discover what plot type and rewards would increase the motivation of our target population, we consulted a speech-language pathologist working in the Center of Speech Pathology and Neurorehabilitation, Moscow, Russia. This gave us an insight into what types of information can capture PWAs' attention, and based on this understanding we opted for adventure as the preferred genre. The protagonist, a tiger (which follows from the abbreviation of our SG), is travelling the world[2], with each area being a separate location (e.g., a country or a continent) with four sub-locations representing various difficulty levels (e.g., different cities in a chosen country or various climate zones).

On its journey, the Tiger learns trivia and interesting facts about the places it visits (e.g., facts concerning local geography, culture, cuisine, etc.). These, in the form of short

---

[2] A survey of persons of over 50 years of age is currently being conducted as to what kind of journey would be more logical and captivating for our target audience, people of age being the group most susceptible to strokes. We have so far collected only a dozen of responses, but the overwhelming majority of our informants embrace the adventure genre with enthusiasm. The opinions, however, are now equally split as to the exact route of this travel: whether it should include the whole world, only the climate zones that tigers inhabit, or only Russia – the birthplace of most of our target audience. The specific locations will be developed based on the feedback obtained from the survey.

text messages and beautiful illustrations, will be presented as a reward for the successful completion of a set of tasks.

Additionally, accomplishing several such sets could lead to another type of reward – a sort of an in-game currency that would allow the user to unlock additional tasks of different types and practise grammatical phenomena not covered in the main areas of the journey. This is, however, only a suggestion, work on which has not been started yet (although it can be implemented later as a series of updates).

## 3  Conclusion

Reviewing data on the existing SGs for aphasia treatment allowed us to identify what the market is lacking at the moment: games targeted at agrammatism rehabilitation, as well as SGs incorporating more game elements, such as a narrative context and an elaborate reward system. In this report, we demonstrated an attempt to improve the current practice and showed work in progress that could potentially raise the quality and attractiveness of mHelath apps for users, which would consequently result in better therapy for PWAs.

**Acknowledgements.** This work is an output of a research project implemented as part of the Basic Research Program at the National Research University Higher School of Economics (HSE University). We are extremely thankful to Ekaterina Zorina for her invaluable feedback.

## References

1. Vos, T., et al.: Global burden of 369 diseases and injuries in 204 countries and territories, 1990–2019: a systematic analysis for the Global Burden of Disease Study 2019. Lancet **396**, 1204–1222 (2020). https://doi.org/10.1016/S0140-6736(20)30925-9
2. Malyutina, S.A., Iskra, E.V.: Public awareness of aphasia: a survey of clinicians. Consilium Medicum **19**(2.1), 56–59 (2017)
3. Repetto, C., Paolillo, M.P., Tuena, C., Bellinzona, F., Riva, G.: Innovative technology-based interventions in aphasia rehabilitation: a systematic review. Aphasiology (2020). https://doi.org/10.1080/02687038.2020.1819957
4. App reviews by the NHS. Northern Devon Healthcare. Best apps for stroke patients – Free NHS guide. https://www.my-therapphy.co.uk/apps/stroke-brain-injury/talking. Accessed 15 May 2023
5. National Aphasia Association. Aphasia apps, https://www.aphasia.org/aphasia-resources/aphasia-apps/. Accessed 15 May 2023
6. Mubin, O., Alnajjar, F., Al Mahmud, A., Jishtu, N., Alsinglawi, B.: Exploring serious games for stroke rehabilitation: a scoping review. Disabil. Rehabil. Assist. Technol. **17**(2), 159–165 (2020). https://doi.org/10.1080/17483107.2020.1768309
7. Ferreira-Brito, F., Fialho, M., Virgolino, A., Neves, I., Miranda, A.C., Sousa-Santos, N., et al.: Game-based interventions for neuropsychological assessment, training and rehabilitation: Which game-elements to use? A systematic review. J. Biomed. Inform. **98** (2019). https://doi.org/10.1016/j.jbi.2019.103287
8. Shklovskiy, V.M., Vizel, T.G.: Restoring the language function in patients with various types of aphasia. Восстановление речевой функции у больных с разными формами афазии. "Defectologist Association", V Sekachov, Moscow, Russia (2000)

9. Edmonds, L., Nadeau, S., Kiran, S.: Effect of Verb Network Strengthening Treatment (VNeST) on lexical retrieval of content words in sentences in persons with aphasia. Aphasiology 23(3), 402–424 (2009). https://doi.org/10.1080/02687030802291339

10. Martin, N., Thompson, C.K., Worrall, L.E.: Aphasia rehabilitation: the impairment and its consequences. Plural Pub, San Diego (2008)

11. Bastiaanse, R., Thompson, C.: Perspectives on Agrammatism (Brain, Behaviour and Cognition). Psychology Press, London (2012)

12. Bastiaanse, R., Hurkmans, J., Links, P.: The training of verb production in Broca's aphasia: A multiple-baseline across-behaviours study. Aphasiology 20(2–4), 298–311 (2006). https://doi.org/10.1080/02687030500474922

13. Akinina, Y., Malyutina, S., Ivanova, M., Iskra, E., Mannova, E., Dragoy, O.: Russian normative data for 375 action pictures and verbs. Behav. Res. Methods 47(3), 691–707 (2015). https://doi.org/10.3758/s13428-014-0492-9

14. Liashevskaya, O.N., Sharov, S.A.: A frequency dictionary of the contemporary Russian language (based on the Russian National Corpus). Частотный словарь современного русского языка (на материалах Национального корпуса русского языка). Azbukovnik, Moscow, Russia (2009)

# A Prototype of a 3D Shooter Game for the Visually Impaired Player

Rogerio Eduardo da Silva[1]([✉])⬤ and Pedro Neves Rito[2]⬤

[1] University of Leicester, Leicester, UK
`rogerio.silva@leicester.ac.uk`
[2] Instituto Politécnico de Viseu, Viseu, Portugal
`rito@esev.ipv.pt`

**Abstract.** Visual impairment refers to a significant loss of vision that cannot be fully corrected with glasses, contact lenses, medication, or surgery. It encompasses a range of conditions, from partial sight to total blindness, and can result from various causes, including congenital conditions, eye diseases, injuries, or neurological disorders. This paper presents an ongoing project of a prototype of a 3D shooter game that is designed to be accessible to people with visual impairments. The game uses a variety of techniques to provide players with information about their surroundings, even if they cannot see. These techniques include audio cues, haptic feedback, and spatial awareness. The prototype's gameplay mechanics are tailored to provide an engaging and intuitive experience. Players rely on auditory cues, such as varying tones, sound effects, and directional audio, to navigate the virtual world, solve puzzles, and overcome challenges. The game mechanics encourage players to use their auditory acuity and critical thinking skills to progress through the game.

**Keywords:** digital entertainment · visual impairment · sound-based games · virtual reality

## 1 Introduction

Video games are a popular form of entertainment for people of all ages. In the work carried out by Cairns et al. (2021) [13], more than 100 players with disabilities were interviewed and one of the results was that video games help them to feel enabled or being on a level footing with non disabled players. Also players with visual impairments often have difficulty playing video games, as they rely on visual information to interact with the game world. This can make it difficult for them to play games that require them to see enemies, obstacles, or other important objects.

In recent years, there has been a growing interest in developing video games that are accessible to people with visual impairments. This is a challenging task, but it is important to ensure that everyone has the opportunity to enjoy the benefits of video games [14].

This paper presents an ongoing project of a prototype of a 3D shooter game that is designed to be accessible to people with visual impairments. The game uses a variety of techniques to provide players with information about their surroundings, even if they cannot see. These techniques include audio cues, haptic feedback, and spatial awareness. At this stage of the work, in addition to collecting information that can help us in development, different technical solutions have also been tested with different software platforms.

## 2   Background

### 2.1   Visual Impairment

Visual impairment refers to a significant loss of vision that cannot be fully corrected with glasses, contact lenses, medication, or surgery. It encompasses a range of conditions, from partial sight to total blindness, and can result from various causes, including congenital conditions, eye diseases, injuries, or neurological disorders. Visual impairment affects individuals of all ages and has a profound impact on their daily lives, including their ability to perform tasks, navigate the environment, and access information [1]. In the report presented by the WHO [2] indicate that about 25% of people have vision problems, of which 13% are serious and very serious problems.

The Designing for Disability Research Project [3] provides information on research prototypes and their significance in exploring innovative approaches to address accessibility challenges. This reference sheds light on the concept of research prototypes in the context of creating inclusive experiences for visually impaired individuals.

There are also other related works where they explore the design of serious games for individuals with visual impairments, highlighting, once again, the importance of research prototypes in this domain. It provides insights into the challenges and considerations specific to developing games for visually impaired individuals [4]. This is also highlighted by [5] where they discusses the development of game accessibility guidelines for players with visual impairments. It emphasizes the need for research prototypes to explore and refine accessible game design principles. The paper provides insights into the potential benefits and challenges of developing research prototypes for visually impaired gamers.

### 2.2   Digital Entertainment

Digital entertainment is a broad term that encompasses any form of entertainment that is delivered in a digital format. This includes, but is not limited to, movies, television shows, music, video games, and e-books. Digital entertainment is typically consumed on a variety of devices, such as computers, smartphones, tablets, and gaming consoles [6].

Digital entertainment is also more accessible than traditional forms of entertainment. For example, people with disabilities can often enjoy digital entertainment more easily than traditional forms of entertainment. This is because digital entertainment can be customized to meet the needs of individual users. For example, people with visual impairments can often use screen readers to access digital content.

Overall, digital entertainment is a convenient, affordable, and accessible form of entertainment that offers a wide variety of options for users. As the popularity of digital entertainment continues to grow, it is likely to become even more important in our lives [7,8].

There are also other details about digital entertainment:

- It is interactive, meaning that users can participate in the experience. This can make it more engaging and immersive than traditional forms of entertainment;
- It is personalized, meaning that users can customize the experience to their own preferences what can make it more enjoyable and relevant;
- It is portable, meaning that users can take it with them wherever they go, making it a convenient option for people who are on the go;
- It is social, meaning that users can share it with others in a fun and rewarding way to connect with friends and family;
- It is a rapidly growing industry, and it is likely to continue to grow in the years to come. This is due to a number of factors, including the increasing availability of high-speed internet, the growing popularity of mobile devices, and the increasing demand for personalized and interactive experiences.

### 2.3  Sound-Based Games

Sound-based games represent a captivating genre within the realm of interactive entertainment, focusing on the integration of audio elements as the primary means of gameplay and player engagement. By leveraging innovative sound design techniques, these games offer unique and immersive experiences that challenge traditional gaming conventions. This abstract explores the concept of sound-based games, highlights the significance of audio in interactive experiences, provides relevant citations to support the discussion, and presents notable examples from the genre [9,10].

We can find some sound-based for visually impaired players:

**A Blind Legend (2015)** Designed explicitly for visually impaired players, this audio-based adventure game provides a rich auditory experience. Through the use of binaural audio, players navigate the game world by relying solely on sound cues, immersing themselves in a story-driven narrative where sound serves as the primary means of interaction and exploration.

**Perception (2017)** In this first-person horror game, players assume the role of a blind protagonist who uses echolocation to navigate the environment. By emitting sound waves and interpreting the returning audio feedback, players uncover their surroundings and solve mysteries. The game offers a unique perspective on sensory perception and highlights the potential for sound-based gameplay to cater to individuals with visual impairments.

**The Nightjar (2018)** This mobile game was specifically developed for visually impaired players and combines spatial audio and touch-based gameplay. Players engage with the game by listening to 3D audio cues and using touch gestures on their device's screen. The immersive sound design allows players to detect and interact with objects and characters in the game world, providing an engaging experience for visually impaired players.

**AudioWizards (2020)** This fantasy-themed sound-based game focuses on rhythm-based combat, where players engage in battles by following audio cues and timing their attacks accordingly. The game provides an accessible gameplay experience by using audio feedback to guide players through the game's challenges, making it suitable for players with visual impairments.

Sound-based games provide a unique and engaging form of interactive entertainment that showcases the power of audio in shaping gameplay and player experiences. By leveraging innovative sound design techniques, these games create immersive environments, challenge traditional gaming norms, and present new avenues for storytelling and player engagement. The examples provided demonstrate the diverse range of possibilities within the sound-based game genre and emphasize the profound impact that audio can have on the gaming landscape [9].

And also, sound-based games offer an inclusive and accessible gaming experience for individuals with visual impairments. By leveraging innovative sound design and audio mechanics, these games provide a means of interactive entertainment that relies primarily on auditory cues, enhancing gameplay experiences for visually impaired players. The examples provided demonstrate the effectiveness of sound-based games in catering to the needs of individuals with visual impairments, highlighting the potential for this genre to bridge accessibility gaps and create engaging gaming experiences for all.

## 3  Prototype Design

### 3.1  The Visually-Impared Player

In the work of Hugill and Pugliese [11] we can find contributions to the understanding and enhancement of the experiences of individuals with visual impairments. The authors' work encompasses various dimensions, including the exploration of the auditory imaginary, solitary auditory hallucination in relation to Shakespearean works, and the sonic experiences of the visually impaired. Their research sheds light on the transformative potential of sound and music in creating rich sensory experiences beyond vision. They also emphasizes the importance of object-based interaction and its impact on engaging visually impaired audiences. By leveraging innovative approaches, This work provides insights into the development of inclusive design principles and strategies that cater to the needs of individuals with visual impairments. Their research contributions in the field of visual impairment are significant and have greatly contributed to our understanding of accessibility, inclusive design, and sensory experiences for individuals with visual impairments

Our work will explore the platform created by Hugill and Pugliese, complementing it with the use of virtual reality, creating an immersive digital environment where the sound will serve as a guide for our player.

## 3.2   The Sound-Based Gameplay

Imagine stepping into a virtual realm where the limitations of visual impairments vanish, and players are transported into a rich and vibrant world solely through the power of sound. The core of this prototype lies in its ability to harness the power of sound to create an accessible gaming experience. Every aspect of the virtual world is intricately designed to generate distinct audio cues, allowing players with visual impairments to navigate, interact, and engage with the game environment [10].

The prototype's gameplay mechanics are tailored to provide an engaging and intuitive experience. Players rely on auditory cues, such as varying tones, sound effects, and directional audio, to navigate the virtual world, solve puzzles, and overcome challenges. The game mechanics encourage players to use their auditory acuity and critical thinking skills to progress through the game. The potential impact of a sound-based virtual world for individuals with visual impairments extends beyond gaming. It opens doors to educational applications, where concepts of spatial awareness, problem-solving, and critical thinking can be seamlessly integrated into gameplay. Moreover, by providing an immersive experience, the prototype fosters empathy and understanding among players, raising awareness about the challenges faced by those with visual impairments.

The sound-based virtual world prototype holds the potential to transform the way we perceive and engage with video games. It is a testament to the power of technology in overcoming barriers and creating meaningful experiences for individuals with visual impairments.

## 3.3   The Game Prototype

Our proposal is the system illustrated in Fig. 1 that should be composed of: (1) a tactile platform that vibrates with sound [12]; (2) an array of speakers to produce surround sound which is the material we have access at the moment. In the future we might consider using a 5.1 sound system [15]; and (3) a VR headset and controllers to allow an intuitive human-centred interface between player and the game environment.

In this setup, the (visually impaired) player will be positioned at the center of the tactile platform, wearing a VR headset (Oculus Rift) and holding controllers for shooting flying targets (e.g. bats). Even considering the player as being visually impaired, it is necessary that the player wears the headset as tracking the controllers positions rely on that.

**Fig. 1.** Proposal for a rig of a sound-based shooting game.

The game prototype should mostly rely on spawning targets that will emit 3D sound (e.g. bat squeaking). These sounds should then be played in the speakers in a way to allow the player to locate it's source. Complementary, the tactile platform generates vibrations that can vary in intensity to indicate the distance from the target. The player should then shoot the target by means of the controllers using a point-and-click fashion.

## 4  Final Remarks

As the digital entertainment industry continues to evolve, it is imperative to prioritize accessibility and inclusivity for individuals with visual impairment. By using sound as the primary medium for gameplay and interaction, sound-based games offer a multi-sensory experience that transcends visual limitations. This approach allows players with visual impairment to immerse themselves in rich narratives, solve puzzles, navigate virtual worlds, and compete with others on an equal footing. The development of prototypes in this field has demonstrated the potential for creating captivating experiences that cater to diverse abilities and preferences.

In addition, user feedback and engagement from the visually impaired community should be at the forefront of these developments. By actively involving users with visual impairment in the design and testing phases, we can ensure that the solutions meet their specific needs, preferences, and expectations.

In conclusion, the integration of sound-based games and prototypes represents a promising step towards a more inclusive future of digital entertainment. While there is still work to be done, the advancements made so far highlight the transformative power of accessible gaming experiences for individuals with visual impairment.

# References

1. World Health Organization (WHO). Visual Impairment and Blindness (2021). https://www.who.int/news-room/fact-sheets/detail/blindness-and-visual-impairment
2. World Health Organization (WHO). World Report on Disability (2011). https://www.who.int/teams/noncommunicable-diseases/sensory-functions-disability-and-rehabilitation/world-report-on-disability
3. Designing for Disability Research Project. Research Prototypes (n.d.). https://designingfordisability.fiu.edu/research-prototypes.html
4. Birkeland, M., Seaborn, K.: Designing serious games for persons with visual impairments: a review of the literature. In: Proceedings of the International Conference on the Foundations of Digital Games (FDG), pp. 1–8 (2016). https://dl.acm.org/doi/10.1145/2897053.2897063
5. Istance, H.O., Benko, H., Wilson, A.D.: Towards game accessibility guidelines for players with visual impairments. In: Proceedings of the 14th International Conference on the Foundations of Digital Games (FDG), pp. 1–6 (2019). https://dl.acm.org/doi/10.1145/3337722.3341867
6. Boyle, E.A., Connolly, T.M., Hainey, T., Boyle, J.M.: Engagement in digital entertainment games: a systematic review. Comput. Hum. Behav. **28**(3), 771–780 (2012). https://doi.org/10.1016/j.chb.2011.11.020
7. Kumar, S.: Consumer engagement in digital entertainment: a systematic review. In: Das, S., Gochhait, S. (eds.) Digital Entertainment. Palgrave Macmillan, Singapore (2021). https://doi.org/10.1007/978-981-15-9724-4_1
8. Dhote, T.P.: Review of consumer engagement and digital entertainment on over the top platforms. In: Das, S., Gochhait, S. (eds.) Digital Entertainment. Palgrave Macmillan, Singapore (2021). https://doi.org/10.1007/978-981-15-9724-4_2
9. Gärdenfors, D.: Designing sound-based computer games. Digit. Creat. **14**(2), 111–114 (2003). https://doi.org/10.1076/digc.14.2.111.27863
10. Friberg, J., Gärdenfors, D.: Audio games: new perspectives on game audio. In: Proceedings of the 2004 ACM SIGCHI International Conference on Advances in Computer Entertainment Technology, pp. 148–154. Association for Computing Machinery (2004)
11. Merritt, T., Ong, C., Chuah, T.L., McGee, K.: Did you notice? Artificial teammates take risks for players. In: Vilhjálmsson, H.H., Kopp, S., Marsella, S., Thórisson, K.R. (eds.) IVA 2011. LNCS (LNAI), vol. 6895, pp. 338–349. Springer, Heidelberg (2011). https://doi.org/10.1007/978-3-642-23974-8_37
12. Hugill, A.: Rethinking the concert experience (2020). https://andrewhugill.com/writings/Rethinking.html. Accessed 15 May 2023
13. Cairns, P., Power, C., Barlet, M., Haynes, G., Kaufman, C., Beeston, J.: Enabled players: the value of accessible digital games. Games Cult. **16**(2), 262–282 (2021). https://doi.org/10.1177/1555412019893877
14. Andrade, R., Rogerson, M.J., Waycott, J., Baker, S., Vetere, F.: Introducing the gamer information-control framework: enabling access to digital games for people with visual impairment. In: Proceedings of the 2020 CHI Conference on Human Factors in Computing Systems (CHI 2020), pp. 1–14. Association for Computing Machinery, New York (2020). https://doi.org/10.1145/3313831.3376211
15. Bratus, A.: An audible environment: production of a generative soundscape device. Master's Programme in New Media, 121 p. (2022) https://aaltodoc.aalto.fi/handle/123456789/114843

# Knowledge Transfer in Disaster Risk Management (DRM)
## Design of a Serious Game

Joachim Schulze(✉), Tom Sauer, Annette Rudolph-Cleff, and Michèle Knodt

Technical University of Darmstadt, Karolinenplatz 5, 64289 Darmstadt, Germany
schulze@stadt.tu-darmstadt.de

**Abstract.** Generally speaking, disaster risk management (DRM) aims to mitigate the impact of disasters and refers to the four stages prior and post to a crisis event namely response, recovery, prevention and preparedness. Measures taken in this context are manifold and apply to the natural and the built environment, governance, economics and society. With no limitation in scale, DRM can raise robustness of entire infrastructures or leverage the preparedness of an individual citizen. In this paper, a serious game entitled *e***HUB**gaming is introduced as a method of DRM. As a means of knowledge transfer, it intends to prepare citizens for the event of a prolonged superregional blackout. As a virtual resident, the player is confronted with a three-day blackout scenario and must get by with a limited amount of energy and react to a series of events taking place. The key research questions are 1) how can such a serious game be designed and 2) how can it incorporate knowledge transfer? *e***HUB**gaming is developed in the context of the LOEWE center emergenCITY as part of the cross-sectional mission *e***HUB** at the Technical University of Darmstadt.

**Keywords:** Serious game · Gamification · Disaster Risk Management (DRM) · Knowledge transfer · Emergency responsive cities

## 1 Introduction

Disaster Risk Management (DRM) as defined by the United Nations (UN) is *"the application of disaster risk reduction policies and strategies to prevent new disaster risk, reduce existing disaster risk and manage residual risk, contributing to the strengthening of resilience and reduction of disaster losses"* [1], p.135]. Structurally, DRM distinguishes between 1) prospective, 2) corrective and 3) compensatory activities. Whereas 1) and 2) predominantly refer to the robustness of infrastructures or lowering the vulnerability of assets or populations at high risk 3) focuses on society by fostering the resilience of individuals to face residual risk through preparedness, response and recovery measures [2]. In this paper, the design of a serious game is presented that has the intention to prepare for the crisis scenario of a prolonged superregional blackout by means of knowledge transfer. It could be distributed by civil protection services and is of interest for any citizen who takes concern in preparedness and coping. Thus, it

M. Haahr et al. (Eds.): JCSG 2023, LNCS 14309, pp. 405–412, 2023.
https://doi.org/10.1007/978-3-031-44751-8_35

can be associated to the compensatory activities in DRM more specifically the phase of preparedness in the common four-part cycle of DRM [3], p. 471].

## 1.1 emergenCITY and the *e*HUB Mission

The serious game entitled *e*HUBgaming is part of the LOEWE center emergenCITY [4], a research center dedicated on research towards the resilience of digital cities at the Technical University of Darmstadt. As the name suggests, the serious game is associated to the cross-sectional mission *e*HUB that revolves around a plus energy building located on the remote campus Lichtwiese of the Technical University Darmstadt [5]. In essence, the mission *e*HUB investigates what role such a plus energy building could play in the context of a prolonged superregional blackout given the fact that it can gain energy even though the power grid is down. Originally, the *e*HUB building was the winning contribution to the 2009 Solar Decathlon, an international competition in which 20 universities competed in fulfilling the task to *"design, build, and operate solar-powered houses that are cost-effective, energy-efficient, and attractive"* [6], p. 3]. Altogether, the *e*HUB building only consumes 30% of the total electrical energy produced enabling a surplus of app. 9590 kWh per year [7], p. 35]. With this amount of energy at the hand, the *e*HUB mission examines how it can be deployed and distributed to assist emergency response and the general public in the case of a blackout. However, research in the mission is not limited to measures of immediate response but also covers the pre-disaster phase namely preparedness. Generally speaking, preparedness is defined as *"the knowledge and capacities developed by [...] individuals to effectively anticipate, respond to and recover from the impacts of likely, imminent or current disasters"* [8], p. 21]. Also referred to as household preparedness [9, 10], Kohler et al. [11], p. 6] outline preparedness as obtaining both *"tangible resources"* in the shape of materials and *"intangible knowledge, skills and behaviours."* Leveraging preparedness through knowledge transfer is the approach investigated in the context of the serious game *e*HUBgaming leading to the following research questions:

1. How can a serious game be designed in the context of DRM?
2. How can such a serious game incorporate knowledge transfer?

## 2 Theoretical Framework

### 2.1 Serious Gaming in the Context of DRM

The initial definition of serious games was given by Abt in 1970. He states that serious games *"[...] have an explicit and carefully thought-out educational purpose and are not intended to be played primarily for amusement. This does not mean that serious games are not, or should not be, entertaining."* [12]. In its essence this definition is still valid today and can be found in a wide variety of contexts [13–16]. When it comes to DRM, the term itself does not appear in the preliminary taxonomy of serious games introduced by Sawyer and Smith in 2008 [15] but there is an underlying linkage to a number of fields listed such as mass casualty response or inform about diseases/risks. Solinska-Nowak, A. et al. [17] provide a comprehensive and profound overview on contemporary serious gaming in the context DRM. In the opening sections of the study the authors elaborate on the relevance of serious gaming as an innovative measure of DRM especially in contrast to common top-down approaches. Essentially, these approaches understand DRM to be mainly in the responsibility of the authorities paying little attention to context and negating the potential of individual or community participation. The emphasis on participation leads to a principle change of perspective in DRM regarding the population more as a contributor rather than just a *"target"* [17], p. 1014]. Serious games are receiving *"increased recognition"* [17], p. 1014] to be applied in these very contexts. Apart from being suited to support a bottom-up approach because they can be easily distributed to a reach a large number of recipients, Solinska-Nowak, A. et al. also outline the didactical potential of serious gaming. Building on a *"shift from authority- and lecturer-based teaching"* [17], p. 1014] serious games require more engagement and activity and by incorporating fun and emotions verifiably information is better received and remembered. This circumstance is confirmed by other sources such as Westera, A. [16]. In conclusion, Solinska-Nowak, A. et al. acknowledge the potential of serious games to act as a complementary tool in the different stages of DRM. This outcome is undermined by a thorough analysis of 45 serious games presented in the main part of the study. Building on the contextual background and theoretical framework described above, the following section provides an overview of *e***HUB**gaming design.

## 3  *e*HUBgaming

### 3.1  State of Development

**Fig. 1.** Exterior and interior view of eHUB (courtesy of Jürgen Schreiter, Darmstadt)

**Conceptual Idea.**  The basic idea of *e***HUB**gaming is the player stepping into the role of the inhabitant of the *e***HUB** building (Fig. 1.) [18] and witnessing a three-day blackout. Being unaware of the duration of the power failure he or she is challenged to get by day by day relying solely on the energy provided by the photovoltaics of the building. In addition, the player owns an electrical vehicle that is connected to the *e***HUB** building providing additional energy. Even though this setting does not resemble the common living conditions of the majority of the German population it is highly beneficial from a game design point of view because it offers a wide variety of gameplay options but still enables universal knowledge transfer that is not unique to the *e***HUB** building. Technically speaking, the game can best be described as a point-and-click adventure

[19, 20] incorporating elements of both role-playing and simulation. Gameplay is based on static perspectives resembling the interior of the *eHUB* building by which the player can navigate to different locations in the house and two main elements which are referred to as activity zones and events. In the activity zones the player can make adjustments to the temperature, the lighting or the level of ventilation and thereby lower the energy consumption. Furthermore, activity zones are meant to satisfy basic needs like hunger, fatigue or personal hygiene. Basic needs and moods of the player are represented by an emoji which first turns yellow and then red whenever an unsatisfactory condition prevails. Turning off the heating completely for example in an attempt to save energy leads to a freezing condition. The player must find a trade-off between lowering energy consumption on the one hand and well-being on the other hand. Events take place based on a fixed schedule and in the most cases involve the player interacting with a fictional neighbor named Mr. Leonwald. Depending on how the player deals with an event taking place subsequent events do or do not occur. Even though the actual intention of the game is knowledge transfer the primary goal for the player is to achieve the highest possible score. Game points are granted whenever knowledge is passed on to the player, certain needs are satisfied or an unsatisfactory mood is relieved. Negative game points on the other hand are subtracted if an unsatisfactory state prevails.

**Fig. 2.** *e*HUBgaming GUI

**Design.** *Grafical User Interface (GUI).* From top to bottom the GUI consists of the upper progress bar, the central perspective, the emoji on the left and the lower status bar (Fig. 2). The progress bar includes a yellow slider that moves from left to right as the day commences with green bars indicating energy gains and red bars indicating energy consumption. It is complemented by a battery symbol showing the state of charge of the electrical vehicle and two thermometers that display inside and outside temperatures. In the middle of the screen the player can navigate to seven different locations in the house by clicking on the upper, right, lower or left border. On the lefthand side of the GUI the emoji is displayed. The current day and the score are included in the lower status bar. In addition, messages appear as a general source of information or when certain events call for the player's attention.

*Activity Zones.* There are four activity zones in the game namely 1) heating & venting, 2) smart panel 3) kitchen and 4) bathroom. These are accessed by clicking on a defined area in the corresponding perspective. In the kitchen the player can have some food, drink a coffee or turn the refrigerator on or off, dimming the light or turning on the sound system is done in an activity zone referred to as the smart panel and in the bathroom the player can take a shower or use the toilette.

*Emojis.* Emojis play an important role in the *e***HUB**gaming. Altogether, there are six emojis representing the conditions of 1) happiness, 2) hunger, 3) freezing, 4) boredom, 5) fatigue and 6) having to use the restroom. The player is advised to take care of his or her needs as soon as possible because they are decisive for scoring.

*Events.* Events introduce an element of story-telling to the game and are the main "carrier" of knowledge transfer. With exception of two events all events involve a character named Mr. Leonwald who is the neighbor living across the street from the *e***HUB** building. Mr. Leonwald first appearance takes place on day 01 at 9:00 h. The player must open the front door upon Mr. Leonwald knocking in order to participate in the event. The first conversation with the neighbor has Mr. Leonwald asking the player if he can charge his cellphone. At this point the player must make a decision that will influence forthcoming events and the possibility to gain extra game points at a later stage. Events appear regularly and call for the player to read the dialogues carefully and offer the possibility of the game to progress in one way or another.

*Knowledge Transfer.* Knowledge transfer in *e***HUB**gaming revolves around three questions: 1) What are the consequences of a blackout, 2) How can one cope with a blackout and 3) How can one prepare for a blackout? The effects of the blackout portrayed in the game are based on the processing of past events [21], publications from the German ministry for civil protection [22] and an assessment commissioned by the German government on the impact of a long-term power failure [23]. In the conversations with the neighbor Mr. Leonwald a number of the adverse effects of a blackout are mentioned e.g. gas stations not being able to provide fuel, traffic lights not running and the general difficulty to communicate or to receive information [24–26]. Measures of preparation and coping are addressed by an official brochure of the German ministry of civil protection [27, 28] that is handed over by Mr. Leonwald to the player. In addition, he recounts having obtained a flashlight, some batteries and stocking some food and water in accordance to the recommendations found in the brochure. He also explains that his old transistor radio would act as a source of information if it were not broken. The question of vulnerability is brought up as well [29–31]. Mr. Leonwald expresses his concern for his elderly mother who lives alone in another part of town. Apart from informing on the far-reaching consequences of a power failure and its impact on everyday life the game also dispels with the apprehension of people panicking and a population engaging in looting and robbing. Mr. Leonwald briefly talks about the predominantly cooperative and pro-social behavior of the population he witnesses which is an observation that corresponds with assessments found in literature [32, 33]. Table 1 outlines what concrete knowledge is intended to be passed on to the players referring to the key questions introduced before.

**Table 1.** eHUBgaming knowledge transfer

| |
|---|
| What are the consequences of a blackout? |
| • Building utilities and technology will not work (e.g. oven, heating and lighting)<br>• Communication infrastructure will break down (e.g. internet, television and cellphones)<br>• Traffic will come to a standstill<br>• Emergency response measures will be delayed<br>• Certain groups of people are vulnerable (e.g. the elderly) |
| How can one cope with a blackout? |
| • If food and water is stocked and one is healthy it is best to stay at home<br>• If a transistor radio is available listen for information there<br>• If one is in need of help or information seek out a police station, the fire department or any centrally-located highly frequented public space |
| How can one prepare for a blackout? |
| • Download federal or state warning Apps<br>• Prepare according to official sources (e.g. stock food and water, transistor radio, flashlight and batteries) |

## 4   Closing Remarks

This paper outlines the theoretical framework, contextual background and design of the serious game *e*HUBgaming. The chosen design of the game is based on the principles established in point-and-click adventures and translates these to the field of serious gaming and DRM. In addition, the emoji is a reference to the iconic Tamagotchi toy whereas energy gains and demands resemble elements common in resource management games. Thus, *e*HUBgaming can be described as a serious game that incorporates and combines gameplay elements that are characteristic for different genres. Knowledge transfer relies mainly on storytelling and the empirical fact that the human brain's receptivity for information is different when engaged in activities such as gaming. This could be acknowledged in a pretest of the game carried out with 45 student participants. As a tool in DRM serious games have great potential. They can be distributed online and other than leaflets can be customized to target different recipients. If disseminated properly serious games are able reach a wide audience and can support civil protection stakeholders in leveraging the preparedness and coping capabilities of the population.

**Acknowledgements.** This work has been funded by the LOEWE initiative (Hesse, Germany) within the emergenCITY center.

## References

1. Kovalenko, O., Velev, D.: Ad-Hoc Architecture of Systems for Disaster Risk Management. In: Murayama, Y., Velev, D., Zlateva, P. (eds.) Information Technology in Disaster Risk Reduction. Springer, Cham (2020). https://doi.org/10.1007/978-3-030-48939-7_12

2. United Nations Office for Desaster Risk Reduction: https://www.undrr.org/terminology/dis aster-risk-management. Accessed 09 Dec 2022

3. Sawalha, I.: A contemporary perspective on the disaster management cycle. Foresight **22**(4), 469–482 (2020)

4. emergenCITY, emergenCITY: https://www.emergencity.de/. Accessed 12 Dec 2022

5. emergenCITY, LOEWE Zentrum emergenCITY - Mission eHUB: https://www.emergencity. de/de/missions/ehub/. Accessed 12 Dec 2022

6. Kamel, E., Memari, A.M.: Energy efficiency and sustainability attributes of the solar decathlon projects. In: Raebel, C.H. (ed.) AEI 2015: Birth and Life of the Integrated Building, Milwaukee (2015)

7. Hegger, M. (ed.): Sunny Prospects: The surPLUShome of Team Germany for the Solar Decathlon 2009, Wuppertal (2010)

8. United Nations General Assembly: Report of the open-ended intergovernmental expert working group on indicators and terminology relating to disaster risk reduction, New York (2016). https://www.preventionweb.net/publication/report-open-ended-intergovernm ental-expert-working-group-indicators-and-terminology

9. Heidenstrøma, N., Hansen, A.: Embodied competences in preparedness for blackouts: mixed methods insights from rural and urban Norwegian households. Energy Res. Soc. Sci. **66** (2020)

10. Brunie, A.: Household disaster preparedness: assessing the importance of relational and community social capital, Chapel Hill (2007)

11. Kohler, K., Hauri, A., Roht, F., Scharte, B.: Risk and resilience report - Measuring Individual Disaster Preparedness, Zürich (2020)

12. Abt, C.: Serious games, New York (1970)

13. Hakulinen, L.: Using serious games in computer science education. In: Korhonen, A. and McCartney, R. (eds.) Koli Calling 2011: Proceedings of the 11th Koli Calling International Conference on Computing Education Research, Koli (2011)

14. Michael, D.R., Chen, S.L.: Serious Games: Games That Educate, Train, and Inform, Boston (2006)

15. Encarnação, L.M.: On the Future of Serious Games in Science and Industry, Kentucky (2009). https://www.researchgate.net/publication/257921847_On_the_Future_of_Ser ious_Games_in_Science_and_Industry

16. Westera, W.: The devil's advocate: identifying persistent problems in serious game design. Int. J. Serious Games **9**(3), 115–124 (2022)

17. Solinska-Nowakb, A.: An overview of serious games for disaster risk management - Prospects and limitations for informing actions to arrest increasing risk. Int. J. Disaster Risk Reduction **31**, 1013–1029 (2018)

18. U.S. Department of Energy Solar Decathlon, Solar Decathlon 2009: http://www.solardeca thlon.gov/past/download/09_construction_docs/manual_germany.zip. Sccessed 23 Dec 2022

19. Bitmap Books (ed.): The Art of Point-and-Click Adventure Games. 3rd. edn, Bath (UK) (2022)

20. Burbach, J.: The Future Perspectives of Point & Click Adventures, Köln (2016)

21. Little, G.R.: Managing the risk of cascading failure in complex urban infrastructure. In: Graham, S. (ed.) Disrupted Cities - When infrastructure fails, New York (2010)

22. Bundesamt für Bevölkerungsschutz und Katastrophenhilfe (ed.): Autarke Notstromver-sorgung der Bevölkerung unterhalb der KRITIS-Schwelle. In: Praxis im Bevölkerungsschutz 19, Hamburg (2015)

23. Petermann, T., Bradke, H., Lüllmann, A., Paetzsch, M., Riehm, U.: Was bei einem Blackout geschieht - Folgen eines langandauernden und großflächigen Stromausfalls, Studien des Büros für Technikfolgen - Abschätzung beim Deutschen Bundestag - 33, Berlin (2011)

24. Hansson, S., et al.: Communication-related vulnerability to disasters: a heuristic framework. In: International Journal of Disaster Risk Reduction, vol. 51 (2020)

25. Bundesamt für Bevölkerungsschutz und Katastrophenhilfe: https://www.bbk.bund.de/DE/Warnung-Vorsorge/Warn-App-NINA/warn-app-nina_node.html. Accessed 23 Dec 2022

26. Bundesamt für Bevölkerungsschutz und Katastrophenhilfe (BBK) (ed.): Resilienz, In: Bevölkerungsschutz 1, Bonn (2020)

27. Bundesamt für Bevölkerungsschutz und Katastrophenhilfe (BBK) (ed.): Stromausfall - Vorsorge und Selbsthilfe. 3rd. edn., Bonn (2019)

28. Bundesamt für Bevölkerungsschutz und Katastrophenhilfe (BBK) (ed.): Kapazitäten der Bevölkerung bei einem Stromausfall - Empirische Untersuchung für das Bezugsgebiet Deutschland, In: Praxis im Bevölkerungsschutz 12, Bonn (2013)

29. Depietri, Y.: Social vulnerability assessment of the Cologne urban area (Germany) to heat waves: links to ecosystem services. Int. J. Disaster Risk Reduction **6**, 98–117 (2013)

30. Ohder, C., Röpcke, J., Sticher, B., Geißler, S., Schweer, B.: Relief needs and willingness to help in the event of long-term power blackout - Results of a citizen survey in three Berlin districts, Berlin (2014). https://opus4.kobv.de/opus4-hwr/frontdoor/deliver/index/docId/417/file/Results+of+a+citizen+survey+(2014).pdf

31. Rudolph-Cleff, A., Knodt, M., Schulze, S., Engel, A.: Crisis communication in a blackout scenario - An assessment considering socio-spatial parameters and the vulnerabilities of the population. Int. J. Disaster Risk Reduction **72** (2022)

32. Rogers, B., Rubin, G.J.: Behavioural and psychological responses of the public during a major power outage: a literature review. Int. J. Disaster Risk Reduction **38**(2) (2019)

33. Helsloot, I., Beerens, R.: Citizens' response to a large electrical power outage in the Netherlands in 2007. J. Contingencies Crisis Manag. **17**(1), 64–68 (2007)

# For Soft Skills, Hard Games! – An Experiment Using Game-Based Methodologies in the Training of Health Students

Emanuel Silva[1] , Nuria Vita-Barrull[2] , Micael Sousa[3] , and Marlene Rosa[4(✉)]

[1] School of Health Sciences, Polytechnic Institute of Leiria, Leiria, Portugal
[2] Faculty of Science Education, Social Work and Psychology, University of Lleida, Lleida, Spain
[3] CITTA, Department of Civil Engineering, University of Coimbra, Coimbra, Portugal
[4] School of Health Sciences, ciTechCare - Center for Innovative Care and Health Technology, Polytechnic Institute of Leiria , Leiria, Portugal
marlene.rosa@ipleiria.pt

**Abstract.** This study sought to characterize the personal perspectives of health students on their experience using different categories of modern board games, modified to become serious games, to develop key transversal skills. Thirty-five students from health degrees were involved in a Serious Game-based Program specially designed to develop key transversal skills in health care. The personal perspectives of participants were collected through a questionnaire filled out by each participant at the end of the individual experience with each game (1–7 scale: 1- "nothing/never"; 7 - "very much/every day"). Participants perceived they were working especially the empathy, communication, and collaboration, followed by innovation (median $\geq 6$), and with a high level of fun ($7 \pm 2$). They reported a lower perception (median $= 5$) of the program's impact on leadership and decision-making. There were differences in scores for almost all transversal skills between game categories. Participants reported a higher perception of the program's impact on communication ($p = .00$). In the narrative games category, the highest average was observed in empathy ($p = .02$).

**Keywords:** Learning · Game-based · Methodologies · Perceptions · Experience

## 1 Introduction

Higher education is facing continuous and substantial changes that intersect with the quality of learning [1].

The need to change and modify education systems, in this case in an area as crucial as health, stems from the importance of a set of skills predominantly referred to as "soft skills," a concept that extends beyond cognitive and/or technical issues to include various intrapersonal and interpersonal skills [2]. Learning soft skills have an impact on students' ability to be awareness of patients' difficulties and/or social asymmetries, using a more holistic point of view [2]. However, few of the pilot studies focusing on

M. Haahr et al. (Eds.): JCSG 2023, LNCS 14309, pp. 413–418, 2023.
https://doi.org/10.1007/978-3-031-44751-8_36

innovative methodologies for training health students in these skills have tested serious games as tools of choice [3].

Simulations using board games can amplify a problem-solving experience, providing a set of hypothetical elements that encourage players to test their decisions while consequently evaluating the results. Besides this aspect of simulation, board games are cheap ways of delivering engaging game experiences for different player profiles [4]. In addition, with the use of this methodology, players will be able to develop not only specific skills for a given context but also skills that can be incorporated so as to be transferrable into other situations, allowing them to avoid, for example, a certain risk [5].

Against this backdrop, the aim of the present study is to examine how students enrolled in a higher education health course perceive the experience of using a board game as a source for the development of skills and competencies, particularly creativity, leadership, decision-making, empathy, communication, and collaboration, while also assessing their perception of fun when playing a particular game.

## 2 Materials and Methods

An experimental study was conducted within the framework of the Gulbenkian Academies for Knowledge, a national program supported by the Calouste Gulbenkian Foundation (CGF). The present study reports the results of the second edition of Gym2BeKind, which was conducted from September to December 2022 and included a specialized selection of modern board games, based on the previously published results of the pilot [6]. About 35 students (age: $18.84 \pm 1.064$; 43.86% female; 54.39% Portuguese nationality) were selected from the courses at the School of Health Sciences of the Polytechnic Institute of Leiria. The criteria for inclusion in the study were: participants would have to be enrolled in a health course at the School of Health Sciences, be 18 years of age or older, and agree to voluntarily participate in an intervention program based on serious games.

### 2.1 Gym2BeKind – Serious Game-Based Program

Gym2beKind defined precise objectives. By playing the games, students should be engaged in an interactive learning and training experience. Although games can provide this, in order for an ortho game [7], i.e., a game made for entertainment, to deliver predefined experiences, modification of that game is required. This is the modding approach, used to transform a commercial entertainment game into a serious game [8–10], a game that can be engaging and achieve purposes beyond enjoyment - in our case, to deliver meaningful experiences to develop essential skills in future health professional. None of the selected competitive games allows direct confrontation in the form of negative interactions between players (e.g., attacking, stealing, player elimination, etc.), which is something modern board games have introduced in the last decades, mainly due to the influence of Eurogames [11]. Games like Ikonikus, Dixit, and Fun Employed require players to build their storytelling from other players' contributions and build up the narrative.

The survey "Game perception questionnaire" was created to evaluate the experience of the game in the context of its use for teaching–learning. Students were invited to rate their learning experience in the following dimensions: generating ideas and innovation, establishing or reinforcing leadership, encouraging decision-making, empathy between participants, communication between participants, collaboration between participants, and fun and motivation. It was an individual assessment (each player assigned a point to each member, without debating with the other participants). A 7-point Likert scale was applied, in which 1 meant "nothing/never" and 7 meant "very much/every day." Each student filled out this questionnaire at the end of his or her individual experience with each game.

## 2.2  Statistical Analysis

To characterize the sample, means and standard deviations of the socio-emotional variables were obtained. The medians and interquartile ranges of each transversal skill were used for each game, game category, and for the overall program in order to know to what degree the students perceived that these skills had been worked on. The game categories were compared in relation to their scores in transversal skills using the Kruskal Wallis test (p-value $< 0.05$).

## 3  Results

The scores of the training program (see Table 1) stand out in empathy and fun (M = 7; IR = 2), followed by communication and collaboration (M = 6; IR = 2). The transversal skill with the lowest median and highest interquartile range was leadership (M = 5; IR = 5).

In communication, the games with the highest scores were Ikonikus (M = 7; IR = .75) and Dixit (M = 7; IR = 1.5). The students gave higher scores to Happy Salmon (M = 7; IR = 0) and Ikonikus (M = 7; IR = .75) in collaboration. In empathy, the games Ikonikus and Funky Chicken (both: M = 7; IR = .75) were rated the highest. In decision-making and leadership, only Ikonikus obtained a score higher than 6 (M = 6.5; IR = 2). In innovation, Fun Employed was the game that most stood out (M = 7: IR = 3), while in fun it was Just One (M = 7; IR = 0). Ikonikus was the game with the highest scores in all transversal skills (M $\geq$ 6.5), followed by Dixit (M $\geq$ 6).

When making comparisons between game categories, significant differences were found for all scored skills (p $\leq$ .02), except for collaboration (p = .28) (see Table 1). Storytelling games scored higher in communication (6.02 $\pm$ 1.34; H = 14.30; p = .00), decision-making (5.37 $\pm$ 1.63; H = 9.54; p = .01), and leadership (4.39 $\pm$ 2.14; H = 11.81; p = .00). In empathy, storytelling (6.08 $\pm$ 1.27) and narrative games (6.09 $\pm$ 1.32) obtained the highest scores (H = 7.81; p = .02). Storytelling (5.73 $\pm$ 1.35) and expression games (5.98 $\pm$ 1.21) scored higher than narrative games in innovation (H = 39.49; p – .00). Finally, the games that scored the highest in terms of fun were the expression games (6.40 $\pm$ .85; H = 7.67; p = .02).

**Table 1.** Descriptive data (median (Interquartile range)) of transversal skills scores for each game and for the complete program.

| Board Games | TS1 | TS2 | TS3 | TS4 | TS5 | TS6 | TS7 |
|---|---|---|---|---|---|---|---|
| Imagidice! | 6 (1) | 5 (2) | 7 (2) | 5 (2) | 4 (4) | 5 (3) | 7 (1) |
| Ikonikus | 7 (.75) | 7 (.75) | 7 (.75) | 6.5 (2) | 6.5 (2) | 6.5 (2) | 7 (1.75) |
| Telestration | 4 (5) | 6 (3) | 6 (3.75) | 4 (1) | 1 (3) | 6.5 (2) | 6 (1.75) |
| The mind | 1.5 (5) | 6.5 (4) | 7 (3.75) | 6 (4) | 3 (4) | 5 (3) | 5.5 (4) |
| Dixit | 7 (1.5) | 7 (2) | 7 (1.5) | 6 (2) | 6 (2) | 6 (2) | 7 (1) |
| Happy Salmon | 7 (2) | 7 (0) | 7 (1) | 2 (2) | 3 (5) | 2 (5) | 7 (1) |
| Fun Employed | 7 (2) | 6 (2.5) | 6 (3) | 5 (3) | 2 (3.5) | 7 (3) | 5 (3) |
| Just One | 6 (1) | 6 (1) | 7 (2) | 5.5 (2) | 5 (1.75) | 6.5 (2) | 7 (0) |
| Codenames | 6 (2) | 6 (2) | 6 (1) | 5 (1.5) | 5 (2.5) | 5 (2) | 5 (3) |
| Funky Chicken | 6 (1) | 7 (1) | 7 (.75) | 5 (1) | 5 (4) | 5 (5) | 7 (1) |

TS (transversal skill) TS1., Communication; TS2., Collaboration; TS3., Empathy; TS4., Decision-making; TS5., Leadership; TS6., Innovation; TS7., Fun/Motivation.

## 4 Discussion

The students perceived that throughout the entire training program they had worked on their empathy, collaboration, communication, and innovation skills, and to a lesser extent on their decision-making and leadership skills, while having a high level of fun.

In communication, we saw that storytelling games scored higher compared to narrative and other types of expression games (e.g., Imagidice!, Ikonikus, Dixit, and Fun Employed). These four games are characterized by the need to create a story from a few elements. Players must, to a large extent, interpret what they see and develop a whole story that gives meaning to the elements that they have. These storytelling games require greater agency. Players must be engaged and establish relationships to support a meaningful and coherent narrative [12, 13].

In the skill of empathy, the expression category scored the lowest compared to storytelling and narrative. Even though Just One and Telestration are games in which players have to guess what their partner means to find out the target word or concept, therefore needing to think about how the other person might think, there were games in the other categories that perhaps required more of this skill to win (e.g., Ikonikus). The experience of studying or working in the health field is considerably associated with emotional challenges related to empathy, and it would probably benefit from there being some distance between the challenge and the player's beliefs [14].

Storytelling board games stood out above the other two categories in decision-making. These results make sense considering that in this category there were games in which the students had to choose between different options to give an appropriate response to each situation. In Ikonikus, they had to choose the card that best fits the emotion that the other person would feel, and in Dixit, the card that best reflected the concept chosen by the active player.

The scores for leadership were low, which can be explained by the nature of the games. Many were collaborative or semi-collaborative, having mechanisms to control emergent leadership, such as controlled communication. Leadership is crucial for positive communication with patients and their families, but also within multiprofessional health teams [15].

Regarding innovation ability, a difference was found between the narrative games, which had lower scores, and the storytelling and other types of expression games, which had higher scores. Innovation is one of the most difficult skills to be worked on by students. This is probably explained by the fact that students define innovation as a mix of competencies, such as tolerance for uncertainty, embracing risk, human-centeredness, awareness of processes, team knowledge, creative confidence, etc. [16].

## 5  Conclusion

Students perceive this methodology based on games as a way to combine the development of their empathy, communication, and collaboration skills with a high level of enjoyment.

Future studies could test the use of different games (for example, games with greater decision-making capacity) as well as different ways of implementing them in the classroom to find the optimal way to work on these skills within the curriculum.

## References

1. Hénard, F., Leprince-Ringuet, S.: The path to quality teaching in higher education (2008)
2. Yorke, M.: Employability in higher education: what it is, what it is not. Higher Education Academy, p. 20 (2006)
3. Sara, M., Gordo, S., Micael, S., Sousa, M., Ricardo, F., Rosa, M.: Critical thinking, empathy and problem solving using a modern board game A learning experience valued by physical therapy students (2021). https://doi.org/10.1145/3486011.3486526
4. Sousa, M., Zagalo, N., Oliveira, A.P.: Mechanics or mechanisms: defining differences in analog games to support game design. In: 2021 IEEE Conference on Games (CoG). IEEE, pp. 1–8 (2021). https://doi.org/10.1109/CoG52621.2021.9619055
5. Linderoth, J.: Beyond the Digital Divide: An Ecological Approach to Game-Play. Transactions of the Digital Games Research Association. 1st ed. (2013)
6. Emanuel, L., Laura, N., Micael, S., Marlene, R.: Inovar em metodologias de aprendizagem de competências sociais em estudantes na área da saúde. Foro Internacional sobre la Evaluación de la Calidad de la Investigación y de la Educación Superior (FECIES) (2022)
7. Vayanou, M., Katifori, A., Ioannidis, Y.: Perspective sharing in culture group games: passing around the social mediator role. In: Proceedings of the ACM on Human-Computer Interaction. ACM New York, NY, USA, vol. 5, pp. 1–24 (2021). https://doi.org/10.1145/3474676
8. Elias, G.S., Garfield, R., Gutschera, K.R.: Characteristics of Games. MIT Press, Cambridge, Massachusetts, USA (2012)
9. Sousa, M., Dias, J.: From learning mechanics to tabletop mechanisms: modding steam board game to be a serious game.In: 21st annual European GAMEON® Conference, GAME-ON®'2020. Eurosis (2020)
10. Sousa, M.: Serious board games: modding existing games for collaborative ideation processes modding board games to be serious games. Int. J. Serious Games **8**, 129–147 (2021). https://doi.org/10.17083/ijsg.v8i2.405

11. Rosa, M., Gordo, S., Sousa, M., Pocinho, R.: Empathy, creativity, and feelings using a modern board game: a learning experience valued by physiotherapy students. In: Ninth International Conference on Technological Ecosystems for Enhancing Multiculturality (TEEM 2021). New York, NY, USA: Association for Computing Machinery, pp. 610–615 (2021). https://doi.org/10.1145/3486011.3486525
12. McDrury, J., Alterio, M.: Learning through storytelling in Higher Education. Taylor & Francis (2004)
13. Long, A., et al.: Storytelling to improve healthcare worker understanding, beliefs, and practices related to LGBTQ + patients: a program evaluation. Eval. Program Plan. **90**, 101979 (2022). https://doi.org/10.1016/j.evalprogplan.2021.101979
14. Jonathan, B., Mary, F.: Designing games to foster empathy. Cogn. Technol. 14 (2022)
15. Ledlow, G.R., Bosworth, M., Maryon, T.: Leadership for health professionals: theory, skills, and applications. Jones & Bartlett Learning (2023)
16. Chen, P.P.Y., Chou, A.C.C.: Teaching health care innovation to medical students. Clini. Teacher **18**, 285–289 (2021). https://doi.org/10.1111/tct.13328

# Narrative-First Design for Language-Learning Games: Insights from *Brendan's Voyage*

Jacob Abell[1]([✉]) [iD] and Lynn Ramey[2] [iD]

[1] Department of Modern Languages and Cultures, Baylor University, Waco, TX 76706, USA
jake_abell@baylor.edu
[2] Department of French and Italian, Vanderbilt University, Nashville, TN 37240, USA

**Abstract.** Teaching "dead" languages and cultures poses unique challenges. *Brendan's Voyage* is a serious game under development for teaching medieval cultures and languages in a narrative context. Developed at the intersection of game-based learning (GBL), communicative language teaching (CLT), and situated (immersive) learning, *Brendan's Voyage* places the user in an environment infused with the art, architecture, and literature of 12th century Europe. After a concise review of important research on language learning using GBL, CLT and immersion, we focus on game narrative, arguing that it ties together the aims of GBL, CLT, and immersion. We outline our narrative-first process in creating *Brendan's Voyage* and show how this method addresses language learning objectives. Finally, we use a completed module to demonstrate the concrete advantages of narrative-based play to teach a fusion of language and historical cultures. To this point, serious games have been designed to teach living languages or to allow a user experience of past cultures. This paper elaborates the project background, the educational objectives of the game, and the specific ways in which our narrative focus provides an enhanced context for teaching medieval culture, history, and language in the form of a web-based game.

**Keywords:** Languages · game-based learning · narrative · situated learning · communicative learning

## 1 Introduction

The role of narrative in video games has long been contentious. While Aarseth, Murray, Juul, and Bogost have all contributed to the "narratology v. ludology" discussion [1–5], the more practical and quantifiable aspects of narrative in serious games remain understudied [6]. Brendan's Voyage is a web-based game in development that teaches the player to speak, read, and write basic medieval French (Anglo-Norman dialect) while also learning key lessons about medieval politics, gender, aesthetics, religious society, and literature. Not only is the game an adaptation of the medieval text The Voyage of Saint Brendan, it also relies on game narrative to accomplish its learning objectives. The development of the game begins with narrative and its active role in language learning, a design approach we call "narrative-first."

M. Haahr et al. (Eds.): JCSG 2023, LNCS 14309, pp. 419–425, 2023.
https://doi.org/10.1007/978-3-031-44751-8_37

Now in its intermediate phase of development, Brendan's Voyage produces a dynamic cultural and linguistic learning experience by drawing on the insights of game-based learning (GBL), communicative language teaching (CLT), and situated learning. Often, these theories are segregated within communities of gaming (and reflection on gaming) associated with language learning on the one hand and reconstructing premodern history on the other. In an effort to combine these approaches, the five learning modules of Brendan's Voyage guide the player to learn substantive language skills and cultural knowledge by placing the player in a narrative-focused environment informed by contemporary language pedagogy and narrative theories.

## 2  Background

Our approach to game design is motivated by existing work in the areas of game-based learning, communicative learning, and situated learning, as applied to language learning.

### 2.1  Game-Based Language Learning

Game-based learning is ideally suited to language acquisition. Citing multiple studies, Constance Steinkuehler and Kurt Squire suggest that language learning is "perhaps the most powerful means to which games have been leveraged to date" [7]. Students often hesitate to speak in class or use their new language skills with other speakers, an imaginary wall called the "affective filter" [8] that they erect due to anxiety, low self-confidence, or lack of motivation. A good learning game environment increases motivation and lowers the affective filter, allowing the student to create an avatar or alternative self with different characteristics like "good at languages" or "outgoing" [9, 10]. Studies of avatar use in second language-learning environments have shown a reduction in anxiety with the selection of customizable avatars [11, 12].

### 2.2  Communicative Language Teaching

Pedagogical approaches to language teaching have changed over the last decades as research studies have helped show what methods work best in different environments. Nonetheless, a consensus has emerged that language pedagogy should aim for communication rather than mastery of complex grammatical structures [13, 14]. While modern and dead languages were previously taught using a focus on written grammar and translation of materials to and from target languages, modern language pedagogy has turned to emphasizing the ways that language learning is linked to communicating with target-language speakers or to accomplish tasks in a target-language environment. This method works well for modern languages, but dead languages (Latin, medieval French, Sumerian, etc.) are still almost exclusively taught using the antiquated grammar-translation model. The use of a communicative model for teaching dead languages can increase student motivation and learning [15].

## 2.3  Situated Learning

From study abroad to immersive classrooms, the success of language acquisition depends upon where the learning takes place. As founding proponents of situated learning assert, "knowledge is not independent but, rather, fundamentally 'situated,' being in part a product of the activity, context, and culture in which it is developed" [16]. Recent work on language teaching has turned to the affordances of technology and/or gaming to provide the situated-ness that enhances learning in all disciplines [17]. Some examples of games that create contexts for language acquisition include an escape room for teaching grammar [18], a VR world to learn Irish [19], and The Sims 4 as a pretext for practicing oral communication skills [14].

## 3  Narrative-First Design and *Brendan's Voyage*

There is no shortage of entertainment-focused games that engage medieval cultures. Assassin's Creed offers elaborate aesthetic designs of medieval Paris among other locations. What is more, the team that designs the Assassin's Creed series includes historians to inform the historical richness of period artifacts and architecture [20]. Nevertheless, the Assassin's Creed series is not "serious," defined as a game that imparts specific learning objectives or skills to its players [21]. The commercial success of Assassin's Creed signals a public appetite for exploring medieval environments, but the game also points to the opportunity to satisfy this clamor with a serious game that actively teaches its players skills and knowledge bases about the Middle Ages.

While still in development, Brendan's Voyage achieves this goal through the game's aesthetic richness and historically informed design while also organizing game play around modules that teach spoken and written medieval French language. The modules provide users with key information about medieval culture, from the importance of female patronage of the arts in Norman England to the process of making manuscripts in medieval monasteries. With few exceptions, games designed to teach the French language are focused on contemporary societies, somewhat ironically, since many students can travel to francophone countries to achieve the immersion that the games provide. With ancient cultures and dead languages, students can only access these worlds through digital recreations.

### 3.1  Defining Narrative in Game Studies

Blyth has observed that AR-generated storytelling environments have begun to serve as a crucial mechanism for intercultural exchange in the context of games that promote foreign language learning [22]. Yet scholars have sometimes objected that such games fail to account for the complexities of embodied language use in the world, which is often, as Blyth suggests, "dynamic, hybrid, and transnational."

Brendan's Voyage takes this concern seriously by emphasizing the dynamism, plasticity, and transnational character of the medieval French dialect spoken in England during the composition of the Brendan story. The player does not learn an idealized standardization of the target language (L2) but instead learns a specific dialect associated with a particular story told in a specific time and place (early twelfth-century

England). Several details of the game design promote the player's awareness of the target language's historical context and fluidity. For instance, in the first module, the player must learn to converse with Lady Adeliza of Louvain, the French-speaking Queen of England who commissions the Brendan story to be translated from Latin into French. This historical context becomes explicit throughout the first game module, emphasizing the time-bound character of the language as a regionally situated dialect associated with a particular narrative tradition, cultural context, and political background.

Additionally, all the modules of Brendan's Voyage position the player as a monolingual character learning a second language (medieval French) in order to culturally assimilate within a bilingual society. Contrary to earlier theories, contemporary second language acquisition research has strongly suggested that England became a diffusely bilingual country after the Norman Conquest. Richard Ingham has argued persuasively that English folk spoke and wrote in both English and French across social demographics, albeit with varying degrees of oral and written fluency [23]. Our game foregrounds this bilingualism by creating conversations between the player and various characters which involve speaking in combinations of medieval French and (contemporary) English.

Written exercises within the game are modeled on extant bilingual medieval texts that used one language for the main body paragraphs and the second language in commentary written around the main text. Relying on this research in medieval studies and historical linguistics, our team has fashioned a game that self-consciously conveys the regionalism and historically dynamic political contexts that gave rise to medieval French spoken in England. This approach realizes Blyth's call for serious games that teach language in ways that acknowledge the dynamic, historical embeddedness of world languages.

### 3.2 Embedded and Emergent Narratives: Maximizing Learning Potential

Sengun has recently drawn attention to the lack of a standardized definition of narrative in discussion of games [24]. Competing definitions of game narrative signal the need for a more sustained discussion of how to distinguish narrative, storytelling, and other related terms that Sengun delineates. Following Jenkins [25], Sengun adopts a useful distinction between "embedded" and "emergent" narratives. Embedded narratives comprise the elements of a game's structure supplied by the designers, whereas emergent narrative refers to the experience of gameplay created by a player as they navigate through the game. Within a given game, the embedded narrative's structure may be more or less defined and rigid, which influences the valence of emergent narratives that a diverse range of players may generate through gameplay. A properly calibrated relationship between these two elements can maximize the language-learning potential that Blyth elucidates [22].

Specifically, Brendan's Voyage offers a game narrative that embodies Sengun's concept of non-sequential autonomy. In such a model of game narration, the player may move in ways that are not fully constrained by prescriptive tasks. While Brendan's Voyage is largely a task-based game experience, the player may migrate freely around spaces in ways that are generally guided by the objectives of specific learning activities. The player's movement, however, is not constricted by those goals. In fact, many of the objectives require players to wander in virtual space.

This is essential for many of the passive cultural learning goals featured in the embedded narrative. For example, in module two, the player finds themself in a medieval English monastic scriptorium where texts were copied and preserved. A discussion with a monk gives the player a specific task. The player must gather specific elements required to copy a text on parchment. This mechanical task immediately implicates the player in a second, subsidiary set of tasks relating to learning medieval French. In order to accomplish the first set of goals, the player must gradually understand and communicate using medieval French language. Crucially, the player may only accomplish both sets of goals by wandering in the visual environment of the space. In this particular module, the player's wandering brings them several times past a detailed visual rendering of a set of tapestries (Fig. 1).

These tapestries are intentionally inspired by the well-known Bayeux tapestries that depict the Norman Conquest of England in 1066. These events are extremely important for the cultural background of the early modules of Brendan's Voyage, since the story of St. Brendan was translated from Latin into French about sixty years after this culturally seismic event. Eventually, the tasks of the module's embedded narrative ask the player to interact with the surface of the tapestries themselves as a kind of giant textbook page. Hence, the virtual tapestries are involved in the learning process as objects of passive cultural learning and active linguistic learning. Similarly, in module three, a player navigating a market space within the castle walls will hear greetings in Dutch, Catalan, and other languages in which the Brendan story circulated through global trade. These audio and visual details of the game's embedded narrative also inform the passive learning opportunities that players variously encounter within their emergent narrative experience of the gameplay.

**Fig. 1.** Player's view of a pair of tapestries inspired by the famous Bayeux Tapestries depicting the Norman Conquest of England. Situated within a virtual medieval scriptorium: Learning Module 2 of Brendan's Voyage.

To summarize, the embedded narrative of Brendan's Voyage imposes certain core aesthetic dimensions, audio-visual experiences, and learning activities that the player must engage. At the same time, each learning module of the game invites the player to explore the space of the medieval gaming environment with a high degree of freedom. This carefully calibrated relationship between embedded and emergent narrative elements serves to optimize both active and passive cultural learning outcomes that accompany the more task-based language learning goals of the game.

## 4  Future Directions and Priorities

With the rise of artificial intelligence and virtual reality, Blyth argues that the future language teacher will be required to use digital technologies to "help learners curate their personalized learning experiences" [22]. Brendan's Voyage realizes this vision for a digital, narrative-based approach to language learning. With our game design partner Causeway Studios, we are in the process of writing, designing, and testing the remaining modules of Brendan's Voyage. We have confidence that our narrative-first design will help position the resulting game as a pedagogically innovative, historically informed, and enjoyable serious game exploring the medieval past.

## References

1. Aarseth, E.: A narrative theory of games. In: Proceedings of the International Conference on the Foundations of Digital Games, Raleigh North Carolina: ACM,  pp. 129–133 (2012)
2. Aarseth, E.J.: Cybertext: Perspectives on Ergodic Literature. Johns Hopkins University Press (1997)
3. Murray, J.H.: The Last Word on Ludology v Narratology (2005), Janet H. Murray: Humanistic Design for an Emerging Medium (2013). https://inventingthemedium.com/2013/06/28/the-last-word-on-ludology-v-narratology-2005-the-slides/
4. Bogost, I.: Video Games Are Better Without Stories. The Atlantic (2017). https://www.theatlantic.com/technology/archive/2017/04/video-games-stories/524148/
5. Juul, J.: A Clash Between Game and Narrative, presented at the Digital Arts and Culture, Bergen, Norway (1998). Accessed: 19 Sep 2019. https://www.jesperjuul.net/text/clash_between_game_and_narrative.html
6. Brenneman, J.S.: Aligning Game Narrative and Learning Outcomes, presented at the Meaningful Play (2022)
7. Steinkuehler, C., Squire, K.: Videogames and learning. In: Sawyer, K. (ed.) Cambridge Handbook of the Learning Sciences, pp. 377–394. Cambridge University Press, Cambridge (2014)
8. Krashen, S.D.: Principles and Practice in Second Language Acquisition. Prentice-Hall (1982)
9. Gee, J.P.: What video games have to teach us about learning and literacy. Comput. Entertain. 1(1), 20 (2003)
10. Ramirez, D., Squire, K.: Gamification for Education Reform, in The Gameful World: Approaches, Issues, Applications, Walz, S.P., Deterding, S. (eds.) Cambridge, Massachusetts: The MIT Press (2015)
11. Harbord, C., Dempster, E.: Avatars: the other side of proteus's mirror: a study into avatar choice regarding perception. In: Entertainment Computing and Serious Games, Van Der Spek, E., Göbel, S., Do, E.Y.-L., Clua, E., Baalsrud Hauge, J. (eds.) in Lecture Notes in Computer Science, vol. 11863. Cham: Springer International Publishing, pp. 412–416 (2019). https://doi.org/10.1007/978-3-030-34644-7_37

12. Peterson, M.: Learner interaction management in an avatar and chat-based virtual world. Comput. Assist. Lang. Learn. **19**(1), 79–103 (2006)
13. Hymes, D.H.: On communicative competence. In: Pride, J.B., Holmes, J. (eds.) Sociolinguistics: Selected Readings, pp. 269–293. Penguin, London (1972)
14. Wang, Q.: The role of classroom-situated game-based language learning in promoting students' communicative competence. Int. J. Comput.-Assist. Lang. Learn. Teach. **10**(2), 59–82 (2020)
15. Djinis, E.: Spoken Latin is making a comeback. Smithsonian Magazine (2023). https://www.smithsonianmag.com/history/why-spoken-latin-is-making-a-comeback-180981621/
16. Brown, J.S., Collins, A., Duguid, P.: Situated cognition and the culture of learning. University of Illinois at Urbana-Champaign, Center for the Study of Reading, Technical, vol. 481 (1989)
17. Schwienhorst, K.: Why virtual, why environments? Implementing virtual reality concepts in computer-assisted language learning. Simul. Gaming **33**(2), 196–209 (2002)
18. Ayman, R., Ayman, R., Sharaf, N.: Catch me if you can: an educational serious game to teach grammatical English rules. In: Söbke, H., Spangenberger, P., Müller, P., Göbel, S. (eds.) Serious Games, JCSG 2022. Lecture Notes in Computer Science, vol. 13476, pp. 198–209. Springer, Cham (2022). https://doi.org/10.1007/978-3-031-15325-9_15
19. Collins, N., Vaughan, B., Cullen, C., Gardner, K.: GaeltechVR: measuring the impact of an immersive virtual environment to promote situated identity in Irish language learning. J. Virt. Worlds Res. **12**(3) (2019)
20. Ramey, L., et al.: Revisioning the global middle ages: immersive environments for teaching medieval languages and culture. Digital Philol. **8**(1), 86–104 (2019)
21. Ibarra, M.J., Ibañez, V., Silveira, I.F., Collazos, C. A., Wallner, G., Rauterberg, M.: Serious games for learning: a quantitative review of literature. In Serious Games, Ma, M., Fletcher, B., Göbel, S., Baalsrud Hauge, J., Marsh, T. (eds.) in Lecture Notes in Computer Science, vol. 12434. Cham: Springer International Publishing, pp. 164–174 (2020). https://doi.org/10.1007/978-3-030-61814-8_13
22. Blyth, C.: Immersive technologies and language learning. Foreign Lang. Ann. **51**(1), 225–232 (2018)
23. Ingham, R.: The transmission of later anglo-norman: some syntactic evidence. In: The Anglo-Norman Language and its Contexts, York Medieval Press, pp. 164–182 (2010)
24. Sengun, S.: Six degrees of videogame narrative. In: Games and Narrative: Theory and Practice, Bostan, B. (ed.) in International Series on Computer Entertainment and Media Technology. Cham: Springer International Publishing, pp. 3–20 (2022). https://doi.org/10.1007/978-3-030-81538-7_1
25. Jenkins, H.: Game design as narrative architecture. In: Wardrip-Fruin, N., Harrigan, P. (eds.) First person: new media as story, performance, and game, pp. 118–130. MIT Press, Cambridge, Mass (2004)

# Educational Video Game for Learning Binary Search Tree

Alberto Rojas-Salazar[1]([✉]) [ID] and Mads Haahr[2] [ID]

[1] Universidad de Costa Rica, San José, Costa Rica
`alberto.rojassalazar@ucr.ac.cr`
[2] Trinity College Dublin, Dublin, Ireland

**Abstract.** This demo paper presents two prototypes of an educational video game for learning Binary Search Tree data structure in higher education environments. The prototypes were used to evaluate the effectiveness of video games to teach abstract non-intuitive conceptual knowledge and the effect of educational video games' perceptual realism on learning gains and motivation. The paper provides a detailed description of the game, focusing on the game's learning aspects, such as the learning theory, pedagogical approach, learning objectives, and learning activities. It also emphasizes how the game elements reflect the learning aspects to facilitate learning complex conceptual knowledge.

**Keywords:** Analogies · Educational Video Game · Binary Search Tree

## 1 Introduction

In this demo paper, we present two prototypes of an educational video game, *DS-Hacker*, designed for learning the Binary Search Tree (BST) data structure in higher education environments. The game aims to evaluate two aspects: (1) the effectiveness of video games in teaching abstract, non-intuitive conceptual knowledge, and (2) the impact of video games' perceptual realism on learning outcomes and motivation.

Regarding the first aspect, *DS-Hacker* adopts a constructivist approach, aiming to facilitate the connection between newly taught information and the learner's existing knowledge. To achieve this, the game uses analogies, which compare parts of structures between two domains [4]. These domains must share symmetrical relations among their components, with the goal of transferring ideas and concepts from a familiar domain (referred to as the source or base) to an unfamiliar one (known as the target) [5].

Concerning perceptual realism, it refers to "how closely objects, environments, and events depicted match those that actually exist" [8]. To evaluate the effects of perceptual realism, two versions of *DS-Hacker* with different levels of perceptual realism were developed. The first version is a 3D adventure PC game, while the second version is a 2D adventure PC game. Both games differ in their dimensionality, graphics, and physics. However, narrative elements, game challenges, levels, and learning aspects remain consistent across both versions of the game.

M. Haahr et al. (Eds.): JCSG 2023, LNCS 14309, pp. 426–432, 2023.
https://doi.org/10.1007/978-3-031-44751-8_38

This demo paper describes the learning aspects and core game concepts of *DS-Hacker* (2D and 3D). We discuss the learning theory and pedagogical approach employed for effective knowledge transmission. Additionally, we list the learning objectives and activities covered by the game. Furthermore, we explain the narrative aspects, aesthetics, and game mechanics used to convey the learning experience.

## 2 Related Work

Educational video games have become popular among computer science educational researchers. In a comprehensive systematic literature review, Petri and Gresse von Wangenheim [9] found 108 games and 117 evaluations related to the computer science field. However, as of 2020, only sixteen educational video games focusing on data structures were reported in the academic literature [11].

Concerning the games that focus on tree data structures, we highlight four. The first one, called *Elemental: The Recurrence*, is a 3D puzzle-coding game that intends to teach the recursive depth-first search (DFS) algorithm of a binary tree [3]. The second game focuses on Adelson-Velsky and Landis (AVL) trees, and it is an adaptation of the classic game *Mario* [14]. The third game, called *AVL Tree Game*, is a mobile casual-puzzle game, and it intends to teach the AVL tree rotation and the add algorithm [13]. More recently, Jiménez-Hernández et al. [6] reported *Tree Legends with UnityChan*, a game for learning tree traversal and search algorithm. The game focuses on binary, ternary, and quaternary trees.

## 3 Game Description

*DS-Hacker* is a PC video game with two versions that vary in their level of perceptual realism. One version of the game is a 3D third-person adventure (Fig. 1) developed with Unity. This version features representational 3D graphics and accurate physics, resulting in complex navigation mechanics that require the player to use the keyboard and mouse. The second version of *DS-Hacker* is a 2D top-down adventure game (Fig. 2) developed with RPG Maker MV. The 2D version has abstract graphics and simple physics, making the navigation mechanics straightforward, with the player moving over a flat surface. Its main controller is the mouse, and the keyboard is optional. Both versions of the game were designed to teach the BST data structure to students enrolled in introductory programming courses in higher education environments. It specifically targets bachelor students in engineering, computer science, or mathematics schools with programming courses. The game's content was selected based on the guidelines for undergraduate degree programs [1], ensuring it aligns with the curricula of many introductory programming or data structures courses.

Regarding the learning aspects, *DS-Hacker* (2D and 3D) was designed from a constructivist stance, which posits that learners build their knowledge by connecting new information with familiar experiences. The assumptions about how people learn were derived from Kolb's experiential learning theory and Kolb's experiential learning cycle [7]. Consequently, the game's learning experience emulates this cycle, linking new information (e.g., BST conceptual knowledge) with familiar knowledge (e.g., previous gaming experiences).

**Fig. 1.** Screenshot of *DS-Hacker 3D* – Level 1.

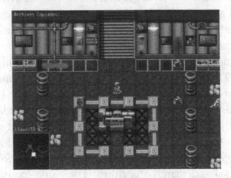

**Fig. 2.** Screenshot of *DS-Hacker 2D* – Level 1.

Regarding the learning content, *DS-Hacker* (2D and 3D) focuses on fundamental concepts of the BST. According to Sedgewick and Wayne [12], a BST is a specific order of a Binary Tree (BT). A BT is a structure made up of objects known as nodes, each of which contains two links that can be null or refer to other nodes. Additionally, each node can be pointed to by just one single node. On the other hand, BST nodes have two additional elements: the comparable key and the associated value. They satisfy the property that "the key in any node is larger than the keys in all nodes in that node's left subtree and smaller than the keys in all nodes in that node's right subtree" [12]. Consequently, the learning objectives (LOs) cover two topics: BT and BST. Table 1 presents the LOs.

Regarding the game genre, the rationale for adopting the adventure genre is its flexibility for teaching purposes. This story-driven genre incorporates conceptual puzzle elements that are ideal for teaching conceptual knowledge. For example, it allows for the introduction and explanation of concepts and theories through the game's narrative elements. Additionally, cognitive and conceptual puzzles can be used to create scenarios where players can practice the concepts taught in the story.

Concerning the game genre, the rationale for adopting the adventure genre is its flexibility for teaching purposes as well as its popularity. This story-driven genre presents conceptual puzzle elements that are ideal to teach conceptual knowledge. For example, it is possible to introduce and explain concepts and theory through the game story using narrative elements. Meanwhile, the cognitive and conceptual puzzles can be used to create scenarios where the player can practice the concepts taught by the story. Finally, the adventure genre is a well-known genre among teenagers and young adults that presents a low learning curve.

The theme of *DS-Hacker* (2D and 3D) is cyberpunk science fiction, and its story follows the Hero's Journey structure [2], a narrative progression used in many myths and classic tales. The game's narrative takes place in a distant future, where a corrupt corporation disrupts society's balance. In the game, the player assumes the role of a robotic hacker, created by activists to infiltrate the computational systems of these corrupt corporations. The robot must traverse several mazes, called *Data Systems*, consisting of interconnected chambers, and extract information stored within each chamber of the computational systems. However, before embarking on the quest, the robot undergoes training and calibration by its creator, Anonymous, a non-player character who guides the player through the game levels. These events mark the beginning of the hero's transformation. The story is presented with appealing graphics, music, sound effects, and a futuristic game environment[1], creating an immersive atmosphere aligned with the game's narrative and designed to increase players' immersion and fantasy, thereby enhancing their intrinsic motivation.

Concerning the game world, *Data Systems* are places where corporations hide and protect their information. The structure of these systems follows the same organization as well-known data structures. Due to the game's learning objectives, the *Data Systems* reflect the structure of BTs and BSTs, and many key elements of the game environment represent important elements of these data structures. For example, a *Data System* that represents a BST consist of a set of rooms that represents the BST nodes. These rooms possess portals, an ID, and a central computer and are organized following the BST property. Portals represent the links that point to other nodes, and deactivated portals represent null values. The room ID represents the BST comparable key, and the information stored in the central computer represents the node's associated values.

Narrative elements play a primary role in teaching the conceptual knowledge of BST. The game's story progresses through monologues delivered by Anonymous, who appears at the beginning of each level or upon completing a challenge. These monologues introduce the missions of each level and the essential BT and BST concepts needed to overcome them. To enhance the understanding of BT and BST concepts, Anonymous employs analogies between the game environment described above and the BT and BST data structures. These analogies aim to facilitate the creation of new knowledge by relating it to the gaming knowledge.

Regarding the User Interface (UI), it is designed to reinforce the BT and BST concepts. For example, the map of the game world serves as a visual representation of a BST. The pause menu includes an option to display cards featuring the concepts taught in the level. This allows players to pause the game and review these concepts to tackle challenges effectively. By incorporating these UI elements, the game reduces the cognitive load on players by providing helpful reminders related to BT and BST concepts.

*DS-Hacker* (2D and 3D) game consists of four levels. Level one serves as a tutorial, introducing players to game controllers, UI, game world, and story. Challenges in this level focus on exploration, allowing novice players to become familiar with game

---

[1] https://www.dropbox.com/s/eoecefxjqx3pnr2/Gameplay%20DS-Hacker%203D.mkv?dl=0.

controls and navigation skills. Additionally, it allows the players to get familiar with the game world. Level two introduces the concept of BT and node structure. Level three

**Table 1.** Levels, topics, intended learning objectives (LOs), and learning activities (LAs) of *DS-Hacker* (2D and 3D).

| Level | Topics | LOs | Learning Activities |
|-------|--------|-----|---------------------|
| Level 1 | No topic | No LOs | No learning activities |
| Level 2 | Binary Tree node | LO1. The student should understand the concept of BT LO2. The student should define the basic elements that compose a BT node | LA1. Read and listen the BT definition LA2. Read and listen the node definition and its basic components LA3. Read and listen the link definition (reference/pointers) LA4. Relate the portals (links) with the concept of reference/pointers LA5. Relate the chambers of the game environment with the BT node structure and components |
| Level 3 | Binary Tree structure | LO3. The student should identify BTs LO4. The student should identify the BT's components | LA6. Read and listen the definition of the left and right child LA7. Read and listen the definition of the parent node LA8. Read and listen the definition of a sub-tree LA9. Identify the left and right child of the BT represented by the game environment LA10. Identify the root node of the BT represented by the game environment |
| Level 4 | Binary Search Tree | LO5. The student should explain the BST property LO6. The student should identify the BSTs LO7. The student should solve problems using the BST property LO8. The student should determine whether the BST property is unfulfilled | LA11. Read and listen the definition of the basic components of a BST LA12. Read and listen the definition of the BST property LA13. Apply the BST property to search for specific nodes |

revisits the BT structure and its component names. Level four introduces the BST data structure, its unique components, and properties. Table 1 summarizes the topics, LOs, and activities for each level.

## 4 Conclusion

This demo paper presented a detailed description of two prototypes of an educational video game for learning BST, called *DS-Hacker* (2D and 3D). Specifically, the paper provided a detailed description of the video game's learning aspects focusing on the learning theory, pedagogical approach, learning objectives and learning activities. Then, the paper described how the learning aspects were reflected in the game elements, such as the game narrative, challenges, and game world. It was expected that the rigorous match between the learning aspects and the game elements increases the video game's potential to convey learning of abstract non-intuitive conceptual knowledge. Moreover, the two versions of DS-Hacker were evaluated in 2020 [10]. Results were promising and showed the potential of the video game's approach.

## References

1. Association for Computing Machinery (ACM) Joint Task Force on Computing Curricula, IEEE Computer Society: Computer Science Curricula 2013: Curriculum Guidelines for Undergraduate Degree Programs in Computer Science. ACM, New York, NY, USA (2013)
2. Campbell, J.: The hero's journey. Harpercollins, New York, NY, vol. 10022 (1991)
3. Chaffin, A., et al.: Eexperimental evaluation of teaching recursion in a video game. In: Proceedings of the 2009 ACM SIGGRAPH Symposium on Video Games, pp. 79–86 ACM, New York, NY, USA (2009). https://doi.org/10.1145/1581073.1581086
4. Duit, R.: On the role of analogies and metaphors in learning science. Sci. Educ. **75**(6), 649–672 (1991)
5. Glynn, S.M.: Teaching Science with Analogies: A Strategy for Teachers and Textbook Authors. Reading Research Report No. 15. ERIC (1994)
6. Jiménez-Hernández, E.M., et al.: Using a serious video game to support the learning of tree traversals. In: 2021 9th International Conference in Software Engineering Research and Innovation (CONISOFT), pp. 238–244 (2021). https://doi.org/10.1109/CONISOFT52520.2021.00040
7. Kolb, D.A.: Experiential Learning: Experience as the source of learning and development. Pearson, New Jersey (2014)
8. McMahan, A.: Immersion, Engagement, and Presence: A Method for Analyzing 3-D Video Games. In: The Video Game Theory Reader. Routledge, New York (2003)
9. Petri, G., Gresse von Wangenheim, C.: How games for computing education are evaluated? A systematic literature review. Comput. Educ. **107**(C), 68–90 (2017). https://doi.org/10.1016/j.compedu.2017.01.004
10. Rojas-Salazar, A.: Game-Based Learning of Data Structures Based on Analogies: Learning Gains and Intrinsic Motivation in Higher Education Environments. Trinity College Dublin (2022)
11. Rojas-Salazar, A., Haahr, M.: Theoretical foundations and evaluations of serious games for learning data structures and recursion: a review. In: Ma, M., et al. (eds.) Serious Games, pp. 135–149. Springer International Publishing, Cham (2020)

12. Sedgewick, R., Wayne, K.: Algorithms. Addison-Wesley (2014)
13. Šuníková, D., et al.: A mobile game to teach AVL trees. In: 2018 16th International Conference on Emerging eLearning Technologies and Applications (ICETA), pp. 541–544 (2018). https://doi.org/10.1109/ICETA.2018.8572263
14. Wassila, D., Tahar, B.: Using serious game to simplify algorithm learning. In: International Conference on Education and e-Learning Innovations, pp. 1–5 (2012). https://doi.org/10.1109/ICEELI.2012.6360569

# BeA-ViR Game: From Virtual Exploration to Simple Gamification

Vittorio Murtas(✉) and Vincenzo Lombardo

Department of Computer Science, University of Turin, Turin, Italy
{vittorio.murtas,vincenzo.lombardo}@unito.it

**Abstract.** Our Cultural Heritage is a treasure trove of human history, consisting of collective knowledge, traditions, and artifacts passed down from our predecessors. Communication of Cultural Heritage in the contemporary digital era can be facilitated through interactive media, such as games, which serve a purpose beyond mere entertainment. Serious Games have evolved as a potent instrument for engaging users in investigating Cultural Heritage. They offer an immersive and intriguing experience transcending mere passive observation, encouraging active participation.

The demo of the BeA-ViR Game presents a work-in-progress Serious Game to emphasize Cultural Heritage content in a virtual environment. To be more specific, simple gamification elements focused on chronological and spatial dimensions are introduced presenting ancient archaeological findings uncovered in Japan in order to engage users with the virtual contents.

**Keywords:** Serious Games · Cultural Heritage · Archaeology

## 1 Introduction

Cultural Heritage Communication (CHComm) is recognized as part of the strategic objectives of UNESCO regarding Cultural Heritage (CH) [12]. Typically, heritage conservation is combined with disseminating heritage to current and future generations. Indeed, heritage conservation is a "communicative act", and public communication is an integral aspect of the conservation process [3]. Nowadays, ubiquitous Internet access and the usage of digital media to communicate CH have drastically altered CHComm. In fact, senders worldwide can include CH meaningful information in a message transmitted via a digital medium.

Among the different media, Serious Games have shown to be a potential instrument in the field of Cultural Heritage and can attract more individuals who are unfamiliar with art [2], history [11], or archaeology [1]. In the archaeology context, they have been designed to boost user interest in remote and inaccessible archaeological sites, raise awareness of these sites, and possibly offer a way to visit them using digital technologies [7]. In these games players can move around reconstruction of archaeological sites and examine 3D artifacts (often

M. Haahr et al. (Eds.): JCSG 2023, LNCS 14309, pp. 433–438, 2023.
https://doi.org/10.1007/978-3-031-44751-8_39

photoscanned). They may rotate, zoom in, and inspect artifacts from various angles to understand their details, significance, and historical context [4]. Most of games in this field are based on the spatial and temporal organization of content, fundamental elements in archaeology. In fact, some Serious Games feature interactive ways to explore content chronologically, allowing players to navigate through different historical eras (e.g. Father and Son Game[1]). This may concern significant events, cultural shifts, and archaeological discoveries, giving players a sense of how civilizations evolved over time. The spatial feature is considered through the use of maps or 3D reconstructions that provide information on the geographic distribution of unearthed artifacts or sites present in the game [10].

The BeA-ViR System [9] enables users to visit and analyze the spatially and temporally organized digitized Japanese sites and artifacts excavated by the BeArchaeo Project[2]. In this demo we present BeA-ViR Game, that relies on exploration and engaging gamification elements based on geographical and chronological dimensions. Gamification may aid users in their reception of cultural information pertaining to Japanese history by promoting an interactive, user-action-based approach that goes beyond the passive presentation of the content.

## 2  BeA-ViR Game

Beyond Archaeology (BeArchaeo, for short) is an archaeological project that employs digital techniques throughout the entire process of excavation, interpretation, and presentation of findings from the Tobiotsuka Kofun, a late 6th-century mounded tomb located in Soja City, Okayama Prefecture, Japan. The project focuses on the excavation activities at Tobiotsuka Kofun as well as the archaeological and archaeometric studies from other sites in the same region (Okayama Prefecture) and nearby prefectures (Shimane and Tottori). Its methodology involves the use of a semantic database that contains comprehensive information on all excavation and analytical activities conducted [5,6]. BeA-ViR is a multi-lingual and multi-platform (desktop, browser and CAVE) system for showing and assessing photoscanned artifacts from the BeArchaeo project. BeA-ViR was presented at the exhibition "The Tale of Be-Archaeo: between Science and Tradition" which was held at the Shimane Museum of Ancient Izumo, Japan, and at the Rectorate Building of the University of Torino, Italy.

Through BeA-ViR, users can view sites and artifacts by interacting with virtual surfaces in various exhibition environments. The application provides three exhibition layouts based on archaeological content: Single Finding Exhibition (which concerns only one finding), Multiple Findings Exhibition (which concerns several findings from multiple related sites), and Site Complex Exhibition (which concerns a virtual representation of an archaeological site and its findings). The entry to the individual environments is controlled by an introductory environment (Main Hall, Fig. 1a) via virtual gates. Users can navigate through the gates

---

[1] Father and Son Game.
[2] BeArchaeo Project Website.

and explore the site-related photoscanned findings in each environment. The controls used by the user are the triggers and buttons on the gamepad or keyboard controller as well as the footboards in the surrounding virtual environment. The footboards allow the user to move from one area to another and activate specific functions related to the archaeological and geographical information of an environment. The controls, standardized to the various target platforms, allow the user to move in first person and also observe the environment from above through a particular action, such as flying or jumping to a greater height before falling with gravity. Finally, users who don't want to explore can use the "guided tour" function that leads them through predetermined paths of exploration, stopping at each specified point of interest. Users can approach each finding in each environment, assess its original size using metric cues, and view the linked information acquired from the BeArchaeo semantic database using graphics panels (Fig. 1b). The facts displayed vary depending on the user; there is more generic information aimed at the general public and more technical information aimed at professionals. In addition to the objects, 3D representations of archaeological sites where the artifacts were discovered are available. In BeA-ViR, spatial and temporal dimensions are crucial. In fact, the contents shown, in addition to the division based on the number and type of artifacts, are grouped from their geographical origin and the period of Japanese history to which they belong. The spatial dimension is highlighted through a 3D map of Japan present in each explorable environment in which the name of archaeological sites from which the artifacts come are shown. The Main Hall is organized as a double-encircled surface, with the inner circle implementing the spatial dimension (with all the gates visible) and the exterior circle representing the time dimension. If the user touches the external circle, the chronological dimension is enabled and a transparent wall appears between them and the gates. This wall works as a timeline and allows exploration of the areas by exploiting the historical period to which the displayed contents belong.

(a) View from the Main Hall        (b) A photoscanned artifact

**Fig. 1.** Screenshots from BeA-ViR.

# 3   Geospace and Chronology Through Interaction

BeA-ViR Game contains simple gamification components, which create a higher level of engagement and immersion when compared to a passive presentation of the CH content. In fact, information about geographical and temporal dimensions is only displayed as a result of the user's exploratory activity, with the goal of fostering discovery and observational abilities. Instead of immediately displaying all the information to the user, the goal is to present it in a playful manner, allowing it to be discovered through exploration. A tight relationship between user engagement and CH dissemination keeps the player engaged in long-term sessions [13] and indicates promising improvements in the learning process, improving user attention and boosting higher-level critical thinking [8].

In conveying the spatial aspects, the gamification approach implemented involves emphasizing the archaeological sites highlighted on the map of Japan. Specifically, as the user approaches a gate, the map of Japan shows a bright beam of light centered on the site related to the gate the user is about to explore. In addition, the name of the site in question is enlarged, placing more emphasis on the user's exploratory choice and geographic information referring to the site (Fig. 2a).

In terms of temporal aspects, the timeline has been the primary focus. To investigate the environments by utilizing the historical eras to which the artifacts and sites belong, the user must access the Main Hall's outer surface. In this manner, the timeline is displayed, and interaction with it requires circumnavigating it. Only the gates that lead to sites that were active in the current chronological era are depicted on the inner surface for each period of Japanese history. On the timeline, historical period names and reference dates are represented by 3D models that are highlighted (via a change in color and size) when the user is in close proximity, in order to elucidate the impact of the timeline on the game environment (Fig. 2b).

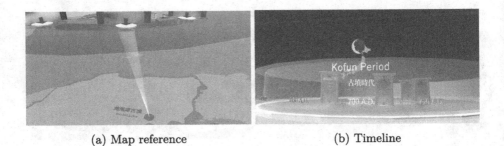

(a) Map reference                    (b) Timeline

**Fig. 2.** Geospace (a) and Cronology Discovery (b).

# 4  Conclusions

This paper presented the demo of the BeA-ViR Game, which is a work-in-progress evolution of the BeA-ViR System. Users of BeA-ViR can interact with multiple exhibition environments, see artifacts and sites digitized by BeArchaeo Project, and access data from the semantic database for a distinctive virtual exploration experience. In BeA-ViR Game, gamification increases user involvement by emphasizing spatial and temporal aspects through interactive exploration. Exploration by users can reveal spatial and temporal information, making learning more pleasurable and productive. This method encourages a greater comprehension of historical and archaeological contexts and strengthens critical thinking.

**Acknowledgements.** The BeArchaeo project is funded by the European Union's Horizon 2020 research and innovation programme under the Marie Skłodowska-Curie, Grant Agreement No 823826. The content of this paper represents the views of the authors only and is their sole responsibility; it cannot be considered to reflect the views of the European Commission and/or the Consumers, Health, Agriculture and Food Executive Agency or any other body of the European Union. The European Commission and the Agency do not accept any responsibility for use that may be made of the information it contains.

# References

1. Antoniou, A., Lepouras, G., Bampatzia, S., Almpanoudi, H.: An approach for serious game development for cultural heritage: case study for an archaeological site and museum. J. Comput. Cult. Heritage (JOCCH) **6**(4), 1–19 (2013)
2. Froschauer, J., Arends, M., Goldfarb, D., Merkl, D.: Towards an online multiplayer serious game providing a joyful experience in learning art history. In: 2011 Third International Conference on Games and Virtual Worlds for Serious Applications, pp. 160–163. IEEE (2011)
3. on Interpretation, I.I.S.C., Presentation: ICOMOS charter for the interpretation and presentation of cultural heritage sites. Technical report. ICOMOS (2008)
4. Liu, Y., Lin, Y., Shi, R., Luo, Y., Liang, H.N.: RelicVR: a virtual reality game for active exploration of archaeological relics. In: Extended Abstracts of the 2021 Annual Symposium on Computer-Human Interaction in Play, pp. 326–332 (2021)
5. Lombardo, V., Damiano, R., Karatas, T., Mattutino, C.: Linking ontological classes and archaeological forms. In: Pan, J.Z., et al. (eds.) ISWC 2020. LNCS, vol. 12507, pp. 700–715. Springer, Cham (2020). https://doi.org/10.1007/978-3-030-62466-8_43
6. Lombardo, V., Karatas, T., Gulmini, M., Guidorzi, L., Angelici, D.: Transdisciplinary approach to archaeological investigations in a semantic web perspective. Semant. Web **14**, 361–383 (2023). https://doi.org/10.3233/SW-223016
7. Mariotti, S.: The use of serious games as an educational and dissemination tool for archaeological heritage. Potential and challenges for the future **2**(1) (2021). https://doi.org/10.30687/mag/2724-3923/2021/03/005
8. Martin, F., Bolliger, D.U.: Engagement matters: student perceptions on the importance of engagement strategies in the online learning environment. Online Learn. **22**(1), 205–222 (2018)

9. Murtas, V., Lauro, V., Lombardo, V.: Virtual archaeology in a multi-platform and multi-lingual setting. In: Adjunct Proceedings of the 31st ACM Conference on User Modeling, Adaptation and Personalization, UMAP 2023 Adjunct, pp. 422–426. Association for Computing Machinery, New York (2023). https://doi.org/10.1145/3563359.3596664

10. Pescarin, S., Fanini, B., Ferdani, D., Mifsud, K., Hamilton, A.: Optimising environmental educational narrative videogames: the case of 'a night in the forum'. J. Comput. Cult. Herit. **13**(4), 1–23 (2020). https://doi.org/10.1145/3424952

11. Šisler, V., Brom, C., Cuhra, J., Činátl, K., Gemrot, J.: *Stories from the history of Czechoslovakia*, a serious game for teaching history of the Czech lands in the 20th century – notes on design concepts and design process. In: Herrlich, M., Malaka, R., Masuch, M. (eds.) ICEC 2012. LNCS, vol. 7522, pp. 67–74. Springer, Heidelberg (2012). https://doi.org/10.1007/978-3-642-33542-6_6

12. UNESCO: UNESCO World Heritage Centre - The World Heritage Convention. UNESCO (2020)

13. Vocaturo, E., Zumpano, E., Caroprese, L., Pagliuso, S.M., Lappano, D.: Educational games for cultural heritage. In: VIPERC@IRCDL (2019). https://api.semanticscholar.org/CorpusID:67865981

# Pervasive Serious Game for Exam Preparation: Exploring the Motivational Effects of Game Narratives

Finn Stoldt[✉][ID], Lea C. Brandl[ID], and Andreas Schrader[ID]

Institute of Telematics, University of Lübeck, Ratzeburger Allee 160,
23562 Lübeck, Germany
f.stoldt@uni-luebeck.de
https://www.itm.uni-luebeck.de/

**Abstract.** German students have a high level of stress due to exam anxiety and performance requirements. Serious games can help improve students' well-being and performance. The principle of pervasive games also brings many opportunities. Regarding the design of such games, there is still no consensus on which game design elements bring positive effects in which contexts. In this paper, we present a new pervasive serious game for exam preparation. The game design was adapted to investigate the relationship between motivation and game narrative. A pilot study's results show that the presence of a game narrative did not affect the subjects' motivation. However, the thematic relationship between the game narrative and learning content seemed to be important for the subjects' motivation. Overall, most of the subjects enjoyed the game and could imagine preparing for exams with such games in the future.

**Keywords:** Serious Game · Pervasive Game · Narrative · Motivation

## 1 Introduction

German students are strongly burdened by exam anxiety and performance requirements [2]. To increase the quality of life of students, learning content can be conveyed or tested playfully. The so-called *gamification* of tasks and processes has many positive effects on the behavior and well-being of users [8,15,19]. If a task is not just augmented by game design elements, but integrated into a full-fledged game, it is called a *Serious Game* [9]. These include increased motivation and attention to the task [4,5,7,10]. By using *Serious Games*, players engage with the learning content for longer [6], and better preparation reduces stress and anxiety related to exams [11]. Thus, it seems logical to use these games for better preparation to reduce stress.

This paper presents a newly developed pervasive serious game. Through the use of Tangible User Interfaces (TUI) as well as light and sound effects, the exam preparation process of students could get more exciting. The experience character is supposed to distract from the stress. To make the game suitable for many

M. Haahr et al. (Eds.): JCSG 2023, LNCS 14309, pp. 439–446, 2023.
https://doi.org/10.1007/978-3-031-44751-8_40

contexts, both the game narrative and the learning content are interchangeable. Therefore, this game was used to investigate the following research questions: *Does (a) the presence of a game narrative and (b) the connection between learning content and game narrative have a positive effect on the players motivation?*

## 2  Background

As introduced, this paper presents a *Pervasive Serious Game*. The term *Pervasive Game* refers to a spatially, temporally, or socially expanded game [17].

In the context of education, serious games have been developed and studied that serve to teach new knowledge [22]. However, games in which already learned knowledge is supposed to be applied are few to be found. One example of these is OSCEGame [11]. It was developed to better prepare dental students for clinical exams and to reduce exam anxiety and stress in this context. Results of the associated study on the usefulness of the game showed that the game reduced exam anxiety in 60% of all participants and promoted time management skills in 65% of all participants.

Another example with a focus on the game narrative is the work of Jemmali et al. [14]. With the 3D puzzle game May's Journey, they investigated the benefits of game narratives within educational games. In several levels, it teaches the basics of programming along a fictional story. To investigate the usefulness of a rich game narrative, they tested the game in a study with two versions of the narrative, one rich and one light. Results of the study indicated that the rich version of the narrative delivered increased engagement and higher performance among testers.

## 3  Game Design and Prototype

Following DIN EN ISO 9241-210 [13], the concept for the developed game was designed in a user-centered way. To understand the usage context, a task and process analysis, a user analysis, as well as a context analysis were carried out according to the suggestion of Preim and Dachselt [18].

### 3.1  Narrative

The so-called Integrated Game Elements, Narrative and Content (IGENAC) model by Theodosiou and Karasavvidis [21] describes the structure of serious games. It tries to synthesize three different but related branches of game design approaches: education-oriented, narrative-oriented, and conventional game design elements. Essentially, it facilitates the instrumental use of resources to overcome obstacles in a principled and contextual manner. In the narrative, the *game's story*, *main characters*, and *environment* are described. *Obstacles* faced by the main characters in pursuit of their *goals* and the *resources* they use in their encounters are also described. Interactions between these game elements are constrained by a set of operational and constitutive *rules*. To investigate the importance of the thematic connection of game narrative and learning content regarding motivation in the evaluation, two game narratives are designed. One is thematically related to the learning content, the other is not.

As the learning content for the evaluation was supposed to be related to medicine, the *environment* of the first narrative (*hospital narrative*) is a Parisian hospital in the future. Using a futuristic laboratory, the *main character* is to help analyze a previously unknown disease (*goal*).

The second narrative (*temple narrative*) takes place in an ancient Mayan temple in the present (*environment*). The *main character*, whose role the player assumes, has the *goal* of using a mystical ritual to gain access to the temple's treasury.

The *resources* include the required expertise as well as a certain physical fitness. These are used in the form of *mechanics*: To operate the laboratory or perform the ritual, cubes must be moved back and forth between pillars. Here, the correct assignment of pillars and cubes is crucial for success. The goal of the game is to analyze the unknown disease or reach the treasury. According to the *rules*, the player plays three different phases on the way there, in which he or she receives different types of tasks. If a phase, consisting of several rounds, is not completed, it must be repeated.

## 3.2 Prototype

To investigate the research questions, a high-fidelity prototype was created. Its structure is described below in terms of hardware and software level.

**Hardware.** An area of approx. $3 \times 4$ m enclosed by a truss was used as the playing field. The legs of the truss were wrapped with fabric and thus used as pillars for the game.

The player makes the essential inputs during the execution of the *mechanics* using cubes, which serve as a TUI. Those support the pervasive game character through spatial expansion. The cubes were made for the game from universal housings of about $10 \times 10$ cm. They were equipped with an Arduino microcontroller [3], a display and a battery. To enable the player to assign the cubes to the pillars, iPads were attached to the truss legs using stands on which the cubes can be placed. The iPads recognize the cubes by unique multi-touch patterns on their undersides. Additional inputs that influence the game flow can be made by the player via a control tablet.

The essential outputs of the system are delivered via a wall-mounted TV, the control tablet, the displays of the cubes, and the iPads of the pillars.

To support the immersion into the game and to improve the experience character of the game, the game is additionally underlined with light and sound effects. For this purpose, LED strips were installed inside the pillars. The sound effects are played back via the TV. Some impressions of the prototype are shown in Fig. 1.

(a) Stage of the Game.          (b) Cube object with embedded display.

**Fig. 1.** Prototypical game setup in a laboratory at the University of Lübeck.

**Software.** The software of the game consists of three components. Node.js was used as the backend framework and Create React App as the front-end framework. TypeScript has been used as the programming language. Communication between distributed components was done via WebSocket and HTTP. The game logic is executed on a local server. Graphic interfaces for the iPads and the TV are provided via web applications that communicate with the game server in real-time. The Arduinos on the cubes receive information from the game server to be displayed on the cubes via the WiFi network. Scripts for those microcontrollers were written in C++.

## 4  Evaluation

To investigate the research questions as well as the acceptance and practical applicability, a summative evaluation of the developed game was conducted as a pilot study. To obtain a homogenous sample with a small number of test persons, the evaluation was focused on medical students, and the content of the game was adapted accordingly. The inclusion criterion was a study related to medicine as well as already acquired knowledge in the field of anatomy, since related questions are used in the game. During the evaluation period, a total of nine test subjects were recruited. These were randomly divided into three groups of equal size. Depending on their group, they were assigned one of the two game narratives or no narrative.

The learning content of the game was compiled with the support of a physiotherapist and a medical student based on content from the AMBOSS [1] learning platform. The result was a question catalog with eight true-false questions, three multiple-choice questions and three matching tasks on the topic of anatomy. These were distributed in three rounds, each played in about five minutes.

Data were collected using three questionnaires [20], one before and two after the game, as well as observations during the game. The first questionnaire (*Questionnaire1*) consisted of eight items to be rated on a 5-point Likert scale [16].

Four items were intended to capture the prior experiences and four to capture the interests of the subjects. During the game, any salient outside observations were documented. After completion of the game, the subjects were presented with the other two questionnaires. The second questionnaire (*Questionnaire2*) was a modification of The Situational Motivation Scale questionnaire by Guay et al. [12]. It is designed to capture situational intrinsic motivation, identified regulation, external regulation, as well as amotivation using 20 items to be rated on a 7-point Likert scale [16]. The modification of the questionnaire included a translation into German and the replacement of the word activity by game. This was intended to make it easier for the subjects to empathize with the statements. The third questionnaire (*Questionnaire3*) consisted of four items to be rated on a 5-point Likert scale [16] and three text fields for positive, negative as well as other comments. Three of the items were used to examine the acceptance. The remaining item was used to investigate practical applicability.

**Motivation and Narrative.** Regarding intrinsic motivation, captured by *Questionnaire2*, the groups did not differ. On average, the value was in the positive range. The subjects' identified regulation of the *temple narrative* group was slightly lower than that of the other groups. External regulation was low across all groups, and amotivation was almost absent. Results are shown in Fig. 2. *Questionnaire3* revealed that liking the game narrative was highly subjective. Although subjects showed liking of the narratives on average, the variance is high. The subjects rated the connection between game narrative and learning content as important.

**Acceptance.** The results from *Questionnaire1* show that five of the nine subjects feel pressure to perform within their studies. Seven indicate that this kind of pressure causes them mental stress. According to *Questionnaire3*, almost all subjects can imagine using a game like this to prepare for exams. All subjects enjoyed the game and most can imagine using games like this for their exam preparation. Through free text, the test subjects praised the immersive experience provided by light and sound effects. The component of physical activity, in particular, excited many players, as it provided a welcome distraction from sitting at a desk. Criticisms included the difficulty of the questions and some usability issues such as an error-prone detection of the cubes and connection problems of the components.

## 5  Discussion and Limitations

The results of the evaluation show an increased intrinsic motivation of all players. Since there were no differences between the groups, for research question *(a)* can be assumed that the test subjects enjoyed the game regardless of whether they played with or without a narrative. Regarding research question *(b)* the notable results of the subscale on the identified regulation lead to the assumption,

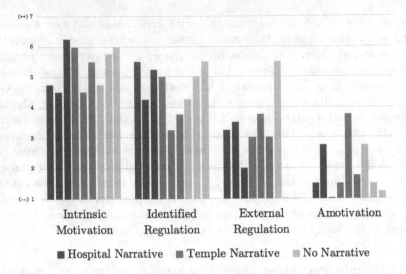

**Fig. 2.** Averaged results subscales of *Questionnaire2* of all subjects rated on a 7-point Likert scale.

that a missing connection between the game narrative and the learning content negatively distracts and lowers personal relevance. As also confirmed by the results of *Questionnaire3*, a thematic connection is therefore useful.

The game could be extended by a more novel game mechanic as well as a social component.

A crucial limitation of the conducted study is the small number of participants. Only nine test subjects could be acquired. On the one hand, this means that the results cannot be statistically evaluated, and on the other hand, negative correlations may be found in the data collected. In addition, usability issues, game rules in need of optimization, and questions that were sometimes too difficult could have hindered immersion in the game narrative. Possible motivational effects could have been distorted in this way. As a next step, the automated generation of pervasive serious games is planned, whereby the combination of different game narratives, learning content and game mechanics will be investigated for suitability for use.

**Contributions of the Authors.** FS, LB, AS: conception of the study, FS: conduct of the study, data collection, data analysis and interpretation; FS, LB: writing of the manuscript, AS substantial revision of the manuscript. All authors have approved the manuscript as submitted and accept responsibility for the scientific integrity of the work.

# References

1. Medizinwissen, auf das man sich verlassen kann | AMBOSS (2022). https://www.amboss.com/de/
2. Arbeitsgruppe Hochschulforschung: 13. Studierendensurvey an Universitäten und Fachhochschulen: Studiensituation und studentische Orientierungen (2017)
3. Arduino - Home (2023). https://www.arduino.cc/. Accessed 05 Dec 2023
4. Barata, G., Gama, S., Fonseca, M.J., Gonçalves, D.: Improving student creativity with gamification and virtual worlds. In: ACM International Conference Proceeding Series, pp. 95–98 (2013). https://doi.org/10.1145/2583008.2583023
5. Barata, G., Gama, S., Jorge, J., Gonçalves, D.: Improving participation and learning with gamification. In: ACM International Conference Proceeding Series pp. 10–17 (2013). https://doi.org/10.1145/2583008.2583010
6. Boeker, M., Andel, P., Vach, W., Frankenschmidt, A.: Game-based E-learning is more effective than a conventional instructional method: a randomized controlled trial with third-year medical students. PLOS One **8**(12) (2013). https://doi.org/10.1371/journal.pone.0082328, https://journals.plos.org/plosone/article?id=10.1371/journal.pone.0082328
7. Buckley, P., Doyle, E.: Gamification and student motivation. Interact. Learn. Environ. **24**, 1162–1175 (2016). https://doi.org/10.1080/10494820.2014.964263
8. Chapman, J.R., Rich, P.J.: Does educational gamification improve students' motivation? If so, which game elements work best? J. Educ. Bus. **93**, 314–321 (2018). https://doi.org/10.1080/08832323.2018.1490687
9. Deterding, S., Dixon, D., Khaled, R., Nacke, L.: From game design elements to gamefulness. In: Proceedings of the 15th International Academic MindTrek Conference on Envisioning Future Media Environments - MindTrek 2011, p. 9 (2011). https://doi.org/10.1145/2181037.2181040
10. Figueiredo, J., Garcia-Penalvo, F.J.: Increasing student motivation in computer programming with gamification. In: 2020 IEEE Global Engineering Education Conference (EDUCON), pp. 997–1000 (2020). https://doi.org/10.1109/EDUCON45650.2020.9125283
11. Germa, A., Gosset, M., et al.: OSCEGame: a serious game for OSCE training. Eur. J. Dent. Educ. **25**, 657–663 (2021). https://doi.org/10.1111/eje.12643
12. Guay, F., Vallerand, R.J., Blanchard, C.: On the assessment of situational intrinsic and extrinsic motivation: the situational motivation scale (SIMS). Motiv. Emot. **24** (2000). https://doi.org/10.1023/A:1005614228250
13. Ergonomie der Mensch-System-Interaktion - Teil 210: Menschzentrierte Gestaltung interaktiver Systeme (ISO 9241-210:2019); Deutsche Fassung (2019). https://doi.org/10.31030/3104744
14. Jemmali, C., Bunian, S., Mambretti, A., El-Nasr, M.S.: Educational game design: an empirical study of the effects of narrative. In: Proceedings of the 13th International Conference on the Foundations of Digital Games pp. 1–10 (2018). https://doi.org/10.1145/3235765.3235783
15. Johnson, D., Deterding, S., Kuhn, K.A., Staneva, A., Stoyanov, S., Hides, L.: Gamification for health and wellbeing: a systematic review of the literature. Internet Interv. **6**, 89–106 (2016). https://doi.org/10.1016/j.invent.2016.10.002
16. Likert, R.: A Technique for the Measurement of Attitudes, 140 edn., pp. 1–55. Archives of Psychology (1932)
17. Montola, M.: Exploring the edge of the magic circle: defining pervasive games. In: Proceedings of DAC, vol. 1966, p. 103 (2005)

18. Preim, B., Dachselt, R.: Interaktive Systeme. Springer, Heidelberg (2015). https://doi.org/10.1007/978-3-642-45247-5
19. Sailer, M.: Die Wirkung von Gamification auf Motivation und Leistung. Springer, Wiesbaden (2016). https://doi.org/10.1007/978-3-658-14309-1
20. Stoldt, F.: Pervasive serious game for exam preparation: exploring the motivational effects of game narratives. Master's thesis, Institute of Telematics at the University of Lübeck, Germany (2022)
21. Theodosiou, S., Karasavvidis, I.: Serious games design: a mapping of the problems novice game designers experience in designing games. J. e-Learn. knowl. Soc. **11**(3) (2015). https://doi.org/10.20368/1971-8829/1071. IGENAC Model
22. Zhonggen, Y.: A meta-analysis of use of serious games in education over a decade. Int. J. Comput. Games Technol. **2019** (2019). https://doi.org/10.1155/2019/4797032

# Challenges in Designing Augmented Reality (AR) in Serious Games and Gamification for Students with Colorblindness

Sundus Fatima[1]([✉]) [ID] and Jannicke Baalsrud Hauge[1,2] [ID]

[1] BIBA- Bremer Institut Für Produktion und Logistik GmbH, Hochschulring. 20, 28359 Bremen, Germany
fat@biba.uni-bremen.de

[2] KTH-Royal Institute of Technology, Kvarnbergagt.12, 15134 Södertälje, Sweden

**Abstract.** Interactive learning espouses a "hands-on" approach, aiming to foster student engagement. In an interactive form of learning, serious games, and gamification have been used in the classrooms to engage students. Nowadays, many serious games and gamification with AR are used in classrooms as it encourages engagement in interactive learning. However, with the usage of such technologies, it remains challenging to engage students with certain impairments as the tools are not designed to accommodate the needs of students with certain impairments. In this poster paper, the focus is on challenges related to red-green color blindness, since this is regularly affecting the learning experience among our students. Making learning content accessible in an AR environment depending on the type and severity of this color blindness is challenging and requires a better understanding of the specific requirements in designing AR in serious games and gamification for red-green colorblindness. To accomplish this, a systematic literature review (SLR) is conducted with the aim of highlighting the existing challenges in designing AR: i) serious games and ii) gamification. The paper also examines the challenges of using AR in interactive learning in a broader context and identified challenges with the key findings discussed.

**Keywords:** Augmented Reality (AR) · Serious Games · Gamification · Color Blindness

## 1 Introduction

Interactive learning promotes active student engagement through hands-on experiences [1], fostering the development of practical skills [2]. Serious games and gamification have been used in classrooms, making the learning process effective [3]. Many of these approaches integrate AR technology to enhance engagement in interactive learning [5]. However, accommodating students with any type of impairment in this interactive form of learning is challenging because there is a lack of tools designed to meet their specific needs [24]. Different types and severities of impairments require tailored solutions [26]. Impairments vary in type (visual, hearing, cognitive, etc.) and have diverse needs based on their type and severity [26]. The central impairment addressed in this paper is red-green colorblindness, a type of visual impairment that affects the ability to distinguish between shades of red and green [22]. Red-green color blindness is prevalent in approximately 8% of males and 0.5% of females [22, 23]. Given that a significant portion of our student population consists of males, this research primarily examines the implications of this impairment.

Apart from challenges in color distinction, students with red-green colorblindness also face difficulties perceiving visual and auditory feedback if not catered to their needs [23, 25]. To overcome these barriers, identifying challenges in designing AR for serious games and gamification is crucial which generates our research question (**RQ**): What actions need to be taken to overcome potential challenges in designing engaging AR in (i) serious games and (ii) gamification applications that take the need of red-green colorblind students into account? The paper aims to investigate design challenges reported in the literature related to AR in (i) serious games and (ii) gamification. To achieve this, a systematic literature review (SLR) is conducted which not only emphasizes the topic but also explores the challenges within the broader context of designing for AR, serious games, and gamification as exploring these challenges is vital for a comprehensive understanding which ensures practical relevance and fosters innovation. Addressing the identified challenges could contribute to a better understanding of the challenges and future research can develop the guidelines to improve the player experience for red-green colorblind learners.

## 2    Research Methodology

A systematic Literature Review (SLR) was conducted, following three stages: planning, conducting, and reporting, based on Tranfield, Denyer, and Smart's approach (2003). The SLR ensures comprehensive research and transparency, benefiting various fields (Thorpe et al., 2005).

### 2.1    Planning the Review

The first stage involves planning the literature review, focusing on AR challenges in (i) serious games and (ii) gamification for red-green color blindness. 'Scopus' and 'Science Direct' databases were chosen as they have sufficient relevant literature in English from 2013 to the present, offering detailed insights into the challenges over the last ten years.

### 2.2    Conducting the Review

The study started by examining AR design challenges in (i) serious games and (ii) gamification for red-green color blindness using specific search queries in each database.

**Serious Games.**    Main search queries were created by using the following keyword groups: (1) Augmented Reality (2) Serious Games (3) Red-Green Color Blindness, Red-Green Color Blind, and Visual Impairment to examine the literature in selected databases based on the formats and rules of selected databases, which are as follows:

*Scopus.* The following string was used to make the search query in all fields, titles, abstracts, and keywords: ALL("augmented reality*" AND "serious games*" AND "design*" AND "red-green color blindness*" OR "visual impairment*"). During stage two, a keyword ("design*") was excluded since it presented vast literature on design only, and to be more specific, we chose the engineering subject area, and the following query was used to perform the next step in the SLR: (A)ALL("augmented reality*" AND "serious games*" AND "red-green color blindness*" OR "visual impairment*") AND ( LIMIT-TO ( SUBJAREA,"ENGI")).

*Science Direct.* The following string was used to make the search query in all fields, titles, abstracts, and keywords: augmented reality AND serious games AND design AND (red-green color blindness OR visual impairment). During stage two, a keyword (design) was excluded since it presented vast literature on design only, and to be more specific, we chose the engineering subject area, and the following query was used to perform the next step in the SLR: (B) augmented reality AND serious games AND (red-green color blindness OR visual impairment).

**Gamification.** Main search queries were created by using the following keyword groups: (1) Augmented Reality (2) Gamification (3) Red-Green Color Blindness, Red-Green Color Blind, and Visual Impairment to examine the literature in selected databases based on the formats and rules of selected databases, which are as follows:

*Scopus.* The following string was used to make the search query in all fields, titles, abstracts, and keywords: ALL("augmented reality*" AND "gamification*" AND "design*" AND "red-green color blindness*" OR "visual impairment*"). During stage two, a keyword ("design*") was excluded since it presented vast literature on design only, and to be more specific, we chose the engineering subject area, and the following query was used to perform the next step in the SLR: (C)ALL("augmented reality*" AND "gamification*" AND "red-green color blindness*" OR "visual impairment*") AND ( LIMIT-TO ( SUBJAREA,"ENGI")).

*Science Direct.* The following string was used to make the search query in all fields, titles, abstracts, and keywords: augmented reality AND gamification AND design AND (red-green color blindness OR visual impairment). During stage two, a keyword (design) was excluded since it presented vast literature on design only, and to be more specific, we restricted our search to the engineering subject area, and the following query was used to perform the next step in the SLR: (D)augmented reality AND serious games AND (red-green color blindness OR visual impairment).

The final stage of the SLR is reporting and dissemination, presented in the next section.

### 2.3 Reporting and Dissemination

In the last stage of the SLR, the results are reported and disseminated in two parts:

- AR in serious games, with separate results from the two databases: (1) The search query (A) for 'Scopus' yielded "36" articles: "32" articles were excluded as they were focused on different technologies and impairments. Only "4" relevant papers are presented in the next Sect. (2) The search query (B) for 'Science Direct' resulted in "40" articles: "34" articles were excluded as they were focused on different technologies and impairments. Only "6" relevant papers are presented in the next section.
- AR in gamification, with separate results from the two databases: (1) The 'Scopus' search query (C) yielded "20" articles: "14" were excluded as they were focused on other domains. Only "6" relevant papers are presented in the next Sect. (2) The 'Science Direct' search query (D) produced "20" articles: "17" were excluded as they were focused on different technologies and impairments. Only "3" relevant papers are presented in the next section.

The final stage provided an overview of identified articles with critical discussions and the next section presents findings, key contributions to research questions, and identified gaps.

## 3    Findings and Discussion

This section presents the findings of the SLR. It highlights the key outcomes and discusses the insights gathered from the existing literature on the topic.

### 3.1    AR in Serious Games

The section presents "10" identified papers from the respective databases (see Table 1).

**AR Design in Serious Games.**    AR in serious games enhances engaging learning experiences through interactive content [9]. For visually impaired users, AR offers improved accessibility features [28]. Challenges include a lack of user inclusion in design [30], high costs, limited customization [10], and unstandardized haptic interaction [11]. Features like screen reader support and voice sign-in exist [13], but may not cover all severe color impairments. Visual interfaces and audio input cater to specific needs [31] [29], while

**Table 1.**  (List of Identified Papers).

| # | Authors and Contributions to the Research Question (Identified Papers) | Ref. |
|---|---|---|
| 1. | Ullah, M., Amin, S. U., Munsif, M., Safaev, U., Khan, H. U., Khan, S., & Ullah, H: Serious Games in Science Education. A Systematic Literature Review. (2022) | [9] |
| 2. | Zallio, M., Clarkson, P. J: A study on inclusion, diversity, equity, accessibility and safety for digital immersive environments. (2022) | [28] |
| 3. | Al-Ansi, A. M., Jaboob, M., Garad, A., Al-Ansi, A: Analyzing augmented reality (AR) and virtual reality (VR) recent development in Education. (2023) | [30] |
| 4. | Žilak, M., Car, Ž., Culjak, I: A Systematic Literature Review of Handheld Augmented Reality Solutions for People with Disabilities. (2022) | [10] |
| 5. | Bhattacharya, P., Verma, A., Prasad, V. K., Tanwar, S., Bhushan, B., Florea, B. C., Taralunga, D. D., Alqahtani, F., Tolba, A: Game-O-meta: Trusted federated learning scheme for P2P gaming metaverse beyond 5G networks. (2023) | [11] |
| 6. | Omary, D., Mehta, G: Mixed reality tailored to the visually-impaired. (2022) | [13] |
| 7. | Pfeuffer, K., Abdrabou, Y., Esteves, A., Rivu, R., Abdelrahman, Y., Meitner, S., Saadi, A., Alt, F: Artention: A design space for gaze-adaptive user interfaces in augmented reality. (2021) | [31] |
| 8. | Garcia, F. E., de Almeida Neris, V. P: Design guidelines for audio games. (2013) | [33] |
| 9. | Lima, C. B., Walton, S., Owen, T: A critical outlook at Augmented Reality and its adoption in education. (2022) | [29] |
| 10. | Herskovitz, J., Wu, J., White, S., Pavel, A., Reyes, G., Guo, A., Bigham, J.P.: Making Mobile Augmented Reality Applications Accessible. (2020) | [12] |

audio notifications improve interaction [33]. Designing inclusive options for various impairments remains challenging [12].

AR in serious games has the potential to enhance learning experiences [9], but achieving this requires overcoming challenges such as understanding the diverse needs of users [31] and with AR addressing hardware limitations is crucial for achieving inclusive design. One significant challenge is the limited involvement of impaired users during design leads to neglect of their specific needs and requirements [30]. Additionally, the currently limited customization options [10] such as color adjustment, and lack of audio/sound support [33] in AR serious games make it difficult to adjust features for such impairment. Efforts have been made to improve accessibility in AR environments, but certain barriers still exist [28]. Haptic interaction, involving touch-based feedback, presents challenges in terms of cost, and user comfort [11]. Despite progress in developing specialized screen readers and voice sign-in features that improve accessibility [13], they may not fully address the range of severe color impairments. Addressing challenges involves incorporating AR visual interfaces with audio feedback to cater to specific user groups [29]. However, designing for multiple impairments with AR in serious games requires careful consideration of diverse accessibility needs [12].

## 3.2  AR in Gamification

The section presents "9" identified papers from the respective databases (see Table 2).

**Table 2.** (List of Identified Papers)

| # | Authors and Contribution to Research Question (Identified Papers) | Ref. |
|---|---|---|
| 1. | Ponis, S. T., Plakas, G., Agalianos, K., Aretoulaki, E., Gayialis, S. P., Andrianopoulos, A.:Augmented reality and gamification to increase productivity and job satisfaction in the warehouse of the future. (2020) | [16] |
| 2. | Ulmer, J., Braun, S., Cheng, C.-T., Dowey, S., Wollert, J.: Adapting augmented reality systems to the users' needs using gamification and error solving methods. (2021) | [17] |
| 3. | Baneres, D., Rodriguez, M. E., Serra, M.: An early feedback prediction system for learners at-risk within a first-year higher education course. (2019) | [14] |
| 4. | Athanasios, M., Paula, B: Gamification of an open access quiz with badges and progress bars: An experimental study with scientists: (2020) | [32] |
| 5. | Mazarakis, A: Using gamification for technology enhanced learning: The case of feedback mechanisms. (2015) | [36] |
| 6. | Mazarakis, A: Gamification reloaded. (2021) | [34] |
| 7. | Sailer, M., Hense, J. U., Mayr, S. K., Mandl, H: How gamification motivates: An experimental study of the effects of specific game design elements on psychological need satisfaction. (2017) | [35] |
| 8. | Garzón, J., Pavón, J., Baldiris, S: Systematic Review and meta-analysis of augmented reality in educational settings. (2019) | [37] |
| 9. | Garzón J.: An Overview of Twenty-Five Years of Augmented Reality in Education. Multimodal Technologies and Interaction. (2021) | [20] |

# 4   Conclusion

AR may enhance active learning in serious games and gamification, but challenges like feedback difficulties, hardware limitations, and customization issues need attention. Tailored visual interfaces, audio support, and effective feedback can improve inclusivity, however; more research is required in this domain. Our research faced limitations due to the scarcity of relevant literature and the focus on other impairments, leading to the exclusion of a significant number of papers. Despite encountering certain limitations, our research partially answered the research question as to some extent we gained an understanding of identified challenges for AR in serious games and gamification in a broader context; however, the research question is not fully answered. Future research can focus on the comprehensive development of guidelines to explore the subject further.

**Acknowledgments.** This work is partly funded by, INCLUDEME (No. 621547-EPP-1-2020-1-RO-EPPA3-IPI-SOC-IN) which is co-funded by the European Commission through the Erasmus+ program, and the work also acknowledges the project DigiLab4U (No.16DHB2113) by German Federal Ministry of Education and Research (BMBF).

# References

1. De Carvalho, C.V., Coelho, A.: Game-based learning, gamification in education and serious games. Computers. **11**(3), 36 (2022). https://doi.org/10.3390/computers11030036

2. Shen, C.W., Ho, J.T.: Technology-enhanced learning in higher education. (2020). https://doi. org/10.1016/J.CHB.2019.106177

3. Becker, K.: What's the difference between gamification, serious games, educational games, and game-based learning? (2021). https://doi.org/10.20935/AL209

4. Laily, A.S., Ismail, A., Mohammad, K.H.: The effectiveness of gamification for students' engagement in technical and vocational education and training (2022). https://doi.org/10. 14569/IJACSA.2022.0130920

5. Avila-Garzon, C., Bacca-Acosta, J., Kinshuk, Duarte, J., Betancourt, J: Augmented Reality in Education (2021). https://doi.org/10.30935/cedtech/10865

6. Lampropoulos, G., Keramopoulos, E., Diamantaras, K., Evangelidis, G: Augmented Reality and Gamification in Education (2022).https://doi.org/10.3390/app12136809

7. Putz-Egger, L.-M., Beil, D., Dopler, S., Diephuis, J: Combining Gamification and Augmented Reality to Raise Interest in Logistics Careers. (2022). https://doi.org/10.3390/app12189066

8. Wei, L., Jin, L., Gong, R., Yang, Y., Zhang, X.: Design of Audio-Augmented-Reality-Based O&M Orientation Training for Visually Impaired Children. (2022). https://doi.org/10.3390/ s22239487

9. Ullah, M., et al.: Serious Games in Science Education (2022). https://doi.org/10.1016/j.vrih. 2022.02.001

10. Žilak, M., Car, Ž., Culjak, I.: A Systematic Literature Review of Handheld Augmented Reality Solutions for People with Disabilities (2022). https://doi.org/10.3390/s22207719

11. Bhattacharya, P., et al.: Game-O-meta: trusted federated learning scheme for P2P gaming metaverse beyond 5G networks (2023). https://doi.org/10.3390/s23094201

12. Herskovitz, J., et al.: Making Mobile Augmented Reality Applications Accessible (2020). https://doi.org/10.1145/3373625.3417006

13. Omary, D., Mehta, G.: Mixed reality tailored to the visually-impaired (2022). https://doi.org/ 10.1109/dcas53974.2022.9845506

14. Baneres, D., Rodriguez, M.E., Serra, M.: An early feedback prediction system for learners at-risk within a first-year higher education course (2019). https://doi.org/10.1109/tlt.2019. 2912167

15. Fatima, S., Baalsrud Hauge, J., Basu, P., Baalsrud Hauge, J., Chowdhury, A., Schurig, A.: Investigating Impact of Augmented Reality on Game Design to Facilitate Learning Experiences in Logistics Operations Using Immersive AR Interfaces (2021). https://doi.org/10. 1007/978-3-030-89394-1_34

16. Ponis, S.T., Plakas, G., Agalianos, K., Aretoulaki, E., Gayialis, S.P., Andrianopoulos, A.: Augmented reality and gamification to increase productivity and job satisfaction in the warehouse of the future (2020). https://doi.org/10.1016/j.promfg.2020.10.226

17. Ulmer, J., Braun, S., Cheng, C.-T., Dowey, S., Wollert, J.: Adapting augmented reality systems to the users' needs using gamification and error solving methods (2021). https://doi.org/10. 1016/j.procir.2021.11.024

18. What Do Color Blind People See? https://www.verywellhealth.com/what-do-color-blind-peo ple-see-5092522. Accessed 09 May 2023

19. Why red green Colorblind individuals are more common? https://iristech.co/why-red-green-colorblind-individuals-are-more-common/. Accessed 09 May 2023

20. Garzón, J.: An overview of twenty-five years of augmented reality in education. Multimodal Technol. Interact. (2021). https://doi.org/10.3390/mti5070037

21. Nature Game. https://sarra-game.hfc.dev/. Accessed 21 Jan 2022

22. Facts About Color Blindness. https://www.nei.nih.gov/learn-about-eye-health/eye-condit ions-and-diseases/color-blindness. Accessed 21 May 2023

23. Colour Vision Deficiency (color blindness). https://www.nhs.uk/conditions/colour-vision-def iciency/. Accessed 21 May 2023

24. Žilak, M., Car, Ž., Čuljak, I.: A systematic literature review of handheld augmented reality solutions for people with disabilities (2022). https://doi.org/10.3390/s22207719
25. Quintero, J., Baldiris, S., Rubira, R., Cerón, J., Velez, G.: Augmented reality in educational inclusion (2019). https://doi.org/10.3389/fpsyg.2019.01835
26. Davis, E.A., Hansen, R., Kett, M., Mincin, J., Twigg, J.: Disability (2013)
27. Coughlan, J.M., Miele, J.: AR4VI: AR as an Accessibility Tool for People with Visual Impairments (2017)
28. Zallio, M., Clarkson, P.J.: Designing the metaverse (2022). https://doi.org/10.1016/j.tele.2022.101909
29. Lima, C.B., Walton, S., Owen, T.: A critical outlook at Augmented Reality and its adoption in education (2022). https://doi.org/10.1016/j.caeo.2022.100103
30. Al-Ansi, A.M., Jaboob, M., Garad, A., Al-Ansi, A.: Analyzing augmented reality (AR) and virtual reality (VR) recent development in Education (2023). https://doi.org/10.1016/j.ssaho.2023.100532
31. Pfeuffer, K., et al.: Artention: a design space for gaze-adaptive user interfaces in augmented reality (2021). https://doi.org/10.1016/j.cag.2021.01.001
32. Athanasios, M., Paula, B.: Gamification of an open access quiz with badges and progress bars: An experimental study with scientists (2020)
33. Garcia, F.E., de Almeida Neris, V.P.: Design guidelines for audio games (2013). https://doi.org/10.1007/978-3-642-39262-7_26
34. Mazarakis, A.: Gamification reloaded (2021). https://doi.org/10.1515/icom-2021-0025
35. Sailer, M., Hense, J.U., Mayr, S.K., Mandl, H: How gamification motivates: an experimental study of the effects of specific game design elements on psychological need satisfaction (2017). https://doi.org/10.1016/j.chb.2016.12.033
36. Mazarakis, A.: Using gamification for technology enhanced learning: the case of feedback mechanisms (2015)
37. Garzón, J., Pavón, J., Baldiris, S.: Systematic Review and meta-analysis of augmented reality in educational settings (2019). https://doi.org/10.1007/s10055-019-00379-9

# Author Index

Printed in the United States
by Baker & Taylor Publisher Services